Revising *Before* You Write a First Draft: Ch. 3, pp. 55–56

Writing Preliminary Drafts: Ch. 3, pp. 57–58

Revising and Editing Preliminary Drafts: Ch. 3, pp. 58–61

Writing Final Drafts

THE WRITER IN PERFORMANCE

THE
WRITER IN
PERFORMANCE

JACK DODDS

William Rainey Harper College

MACMILLAN PUBLISHING COMPANY

New York

Macmillan Publishing Company
866 Third Avenue, New York, New York 10022

Library of Congress Cataloging in Publication Data

Dodds, Jack.
  The writer in performance.

  Includes index.
  1. English language—Rhetoric.   I. Title.
PE1408.D585   1986   808′.042   85–7254
ISBN 0–02–330380–8

Printing: 1 2 3 4 5 6 7 8   Year: 6 7 8 9 0 1 2 3 4 5

Acknowledgments

Garry Wills. "Education elitist? You bet!" is taken from his column "Outrider." Copyright © 1983, Universal Press Syndicate. Reprinted by permission. All rights reserved.

Thomas H. Middleton. "I Share Your Concern—Very Much." *Saturday Review*, November 1981. Reprinted by permission.

Sydney J. Harris. "Boiled, mashed, duchesse, fried, baked, scalloped . . ." Copyright © News Group Chicago, Inc., 1978. Excerpted from a column by Sydney J. Harris. Reprinted by permission of the Chicago Sun-Times.

Gurney Breckenfeld. "The New Entrepreneur: Romantic Hero of American Business." *Saturday Review*, July 22, 1978. Reprinted by permission.

Leon Botstein. "Why Jonathan Can't Read." Reprinted by permission of The New Republic. Copyright © 1983, The New Republic, Inc.

Carll Tucker. "Image." *Saturday Review*, February 18, 1978. Reprinted by permission.

Sydney J. Harris. From "War is Cancer of Mankind," *The Best of Sydney J. Harris* by Sidney J. Harris. Copyright © 1975 by Sydney J. Harris. Reprinted by permission of Houghton Mifflin Company.

Thomas H. Middleton. "Endangered Words." *Saturday Review*, October 14, 1978. Reprinted by permission.

ISBN 0-02-330380-8

Henry Fairlie. "Lust or Luxuria." Reprinted by permission of The New Republic. Copyright © 1977, The New Republic, Inc.

Sydney J. Harris. From "Of Loving and Liking," *Pieces of Eight* by Sydney J. Harris. Copyright © 1982 by Houghton Mifflin Company. Copyright © 1975, 1976, 1977, 1978, 1980, 1981 by the Chicago Daily News, The Chicago Sun-Times, Field Newspaper, and Sydney J. Harris. Reprinted by permission of Houghton Mifflin Company.

Susan Schiefelbein. "Children and Cancer; New Hope for Survival." *Saturday Review*, April 14, 1979. Reprinted by permission.

Ellen Goodman. "Telephone keeps us in touch—but isolates, too." Copyright © 1983, The Boston Globe Newspaper Company/Washington Post Writers Group. Reprinted by permission.

Michael Davis. Copyright © News Group Chicago, Inc., 1983. Excerpted from an article by Michael Davis. Reprinted by permission of the Chicago Sun-Times.

James Traub. "God and Man in Guatemala." *Saturday Review*, October 14, 1978. Reprinted by permission.

Richard Selzer. "The Discus Thrower." Reprinted by permission of Georges Borchardt, Inc. and the author. Copyright © 1977 by Richard Selzer.

Haiku from *Japanese Haiku* and *Cherry Blossoms*, Series I–IV. Copyright © Peter Pauper Press, 1956, 1958, 1960, and 1962. Reprinted by permission.

"Mustard Gas." *The New Columbia Encyclopedia*. Copyright © 1975, Columbia University Press. Reprinted by permission.

Wilfred Owen, *Collected Poems*. Copyright © 1963 by Chatto & Windus Ltd. Reprinted by permission of New Directions Publishing Corporation.

James Alexander Thom. "The Perfect Picture." Reprinted by permission, from August 1976 *Reader's Digest*. Copyright © 1976 by the Reader's Digest Association, Inc.

Henry Fairlie. "Too Rich for Heroes." Copyright © 1978 by *Harper's* Magazine. All rights reserved. Reprinted from the November, 1978 issue by special permission.

"Personal Computers." *1984 Buying Guide Issue*. Copyright © 1983 by Consumers Union of United States, Inc., Mount Vernon, NY. Reprinted by permission, from *Consumer Reports*, December 1983.

Frank Trippett. "The Great American Cooling Machine." Copyright © 1979 Time, Inc. All rights reserved. Reprinted by permission of Time, Inc.

M. M. K. "Just for You, Barbara." Reprinted by permission of The New Republic. Copyright © 1977, The New Republic, Inc.

Sydney J. Harris. From "Guilt Gives Rise to Double Talk," *The Best of Sydney J. Harris* by Sydney J. Harris. Copyright © 1975 by Sydney J. Harris. Reprinted by permission of Houghton Mifflin Company.

Barbara Lawrence. "Four-Letter Words Can Hurt You." Copyright © 1973 by the New York Times Company. Reprinted with permission.

Colin Westerbeck. "Good Fast Food." Reprinted by permission of *Esquire*. Copyright © 1983 by Colin Westerbeck.

Thomas H. Middleton. "On Learning the Rules." *Saturday Review*, January 21, 1978. Reprinted by permission.

David Owen. "Boycott Cocaine." Copyright © 1982 by *Harper's* Magazine. All rights reserved. Reprinted from the December, 1982 issue by special permission.

Henry Fairlie. "Why I Love America." Reprinted by permission of The New Republic. Copyright © 1983, The New Republic, Inc.

Michael V. DiSalle. "Capital Punishment: The Barbaric Anachronism." Originally appeared in *Playboy* Magazine. Copyright © 1966 by *Playboy*. Reprinted by permission of Anita Diamant Literary Agency.

Walter Berns. *For Capital Punishment*. Copyright © 1979 by Walter Berns. Reprinted by permission of Basic Books, Inc., Publishers.

Franklin Zimring. "Capital punishment's getting a bad name lately—and it should." Copyright © News Group Chicago, Inc., 1983. Article by Franklin Zimring. Reprinted by permission of the Chicago Sun-Times.

Robert di Grazia. "Limiting Handguns." Copyright © 1974 by The New York Times Company. Reprinted by permission.

Katherine Mansfield. "The Garden Party." Copyright © 1922 by Alfred A. Knopf, Inc., and renewed 1950 by John Middleton Murry. Reprinted from *The Short Stories of Katherine Mansfield*, by permission of the publisher.

Data (for diagram) based on hierarchy of needs in "A Theory of Motivation" *Motivation and Personality*, 2nd ed., by Abraham H. Maslow. Copyright © 1970 by Abraham H. Maslow. Reprinted by permission of Harper and Row, Publishers, Inc.

"Comparative Evaluation of Fast-Food French Fries." Copyright © 1984 by Consumers Union of United Sates, Inc., Mount Vernon, NY. Reprinted by permission, from *Consumer Reports*, July 1984.

Tennessee Williams. *A Streetcar Named Desire*. Copyright © 1947 by Tennessee Williams. Reprinted by permission of New Directions Publishing Corporation.

Sydney J. Harris. "Human tragedy: knowing the best but doing the worst." Copyright © News Group Chicago, Inc., 1983. Excerpted from a column by Sydney J. Harris. Reprinted by permission of the Chicago Sun-Times.

Ben Yagoda. "What Every Man Should Know." Reprinted by permission of *Esquire*. Copyright 1983 by Ben Yagoda.

Reader's Guide to Periodical Literature. Copyright © 1984 by The H. W. Wilson Company. Material reproduced by permission of the publisher.

New York Times Index. Copyright © 1980 by The New York Times Company. Reprinted by permission.

Reprinted by permission of the Modern Language Association of America, from the *1983 MLA International Bibliography of Books and Articles on the Modern Languages and Literatures*, Volumes I–V: Classified Listings with Author Index. Copyright © 1984.

Warren S. Walker. Acknowledgment is made to The Shoe String Press, Inc. for excerpts from *Twentieth Century Short Story Explication*, Third Edition by Warren S. Walker. Copyright © 1977 by The Shoe String Press, Inc. Reprinted by permission.

PREFACE

IN MOST PERFORMANCES, whether artistic, athletic, or practical, three things are happening. First is the performer performing: the actor acting, the ballplayer playing ball, or the writer writing. On stage, in the outfield, or at their desks, performers have their own physical, emotional, and intellectual challenges; their own rituals and rhythms; their own perspectives and pleasures that make their experience of their performance very different from their audience's. In their eyes, a good performance is one in which they master its rituals, move to the rhythms of play, and meet the challenges of the moment.

Second is the occasion exerting its influence. Whether performing "live," in a studio, or alone at a desk, successful performers feel this influence and rise to the occasion. A ballplayer plays one way in front of fifty-thousand fans during the World Series and a different way in the backyard with his kids. A jazz musician may turn his back in disregard of his audience but does so in relation to that audience. An actress plays to the camera's lens. And a writer decides what to say and how to say it on the basis of rhetorical intentions and assumptions about her readers.

Third is the audience responding: in its own way, apart from the performer's experience of the event, sometimes contrary to the performer's best intentions. Audiences, too, have their own challenges to meet, their own rituals and rhythms of attention, their own perspectives and pleasures. Aware of these differences, successful performers often adjust their performances to help audiences respond in appropriate ways. This an actor does during rehearsal when he exaggerates a gesture or modifies his voice to see how it plays at the back of the theater. A writer does the same when she reads her draft as readers might.

The Writer in Performance takes for its subjects these three dimensions of writers performing. It treats writing as both a process and a product, a product that stimulates and aids another process: reading. It emphasizes writers writing in public contexts, shaping their writing for the sake of their message and their readers.

This approach puts *The Writer in Performance* somewhere near the middle of the spectrum of current composition pedagogies, comfortable with the pedagogies on either hand. On the one hand, it makes use of much recent research into the processes of writing and reading. It teaches the importance of prewriting. Writing does not simply express a thought; it may also create it, in a process that is recursive and evolutionary. It teaches, too, the extent to which readers create meaning as they read, in their own way "composing" a text in their minds, depending on writers to guide their process. On the other hand, *The Writer in Performance* depends heavily on the principles of traditional rhetoric. It teaches that rhetorical strategies shape the writing process and that the traditional modes and constituents of writing express a writer's purpose. And it teaches the usage conventions of edited American English as the etiquette proper to most public writing, a matter of the persona of a writing as well as its meaning.

However, if *The Writer in Performance* is at all the book I have in mind, it will be more than a crowding of the two ends of the pedagogical spectrum into some kind of compromise; it will be a harmonious union of the two into one new program to help students meet the divided demands of public writing. What makes possible this synthesis of the new and the traditional is a design based on the hierarchy of choices writers face whenever they sit before a blank sheet of paper. Writers don't always make these choices in the same order, but we all make the same kinds of choices when we write. And once we make the cardinal choices about subject, audience, persona, and purpose, the subordinate choices about details, organization, paragraphing, syntax, and language come more easily. To design a textbook in this way—cardinal choices first, subordinate choices following—emphasizes not the process of writing, nor the product, but the strategies by which writers make meaning for themselves and their readers.

In the course of its descent through this hierarchy, *The Writer in Performance* helps students learn to make that shift in attention characteristic of successful writers. Early chapters emphasize writers writing for themselves, either personal response writing or narration; later chapters emphasize writers writing for readers, through exposition, evaluation, or persuasion. The exercises of early chapters teach invention and the creation of rhetorical strategies; in later chapters the exercises teach revision and copyediting. At each chapter's end, however, the major writing assignments lead students through the entire composing process. In sum, as *The Writer in Performance* takes student writers, chapter by chapter, deeper into the texts they create, it also leads them out of themselves into the world around them, a world of potential readers with their own perspectives and needs.

A part-by-part summary of *The Writer in Performance* follows:

PART I: STARTING POINTS (Chapters 1 and 2)

These chapters are introductory in both senses of the word. They set the tone and pattern for the book, and by summarizing the effects writers aim for and the most important devices for achieving those effects—role, persona, audience, and thesis—they provide the point of view from which students will view all the writing they do.

PART II: WRITING FOR DISCOVERY (Chapters 3–5)

Presenting the writing process, these chapters show students how to discover ideas and develop them in ways appropriate to their intentions and audience.

PART III: WRITING FOR READERS (Chapters 6–10)

These chapters show students, first, how to plan a communications strategy that will help them organize and express their subjects and, later, help their readers read. Second, they show students how to revise and edit their writing to make it as readable as possible. The subjects of these chapters are patterns of organization, introductions and conclusions, paragraphs, sentence structure, and diction.

PART IV: WRITING FOR STYLE (Chapters 11–12)

The subjects here are those devices of sound, rhythm, stress, sentence structure, and point of view that hold reader interest, shade emphasis, and give pleasure to writer and reader alike.

PART V: A GUIDE TO PUBLIC WRITING (Chapters 13–17)

These chapters introduce students to the most common forms of academic and public writing: business letters, essays, reports, critiques, literary analysis, and research projects. Part V is intended to be a reference section, supplementing Parts I–IV. The varied kinds of writing described here will allow instructors to adapt *The Writer in Performance* to the needs of their students and the requirements of their courses.

PART VI: A HANDBOOK FOR COLLEGE WRITERS (Chapter 18)

Included in Chapter 18 are the conventions of edited American English and exercises on the most troublesome issues of standard English usage.

The accompanying instructor's manual, *The Teacher in Performance*, contains the following: (1) an extended description of the text and its design, (2) sample syllabuses for a variety of courses, (3) suggestions for using this text with peer editing groups, (4) chapter-by-chapter summaries, complete with teaching strategies and answer keys for the short-answer exercises.

As the preceding description implies, a performance is almost always a collaboration of one sort or another. That's especially true of the writing-a-textbook performance. To my many friends and associates who gave their support and advice during the writing of *The Writer in Performance*, I owe a debt of gratitude. Whatever virtues this book possesses are largely due to their assistance. I am most grateful to two of my colleagues at Harper College, Joseph Sternberg and Peter Sherer, who cheerfully read my manuscript from start to finish, draft after draft. The criticism they offered was unfailingly insightful and constructive. I am grateful, as well, for the careful and helpful reading of my reviewers: E. Jean Amman, Ball State University; Lynn Z. Bloom, Virginia Commonwealth University; Richard Fulkerson, East Texas State University; Richard Gebhardt, Findlay College; Kris Gutierrez, University of Colorado; Michael Hogan, University of New Mexico; Lorraine M. Murphy, University of Dayton; Ron Strahl, Indiana University–Purdue University at Indianapolis; and Josephine Koster Tarvers and J. Randal Woodland, University of North Carolina at Chapel Hill. To all those at Macmillan who gave me their enterprise and patience, I owe thanks: Susan Didriksen, Carol Summerfield, Eben Ludlow, Wendy Polhemus, and Tucker Jones. Thanks to Linda Glover, Jerome Stone, John Muchmore, and John Tobin of Harper College for their helpful advice and assistance. Thanks to Lynda Sanford of the Chicago Public Library. A special thanks to Marcy Brandt of Harper College and William Winschief of Macmillan, who encouraged this book in its early stages. Thanks to my wife Judy for her constant support. Thanks, finally, to my students, the first readers of this book and the audience who gave me my voice.

J. D.

BRIEF CONTENTS

DETAILED CONTENTS

Chapter 4   Development: Unwrapping a Subject   67

Chapter 5   Development: Seeing Is Believing   86

PART III   WRITING FOR READERS

Chapter 6   Predictable Patterns: Maps for Writing and Reading   109

PART IV ❧ WRITING FOR STYLE

Chapter 11 Interest: "It Don't Mean A Thing If It Ain't Got That Swing" 225

Chapter 12 Interest: Variety's the Spice of Life— and of Good Writing, Too 247

PART V ❧ A GUIDE TO PUBLIC WRITING

Chapter 13 Four Kinds of Public Writing: The Letter, the Essay, the Report, and the Critique 271

Chapter 14 **The Persuasive Essay**   307

Chapter 15 **The Literary Essay**   369

Chapter 16 The Research Project: Searching and Re-Searching 396

Chapter 17 **The Research Project: Writing and Revising** 438

PART VI 🐿 A HANDBOOK FOR COLLEGE WRITERS

Appendix Bibliographies, Indexes, and Reference Books: A Brief Guide to Who, What, When, Where, Why, and How   539

Index   553

PART I

STARTING
POINTS

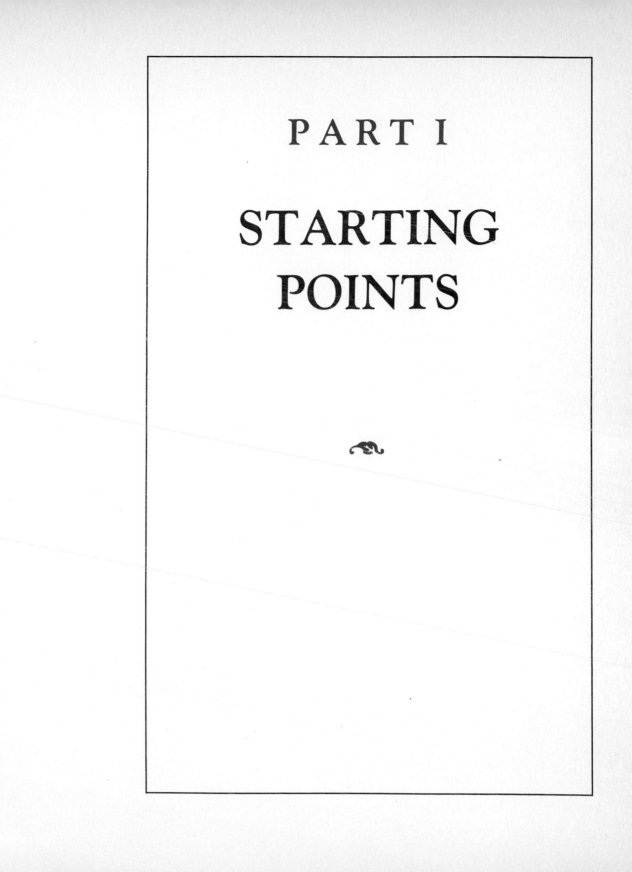

Chapter 1
What Is Good Writing?

Many people—perhaps you're one of them—think that writing well is a murky mystery, something only other people do and then as much by chance as by skill. Remember some of the writing projects you've wrestled with, a paper for school, say, or an important letter? Remember how hard it was to get started or put your ideas together? Remember, too, your quandaries about what words to use and what the rules were for using them? Why doesn't writing come as easily as speaking? you may have wondered. Remember that sinking feeling, knowing that something wasn't quite right but not knowing where to look for the problem? The more important a project is, it seems, the more trouble we have setting our words down on paper. "Murky mystery" barely begins to describe the ordeal of the blank page that lies before us, sullen, scornful, refusing to be filled. No wonder so many of us conclude that only geniuses with a knack for words can write well, surely not we, not even after years of school and semesters of English classes.

If you're one who thinks this way, even only occasionally, this book is written for you. Its purpose is to show you that writing well is something worth doing and something almost any of us can do, neither as difficult nor mysterious as many think. We can begin to demystify it just a little by thinking of it as a game. I know, I know: *game* is hardly the word for the subject of a book this thick and certainly inappropriate for college work. This is serious business. Still, as I hope to show, comparing writing to a game is a useful analogy. Let's start here: when you're first introduced to a new game, one question you ask right away is the point of the game. You want to know what the object is, what you have to do to win. To ask this about the writing game is to ask what we mean by "good writing." What do good writers aim to do when they write, and how do they know when

3

MISS PEACH

MISS PEACH by Mell Lazarus. Courtesy of Mell Lazarus and News Group Chicago, Inc.

their writing is "good"? And what about readers, the spectators of the writing game; what makes them call a piece of writing "good"? Here are their answers, along with a few other things you need to know at the outset about the college writing game.

GOOD WRITING SPEAKS AUTHENTICALLY, ONE HUMAN BEING TO ANOTHER

Every good writing has its own fully human voice. Listen:

> Going from high school to college is like having to jump into a pool without knowing in advance how cold the water is; it's a hot day and I know I want to . . . sure, why not! Hey, that wasn't too bad—as a matter of fact, it feels pretty good. I've got more responsibilities but no more mandatory attendance policy—and no kiddie cops in the halls asking me for my I.D.
> —Eric Olson

> What do you say to one of your best friends who has just lost her husband? How do you express the sorrow you feel for her? This happened to me recently and I am not sure whether I handled it well or not. Never in my life have I found myself kicking my toe on the ground and staring into space. But my mouth and my brain and my heart could not seem to work together and express to my friend what I truly wanted to say.
> —Erica Cohen

> On my last trip from my study I glanced at the hall mirror as I passed. What I saw there stopped me in my tracks. My face was drawn into a wrinkled frown that would put any California prune to shame, and my hair hung down in my face with that shaggy sheepdog look. As I stood there contemplating my outlandish reflection, I realized this was no way to write an essay. At the rate I was going, my family would soon toss me out in the rain or lock me in the garage for the night.

Studying that wretched creature in the mirror, I decided I needed a good lecture. Pulling the hair out of my eyes so I could see who I was talking to, I said to myself, "Kid, get a grip on yourself. You've had tougher assignments than this one; you've always pulled through and you can do it again. So straighten up those hunched-over shoulders, put a smile on your face, make an appointment at the beauty shop for that hair, and go out and knock them over with your charm."

I took my advice. I unplugged my typewriter, threw out all my half-finished rough drafts, and went out to my family and announced, "Hi, everyone, I'm home. Did you miss me?" The entire house seemed to breathe a sigh of relief as I planted myself in the overstuffed easy chair for a relaxing evening of TV reruns.

—Colleen Feilen

Did you hear these voices, by turn delighted, dismayed, and defiant? Voice is the characteristic good writers listen for first and last in the writing they do. Once they hear it in their writing they can be confident that almost everything else will come out all right. But it can't be just any old voice. It may be their student voice or business voice in an essay or letter, their private voice in a personal essay or diary, or their funny voice in a note to a friend, but it must be *their* voice. They never want to feel their writing has been voted on by a committee or punched out of a machine. Their best writing is what best creates and speaks for them.

Readers, in contrast, are less concerned with *who* is speaking than *how* a writer sounds. They want to read a voice that speaks to *them*, directly. They want it to sound sincere above all, warm, and concerned for their well-being. Writing that is phony, condescending, time-wasting or manipulative is almost never good—no matter how fluent, well-spoken, or intelligent—because it breaches the social contract that any communication makes between speaker and audience. Good writing never does this. Even when it criticizes, satirizes, or rages, it acknowledges readers' integrity and pays the respect due them as human beings.

GOOD WRITING TELLS THE TRUTH

What writers aim for when they write is fidelity, words that are truthful to their sense of themselves and the world as they see it. They want to get it *right*, whatever it is: the sound of the rain, a woman's confusion, the aftermath of an auto accident. Listen again:

I drifted to sleep accompanied by the strange music of water banging into pans and buckets, like a child making a drum out of a coffee can.
—Anita Santoro

Her husband's abuse had so eroded her self-respect that her life seemed to be a sweater six sizes too large. She couldn't find where her arms should go, and even if she did manage to get it on, it would never fit right.
—Mary Anderson

I don't remember the accident happening. I remember what seemed immediately afterward. A frantic lady was coming at me through the smashed and scattered window of what used to be a car. She was gone. Bob had somehow gotten out. Feeling no pain, I lifted myself from the floor of the car, shaking off the pieces of glass from my torn slacks. I looked in the rearview mirror (which strangely was unbroken). Blood was all over my face. My only worry at this point was how to explain to my mother that my clothes were ripped and my face, my arms, and legs were bleeding. Amazingly, I spotted my tooth among the ruins on the floor of the car. I reached for it, suddenly aware of the pain in my head. Bob was talking to some man from the ambulance. Why isn't anyone talking to me? I held out my tooth. "Keep that," he said. "They might be able to fix it." Clutching my tooth, I passed out while the funny-looking man wrapped my head.
—Denise Seretis

There is also another way writers aim for truth. Because their writing is one of the ways they act in the world, they hold it to the same standard of conduct they hold themselves to in the rest of their lives. When their writing is good, it speaks with integrity in some ethical context. This is not to say that all good writing holds to the same morality, only that we hear a voice resonant with moral value in writing that is good. For example:

I have just finished my Criminal Law homework. God, I can't begin to imagine all the schooling required to be a lawyer. And it seems kind of strange that all my schooling and practical experience will be teaching me how to lie, stretch the truth, or get around things by double-talking. Lawyers can't be 100 percent honest or they would be 100 percent broke.
—David Barts

God's partiality is even seen in the contrasts among nations. There is so much poverty in underdeveloped countries like India and Pakistan, it's shocking! Unbelievable! One out of every three persons roams about half-naked in the streets, looking in every nook and corner and garbage can for a little food for his stomach. The houses these people live in are not fit even for animals. And many of them don't have that. In sickness they lie unattended, and in misery and pain they die, welcoming death.
—Saadia Masood

What readers listen for when they read is not just *a* truth, but *the* truth, the whole truth and nothing but. And what catches their ears is not only fidelity but honesty; they want their reading to lay everything out clearly before them, never twisting facts or stealing another's words or ideas. A writer's voice creates that social contract I spoke of, but honesty keeps it in force.

❧ GOOD WRITING IS EFFECTIVE

Whenever writers put pen to paper, even on the most casual or personal occasions, they have reasons for doing so, and they judge their writing by how well it fulfills their intentions. Good writing does what they want it to. That means that learning to write is learning to please ourselves, learning all the things we can do with words, how to do them, and how to know when we've done them. How can we write effectively and satisfy others— even teachers—unless we first write effectively for ourselves? Any doubt or dissatisfaction we feel about our words is bound to show, corroding our effect. The applause that matters most is the applause of one, a writer's self-congratulation for a job well done.

But the applause of readers matters, too, of course, and they give it when their reading keeps the promises it makes to them. The whole effect of a piece of writing is always worth more than the sum of its individual excellencies of style or content. After all, how good can entertaining writing be if no one laughs or smiles, gets chills of excitement, or weeps those paradoxical tears of pleasurable sadness? What good is an informative piece of writing, no matter how well informed, if the reader asks, "What's going on here?" And how good can the persuasive letter be that does not persuade, or the expressive letter that gives the wrong impression? Writers, like the players of any game, take pleasure simply in writing, because it expresses and fulfills them. But to win, really to win, they have to satisfy their spectators.

❧ GOOD WRITING IS READABLE

Because so much writing is addressed to people who are more or less strangers, it has to be readable to be good. Most readers won't get the drift of a vaguely written piece that doesn't speak their language or make special effort to understand. Therefore, writers are the ones who must make the effort to put their ideas in a style interesting and appropriate to a particular audience. Usually their readers should not have to circle back and reread just to get the point. If they do reread, it should be to enjoy the "good parts" once more. I don't want to imply that a simple "See Spot run" style is what we ought to aim for when we write; a "simple" style is not necessarily the most readable style and not always possible. Often we have complex things to say or many things to say at once: some we want to make obvious, some we want only to suggest. But when two pieces of writing treat the same subject for the same audience, the one that is read with greater ease and attention is probably the better of the two. It's that business of the social contract again. Writers want readers to get their point—they *deserve* to get it—and good writers will do what they can for them. All they ask is that readers pay attention and not expect from them what they don't promise to do.

❧ MORE PRECISELY, WHAT IS GOOD COLLEGE WRITING?

Your most important college readers, your instructors, begin with the same expectations other readers do. But because of their special position as teachers, they bring an extra set of expectations to their reading. They may ask you to write an explanation of something, defend an opinion, give some information in a report, or narrate a personal experience, but you know they want to read more than an explanation, argument, report, or story. These are almost always pretexts for the real business at hand: showing your stuff, letting them know that you know what they're trying to teach.

The real purpose of almost all college writing is *demonstration.* No matter what else it does, good college writing demonstrates mastery: of a subject, a language for speaking about that subject, a manner of thinking about it, a method of organizing it, and a style suitable to it. You have been asked not simply to tell what you know about the causes of the Civil War, why economic recessions occur, or why children rebel against their parents; you have been asked to write like a historian, think like an economist, and sound like a psychologist. College writing is not, in the end, only about facts; it is about a particular way of looking at them: not only about knowledge but how we know.

Therefore, good college writing is generally

- Detailed and specific.
- Eager to support theory with the facts of experience.
- Precise in language.
- Systematic in organization.
- Careful to acknowledge sources of information.
- Quick to qualify statements (*might, seems, perhaps*) and slow to make categorical statements (*all, never, always, none*).
- Skeptical about accepted opinions but always open to new ones.
- Sensitive to questions by its readers.
- Conventional in format, grammar, spelling, and punctuation.

As well as a little bit humble about knowing so much yet having so much more to learn. Also, good college writing is seldom—sad to say—humorous. It may be witty, but the wit is usually dry, working more through understatement than overstatement.

This double responsibility, to know a subject and how to present it, makes college writing as difficult as any other writing you will do. Its range will probably challenge more of your powers of reason and feeling than almost any other, and some temperaments will find its conventions more difficult to master than others. But when you are finished, degree in hand, all your college writing tucked away in folders, not only will you have stocked your mind with some of the best that humankind has thought and felt, you probably will have transformed the way you think and feel. College writing is well worth the mastery.

THREE HALF-RIGHT ASSUMPTIONS ABOUT GOOD WRITING

Useful though it is for promoting good writing, college does have one unfortunate side effect. It leads some writers to a kind of double standard; in the classroom they rank high certain qualities that they don't give much thought to when they're outside in the real world. For one, when they walk into an English class or open a book like this, right away they begin to equate good writing with correct writing and assume that good writers are good chiefly because they remember all those intricate rules the rest of us forgot fifteen minutes after the test. Now it is true that good public writing is almost always grammatically correct, but it is also true that writing can be grammatical without being good and good without being strictly grammatical. Contrast these two passages about the human condition, the first by a PhD, the second by a college freshman. Is there any doubt which is better, even though the first is grammatically correct and the second not?

> To clearly, totally understand and categorically explain the process or facet of behavior called juvenile delinquency would, indeed, require a magnitude of understanding which, if attained, would be tantamount to omniscience. Nevertheless, a sound understanding of juvenile delinquency and its psychosocial ramifications enables us to approach this area with theoretical concepts and ideas that stimulate the formation of certain programmatic and therapeutic methods of mitigating a problem which very often thwarts youth from fully self-actualizing themselves. . . .

> If you take time to know a single person, you learn they are wrapped up in their lonliness. Every one of them have toothaches, hangnails, sore toes, arthritis, bursitis, colds, headaches, a temperture, a lump on their breasts. Maybe

they aren't able to take care of themselves, perhaps they want a mama to mother them. Or just someone to nag them and keep their minds off themselves.

Yes, the second paragraph makes lots of mistakes: it shifts from singular to plural for no reason (*person/they, every one/have*—a construction called an agreement error). The third sentence is really two sentences punctuated as one; the last is not a sentence at all but a fragment. And there are two misspellings (*loneliness* and *temperature*). Still, with all its errors, how much more vividly it describes loneliness than the first describes juvenile delinquency. We see and feel what the second writer is writing about; what the first has for us deep inside these shapeless and interminable sentences, we can't quite say, except that the grammar is correct.

To confuse good grammar with good writing is like confusing regulations for the size of the baseball, the distance from the pitcher's mound to home plate, and the number and positions of the ballplayers with an extra-inning World Series game. The rules that organize a game enable us to play but don't tell us *how;* nor do they help us tell a well-played game from a poorly played one. The same is true with grammar. The rules of a language are not the same as the conventions, common sense, and artistry of the users of that language. It is these that make for good writing. Certainly, grammar is worth knowing, as most human subjects are worth knowing. It will show you how language works and give you words for talking about certain parts of your writing. Later this book will describe some of the grammatical principles most important for writers. Knowing them will make you a more informed, more correct writer, but not automatically a better one.

A second misassumption is that good writing is "artistic" writing. We may have gotten this idea from our literature classes, when we've read richly descriptive, thickly emotional, complex poems, stories, and novels. Believing that this is *the* model for good writing almost always leads us to a related assumption: that we can never become good writers. Who can match a Shakespeare, Hemingway, or even J. D. Salinger? Two qualifications are in order here: First, artistic writing is *one* form of good writing; our writing would be better if we picked up some of the tricks used by the "great" writers, and had some of their insights, too. But "great art" writing is not the only kind. We're surrounded by good writing every day in our newspapers and magazines; in letters, memos, and reports; in the writing of the students that sit next to us. All we have to do is train our eyes to see it. You may even discover authentic, effective, readable writing in what you've done. If others, people like you, with much the same skill and intelligence, can learn to write well, why not you? You should know, by the way, that all the examples of good writing in this chapter were written by college students. Pretty good, don't you think? To say we can never write well is like saying we can't play baseball because we don't have the gifts of a Babe Ruth or Henry Aaron. We may never reach the greatness of the greats. Who does? But we can learn from them and write with our own sensitivity, skill, artistry, and pleasure.

Like this second misassumption is a third, that good writing is highfalutin, impressively difficult, filled with big words and bigger sentences. This may be the mistake made by the PhD I quoted previously. We are offered so many big books filled with big words about big ideas that it's no wonder we assume the quality of writing can be measured by the pound. But if you examine the writings of a good writer who has been at the craft for a long time, you almost always discover an arc in that career. The longer a writer writes, the simpler the writing becomes in language and style. Most practiced writers discover ways to make the hard seem easy, the complex seem simple. Like athletes at the top of their form, they perform economically, doing more with less effort because they know the game so well and have trained themselves to its demands. Remember your readers and the principle of readability. There will be occasions that require big words and complex sentences, and you will want to expand the range of your style to be ready for them. But just as often a clear, economical, direct style will be the best.

USING THIS BOOK TO IMPROVE YOUR WRITING

This is a book about good writing and writing well, about what makes writing good and how to make it that way, about writing for ourselves and writing for others. It aims to help you please yourself and others with your writing. The early chapters explore how successful writers find things they want to say and a style for saying them. The later chapters recognize that the good writer is also the good editor, one who knows how to prepare a writing for its readers. In sum, this is a book of options. The exercises and topics accompanying each chapter will give you the opportunity to explore the strategies successful writers use and help you develop the writing style that is right for you. This is a book for playing around in, trying things out, experimenting, succeeding, and then experimenting some more. No two writers write alike, and there is no single method for writing well. You have to find what works for you, and this book will help.

WHY BOTHER?

Among our large store of proverbs about life there is one that suggests writing well is not very important: "It's the thought that counts." Not so. This book will try to show you that thoughts *never* count without the right words and an effective style to express them. It is good writing that counts. For one thing, it counts on the job. Careers in business, law, education, medicine, and the social sciences require a high level of verbal skills. A recent survey discovered that "people in professional and technical occupations—the types of occupations in which over half of college-trained people are employed—on the average write nearly 30 percent of total work time."[1] Did you get that? Thirty percent. That's almost two full days of writing every workweek! With so much writing to do, a person has to be a practiced writer to work efficiently. More importantly, promotion seems to depend on those skills. In response to another survey, the "senior vice president of a computer company wrote a long letter saying that the difference between the winners and the also-rans at the top levels of business was the ability to communicate effectively."[2] Still a third survey has discovered that people with well-developed verbal skills are preferred for jobs, *even* when language skills have nothing to do with the job they're being hired for![3] It may not be fair that employers—and almost everyone else—respond this way. But there it is. What are you going to do?

For another thing, writing well counts personally. If writing on the job is a kind of power, so it is in everyday life. Using words well, confident we can find the right one for almost every occasion, we give a great boost to our self-esteem. Knowing that we don't have to be at a loss for words is also knowing that we can live our lives just that much more successfully. This capacity for language—to speak it, write it, and read it—is one of our defining characteristics as human beings. We are preeminently language-making creatures, creating and created by the language we use. What is a feeling, a thought, or an urge without a word to express it? Little more than *brute* force. To grow as writers, therefore, is to grow as human beings, into greater self-awareness, greater intellectual power, greater sensitivity, greater capacity for pleasure.

EXERCISE

Bring to class a piece of writing that you think is good. It may be a complete piece, if it is short, or an excerpt from something longer. It may be fact or fiction, poetry or prose. It may even be something you've written. Write a paragraph explaining why you like it and what parts are good.

END NOTES

1. Lester Faigley and Thomas P. Miller, "What We Learn from Writing on the Job," *College English* 44 (Oct., 1982): 564.
2. Maxine Hairston, "Not All Errors Are Created Equal," *College English* 43 (Dec., 1981): 798.
3. Edward Anderson, "Language and Success," *College English* 43 (Dec., 1981): 807–12.

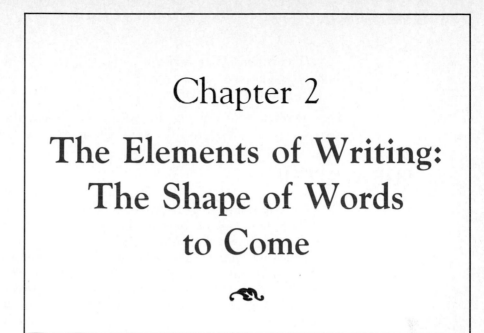

Chapter 2

The Elements of Writing: The Shape of Words to Come

The poet's eye, in a fine frenzy rolling,
Doth glance from heaven to earth, from earth to heaven;
And, as the imagination bodies forth
The forms of things unknown, the poet's pen
Turns them to shapes, and gives to airy nothing
A local habitation and a name.
 (William Shakespeare, A *Midsummer Night's Dream*)

What William Shakespeare says of his poet is true of all writers. We take the "airy nothings" of ideas, facts, and feelings and turn them into "solid somethings." Think of the ways we talk about writing as if it had weight, texture, color, sound, taste, sometimes even a smell. "That's heavy stuff," we say, or "deep," or if we're serious, "That's substantial." It "sparkles" and "shines." It "flows." It's "spicy," "sharp," "crisp," or "spongy." If we're having trouble with it, it's "fuzzy" or "cloudy." Sometimes it's "shallow." Other times, it plain "stinks." You know what I mean if you've ever been *moved* by a story, *tickled* by a joke, *illuminated* by an informative essay, or *rubbed the wrong way* by a newspaper editorial. Writing seems far more real than those tiny black squiggles on the page. What gives these airy nothings their particular heft, shape, and feel and provides them with "a local habitation and a name"? For much of the writing we do there are three answers to this question:

1. The writer.
2. The audience.
3. The thesis.

Here is where a writing begins. Singly or together, these three elements give a writing its individual look, sound, mood, and design.

THE WRITER

Before you read any further, take a few minutes to write a brief paragraph describing the following cartoon. Do it in any way you wish. You'll use your description as you continue reading.

"Le style est l'homme même [style is the man himself]," said the eighteenth-century naturalist Georges Buffon. Our *style,* the choices we make when we write, is the signature of our personalities; even objective writing in school or on the job bears the mark of its author in one way or another. Look for a moment at your cartoon description. Did you write factually, as if you were doing a school assignment, or imaginatively, to have some fun? Did you first put the picture inside a frame and call it a cartoon or jump right into the description? Did you refer to yourself, an "I"? Where did you begin, with the man, the animal in the maze, or the creature in the cage? What is that first animal, mouse or rat? And the second, ape or monkey? Is the man in the white coat a scientist or researcher? What is

Used by permission of Don Dougherty and *Saturday Review.*

he doing? What is the caged creature doing? Did you mention the timer or the door? The pencil or the clipboard? How many sentences did you write? How many words in each? Were they big or little words?

Each of these choices put a little bit of you onto paper. You can no more avoid expressing yourself when you write than you can avoid breathing. Oh, you can create a false self, and if you're clever, few will notice, but even that false self will be your choice and an ironic reflection of your character. Since, therefore, we figure in our writing no matter what we do, even when there is no "I" in it, we ought to capitalize on our presence and turn it to good advantage. The two most potent ways to do this are the roles we play and the personas we create.

Role

In the last chapter I spoke of writers as players of a game. Here I want you to imagine them as players in the theatrical sense. What an actor does when he steps on a stage is play a role; what a writer does when she sits down at her desk, her stage, is much the same. When an actor acts a role, he brings a script to life by giving those words on the page a dramatic interpretation. He does something *to* a script *for* his audience. When a writer plays a role, she does something to a *subject* for her audience, using her knowledge and experience to give that subject shape and substance. A role is a writer's purpose put into action as the writer writes; it consists of a subject at the center of attention, a particular audience to perform for, and something to do to that subject. Following are the writer's most common roles.

Reporter   Remember "show and tell" back in grammar school? That's what a reporter aims to do: accurately present a subject to an audience. What the writer feels about the subject is less important than the who, what, when, where, and why of it. As she writes, she pays scant attention to herself and only slightly more to her audience. A reporter writing about our scientist cartoon might say: "A researcher appears to be timing a mouse as it runs a maze. While his back is turned, a monkey in a cage directs the mouse to the exit."

Critic   The critic's role is to evaluate a subject, sifting, weighing, and ranking; praising or condemning. Because her writing argues for her opinion, a critic is more involved with a subject than a reporter is. An example: "In this mildly amusing cartoon, a scientist fails to see that his experiment is being ruined by a foolish-looking monkey. The cartoon might be more effective if the monkey's gesturing paw were drawn skillfully."

Poet   The word *poet* comes from the Greek word for "maker." What a poet—or any artist, for that matter—does is make up things according to her powers of imagination. The poet is the writer as storyteller, dramatist, and versifier. Her aim is not so much accuracy or judgment as pleasure. "Professor Edwin Schmaltz scribbles frantically on his notepad. Behind him his tidy scientific universe is about to crumble. 'Let's see,' he pauses, pencil in hand, 'I need two dozen eggs, a loaf of bread, and a bottle of Worcestershire sauce. Is the supermarket still open?' "

Participant   In this role the writer becomes the subject of her writing. She is a kind of seismograph, recording all the shocks of feeling or insight that something—an idea, person, or event—gives her. "I can't figure out what the silly-looking ape is doing. Is he showing the rat how to get home free or reaching for some lunch? I'll bet the scientist is going to be angry when he finds what a botch his experiment has become."

Teacher   The teacher aims to help her audience understand a subject. Information and accuracy alone are not sufficient. What matters is not simply the ingredients for baking bread but learning how to bake it; not simply dates, persons, and places from the Civil War but a meaningful portrait of the event; not simply the details of a cartoon but its message. "The cartoon implies that life is always just about to play a big joke on us. We dare not turn our backs or relax even for a moment."

Persuader   This writer aims to change her audience's thinking or behavior. Explicitly or implicitly the persuasive writer bases her writing on an "ought": "You ought to believe this" or "You shouldn't do that." For example: "Life is always about to play a big joke on us. This the cartoon makes clear. Don't turn your back or relax, even for a moment."

Friend or Enemy   The writer's audience becomes her subject, and her aim is to change its self-image by what she writes. She gives verbal strokes or strikes, praising or sympathizing on the one hand, or denouncing, scorning, and belittling on the other: "If you can't figure out what that ape is doing, you're less intelligent than he is!"

What role did you use to write your description? Identify it in the margin next to your paragraph. If you're like most writers, you played more than one role at once: reporter-critic, poet-participant, reporter-teacher-critic. That is the natural thing to do but also part of what makes writing difficult. Here is a reporter-participant-teacher-critic:

> In this cartoon a monkey is guiding a mouse through a maze while a scientist's back is turned. I suppose most people root for the monkey and hope he gets the mouse through the maze before the scientist turns around. Not me. I wanted someone to come through that door and wake him up. He looks dazed. I suppose my sympathies have been shaped by the crown of my own balding head. Baldies are always portrayed as wimps or villains, and I don't like it.

Complex though your multirole performance may have been, you probably didn't spend much time planning how to write it. You just followed your instincts about what the occasion called for. As you should. There are times, however, when you'll want to consider your roles with care: when the subject is difficult, the audience unfamiliar, or the occasion important. Fail to match yourself to the subject and occasion and you'll end up developing your subject inappropriately. This happens in college writing when writers take too narrow a view of their assignments. They assume their assignments call upon them to be reporters only, but they are also often asked to be teachers, critics, even participants.

Here are three simple questions to help you choose the right roles for every situation:

1. What roles am I qualified by knowledge or experience to play with this subject?
2. What roles does my audience expect me to play?
3. What roles will enable me to write most interestingly and significantly about this subject?

If you can identify your roles early in a writing project you'll have a better idea of how to prepare, what parts of your subject to write about, how to write about them, and sometimes even how to organize them.

EXERCISES

1. Below are five passages about education. Identify the roles each writer is playing and be able to explain how you made your decisions.

a. Back in the days when everyone was old and stupid or young and foolish and me and Sugar were the only ones just right, this lady moved on our block with nappy hair and proper speech and no makeup. And quite naturally we laughed at her, laughed the way we did at the junk man who went about his business like he was some big-time president and his sorry-ass horse his secretary. And we kinda hated her too, hated the way we did the winos who cluttered up our parks and pissed on our handball walls and stank up our hallways and stairs so you couldn't halfway play hide-and-seek without a goddamn gas mask. Miss Moore was her name. The only woman on the block with no first name. And she was black as hell, cept for her feet, which were fish-white and spooky. And she was always planning these boring-ass things for us to do, us being my cousin, mostly, who lived on the block cause we all moved North the same time and to the same apartment then spread out gradual to breathe. And our parents would yank our heads into some kinda shape and crisp up our clothes so we'd be presentable to travel with Miss Moore, who always looked like she was going to church, though she never did. Which is just one of the things the grownups talked about when they talked behind her back like a dog. But when she came calling with some sachet she'd sewed up or some gingerbread she'd made or some book, why then they'd all be too embarrassed to turn her down and we'd get handed over all spruced up. She'd been to college and said it was only right that she should take responsibility for the young ones' education, and she not even related by marriage or blood. So they'd go for it.

(Toni Cade Bambara, *Gorilla My Love* [New York: Random, 1972])

b. One cannot believe in education and not believe in excellence. The mark of true learning is that one knows what one does not know, with the corollary that one always wants to know more. If knowledge is itself good, is a basic human hunger, like that for food, then it should spur some to excel, to learn what others do not know, to find ways of spending more time learning more things, endlessly.

(Garry Wills, "Education elitist? You bet!" *Chicago Sun-Times* 10 May 1983)

c. Except for the fragmentary and specialized knowledge associated with our work, we have only the most superficial information about the world. We do not read well and we do not read books. Except for a few childish folk tales, we know nothing whatever about history, and being ignorant of the past, we have no realistic idea of the future. We are surrounded by, and entirely dependent on, a technology which we cannot understand. We are intellectually *passive*, watching and listening but never understanding or remembering. Our memories are so weak that the introduction of a simple zip code causes a near panic and evokes angry howls of "I don't like it." We remember only that we are Americans, so we must therefore be educated. But can you identify, even vaguely, Charlemagne? Can you extract a simple square root? Do you know what a square root *is*? What is the capital of Illinois? Who were, in order, the last six Presidents of the United States? How much is eight times eight?

(Roger Price, *The Great Roob Revolution* [New York: Random, 1970])

d. Last September, with the aid of an unusually generous fellowship, I enrolled in a doctoral program in Italian Renaissance art history. Although I had selected this particular career path as a college freshman and had never seriously considered any alternatives, I experienced severe doubts as I packed my bags and prepared to re-enter the academic life after a year away. For although my return to school elicited a few wistful wishes for happiness and success, it primarily provoked a chorus of lugubrious [mournful] warnings about the "lack of relevance" of my chosen field and the uncertainty of my professional and financial future.

I coped easily with the tired jokes about Ph.D.'s driving cabs from the lawyers, doctors and M.B.A.'s of my acquaintance. But when a professor who had encouraged me to apply for graduate study sat me down and described in lurid detail his 20 years of frustration and comparative poverty as an academic, I began to be disturbed. And it was something of a shock to hear him say, as he leafed through the pages of his latest book, "I spent 10 years of my life on this thing, and what do I get? A thousand bucks and a pat on the back from a couple of colleagues. Sometimes I think it isn't worth it anymore."

(Leslie S. P. Brown, "Who Cares About the Renaissance," *Newsweek* 11 Apr. 1983)

e. A liberal education is at the heart of a civil society, and at the heart of a liberal education is the act of teaching. To speak directly of how a liberal education prepares students for a civic role, I must begin with the teacher.

The teacher chooses. The teacher chooses how to structure choice. The teacher's power and responsibility lie in choosing where everyone will begin and how, from that beginning, the end will be shaped. The choice of that final form lies in the teacher's initial act. The phrase *final form* sounds more arbitrary and imposing than it should. No good teacher ever wants to control the contour of another's mind. That would not be teaching, it would be a form of terrorism. But no good teacher wants the contour of another's mind to be blurred. Somehow the line between encouraging a design and imposing a specific stamp must be found and clarified. That is where the teacher first begins to choose.

(A. Bartlett Giametti, "The American Teacher," *Harper's* July 1980)

2. Imagine you are going to write on the following subjects. What roles are you qualified by knowledge or experience to take for each one? List them. If you're not qualified to write on a subject, write *none*.

a. Automobiles.
b. Parents.
c. Racial integration.
d. Skiing.
e. Big cities.
f. Suburbia.
g. Freedom.
h. Poverty.
i. Death.
j. The feminist movement.

3. Choose one of the preceding subjects for which you have listed at least two roles and write a separate paragraph in each of those roles.

4. Explain what roles the following subjects and occasions require.

a. An essay on skiing for a freshman English class.
b. A report on racial integration for a sociology class.
c. A letter about automobiles to a newspaper editor.
d. A letter to someone whose spouse has just died.
e. An article on parents for *Parents' Magazine*.
f. A movie review for the campus newspaper.
g. A letter of application for a job.
h. An essay about a novel for a literature class.
i. A "Dear John" letter.
j. A letter to the President of the United States.

Persona

The voice we hear speaking in a piece of writing has a name: *persona*. The word is Latin and originally referred to the masks worn by the ancient Greek and Roman actors. Crafted in bold smiles, frowns, or grimaces, these masks fixed the personalities of the characters and projected their emotions and attitudes so that even spectators back in the cheap seats could see them. There were even tin mouthpieces built into them to help amplify the actor's voice. The persona in a writing does much the same thing for a writer.

Whenever we write, we are like the ancient actors. We im-person-ate ourselves, projecting part of our personalities through our language. I know that sounds suspicious in an age that made popular a song titled "I Gotta Be Me." But it's true. Writing requires impersonation. Complex as we are, we can never be all of ourselves at once. We have to choose, consciously or unconsciously, how we shall appear, and these choices create the person the world sees, one of the masks of our social self, true or false to what we really are, right or wrong for the occasion. From what word do you think we have derived our words *person* and *personality?* In our writing, these choices create a persona, one mask among many in our repertoire of verbal selves. The choices that create this persona concern the distance we put between ourselves and our audiences and the attitudes we take to our subjects.[1]

Distance   Between ourselves and others we keep a certain distance. People who know each other well are "close"; they "keep in touch." Those who are only acquaintances or brought together by business separate themselves by real space, in the United States often a full yard. Many times a physical barrier divides them: the lectern between teacher and students, the counter between customer and sales person, the desk between boss and employee. But the greatest distance is that between speaker and listener on some ceremonial occasion. The speaker's voice is frequently amplified or recorded, he doesn't know his listeners, and he speaks to them, often across great physical space, not as individuals but as an assembly.

We create similar distances in our writing when we sense differences between ourselves and our audience: differences in age, knowledge, class, culture, or era. The closer a writer feels herself to her audience, the more conversational her writing sounds, almost as if she were talking rather than writing. The more distant she feels, the more her writing sounds like just that, like writing between strangers. Here is the first of three descriptions of our scientist cartoon. Watch what happens to the relations between writer and reader in each one:

> After studying this cartoon for twenty minutes, I think I've finally figured out what the monkey is doing. It is a monkey, don't you think? Actually, I thought it looked more like Grover from "Sesame Street." That made this picture a little hard to understand. Why would Grover be in a cage, and is he pointing or trying to grab the mouse?
>
> But anyway, I think that since Bonzo is pointing the way for the very bewildered mouse while the brilliant scientist foolishly has his back turned on them, the chimp is obviously making a fool out of the man. Einstein will think he has a very smart mouse, who got through the maze in record time, when in fact what he has is a wise guy version of Cheetah.

In a clear example of "talker-style" writing this writer makes us feel as if we're listening to her rather than reading her. Her continual self-reference, her questions to her audience, her use of contractions and slang, her sentences that seem to meander from point to point, her "but anyway" that gets her back on track—all these make her sound as if she is thinking out loud for us. She takes for granted that we know what cartoon she's describing, what "Sesame Street" is, and who Grover, Bonzo, Cheetah, and Einstein are; in other words, she assumes we have had the same education she has and know children's television and Tarzan movies. She feels close to her readers and comfortable with them. We can identify this distance by a little diagram:

Intimate←——The Writer

The distance widens somewhat in the second example:

> While Dr. Frankenstein, no doubt a behavioral psychologist, is busily recording "observable and measurable" behavior, Bongo the ape exhibits what appears to be some sort of "cognitive activity." Old Frankenstein's close attention prevents him from noticing some interesting phenomena. His hairy test subject appears either about to add variety to his diet or amuse himself by directing a wide-eyed, perhaps scared rat through the maze. So much for the good doctor's findings.

This writer, too, assumes we know what cartoon he's writing about, and that brings him close to his readers, as do his name-calling, his closing sentence fragment, and the quotation marks he puts around the phrases *observable and measurable* and *cognitive activity* to let us know he is playing with the jargon of behaviorist psychology. But he never refers directly to himself or his audience. His language is familiar but not casual or slangy. And his sentences don't wander as the first writer's do. See how the main clause of the first sentence comes in the middle, ". . . Bongo the ape exhibits . . ." and how in the next to last sentence one part is balanced against another: "about to *add* variety to his diet or *amuse* himself"? These kinds of sentences take some planning, not what you often hear when one person talks to another. This writer is performing in public for an audience he doesn't know well. He feels comfortable with them, but he's thought for a moment at least about his performance, as a public writer should. His version is a combination of "writer-style" and "talker-style."

Public←————————The Writer

The last writer takes nothing for granted:

> The scientist in the cartoon is conducting an experiment to see how long it takes a mouse to traverse a maze. Another research animal, a monkey, gestures from a cage suspended above the mouse. While the scientist's back is turned, the monkey shows the mouse the quickest way through the maze and alters thereby the outcome of the experiment. If the cartoon has a message, it is the seeming conspiracy of the subjects of science against the scientist, actively opposing him, betraying his experiments, and confounding his theories. Reality resists our knowing.

This writer isn't speaking to us; he is *writing* to everyone for everyone. The *our* in the last sentence is all humankind. Accordingly, he tells everything: what his subject is, what is in the cartoon, and what it all adds up to. His language befits someone writing for all time. No slang here. It is less familiar and more precise than in the preceding examples. There is nothing conversational about words like *traverse, conducting,* or *conspiracy.* The only time his language lets down its hair, even a little bit, is in the repeated sounds of *reality resists,* but this, too, has a ceremonial formality about it. As do his sentences. In sentences three and four, introductions delay the main clauses:

> While the scientist's back is turned,
> the monkey shows the mouse the quickest way. . . .

> If the cartoon has a message,
> it is the seeming conspiracy of the subjects of science. . . .

Both sentences also contain balanced structures:

> the monkey shows . . . and alters

> actively opposing . . . betraying . . . and confounding his theories.

Its careful and slightly self-conscious craftsmanship makes the writing seem premeditated and the writer detached from his audience.

Ceremonial◄────────────────The Writer

In sum, the way to vary the distance between you and your reader—and change your persona in the process—is to manipulate the four variables that distinguish writer-style from talker-style: (1) your presence and that of your readers, (2) what you assume your reader knows about you and your subject, (3) your language, and (4) sentence style.

Ceremonial◄──────Public◄──────Intimate◄──────The Writer

Writer-style	*Talker-style*
No *I* or *you*	*I* or *you*
The writer assumes the reader knows little	The writer assumes the reader knows much
Less familiar words, very precise words	Slang, contractions, familiar words
Main clauses late, complete sentences, balanced parts	Main clauses early, fragments permitted, add-on style

Where would you place your cartoon description on this diagram, and what helped you make up your mind? Write a sentence or two of explanation. If your writing has several features from the left list and repeats them frequently, you have written writer-style and sound formal and relatively far away from your readers. Several from the right list, and you have written talker-style, narrowing your distance by an intimate, casual voice. If you have mixed the features—familiar but precise words, few contractions, occasional references to yourself or your readers, sentences that begin with main clauses but balance some of their parts—you have produced public writing of the kind you do for school or on the job.

Attitude The second way we create a persona is by expressing our feelings about a subject: positive, negative, or neutral. These feelings may be moderate or intense, subdued or forceful, depending upon how charged our language is. In expressions of attitude, language is everything, words positive, negative, or somewhere in between. We can represent these possible attitudes with another diagram:

Words positive in their feelings we call *honorific* terms. Those that are negative are *pejorative* terms. These words, adjectives and adverbs mostly, make explicit judgments:

Honorific: The *knowledgeable* or *intelligent* scientist

vs.

Pejorative: The *ignorant* or *dull-witted* scientist

Other words carry their attitude as a kind of emotional baggage. We call these emotional associations the *connotative meaning* of a word (its connotation). They become associated with the definition of a word by the ways in which that word has been used. Consider the words *brilliant* and *cunning*. They both describe someone of keen intelligence, but most people would rather be known as *brilliant* than *cunning*, even though the latter word originally meant "to know." The reason is the difference in connotations. *Cunning* was so often associated with guile—intelligence in the cause of deception—that the word gradually acquired the negative connotation it has today. Likewise, we distinguish among persons who are *astute*, *brainy*, and *clever*, but the differences lie more in our feelings about them than in their respective IQs. We express our different feelings in words with different connotations.

If we put both kinds of words together, those explicit in attitude with those that make implicit judgments, we get something like this:

Positive
   A stout scientist is conducting an experiment to discover how quickly a mouse can scamper through a maze.

The Writer ——— + attitude

Neutral

A heavy researcher is making an investigation to determine how long it takes a laboratory animal to run a maze.

The Writer ————— Neutral attitude

Negative

Some fat egghead has concocted a scheme to see how fast a rat can race through a maze.

The Writer ———
                   — attitude

Now examine your description of the cartoon. <u>Underline</u> any positive terms, (circle) negative ones, [bracket] neutral terms. <u>Draw a diagram</u> like the ones shown to illustrate your overall attitude.

Creating a Persona When you sit down at your desk you don't have a choice of whether to wear a mask or bare your soul to the world. You choose to wear your "baring my soul" mask or some other, true or false to you, but wear a mask you must. The trick is choosing the right one, right for you and the occasion. It is hard for writers to see and hear the personality they create with their words, but the right choice of persona is almost everything in public writing. Bring your audience in too close or be too strenuous in your attitudes and you'll sound presumptuous or shrill. "Keep your distance!" they'll want to respond; "Get off my back!" Hold them too far away or be too cool in your attitudes and they'll think you "standoffish," a strange species of cold fish.

You probably didn't plan for distance and attitude as you thought about describing the cartoon, any more than you thought about what role to take. For some kinds of writing—usually spontaneous, personal, or casual—we put on the right mask so easily we don't have to worry about our choices. But whenever there is important public writing to be done, you ought to have some strategies to help you find which persona is best for you and your audience. One strategy is to start right in on your writing project, but *listen* to what you're writing; recognize that it won't be effective until you hear the right voice. Imagine a movie actor or actress reading your writing. Who would that be? Does it sound like the kind of person who should be reading about your subject to your audience?

A second strategy is to combine the two diagrams presented previously and draw the persona you want to create. "See" your mask before you turn it into words. Here are the options you have to choose from as you draw your diagram:

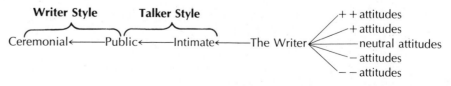

A third strategy is to revise for persona. Do your writing, and when you've finished, examine it for those features that create distance and attitude. *Then* draw your persona diagram. Reread. Any words or sentences that do not conform to your diagram you will want to change. No matter how you proceed, however, you should never write anything that you can't imagine yourself saying. That doesn't mean you actually would say it, and it won't really be speech, but it should *sound* like it, humorous speech or serious, formal or informal.

EXERCISES

1. Arrange the following passages according to the distance between writer and reader, from near to far, talker-style to writer-style. Be able to explain your ranking according to the four variables that create distance: (1) the presence of writer and reader, (2) what the writer assumes about the audience's knowledge, (3) sentence style, and (4) language.[2]

a. The Colombia-Excelsior, like many old-fashioned luxury hotels, faces the train station. In the lobby, scruffy, animated young men in jeans and sneakers sprawled on the green baise furniture, hunkered down on the double stairway that curved away to the mezzanine, and loitered beneath an enormous chandelier, talking loudly enough to set its cut glass quivering. Professional tennis players, they had gathered in Genoa in February 1982 for the Bitti Mergamo Memorial Tournament, one of twenty-two events on the World Championship Tennis circuit, which offers $8 million in prize money.

(Michael Mewshaw, "Say it ain't so, Bjorn," *Harper's* June 1983)

b. There is something suicidal in retirement, just as there is something suicidal in society's callousness toward the old. So forget the young. You worked to get what you have. Keep it; enjoy it. They are young and strong; let them struggle. It isn't your problem, you shouldn't take the rap. Don't leave your job one minute before you have to—even if you hate it—unless you can't get out of bed. You have something to give. It isn't true that to be old is to be incompetent. Fight. Don't quit. Elect your own to legislative office. Band together: the old-age party, the life party. Don't let them convince you that the "golden years" await you. It's a lie. No one should go down without a struggle. Kick. Scream. Be heard all the way to Washington. You have nothing to lose but your dignity and your life.

(Kenneth Bernard, "The First Step to the Cemetery," *Newsweek* 22 Feb. 1982)

c. Technology is applied science. Engineers are the people who make the applications. They are by nature not dreamers but doers—builders, tinkerers, realists. Typically they are people who showed a fascination with gadgetry from an early age, who pulled radios apart and put them back together while other kids were shooting marbles. When they get to engineering school, they are taught to think rationally and to express themselves in mathematical terms. They learn to reason analytically, to pull a problem apart and examine it logically and resolve it with precision. They learn that there is a single right answer to every question. They learn about elegance and simplicity, but not about subtlety or ambiguity.

(Frank Rose, "The Mass Production of Engineers,"
Esquire May 1983)

d. People by and large use the language they are exposed to, and the growth of what to you and me might be an objectionable rhetorical style is almost impossible to stunt. If most of your co-workers are talking about parameters, interfacing, areas and subareas, modules, cognitive transformations, and the like, it probably won't be long before you, too, start talking about these strange intangibles. The human mind being what it is, you might even start constructing large verbal edifices of pure gobbledygook yourself. There are thousands of people in government and academia who specialize in turning out unsightly cathedrals of verbiage, and these people give the impression that they understand one another, though common folk like me haven't the vaguest notion of what they are talking about.

(Thomas H. Middleton, "I Share Your Concern—
Very Much," *Saturday Review* Nov. 1981)

e. As a man who has resolutely been trying to take off weight for a year or so, I resent the low estate into which the potato has fallen in the eyes of diet-regulators. They have been flagrantly unfair to my favorite dinner food.

Actually the potato has been much maligned—denigrated as a source of vitamins and minerals, and inflated as a source of calories. The fact is that the potato *au naturel* contains no more calories than a raw apple and is just as nourishing.

(Sydney J. Harris, "Boiled, mashed, duchesse, fried,
baked, scalloped . . ." *Chicago Sun-Times* 12 Dec.
1978)

2. Choose one of the topics from Role Exercise 2, page 19, and one of the roles you have listed for it. Write a paragraph about it to the members of your class, sharing your knowledge, experiences, or feelings. When you have finished, diagram the persona you have created by your style of writing; use the model on page 24 to guide you. Then write another version of the paragraph. Don't change your subject but do change your message about that subject by changing your persona. Shift your distance and attitude: change from writer-style to talker-style or vice-versa; change your attitude from positive to negative or negative to positive. Use a thesaurus, if necessary, to help you find the right words. Draw a diagram of this new persona. Here's an example:

I and *you* contractions

Negative attitude

Sentence fragments

Familiar words

You say you're thinking about buying a new car soon? Well, I advise you to think long and hard before buying a car like mine. It's put together with the cheapest materials available to man, and it's the most annoying car you'll ever drive. Open the paper-thin doors and check the shoddy interior, complete with unreadable gauges and impossible-to-control switches. Turn the key and start the engine. Wait. Give it one more chance. There! The noisy, underpowered engine has finally decided to turn over. Driving down the road you'll hear squeaks and rattles you never thought possible. Sure, the car gets forty miles to the gallon, but the dealer forgot to tell you the engine runs only on expensive premium-unleaded gas. So much for economy! Take my advice: buy any other kind of car.

—Steve Duda

Intimate——The Writer
— — Negative

Writer-style sentences:
Main clauses late and
balanced patterns
No *I* or *you*
Less familiar words

Positive attitude

No contractions

If the purchase of a new automobile lies in his future, a wise investor should consider very carefully an automobile like this writer's. It is the least expensive automobile being driven today and one that will fill his day with one astonishment after another. Upon opening the doors refined to elegant thinness, he will observe an interior laid out by relaxed craftsmen, complete with gauges and levers that challenge his visual acuity and manual dexterity. While he turns the ignition repeatedly to start the automobile, he will enjoy a brief interlude. Then, at last, he will hear the robust sound of the economy-sized engine. Once under way, he will experience the sounds of driving as he has never experienced them before. Yes, this automobile has a mileage rating of forty miles per gallon; however, the man of means will be pleased to know that it consumes a premium fuel appropriate to his position. This is one automobile, therefore, that allows for both economy and conspicuous consumption. If one is wise, he will compare this automobile with others before making his purchase.

+ Positive
Ceremonial————————The Writer

3. Write a memo or brief letter in response to one of the following situations. In each instance, the persona you choose and the way you create it will be crucial to the success of your writing.

a. You are a reasonably conscientious composition student who would like to do well in your English class. And you *need* to do well—at least a B—to keep your scholarship. Doing well means, in part, keeping in the good graces of your instructor.

But you have a problem. You've just been offered an all-expenses-paid one-week dirigible tour of the Bahamas that leaves tomorrow. You imagine your dirigible drifting lazily from one green island to the next. You can see yourself swimming in the warm blue Atlantic or lying on a long white beach under a cloudless sky, sipping a tall, cool drink. One thing is sure: you want desperately to take this trip. You work part-time, go to school full-time, and haven't had a day off the whole term. The weather outside is awful. This will be the vacation of a lifetime.

Unfortunately, you recognize your instructor will not look kindly upon frivolous absences from class, certainly not vacations in the middle of the term. You stop by your instructor's office to explain your impending absence, but he/she is nowhere to be found. You can't wait, and you can't come back—the blimp is about to leave. But you can't just disappear. Your instructor will wonder where you are—you haven't missed a class so far. You decide to leave a note. Write that note. Oh, by the way, you are a scrupulously honest person who *never* lies.

b. You have an acquaintance by the name of I. M. Leach, who thinks you are the greatest person in the world. Poor Leach, however, is an over-sensitive, ill-tempered, slovenly misfit. He has no friends, not even you; nevertheless, he is a human being and you don't want to hurt his feelings if you can help it. He has enough troubles. But you can't agree to his plea to accompany you on your Bahamas trip. He has left an eager, excited letter in your mailbox, begging to be included. Human decency demands a response. Write a return in which you refuse his plea. Again, you would never lie, not even to Leach.

c. Buzz Burrdock, blimp-owner and captain, has posted a summer job opening for blimp-holders in your school's employment office. A blimp-holder is one of those people who grab the lines when a dirigible lands and hold the ship until it can be moored. The only requirement is that employees must weigh 100 pounds. A bag of sand would be perfect for the job if it could reach up and grab the line. No other skills or intellectual abilities are needed. You recognize that this is your opportunity to see the world, to begin living life in the fast lane, to move with, well, if not the jet-set, then the blimp set. But how will you distinguish yourself from the hundreds of others who are also sure to apply for this job? Write a letter of application that will get you noticed and persuade Captain Burrdock to hire you. Again, you would never lie.

4. Write a 500-word letter introducing you to the members of your composition class. You can't say everything about yourself in the space you have, so give your letter unity and focus by making it a "Dear Class: Here's what it's like being a . . ." letter. Pick some part of your life and use that as the vantage point for describing yourself and your world. What does it feel like to be a college freshman? And how does the world look to a college freshman? What is it like doing the job you do or living where you live, and what does the world look like from your job or address? What is it like being eighteen or nineteen, twenty-nine or fifty-nine? What is it like being a southerner, a Minnesotan, or a student from another country? Whatever perspective you choose, create a persona comfortable to you and appropriate to the occasion. Draw a persona diagram (see p. 24) of the personality you'd like to project; this will guide you as you write and revise.

5. Analyze the narrator of something you've read recently, fact or fiction: first draw a diagram of the narrator's persona (see p. 24); then write a brief 500-word essay explaining the narrator's role, distance, and attitude. To prepare for your essay, look closely at the narrator's relationship with his or her readers, sentence style, and language.

❧ THE AUDIENCE

Most writers prefer to work alone. The presence of others, especially those who want to peer over our shoulders, is a distraction. So we shut ourselves up, in a cabin in the woods if we can afford it, in an office, a spare room, or some quiet corner of the library. The silence and solitude help us concentrate; unfortunately they bring with them troubles of their own. Compare writing and talking. When you talk to someone, that person is there in front of you or at least you hear a voice at the other end of the line. You have only to hold up your end of the conversation; he does the rest. While you're talking you can judge by his gestures or tone of voice whether you've got his attention or you're getting through. But when you write, you have no listener to help you. You're all alone, remember? You have to hold up *both* ends of the conversation. That's the first thing to be understood about a writer's audience.

Audiences and Readers

The second is that the audience for a writing and the actual readers of that writing are not necessarily the same. Imagine for a moment that you've just finished a history paper for school. There it sits, neatly typed, on the edge of your desk. A friend sees it, picks it up, and caught by its title, begins to read. Now she is certainly a reader of your writing but just as certainly *not* the audience for that writing. Your history teacher is. Eventually, unless he quits, retires, or dies, this audience will become one of your readers, but the two are not always the same.

There is one more wrinkle in the problem of the writer's audience. You have written a paper for your history teacher, but who exactly is that audience? You see him for three hours each week and occasionally after class. You know what he looks and sounds like. You know he wears ties with tiny animals on them and that his shoes need shining. You know he likes southern cooking, because he said so during a lecture on the Civil War, and what his opinions of Lincoln's presidency are, because you took notes. But what does this add up to? You know next to nothing about this man, yet you've written a paper for him anyway. How is that possible?

What you have done, whether you've thought about it or not, is combine your fragmentary knowledge of your real history teacher with hunches about history teachers in general. The audience for your history paper, and for most public writing you do, exists as much in your mind as in the real world. This is a third thing to know about a writer's audience: it is a fiction, a mental image made up to substitute for the real audience you would have before you if you were talking to someone. Your imaginary "my history teacher" audience has given you someone to talk to on paper and made it easier for you to write. Good writers have to be like good movie or television actors. Neither have real audiences. Just as actors play to the camera, writers play to the audience in their mind's eye.

Consider this excerpt from an essay published in *Newsweek* magazine:

We Americans are a charitable and humane people: we have institutions devoted to every good cause from rescuing homeless cats to preventing World

War III. But what have we done to promote the art of thinking? Certainly we make no room for thought in our daily lives. Suppose a man were to say to his friends, "I'm not going to PTA tonight (or choir practice or the baseball game) because I need some time to myself, some time to think"? Such a man would be shunned by his neighbors; his family would be ashamed of him. What if a teen-ager were to say, "I'm not going to the dance tonight because I need some time to think"? His parents would immediately start looking in the Yellow Pages for a psychiatrist. We are all too much like Julius Caesar: we fear and distrust people who think too much. We believe that almost anything is more important than thinking. . . .

It is easy to understand the causes of this prejudice against thinking. One problem is that to most of us, thinking looks suspiciously like loafing. Homo sapiens in deep thought is an uninspiring sight. He leans back in his chair, props up his feet, puffs on his pipe and stares into space. He gives every appearance of wasting time; he reminds us more of Dagwood and Beetle Bailey than of Shakespeare and Einstein. We wish he would get up and *do* something; mow the lawn, maybe, or wash the car. Our resentment is natural.

(Carolyn Kane, "Thinking: A Neglected Art," *Newsweek* 14 Dec. 1981)

Catch the audience here? This writer is speaking to the fabled Middle Americans of song, story, and stereotype. The *we* she addresses have lawns to mow and cars to wash. *We* are motivated by a strong dose of the work ethic. *We* are concerned citizens and parents; *we* are religious. *We* go to church and PTA meetings and give to our favorite charities. *We* are educated enough to know who Einstein is and see the allusion to Shakespeare's *Julius Caesar:* "Yond Cassius has a lean and hungry look;/He thinks too much: such men are dangerous." But *we* also read the funny papers and get the references to Dagwood and Beetle Bailey. Does such an audience actually exist? Well, perhaps, but the actual readership for *Newsweek* is certainly more diverse than this. What Carolyn Kane has done is to *make up* an audience that will provide a focus for her protest. The majority of her real-life readers probably share just enough characteristics with her fictional audience—where they live, their pastimes, their education, lifestyles, or values—that they can envision themselves as members of that audience and take her message to heart.

Imagining an Audience

Audience works both ways. It helps writers find a role, persona, and something to say, but it also draws real readers into a writing and helps them read. This means that we have to be realistic and make accurate assessments of our potential readers as we create an audience in our imaginations. If we pitch our writing too high, to an audience better educated than our real readers or educated differently, these real readers will think we're writing gobbledygook. If we pitch our writing too low, our readers will think us condescending or, worse, simpleminded. Readers call writing good when they can read it with unself-conscious ease. You will put them at ease and go far to create the audience in your mind's eye if you can answer the following questions as you work through a writing project:

1. How much does my audience know about me and my subject?
2. Why are they reading?
3. How much time do they have for their reading?
4. Where are they doing their reading?
5. How do they see themselves as they read?

That last question needs some comment. Your real readers see themselves in two lights, as you imagine them in your audience image and as they imagine themselves. If you imagine them in an unflattering light, they will see themselves portrayed that way in your prose, an image that conflicts with their own more positive self-appraisal. If you want to make them uncomfortable, fine. If not, you run the risk of losing your readers as they slap your writing down in a huff. What to do? Imagine the best version of your audience you can. This does not mean you should toady to your readers; it does mean you should be realistic about others' self-image. Doing so calls upon them to be true to their highest ideals for themselves. The Golden Rule applies to writers as well as everyone else: Write unto others as you would have them write unto you.

EXERCISES

1. Write one-paragraph audience sketches for three of the following, but make each sketch a comparison-contrast. Imagine these readers as *you* think they are and then as you suspect *they* imagine themselves. Describe their attitudes toward themselves and others, their characteristic moods, their feeling about their jobs and life in general, their pet peeves and greatest pleasures. Visualize them by setting them in a scene and putting clothes on their backs. Imagine any quirks they might have.

a. English teachers or some other kind of teacher.
b. The President of the United States or another politician.
c. A famous person no longer living who has influenced the present.
d. A famous person you would like to meet.
e. Americans or some other nationality or ethnic group.
f. The author of something you've read recently.

2. Letter writing.

a. Write two letters of complaint, one in which you sound off and let your readers know how you really feel, the second in which you try to get them to settle your complaint.
b. Write a letter of mixed feelings to a boss, subordinate, friend, spouse, teacher, parent, child, or anyone. Write what you might actually say, then immediately following it put into brackets [ ] what you're really thinking but would never write.[3]

    c. Write an open letter of praise or condemnation to one of the persons or groups named in Exercise 1. Your audience will be the addressee; your readers will be your English instructor and the members of your class.

∾ THE THESIS

The thesis is the point of a writing. Of course, not every writing tries to make a point. In news stories, for example; in certain kinds of business writing; in reports; in instructions; in the stories we tell and the literature we read, the aims are often to inform or give pleasure. These writings are given their shape by a main idea—they don't need a point. But in much of the writing we do and in much that is most complex, we aim to make and prove a point. This point may be important or not, controversial or uncontroversial, arguable or unarguable: "Drivers twice-convicted of drunk driving should lose their licenses forever" or "My vacation in Idaho was the most fun I've ever had." This point, the thesis, is the *central controlling assertion* of every writing in which it appears:

1. It is the single most important part of the writing.
2. It is an umbrella generalization that covers everything a writing says.
3. Everything leads to or follows from the thesis.
4. It is a declarative statement (not a question). In some writings it is a single declarative sentence or part of one; in others it may be a paragraph or even longer. A thesis has no fixed length.

Don't confuse a thesis with a statement of purpose. A *purpose statement* makes an assertion about the writing itself. Writers sometimes begin with a purpose statement for the sake of clarity. Here's one:

> The campaign to educate us about the benefits of the 55-mph limit has been strident and persistent. Somehow this new wonder drug, the 55 limit, is supposed to cure our national energy problem, save lives and cause us all to pursue a more virtuous existence. But wonder drugs often have unfortunate side effects, and this one is no exception. I want to focus your attention on some of these undesirable side effects.
>
> (Charles A. Lave, "The Costs of Going 55,"
> *Newsweek* 23 Oct. 1978)

After proposing to focus his readers' attention on the undesirable side effects of the 55-mph limit, Charles Lave does just that throughout his essay until the end, where he comes at last to his thesis, an assertion about his subject:

> The point is simple: if we are going to insist on manipulating the speed limit to affect energy conservation, then let's at least manipulate it in an effective way.

A thesis may be any kind of assertion:

1. A *persuasive thesis:* We live in an age of such disorienting change and mobility that every social unit is threatened: families, communities, whole regions, even the nation itself. We must direct this change in healthy, productive ways or decline as a nation.
2. A *fact thesis:* We live in an age of change and mobility.
3. A *value judgment:* Technological change and geographic mobility are the most important social phenomena of the twentieth century.
4. A *comparison or contrast thesis:* Not since the turn of the century have we lived through a period of such disorienting technological change and social mobility.
5. A *cause and effect thesis:* The civil rights movement and the growth of large multinational corporations have made ours an age of change and mobility.

The Parts of a Thesis

No matter what it asserts, no matter how it is written, every thesis has at least two parts, a *subject* and an assertion about that subject, called *the key idea:*

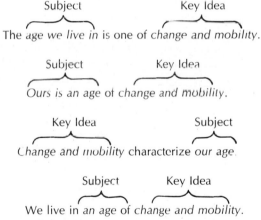

Often, however, a thesis will make an assertion complex enough that it requires an additional statement if it is to be clear and complete. Generally this will be an *explanatory statement* of how, what, or why.

> My premise, which is not amenable to statistics, is that *we are all,* as a whole, as a nation, *dumb.* We simply don't know very much. We are educated only in the way that a chimpanzee who sits at a table and drinks from a saucer is educated compared to a baboon. Our schools have trained us in the technique of modern living, they have turned out excellent technologists, engineers, professional people, but they have not educated us.
> (Roger Price, *The Great Roob Revolution* [New York: Random, 1970])

The subject here is *we* Americans; the key idea to be proved, that we are *dumb*. The first two sentences following the thesis are "what" statements: they describe what the author means by *dumb*. The final sentence, a "why" statement, explains what the author believes to be the cause of our dumbness. We may not agree with his thesis, but we can be sure we understand it and what direction he will take to prove his point. These are the virtues of explanatory statements. They are as useful for a writer figuring out how to support a thesis as they are for a reader wondering what a writer means by an assertion.

Occasionally a writer must follow a thesis with a *qualification* to modify or sharpen the broad claims of the thesis proper. Here is another thesis, complete with the introduction that leads to it and the qualifying statement that follows:

> "The average Yaleman, Class of '24," *Time* magazine reported last year, "makes $25,111 a year [this was written in 1950].
>
> Well, good for him!
>
> But, come to think of it, what does this improbably precise and salubrious [wholesome, healthy] figure mean? Is it, as it appears to be, evidence that if you send your boy to Yale you won't have to work in your old age and neither will he? Is this average a mean or is it a median? What kind of sample is it based on? You could lump one Texas oilman with two hundred hungry free-lance writers and report *their* average income as $25,000-odd a year. The arithmetic is impeccable, the figure is convincingly precise, and the amount of meaning there is in it you could put in your eye.
>
> In just such ways is the secret language of statistics, so appealing in a fact-minded culture, being used to sensationalize, inflate, confuse, and over-simplify. Statistical terms are necessary in reporting the mass data of social and economic trends, business conditions, "opinion" polls, this year's census. But without writers who use the words with honesty and understanding and readers who know what they mean, the result can only be semantic nonsense.
>
> (Darrell Huff, "How to Lie with Statistics," *Harper's* Aug. 1950)

At the beginning of his fourth paragraph, Huff announces his general subject, "the secret language of statistics," and then asserts his key idea, that this language "is being used to sensationalize, inflate, confuse, and over-simplify." But to be sure that we don't assume he is against *all* statistics, he follows his generalization with a qualification recognizing their importance and declaring how they ought to be used.

Where to Put Thesis Statements

If you've studied thesis statements before, you may have been taught to put them at the beginning of a writing. It's true they often do come early, sometimes in the opening line if the assertions are dramatic and can be understood by themselves. More often they come near the end of an introduction that prepares their way. If you write it early, your thesis will act as a reference point while you finish your writing; you can always look back to it to see whether you are sticking to your subject. When your readers come to your writing, a thesis placed early will be like a map, showing them at the outset where you're taking them, perhaps even how you will get there.

But a thesis may just as well come near the end of a writing, perhaps as the last line. If the subject matter and organization are clear, developing consistently in one direction, a thesis at the end will act as a conclusion, pulling together all you have written. For your readers the effect will be like taking an exploratory journey, led by an expert guide, and coming finally to the journey's end at a place they were unsure of but never doubted they would reach. This kind of writing is harder to do because you, the writer, first must take that exploratory journey yourself, making your map as you write. You may get lost and end up losing your reader. But this risk is no reason you shouldn't learn to organize this way. With a little practice you'll become a master guide.

Occasionally you won't want to put your thesis in your writing. You'll have a point to make and you may have written out a thesis for yourself, but to put an explicit thesis statement into your writing may belabor the obvious. This is especially true of stories, description, and satire in which the point is made implicitly by the movement of the piece or emerges from its details. Do take care, however, to be clear to yourself about your point. If you aren't, you can be sure your readers won't be.

Writing Thesis Statements

You might think something as important as thesis statements would be difficult to write. But they aren't if you remember this simple formula:

> My point is that . . .
> What I mean to say is that . . .
> My point is that we live in an age of disorienting change and mobility.
> What I mean to say is that this change and mobility have brought upset and confusion to the members of every social unit: families, communities, whole regions, even the nation itself.

The first part of the formula requires you to state a subject and assert a key idea about it. The second requires you to explain the first, to break it down so that you understand it and see all its parts. You can modify the language of the formula to suit a particular subject and role, for example:

> I want to explain/show/demonstrate how . . .
> I want to persuade ____(the name of an audience)____ to . . .
> I want to prove/argue that . . .

Once the formula has done its work, put it aside and omit it from your final draft. It has helped you find a point to make, but it won't help your readers read. Do what the writers of the preceding examples have done and work your thesis into the design of your writing so that it doesn't stand out from the surrounding sentences. Your readers should read smoothly into and out of your thesis, getting your point but not stumbling over it.

You can use this formula at any stage of the writing process. In the beginning, try as many versions as you need to discover your point and get it right.

> My point is that growing up in a small town was not all bad. What I mean to say is that it had its advantages and disadvantages.

> My point is that Lund's Crossing was a great place to be a kid but not an adult. What I mean to say is that its size and isolation sheltered children and protected them from the ways of the world, but it was a boring place to be an adult.

> My point is that I used to think Lund's Crossing, a small country town, was another "Little House on the Prairie," a great place to grow up, but then I began to realize that its isolation didn't prepare children for adulthood and often made life miserable for those who stayed behind when they reached adulthood. What I mean to say is that until recently I believed all the myths of small-town America sold on television and didn't understand what real-life small towns did to many children and their parents.

After you've finished a draft, write another version to see whether it sums up what you've actually written. If it doesn't, shape your thesis to fit your writing or rewrite to fit the thesis you started with.

As easy as they are to write, however, thesis statements may still go awry in three ways. For one, they may be too general. Although they are generalizations, the best thesis statements are as specific as possible.

Not
> Things aren't the same in my town anymore.

But
> My home town has changed in these thirty years of the American story. It is changing now, will go changing as America changes. Its biography, I suspect, would read much the same as that of all other home towns. Depression and war and prosperity have all left their marks; modern science, modern tastes, manners, philosophies, fears and ambitions have touched my town as indelibly as they have touched New York or Panama City.
> (Eric Sevareid, *This Is Eric Sevareid* [New York: McGraw, 1964])

The more precise you are, the easier it will be to find support for your thesis and easier for your readers to know where you're taking them.

Beware of "So?" thesis statements. They seem to make a point but don't. "The Civil War was long and bloody" asserts a fact, but "So?" That's what your readers will ask: "So what's your point?" A statement of fact almost always requires another assertion about the causes, consequences, or significance of that fact. "The Civil War was long and bloody but would have been even longer and bloodier were it not for the success of the Union blockade of the Confederate coastline." Now there is a real point to support, that the blockade shortened the war.

Finally, beware of the misleading conclusion. Occasionally a writer will start writing, not sure where he's going. It's perfectly all right to work this way as long as he knows he doesn't know. Then his writing is not a draft so much as an exploration of a subject. Too often, however, a writer *thinks* he's got a pretty good idea what he wants to say, and so he starts writing. He writes until a voice inside him says "Aha!" He assumes that voice is telling him he's reached a conclusion, and so he stops, neatens everything up, and believes he's finished. But he may be mistaken. Often that "Aha!" signals not a conclusion but the discovery, at last, of a thesis. What he has found is not the end of a writing but the beginning. It's a lot of work, I know, to take that thesis and begin anew, rewriting to make all that you have said support this lately discovered thesis, but your writing will be clearer, more focused, and more readable for your pains. Writers should trust their inner voices, but first they have to be sure of what these voices are saying.

EXERCISES

1. In each of the following identify the parts of the thesis: subject, key idea, and explanation or qualification. The subject and key idea are underlined.

a. *All Our Children* is a valuable book. It forces one to see how poorly we have done by the citizens who need us most.
          (Carll Tucker, "The Citizens Who Need Us Most,"
          Saturday Review 15 Oct. 1977, emphasis added)

b. Several years ago, André Hodeir, an eminent French jazz critic, observed that the music he loved seemed to have retraced in 50 years the path that European classical music had required 10 centuries to cover—the path of birth, development, maturity, and decline. These days, a stroll through a record store or a twist of the radio dial (AM or FM, it no longer matters which) brings similar thoughts to mind about rock music—except that rock's life cycle seems to have been only half as long as that of jazz. Music—at least popular music—is in a sorry, and possibly terminal state.
          (Barry Gewen, "Bone-dry in the '70s," *Saturday*
          Review 1 Apr. 1978, emphasis added)

c. All women—and men, and legislators, lobbyists and employers—need to understand that a parent's job *as a parent* is important, that something is lost when a parent is not there, that every parent has a right to be raising his or her own child and that business and government should look for ways to make that possible.
          (Deborah Fallows, "What Day Care Can't Do,"
          Newsweek 10 Jan. 1983, emphasis added)

   d. <u>Television's real crime is not that it incites passion, but that it purveys pab-</u> <u>lum, intellectual paste and emotional puree.</u> Can anyone hooked on the Fonz or Charlie's Angels possibly weep for Othello and Desdemona? If you get used to thinking that Farrah Fawcett-Majors is a star, what taste do you have left with which to appreciate Bette Davis?

                    (M. M. K., "Just for You, Barbara," *The New Republic* 10 Dec. 1977, emphasis added)

   e. <u>Americans have a sense of space, not of place. . . . the Chinese is rooted</u> <u>in his place.</u>

                    (Yi-Fu Tuan, "American Space, Chinese Place," *Harper's* July 1974, emphasis added)

2. Locate the thesis and identify its parts in each of the following introductions. Begin by looking for a generalization that needs support; that will be the subject plus key idea assertion.

   a. A 3,600-mile walk has proved to me that America is not as dangerous as many people think.

     Last May, I set out on foot from Boston. Eight months later, I walked into San Diego, having accepted no rides en route. But it was not the hike's length that astonished many of the back-porch and lunch-counter acquaintances that I made along the way; it was the fact that I had not been mugged.

     Said a waitress in North Texas: "You mean you don't carry no *gun?*"

                  (Gary Moore, "What America Is Really Like," *Newsweek* 10 Apr. 1978)

   b. The prevailing vision of the good life in America has for some time included early retirement. Numerous voices speak in its behalf, from insurance companies to unions to government agencies. Quit while you're ahead, still healthy and young enough to enjoy a generous spread of the sunset years. Not only should you enjoy the fruit of your labors in the most bountiful of countries, say the many voices, but you should also give the young folk their chance to move up by exiting gracefully. There are, you are told, numerous benefits—tax, medical, recreational, psychological. It is not only foolish to overlook the opportunity; it is downright un-American. So why not do it? Why not? Because it will probably be the worst decision you have ever made.

                  (Kenneth Bernard, "The First Step to the Cemetery," *Newsweek* 22 Feb. 1982)

   c. Our fabulously successful economy has always been powered by entrepreneurs—people of vision and daring whose drive to make a fortune has also helped to enrich the nation. In recent years though, the notion has taken root that opportunities for entrepreneurs to be a productive force in America have dwindled. The charge is heard that confiscatory taxes, jaded consumer appetites, and cut-throat competition from giant corporations have closed the road to success for would-be innovators. The proposition is wrong on all counts: The nation still abounds with entrepreneurial opportunities—especially in real estate development, new kinds of services, and electronics technology—and every year thousands seize these opportunities.

     Last year, 475,388 new companies were incorporated—more than double the number 20 years earlier. Each year since 1960 (except for the recession year 1974), the number of business corporations has steadily increased.

(Gurney Breckenfeld, "The New Entrepreneur: Romantic Hero of American Business," *Saturday Review* 22 July 1978)

d. Your eyes are sore, your muscles ache, your skin turns clammy. Your temperature is 101. Self-diagnosis: flu. Self-prescription: take two aspirins and *maybe* call the doctor in the morning. You open the medicine cabinet and reach for the aspirin bottle. You may be making a mistake.

Some recent research suggests that fever itself plays a useful part in fighting disease and that bringing the temperature down may prolong the misery.

("How a Fever Can Help You," *Newsweek* 9 May 1983)

e. Tom Wolfe has christened today's young adults the "me" generation, and the 1970s—obsessed with things like consciousness expansion and self-awareness—have been described as the decade of the new narcissism. The cult of "I," in fact, has taken hold with the strength and impetus of a new religion. But the joker in the pack is that it is all based on a false idea.

The false idea is that inside every human being, however unprepossessing, there is a glorious, talented and overwhelmingly attractive personality. This personality—so runs the erroneous belief—will be revealed in all its splendor if the individual just forgets about courtesy, cooperativeness and consideration for others and proceeds to do exactly what he or she feels like doing.

Nonsense.

(Margaret Halsey, "What's Wrong With 'Me, Me, Me,' " *Newsweek* 17 Apr. 1978)

3. Write a thesis statement of one to three sentences for each of the following. Be specific and complete. Begin with the formula "My point is that . . . What I mean to say is that . . ." Then, when you've decided exactly what point you want to make, write a final draft of your complete thesis *without* using the formula.

a. Write a thesis about the purposes of a college education.
b. Make an evaluation of a book you've read recently or a movie you've just seen.
c. Evaluate the quality of some aspect of life in your community (housing, transportation, recreational facilities, or cultural events, and so on).
d. Make a judgment about young people today.
e. Write a thesis about the chief components of "the good life."

4. Write an open letter of approximately 500 words to those who matter most to you, explaining how you're living your life and what you're living for: your most important beliefs and dreams. You will be addressing your audience by name—those who matter most—but your actual readers will be the members of your composition class, so be careful to explain any references your classmates may not understand. Use footnotes if these explanations cannot be worked smoothly into the body of your letter. Consider carefully your role, persona, audience, and thesis before you begin.

5. Your high school principal has asked you to represent the members of your high school graduating class and write a 500-word letter to *next* year's graduating class. This letter, which will be framed and hung in your alma mater's entrance hall, should contain whatever wisdom you have to give from your generation to those coming up behind you. You can't give all your wisdom, so make your thesis the single most important piece of wisdom you have to offer. Consider your audience and persona carefully: seventeen- and eighteen-year-olds don't like to be preached to or talked down to. You may write seriously or humorously.

6. NASA, the National Aeronautics and Space Administration, has decided to launch another *Pioneer* spacecraft to search the galaxy for intelligent life forms. You have been nominated to speak for all earthlings to those whom the ship may encounter. Write a 500-word message to be bronzed and affixed to the ship's hull. Assume that those who read your message will have already found the first *Pioneer* craft and read the message affixed to it. They know, therefore, where earth is located, who lives here, and something about the advancement of our civilization. What is the most important thing they have yet to learn about us and our planet, especially if they plan a visit? What persona will you use to talk to beings from another world? You may write seriously or humorously.

END NOTES

1. For much that I say about persona I am indebted to Walker Gibson's *Persona* (New York: Random, 1969).
2. For this exercise I am indebted to Walker Gibson's *Persona* (New York: Random, 1969).
3. For this exercise I am indebted to Walker Gibson's *Persona* (New York: Random, 1969).

PART II

WRITING
FOR
DISCOVERY

Chapter 3

The Writing Process: Good Writing Means Writing Well

EXERCISE

Here is another brief introductory writing project like the cartoon description you wrote in the last chapter. Spend ten or fifteen minutes writing a profile of your experiences as a writer. You'll use it to compare yourself with other writers and to act as a reference point for reading the rest of the chapter.

1. Describe what you do when faced with an important writing assignment at school, on the job, or at home. Where do you write? How do you prepare? How do you write? What do you do after you have finished a draft of your writing?
2. Describe the kind of person you are when you're doing your best writing. What's happening? And what does it feel like when you're doing writing that dissatisfies you?

THE WAY WRITERS WRITE

If you're anything like the other student writers who have completed this writer's profile, you can't be neatly pigeonholed. No two writers, professional or student, are alike, even though they may share some of their habits and techniques. Take, for instance, the environment in which we write. None of us would go to the length the French writer Marcel Proust did and build a cork-lined room to wall out noise and visitors, but most of us do require quiet and privacy for our work:

> I tell myself that I write better with the TV set on, but of course this isn't true. I write better in total silence with my dogs flat on the floor under the table.

A much smaller number are like the German novelist Günter Grass, who built a small loft in his living room just so he could write with the stimulating noise of his children swirling beneath him. In what environment do you write best?

How do you prepare for your writing? When a few hardy souls are given a writing assignment, they jump right in and start to work. Most procrastinate, however, using the delay to think—or worry—and incubate their ideas. Finally, after an hour, a day, or a week, the pressures of a deadline propel them into composing.

> When I have to write, I sit down at my desk and get out a sheet of paper. After the sheet is out, I sit and stare at it for about five minutes; then I start to stare at the television set that seems so strangely quiet. When I finish staring, I glance over at the stereo, then say, "The hell with this, I'd better go to the library." I grab my books, run out to the car, and head that way. Somehow I always manage to get lost in the stereo or the responsiveness of my car.
>
> A good hour later I finally show up at the library, put my books on a table, and sit down. Then I get up, get a drink of water, and walk around to see anyone I know. When I finally get through with that little ritual, I sit down to start my writing. After some contemplation, an idea pops into my brain, I jot it down, then go back home and do the actual writing.

Few have creative rituals as elaborate as this, or the even more elaborate rituals of two French writers, one who couldn't write unless dressed in a monk's habit, the other who required the smell of apples rotting in a desk drawer to set him composing. But most writers do have little quirks that help put them into a creative mood, like Ernest Hemingway's habit of sharpening exactly eight pencils before beginning another working day.

> When I write, I need to be sitting at a desk or table with a glass of cola and my cigarettes. Everything else—paper, pen, pencils, and so on—has to be at arm's length. I don't like getting up once I sit down.

When they begin, writers seem to find their ideas in at least five places. Where do you look? Some begin by (1) thinking about a subject until their ideas are so complex they can't be held inside any longer and have to spill into writing.

> Serious writing, which means school work, my job, or personal business, is dictated by my inspiration. Normally ideas fester in my mind for a few days until I classify, clarify, and organize my thoughts into writing. Generally writ-

ing isn't a structured event for me; I remain a puppet of inspiration. If I fail to get inspired, I sit down in a library or other quiet place and try to feel emotional about my topic.

Others begin by (2) making lists, (3) compiling notecards, or (4) writing exploratory drafts. A few are like the professional writer who said that if he had but one week to live, he'd spend the first three-and-a-half days (5) reading, the second three-and-a-half writing. For those in this small group, reading provides not only ideas but a mood and style to write in.

When it comes to organizing, most writers turn to outlines, usually simple sketch outlines. Some outline in great detail, with the spirit if not the length of the outline that the southern novelist William Faulkner prepared for one of his novels. He put up brown butcher paper on each wall of his study, outlined the novel on the paper in exhaustive detail, and then wrote the novel, gradually working his way around the room. How do you structure your writing?

A sizable group of writers will have nothing to do with outlines. As soon as they've got something to say, they proceed right to a trial draft. Some, like the American writer William Zinsser, perfect their design and style as they go along. Every paragraph has to be "right" before they can go to the next. Others postpone organization until they revise:

1. Trying to put my thoughts into some logical flow, I start writing. This is the most time-consuming part, for I write and rewrite, drawing arrows all over and scratching out everywhere.

2. At last I put my many thoughts on paper, in most cases typing them. I read through them all again and again and cut this pile of thoughts apart—literally—and reassemble them to make a first draft, revising as I retype. It usually takes me at least three times through my materials for me to be happy with them.

And there you have the writing process, or most of it, anyway, as practiced by students and professionals alike. What they do when they revise I'll have more to say about later in this chapter. What does this description add up to? Just this: there is no single "correct" method of writing that works for every writer, no single set of inflexible instructions that can be packaged and sold in a textbook like this one. Almost any process, it seems, is potentially a good one. The only bad one is the one not followed in all its implications to a natural conclusion. To write well, you have to find what works for you, perhaps only for you, and practice it until you've perfected it.

As for the answers to the second question in your profile, it is easier to find agreement. Differ though they may in their methods, most writers are in remarkable harmony about what happens when they're writing well and not so well. Listen:

When writing a good paper, I am writing about something I know well enough to express my own views. I have a clear picture of my subject. I am able to keep writing and don't have to stop to think whether I'm saying the right thing or not. I'm flowing freely. . . . When writing a poor paper, I'm in the dark, struggling to get enough down to make sense and prove my point.

When I write well, I'm at ease, not distracted, but smooth. I may scramble and grab, but I am able to latch onto a thought and not let it slip away. I'm not cutting ideas before they get to my paper.

When things are going well, I am more carefree about my writing. . . . I don't worry about spelling certain words or choosing the right one.

Sometimes I'm pleasantly surprised when I discover I've been doing something I hadn't realized while writing on and on, adding knowledge to my subject matter. . . . I can shut out the noise around me; I see only the pen and my hand moving, no other part of my body.

When I am writing good stuff, I become a very comfortable and creative writer. This is the time when nothing can go wrong. My ideas are present and my writing is fluent. It's almost as if I'm in a fantasy and no one can penetrate my little writing world. . . . When my writing is not as good, I feel like I am a prisoner locked in a writing room and I want to break out of that room.

When my writing is good, I don't concern myself with structure; I take a relaxed view of the project and draft, draft, draft until it is finished. When my writing is bad, I usually think too hard about writing instead of just writing what comes to mind. At these times I end up looking at the paper in front of me longer than the time I actually spend writing.

When I don't like a subject, the flow of my pen really runs out of gas.

I'm very proud of myself and very confident when I write something I am satisfied with. I can almost understand what it feels like to invent something.

When the work is flowing free and easy I feel smart. Intelligent. When I don't like the work, I'm a disgusted person who sits at a table with an unpleasant look on her face, hoping and praying that suddenly a flash of ideas will strike. I feel tension in my neck and anxiety all the way to my toes. This person is stiff; her whole body feels stiff.

When I'm writing well, I am a commentator. My role is omnipresent in my mind. My point of view is part of everything I write. I have an attitude of complete confidence. When I'm not writing well, I can't picture myself as anyone but myself.

Time and again these writers agree about what it feels like to do good and bad writing:

Doing Good Writing	Doing Poor Writing
Well-prepared, clear picture of the subject.	In the dark.
No need to stop and think.	Struggling.

Relaxed, carefree.	Concerned with mechanics, structure.
Concentrating, creative, self-confident, intelligent.	Self-censoring, uncreative, bored, confused.
Writing fluently.	Writing choppily.

Perhaps you see in these characteristics the same connections I do, two formulas for successful writing:

1. Preparation + understanding = relaxed attitude + confidence.
2. Relaxed attitude + confidence = concentration + creativity + fluent writing.

What the remainder of this chapter and the book proposes to do is give you techniques to help you perfect your individual writing style, so that it follows these formulas for successful writing. Find out what works. Try as many of the techniques as you can. Experiment and practice. When you've finished with this book, well on your way to developing your style and becoming a master of the writing process, you will keep what works for you and discard what doesn't. In this chapter these techniques are presented according to the three stages of the writing process.

1. Writing-in-progress.
    a. Exploring and developing techniques.
    b. Planning a communications strategy.
    c. Revising techniques.
2. Writing a preliminary draft.
3. Rewriting.
    a. Revising techniques.
    b. Copyediting techniques.
    c. Proofreading techniques.

✎ WRITING-IN-PROGRESS

Exploring and Developing

The preparatory period before we write the first draft of a project is *not* a time for speaking our minds; it is a time for making them up. The crucial truth of this stage is that writing not only expresses thought; it creates it as well. This the British novelist E. M. Forster understood perfectly when he asked, "How can I know what I think till I see what I say?" Writing is a kind of seventh sense, a way of knowing, a means of discovery. You know what I mean if you've ever thought of something to say, written it down, and then found you had written something different. You know what I mean, too, if you've ever gotten going on a writing project and found yourself putting down words without having to think of them in advance, expressing thoughts and feelings you never knew you had. Writing is less like sausage stuffing, cramming a prepared shape with premixed mush, and more like the formation of a pearl from a grain of sand, the growth of a tree from a small seed, or the transformation of a butterfly from a caterpiller and chrysalis: what is created often ends up very different from what it was in the beginning.

What follows are a number of exploring and developing techniques. Their aim can be summed up in an anecdote about the scientist Linus Pauling, the only person ever to win the Nobel Prize in two different fields. He was once asked what it takes to be a genius, and he answered, "A genius is someone who knows how to have a great many ideas and then how to tell the good ones from the bad." A good writer, the genius of the writing process, is someone who knows how to produce a great many *words* and then how to tell the good ones from the bad. These exploring and developing techniques will take you halfway to being a genius of the writing process; each one will help you produce a great many words about a subject.

Exploratory Writing   Exploratory writing is just that, looking around inside your mind to see what's there. Practiced writers know that you can't force ideas into mind; you can only create the conditions that will allow them to come. Exploratory writing does this. Because it differs fundamentally from the writing you are used to doing, the following guidelines are in order.

Don't stop. The aim of the writing you normally do is to say something; the aim of exploratory writing is to not stop, to put your hand in touch with your mind and get the words—any words—flowing. Do your exploring at a place and time that are interruption-proof. Set yourself a time limit of seven to ten minutes and start to write. At first this period will seem an eternity, but as you begin to feel comfortable with exploratory writing, you'll probably want to expand it. Inevitably—especially in the beginning—your mind will suddenly go blank. When it does, *don't stop.* Instead, write just that—*blank, blank, blank, blank, blank*—until something comes to mind. I know, it sounds foolish, and you're going to feel silly the first time you write *blank, blank, blank* down a page, but you don't want to break the connection between mind and hand. Keep writing. You won't write *blank* many times before the words start flowing anew.

Don't censor anything. Write whatever comes to mind, no matter how it sounds. Most of us are so self-protective, so fearful of exposure and embarrassment, that we don't like to reveal ourselves even to ourselves. Exploratory writing runs that risk. But remember, it's only exploration. If when you finish you don't like what you've written, or if you've told more truth than you'd rather tell, you can always throw it away. However, you just may discover things worth keeping. You won't know till you go looking.

Don't change anything. This is a version of the "Don't Censor" rule. Don't tempt yourself to stop writing by worrying whether this or that is the right word. If you write something in one way and think of another way to say it, put a slash (/), write the second version, and third and fourth if they come to mind, then keep going. You'll have plenty of opportunity later to choose the best among them.

Don't make corrections. We all make mistakes when we write, even the most polished among us. Often we see these mistakes as soon as we've made them. Now is not the time to check spelling, to ponder whether commas are correct or whether subjects agree with their verbs. An exploration is not written for publication or a grade. All that really matters is getting words onto paper and keeping them coming. You'll have time for copyediting later.

The easiest exploration to make is the *free association,* nothing more than a list of words, phrases, or clauses running down a page. The idea, image, or feeling in one item leads by association to the next, and so on. Here is a free association done one midwinter day:

cold
blanket
warm
days and nights
drizzle
London
fog
cars
Plymouth
taxicabs
black
London cabs—high, dowdy, passengers look regally down on pedes-
    trians
"Where to, guv'nor?"
The drivers really say that!
St. Paul's Cathedral
whispering gallery high in its dome
looking down from 100 feet I see cold marble, but warm gold in the
    center of the floor, a sun in the middle
"unto us a sun is born"
whispering
secrets
who knows?
what is the secret?
green grass in winter, how can it be? Illinois so cold and brown
a contradiction

a whole host of them
London

Now, this list may sound like gibberish to you, but it doesn't have to make sense to anyone but the writer who wrote it. Explorations are private journeys. We can see, however, that in this free association the writer is shaking off the sensations of the moment and escaping first to his memories of a London vacation and then to something deeper, his dominant impression of the city.

A second version of the exploratory list is the *focused free association*. The writer concentrates on one particular subject and writes down whatever comes to mind about it. Here is a focused free association that grew from the preceding list:

Contradictions
green grass in winter, brilliant green lawns and fields framed by leafless trees and brown hedgerows
churches—monuments to heroes, politicians, and kings; Christ hidden by marble and gold statuary
churchgoers, eyes downcast, not heavenward, reading marble grave markers in the floors
American tourists thronging London, admiring the marble bones of this old empire
shoppers profit from England's woes; the worse the economy, the cheaper the prices, the more crowded the streets
scaffolding erected on every block, rebuilding monuments to the old dead time
London is a monument to dead time, filled with marble, brick, granite memorials to the old time, but the clocks work perfectly—Big Ben loses only 4/5s of a sec. every 20 hrs.
All this life in a city so dedicated to celebrating the past
The contraction of an empire—narrow streets filled with subjects of the old Commonwealth: Indians, Africans, Jamaicans
spice from the Orient now the spice of London's street life
London surviving—huge city—thriving on the old dead time

The second kind of exploratory writing, *freewriting*, looks more like the writing you are used to doing. It is written in more or less complete sentences, breaks for paragraphs, and fills whole pages. But the aim, again, is not to produce polished writing; the aim is to get words and ideas flowing. Like free association, freewriting may be *unfocused* or *focused*.

Unfocused Freewriting
 1. I stopped at my high school the other day. Everything has changed—they put walls up where they weren't when I graduated. I spent four years there—

and I got lost—I had to ask someone where this particular class was meeting so I could say hello to an old teacher/friend. The students are so different now. They look small—let me tell you, the H.S. years are really a breeze. Funny, though, you never think that until you look back. 16 years old—dying to be 18—now I'm dying to be 21. Funny saying, "dying to be something"—it's a little morbid if you think about it. Work, work, work—seems to be piling up. Once I get caught up, something else gets thrown in. It's one vicious circle—silence is golden—bull!—silence is nice once in awhile, but if you think about it, there's never silence. It can be so quiet and my mind seems so loud. Do you ever think about this? blank blank blank can't think—yes, I can—I'm arguing with myself again. Sound like a psycho.

Focused Freewriting

2. 7:15 in the morning on the 1 day I don't have to get up until 10:00, and my little brother has to blow his new trumpet. I just laid in bed for awhile pretending it wasn't happening. My older brother—who is 20 going on 7—decided to show the kid how inconsiderate it was to blow his flugel horn in the A.M.'s, so he plugged in his electric guitar and blasted through a fractured version of "Close to the Edge." The whole thing backfired, though, because in his fury he popped a string and ended up screaming at the kid and blaming the whole thing on him. Eventually, they compromised, I turned over in my bed and peace was again restored. It lasted for a whole three minutes. It turned out that their deal was for the kid to blow his brains out in the rec-room, which just happens to be directly under my room. The rest of the day floated by like a nightmare.

3. What subject shall I write about? I think I want to write my own "Roots" saga, but not about my family. When I think about my roots I think about the tiny country town where I grew up, Lund's Crossing. Blank, blank, blank, blank, in my memories it's always late October in Lund's Crossing after the first frost. The waist-high weeds beside the roads have turned to brown sticks; the corn stalks are pale yellow. The air is still warm, but you can tell winter's coming. You can feel it in the northwest wind and in the light that seems to grow thin. When I lived there, up to my freshman year of high school, I could look out my bedroom window and see for seven miles across the fields—green, shimmering corn fields one summer, crackling at night (it's true, you can actually hear corn grow), rustling soybeans the next summer, fragrant clover the summer after that. Fields filled with growing plants, but they looked so empty. I remember slaughtering time at the Staeffeldts'. Pigs and cows hanging, one at a time, upside down in the barn door, entrails hanging. Pink was the color I remember, not the bloody scarlet of Hollywood movies. A fascinating sight for a ten-year-old to watch. I remember the silence in which the butchers worked preparing the carcasses, only the sounds of knives and saws.

Sometimes freewriting goes nowhere and does nothing more than capture in words the details and feelings of a moment. But more often and with no greater effort, freewritings lead to materials that could be developed, shaped, and polished into an interesting public writing:

- *Significant ideas*, which the first writer discovers as she meditates on her high school years.
- *Telling details*, as when the third writer describes the silence in which the farmers butchered their animals.
- *Authentic voices and roles*, as the second writer creates in his description of one "nightmare" morning.
- *Vivid language*, as the third writer describes the fields around his boyhood home.

Freewriting is like an endless mother lode in a bottomless gold mine of good things for writers. We can't always be sure when we begin whether that freewriting will lead to anything valuable, or even where, exactly, it will lead; that's part of the excitement of exploration. If one freewriting plays out or leads nowhere, what has it cost but ten minutes of time and one sheet of paper? We can put it aside and try another—and another and another, until we know all that we want to say. Term after term, year after year, my students tell me that exploratory writing has made their writing easier to do, better developed, and more interesting. It is, they say, one of the most valuable skills they've acquired in college composition. I hope you agree.

Notes   Once you have a subject fixed clearly in your mind, especially if it is complex or involved, take *notes* freewriting style. On several pieces of notebook paper, draw two intersecting lines, and you have ready-made note slips. Later you can cut these quartered sheets into the individual notes you'll arrange to write a preliminary draft. As you take notes, don't write very much on each slip, leave wide margins to add things later, and don't worry about the wording or how everything will fit. Simply aim to get as much of your subject as you can think of down on paper: in single words, phrases, sentences, or short paragraphs.

Walk-Around Notes   If you have a subject but are unsure what angle to take on it or how to develop it, take walk-around notes in answer to the following questions:

- What is my subject, exactly? What is it for?
- What does it belong to? How is it alike or different from the things it belongs to?
- What are its parts? Explain how they fit together.
- What is it doing? Is that what it's supposed to do? How is it changing?
- What good is it? For whom?

Your answers to these questions will help you walk around a subject, look at it from several angles, discover what you know about it, and equally important, what you don't. Here's an example:

My *subject* is a small country town, Lund's Crossing, population 165 people and hundreds more cattle, sheep, pigs, and chickens. A farm on one side of the town's main street, a railroad at the south end, one general store with a rusty gas pump out front, a tiny one-room post office on skids that was towed from one postmaster's front lawn to the next, a canning factory next to the railroad that employed half the people in town, two parallel streets running north to south, an alley between them, two side streets at each end, twenty or thirty houses, and that was all.

What is it for? When I lived there, it sure didn't seem to be a community. Everyone knew everyone else, of course, but except for childhood friendships, I don't remember the adults being companions of one another. What was it for? For shelter, I guess, but surely not for community.

What does it belong to? The past, mine, because the life I live now is nothing like the life I lived then. I don't know whether it is different from other small towns because my family moved to a middle-sized city, and me with them. But I do know it's different from the small towns you see on television. It was not picturesque—not ugly, either—not homey, not very civic-minded. It was a town in name only, since it never even bothered to incorporate itself.

What are its parts, and how do they fit together? Well, it looked like a town and had most of the geographical features of a little village, but the parts didn't fit together, because everyone went his own way.

What is it doing? Now, I couldn't say, since I don't live there anymore, but what it did to me was to make me a little too open about people, made me take too many of them at face value. There were no secrets in that town—at least I don't think there were—and people were pretty much what they seemed to be. I think a community ought to prepare its children better for the adult world they'll have to live in.

What good is it? It was a good place for kids to play—open spaces and all that—and it was good for anybody looking to escape from the world, but that's about it. I'm glad to be living in a city now.

Freewriting Letter Another way to develop a subject you're unsure of is to write a freewriting letter to your audience. Introduce yourself, give your credentials for writing about your subject and your reasons. Tell your readers why they ought to know about your subject, what you have to tell them, and anything in their experience and beliefs that will affect their response to your writing. Often, of course, this letter will provide you with a role and persona. An example:

Dear Urbanites and Suburbanites, My roots are in a tiny country town and I want to tell you about them. I'll bet you don't know much about small towns, except what you see on television and vacation. That won't tell you much. You probably think small towns are like "Little House on the Prairie": pretty places, wonderful places to live, close to nature. Well, you're close to nature, but that's about all you're close to. You're sure far from people and the excitement that crowds of people in large cities can create. I think many of the adults who lived in my small town were like a lot of the people I meet today. They don't see any way to solve the big human problems like crime, poverty, and hatred, and so they say, "The hell with it. I'm getting out." You see a lot of people like that in small towns, their backs turned. That's the small town life I'd like to show you.

EXERCISES

1. Try your hand at exploratory writing. Set aside a time of day when you won't be interrupted and do one free association or freewriting for as many days as your instructor assigns. Write for ten minutes about whatever comes to mind. Don't stop, don't censor, don't change anything, don't correct anything. Your only aims are exploration and discovery.

2. Do a *focused* freewriting on each of the following topics. Follow the instructions in Exercise 1.

a. Write about something big or little, important or unimportant.

b. Write about what it feels like to have an experience (proposing marriage, stubbing your toe, diving from a three-meter board, anything). Aim to re-create your experience in words.

c. Write about some human condition you know or can imagine (e.g., debt, happiness, discontent, achievement, friendship).

d. Write about an idea (virtue, justice, infinity, merit, forgiveness, square roots, social change, education, and so on).

3. Choose one of the writing topics from the end of this chapter (pages 64–65), or come up with a subject of your own. Explore and develop it.

a. Do a series of three exploratory freewritings about it. If you find that you start to repeat yourself, either narrow your focus and explore your subtopics or let your present freewriting turn into an exploratory first draft of your essay.

b. Take walk-around notes:
- What is this subject, exactly? What is it for?
- What does it belong to? How is it alike or different from the things it belongs to?
- What are its parts? Explain how they fit together.
- What is it doing? Is that what it's supposed to do? How is it changing?
- What good is it? For whom?

c. Write a letter or two to your audience.

4. Keep a freewriting journal for two weeks. Set aside the same ten-minute period each day, then write freely about whatever comes to mind. But aim to make your journal more than a diary. Explore in writing whatever is important to you on that day from your thoughts, feelings, and experiences. Try to capture in small time capsules the flavor of this time in your life.

Planning a Communications Strategy

Within the last decade or so researchers have begun systematically to study writers to discover what the good ones do that makes them good. One of their discoveries concerns the attention writers pay to their prospective audience. In the beginning, they focus on themselves and their subject matter and write primarily for their own understanding and satisfaction. This explains the character of most exploratory writing. At some point, however, they shift attention from themselves to their audience and begin to write and revise for them.

What separates professional from novice writers is that the professionals shift their attention sooner, concentrate longer on their audience, and plan for them in more varied and detailed ways. While novice writers are worrying about how to get their ideas down into words, the professionals are planning how to communicate those ideas to a particular audience. They understand that the writing process involves a hierarchy of choices from big to little, and that the big ones about role, persona, audience, and thesis help shape the lesser ones about design, paragraphing, sentence structure, and language. If the big choices that make up their communications strategy aren't right, the smaller ones won't be, either. Therefore, whatever attention they do give the smaller choices about language and sentence style is given to help them make their more important choices.

You will write more effectively and interestingly when you do what the professionals do and plan a communications strategy as you explore and develop your subject. There is no "correct" order for finding the elements of this strategy nor one element that is always more important than others. Some writers habitually begin with a thesis, others by listening for their voice, still others by working out a role appropriate to the occasion. In the beginning you will have to give your strategy deliberate, even self-conscious, effort because it is hard to get outside your own frame of reference and see a subject from your audience's point of view. But as your skills increase, you'll find that planning for your readers has become second nature. It will begin at the beginning of a project and continue through to its conclusion.

Revising

Most of us assume that revision is what happens *after* we've produced a "rough" draft. The word *revise* does come from a Latin word, *revisere*, meaning "to look back at; to see again; to revisit." But practiced writers know they have to revisit their writing throughout the process, from *the beginning to the end*. They know that an idea almost never comes to mind full-blown and well formed, so they have to look at it and work on it again and again, not just after they've produced a draft. It is here that in Linus Pauling's words these geniuses of the writing process begin to tell the good ideas from the bad, the right words from the wrong.

Revision, then, means reconsidering. But that is difficult to do. We've had to work hard for our words and ideas, and we're glad for what we've got. How can we imagine them any other way? Let well enough alone is our impulse. After all, revision may just make them worse; why risk it? Practiced writers, however, take that chance. They challenge themselves, defying their own ideas by creating rough spots in them, frictions that have to be smoothed out before they're finished. They force themselves into arguments with themselves that test the quality of their ideas and often bring them to deeper insights and fresher perspectives. Here are some formula expressions to help you reconsider your thinking. Try any that fits your subject. You're not necessarily forcing a change of mind so much as gaining the perspective necessary to see whether you should change your mind.

Not only ____(a statement about your subject)____ but also . . .

Example
Not only is London the capital of a shrunken empire, it is also the center of vigorous commercial and artistic growth.

On the one hand ____(a statement about your subject)____ ; on the other hand . . .

Example
On the one hand Lund's Crossing is not a town I'd ever want to live in again, but I did enjoy living there as a child, and my memories of the town are still very vivid.

____(Your subject)____ is not like _____ but is similar to _____.

Example
Drunk driving is not viewed as a crime by most people but is seen more as a common human failing, like baldness, falling arches, something that could happen to anyone.

Here are two more tactics to provoke a reappraisal of your ideas. One, write a contradiction of your thesis. Is there any situation in which this contradiction might be true or plausible? Two, ask yourself how people who disagree with you would see your subject. Explain to yourself why they see it that way.

EXERCISES

1. Plan a preliminary communications strategy for the subject you explored and developed in Exercise 3, page 54. Whom will you write to? What will your role and persona be? What point do you want to make about your subject, or, if your writing doesn't need a thesis, what is your main idea or the feeling you want to convey? Your answers to these questions will not be the final word on your strategy; you've barely just begun. But they are a beginning and you will have created options for yourself you've never had before.

Role
a. What roles am I qualified by knowledge or experience to play with this subject?
b. What roles does my audience expect me to play?
c. What roles will enable me to write most interestingly and significantly about this subject?

Persona

$$\text{Distance} \longleftrightarrow \text{Writer} \begin{array}{l} \longrightarrow \text{Positive attitudes} \\ \longrightarrow \text{Neutral} \\ \longrightarrow \text{Negative} \end{array}$$

Audience
a. How much does my audience know about me and my subject?
b. Why are they reading?
c. How much time do they have for their reading?
d. Where are they doing their reading?
e. How do they see themselves as they read?

Thesis
My point is that . . .
What I mean to say is that . . .
[If a thesis is not needed: My main idea is . . .]

2. Create frictions in your thinking about your subject by trying two or three of the preceding revision formulas: Not only ＿＿＿ but also ＿＿＿. On the one hand, ＿＿＿; on the other, ＿＿＿. ＿＿(My subject)＿＿ is not like ＿＿＿ but is similar to ＿＿＿. Contradict your thesis. Write down what your opponents would say about your subject. Then, if necessary, smooth out these frictions by a freewriting that harmonizes your new thinking with your old or that exchanges one view for the other.

3. How will you organize your essay? Plan your design in either an outline or brief freewriting.

4. Circle important words in your thesis, notes, or freewritings. Do they say exactly what you want? Do they create the appropriate distance and attitude for your persona?

✍ WRITING A PRELIMINARY DRAFT

When you write a first draft, let yourself go. It should feel, once you get started, as if you are doing a freewriting. You understand your subject well, you've developed it thoroughly, you've elaborated your communications strategy; now you want to make a kind of dress rehearsal to see whether everything plays together, a harmonious company of ideas. Surely you can be confident that you'll have no trouble getting words down onto paper. Here are guidelines for getting these words onto paper. Just as there are good and not-so-good final drafts, so are there also good and not-so-good first drafts. These will make your first draft a good one, which is to say a productive one.

Keep going. Some writers plan their openings very carefully so they can get going easily. If you are unable to find a good place to begin, start with the body of your writing. You can come back to the introduction later. Once you get going, keep going. While working on their projects, professional writers seldom take long breaks. They do, however, pause briefly and often to read the lines they've just written. This maintains the thread of their ideas and keeps them on course.

Leave lots of white space. Make wide margins, two inches on the top, bottom, and sides of your pages. Double- or even triple-space between lines. If you fill up a page from left to right and top to bottom, you will prevent yourself from making any but the most minor changes. Paper is still inexpensive, and trees sacrifice themselves willingly for good writing.

Don't bother copyediting or correcting. If you're unsure of a word, phrase, or whole sentence, write out several possible choices separated by slashes [/]. Then put a check [√] in the margin and keep going. Do the same if you're unsure of spelling or the grammar of a sentence. Don't break your concentration.

EXERCISE

Write the first draft of your writing project according to the instructions given previously. If you find many new ideas coming to mind that don't fit snugly into your plans, your draft is turning into an exploratory writing. This happens sometimes. Finish it as if you were doing a long freewriting, rethink your communications strategy, and begin again.

🐾 REVISING, EDITING, AND REWRITING

Because this is the spot most people associate with revision—after a preliminary draft has been completed—a few more words about it are in order, especially because for so many it carries such a bad odor. Some novice writers don't even bother to revise. Frankly, they don't care very much for their writing or don't want to take the time. If you're one of these, you should know that professionals don't always revise their writing, either.[1] This is especially true of routine writing requiring little thought or organization. There are even a few professionals (the novelist Truman Capote was one) who claim never to revise. These make a tiny minority, however. The great majority revises extensively, especially in important or original writing that has required large investments of thought and time. It is not unusual for authors to revise book-length manuscripts thoroughly three, four, even five times! Most of the public writing you do for college falls into this "important writing" category. It deserves whatever time and effort of revision you can give it—at least your instructors think so.

Other novice writers don't revise because revision seems unnatural. We don't revise when we talk, they observe, so why do it when we write? It seems to quash spontaneity, muffle their natural voices, and rob them of their own words. But remember, writing is not just expression; it is the creation of meaning, and meaning is never made in a straight line. Recall your serious discussions with friends about complex and important issues. They never went straight ahead, one speaker saying all she had to say and getting it right the first time, the second having his say and saying it perfectly, and so on. Rather, it was through give and take, interchange and interaction, that each of you arrived at your own understanding. The same is true in the dialogue of writing and revising, finding words to say and ways to make them right. It is a curious paradox of much public writing that the most spontaneous, natural-sounding writing is often the most carefully revised. The "spontaneity" is revised in. Thus the truth of the old proverb: "Hard writing makes for easy reading." To learn to write is to learn to revise.

Some novice writers do want to revise, but they're more than a little afraid they may botch it. To you I say, think of all you've done to bring your writing this far. Think of the revising you've already done as you've thought your way into your subject, considering, weighing, choosing, adding, and discarding. Think of your well-developed communications strategy that has helped you "see" your promises to yourself and your readers. Think of the preliminary draft you've written and the writing that led to that. You have reasons to be confident of your powers.

There is, finally, that largest group of writers, those who do at least some revising. The revising they do, however, is too often touch-up work more than anything else, rereading for misspellings or repeated words. Touch-up artists don't like to see too many *I*'s on a page. They pick hesitantly at other words, perhaps check a thesaurus, choose impulsively, and then proceed. Now don't get me wrong; you *should* check your spelling, *should* avoid certain kinds of repetition, *should* weigh your words carefully. But you should do it at the right time, *after* you've finished revising. The touch-up work that too many of us call revision is not really revision at all but copyediting.

Before copyediting comes the serious "looking again" and its companion activities that are the soul of revision. Following are guidelines to serious, genuine revision of the kind professionals do.

Let your writing get cold. The ancient Roman writer Horace recommended putting a writing away for nine years. If you followed his advice you'd never graduate, but any time you can allow between drafting and revising will help cool your ardor for your words. We're often elated when we've just finished a project, happy at finding words and getting them down, and it is easy to mistake that elation for a judgment of our writing's worth. A few hours or days will give the fresh critical perspective necessary to reveal flaws and the ways improvements could be made.

Be a zoom lens. Begin with the lens fully opened; take in your whole writing in a quick read-through. Does it seem unified and complete? Does everything fit? Are there any gaps? Does everything make sense? This first reading will help you spot any major problems. It is pointless to work on small problems before the big ones are solved. Once they are, close up the lens of your critical eye and zoom in on the smaller parts of your writing: paragraphs, sentences, and individual words. You will make four changes as you reread:

1. Adding.
2. Deleting.
3. Substituting.
4. Rearranging.

To give you an idea how this process looks, below is one stage in my revision of a paragraph that appears earlier in this chapter (page 57). Sure, it looks like messy business, but this experimental cutting, adding, and shuffling is the way effective writing works.

Consider certain parts with special care. Except for your thesis, your opening is the most important part of your writing. First impressions last. Give the wrong first impression and you risk losing your reader before you've begun. Professionals spend much time on their openings, and so should

```
     When you write a first draft, let yourself go.  It should feel,
                                      dress rehearsal        free
once you get going, [almost] as if you are doing a [preliminary] writing.  You

understand your subject well, you've developed it thoroughly, you've
            now you want to see if everything plays together, an harmonious company of ideas
elaborated your communications strategy, surely you can trust [that] you'll
                                                                  worry
have no trouble getting words down on paper.  Don't [trouble] yourself too
           about
much [with] finding the right words; you're not after perfection [on
                                              now, anyway, not
the first draft.]  That almost never happens, even to the best prepared among
                                      be prepared
us, perhaps especially not to them.  Just [get going and then let yourself
            to follow
go, free to allow] the inspiration [to strike] that almost always comes after

careful preparation.  You'll probably be struck by all sorts of new ideas,

details, and ways of saying things.  Write them down. [They are your

inspiration.]  If any don't fit, you can always cut them later.  All

you are aiming to do now is bring your materials to life and give them

continuity, an harmonious community of ideas.
```

you. Spend time, too, with your supporting paragraphs. Weight your opinions and generalizations with telling facts, details, and dramatic illustrations.

Write for your audience; revise for your readers. Successful revising depends upon your ability to see your writing through your readers' eyes, anticipating their questions, responses, and problems.

Cut in two places. The part of your writing you like best is probably what you should cut first. That's right, the part you like best. It may be there not because it does something for your subject but because you like it. If that's the case, cut it. And then try to cut at least one word *from each of your sentences.* See how the preceding sentence might read: "And then try to cut at least one word *from each sentence."* A small revision, perhaps, but over the course of a long writing, those small cuts will add up to writing that is more compact and emphatic.

Trust yourself. Don't be afraid to ask others to read your writing and give you advice. But all the advice in the world is no good if it's not right for you. You're not doing *their* writing. Before you can follow their advice, you have to meet your standards.

When you've finished revising, you're ready to do the copyediting some confuse with genuine revision. What you're looking for now are mechanical errors. Everyone, even the most polished writer, makes mistakes, usually the same errors repeated in writing after writing; you know what yours are better than your English teacher ever will. Reread your draft looking for these errors of language, grammar, spelling, or punctuation. They may seem to be small matters, hardly worth your trouble. After all, they don't affect the quality of your ideas; nor do they prevent your readers from reading. True. But giving your public an unedited manuscript is like going out your front door in your underwear. It's something most would do only in an emergency.

Preparing the Final Draft and Proofreading

Copy out your finial draft as carefully and neatly as possible. (See Chapter 18, pages 511–512, for the manuscript conventions for college writing. If you can, type your writing. It will be more readable and look more professonal. Then proofread it. Human beings being the the falliable creatures they are can't even copy without making mistaeks. Proofreading gives the final finishing touch to your work. There is an art too proofreading, however.

See what I mean? How many errors did you spot as you read the preceding paragraph? One or two? Three or four? There are eight. If you didn't spot more than a few, that was because you were reading normally. Reading in this way, our eyes move across the page in jumps, called saccades. We see only what our eyes take in during the instant they are at rest. Thus, if you read the first sentence of the above paragraph like this,

Copy out your finial draft *as carefully and neatly* as possible,

you missed the errors in *finial* and *possable.* What proofreaders must do is defeat their attempt to read normally for the sense of a passage and read instead for its "look."

To proofread, take a pencil eraser and point at *each* word or lay a ruler on the page beneath each line. When you spot an error, stop and correct it, but *don't* begin reading again at the point of the error. Go back to the beginning of the line. It is not unusual for a proofreader to spot an error out of the corner of her eye and saccade over to it, missing another error on the way. Beginning at the beginning of a line prevents that. If poor spelling is your problem, read your writing backward; you'll force yourself to look at the words instead of reading them. Only when you have proofread carefully are you finally finished with a writing project.

EXERCISE

Revise your writing project—adding, deleting, substituting, rearranging, correcting, and proofreading—according to the preceding guidelines.

A POSTSCRIPT: WRITING WITH MACHINES

No discussion of the writing process is complete without some comment on the ways writers produce their texts. The tools they write with affect the process itself, how much they write, the time they take, how they revise, and, ultimately, the quality of the finished product. Most writers, of course, do at least part of every writing project with paper and pen or pencil. And some celebrate the manual labor of writing by hand as the only completely human way to write. Well, perhaps. Most of us lack the dexterity for handwriting that has anything like the dignity and beauty of calligraphy. But we all have known the pleasures given by the feel of high-quality paper under our hand, the weight of a good pen, or the bold swash of fresh ink on a white background. A personal letter or thank you note written in our best hand may be a small gesture of human self-expression, but a satisfying one nonetheless.

The trouble is that most us of don't have time for our best handwriting when we do routine writing for school or work; besides, most of these projects are large enough that the physical pleasures of doing them evaporate before we're half-done. We've all tried to shake off a bad case of writer's cramp, felt our biceps sag with fatigue, or winced with the feeling that someone has driven an umbrella point into our shoulder blades. Handwriting can be hard, painful work. And so we look for less painful and tedious alternatives. What follows is a commercial in praise of the machines we turn to. Used rightly they shorten our writing time, make writing easier to do, and may even make it better.

Tape Recorders

Tape recorders would seem to be the ultimate labor-saving device, especially when there is someone to transcribe what the writer records. Even for those who don't have secretaries, recorders offer writers speed, ease, and portability. What a joy to "write" lying down, relaxing in a recliner, out for a walk, or at the beach! With a footpedal to turn the machine on and off, transcription is simple and efficient. Unfortunately, recorders do have serious drawbacks. Eventually the spoken word *does* have to be transcribed and there goes the time-saving. And some people are distracted by hearing the sound of their own voices. More importantly, recorders seem to work best for those who can formulate fairly well polished sentences in mind before they speak or those who write short pieces with standard formats, such as business letters or memos. Most writers find them inefficient for original or complex writing, because our short-term memories will not hold all that we need to compose an effective sentence. The tape recorder is a special tool with limited uses.

Typewriters

Not so the typewriter. For all college students, but especially those who plan careers that require writing, the ability to type is a nearly indispensable tool. If you are serious about writing, you must know how to type; it's as simple as that. Especially now that we have self-correcting typewriters, typing speeds our work by half and makes it look more professional and readable to our readers. As valuable as these public relations virtues are, however, even more valuable is the critical distance that cold, black type puts between writers and their words. Typed words no longer seem quite as much the writer's own, and so he can begin to see them through his readers' eyes. The only drawbacks to typewriters are the expense of the good ones and the difficulty of revising while composing. To do this you have to be sure to triple-space and then roll the platen backward and forward, from the spot where you're typing to the place you want to make a change and back again. It's an especially clumsy procedure if you have no more room to type and want to write by hand on the page without removing it from the typewriter. Still, it is a minor and infrequent annoyance. Typing skill is invaluable.

Computers and Word Processors

Computers are no longer the wave of the future. They and their relatives the word processors (computers built to handle only language) are here now, in daily use on the job, in schools, in homes; with the rapidly expanding applications for personal home computers, the ability to use these machines will soon be as essential as typing skill. Increasingly, job placement and advancement depend on computer literacy. For writers, these sophisticated machines are especially useful, both on the job and off, enabling them to do more quickly and efficiently everything they can do on a typewriter and much more.

A writer can type a draft into a computer, revise it on the monitor screen in front of her, or, if she prefers, print it out on paper (called hard copy) to work on it there. She can add words, phrases, sentences, paragraphs, or whole pages of material, and the computer will accept all her additions and fit them neatly into place on the screen or page. She can delete or substitute, and the machine will pull her text together and fill up the gaps. If she wants to change the order of her text, no longer does she have to cut and paste or draw arrows to follow when she types the next draft. All she has to do is type in a few simple commands, and the computer will scoop up what she wants to move and move it for her. If she's not really sure where she wants to put part of her text, she can divide the monitor screen, put the passage in two places at once, consider them both, and then choose. Or she can take part of a text off the screen, save it, consider her text without it, and then, if she prefers, put it back.

No longer does she have to recopy after each round of revision, although she can tell her printer to give her a fresh, neat copy of her latest version if she wants one, printed faster than any human can type. Usually, however, she saves her drafts on a small plastic disk for future writing and revision: no more wastebaskets full of scrapped or reworked pages. When she finally decides she is finished with a project, she can tell the computer to print it for her, and it will do so perfectly, counting all her pages, centering titles, checking margins, lining up columns of figures, drawing graphs, and measuring in footnotes at the bottom of pages. If she has the appropriate word processing program, her computer will even check her spelling and grammar. Computers can't do everything, of course. The writer still has to do all the thinking, choose the right words, organize effectively, and give the computer the proper commands. If she makes an error in logic, misorganizes, or writes an ungraceful sentence, the computer will faithfully reproduce her error. It is, despite all its sophistication, nothing more than a very powerful, very loyal, but not very intelligent servant. However, by taking away much of the drudgery of writing, revising, and layout, the computer frees writers for more important work, allowing them the time for and even encouraging the playful experimentation essential to all good writing. If you don't already know how to use one, you need to learn.

WRITING PROJECTS

Topics

1. Write a three- to five-page personal experience essay in which you share with your composition class an important event or period in your life. Here are several options:

a. The event that has made the biggest difference in your life.
b. The event that has taught you the most about life.
c. The time you grew up all at once.
d. A dramatic, significant, or humorous experience.

For this kind of writing you may not need a thesis. You'll develop your subject according to a main idea instead. In either case, don't feel you have to give your story a "moral," unless there really is a moral to be given. Chapter 13, pages 278–279, will introduce you to personal essays.

2. Write your own three- to five-page "Roots" saga addressed to your family. Record the history of your family *for* your family, but aim to make it more than a report. Look for characteristics, beliefs, ideals, traits, or habits that have recurred from one generation to the next. How are you alike or different from your forebears? What explains how your family has come to the point where you find yourself? Answering these questions will give your saga a thesis or main idea. You probably won't be able to say everything about your family; include only those persons, places, events, and details that help make your point. Unless you have a good reason not to, you will organize your saga in story form.

3. Write a three- to five-page essay explaining a character in a story or narrative you've read recently. What are the character's appearance and behavior, and what do they reveal about his or her personality and values? What is this person's ruling passion or most important motive? What are his or her conflicts? How are they resolved? Answering these questions will give you a point to make about the character (your thesis). The body of your essay will support this thesis with evidence and your explanation of it.

THE WRITING PROCESS

Here are the techniques of the writing process that you have studied in this chapter. If you haven't done the exercises while reading the chapter, follow the process as it is repeated in the following outline. Experiment with the techniques, test them, and adapt them to your own writing style. Future chapters will add new techniques to the process.

1. Writing-in-progress.
   a. *Exploring and developing:* Do free associations and freewritings, focused or unfocused, to find a subject and think your way into it. Take notes, especially walk-around notes; write a letter to your audience about your project (see pages 47–54).
   b. *Planning a communications strategy:* As you explore and develop your subject, plan in writing how you will communicate it. Decide on your role, persona, thesis, and design (see pages 54–55).
   c. *Revising:* Reconsider your ideas and communications strategy; create frictions in your thinking (see pages 55–56).
2. Writing: Write the preliminary draft of your project. Write freely, don't stop except to reread, give yourself room to revise (see pages 57–58).
3. Rewriting (see pages 58–61).
   a. Be a zoom lens when you revise: work on the big parts first, then the smaller ones.

    b. Add, delete, substitute, and rearrange.

    c. Carefully consider your opening and supporting details.

    d. Cut what you like best; cut a word from every sentence.

    e. Copyedit for mechanical errors, recopy according to conventional manuscript form (see pages 61–62), and proofread.

4. Self-evaluation: From the beginning to the end of your project, you have been its first reader. You ought to be the first to evaluate it. Do so in a freewriting that responds to the following questions.

    a. What are your intentions in this writing?

    b. What process did you follow?

    c. Did you try anything you hadn't tried before? If so, how did it work?

    d. What was the easiest? The most difficult? What did you enjoy most? Least?

    e. What is best about this writing? What one change would most improve it? How could that change be made?

END NOTE

1. For much of my information on the revising practices of professional writers I am indebted to Maxine Hairston and the research she reported in her paper, "Challenging the Conventional Wisdom about Writing and Rewriting," given 18 Mar. 1983 at the Conference on College Composition and Communication, Detroit, MI.

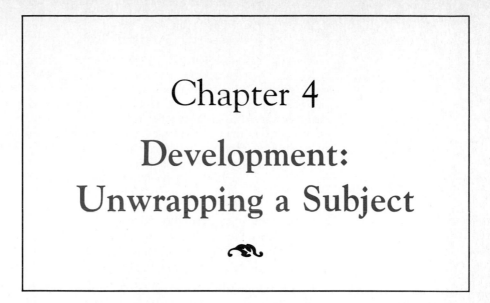

Chapter 4

Development: Unwrapping a Subject

Here is an introduction to an essay about America's health and fitness fads:

> Beware: living may be hazardous to your health. Each of us every day exposes himself to countless risks. Most of us are aware of these risks and yet few of us actually stop taking them.
>
> Is this the expression of some subliminal death wish? Perhaps, but it is probably safe to say that for most people who engage in risk taking, there are benefits that seem to outweigh the risks. These benefits may consist of nothing more nor less than the satisfaction of some basic urge, but I suspect that we cannot eliminate the risky behavior that provides these slight benefits.

This opening does have its virtues: the paradox in the first line is dramatic, the ideas are fresh and interesting, and the style is clear and readable. But how little these paragraphs communicate! Are they intended for us? We can't be sure because we don't know what risks are referred to. Are they the risks we take? Is the thesis sound? We can't be sure about that, either; we have nothing to test it with. We can't even be entirely sure what the sentences mean—no matter how clear the language. All we have is a string of unsupported and unexplained generalizations.

Now contrast this opening with another version, the original:

> Beware: living may be hazardous to your health. Each of us every day exposes himself to countless risks to his health—some known, many suspected, and innumerable others yet to be uncovered. The cigarettes we smoke, the alcohol we drink, the diet we eat, the automobiles we drive, perhaps even the air we breathe may represent substantial health risks. Most of us are aware of these risks and yet few of us actually stop smoking or drinking, stay off the

highways, or lose weight. Not even the most health-conscious among us has decided to stop breathing.

Is this the expression of some subliminal death wish? Perhaps, but it is probably safe to say that for most people who engage in risk-taking, there are benefits that seem to outweigh the risks. These benefits may consist of nothing more nor less than the satisfaction of some basic urge, but I suspect that we can no more eliminate smoking, drinking or gluttony by appealing to a desire for "good health" than we can eliminate lust by declaring sex immoral.

(Michael S. Kramer, M.D., "The Risks of Health," *Newsweek* 6 Feb. 1978)

The differences between the two versions are few: three lists of clarifying illustrations in the first paragraph and a humorous comparison at the end of the second. But how much more the second version tells us! Now we know whether these paragraphs are intended for us. If we smoke, drink, overeat, drive unsafe cars, or breathe polluted air, they are. Now we know exactly what Dr. Kramer means by health risks and whether his opinions are sound. If his examples prove his assertions—if smoking, drinking, overeating, and driving are risky, and if we refuse to stop doing them even though we know they're risky—he has made his point. The second version of this introduction is better than the first, even though the ideas are exactly the same, because in the second those ideas are *developed*.

The word *develop* comes from the Latin *disvoloper*, meaning "to unwrap or unroll." A writer develops a subject by unwrapping it and laying it out, first for himself as he discovers it and then for his readers. What is inside the package of our ideas is the substance of every writing: what we're really writing for and what our readers are really reading for. It is development that proves an argument, that supports an opinion, or explains a generalization; development that makes an idea vivid, puts us into the middle of a scene, or presents a person so dramatically we forget we're only reading words. A thesis *tells*; development *shows*. It is indispensable to good writing. Everything else about our writing may be perfect, but if neither we nor our readers ever say "I see!" what have we achieved? Here are six methods skilled writers use to unfold their subjects.

✒ METHODS OF DEVELOPMENT

Facts and Statistics

"Matters of fact," the seventeenth-century Englishman Matthew Tindal observed, "are very stubborn things." There's no getting around them. That may be why Tindal's countryman Winston Churchill declared, "Facts are better than dreams" and why facts and statistics are what first come to mind when we think about developing a subject. We can get our hands on them; they are rock hard; they won't evaporate on us. Also, they are easy to use. All we have to do is follow a few simple conventions, as does the following report on literacy in America.

Give the point of your information

The crisis of literacy is no fiction. Most young Americans now complete high school and at least attend college, yet few can read and write with a sophistication sufficient to justify twelve to sixteen years of schooling. At even the most elite colleges, a low standard of reading and writing among entering freshmen has come to be taken for granted.

Explain what statistics show

Give the source of the information

Over the past decade, young Americans' command of English has consistently declined, from a standard that was none too spectacular to begin with. In 1973, 69 percent of 13-year-olds were able to write a "persuasive" letter as defined by the National Assessment of Educational Progress, mandated by Congress to monitor educational attainment around the nation; in 1978, 64 percent could demonstrate this very basic and trivial example of command of written language.

Give the author and title of a source

Weave the information into your writing

As studies by the National Assessment and by John Goodlad, the author of *A Place Called School*, have shown, little writing is demanded of pupils in elementary and secondary school. The emphasis, in Goodlad's words, is on "mechanics—capitalization, punctuation, paragraphs, syllabication, synonyms, homonyms, antonyms, parts of speech—if teachers gave tests involving writing paragraphs or essays, they seldom so indicated." Tests ask students merely for single words or short answers—identifications, "circle-the-verb" requests and the like. The result is that pupils don't develop the habit of commanding language to express complex feelings or ideas, either in speech or in writing.

Explain the significance of facts

(Leon Botstein, "Why Jonathan Can't Read," *The New Republic* 7 Nov. 1983)

Easy though they may be to use, facts and statistics do contain several pitfalls you should beware of:

- *Mistaking assumptions for facts.* A fact is something demonstrably true; an assumption, the *belief* that something is true. It is a fact that many students today don't write as well as their older brothers and sisters did at the same age. It would be an assumption to conclude that today's students have less aptitude—there are no facts to support it. It may feel like a fact to some people, but an assumption stands by itself, without facts. To base informative writing on assumptions alone is to build on sand. The first wave of facts from one who is informed may dash your fine ideas.
- *Undependable sources of information.* Beware of those that are excessively biased or unqualified and those that are out of date.
- *Overwhelming your readers with information.* If you blind your readers with a blizzard of facts and figures, more than they can understand or use in the time they have for your writing, they won't see your point.

EXERCISES

1. Write a paragraph presenting important information about some feature of your community: facts and statistics about population (age distribution, races, ethnic groups), income, employment, housing, recreational opportunities, geography, education, crime, or community history. Gather the information wherever you can find it (the library, local government, the news media, interviews), introduce it, explain what it shows about life in your community, and document your sources.

2. Write a paragraph telling your composition class how to find little-known but important places in your community that reveal its spirit or values, or that offer interesting things to do or see. You may have to explain what your readers should look for at the end of their journeys.

3. Write a paragraph of instructions telling your readers how to do something customary in your community: how to cook a particular dish, play a game, or practice a custom. Be original: choose a subject that distinguishes your community from others.

Examples

An example presents a typical member of a class or group (of people, events, conditions, objects, or ideas) in order to explain the whole class. Here is an example of an example:

The main idea to be illustrated
The class illustrated: "Certain jobs" held by women
Introductory phrase
Example

> In the marketplace, women have passed the point of insisting on "equal pay for equal work" and are demanding something more: "equal pay for work of equal value." Certain jobs such as secretary or nurse often pay less for the very reason that women hold most of them—yet the work is as valuable as that performed by men with different responsibilities. In Pittsfield, Mass., for instance, the school board recently agreed to pay female "housekeepers" at the same rate it pays male "custodians."
>
> ("The Battle of the Sexes," *Newsweek* 30 Apr. 1979)

Sometimes, however, writers can't find actual examples to explain a subject, or the ones they do have may not be familiar to their audience. What to do? Make up a *hypothetical example*, a plausible illustration invented for the occasion.

The class illustrated: Stereotypes

Hypothetical examples

Explanation of the illustration

> No human being is as uncomplicated as his image. . . . For the sake of order we confine complex individuals to the cubicle of an image. We do this not only to public figures but, to some extent, to every person of our acquaintance. Old Jack is the perennial optimist; Miss Nit, a desiccated spinster; Billy, a jock; Alphonse, a lush; and so forth. Even those we know best and love most—for that matter, even our own selves—we simplify into an image for the sake of comprehension. The human being is the only creature who can "surprise" himself because he is the only creature who holds in his mind an image of himself that he can confute.
>
> (Carll Tucker, "Image," *Saturday Review* 25 Nov. 1978)

The foregoing paragraph also illustrates *multiple examples.* If a subject is too broad or complex to be explained by only one example—in this instance, the stereotypes we create to simplify our understanding—then we must supply more than one.

Anecdotes

An anecdote is an illustration in story form, a brief narrative told to make a point about a subject. Here an anecdote disputes the belief of many Americans that their country is filled with murderous lunatics ready to commit mayhem at the slightest provocation. Notice how carefully it follows the conventions for good story telling:

Setting or background

The fallacies of the murderous-lunatic syndrome can be summed up by an incident that happened to me in St. Louis, on a bus-stop bench. I had stopped there to rest my pack, and was soon joined by a small man of middle age. He was wearing a football-referee's cap.

The anecdote itself

He seemed to think that because I carried a backpack, I was hitchhiking, and he told me that he just did not see where I got the courage to get into other people's cars. Why, every day he saw bus seats that had been carved on with *knives.* I should watch my step, he said, for the world was definitely full of dangerous weirdos.

This rankled me, and I gruffly told my new companion that he was wrong—especially about the abundance of weirdos. The rebuff seemed to stun him like a physical blow—sending him into shock. For a moment, he stared into space, then suddenly he whipped off his referee's cap, snatched a silver whistle from underneath it, blew the whistle, replaced the whistle on his head, replaced the cap on the whistle, and after another pause he began, as if nothing had happened, to talk cooperatively about how safe the country was.

Explanation of the anecdote

Slowly I realized that when he had first sat down, he had been afraid of me. His unusual behavior was just his way of coping with the hostility he expected to find. But in fact, I was rather harmless, and so was he.

(Gary Moore, "What America Is Really Like," *Newsweek* 10 Apr. 1978)

EXERCISE

What values, attitudes, or beliefs are characteristic in your community? Write a brief free association to discover them. From your list choose the two most important or least recognized and write a brief paragraph about each, using examples or anecdotes as illustrations. If, for example, you decide that fear characterizes large numbers of your neighbors, you may illustrate it by citing the measures some have taken to secure their homes. Introduce your subject in a sentence. Follow it with your examples or anecdote. Conclude, if necessary, by explaining the point of your illustration.

Analogies   An analogy compares a simple or familiar subject to one that is complex or unfamiliar in order to explain the latter. Often the comparison is signaled by transitional phrases: *like, as if, just as . . . so.*

> Like a person doing exercises in front of a mirror to develop his back, leg, and stomach muscles, a Muslim at prayer first stands, then bends in half, kneels, and touches his forehead to the floor.
> —Abdullah Hamidani

$$\frac{\text{The familiar}}{\text{(Exercising before a mirror)}} = \frac{\text{The unfamiliar}}{\text{(A Muslim at prayer)}}$$

The illuminating power of analogy increases when the subjects compared are completely different *except* for the points of comparison. Consider this analogy exploring the effects of special interest groups on America's national unity:

The familiar (the effect of a solvent) = The unfamiliar (the effect of special interest groups)

It's as if the nation had swallowed a solvent and we were breaking up into our constituent parts—or, to be chemically more consistent about it, coming unglued. I can't remember a time in Washington when interest-group issues and politics so dominated events. And every day the units of protest and concern seem to be subdividing into even smaller and more specialized groupings—these miners, those farmers, certain public employees, some gas-producers and so forth.

Explanation of the analogy

(Meg Greenfield, "Thinking Small," *Newsweek* 24 Apr. 1978)

A special interest group like a miner's union has nothing in common with a solvent—nothing, that is, except its divisive powers. And there lies the power of analogy. The vast differences between union and solvent make their sole similarity that much more dramatic and revealing. Analogy is one of the most valuable methods of development, first, because it is such a vivid device for discovering a subject; second, because it helps readers understand so clearly; and third, because for writers and readers alike it begins where they are, with the familiar—what they already know—and then leads them to the unfamiliar.

When a subject is especially complex or unfamiliar, a writer may not only have to explain the analogy, as Meg Greenfield does, but also develop an extended point-by-point comparison between its halves.

A question that needs answering

We say that the aim of life is self-preservation, if not for the individual, at least for the species. Granted that every organism seeks this end, does every organism know what is best for its self-preservation?

One half of the analogical comparison
First characteristic of cancer cells

Consider cancer cells and noncancer cells in the human body. The normal cells are aimed at reproducing and functioning in a way that is beneficial to the body. Cancer cells, on the other hand, spread in a way that threatens and ultimately destroys the whole body.

Normal cells work harmoniously, because they "know," in a sense, that their preservation depends upon the health of the body they inhabit. While they are organisms in themselves, they also act as part of a substructure, directed at the good of the whole body.

Second characteristic of cancer cells

We might say, metaphorically, that cancer cells do not know enough about self-preservation; they are, biologically, more ignorant than normal cells. The aim of cancer cells is to spread throughout the body, to conquer all the normal cells—and when they reach their aim, the body is dead. And so are the cancer cells.

Third characteristic of cancer cells

For cancer cells destroy not only all rival cells, in their ruthless biological warfare, but also destroy the large organization—the body itself—signing their own suicide warrant.

The second half of the analogical comparison

The same is true of war, especially in the modern world. War is the social cancer of mankind. It is a pernicious form of ignorance, for it destroys not only its "enemies," but also the whole superstructure of which it is a part—and thus eventually it defeats itself.

Explanation of similarities to show that cancer and war are, indeed, analogous

Nations live in a state of anarchy, not in a state of law. And, like cancer cells, nations do not know that their ultimate self-interest lies in preserving the health and harmony of the whole body (that is, the community of man), for if that body is mortally wounded, then no nation can survive and flourish.

(Sydney J. Harris, "War is Cancer of Mankind," *The Best of Sydney J. Harris* [Boston: Houghton, 1975])

EXERCISES

1. Invent analogies to dramatize the similarities and differences between the members of four of the following pairs. Make sure you find *related* imaginative words or phrases to illuminate the relationship between the members of each pair. Try several versions until you find analogies that are just right. If necessary, explain your comparison in a brief sentence.

    a. To be a man is to be _____. To be a woman is to be _____.
    b. Employee/boss.
    c. Parent/child.
    d. Student/teacher.
    e. City dweller/country dweller.
    f. Young/old.

Examples

To be a man is to be an incurable disease; to be a woman is to be a scientist looking for a cure.
    —Celeste Cross

To be a man is to be a cup of coffee; to be a woman is to be the cream and sugar.
    —David Lopez

To be a city dweller is to be boxcake; to be a country dweller is to be home-made.
> —Joan Pacholski

To be a parent is to be an artist; to be a child is to be an unfinished picture.
> —Mollie McMahon

2. Here are more complex or abstract subjects. Choose four and invent an analogy to explain and dramatize each. If necessary add a line or two to make your comparison clear.

a. Music is like _____.
b. America
c. Innocence or guilt.
d. Solitude.
e. Mercy.
f. Thinking.
g. A friend.
h. Being powerful or powerless.
i. Marriage.
j. Progress.

Example
Rock music is like Mexican food, some spicy hot, some mellow mild. You can't judge all Mexican food by one dish filled with jalapeño peppers, and you can't judge all rock by hard rock standards alone. Taste, experiment—in both you'll find flavors to enjoy.
> —Lisa Wood

3. Choose one pair of analogies from Exercise 1 and one analogy from Exercise 2. Expand each into a one-paragraph extended analogy. In both, explore all the similarities between the familiar or simple terms and the unfamiliar or complex terms, as Sydney Harris does in the preceding example (pages 72–73).

Definitions

When you define a word or phrase, you tell not only what the term means but also how to use it. The word *definition* comes to us from the Latin *definere*, "to limit," "to set a boundary to." The most common form of definition is the one we associate with dictionaries, *formal definition*. A formal definition first puts a term into a class of related words called the *genus*, and then distinguishes it from every other member of the class by details known as the *differentia*. For example, *democracy* may be defined as

Genus
A form of government . . .

Differentia
in which the supreme power is vested in the people and exercised by them or by their elected agents under a free electoral system.
> (*The Random House Dictionary*, College Edition, 1969 ed.)

Comparison/contrast defines by comparing an unfamiliar to a familiar term, as in the following example comparing the uncommon word *healthful* to the common *healthy*:

Healthful means "conducive to health; wholesome or salutary." The trouble is that *healthy* can *also* mean "conducive to health; wholesome or salutary," as well as "in good health." *Healthy* can play both sides of the street, and it seems to be elbowing old *healthful* right out of the picture. I think this is a shame. We have a very healthy oleander in our backyard. In this case, *healthy* definitely doesn't mean healthful. Anyone who thought it did might make a fatal error. "Nice healthy water hemlock you got there, lady." "Thank you, sir. Would you like a nice healthy cup of hemlock tea?"

Healthy germs can be extremely unhealthful, and the health of the germs will be in direct proportion to their unhealthfulness.

(Thomas H. Middleton, "Endangered Words," *Saturday Review* 14 Oct. 1978)

A *functional definition* describes how something works, as in the following definition of *poortalk.*

A debilitating idea afflicts American thinking. It is highly contagious, perhaps because people enjoy having it. Moreover, once it starts to spread, people quickly try to one-up each other to see who has it the worst. The ailment contaminates people at all levels of income and education—college faculty, union workers, business executives.

We call this affliction *poortalk.* As people's spending outstrips their income, they feel and proclaim that they are underpaid, defeated by inflation and taxes, and incapable of affording their family's needs. Workers complain they cannot make ends meet on their inadequate salaries. Friends grouse to one another about rising costs and find bittersweet pleasure in itemizing what they cannot afford. People living in lavish homes bemoan the cost of trivial items.

(David Myers and Thomas Ludwig, "Let's Cut the Poortalk," *Saturday Review* 28 Oct. 1978)

Definition by origins or etymology tells the history of a term, tracing it to its source.

I shall try to enlist you in the struggle to give elitism a good name. If I believe anything, it is this: there can be neither true culture nor true art without elitism. And yet "elitism" is a word that seems to get dirtier every day in the mouths of Americans, and may already be beyond the ministrations of our most miraculous detergents.

What does this dirty word actually mean? It comes from "elite," obviously, which means the elect, deriving from the latin *eligere,* to elect, wherefrom, through the Old French feminine past participle *elite* (elected), we get the modern French and English nouns. The elite, then, are the elected or elect, and elitism is belief in the superior wisdom or ability of such a group.

(John Simon, "In Defense of Elitism," *The Atlantic* Dec. 1978)

If a term is especially complex, unfamiliar, or often misunderstood, a writer may have to combine methods and define at length and in detail:

an extended definition. Here is an extended redefinition of *lust,* one of the seven deadly sins, for a contemporary audience:

Functional definition

Listing characteristics
Connotative definition
(attitudes associated
with the term)
Functional definition

Comparison and
contrast

Formal definition

Functional definition

Lust is not interested in its partners, but only in the gratification of its own craving: not even in the satisfaction of our whole natures, but in the appeasement merely of an appetite which we are unable to subdue. It is therefore a form of self-subjection; in fact of self-emptying. The sign it wears is: "This property is vacant." Anyone may take possession of it for a while. Lustful people may think that they can choose a partner at will for sexual gratification. But they do not really choose; they accept what is available. Lust accepts any partner for a momentary service; anyone may squat in its groin.

Love has meaning only insofar as it includes the idea of its continuance. Even what we rather glibly call a love affair, if it comes to an end, may continue as a memory that is pleasing in our lives, and we can still renew the sense of privilege and reward of having been allowed to know someone with such intimacy and sharing. But Lust dies at the next dawn and, when it returns in the evening, to search where it may, it is with its own past erased. Love wants to enjoy in other ways the human being whom it has enjoyed in bed. But in the morning Lust is always furtive. It dresses as mechanically as it undressed and heads straight for the door, to return to its own solitude. Like all the sins, it makes us solitary. It is a self-abdication, at the very heart of one's own being, of our need and ability to give and receive. . . .

Lust is not a sin *of* the flesh so much as a sin *against* it. We are present in it to each other, revealing and exposing, sensitive to others and even vulnerable to them. When one hears people talk today of the sexual act as if it were rather like emptying one's bladder, one wishes to remind them that people still get hurt. They get hurt in their bodies, not merely from slappings and beatings and whippings, but from more subtle humiliations of which our sexual feelings are registers. Lust is a humiliation of the flesh, of another's and of one's own; and it is a perversity of our time that, in the name of a freedom which is delusive, we not only tolerate this humiliation but exalt it as a wonder of the modern age.

(Henry Fairlie, "Lust or Luxuria," *The New Republic* 8 Oct. 1977)

Defining well is not only a matter of knowing *how* to define but also *when.* Obviously definition is in order whenever you use terms you suspect will be unfamiliar to your audience. But you will also want to define the following types of terms.

Specialized Terms   Specialized terms may be unfamiliar to readers in general. Here, for example, are functional definitions of two terms unique to the black neighborhoods of Brooklyn:

In Brooklyn you fall into one of two categories when you start growing up. The names for the categories may be different in other cities, but the categories are the same. First, there's the minority of the minority, the "ducks," or suckers. These are the kids who go to school every day. They even want to go to college. Imagine that! School after high school! They don't smoke cheeb (marijuana) and they get zooted (intoxicated) after only one can of beer. They're wasting their lives waiting for a dream that won't come true.

The ducks are usually the ones getting beat up on by the majority group—the "hard rocks." If you're a real hard rock you have no worries, no cares. Getting high is as easy as breathing. You just rip off some duck. You don't bother going to school; it's not necessary.

> (Deairich Hunter, "Ducks vs. Hard Rocks," *Newsweek* 18 Aug. 1980)

Ambiguous Terms   Words may at once have several meanings. Clear writing must stipulate which meaning is intended.

A large part of the confusion about [the meaning of the word "love"] springs from the fact that English, unlike some other languages, does not distinguish among different types of love. Ancient Greek, as we know, had three forms: *eros* for sexual and emotional love, *philia* for brotherly love and *agape* for love of God.

When we are commanded, in all the bibles of the world, to "love our neighbor," it is the latter two forms of the word *love* that are being enjoined, not the first. For we cannot be commanded to love emotionally, since this kind of love is a feeling and not an act of the will.

> (Sydney J. Harris, "Of Loving and Liking," *Pieces of Eight* [Boston: Houghton, 1982])

Relative Terms   Some words have different meanings in different places. *Poverty*, for example, refers to one set of income figures when it describes life in a large northern city and quite a different set when applied to life in a small southern town where less money may be required for the same standard of living. Effective writing tells what a relative term means within a particular context.

EXERCISES

1. Following are pairs of words that need redefinition by each generation. Choose four pairs and, without using a dictionary, redefine them. The meaning of one term in a pair should exclude, as far as possible, the meaning of the other term. Use as many kinds of definition as you need to make your point.

Training/education.	Art/craft.
College/community college.	Profession/job.
Happiness/joy.	Youthfulness/
Self-fulfillment/selfishness.	immaturity.
Work/play.	Adulthood/maturity.

Freedom/anarchy.
Feminine/female.
Masculine/male.

Intelligence/wisdom.
Equality/identity.
Justice/fairness.
Good/evil.

Example
Training is a process of bending and shaping. For example, we train a vine to grow upward. Training enforces conformity of one sort or another, as when a mother toilet trains her child. We train in order to prompt a particular response, as Pavlov did when he trained dogs to salivate at the sound of a bell. Education, on the other hand, requires the will of the learner. It is not passive, mere response, but the acquisition of knowledge, either through schooling or by learning on one's own. Education requires understanding. You can train animals, but you don't educate them.

—Joan Rotonda

2. Invent and then define four terms that do not now exist but are needed to make sense of some feature of your life or community. Your terms may refer to people, events, problems, objects, ideas, buildings, institutions, or emotions. You may make up words or combine parts of words. Try to make the sound fit the meaning. You may write humorously or seriously.

Examples
Roadent: One who lives on the road, e.g., truckers or bikers.

—Zackary Lowing

Mega-opted: An event that occurs when you're eighteen, you have your whole life before you with unlimited options to choose from, yet your elders still insist on choosing for you.

—Scott Crossland

The Words of Others (*Quotation and Allusion*)

One of the most straightforward ways to develop a subject is to draw from the words of others and quote, summarize, or make allusions. When writing about people, you'll write more vividly and dramatically if you let them speak for themselves, especially at crucial moments. Their words will bring your writing to life and dramatize its themes. Here, in an excerpt about childhood cancer, quotations dramatize the anxiety and strength of a mother and daughter, as well as supporting the topic sentence of the first paragraph.

Not all the children who are told falsified diagnoses of their cancer are defeated by loneliness if they later hear the truth; some react in strength, often to protect their parents. One such situation was experienced by the Chapmans, who—like many parents—found it emotionally impossible to tell the full diagnosis to their child, Jill, who was 14 when she contracted Hodgkin's disease five years ago. "We told her she had Hodgkin's disease," says Mrs. Chapman, "but we didn't tell her that Hodgkin's is a cancer. I felt very protective of her and I didn't know how much she understood. I was shocked and scared that she might not live, and I think because I was so frightened, she was too."

And Jill Chapman was. "After a few months," she told me recently, "I realized that something was strange about the reactions of my parents, friends, teachers, and I thought, 'I'd better find out what this is.' I looked it up in the encyclopedia and saw that it was cancer. I was shocked. Nobody had said anything about that. But there it was in print, 'A cancerous disease.' I cried myself to sleep that night. But I didn't go to my parents. I had to understand myself and my own feelings before I could go to them. My mother would have said, 'Don't worry about it.' It would have upset her, and it wouldn't have helped. Nothing would help unless I came to grips with it myself."

She did; and eventually she told her mother that she knew. Today they both say their relationship is stronger than ever. . . .

(Susan Schiefelbein, "Children and Cancer; New
Hope for Survival," Saturday Review 4 Apr. 1979)

When you want to prove a point or explain something complex or controversial, quote authorities for support. Just be sure to observe the conventions for borrowing someone else's words:

Introduce the authority and give his or her credentials
Weave the quotation into the fabric of your own ideas

John Staudenmaier, a Jesuit and visiting professor at MIT's center for Science, Technology and Society, talks about the birth of the phone in 1876 as "the first time in human history that we could split voice from sight, touch, smell and taste."

What does that mean? That we no longer have to be in the same room to talk to each other. That we can choose friends across space and keep friends over distance.

Explain your quotations

But doesn't it also mean that we can ignore the people who live in our hallway? In some ways, the same machine that offers us a handy shortcut through loneliness may also make it more likely for us to live alone.

(Ellen Goodman, "Telephone keeps us in touch—but
isolates, too," Chicago Sun-Times 29 Mar. 1983)

Whenever you quote, be as *brief* as possible. Few people read long quotations unless they're reading an assignment in a textbook like this—and sometimes, truth to tell, not even then. Your readers expect that every quoted word will have meaning or significance. If you quote 150 words but need only the 25 in the middle, you will mislead them and leave them wondering just what is the point of your quotation. Besides, brief quotations are more emphatic than long ones and less likely to interrupt the flow of your ideas. What to quote?

- The apt or striking phrase.
- The idea that is better put than you can put it.
- The line whose feeling would be lost in summary or paraphrase.
- The famous line (Who would paraphrase Hamlet's "To be or not to be" as "Should I or shouldn't I?").

Whenever you take words from books or magazines, remember to document your borrowing by giving the author's name in your text and full publication information at the end. (For complete information on documentation, see Chapter 17, The Research Project, Step 6, pages 455–463.)

An *allusion* makes a veiled reference to the words or sometimes the deeds of another, often to the words of a famous speech or literary work. It adds a new dimension to a piece of writing, supporting direct statement by the implications of indirect statement. By putting familiar words into unfamiliar contexts and making them resonate with new meaning, we make our ideas and persona more complex and interesting. For example, in an essay chronicling her reluctant conversion to the ranks of nonsmokers, this writer alludes to the biblical Book of Daniel, remarking that,

> in any case, for smokers the handwriting is, quite literally, on the wall: an epidemic of "No Smoking" signs that point to a day when puffing and dragging in public places will be forbidden altogether.
> (Meg Greenfield, "Two Cheers for the Unfit,"
> *Newsweek* 2 Jan. 1978)

Do you remember the story behind this oft-made allusion? The hand of God wrote on a palace wall, warning the Chaldean king that his days were numbered. The writer counts on her readers' memory of this famous incident to give ironic meaning to her tale of No Smoking signs. The signs, she suggests, do more than command smokers not to smoke; just as the king was warned of his imminent death, smokers are warned of a grim future of enforced self-denial.

The following opening to an essay on test-tube babies employs allusion for more serious ends, to criticize quietly those doctors and scientists who engineer where the author believes they have no right.

> Medical scientists work in mysterious ways their miracles to perform. For instance, the test-tube baby.
> (Goodman Ace, "You've Come a Long Way, Baby,"
> *Saturday Review* 14 Oct. 1978)

The source of the allusion is a poem by William Cowper (1731–1800), "Light Shining out of Darkness":

> God moves in a mysterious way,
> His wonders to perform;
> He plants his footsteps in the sea,
> And rides upon the storm.

Now, most readers are probably not familiar with this poem and so probably wouldn't get the allusion directly. But they have heard the poem's opening lines so many times in other allusions that when they hear them again in this introduction, their memory helps reinforce the writer's point.

MISS PEACH

MISS PEACH by Mell Lazarus. Courtesy of Mell Lazarus and News Group Chicago, Inc.

By substituting scientists for God, the writer suggests their power and his opinion that they are playing God, usurping a power they have no right to use. The allusion adds an ironic undercurrent of contradiction to what at first seems a direct statement of praise.

Whether your purposes are straightforward or ironic, humorous or serious, allusion will give depth to your subjects and subtlety to your style. It can make even the most serious writing interesting to read. One caution: your allusion and its point are lost if readers aren't familiar with the original quotation you're alluding to. If you doubt they will remember the source, introduce your allusion, but be brief. The best allusions are like the knowing looks that pass between friends, given without comment.

If the Atlanta Braves are America's Team, then their center fielder, Dale Murphy, is the Greatest American Hero.

Murphy does everything but leap tall buildings in this metropolis, which after suffering almost 15 years of baseball mediocrity, has a Brave new world to contemplate.

(Michael Davis, *Chicago Sun-Times* 17 May 1983)

EXERCISES

1. Write a brief revealing dialogue, fact or fiction, between two or more members of your community. They should talk the way people in your community talk about subjects that interest them. If necessary, describe the scene and speakers; use verbs of saying (*he said, she blurted, he sighed,* and so on), but use them sparingly. Try to make the speeches identify the speakers and reveal their attitudes. (See Chapter 18, pages 529–530, for information about direct quotations.)

2. Make a list of famous lines from literature, music, movies, sports, politics, current events, and advertising that the members of your class would be sure to know. Then write a paragraph about some feature of life in your community, turning several of these quotations into allusions. Don't overuse allusions; use just enough to help make your point.

DEVELOPING A SUBJECT

Too much writing, both in school and out, is underdeveloped and unimpressive. One reason is that we speak more than we write. We're used to depending upon gesture, the inflection of our voices, and our listeners to help make our meaning. If we don't say enough or say it clearly, our listeners will tell us. Unfortunately we don't have these resources when we write. Another reason is that we're afraid of boring our readers. We want just to make our point and be done with it, sparing them the tedium of unnecessary words. And so we make it short and simple and hope that will be enough. Or we may not know very much about our subjects or lack the words to say what we want. No wonder our writing often does little more than cast the shadow of our subjects.

But try for a minute to see your writing from your readers' points of view. They don't have you there to explain yourself to them. Therefore, nothing is more important than the details you provide. Nothing makes your writing more interesting to read or easier to understand. When was the last time you read a novel or short story primarily for its theme? You read for the color of the sky, the swagger of the hero's walk, the action of the chase, the good feeling that comes when everybody lives happily ever after. What pleased you were the details. Or when did you ever read a recipe just to hear how a pie tasted? Never. You read for all the details of ingredients, mixing instructions, and baking time so you could bake your own pie and taste it for yourself. Your readers read your writing for the same reasons, "to *see* what you have to say."

Now forget your readers for the moment and consider the way *you* read your writing. Put aside the practical reason of writing to satisfy readers at school or on the job. Where do *you* find pleasure and satisfaction in your writing? Where do you find the parts worth rereading? Why, in the details, of course. The pleasure comes in discovering the details that bring a subject to life and the satisfaction in tinkering with them until they're worded just right. Developing a subject well is as important to us as to our readers. Remember E. M. Forster's paradoxical question quoted in the last chapter: "How do I know what I think till I see what I say?" We write for the same reason our readers read our writing, to *see* what we have to say.

That we almost never see our subjects whole at the beginning of a project is one reason for taking notes. And because you never can tell when you'll discover something new to say, you ought to get in the habit of keeping pen and paper handy throughout the project, in your car, by your bed, in a pocket or purse. Don't worry about writing too much. You can't know in the beginning what you'll need at the end; it's always easier to cut than find something new. Just aim to lay out all your facts, figures, and explanations on paper. Later, out of these fragmentary details, you'll create "the big picture," your fully developed subject.

Drawing a Subject

How much detail you include in this finished picture depends upon how much your readers want to know of your subject. How can you make an intelligent guess about that? One way is to draw your subject. That's right, *draw* the subject you're writing about.[1] We don't always think in words; why should we prepare to write by using words alone? Einstein began his scientific speculation not with words or numbers but with an image. William Faulkner, the southern novelist, began thinking about his greatest novel with the image of a little girl in a tree. Many writers work this way, from a picture rather than an idea, first *seeing* their subject—literally— then translating it into words. The next time you have a writing project to do, try drawing it before you write a preliminary draft. You don't have to be a skillful artist, and your picture need not be—possibly shouldn't be—a realistic representation. How could you draw a realistic picture of "Justice," for example? All you have to do is draw your subject as you imagine it in your mind's eye.

1. Make an abstract or symbolic drawing, a doodle, a diagram, a cartoon, or rough sketch: anything that represents your subject to you.
2. Then circle those parts that are least clear to you or that your readers will find hardest to imagine or understand. On those parts you'll lavish the most attention and detail.

Here's a doodle one writer made while preparing to write an essay about his childhood hometown.

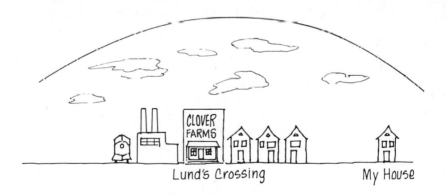

EXERCISE

Make a drawing of your community that expresses your most important opinions of it. Your drawing need not be realistic; make it abstract or symbolic, a doodle, diagram, or a cartoon. Circle those parts your readers might not understand or notice if they traveled to your community.

WRITING PROJECTS

Topics

1. That circle of faces:

    a. Write an informative and evaluative essay of three to five pages about a problem in your community that needs quick attention. Address your essay to the citizens of your community. What is this problem? Give full details. What caused it? What will be the consequences if no one does anything about it?

    b. Write a three- to five-page informative and evaluative essay telling the members of your composition class about the institution, place, or event that gives your community its identity. What is it? Where is it? Give full details about it. How does it express or shape the spirit of your community?

    c. Write a three- to five-page informative essay about some group (social, racial, or ethnic) in your community that your readers may not be aware of. Aim to introduce your readers to them by telling where and how they live, their most important values, customs, and beliefs. Write to the majority group in your community.

2. If you have been doing the exercises in this chapter that ask you to explore your community, revise and assemble them into a three- to five-page community profile. This will be an informative report in which you try to explain its geography, its citizens, what makes them a community, community resources, opportunities, problems, and the outlook for the future. Address your report to your fellow citizens; describe their community for them. If your community is large or if you have a lot of information, you will have to be selective, giving the most important information about its most important features. Chapter 13, pages 287–298, will show you how to prepare a report. You will probably organize the body of your report according to the list of subjects in the second sentence of this topic.

3. Write a three- to five-page extended definition of that primary community, the family. Address your family. What is a family, exactly? What are its functions? How has it changed from earlier times? For better or worse? What are its virtues and vices? Under what circumstances does it function best? What are the greatest threats to it? How does your family measure up to the standards of your definition? What would improve the quality of your family life? You will probably organize your essay according to the order of the preceding questions. Omit any that don't help you make your definition.

4. Write a three- to five-page extended analogy essay that makes sense of some feature of your community: its geography, architecture, social life, economy, values, changes, growth or decline, or prospects for the future. Choose this feature, then find an analogy to help you understand it. Write to the members of your community; help them understand. Organize your essay as a detailed comparison between your subject and the object of comparison in your analogy.

5. Write a three- to five-page essay explaining how an essay you've read recently has used methods of development to support a thesis. What is the thesis? What methods are used to support it? How are they used? Which provide the best support? Are any methods unpersuasive, incomplete, or inaccurate?

The Writing Process

1. Writing-in-progress.
    a. *Exploring:* Free association and freewriting.
    b. *Developing.*
        i. Take notes and freewrite to discover what you will say, take walk-around notes, or write a letter to your audience (see pages 47–54).
        ii. *New in this chapter:*
            List facts and statistics.
            Illustrate your ideas: *For example* . . .
            Write anecdotes: *Once* . . .
            Write analogies: *To be* _____ *is to be* _____.
            Define your key terms: _____ = *genus* + *differentia.*
            Quote the right people.
            Gather famous sayings for allusions to your subject.
            Draw your subject.
    c. *Planning a communications strategy:* Decide on a role, persona (distance and attitude), thesis (*My point is that* . . . *What I mean to say is that* . . .), and design.
    d. *Revising:* Reconsider your ideas and communications strategy; create frictions in your thinking (see pages 55–56).
2. Writing: Write the preliminary draft of your project. Write freely, don't stop except to reread, give yourself room to revise (see pages 57–58).
3. Rewriting.
    a. Be a zoom lens as you revise; add, delete, substitute, rearrange.
    b. Consider your opening and supporting details especially; cut what you like best; cut a word from each sentence (see pages 60–61).
    c. Copyedit for mechanical errors, recopy, and proofread (see pages 61–62).
4. Self-evaluation (when you have finished your project).
    a. Summarize your readers' responses to your last writing.
    b. Which of them do you disagree with or not understand? Which do you agree with? Should they have done anything they did not do?
    c. Did you learn anything from your last writing that you tried to apply in this writing?
    d. What are your intentions in this writing?
    e. What was most difficult about it? Do you see any parts you don't like? How might they be improved?
    f. What do you like best about it?

End Note

1. I am indebted for this composing strategy to Nancy Mack and her paper on right brain/left brain enhancing strategies, "Brain Hemisphere Lateralization: Helping the Writer Choose the Appropriate Composing Strategy," Conference on College Composition and Communication, Detroit, MI, 18 Mar. 1983.

Chapter 5

Development: Seeing Is Believing

❧

❧ TWO METHODS OF DEVELOPMENT

Description   More than any other method of development, description enables us to *see* a subject. It presents the impression a subject makes on our senses of sight, hearing, touch, taste, and smell. There are two kinds. With the first, *imaginative description,* we aim to recreate a subject in words and then help readers experience it just as we have. Good imaginative description exercises all our senses, turning words into eyes, ears, fingers, tongues, and noses. See how many senses this writer uses to describe the villagers living beside Lake Atitlán in central Guatemala:

Santiago, like the other lakeside towns, bears no trace of the influence of the Spanish, who appear, fortunately, never to have found this cradled paradise. On either side of the broad, cobbled street that leads into town, *Sight*   Indian women sell parti-colored shirts and immense blouses, brilliant, tie-dyed material for skirts, and candy-striped pants. Guatemalan Indians are the world's flashiest dressers. The women wear a huge, square-cut blouse called a *huipil,* striped in every color of the rainbow. Every village has its own fashion in *huipiles:* some have vertical stripes, some horizontal, some have diamonds or squares, some checks, some feature a red-orange-yellow progression, some blue-green. Nor does it stop there: flouting all the known laws of *chic,* women wear skirts and shawls as vivid as their blouses, giving them the look of impossibly decorated butterflies. . . .

Elsewhere on Santiago's mercantile boulevard, a toothless hag tries to sell *Sound*   a spool of brown cotton, which she spins ceaselessly as she hectors the crowd.

Sight
Sound

Sight

Touch
Taste
Smell

A gang of tiny girls hawks equally tiny ceramic ducks, most of them with their flying apparatus already fractured, but with the compensation that they produce music as gracefully as a kazoo. . . .

The principal feature of the town itself is the municipal market, where rows of stolid, unsmiling Indian women sit behind baskets and bushels filled with numberless varieties of peppers and bananas, paprika, yucca, grains, corn—white, yellow, and black; large and small; hard and soft. And then the tropical fruits, swaddling the buyer in their sweet, riotous perfume— watermelon, pineapple, canteloupe, papaya, and guava. Also, alas, metal watchbands, flashlights, and plastic urns from Japan. No one is immune.

(James Traub, "God and Man in Guatemala," *Saturday Review* 14 Oct. 1978)

Good imaginative description also uses the right number of the right kinds of details. It doesn't belabor the obvious and tell everything but invites readers to participate in the description and create a subject from their *own* store of details, memories, and ideas. In the preceding passage, James Traub sketches in the outline of his scene: a village without Spanish architecture, a broad cobbled street, "a toothless hag," "a gang of tiny girls," a market place, Indian women, fruits and vegetables. But he depends on us to use our imaginations and fill in the scene with details about Central American villages, old women, young girls, and marketplaces. What details he *does* provide are almost always the ones we can't imagine by ourselves or small details we might miss without his guidance: the *huipil*, the toothless hag's spool of cotton, the little girls' broken ceramic ducks, and the textures and smells of fruits and vegetables.

With *technical description,* on the other hand, we aim not so much at the imagination as the intellect. We use sensory information to discover a subject and then to help readers understand it as we do. Here is James Traub's chiefly technical description of an ancient Mayan city that archeologists are gradually reclaiming from the Guatemalan jungle:

The only part of Tikal (whose name, my guide explained logically, is similar to the Mayan words for "sound" and "twenty," "so we conjecture that it means 'the place of voices' ") that has been fully explored is the grand plaza. It's here that we can begin to imagine the grandeur of this vanished civilization: two towering, vertiginous [dizzying] temples, one of them 170 feet tall, square off against one another to the east and west, while north and south are occupied by twin acropolises [citadels]. The temples are as steep as a sorcerer's hat, perhaps to encourage humility in the climbing aspirant; they must be ascended sidewise.

The acropolises are as complex as the temples are simple. The Mayas simply built one civilization atop another, so that each acropolis is a vast, labyrinthine honeycomb of apartments from 10 different centuries, each one squatting on the one beneath it. And these, in turn, stretch back into neighborhoods, courtyards, more temples; and at the crown of a nearby summit stands the observatory, almost all of whose abstruse [difficult to understand] calculations are lost to us today.

(James Traub, "God and Man in Guatemala,"
Saturday Review 14 Oct. 1978)

It is not just the temples' height that interests Traub but *how* high they are, how many there are, where they stand, what the acropolises look like, how they came to be built, how long they have stood. Concerned that we understand as well as see these ruins, the writer has created a verbal map as part of his description.

As this example makes clear, technical description need not be impersonal or wholly objective. Most description, imaginative or technical, conveys two messages at once, what a writer *feels* about a subject as well as what he has perceived. This emotional message is known as *the dominant impression,* the mood or judgment evoked by the details a writer describes and by the way he describes them. The dominant impression gives feeling and meaning to raw sensory impressions. The Mayan ruins of Tikal were just ruins and nothing more until James Traub saw them, felt their mystery—his dominant impression—and tried to suggest it by phrases like these:

steep as a sorcerer's hat
vast, labyrinthine honeycomb
the observatory, almost all of whose abstruse calculations are lost to us today

The ruins mystified James Traub, and if he has described well, they mystify his readers.

The key to good dominant impression writing is *selection:* presenting those details that create the impression and leaving out any that detract from it. Imagine the civilizing presence of a tourist bus parked beneath Tikal's ruined temples; tourists, cameras slung over their shoulders, trooping up the monuments; and all the paraphernalia of an archeological dig. These details actually may have been there when Traub visited Tikal, but when he sat down to describe it he left them out because they would rob the place of the mystery he felt. Effective writers choose language true to their subjects *and* to their feelings about it.

EXERCISES

1. When you think of your community, what building, monument, person, place, or event comes to mind? If possible, go observe it and then write two descriptive paragraphs. Make the first primarily technical. Aim to inform through descriptive details. Make the second primarily imaginative and convey a dominant impression. Decide how you feel about your subject, then select and present your details to create that feeling. Use as many senses as possible.

2. The Zoom Game: Imagine you are making a movie of your community. You want to open with a shot of the building, monument, person, place, or event that best characterizes it. You want this opening to create a mood for your film, so it must register a dominant impression of your subject. Your camera has three lens openings:

Panoramic.
Middle distance.
Close focus.

It can move up and down, back and forth. You have allowed only thirty seconds for your opening, and that gives you just six camera moves. Write a film script for that opening. For each "scene," identify the lens opening and the camera movement from the preceding scene; then describe in detail what your camera and microphones will record. Use sounds and pictures to create your dominant impression and evoke other senses—taste, touch, and smell.

Figurative Language

Figurative language, like description, helps us see a subject. It is also a form of comparison similar to analogy. In fact, figurative language and analogy are often so close we can't tell them apart, but in one respect they are different: analogy appeals to the intellect; figurative language appeals to the imagination. Analogy aims to inform; figurative language aims to dramatize. Analogy compares to help readers understand; figurative language compares to help them see and feel. Consider how the figurative language in the following passage helps us see the dying patient and then creates our feelings for him.

Brown skin = Rust
Blind eyes = Frosted windows of a snowbound cottage

Legless = Bonsai tree

Legless body = Rotting log
Legless body = Sailor on a slanting deck

From the doorway of Room 542 the man in the bed seems deeply tanned. Blue eyes and close-cropped white hair give him the appearance of vigor and good health. But I know that his skin is not brown from the sun. It is rusted, rather, in the last stage of containing the vile repose within. And the blue eyes are frosted, looking inward like the windows of a snowbound cottage. This man is blind. This man is also legless—the right leg missing from midthigh down, the left from just below the knee. It gives him the look of a bonsai, roots and branches pruned into the dwarfed facsimile of a great tree. . . .

What is he thinking behind those lids that do not blink? Is he remembering a time when he was whole? Does he dream of feet? Of when his body was not a rotting log?

He lies solid and inert. In spite of everything, he remains impressive, as though he were a sailor standing athwart a slanting deck.

(Richard Selzer, "The Discus Thrower," *Harper's* Nov. 1977)

The images of rust, the frosted cottage windows, the dwarfed bonsai tree, the rotting log, and the sailor on the storm-tossed ship paint *pictures* of a man ravaged by disease that play on our feelings. The rust and rotting log make us want to turn away from the man's terrible suffering, but the cottage windows, the bonsai tree, and the sailor image hold our gaze. Snowbound cottages, after all, are often places of warmth and refuge. Bonsai trees are tortured into works of beauty. And sailors athwart slanting decks have courage and poise. As we study this man through the overlaying images of figurative comparison, we begin to admire his endurance and strength showing poignantly through the isolation and pain. These feelings come to us, the readers, as we transfer emotional associations from the descriptive half of the comparison (often called the *vehicle*) to the actual subject of the writing (often called the *tenor*). The passage is about the dying man, but we see him in terms of our feelings for rust, window, tree, log, and sailor. The three figures of speech we create most frequently are simile, metaphor, and personification.

Simile   A simile compares "tenor" and "vehicle" explicitly, using *like, as, as if,* or *as though.*

Tenor		*Vehicle*
blind blue eyes	——look like——	the frosted windows of a snowbound cottage
the legless man	——has the look of——	a bonsai tree
he remains impressive	——as though——	a sailor standing athwart a slanting deck

Metaphor   A metaphor, on the other hand, compares implicitly, not "*X* is like *Y*" but "*X* is *Y*."

Tenor		*Vehicle*
brown skin	——is——	rusted [metal]
"it is not brown from the sun"		"it is rusted rather"
the sick man's body	——is——	a rotting log

Tenor and vehicle are fused. The features of the vehicle are *not*, as in a simile, transferred from vehicle to tenor; instead, by verbal prestidigitation one subject, the tenor, *becomes* the vehicle, something else radically different yet similar in key respects. Here's another metaphor:

> Superstition seems to run, a submerged river of crude religion, below the surface of human consciousness.
>
> (Robertson Davies, "A Few Kind Words for Superstition," *Newsweek* 20 Nov. 1978)

Tenor		*Vehicle*
superstition	——becomes——	a submerged river

By this fusion, the subject, superstition, acquires all of the underground river's characteristics: the forbidding depth, the darkness, the cold power. Through metaphor we see and feel the irrational strength of superstition as we might not otherwise.

Personification   Personification is a special kind of metaphor. When we personify a subject, we give it human characteristics and describe it as if it were a person. Consider the human traits in this description of two Guatemalan volcanoes:

> For all their *stolidity* [showing little emotion], the volcanoes lead a *moody* life: *peaceful and protective* in the clear light of the morning; *brooding and withdrawn* when the afternoon clouds sail in from the north, creeping up the *shoulders* of the peaks toward their summit; and at night, in the rainy season, when the sheet lightning flashes across the surface of the lake, *splendid* and *terrifying* in a moment of white light.
>
> (James Traub, "God and Man in Guatemala,"
> *Saturday Review* 14 Oct. 1978, emphasis added)

Creating Figures of Speech   Use figurative language often when you write; its glimmers of insight will make your style clearer, more dramatic, and more interesting. But be original; don't write clichés. A *cliché* is a figure of speech that, through time and overuse, has lost its freshness and power to communicate; it is darkness and dead air where a flower should be blooming fragrantly. The simile *stubborn as a mule* and the metaphor *life is just a bowl of cherries* must have once been lively expressions of stubbornness and life's sweetness. But after years—decades, centuries, even—of popularity, the mule has died and cherries come in cans. These comparisons are now little more than verbal shorthand for judgments made without thinking.

Especially beware, therefore, of borrowing figurative language. Chances are the catchy metaphor or simile you've just heard is stooped with age, well on its way to the cliché graveyard. Even the figurative language you see in print, though new to you, may be a middleaged cliché to millions of others. Create your own figures of speech; make them new and make them true. Here is a simple formula called a *figurative free association* that will help you write fresh analogies, similes, and metaphors: If __(1)__ were a __(2)__, it would/wouldn't be a __(3)__. Put your subject into the first blank and a term from one of the following lists into the second; for the third blank, supply an image that completes the sentence.

a means of transportation	a piece of furniture	a beverage
a place	a movement	a building
a toy	a musical instrument	a color

the weather	a tool or device	a smell
a plant or tree	a sound	a shape
an animal	an article of clothing	
food	a road	

Example

If *sky diving* were a *movement,* it would be a *dandelion seed drifting in the wind.*

Whenever you have a writing project use this formula to explore your feelings about a subject and discover vivid details to dramatize it. But later, when you write the preliminary draft of your project, drop the formula and weave your figure of speech into the fabric of your writing.

As soon as the chute opened above me, I lost my pre-jump jitters, relaxed, and suddenly realized how graceful I was, floating as softly as a dandelion seed drifting in the wind.

—Nancy Lee

EXERCISES

1. Illustrate your feelings about your life in two figurative free associations: If I were a ___(choose from one of the preceding lists)___, I would/wouldn't be a ___(make up an image to complete the formula)___.

If I were the weather, I'd want to be a horrible snowstorm that would be remembered for years. After all, who remembers the winter we had the most sunshine?

—Micki Richmond

If I were food, I'd be an open-faced avocado sandwich piled high with crisp green scallions and melted cheddar and mozzarella cheese, then sprinkled lightly with seasoned salt.

—Wayne Deering

2. Illustrate your feelings about your community in two figurative free associations: If ___(my community)___ were a _____, it would/wouldn't be a _____.

If Wheeling were an article of clothing, it would be bell-bottom jeans, a bit behind the times but not aware of it.

—Barry Bruno

If Palatine were an automobile, it would be a four-door Chevy Impala with an A.M. radio—boring, dull, and boxy, without style, grace, or excitement.

—Steve Duda

3. Here is a list of terms important to human and communal life. Choose four and write a figurative free association for each.

Marriage.	Politics.	Families.
Work.	Recreation.	Growing old.
Being a child.	Being a teenager.	Integration.
Being a minority.	Compassion.	Charity.

Transportation.	Class divisions.	The wrong side of the tracks.
Education.	Food.	Clothing.
Shelter.	Hang-outs.	Hanging out.
Streets.	Neighborhoods.	Houses and other buildings.
Neighbors.	Strangers.	Law and order.

4. Choose three figurative free associations, one each from Exercises 1, 2, and 3. Expand them into an extended analogy or figure of speech: Write a brief paragraph exploring all the similarities between the tenor (your subject) and vehicle (your imaginative object of comparison).

❧ WORDS TO SEE BY

Here are two more paragraphs to compare:

At Sealdah Station, in Calcutta, one of India's largest cities, there is poverty everywhere. In the station, homeless families stand around their few possessions. Outside, dusty streets run away in every direction, lined with small dilapidated buildings of metal, wood, and cloth. Inside these dark houses, small fires burn, and faces look out through the smoke at children playing in the dirty, smelly streets. In a short time the children who survive these terrible conditions will stop playing and become poverty-stricken, apathetic, starving adults. This is not a bright future, but it is the only one many of these children can expect.

At Sealdah Station, Calcutta, misery radiates outward. In the station, displaced families from East Pakistan hover around little piles of possessions. Outside, dusty streets straggle away in every direction, lined with tiny shacks of metal scraps, pieces of old baskets, strips of wood, and gunny sacks. In the dark interiors of the shacks, small fires glow through the smoke, and dark faces gaze out at children playing in the urinous-smelling, fly-infested streets. In a few years the children who survive these conditions will stop playing and become adults; that is, they will grow taller and thinner and stand in the streets like ragged skeletons, barefoot, hollow-eyed, blinking their apathetic stares out of gray, dusty faces. That is not a bright future, but it is the only one many of these children can expect.

(Philip Appleman, *The Silent Explosion* [Boston: Beacon, 1965])

Both of these paragraphs are adequately developed; each uses description to dramatize the poverty of urban India. Yet what differences between them! The first seems flat, even though filled with details, facts, and opinions; the second swells with painful, alarming life. The first gives us the idea of poverty; the second, an image that hurts our eyes, burns our nostrils, grates on our ears, and wounds our pity. The difference between the two lies, of course, in the language. Effective development of a subject— whatever the method—depends not only on how much we say but also on the words that express those details.

General and Specific Words

We can classify many words by whether they are general or specific. *General words* are umbrella terms that refer at once to many things:

"India's largest cities."
"Homeless families."
"Dirty, smelly streets."
"Small delapidated buildings of metal, wood, and cloth."

There are many large cities in India; many homeless families; many kinds of dirty, smelly streets; many kinds of small delapidated buildings. By contrast, *specific words* refer to fewer things; they are more precise:

"Calcutta."
"Displaced families from East Pakistan."
"Urinous-smelling, fly-infested streets."
"Tiny shacks of metal scraps, pieces of old baskets, strips of wood, and gunny sacks."

These words refer to a specific city, an especially painful kind of homelessness, a specific smell, specific vermin, and a specific kind of building.

You may already see the value of specific words: they help us focus on particulars and by so doing make a subject clearer and easier to grasp. The second paragraph on Sealdah Station is better than the first because its details are more specific. You can't avoid general terms in your writing, and you wouldn't want to. We use them to categorize things, people, places, ideas, sensations, and actions: to draw an outline, as it were, around a subject. But specific terms fill in that outline and turn it into a picture with depth and shade, highlights and details. General terms classify; specific terms individualize.

Abstract and Concrete Words

If we look at a red shoe and are not color-blind, we see pretty much what everyone does. If we eat a plum, we taste its tartness with everyone else. And if our hearing is not impaired and a fire truck passes, we all hear the same siren. These are sensuous reactions, and the words that describe them are concrete words. *Concrete words* refer to things we perceive with our five senses. Now consider words like *democracy, fear,* or the *misery* of Sealdah Station. We can see a voter going into a voting booth, feel our clammy palms when we're afraid, or smell the odors of a street, but we don't actually *see* democracy, *feel* fear, or *smell* misery. We see, feel, and smell their physical attributes. *Democracy, fear,* and *misery* are *abstractions,* words that refer to qualities or conditions that cannot be perceived by the senses.

We need abstractions just as we do generalizations. They energize our thinking and justify our actions. We couldn't live fully human lives without abstract concepts like justice, mercy, right, and wrong. But because they can't be perceived by our senses, abstractions are wispy terms and often mean very different things to different people. Sometimes they seem not to mean much at all. To be brought to life they must be anchored to concrete words and the real world of things we can see, hear, taste, touch, and smell. Ralph Waldo Emerson, the nineteenth-century American philosopher, gives this counsel: "But wise men pierce this rotten diction [of abstraction] and fasten words again to visible things."

The second paragraph about Sealdah Station is better than the first because it fastens its *misery* to the smell of urine and the feel of flies. It fastens *poverty* to *tiny shacks of metal scraps, pieces of old baskets, strips of wood, and gunny sacks.* It fastens *starvation* to *ragged skeletons, barefoot, hollow-eyed, blinking their apathetic stares out of gray, dusty faces.* Effective development alternates rhythmically between the generalizations and abstractions that express our understanding and the concrete particulars that our understanding depends upon. This rhythm guarantees that writing is lively and that all its life has meaning and purpose.

Denotation and Connotation

Many words have two kinds of meaning. The *denotative meaning* of a word is what the word denotes or points to in the real world, its dictionary definition. The denotative meaning of *misery* in the second sample paragraph above is "prolonged or extreme suffering; a state of great mental, emotional, or physical pain; wretchedness" (*The American Heritage Dictionary*).

The *connotative meaning* of a word, as you know from your study of persona in Chapter 2, is the cluster of emotional associations that a word acquires because of the way it is used. What is true of writing that dramatizes our persona and true as well of description that creates a dominant impression is also true of other well-developed writing. We write not only to produce understanding, our readers' and our own, but also to convey our judgments and feelings about a subject. We do both by the words we choose. In the second paragraph about Sealdah Station, the writer chooses

Used by permission of Johnny Hart and News America Syndicate.

the word *hover* rather than *stand* in the phrase *hover around little piles of possessions* because *hover* connotes anxiety, the nervous energy that would characterize the displaced Pakistanis. In the miserable world of the second paragraph, streets don't *run*, they *struggle away in every direction*, without purpose it seems, enervated, like their inhabitants. They are *fly-infested* rather than fly-filled because *infested* calls to mind rot and disease. And dust swirls throughout this scene, not only suggesting the filth that accompanies such poverty but also foreshadowing the death too soon to come to the children, *ragged skeletons . . . hollow-eyed* corpses-to-be. "Ashes to ashes and dust to dust" plays in the backs of our minds as we read. This paragraph is better than the first because here we see the misery but also *feel* it and are *moved* by it.

EXERCISES

1. We are surrounded by "thingumajigs." These are things, tools, events, people, jobs, or places we encounter every day that many of us don't know what to call. They influence our lives by their presence or the way we use them: they help us cook our food or communicate with others; they are hidden in our clothing and in plain sight in our environment; they teach us and do jobs for us. Drawing upon your own experiences and expertise, list the actual names for three thingumajigs that you know about but that the members of your composition class may not know. Then describe and explain each in a brief paragraph; use as many methods of development as necessary. Be so concrete and specific that your readers will be able to identify your thingumajig even if they don't know its name.

2. The *haiku* is a tiny Japanese verse form hundreds of years old. Generally a form of nature poetry, it captures in concrete, specific, connotative language the sensations and feelings of a season of the year. Either the season is mentioned directly, or some detail from natural or human life is presented that suggests the season. The trick of haiku writing is this: the poem has only three lines and seventeen syllables, five in the first line, seven in the second, five in the third. Write a haiku for each of the seasons, suiting your descriptions to the seasons where you live. Be serious or playful. Avoid clichés and trite description. Be as concrete and specific as you can. Some examples:

In silent mid-night
Our old scarecrow topples down . . .
Weird hollow echo.

Ballet in the air . . .
Twin butterflies until, twice white
They meet, they mate.

Under cherry-trees
Soup, the salad, fish and all . . .
Seasoned with petals.

Stupid hot melons
Rolling like fat idiots
Out from leafy shade.

Deep in dark forest
A woodcutter's dull ax talking . . .
And a woodcutter.

Shocking . . . the red of
Lacquered fingernails against
A white chrysanthemum.

November sunrise . . .
Uncertain, the cold storks stand . . .
Bare sticks in water.

Bony brushwood twigs
Cut down and stacked in
    bunches . . .
Yet bravely budding.

(*Japanese Haiku* and *Cherry Blossoms* [Mount Vernon, NY: Peter Pauper Press, 1956, 1960])

3. Identify the synonym that best fits each of the following sentences and then explain how its connotation differs from those of its relatives.[1]

    a. Those in your community who have money are (*affluent, prosperous, opulent, flush, rolling in money*).

    b. Those in your community who have little money are (*indigent, impoverished, needy, insolvent, impecunious*).

    c. Those in between earn an income that is (*middling, moderate, mediocre, so-so*).

    d. You have come to college to (*reform, better, redeem, improve*) yourself.

    e. Your teachers (*enlighten, indoctrinate, drill, educate, train*) you.

    f. If a police officer in your community arrests a young drunk driver, the officer is likely to (*grab, grip, clutch, snare, hold*) the offender and (*lead, escort, shove, hurry*) him or her to the squad car.

    g. The traffic in your community makes a (*clamor, din, racket, rumble, uproar, pandemonium*).

    h. People over sixty-five are (*senior citizens, golden agers, moms and pops, fossils, the elderly, oldsters*).

    i. People in your community who don't behave like the majority are (*idiosyncratic, nonconformist, eccentric, odd, weird, queer*).

    j. The flowers at the mall are (*imitation, fake, phony, artificial*).

    k. Those in your community who favor racial and social integration would (*herald, embrace, greet, kow tow to, toady to, cater to*) minorities. Those not in favor of integration are a (*pack, crowd, group, assembly, congregation*) who (*reject, exclude, repudiate, spurn, shut out, disapprove of*) these new arrivals.

4. *The connotative mirror.* Write a one-paragraph character sketch of yourself, contrasting your self-impressions with those your enemies may have. Create this double picture by using denotative synonyms that have different connotations, those that flatter and those that criticize. Use a dictionary and thesaurus if necessary. Describe your personality traits, behavior, life-style, habits of mind and feeling, home, political or religious beliefs, entertainment preferences: whatever is most important to your sense of identity. As you write, keep in mind the lines from the Scottish poet Robert Burns: "O wad [would] some Pow'r the giftie gie us/To see oursels as others see us!"

Examples

    I say I'm firm; my enemies say I'm hard-headed. I say I stand for principles; they say I'm dogmatic. I say I'm zealous in the defense of my principles; they say I'm fanatical. I say the wrongs of this world prompt my righteous indignation; they say I've got a holier-than-thou attitude.

I say I was an underachiever in high school algebra; my math teacher called me stupid. Now I'm all a-quiver with animal vitality; my parents say I'm hyperactive. Lately I've begun to put on a few pounds; my enemies say I'm getting as big as a house.

❧ DEVELOPING A SUBJECT EFFECTIVELY

Choosing the Right Methods of Development

In this chapter and the preceding, you've studied eight methods of development: facts and statistics, examples, anecdotes, analogies, definitions, the words of others, description, and figurative language. Which methods you choose for a particular project depend on your purposes. If you write for your own understanding or to inform readers, the case with most college writing, you'll probably develop your subject with *hard support,* those methods of development that appeal primarily to the intellect: technical description, facts and statistics, the words of authorities, definitions, examples, and analogies. If, on the other hand, you write to express your experiences or to move an audience, sweet reason and the evidence of "hard support" may not be enough. You'll turn to *soft support,* methods of development whose appeal is primarily imaginative and emotional: imaginative description, anecdotes, figurative language, certain kinds of examples and definitions, and allusion. At their extremes, the differences between hard and soft support are the differences in purpose, form, and content between an encyclopedia entry and a poem:

Definition
Comparison

Description
Facts
Description

Facts

Mustard gas, chemical compound used as a *Poison gas* in World War I. The burning sensation it causes on contact with the skin is similar to that caused by oil from black mustard seeds. The compound is not a gas but a colorless, oily liquid with a somewhat sweet, agreeable odor; it boils at 217°C. A powerful vesicant, mustard gas causes severe blistering even in small quantities. Highly irritating to the eyes, it quickly causes conjunctivitis and blindness. If inhaled, it attacks the respiratory tract and lungs, causing pulmonary edema. Some effects of exposure to mustard gas are delayed up to 12 hr; death may result several days after exposure. Mustard gas was introduced by the Germans in warfare against the British at Ypres, Belgium, in July, 1917, and took a heavy toll of casualties. It is dispersed as an aerosol by a bursting shell.

(The New Columbia Encyclopedia)

Dulce et Decorum Est

Anecdote
Simile
Description

Bent double, like old beggars under sacks,
Knock-kneed, coughing like hags, we cursed through sludge,
Till on the haunting flares we turned our backs,

	And towards our distant rest began to trudge.
Facts	Men marched asleep. Many had lost their boots,
	But limped on, blood-shod. All went lame, all blind;
Metaphor	Drunk with fatigue; deaf even to the hoots
	of gas-shells dropping softly behind.
Quotation	Gas! Gas! Quick, boys—An ecstasy of fumbling,
	Fitting the clumsy helmets just in time,
Description	But someone still was yelling out and stumbling
Analogy	And floundering like a man in fire or lime.—
	Dim through the misty panes and thick green light,
Simile	As under a green sea, I saw him drowning.
	In all my dreams before my helpless sight
Description	He plunges at me, guttering, choking, drowning.
Metaphor	If in some smothering dreams, you too could pace
Description	Behind the wagon that we flung him in,
	And watch the white eyes writhing in his face,
Simile	His hanging face, like a devil's sick of sin;
	If you could hear, at every jolt, the blood
Metaphor	Come gargling from the froth-corrupted lungs,
Simile	Bitter as the cud
	Of vile, incurable sores on innocent tongues,
	My friend, you would not tell with such high zest
	To children ardent for some desperate glory,
Allusion	The old Lie: Dulce et decorum est
	Pro patria mori ["It is sweet and fitting to die for one's country"—Horace].

(Wilfred Owen)

Between these two extremes, where you do most of your writing, you will have to balance hard and soft support, appealing both to intelligence and emotions. The key to an artful balance is remembering that in good writing no detail exists for its own sake. No matter what satisfaction you had discovering a fact or creating an analogy, no matter how vivid a descriptive paragraph or figure of speech might be, each must help fulfill your larger purposes of persuasion, information, instruction, or self-expression. This advice is especially important to remember when you use methods of development that appeal to the senses: description, figurative language, analogy, and anecdote. Often they are the most compelling parts of our writing, and it's easy to believe we'll steal the life from it by cutting them. But remember the advice from Chapter 3: You should probably cut what you like best. It may be there for its own sake alone. We cut irrelevant parts from our writing for the same reason a gardener prunes a bush: to give it shape, proportion, and new vitality.

Choosing the Right Words

If you develop your subject while you're planning, so you see it in detail, you shouldn't have to worry about your language while you're drafting. Any changes you make trying to tell the truth will help make it "right." But when you've finished that preliminary draft and turn to revision, give yourself enough time to consider with special care your nouns and verbs. Novice writers say they worry most about their adjectives. Skilled writers, however, understand with the French writer Voltaire that adjectives are the enemy of nouns. Often they are empty abstractions that obscure rather than aid a reader's vision.

Even when they aren't abstract, adjectives by their mere presence drain energy from the nouns that are the eyes, ears, hands, nose, and tongue of a sentence and so sap its life. We need adjectives, of course, and write them in almost every sentence, but if you begin to emphasize your nouns by making them concrete and specific, you'll need fewer adjectives *and* write more vividly. Consider:

> When a boy, you fished as a boy: you put some *bread* on a hook tied to a line sturdy enough to pull in a *car,* which in turn ran around a heavy reel connected to a *sturdy fishing rod.*

All we have to do here is substitute more specific nouns and we can see the subjects clearly:

> When a boy, you fished as a boy: you put *a piece of Wonder Bread* on a hook tied to a line sturdy enough to pull in a *Buick,* which in turn ran around a reel heavy enough to pull *a small truck,* which was connected to a *fiber glass rod only a pole vaulter could love.*

Not all nouns, however, come to us with such power. Beware when you revise of the "seven deadly nouns," nouns so general, so abstract, so vague, that they say almost nothing:

BLOOM COUNTY

Copyright © 1984, Washington Post Writers Group. Used by permission.

Situation.
Type.
Thing.
Area.
Field.
Factor.
Experience.

> Things can be factors producing certain experiences or situations in almost any type of field or area where they appear.

What was that again? Using these when other, more specific, concrete nouns are at hand will pull down the blinds on your subject.

If its nouns provide a sentence with eyes, ears, and hands, its verbs give it heart and muscle and rouse it to action. Allow verbs as much revision time as you do nouns. Let's consider the verbs in our sample sentence:

> When a boy, you *fished* as a boy: you *put* a piece of Wonder Bread on a hook tied to a line sturdy enough *to pull* in a Buick, which in turn *ran* around a reel heavy enough *to pull* a small truck, which *was connected* to a fiber glass rod only a pole-vaulter could *love*.

Not bad. Most of the verbs are concrete and specific. A few could be made more lively, however. Here is the finished version of our test sentence as it appears in print:

> When a boy, you fished as a boy: you *soaked* a piece of Wonder Bread, *mushed* it on a hook tied to a line sturdy enough *to haul* in a Buick, which in turn *was wound* around a reel heavy enough *to tow* a small truck, which *was screwed* to a fiber glass rod only a pole-vaulter could love.
>
> (Lee Eisenberg, "Fishing for an Education," *Esquire* May 1983, emphasis added)

Now there's a sentence with life and action.

One verb deserves special attention during revision, *to be* and all its forms: *am, are, is, was,* and *were.* We use many *to-be* verbs for the same reason we use so many adjectives: because we need them. In one of their functions they link a subject with information about the subject (thus their name, a *linking* verb):

> Marion *is* a champion tennis player.

There is nothing wrong with this sentence or countless others like it. The trouble comes when we use *to be* in place of more concrete, lively verbs:

> College *is* a challenge to Luther and Wilma.

What should be the mover and shaker of this sentence, *challenge*, has been transformed from a verb to a noun, leaving an empty space where we expect action. As you revise, look for the important action in each sentence and, if possible, rewrite so the action occurs *within* the verb.

> College *challenges* Luther and Wilma.

Now there's a sentence that moves. Here's one more:

Original
> The Social Security Administration *is now lacking in its ability to guarantee* that the money *we're* putting into the system will *be* there when we retire.

Revision
> The Social Security Administration *cannot guarantee* that the money *we put* into the system will *be* there when we retire.

The original sentence contains three *to be* verbs. It needs only the last. See how emphatic it becomes when the first two are transformed?

EXERCISES

Rewrite the following sentences to make them more concrete and specific. Consider especially the underlined nouns and verbs. Feel free to invent details or add from your own experience: whatever will make your language as lively as possible.

1. Lake ____ (the name of a lake you're familiar with) ____ 's beaches are getting cleaner every year, and things are being kept up for the most part.
2. Our drive to the mountains took only a couple of hours—not long, but long enough to relax and enjoy the gorgeous scenic view of the spacious landscape along the way.
3. Strangers do not behave as civilly to one another as they once did. A perfect example of this type of situation is the expressway during rush hour.
4. Sally was a poor type of student. It was only a matter of time before things in the academic and social areas of her life would become factors producing an untenable academic situation.
5. A mistaken assumption that many of Fred's friends make, one that leads them to think him a failure, is that he is an unambitious person, at the same place now as he was fifteen years ago.
6. Finally, the skyline is visible and the interesting sights really begin. It may not be as inspiring as a mountain range, but as a visual experience a drive into Manhattan is quite a pleasure.
7. Crater Lake presents a green punchbowl effect.
8. The murder in question was the consequence of a robbery of an elderly couple by four hoodlums wearing plaid knickers, sport shoes, and rock tour T-shirts.
9. Our schools are suffering from a lack of funds. It is clear that this situation is being caused by unfortunate tax factors.
10. Only when the lines are at gas stations once more, power brownouts are more common, and electrical companies are seeking huge rate increases

will Americans come to the realization that we are nearing the upper limit in the area of the earth's energy resources.

WRITING PROJECTS

Topics

1. That circle of faces.

   a. Write a three- to five-page descriptive critique of the best (or worst) restaurant or fast-food place in your community. Write so vividly your mouth waters—or puckers. Give any background information your audience will need about menu, location, hours, and prices. Your recommendation will be your thesis. Write to the members of your composition class or the readers of your community newspaper. Chapter 13, pages 299–306, will show you how to write a critique.

   b. Write a three- to five-page descriptive critique of the best (or worst) place in your community to hang out, relax, have fun. Put yourself into the picture and bring your readers, the members of your composition class, along with you. Make them feel what the place is like. Chapter 13, pages 299–306, will show you how to write a critique.

   c. Write a three- to five-page descriptive and informative essay about the "right [or wrong] side of the tracks" in your community. Aim to reveal the quality of life in this community by taking your readers on a guided tour. Write with your eyes open to irony. What's wrong with the right side of the tracks or right on the wrong side? Address your essay to people who live on the *other* side of the tracks from the one you are writing about. Organize your essay chronologically, as you would if you were taking a tour, or logically, according to your subject's most important features.

2. The travelogue: Have you been to some place near or far where most of the members of your composition class have not, or some place most of them may not have visited recently? Write a three- to five-page descriptive and evaluative essay about it. Should your readers travel there? Why or why not? Your recommendation will be your thesis. Don't waste time telling about the trip there, unless the trip is important. Tell instead about the place itself, its people, their customs, food, where to stay, what to see—or not. Create a dominant impression that evokes the spirit of the place. Organize your description and evaluation according to a systematic plan, either chronologically, as an actual traveler would experience the place, or logically, according to the most important features of your subject.

3. Pick a nonverbal work of art, a painting, sculpture, dance, piece of music without words, or some other less traditional work of art, including architecture. Write a three- to five-page descriptive and evaluative essay in which you aim to explain the work to your composition class and to convey your dominant impression of it. Study the work in detail, form your dominant impression, decide on some vantage point for viewing or experiencing the work, and create a systematic pattern for describing it. The details of your description should explain the work and suggest your feelings about it. As you write, don't forget the power of figurative language simultaneously to convey sense impressions, emotions, and judgments.

4. Pick a short story, novel, or poem you've read recently and write a three- to five-page essay explaining how it uses description and figurative language. How do these methods of development create the mood of the piece, present character or conflict, and suggest theme?

THE WRITING PROCESS

1. Writing-in-progress.
   a. *Exploring:* free association and freewriting.
   b. *Developing.*
      i. Take notes and freewrite to discover what you will say, take walk-around notes, write a letter to your audience (see pages 47–54).
      ii. List facts and statistics.
         Illustrate your ideas: *For example* . . .
         Write anecdotes: *Once* . . .
         Write analogies: To be _____ is to be _____.
         Define your key terms: _____ = *genus + differentia.*
         Quote the right people.
         Gather famous sayings for allusions to your subject.
         Draw your subject.
   ——→iii. *New in this chapter:*
         Do a descriptive freewriting, imaginative or technical; create a dominant impression.
         Try several figurative free associations: If _____ were a _____ it would/wouldn't be a _____. (See pages 91–92.)
   c. *Planning a communications strategy:* Decide on a role, persona (distance and attitude), thesis (*My point is that . . . What I mean to say is that . . .*), and design.
   d. *Revising:* Reconsider your ideas and communications strategy; create frictions in your thinking (see pages 55–56).
2. Writing: Write the preliminary draft of your project. Write freely, don't stop except to reread, give yourself room to revise (see pages 57–58).
3. Rewriting.
   a. Be a zoom lens as you revise; add, delete, substitute, rearrange.
   b. Consider your opening and supporting details especially; cut what you like best; cut a word from each sentence (see pages 60–61).
   ——→c. *New in this chapter:* Make your nouns and verbs as concrete and specific as possible (see pages 100–102).
   d. Copyedit for mechanical errors, recopy, and proofread (see pages 61–62).
4. Self-evaluation (when you have finished your project).
   a. Summarize your readers' responses to your last writing.
   b. Which of them do you disagree with or not understand? Which do you agree with? Should they have done anything they did not do?
   c. Did you learn anything from your last writing that you tried to apply in this writing?
   d. What are your intentions in this writing?

e. What was most difficult about it? Do you see any parts you don't like? How might they be improved?

f. What do you like best about it?

END NOTE

1. For the idea of this exercise I am grateful to Thomas Whissen, *A Way with Words* (New York: Oxford UP, 1982).

PART III

WRITING
FOR
READERS

Chapter 6

Predictable Patterns: Maps for Writing and Reading

Imagine a lost hiker picking her way along a seldom-traveled mountain trail. She has no map or compass; she hasn't seen a trail marker for miles. All she has to guide her is the faint path ahead, leading who knows where, threatening to disappear at any moment. She came to see the scenery: the mountains above her, the trees, and the river below. But now she is scarcely aware of them; she can't afford the luxury of sightseeing. All her concentration is devoted to finding out where she is and where she's going.

If you've ever tried to write something and been uncertain of your plans, you know just how this hiker feels. We even use journey metaphors to describe our frustration. "I'm lost," we say, or "I don't know where I'm headed." We have nothing in mind or on paper to guide us, nothing to show us where to go or how to get there. The end of every paragraph plunges us over another precipice of broken, disconnected thought. And so, distracted and confused, we spend more energy trying to find our way than we do actually writing—that is, unless we give up our search and stop writing altogether. Just as our lost hiker failed to see the scenery she came for, we fail to say what we intended or say it so confusedly our readers are as lost as we are.

Now turn the analogy around. Imagine a hiker who has detailed maps, a good compass, and a well-marked path. She may never have traveled this trail before, but with all these aids to guide her, she has a good idea where it will take her and how it will take her there. Knowing where she is and able to anticipate the course of her journey, she can relax and enjoy the scenery she came to see. The same is true of skilled writers. They prepare maps and other travel guides to start them writing, head them in the right direction, and help them find their way if they stray or find new territory worth exploring. In this way they smooth their journey from draft to draft—and guarantee, as well, a smooth journey for their readers. For skilled writers know that readers also depend on these maps and guides. With their aid, readers are able to anticipate where a writer is taking them, and once they have a feeling for the writer's purpose and design, they can relax and pay attention to the subject matter. Simply put, skilled writers make their writing *predictable*. Its maps and travel guides—called *prediction devices*—make writing easier to do and easier to read.

One important qualification: The principle of predictability does *not* mean that writers should give away all their secrets in the beginning or that good writing is without surprise. If a writing were entirely predictable, it would soon become monotonous, boring, and as difficult to write and read as unpredictable writing. Imagine hiking a trail with destination, distance, and direction signs nailed to nearly every tree. You'd know where you were going, all right, but the trip would be so obvious, and so distracting in its obviousness, that you wouldn't much enjoy it. Too much direction can be as troublesome as too little. The principle of predictability means only that writers should do whatever necessary to keep themselves and their readers oriented and, therefore, free to satisfy their reasons for writing or reading.

So go ahead, if you wish, and surprise your readers with fresh ideas, delightful twists, and vivid language. Chapters 11 and 12 will show you still more ways to create surprises in your writing. Just make sure you put them there on purpose—pleasant surprises—not the confusing, unpleasant kind. Once you've discovered what you want to say, help your readers make the same discoveries. The prediction devices that enable them to do this are among the gestures of respect we pay readers and one of the ways we draw the community circle that unites them with us. The most obvious of these devices, the main idea and the thesis statement, you already know well. The next, patterns of organization, are the subject of this chapter. The remainder—introductions, conclusions, and paragraphs—are the subjects of Chapter 7.

PATTERNS OF ORGANIZATION

Organization is the most important prediction device. When we organize a subject, we put its parts in order according to some ordering principle or discover the pattern already there within a subject. A pattern of organization provides the map that we and our readers follow. Using it, we know what to write next, even how to write it, and our readers are able to anticipate what's coming. If a sentence opens *In the beginning . . .* , we expect to write a story—or read one. If a sentence opens *First . . .* , we expect a *Second. . . .* If *On the one hand . . .* , we expect an *on the other hand. . . .* Using the map a pattern gives us, comfortable with its layout, knowing that everything has a place and a sequence, we're free to turn our attention where it properly belongs, to the subject itself. We organize our writing according to three primary patterns: narrative, spatial, and logical order.

Narrative Order

Narrative order arranges actions in time, chronologically. It is the pattern of the story, the one you probably followed if you wrote the personal experience essay assigned in Chapter 3 or the travelogue in Chapter 5. We also use narrative order to explain a process—how something works or how something happened—and to give directions. Narrative order is one of the easiest patterns to create, the one we're most familiar with. After all, we've been listening to stories and telling them since early childhood, and we've been giving and receiving directions for nearly that long. But telling stories easily does not necessarily mean telling them well—as you know from listening to the anecdotes of long-winded relatives. Nor will the fact that you've heard thousands of directions in your lifetime guarantee that you'll be clear when asked to give your favorite recipe or the tricks of successful slalom skiing. To use narrative order effectively, you need to know the three principles of effective narration.

Selection   What you include in a narrative depends upon your purpose, point, audience, and occasion. For example, you probably don't have time to write all you could about the difficult passage through adolescence. Nor would every detail about the eruption of Mt. Vesuvius be appropriate to a paper written for a world history class. And what younger brother or sister would need every piece of advice you could give from your expertise about automobiles? Select only those details of fact, action, and instruction that will help you fulfill your narrative intentions for your particular readers.

Sequence   All narratives have a beginning, middle, and end marking the stages of their action. More often than not, a good narration begins at a moment of instability, when something is about to happen: You've just suffered a devastating loss—how did you react? Import quotas on Japanese automobiles have recently been eliminated—what will happen to American auto production? Your neighbor asks how to refinish the antique chair he's just bought. Frequently this *beginning* presents the background necessary to understand the impending action or follow the directions about to be given. The *middle* presents the action itself, usually a process of change: your attempts to cope with your loss; the changes in American auto design, production, and pricing; step-by-step refinishing instructions. The *end* presents the culmination of the process. Events have run their course, change is complete, steps have been followed to their conclusion, and conflicts or tensions have been resolved. Not all narratives, of course, follow this strict chronological pattern. Sometimes, to stimulate interest, a writer will begin in the middle of things, at a dramatic moment, and when the reader is hooked, make a *flashback* to the beginning of the narrative.

Pace Narratives seldom unfold at the speed of real time. They speed up or slow down according to the importance of what is being told. In your narratives you'll quickly summarize unimportant or background events, but important events you'll dramatize deliberately and in detail.

Here are examples of each kind of narration: a story, a process analysis, and directions. Each writer writes for reasons and audiences quite different from the other writers, but watch how all three follow the same principles of narration—selection, sequence, and pace—to fulfill their intentions. In the first example, a *story*, the writer dramatizes a discovery about himself and his job.

The Perfect Picture

Beginning: Setting the scene—a spring day and a green reporter

It was early in the spring about 15 years ago—a day of pale sunlight and trees just beginning to bud. I was a young police reporter, driving to a scene I didn't want to see. A man, the police-dispatcher's broadcast said, had accidently backed his pickup truck over his baby granddaughter in the driveway of the family home. It was a fatality.

Middle: The narrator's quest for the perfect picture
Selection: Details to reveal the old man's grief

As I parked among police cars and TV-news cruisers, I saw a stocky, white-haired man in cotton work clothes standing near a pickup. Cameras were trained on him, and reporters were sticking microphones in his face. Looking totally bewildered, he was trying to answer their questions. Mostly he was only moving his lips, blinking, and choking up.

Pace: Deliberate so the writer can describe in detail

After a while the reporters gave up on him and followed the police into the small white house. I can still see in my mind's eye that devastated old man looking down at the place in the driveway where the child had been. Beside the house was a freshly spaded flower bed, and nearby a pile of dark, rich earth.

Selection: Revealing dialogue

"I was just backing up there to spread that good dirt," he said to me, though I had not asked him anything. "I didn't even know she was outdoors." He stretched his hand toward the flower bed, then let it flop to his side. He lapsed back into his thoughts, and I, like a good reporter, went into the house to find someone who could provide a recent photo of the toddler.

Pace: A change of scene summarized quickly

A few minutes later, with all the details in my notebook and a three-by-five studio portrait of the cherubic child tucked in my jacket pocket, I went toward the kitchen where the police had said the body was.

Selection: Details of
the camera that will
affect the narrator's
action

I had brought a camera in with me—the big, bulky Speed Graphic which used to be the newspaper reporter's trademark. Everybody had drifted back out of the house together—family, police, reporters and photographers. Entering the kitchen, I came upon this scene.

Pace: Deliberate
description of the
climactic scene

On a Formica-topped table, backlighted by a frilly curtained window, lay the tiny body, wrapped in a clean white sheet. Somehow the grandfather had managed to stay away from the crowd. He was sitting on a chair beside the table, in profile to me and unaware of my presence, looking uncomprehendingly at the swaddled corpse.

Selection: Details that
evoke the old man's
grief

The house was very quiet. A clock ticked. As I watched, the grandfather slowly leaned forward, curved his arms like parentheses around the head and feet of the little form, then pressed his face to the shroud and remained motionless.

Selection: Details of
the shot that create
the narrator's conflict

In that hushed moment I recognized the makings of a prize-winning news photograph. I appraised the light, adjusted the lens setting and distance, locked a bulb in the flashgun, raised the camera and composed the scene in the viewfinder.

Every element of the picture was perfect: the grandfather in his plain work clothes, his white hair backlighted by sunshine, the child's form wrapped in the sheet, the atmosphere of the simple home suggested by black iron trivets and World's Fair souvenir plates on the walls flanking the window. Outside, the police could be seen inspecting the fatal rear wheel of the pickup while the child's mother and father leaned in each other's arms.

The moment of crisis

I don't know how many seconds I stood there, unable to snap that shutter. I was keenly aware of the powerful story-telling value that photo would have, and my professional conscience told me to take it. Yet I couldn't make my hand fire that flashbulb and intrude on the poor man's island of grief.

End: The narrator
makes a decision and
resolves his conflict

At length I lowered the camera and crept away, shaken with doubt about my suitability for the journalistic profession. Of course I never told the city editor or any fellow reporters about that missed opportunity for a perfect news picture.

The point of the story:
The narrator chooses
human feeling over
professional
responsibility

Every day, on the newscasts and in the papers, we see pictures of people in extreme conditions of grief and despair. Human suffering has become a spectator sport. And sometimes, as I'm watching news film, I remember that day.

I still feel right about what I did.

(James Alexander Thom, *Reader's Digest* Aug. 1976)

In this next example, a *process analysis*, the writer charts the rhythmic growth and decline of rock 'n' roll. Because this writer intends to explain an event rather than dramatize it, the "what," the details of the narrative, are less important than the "how," its stages. The principles of selection, sequence, and pace are the same as they would be in a story, but different intentions lead to a narrative different in attitude, emphasis, and meaning.

Beginning: Stage one,
the era in which
Rock arose

Selection: Examples
from jazz and the 50s
that contrast most
vividly with rock

Middle: Stage two

Pace: Rock's golden
era passed over quickly
in order to move on to
the second decline in
popular music

Selection: Details that
emphasize the decline
of rock 'n' roll

The end: Stage three

Selection: Details that
emphasize the third
decline of American
popular music

. . . Rock itself arose during a lull in the early Fifties. At that time jazz had turned into an exclusive club, practically Ptolemaic in its structure of circles within circles: white cultists on the outer rim, contemptuous of the straight majority that had given its heart to Eisenhower; black hipsters in the second circle, mutely disdainful of the white hangers-on; and jazzmen at the cool-blue center, scorning everything but the Inner Voice and showing what they felt for their fans by playing concerts with their backs to the audience. The "Top 40," meanwhile, contented itself with the musical dregs of a flabby Broadway—which had not yet given itself over to live sex shows—performed by a colorless parade of Perrys and Pattis and Eddies and Tonys and Rosemarys. Then Elvis arrived, and "How Much Is That Doggie in the Window?" was never heard from again.

A second dry spell began around 1959 and lasted until the arrival of the Beatles at the end of 1963. Rock 'n' roll, which for five years had overwhelmed everything in sight, lost its vitality at the end of the decade and sought sustenance in the weighty issues of high school proms, teachers' pets, and acne control. One by one, the music's luminaries passed from the scene: Buddy Holly died in a plane crash; Chuck Berry was sent up on a morals charge; Little Richard entered the ministry; Frankie Lymon drifted into drugs and self-destruction; Elvis himself went into the army and came out with more than his hair cut off. At the same time, the vultures descended—modern-day alchemists who turned plastic into gold by means of fabricated talents like Frankie Avalon and Fabian. Commercialism and cynicism did their worst, and for four years the people dwelt in darkness—until Britain sent a great light.

The music entered a slough for the third time about 1968, and it is one that we are still wading through. The strongest indication of a decline from the rock heights of the mid-Sixties was, obviously, the breakup of the Beatles in 1970, but before that explosion there had occurred the eerily appropriate deaths of Jimi Hendrix and Janis Joplin, two performers who specialized in a kind of demonic abandon and whose end seemed to mark a certain drawing of limits. There had been, as well, the ugliness and violence of Altamont, after which, consciously or unconsciously, Mick Jagger's satanic majesty transmuted into an androgynous theatricality that spawned a legion of disingenuous transvestites, the pop heroes of teen-agers who in the Seventies have made a style out of decadence.

(Barry Gewen, "Bone-dry in the '70s," *Saturday Review* 1 Apr. 1978)

The third example of narration is a series of *directions* telling how to do something well that seems simpler than it is: hammering a nail. At first glance, these instructions may seem to have little in common with the first two narratives, but because instructions usually require actions taken in chronological order, we organize them using the same principles of narration.

Beginning: Background information necessary to use a hammer effectively

For extensive nailing, use a hammer that feels comfortable when you swing it. And keep it clean—a smudge on the face can be transferred almost indelibly to the work. If you should bend a nail in driving it, place a thin block of scrap wood under the hammer head to protect the work as you start pulling the nail; change to a thicker block to get extra leverage at the finish.

Middle: Instructions
Step 1
Step 2
Step 3
Step 4

To drive a nail, hold it upright on the wood between the thumb and forefinger of your left hand. Hold the hammer near the end of the handle with your right hand and tap (don't bang) the nail a few times to drive it just far enough to stand up by itself. With the nail standing up, take your fingers away, and swing the hammer a little harder, but only a little. Don't use really heavy strokes until the nail is about an inch into the wood; a glancing blow can send it ricocheting, with possible injury to you.

Step 5: Alternative instructions
Pace: Narrative slows for alternative instructions

Additional equipment needed

If you're driving common nails in rough work, such as house framing, drive the heads in flush with the surface and don't bother to be careful about hammer marks. If you're driving finishing nails in work where appearance counts, stop when the head is just above the surface, and then sink it with a nail set. When you work with hardened nails (many modern flooring and special-purpose types are hardened), always wear goggles. Such nails sometimes break instead of bending. The goggles will protect your eyes against flying pieces.

(*Reader's Digest Complete Do-It-Yourself Manual*
[Pleasantville, NY: Reader's Digest Assn., 1973])

EXERCISES

1. When you were a child you heard all kinds of fables, nursery rhymes, and bedtime stories that taught you the wisdom of life: the three little pigs, Hansel and Gretel, the old woman who lived in a shoe. Choose one of these brief stories with a moral that might be updated and applied to contemporary life; in a paragraph or two retell it for adults. Imagine, for example, a tale titled "The Three Little Freshmen." Make your tale illustrate in a pointed fashion the ideals, delusions, foibles, or values of our time. Write to the members of your composition class.

2. Write a one or two paragraph process analysis of some aspect of contemporary romantic life. How do lovers behave nowadays? Make some observations. How do they kiss, hold hands, or exchange other forms of endearment? How do they fight, talk, propose marriage or other forms of cohabitation? Write to your composition class.

3. Write a long paragraph of directions to the modern lovers mentioned in Exercise 2. Identify one part of their relationship that they handle badly. Tell them what's wrong with their behavior and the consequences of it. Then give them step-by-step instructions for behaving well. For example, how do the lovers you know fight? How should they fight so they don't ruin their relationship? Be specific and systematic. You may, if you wish, address one half of the relationship, men or women, and instruct them alone.

Spatial Order Spatial order is the pattern we use for description. It arranges physical objects, people, or scenes in space. In contrast to narrative order, it is seldom the primary pattern for organizing a writing. More often than not we give spatial order a subordinate role, organizing individual paragraphs that set the scene for the action or explanation to come. Like narrative order, however, effective spatial order takes its shape from its own three principles of design.

Descriptive Point of View

This term refers to the physical point from which a writer views a scene. Recall a scene from the photographer's story you read earlier:

> Entering the kitchen I came upon this scene.
>
> On a Formica-topped table, backlighted by a frilly curtained window, lay the tiny body, wrapped in a clean white sheet. Somehow the grandfather had managed to stay away from the crowd. He was sitting on a chair beside the table, in profile to me and unaware of my presence, looking uncomprehendingly at the swaddled corpse.

The writer's descriptive point of view is the kitchen doorway. He looks into the kitchen, the rest of the house behind him. This point of view determines what he can see and hear and, therefore, what he describes. Had he entered from another direction, his point of view would have been different and he might not have seen the grandfather "in profile." By controlling what we see, point of view helps us organize a description. The more consistent your point of view when you describe, the more predictable and readable your description will be.

Psychological Point of View

An observer, however, is more than a camera recording images that strike him. An observer brings particular interests and feelings to his subjects. These help determine what he sees, how he sees, even the order of his perception. Recall another paragraph from "The Perfect Picture":

> I don't know how many seconds I stood there, unable to snap that shutter. I was keenly aware of the powerful story-telling value that photo would have, and my professional conscience told me to take it. Yet I couldn't make my hand fire that flashbulb and intrude on the poor man's island of grief.

The writer's psychological point of view is that of a man divided between his professional and human responses. He sees what a photographer would see but also what a compassionate human being would see, and this divided psychological point of view gives him his dominant impression of his subject, the old man's "island of grief" that prevents him from shooting the picture.

Pattern Effective description rarely arranges physical details in a random order. How they are arranged depends on a writer's intentions, interests, and some conventional pattern. That pattern may be thematic—based on an idea or emotion—and the writer will first describe what is most important to him. Or it may be linear: top to bottom, left to right, foreground to background, center to periphery, and so on. The writer of "The Perfect Picture" describes the grandfather and the kitchen thematically and from foreground to background.

> Every element of the picture was perfect: the grandfather in his plain work clothes, his white hair backlighted by sunshine, the child's form wrapped in the sheet, the atmosphere of the simple home suggested by black iron trivets and World's Fair souvenir plates on the walls flanking the window. Outside, the police could be seen inspecting the fatal rear wheel of the pickup while the child's mother and father leaned in each other's arms.

This pattern enables the writer to emphasize the grandfather's loss and grief as well as his isolation from the domestic and professional life continuing behind him. Pattern reinforces the dominant impression.

EXERCISES

1. Write a paragraph or two describing the place you most call your own: a room, a building, or some natural place. Select a specific physical point of view and a specific dominant impression (psychological point of view) that will help you choose your details. Arrange and present your description to suggest your feelings for the place and what is most important about it. Write to your composition class.

2. Choose one of the following faces and write a long descriptive paragraph. Select a physical and psychological point of view best suited to reveal your feelings about the face and trait in question. Organize your description thematically or linearly, leading to a dramatic, telling detail. Write to the person whose face you describe.

A liar's face.	A lover's face.
A hateful face.	A world-weary face.
An innocent face.	A naive face.
An insensitive face.	A compassionate face.
The face of a dullard.	

Logical Order

When we organize logically, we organize ideas, people, objects, and events according to some interest that we bring to our subjects. More clearly than narrative and spatial order, *logical order* is the pattern of the human mind at work—responding to the world, thinking, discriminating, ranking, sorting, and explaining. Here are six common logical patterns, some you already use in your writing, others you can easily learn to use.

Order of Importance   Order of importance is the simplest logical order. We use it to arrange subjects in two ways. In *descending order*, we put the most important subject first, then the next most important, and so on until the least important. *Ascending order* is precisely the opposite: we put the least important subject first, the most important, last. In practice, you will soon discover ways to modify ascending order to present subjects in more interesting and complex ways. You may arrange a subject from its superficial and insignificant aspects to its underlying and significant aspects. You may present appearances first, the way things *seem* to be, and then the reality, the way things really are. Or you may move from the background to the foreground, from general information about a subject that gives its context to specific and detailed information. Such arrangements will help you build to an emphatic conclusion, as in this contrast of two generations of American business people:

The least important contrast

Today's successful entrepreneurs differ in numerous ways, some obvious, some subtle, from the industrial tycoons of a century or half a century ago. . . . On average, the modern business leaders are less flamboyant, more anonymous, and very possibly harder working. Nowadays, many persons who run their own businesses seem driven by a compulsive desire to succeed. The challenge of overcoming obstacles is more of a goad to their efforts than the prospect that new wealth will let them indulge sybaritic [luxurious] fantasies. "The fear of being a failure is what drives me," observes Ken Brown, thirty-three, a college dropout who was recently grossing some $3.5 million a year from various motorcycle ventures. "Money is just a way of keeping score."

A second contrast

Another big difference between nineteenth- and twentieth-century magnates: Today remarkably few big-money men, even the wealthiest of them, live ostentatiously—and this trend seems likely to endure at a time when the rich must again worry about kidnapping and other threats to their personal safety. But a second home and a taste for fancy automobiles are of course commonplace.

The most important contrast

The biggest difference between today's and yesterday's entrepreneur has to do with his or her field of endeavor. As the nation moves into the post-industrial era, the main action no longer lies in steel, autos, railroads, shipping, and other basic industries or heavy manufacturing but in advanced technologies, in new kinds of services, and even in the arts. Despite inflation and recessions, the nation's economic growth creates enormous needs and challenges. Changing trends in business, new legislation, demographic shifts, and new scientific discoveries give risk takers a bedazzling array of fresh chances. Quantum leaps in technology—notably in electronics—have opened dozens of new industries over the past several years. And the pace of change grows faster every decade.

> (Gurney Breckenfeld, "The New Entrepreneur: Romantic Hero of American Business," *Saturday Review* 22 July 1978)

EXERCISES

1. Write a long paragraph about the names you are known by. How did you get them? What do you feel about them? Which tells the most truth about you? Imagine all the people who gave you these names gathered in one room; write to them. Organize your description according to one of the order-of-importance patterns.

2. Write a paragraph or two addressing a person or group of people guilty of fooling themselves. They may be kidding themselves about their personalities, the way the world is, their prospects for the future, or what others think of them. First describe what they think and then the way things really are.

Comparison/Contrast   By arranging subjects according to their similarities, their differences, or both, we can explain them, evaluate them, or evoke a reader's feelings about them. Here an evaluative contrast helps make a larger point about the depersonalization that so often characterizes our age.

The point of the contrast

The customer of an independent businessman

The customer of a department store

Significant differences between the customer's relationship to the two stores

The insignificance of the individual in our era concerns not only his role as a businessman, employee, or manual laborer, but also his role as a customer. A drastic change has occurred in the role of the customer in the last decades. The customer who went into a retail store owned by an independent businessman was sure to get personal attention: his individual purchase was important to the owner of the store; he was received like somebody who mattered, his wishes were studied; the very act of buying gave him a feeling of importance and dignity. How different is the relationship of a customer to a department store. He is impressed by the vastness of the building, the number of employees, the profusion of commodities displayed; all this makes him feel small and unimportant by comparison. As an individual he is of no importance to the department store. He is important as "a" customer; the store does not want to lose him, because this would indicate that there was something wrong and it might mean that the store would lose other customers for the same reason. As an abstract customer he is important; as a concrete customer he is utterly unimportant. There is nobody who is glad about his coming, nobody who is particularly concerned about his wishes. The act of buying has become similar to going to the post office and buying stamps.

> (Erich Fromm, *Escape from Freedom*, [New York: Holt, 1941, 1969])

You can organize a comparison/contrast in two basic ways. Erich Fromm's paragraph above is a *block comparison,* one subject presented entirely before the second, a customer's reception in an independent retail store and then in a chain department store. *Point-by-point comparison* moves back and forth between subjects, first to one point of comparison, then to the next, and so on. Here is a point-by-point contrast of our generation's skepticism and the previous generation's optimism:

Exploration then and now

Religion

Science

National defense

Politics

Art

We no longer believe in the mission of our civilization. We once believed that it should explore, so that we could see Lindbergh as a hero, but we no longer do: Hillary [first to climb Mt. Everest] was not a hero. We once believed that it should go to the bounds of the earth, but we do not believe in it going to the boundaries of the universe, and so we regard our astronauts as little more than acrobats. We once believed that it should teach and hear, so missionaries such as Livingstone and Schweitzer were heroes, but now when we read that some missionaries have been massacred we tend to think that they may have deserved it. We once believed in our science, so that in the Golden Age of Physics, men such as Einstein and Rutherford and Bohr were heroes, but now we do not believe in it, and out of all the scientific advances of recent years not one scientist's name is a household word. We used to think that our civilization should be guarded, and even that at times it should advance, so that our soldiers were heroes, but now we think of our generals only as stupid and knavish and war-hungry. We used to believe that our civilization should act with great authority in the world, so that we found heroes among our politicians to speak for it, but now we regard our politicians only as petty and self-serving. We once believed that our writers and artists should speak of and to the common values of our civilization and be bearers of it, so that we found heroes among them even down to the 1930s, but now we think that our writers and artists should stay on the margins and entertain us.

(Henry Fairlie, "Too Rich for Heroes," *Harper's* Nov. 1978)

Pro/Con The pro/con pattern is similar to comparison/contrast. The human mind feels comfortable, it seems, working with pairs—either pairs of subjects, as in a comparison/contrast, or two views of a subject. The *pro/con pattern* organizes these views in four ways: (1) two conflicting views of a subject *(on the one hand . . . on the other . . .);* (2) a writer's concessions and reservations *(yes, but);* (3) paradoxes (two contradictory views simultaneously true); or (4) what is favorable and unfavorable about a subject. We use this pattern frequently in arguments to counter our opponents, as this writer does to criticize the excessive claims made by some joggers:

The benefits of running on the one hand (Pro)

It's easy enough to see how running got confused with religion. Running can, it's true, make you imagine yourself a better person than you are. Yesterday, I ran for an hour through a seaside park near my home in Connecticut. The last of the leaves were tumbling in the wind. I ran past three imperturbable skunks, a raccoon, a family of squirrels busily laying in a winter's supplies. A pheasant noisily took to the air at the sound of running shoes on gravel. By the time I got home, I felt refreshed and beatified. I know of no human activity, except perhaps sex, that can do so much in so brief a time, and do it so wonderfully.

The limitations of jogging on the other (Con)

Think, on the other hand, of what running can't do. Running has nothing, absolutely nothing, to do with caring about other people, or with compassion or with self-sacrifice. On the contrary, devotees of the sport are likely to be incorrigible loners, sufficient unto themselves in their sweaty enjoyments. To the extent, therefore, that we let ourselves equate those enjoyments with the traditional pursuits and hard-won satisfactions of religion, we deflect our attention from concerns that are far more important than getting into a pair of Adidases and breathing hard before breakfast.

(James Fixx, "What Running Can't Do For You," *Newsweek* 18 Dec. 1978)

EXERCISES

1. Write two paragraphs of comparison/contrast about the ways men and women do something, e.g., the way they think, speak, argue, make judgments, play, sleep, or eat. You may have to make first-hand observations before you begin to write. Organize one paragraph according to the block pattern, the other point-by-point. You may write two separate paragraphs about different subjects or consecutive paragraphs about one subject. Write to your composition class.

2. Write two pro/con paragraphs, one describing important features of your generation and one describing important features of the preceding generation, that of your older brothers and sisters or your parents. Avoid broad generalizations; write about what you have observed or know for sure. Make your first paragraph an *on the one hand . . . on the other* address to your generation. Make the second a *Yes, but* address to the older generation.

Classification   Classification organizes subjects into groups or classes according to the characteristics they share. Here the Canadian novelist Robertson Davies sorts his academic colleagues according to their superstitions:

The principle of classification

Few people will admit to being superstitious; it implies naïveté or ignorance. But I live in the middle of a large university, and I see superstition in its four manifestations, alive and flourishing among people who are indisputably rational and learned.

You did not know that superstition takes four forms? Theologians assure

The first class: Vain observances

One member of this class

us that it does. First is what they call Vain Observances, such as not walking under a ladder, and that kind of thing. Yet I saw a deeply learned professor of anthropology, who had spilled some salt, throwing a pinch of it over his left shoulder; when I asked him why, he replied, with a wink, that it was "to hit the Devil in the eye." I did not question him further about his belief in the Devil: but I noticed that he did not smile until I asked him what he was doing.

The second: Divination

The second form is Divination, or consulting oracles. Another learned professor I know, who would scorn to settle a problem by tossing a coin (which is a humble appeal to Fate to declare itself), told me quite seriously that he had resolved a matter related to university affairs by consulting the *I Ching.* And why not? There are thousands of people on this continent who appeal to the I Ching and their general level of education seems to absolve them of superstition. Almost, but not quite. The I Ching, to the embarrassment of rationalists, often gives excellent advice.

The third: Idolatry

Signs of this class

The third form is Idolatry, and universities can show plenty of that. If you have ever supervised a large examination room, you know how many jujus, lucky coins and other bringers of luck are placed on the desks of the candidates. Modest idolatry, but what else can you call it?

The fourth: Improper worship

The fourth form is Improper Worship of the True God. A while ago, I learned that every day, for several days, a $2 bill (in Canada we have $2 bills, regarded by some people as unlucky) had been tucked under a candlestick on the altar of a college chapel. Investigation revealed that an engineering student, worried about a girl, thought that bribery of the Deity might help. When I talked with him, he did not think he was pricing God cheap, because he could afford no more. A reasonable argument, but perhaps God was proud that week, for the scientific oracle went against him.

(Robertson Davies, "A Few Kind Words for Superstition," *Newsweek* 20 Nov. 1978)

The members in each of these classes are grouped because they share a characteristic with other members of their class, namely, that they practice the same form of superstition. What comprises a class and determines a classification scheme depends upon a writer's interests. If you were interested in religious affiliations instead of superstition, you might classify the members of your college community into two most inclusive classes, the religious and nonreligious. The religious you might then classify into Christians and non-Christians, the Christians into Catholics and Protestants, and so on, grouping and subdividing until you had reached the smallest subclass, individual faculty or students with individual religious beliefs.

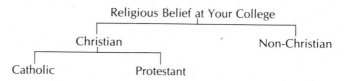

But you can apply only *one* principle of classification at a time. A scheme such as this would be illogical:

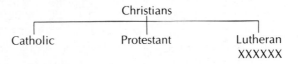

Here two principles of classification, church membership and denominational affiliation, are at work in one scheme. They make it appear that someone cannot be both a Protestant and a Lutheran, although, of course, the Lutheran church is one denomination, a subclassification, of Protestantism. Classification is the *systematic* dividing up of members of a group, one principle at a time.

EXERCISES

1. Write a long paragraph classifying one of the following groups of people: teachers, members of the opposite sex, workers, bosses, parents, children, Americans, or nations. Make your classification scheme original and insightful. What primary interest will you use to divide your group into classes: their values, habits, hopes, fears, possessions, or behavior? Can any of your classes be subclassified into smaller groups? Use examples, facts, and description to distinguish one class from another. Arrange your classes in a significant order, probably one variation of the order of importance. Write to the group you are classifying.

2. When you think of the movies we see, the music we enjoy, the tools we use, the objects we treasure, the houses we live in or the style of our dress, ready-made classifications come quickly to mind. Choose one of these subjects and write a long paragraph classifying its members, but devise a new classification scheme, one your readers—your composition class—may not have thought of. For example, aim to classify movies in ways other than G-, PG-, PG-13-, R-, and X-rated movies or as adventures, comedies, horror films, spy movies, art films, and so on. Use examples, facts, and description to distinguish one class from another. Arrange your classes in a systematic order, probably one variation of the order of importance.

Descriptive Analysis   As classification gathers things together to show what they have in common, descriptive analysis divides a subject into its parts. If you were classifying automobiles, for example, one way to classify a luxury car, would be to group it with other large luxury cars. But if you wanted to analyze that luxury car, you would disassemble it systematically and describe its parts—and often the relationship among those parts, the way they work together to make the car perform as a luxury car should. Classification organizes according to shared characteristics; analysis, according to parts and their relationships. We can analyze anything with parts that fit or work together in some systematic way:

- An object (e.g., the parts of a machine, tree, or musical instrument).
- A person (psychology or physiology).
- An institution (its operation, goals, methods).
- A book (its design, themes, characters, language).
- An event (the stages of the event, their relationships, their causes).
- An idea (its components, origins, effects).
- A group, provided its members work together (e.g., an office staff).

Here is a descriptive analysis of a machine, the personal computer, as it appeared in *Consumer Reports* magazine.

The primary component of a computer, the CPU

The "brain" of every computer is its central processing unit (CPU), the chips that do all the work. They're always mated with one or several chips that contain memory. Part of the memory is permanent, installed by the maker to give the CPU an elementary ability to do its work; that part is called read-only memory, or ROM. The rest of the memory is available for your use. It can store information and the instructions for what you want done with it (a "program"). That part is called random-access memory, or RAM, and its size has a strong bearing on what you will be able to do with the computer. (The size of memory is measured in units called kilobytes—thousands of bytes. One byte stores a single character, so one kilobyte can contain up to about 1000 letters or digits.)

An analysis of the major part of the CPU, its memory

The parts of memory: ROM and RAM

The second component: A storage device

Everything in the RAM is transient. It can be altered easily and it disappears when the computer is turned off. Therefore, a computer needs a storage device to preserve programs and data for when they are wanted again. With the computers we're considering, there are two types of storage devices. One is a simple cassette tape recorder, which is cheap, but comparatively slow and inconvenient. The other, called a disk drive, is very fast but much more costly. . . .

The third component: An input device

To give you some way to put information into the computer, you need what's called an "input device." For a computerized game, the input device might be a joystick, but for just about everything else you'd use something that looks and works very much like a typewriter keyboard. The type and quality of the keyboard can have a lot to do with which computer you might select.

The fourth component: Output devices

Finally, you'd need some way to see what's going on in the computer and to obtain any results, or "output." For that you'd probably use two "output devices"—a video screen and a printer.

These few pieces, assembled in different ways, make up the whole computer system. You don't really have to know how any of them work internally, any more than you have to understand the inner workings of hi-fi components, but you should assemble a system of suitably matched parts in order to get the most out of each piece.

(*1984 Buying Guide Issue* [Mount Vernon, NY: Consumers Union of the United States, 1983])

What determines the parts of an analysis are the writer's intentions. These writers explain the parts of a computer and how they work together because they want their readers to understand the ratings of the various brands they will evaluate. If they had intended to explain how to use a computer and wished to write a series of directions, they would have looked at the components from a different point of view, explained them in another way, and organized their explanation differently. Intentions determine both the content and design of a writing.

EXERCISES

1. Write a long paragraph analyzing a current fad for your composition class. Describe its parts or features in a systematic way and then explain what it shows about its practitioner's interests or values.

2. Write a two or three paragraph character sketch of the most unforgettable person you have known or observed. What are the "parts" of this person that make him or her unforgettable? Write to your composition class.

Causal Analysis   Causal (that's *causal*, not *casual*) analysis does what its name implies, divides an event into causes and effects or conditions and consequences. To use causal analysis effectively, you must account for the remote, underlying causes of an event as well as the immediate, obvious causes. Often you'll detect the simultaneous influence of multiple causes or multiple effects produced by a single cause. Sometimes you'll have to distinguish between causes that can create effects by themselves—the dropped cigarettes that start forest fires (called *sufficient causes*)—and those that merely contribute to the effects—the droughts that turn forests to tinder (*contributory causes*). Consider how the following causal analysis accounts for all effects of modern air conditioning technology, from immediate to remote.

Air conditioning is a contributory cause of multiple immediate effects

Effects that become causes

Multiple remote effects:
1.
2.
3.

4.

Many of its byproducts are so conspicuous that they are scarcely noticed. To begin with, air conditioning transformed the face of urban America by making possible those glassy, boxy, sealed-in skyscrapers on which the once humane geometries of places like San Francisco, Boston, and Manhattan have been impaled. It has been indispensable, no less, to the functioning of sensitive advanced computers, whose high operating temperatures require that they be constantly cooled. Thus, in a very real way, air conditioning has made possible the ascendancy of computerized civilization. Its cooling protection has given rise not only to moon landings, space shuttles and Skylabs but to the depersonalized punch-cardification of society that regularly gets people hot under the collar even in swelter-proof environments. It has also reshaped the national economy and redistributed political power simply by encouraging the burgeoning of the sultry southerly swatch of the country, profoundly influencing major migration trends of people and industry. Sun-

belt cities like Phoenix, Atlanta, Dallas and Houston (where shivering in-
door frigidity became a mark of status) could never have mushroomed so
prosperously without air conditioning; some communities—Las Vegas in the
Nevada desert and Lake Havasu City on the Arizona-California border—
would shrivel and die overnight if it were turned off.

(Frank Trippett: "The Great American Cooling
Machine," *Time* 13 Aug. 1979)

EXERCISES

1. Write a long paragraph to your family giving the most important influence
in your life and explaining how it has shaped your character. Share with them
some facts about your growth they may not know. Organize your analysis either
from cause (influence) to effect (a description of your character as it is now) or
from effect (your character as it is now) back to cause (influence).

2. Write a long paragraph analyzing the two most important contributors to
individual human happiness. What are they? How do they create human happiness? Besides human happiness do they cause unintended or unrecognized effects?
Write to your composition class. You may organize your analysis one contributor
at a time, first one cause and then the next, or, if they are related, you may trace
their influence simultaneously, multiple causes leading to one effect.

Mixed Patterns of Organization

Seldom when we write do we use only one pattern of organization. If a
subject is complex and we write at length, we almost always need a mixed
pattern. A mixed pattern is a hierarchy of designs, pattern within pattern,
one pattern of organization in the service of another. Earlier you studied
spatial order and saw that pattern contained, as it so often is, within narrative order. Stories, after all, wouldn't have much life without description of setting, character, and action. But these descriptive paragraphs are
never organized for themselves alone; they are organized to help tell a story.
Spatial order is subordinate to story order.

So, too, with other patterns. Order of importance, comparison, pro/con,
classification, or analysis may provide the outline for a writing, but other
methods determine the design within individual paragraphs. Look once more
at Gurney Breckenfeld's descending-order paragraphs about contemporary
business people (pages 118–119). The order *within* each paragraph is com-
parison/contrast.

    I. Least-important contrasts between tycoons of this age and the last.
       A. Their flamboyance.
       B. Their energy.
   II. A second contrast: their life-styles.
  III. The most important contrast: their fields of endeavor.

Or consider James Fixx's first pro/con paragraph criticizing those who have made running a religion (page 121). Running's benefits are dramatized by an anecdote arranged in chronological order:

I. The benefits of running confused with those of religion.
   A. Topic sentence.
   B. One reason for the confusion: running makes runners feel so good.
   C. An illustrative anecdote: running through a seaside park.
      1. Watching the leaves fall, feeling the wind.
      2. Watching the animals.
      3. The feeling of beatification and refreshment at the end of the run.
   D. A closing comparison of running and sex.

The second paragraph in this pro/con argument is really a kind of causal analysis: what running cannot do (the effects it cannot have) and the unfavorable consequences of confusing it with religion.

Mixed patterns are almost always put together for a particular occasion, and for this reason you can rarely tell beforehand what patterns you'll combine. There are, however, two mixed patterns that have almost achieved independent status. We bring them to our writing ready-mixed, so to speak. The first, the "What is it?" pattern, is appropriate to extended definition and descriptive analysis. Often it looks like this:

I. Definition of the subject (order of importance, classification, or analysis).
II. Descriptive analysis of its parts.
III. Process analysis of its function or uses.
IV. Its value, significance, or problems associated with it (order of importance, comparison/contrast, pro/con, or analysis).

The second is the "Problem/Solution" pattern:

I. Descriptive analysis of the problem.
II. Analysis of its causes.
III. Its consequences if untreated or unsolved.
IV. Solutions (order of importance, comparison/contrast, pro/con, or analysis).

Often the parts of these patterns are rearranged slightly to fit particular subjects or situations, and when parts are unnecessary or irrelevant, they are omitted. Despite such minor alterations, however, these patterns are used so frequently that they have become predictable patterns for writers and readers alike.

✎ GETTING ORGANIZED

Skilled writers often organize their writing instinctively but never at random. A design is not a cookie cutter, one shape selected whimsically from the many you've studied in this chapter and pressed upon the formless dough of an idea. A design may, it is true, come to us by convention—the format for a business letter, for example—but in our best writing we never force that design on a subject. Design is *organic*, in at least two senses of the word. In the first sense, the design of a writing, like the shape of flower and tree, is contained in its seed. It is there from the beginning, implied by the subject itself, the writer's role, the occasion, or the thesis. When you think of organizing a writing project, begin your search for a design there, within that communication network:

- Is my role to inform, dramatize, explain, or persuade?
- How many assertions do I make in my thesis and what is their logical order?
- What does my audience expect from me?
- What conventions do writers usually follow on occasions like this?

The second sense in which design is organic has to do with our discovery of it. A pattern may lie in our material from the very beginning, but we almost never find it finished and whole, a perfect pattern. It grows as our understanding of our subject grows. Design and content influence each other in a process of give and take, one creating the other. A subject gives us materials to organize and suggests the form they should take; our search for order gives us lists and outlines with blank spaces to be filled, empty pigeonholes that draw our subject out of itself. Because of this mutual influence you should be concerned with organization throughout a project, not just at the beginning or end, and you should be cautious about sticking with the first pattern that comes to mind. You don't want to finish the map for your writing before you complete the exploratory journey through your ideas.

And that brings us to outlining, the only device many of us have for creating order. Outlines are wonderful for getting organized: lists and brief sketch outlines for sorting ideas and testing logic, and more detailed working outlines for mapping our drafts. If you've never learned how to write them, Chapter 17, "The Research Project," Step 5, pages 444–449, will show you. But, and this is an important *but*, outlines do have drawbacks, especially if you depend on them exclusively. For one thing, they may organize an idea, but they don't communicate it. They can make an idea logical, but they can't make it appealing to readers. They can give it a skeleton to stand by itself, but they can't clothe it in vivid language or a winsome persona. An outline without a communications strategy to go with it is sure to produce rigid, hollow-sounding prose.

For another thing, some writers find it impossible to make outlines work, even though they understand perfectly well, in theory, how outlines are supposed to work. Instead of liberating them from the often frustrating search for form, outlines seem always to transform the light, bright gem of their latest idea into a heavy, gray cinder block. These writers, like those who depend exclusively on outlines for their communications strategies, need other ways to discover predictable yet lively designs, designs that will help them communicate as well as organize their ideas. Here are several; try them and see which work for you.

Alternative Outline Strategies

Outline your thesis to discover a design. Often the pattern for a writing is contained within the language and logic of its central assertion.

> Three passions, simple but overwhelmingly strong, have governed my life: the longing for love, the search for knowledge, and unbearable pity for the suffering of mankind. These passions, like great winds, have blown me hither and thither, in a wayward course, over a deep ocean of anguish, reaching to the very verge of despair.
>
> (Bertrand Russell, *The Autobiography of Bertrand Russell, 1872–1914* [Boston: Little, 1951, 1967])

   I. The longing for love.
  II. The search for knowledge.
 III. The unbearable pity for the suffering of mankind.

Sometimes a thesis provides if not an outline for a subject then at least an organizing principle:

> Obviously, it is futile to talk of accuracy or inaccuracy, authority or lack of authority, with reference to the newspaper as a whole. The newspaper cannot be dismissed with either a blanket endorsement or a blanket condemnation. It cannot be used as if all its parts had equal value or authenticity. The first duty of the historical student of the newspaper is to discriminate. He must weigh every separate department, every article, every writer, for what the department or article or writer seems to be worth.
>
> (Allan Nevins, *Allan Nevins on History*, ed. by Ray Allan Billington [New York: Scribner's, 1975])

This combination thesis-purpose statement commits the writer to a section-by-section analysis and evaluation of a newspaper's contents.

Do a freewriting letter giving your reasons for writing and outline that. Here's the letter you read in Chapter 3 and the pattern it contains:

> Dear Urbanites and Suburbanites, My roots are in a tiny country town and I want to tell you about them. I'll bet you don't know much about small towns, except what you see on television and vacation. That won't tell you much. You probably think small towns are like "Little House on the Prairie"—pretty

places, wonderful places to live, close to nature. Well, you're close to nature, but that's about all you're close to. You're sure far from people and the excitement that crowds of people in large cities can create. I think many of the adults who lived in my small town were like a lot of the people I meet today. They don't see any way to solve the big human problems like crime, poverty, and hatred, and so they say, "The hell with it, I'm getting out." You see a lot of people like that in small towns, their backs turned. That's the small town life I'd like to show you.

I. How urbanites and suburbanites imagine small-town life.
II. The truth in their image (the *Yes, but* pattern).
  A. Life lived close to nature.
  B. Life lived far from crowds and cities.
III. The more important truth these people fail to see.
  A. The boredom of small-town life.
  B. Small towns as places of escape and denial.

Write an exploratory or preliminary draft, outline it, and revise in light of that outline. Often we already have a predictable pattern that just needs to be written out so we can see it in the natural terrain of our subject. But as you write this exploratory draft, remember it's just that. It may give you a pattern you can use, but don't assume that writing out your ideas will automatically organize them. Nor should you assume that the pattern of ideas in a freewriting is the only pattern they can take. You're only experimenting.

Alternatives to Outlining

Pie Charts and Flowcharts   Outlines are not the only logical scheme for organizing a subject. Try *pie charts* to discover the proportions among sub-topics, their order, and how much space you'll have to give to each. Try *flowcharts* to indicate all the things you have to do at the same time while you write. (See the diagrams at the top of page 131.)

A Drawing   Use a little imagination. In Chapter 4 you learned to draw your subject to help you develop it. That doodle or sketch may also give you a *map*. Use it as a guide. Where would you start your journey through your sketch? Are there places where you have to jump from one part of the picture to another? How will you bridge those gaps for your readers? Where will you end your journey? Apparently the great movie director Alfred Hitchcock worked this way, first imagining a movie from a single visual image and then working with a screen writer to devise a plot to fit the image. Remember the writer's doodle of his hometown in Chapter 4? It appears again at the bottom of page 131 with a map through it, leading from the general isolation of the town to his special further isolation at the town's edge.[1]

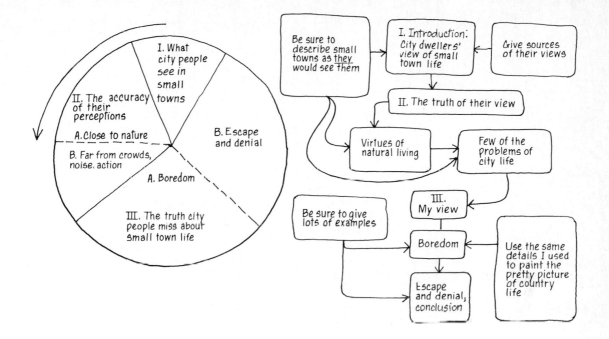

The House Tour   If you divided up your subject and put the parts into each room of your house, where would you put them? What would go into the living room, the dining room, kitchen, basement, attic, and so on? And if you were going to give your readers a guided tour, where would you begin and end?

The Gimmick   If it is a suitable occasion, think of an organizing pretext, some gimmick that brings a pattern of organization along with it. Do

your writing in the form of a letter, travelogue, diary, or some other conventional format.

EXERCISES

1. From the preceding exercises in this chapter, choose two. Follow the instructions for each exercise, but instead of writing a paragraph, do a one page freewriting to discover what you will say and then write a conventional outline to organize your ideas. You may write an outline that reflects the order of ideas as you actually wrote them in your freewriting, or you may use your outline to organize those ideas in a more logical way. For a guide to outlining see Chapter 17, "The Research Project," Step 5, pages 444–449.

2. From the preceding exercises in this chapter, choose two. Follow the instructions for each exercise, but instead of writing a paragraph, do a one page freewriting. Then try one of the alternative organizing strategies to organize your discoveries: a pie chart, flowchart, doodle, house tour, or gimmick. You may organize your ideas in the order they appear in your freewriting, or you may use one of these alternative organizing strategies to put your ideas in a more logical order.

WRITING PROJECTS

Topics

1. Choose one of the paragraphs you have written for this chapter's organization exercises and use it as the foundation for a full-length three- to five-page essay. You may expand your exercise paragraph into an essay, fit it into one part of your essay, or use it as an exploratory writing for an essay that contains its ideas, if not its language and design. Explore the subject in more detail, find a thesis, develop it, find a communications strategy, and organize your presentation in whatever pattern seems most appropriate. Write to the audience identified in the exercise.

2. Choose a year ten, twenty, thirty, forty, or fifty years from last year. Or choose the year of your birth. Then choose a subject that you guess was as important in the past as it was last year, e.g., exploration, a specific technology, sports, medicine, fashion, the movies and other arts, education, employment, the economy, justice, social relations, and so on. Look up your subject in the two appropriately dated volumes of *The Reader's Guide to Periodical Literature.* List three or four magazine articles from each volume relevant to your subject. Look them up, read them, and take notes. Then write a three- to five-page comparison/contrast essay. Write to people your own age, and aim to share this two-compartment time capsule with them. Ask yourself these questions: With respect to your subject, how are things different between last year and the earlier year? How are they the same? What differences in values, attitudes, technologies, and abilities are revealed by the contrasts you discover?

3. The how-to essay: In three to five pages tell your composition class how to do something they should know how to do or something they would enjoy doing. Before you decide on a subject, consider whether your readers could actually use your instructions. Of how much use, for example, is a set of written instructions

for learning to water ski. They'd better be brief—and waterproof! Your introduction should show how important and useful your chosen activity is or dramatize how enjoyable it is. The body of your essay will, of course, be a series of directions presented clearly, systematically, and in detail. Aim not only to instruct your readers but also to encourage them.

4. Write a three- to five-page essay analyzing the design of some essay or literary work you've read recently. Divide it into its major parts and explain how each part serves to advance the writer's theme or prove the thesis. You'll probably organize your essay as a process analysis.

THE WRITING PROCESS

1. Writing-in-progress.
   a. *Exploring:* Free association and freewriting.
   b. *Developing.*
      i. Take notes and freewrite to discover what you will say, take walk-around notes, write a letter to your audience (see pages 47–54).
      ii. Use whatever methods of development are appropriate: facts and statistics, examples, anecdotes, analogies, definitions, quotations, allusions, description.
      Try several figurative free associations. If _____ were a _____ it would/wouldn't be a _____. (See pages 91–92.)
      Draw a picture of your subject; circle those parts your readers may not notice or understand (see page 83).
   c. *Planning a communications strategy:* Decide on a role, persona (distance and attitude), and thesis (*My point is that . . . What I mean to say is that . . .*).
   ————→d. *New in this chapter:* Organize your essay according to one of the patterns of order—narrative, spatial, order of importance, comparison/contrast, pro/con, classification, descriptive analysis, causal analysis—or devise an appropriate mixed pattern. Discover your pattern by writing outlines, pie charts, flowcharts, sketches, or house tours (see pages 128–132).
   e. *Revising:* Reconsider your ideas and communications strategy; create frictions in your thinking (see pages 55–56).
2. Writing: Write a preliminary draft of your project. Write freely, don't stop except to reread, give yourself room to revise (see pages 57–58).
3. Rewriting.
   a. Be a zoom lens as you revise; add, delete, substitute, rearrange.
   b. Make your nouns and verbs as concrete and specific as possible (see pages 100–102).
   c. Copyedit for mechanical errors, recopy, and proofread (see pages 61–62).
4. Self-evaluation.
   a. What is your intention in this writing?
   b. What is your thesis?
   c. What did you do to help your readers read this writing? Will any parts be hard to follow? If so why? What would make them more readable?

  d. What do you like best about this writing?
  e. Did you try anything here that you hadn't tried before?
  f. What one change would most improve this writing?

END NOTE

  1. I am indebted for this organizing strategy to Nancy Mack and her paper on right brain/left brain enhancing strategies, "Brain Hemisphere Lateralization: Helping the Writer Choose the Appropriate Composing Strategy," Conference on College Composition and Communication, Detroit, MI, 18 Mar. 1983.

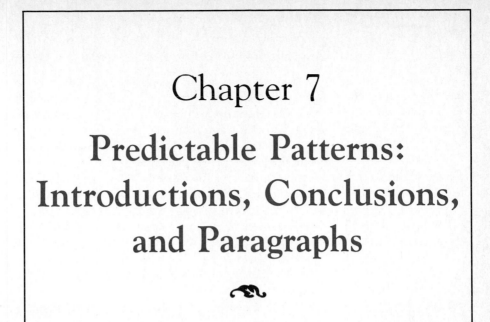

Chapter 7

Predictable Patterns: Introductions, Conclusions, and Paragraphs

INTRODUCTIONS AND CONCLUSIONS

In the last chapter I suggested that writing and reading were like taking a journey. That analogy applies not only to the design of a writing but also to its introduction, conclusion, and paragraphs. If patterns of organization provide maps for your writing, introductions provide a compass to travel by, and conclusions and paragraphs mark the stages of the journey through your writing, both for you and your readers. Titles and introductions are the prediction devices readers encounter first, of course, and for that reason alone they often make the most lasting impressions. That's why professional writers spend so much time on them, making sure they get their readers well launched. A good opening prepares readers for their reading in three ways. First, it turns their attention. That word *turn* best describes the power of a good opening to draw readers from the real world into the writer's world of words. Then the good introduction focuses the attention of those readers on the subject at hand and gives them reasons to read on. Finally, it builds a bridge into the body of the writing, either through a thesis or some transitional statement, suggesting the subject, the writer's persona, and, often, the design of writing that follows. The more effectively your introductions capture, narrow, and focus your readers' attention, the more likely they'll read what you say with interest and understanding.

Consider how this multiparagraph opening works on its readers:

A dramatic opening line that captures the attention of those interested in public education

Dramatic details that create an urgent mood

Survival, rather than education, would seem to be the order of the day at many New York City public high schools. Last year, New York public schools reported 1,673 assaults, 1,635 weapons offenses, and 1,151 robberies—and that was a good year. At Thomas Jefferson High School in Brooklyn, a recent surprise search of the student body uncovered bats, long knives, and Kung Fu-style wooden clubs. It also set off a minor riot that culminated in the trashing of the cafeteria. The lone teacher bold enough to stand in the students' way had his nose broken in several places.

The topic of school order narrowed to a specific school

Louis D. Brandeis High School, on Manhattan's Upper West Side, ought to be no less harrowing. Virtually all of its 3,600 students come from poor minority families in West Harlem. 60 percent of them speak Spanish as a first language. A Hispanic gang, the Ballbusters, enrolls many of its members at Brandeis, as to a lesser extent do La Familia and the black Zulu Nation.

Dramatic details make readers expect a "human interest" approach and anecdotal style

Yet Brandeis has gone about the business of education in an orderly and unperturbed, though sometimes discouraging manner. Gang members may slaughter one another on their home turfs, but they behave themselves in school. The million tiny raids students conduct against authority (turning on a radio for a second, strutting into class fifteen minutes late with a truculent expression), which make many schools ungovernable and many teachers prematurely gray, are kept in check at Brandeis, though scarcely eliminated. Attendance levels, around 79 percent, are above the city average. Even the school's appalling dropout rate of roughly 50 percent is merely average for New York's public high schools.

The difference that makes this school worth reading about

The subject narrowed to the center of focus, the cause of the differences between this school and others

The chief reason, it is generally agreed, for these modest successes in the face of apparently insuperable obstacles is the sixty-seven-year-old principal of Brandeis, Murray Cohn. . . .

(James Traub, "Principals in Action," *Harper's* May 1983)

Almost any introductory strategy is potentially a good one. Whether it fulfills its potential depends upon the subject, the writer's purpose, and the audience. To aim to write seriously about teenage alcoholism, for example, yet begin with a humorous anecdote about a high school party is almost sure to fail. Who would take such an essay seriously? Or consider what would happen to a writer trying to win over a hostile or skeptical audience who began by hurling controversial opinions at them. The good opening grows out of the attempt to create an effective communications strategy, and as often as not, openings suggest themselves naturally, as part of the exploring, developing, and shaping process that precedes a preliminary draft. But not always. Sometimes writers can't find a way to begin. That's when the following conventional openings are useful. Familiarize yourself with them; you'll find them useful, too.

Eleven Ways to Begin

The Anecdote   Begin with a brief story that dramatizes your subject and introduces your thesis or main idea. Anecdotes are especially useful for humanizing abstract, complex subjects and for human-interest writing. Don't take your anecdote for granted, however; you may have to explain its meaning and how it pertains to your subject.

The anecdote

My eight-year-old daughter and I were out walking our dog the other day when the dog saw a cat and bolted across a busy street. The dog didn't get hit by a car and was waiting when we arrived to grab her leash. We were delighted the dog hadn't been killed. My daughter, television's child as much as mine, remarked: "Plop. Plop. Fizz. Fizz. Oh, what a relief it is."

Explanation of the anecdote

My daughter, thinking in jingles? I was appalled, of course, but I was also secretly satisfied. Part of me hates and fears television, and what could be better evidence of its malevolent effects on the youth of America? Contrary to widespread claims and parents' worries, violence and sex are not what's wrong with television. Johnny Mack Brown and Lash Larue, the old-time Saturday afternoon Western heroes, wasted their enemies with even less compunction than Baretta or Kojack show on the tube. There always have been more cheap sexual thrills available to even the semi-literate in *True Confessions*—never mind *Penthouse* and *Hustler*—than will ever get past the

Thesis

FCC. Television's real crime is not that it incites passion, but that it purveys pablum, intellectual paste and emotional puree.

(M. M. K., "Just for You, Barbara," *The New Republic* 10 Dec. 1977)

The Setting or Background   Begin by setting the scene for the narrative to follow or by providing background information necessary to understand a subject or problem. The following example sets the scene for a descriptive analysis and evokes a feeling for its subject.

The general scene and background

There are some fifty square blocks of pre-World War II apartment buildings in what used to be one of the most genteel neighborhoods of New York City, near Columbia University, where things have gone slightly, delicately, to seed. The area is called Morningside Heights, and many old ladies live there. Inside front hallways, the polished tables are scratched and the Tiffany lampshades have a panel or two of their stained glass missing. On the outside, the creamwhite stones have graffiti on them and the wrought-iron railings of the buildings are surrounded by weeds.

The specific scene

The old ladies' apartments are all different, but all alike—multi-roomed, dark, large, meticulously kept; the way professional people lived forty years ago; not an appliance less than thirty years old; walls hung with prints of Bavaria in the 1890s, or of India, or Japan, and the dark corners crowded with knickknacks: shells, Mexican rattles, Japanese netsukes, oils by artists

Mood-setting details

whose careers never flowered, oak music boxes, bronze vases, porcelain peasant children; dark shelves with yellow postcards, art prints, polished wood, dusty books, letters, photographs, souvenirs. The smell of their apartments is of good, clean dust relieved by an occasional whiff of perfume or beeswax polish.

(Paul Malamud, "Rented Rooms," *The Atlantic* July 1978)

In Medias Res ("in the Middle of Things")

If you're writing a narrative, begin in the middle of things, perhaps at a moment of suspense, crisis, or climax. Once you've captured your readers' interest, flash back to the actual beginning of the story and pick up its thread there.

The money looked good. There were tall stacks of it, mostly tens and twenties, just for the taking. There was no casing of the joint and no gunplay. The job was done in less than 60 seconds, and the total take came to $1,444. Not bad wages for one minute's work. Of course, it also cost me another two years in prison, as well as additional time for my parole violation. The fact that this is my third prison stint shouldn't pose any problem. But it gets harder, especially now that my wife has told me to make arrangements to have my things moved out of the house. She cannot take it any longer, and I do not blame her.

(Marcus W. Koechig, "Paying My Debt to Society," *Newsweek* 15 Nov. 1983)

Sensational Details

Using sensational details is a strategy much like the *in medias res* opening. It grips the readers' interest in a dramatic writing that may not otherwise begin very dramatically.

My father died when his heart could no longer manage to pump blood through his embolismic lungs. He had a pulmonary embolism because most of his lungs' healthy tissue was covered with a swamp of killer cells. My father was not without blame for this, as he had smoked a pack of cigarettes a day for thirty-five years. He gave up smoking thirteen years ago because he was by then convinced that it wasn't good for him.

(Eric Lax, "The Death of My Father," *The Atlantic* July 1978)

Notice how the clinically precise details, the ironic statement of the cancer's cause, and the matter-of-fact tone make us expect that the writer will portray his father without sentiment, as objectively as possible.

A Well-known or Appropriate Quotation

Introduce the quotation with its author and source, then, if necessary, explain how the quotation sums up the theme of your writing.

"Hypocrisy," said La Rochefoucauld [the seventeenth-century French author] a long time ago, "is the homage that vice pays to virtue." And so it is with language—for those groups that are the most ruthless in their acts are also the most devious in their speech.

Totalitarian governments do not "kill" dissenters and heretics; they "liqui-date" them. Goering did not speak of "gassing" the German Jews; he spoke of "the final solution" to the Jewish problem.

The fine art of double-talk has been raised to the ultimate degree by modern communist and fascist governments; and the more vicious their policies, the more they seem to feel the need to use the soft word.

(Sydney J. Harris, "Guilt Gives Rise to Double Talk," *The Best of Sydney J. Harris* [Boston: Houghton, 1975])

The Strong Statement   If a subject contains its own drama or impor-tance, you may not have to work very hard for your readers' attention. Begin with your dramatic thesis.

Two recent studies, one conducted by the esteemed New York Stock Ex-change and the other by W. R. Grace & Co., make this observation painfully obvious: You have to have rocks in your head to invest in the stock market these days.

(William Flanagan, "Pilloried in Stocks," *Esquire* 15 Aug. 1978)

A Warning   A version of the strong statement opening, a warning is not only dramatic; it is also a way to register readers' involvement with a subject, even their responsibility for it. They are, after all, the ones being warned. The following example aims to increase public pressure for re-form, pressure that will, in turn, provoke political action.

Something fundamental must be done—and done soon—if America is not to default on its national commitment to equal educational opportunity. Un-less comprehensive steps are taken in the financing of higher education—steps comparable in scope to the Morrill Act of 1862 establishing land grant col-leges, or the Servicemen's Readjustment Act of 1944 establishing the GI Bill—increasing numbers of academically qualified students will be denied access and choice in higher education simply because the costs will prove unmanageable.

(John R. Silber, "The Tuition Dilemma," *The Atlantic* July 1978)

A Question or Problem   Ask real questions requiring real answers. Avoid those that can be answered by a simple yes or no; once your readers have answered yes or no they have no need to read further. For much the same reason, avoid posing problems with self-evident solutions.

Why should any words be called obscene? Don't they all describe natural human functions? Am I trying to tell them, my students demand, that the "strong, earthy, gut-honest"—or, if they are fans of Norman Mailer, the "rich, liberating, existential"—language they use to describe sexual activity isn't pref-erable to "phony-sounding, middle-class words like 'intercourse' and 'copulate'?" "Cop You Late!" they say with fancy inflections and gagging grimaces. "Now what is *that* supposed to mean?"

Well, what is it supposed to mean? And why indeed should one group of words describing human functions and human organs be acceptable in ordinary conversation and another, describing presumably the same organs and functions, be tabooed—so much so, in fact, that some of these words still cannot appear in print in many parts of the English-speaking world?

(Barbara Lawrence, "Four-Letter Words Can Hurt You," *The New York Times* 27 Oct. 1973)

The Rebuttal   Begin by giving your opponents' position or some commonly held opinion. By presenting generally held opinions first, a writer with a new or opposing view woos readers who hold those opinions. Once they have been attracted by the restatement of their beliefs, the writer can present his or her opposing opinion. This opening provokes readers to read on, either because they have been captivated by this view or because they want to follow to its end the writer's quarrel with them.

There is a belief, widely held among both sexes, that whereas men are irked by monogamy women are suited to it by nature.

Even on the face of it, this seems fishy. After all, monogamy is what we actually have; and the social, religious and legal systems which gave it to us were all invented, and until recently run, by men. I can well believe men were masochistic enough to impose monogamy on themselves as a hairshirt, but I find it a touch implausible that the hairshirt designed for the husband just happened to be a comfortable and perfectly fitting garment for the wife.

And indeed I suspect that, if you scrutinize the notion that women are naturally monogamous, it turns out to be based on no sounder authority than that rhyme which begins "higamus hogamus, woman is monogamous," and no more cogent evidence than a one-eyed view of biology which is in fact about as good science as "higamus hogamus" is good Latin.

(Brigid Brophy, "Monogamy," *Don't Never Forget* [London: Jonathan Cape, 1966])

The Generalization   Open with a general truth that you use to illuminate a specific subject. But beware of overgeneralizing. The general truth should fit your specific subject closely.

The entertainment we enjoy is a measure of who we are. Two recently ballyhooed movies—last summer's *Star Wars* and November's *Close Encounters of the Third Kind*—suggest that Americans are both fascinated with and horrified by the technological world we have shaped.

(Carll Tucker, "Our Love-Hate Affair with Technology," *Saturday Review* 10 Dec. 1977)

The first sentence offers a truth few would quarrel with. The second applies it to two movies to see what they tell us about ourselves. This pattern reveals how a narrow, specific subject is part of a larger issue and gives that specific subject an importance it might not otherwise have.

The Definition   If your subject is unfamiliar or unclear to your audience, if it is likely to be confused with another subject, or if you want to suggest a new way of looking at it, open with a definition of key terms. But avoid the overworked lead-in *Webster's Dictionary defines. . . .*

> I'm not a gourmet. I'm a gourmand. It's a subtle distinction. A gourmet eats only the very best food. A gourmand prefers that as well, but he'll eat what he can get, or afford. The main thing is that he likes to eat and will try anything, even fast food. I've taken my chances with them all—Arby's, Pizza Hut, Kentucky Fried, Tico Taco Toeco.
>
> (Colin L. Westerbeck, Jr., "Good Fast Food," *Esquire* May 1983)

Only by defining *gourmand* and distinguishing it from the finickier *gourmet* does this writer establish his credentials for judging fast food. Once he has made his definition, we are more likely to trust the opinions that form the body of his essay.

Eight Ways to Conclude

For most writers conclusions are easier to write than introductions, if only because stopping is easier than starting. Yet a conclusion is more than a convenient stopping place. The good conclusion does two things: first, it marks the end of a journey; it completes the last of the expectations raised in the beginning and gives the writing, thereby, a satisfying sense of wholeness and unity. Second, it releases readers from the writer's world of words and sends them back to the real world, often with something new to think about or do.

Almost always the good conclusion grows naturally from the writing that precedes it. By the time we near the end of a writing we have a feel for its rhythm and flow; we know where and how to tie everything up. If you can't find a way to finish, however, here are eight conventional endings. Whether one is right for you depends, as always, on your interests and attitudes, your subject, and your audience.

The Concluding Thesis   Arrange your materials so they lead clearly and inevitably to a closing opinion. This is not the restatement of an opening thesis; rather, it is the goal toward which a writing has aimed throughout. Here is the conclusion-thesis to an essay arguing the importance of grammar instruction:

> I can't accept the theory that learning has to be fun. If it is fun, so much the better. Certainly, it *can* be fun. Equally certainly, learning can be tedious.

But even when it is drudgery, learning something and understanding what has been gained on the way brings a sense of satisfaction that frequently leads to a desire for further achievement, however painful the process.

The rules are there to be used or to be broken. Often the breaking of grammatical rules enhances style and clarity. But the knowledge of the rules and of how and why they work is *always* a tremendous asset. The important thing is to know that they are your tools, not your master.

(Thomas Middleton, "On Learning the Rules,"
Saturday Review 21 Jan. 1978)

A Question   Leave your readers thinking about your subject or ask them to apply what you've written to their own lives. But gauge carefully the attitude of your question. Condescension, hostility, or sarcasm will undoubtedly defeat your purposes. Ask questions that prompt rather than stop thought. Here is the close to an essay about the reception given veterans on their return from the Vietnam War:

It does the Vietnam veteran no good to talk about how different his war was. In some ways, in fact, such comparisons tend to deflect attention from the truly important moral issues: Was the war *wrong*, not just "different"? Was the veteran's sacrifice, however real, cheapened by a mistaken cause? Did we abuse the Vietnam veteran not by the treatment we gave him upon his return home but rather by sending him to war in the first place?

(Tim O'Brien, "The Violent Vet," *Esquire* Dec. 1979)

A Strong Challenge   Move your readers to change their beliefs or behavior. Dare their response, as does this conclusion to an essay on violence in the cocaine trade:

The victims are not all rival businessmen, who might only be getting what they deserve. Cocaine hit men tend to be casual in their aim. "Children have been killed in cross fires, and so have innocent adults," says Brent Eaton, a special agent in the Miami division of the Drug Enforcement Administration. "We've had machine-gun fights as people were driving down expressways here in town. We've had people riddled with machine-gun bullets as they were waiting for traffic lights."

At the very least, cocaine has rent the social fabric and economic fabric of two South American countries and fueled the decay of considerable sections of the United States. To buy cocaine is to subsidize a network of death and despair. Snorting cocaine is at least as bad for the planet as wearing a coat made from an endangered species. Join the cause. Boycott cocaine.

(David Owen, "Boycott Cocaine," *Harper's* Dec. 1982)

A Quotation   Use a quotation to illustrate or encapsulate the point of your writing. Introduce and explain it if necessary. Here is the conclusion to an essay criticizing egocentrics' excessive preoccupation with themselves:

> The current glorification of self-love will turn out in the end to be a no-win proposition, because in questions of personality or "identity," what counts is not who you are, but what you do. "By their fruits, ye shall know them." And by their fruits, they shall know themselves.
>
> (Margaret Halsey, "What's Wrong With 'Me, Me, Me,' " *Newsweek* 17 Apr. 1978)

An Anecdote   Tell a story to summarize and dramatize the point of your writing, as this conclusion does to an essay arguing against those who exclude children from their communities:

> Some months ago there was a knock on my door late in the evening. It was my neighbor's 12-year-old. He walked into the kitchen, sat down and said, "*Alison. What is the soul?*" That question was worth a week in the country with the guru of your choice. Who can afford to say, "Suffer the little children to stay the hell away from me?" When I was a child, my elderly next-door neighbor taught me what the phrase "live and let live" means—along with many other lessons in generosity and how to help rear the kids next door. I like to think that what she knew about tolerance was augmented by long association with kids to whom a fence was something expressly designed to be climbed over. We, on the other hand, also learned to respect our elders by having one around who was indeed our better.
>
> The high price of the company of children is only a small measure of its worth. Excluding them from our neighborhoods is a life-defying act.
>
> (Alison Kilgour, "What's Wrong With Kids?" *Newsweek* 5 June 1978)

The Hook   Return to the materials of your introduction and comment on them in light of all that you have written in the body of your essay. No other close gives a writing quite the same feeling of wholeness. Notice, however, that the hook is not a summarizing device but a way to round out an idea. Here is an opening anecdote to an essay analyzing the apparent miseducation taking place in many American colleges:

> During the Spanish Civil War, the Rector of the University of Salamanca, the writer and philosopher Miguel de Unamuno, came to the window of his study to find a fascist demonstration in the courtyard. "Down with intelligence," shouted the fascists. "Long live death." Unamuno responded to the demonstrators, "No. Long live intelligence." There are few real fascists in the courtyards of our universities today, but a trail for them is being blazed, most obviously and notoriously, by the men and women of intellect who sell the legacy of intellect to the CIA and the Pentagon. Much less noticeable are their accomplices, the innocent students, pitiful in their eighteen-year-old cynicism,

the offspring of a society where youth no longer enjoys the luxury of the cheapest idealism.

> (Harry Brent, "Long Live Intelligence," *Rhetorical Considerations*, ed. Harry Brent and William Lutz [Cambridge, MA.: Winthrop, 1977])

Having explored in the body of his essay how teachers have sold this "legacy of intellect," how their students aided them in this betrayal, and what he believes to be the anti-intellectual bias of some in higher education, the author recalls in his conclusion his opening anecdote but adapts it to apply to contemporary American students. Students

> from the slums, and increasingly from middle-class suburbia are passed along and given degrees by liberal-minded educators. They may even get into law school or Wharton [Business School] on minority admittance programs (unless they happen to be poor white males) and end up as window dressing at IBM, comfortably ensconced behind the portals of power, but without power, waiting to join their brothers and sisters who have been taught the irrelevancy of intellect in taking up the banner of some new leader, waiting to follow him or her into the future, shouting "Down with intelligence; long live death."

A Warning   Here is the close to another essay decrying people's ignorance of the way language works. Notice how the warning connects the immediate subject to larger, more important ones.

> We are in trouble. When writers don't know the rules, their writing usually turns to mush. When writing turns to mush, thought, which feeds on writing, suffers from malnutrition and is incapable of clear development or expression.
> When that happens, the perils of this complex world become overwhelming.

> (Thomas Middleton, "Less Than Words Can Say," *Saturday Review* 24 Nov. 1979)

A Generalization   Open your writing outward at its end. Apply the point of your writing to some larger or related issue. Show how your subject is part of the big picture, that what applies in one instance applies in others, or that your subject has implications. Here is the close to an essay criticizing the reluctance of some schools to fail students who have not learned their lessons:

> The young people are interested, I think, in taking their knocks, just as adults must take theirs. Students deserve a fair chance, and, failing to take advantage of that chance, a straightforward dismissal. It has been said that government must guarantee equal opportunity, not equal results. I like that. Through the theoretical fog that has clouded our perceptions and blanketed our minds, we know what is equitable and right. Mother put it another way.

She always said, "Life is real; life is earnest." Incidentally, she taught me Latin and never gave me air in a jug. I had to breathe on my own. So do we all.
(Suzanne Britt Jordan, "I Wants to Go to the Prose," *Newsweek* 14 Nov. 1977)

Creating Effective Introductions and Conclusions

I wrote earlier as if introductions were for the primary use of readers, but that's not quite right. Openings are just as valuable for writers. Some writers are not comfortable until they find the perfect title or opening lines. Their concern is not misspent. Titles and opening lines give them a feel not only for their subject matter but also for their attitude, role, and style. If you're having trouble finding that just-right opening:

- Imagine your ideas in a box, all of them tied together on a string. If you started to pull on that string, what would appear first? Thinking in this way, you might discover a logical starting point.
- If your readers met your subject on the street, what's the first question they'd ask? Here you see your subject from your readers' point of view.
- Look up your subject, a synonym for it, or something associated with it in a book of proverbs or quotations.

However you begin, check for two problems when you revise. Writers often begin ahead of themselves, writing a line, paragraph, or page of related but largely irrelevant matter before they get down to business. This writing is often invaluable for getting them warmed up but useless to readers and should be cut in revision. Such cuts will make your writing clearer, more emphatic, and more predictable. So, too, should you eliminate any self-consciousness from your openings. Often writers begin a preliminary draft unsure of their direction or purpose and try to force issues with bald statements like *In this essay I intend to. . . .* There's nothing wrong with such statements, so long as writers remember they're talking to themselves and not their readers. When these statements linger into the final draft, they can be distracting, focusing the readers' attention on the writer instead of the subject.

When it comes time to close your writing, avoid restating your thesis unless the conventions you're following require it. Recapitulation is the easiest way to announce that you have fulfilled the expectations created in your introduction, but unless your writing is long or complex, readers will find it self-conscious, repetitive, and unimaginative. Also beware of stopping too soon, of stopping rather than concluding. Because a writer's energies often flag near the end, it's important to take care here. Make sure you have developed your subject completely and followed your pattern through to its finish. But when you have finished, stop. Beware of trailing off into irrelevancies or opening new issues.

EXERCISES

1. You have decided to write and publish an essay giving your impressions and evaluations of the spirit of this decade. Your aim is to help your readers make sense of an era. Do a ten-minute freewriting to discover what you think are this decade's mood, most important characteristics, and outlook. Then, using the suggestions and models in this chapter, write an appropriate title and introductory paragraph for two of the following situations. Identify the magazine you're writing for. To make sure your opening is appropriate you may have to examine copies of the magazines in question to see how their pieces begin.

   a. You want to publish your essay in *Rolling Stone* or some other magazine appealing to young men and women. Write an introduction to engage this audience.

   b. You want to publish your essay in *Life, Saturday Evening Post, Reader's Digest,* or some other magazine appealing to middle-class, middle-aged, middle-brow readers.

   c. You want to publish your essay in some magazine, like *Ebony,* aimed for a minority or ethnic audience.

   d. You are writing for a magazine like *Modern Maturity,* read by people in their fifties and beyond.

   e. You are writing for a woman's magazine like either *Ms.* or *Woman's Day.*

   f. You are writing for a man's magazine like *Esquire* or *Playboy.*

   g. You are writing for a magazine for children twelve and under, like *Jack and Jill* or *Junior Scholastic.*

2. Choose one of your previous writing projects and, using what you know about introductions and conclusions, revise the introductory and concluding paragraphs of that essay. Then write two *new* introductions and conclusions for your essay based on strategies from the preceding pages.

PARAGRAPHING

By definition paragraphs are prediction devices. Whenever we make the indentation that signals a new paragraph, we mark a boundary dividing subjects and create in our readers definite expectations that a change of one sort or another is about to occur.

A Change in Subject Matter

A paragraph is a unit of meaning. Like an individual sentence, it is complete in itself, although it may be and often is part of some larger pattern. It develops a complete idea, action, or description. This definition means that, whenever possible, the parts of a subject or related subjects should be put together in one paragraph. See how the paragraphs in the following excerpt classify restaurants everyone ought to avoid?

Subject: Restaurants to avoid

I love restaurants. I can spend hours in them. I collect them—their style, shape, size and syntax, their decor and dress—and I can spot at a glance the sure signs of a lousy one.

Subtopic: Restaurants known by their architecture

Some restaurants are easy to avoid. You know better than to enter an eatery shaped like a doughnut or bowler, right? Well, the same rule applies to ethnic architecture—Chinese pagodas, Dutch windmills, mini-Mount Vernons, mock Elizabethans and too-tall A-frames.

Subtopic: The views

Restaurants with skyline views have reached a new low in highs. Every urban center now has something at the top of a skyscraper, usually twirling, where the vistas look good enough to eat, but the victuals are not. Views of any kind, in fact, sky- or eye-level, generally attract customers who are there to oo-ah, not to nosh.

Subtopic: Fancy names

While you are still safely on the outside looking in, think twice about over-Anglicized country inns called The Ye-Olde-Anything, particularly if any combination of the words crown, Sussex, feather, shield, squire, oak, cork, or York appears in the name. They are apt to serve defrosted flounder, pink chicken, wet steak and dead duck.

Subtopic: Novelty restaurants

Also potentially hazardous is the epidemic of novelty restaurants, often in spiffy old-town restorations and hopelessly indigenous to waterfront developments. Here a severe case of the cutes is contagious. The ice-cream parlor is called Scoopy-Doo and the candy shop, Oh, Fudge. Down the cobblestone lane, there's Honky Dorry, Polly Wog's, Once Upon a Stove and Bonnie View. *Nouvelle cuisine*, where the food is not so much prepared as it is arranged, often fits the novelty category. Photograph it, if you like, then get out while the getting's good.

(Curtiss Anderson, "Dinner at the Make-Sick Restaurant," *Newsweek* 13 June 1983)

A Change in Function

Emphasis Paragraphs   Every paragraph has a specific job to perform, and an indented first line often signals a change in function from one paragraph to the next. You've already studied paragraphs designed to introduce or conclude. Others are designed for emphasis. Often brief, they set their subjects apart from the discussion that leads to or from them. Sometimes they are only one sentence long, sometimes shorter.

The false idea is that inside every human being, however unprepossessing, there is a glorious, talented and overwhelmingly attractive personality. This personality—so runs the erroneous belief—will be revealed in all its splendor if the individual just forgets about courtesy, cooperativeness and consideration for others and proceeds to do exactly what he or she feels like doing.

Nonsense.

Inside each of us is a mess of unruly primitive impulses, and these can sometimes, under the strenuous self-discipline and dedication of art, result in notable creativity. But there is no such thing as a pure, crystalline and well-organized "native" personality, though a host of trendy human-potential groups trade on the mistaken assumption that there is.

(Margaret Halsey, "What's Wrong with 'Me, Me, Me,' "
Newsweek 17 Apr. 1978)

Thesis Paragraphs In longer or more complex writings, a thesis may be set off from the introduction and body in its own paragraph. The message of such separation is clear: here is the point of the writing, where we get down to business.

It seems to be the fashion these days to equate a lower standard of living with a better way of life. We are told by the oracles of press and television how much more rewarding our lives will be when we drive little shift cars, eat food without preservatives, dwell in Spartanly heated homes, wear natural fibers and abandon energy-guzzling appliances.

Well, I've just wound up two years of living in exactly that style and, let me tell you, it's no fun.

Our family recently spent two years in Sydney, Australia, where people live pretty much as they say Americans will live in the next decade. They drive little shift cars, bundle up in unheated homes, eat unpreserved foods, wear natural fibers, make do with a minimum of appliances and enjoy hot showers only during off-peak hours. This may be heresy, but it isn't exactly terrific.

(Bernard Sloan, "The Future Doesn't Work,"
Newsweek 19 Sept. 1977)

Transitional Paragraphs Transitional paragraphs create bridges between major sections of a writing. Often they are as brief as emphatic paragraphs.

If we no longer have any heroes, it may not be because no one is fit to be a hero, but because we are not fit to recognize one. It may even be that the powers-that-be in our societies do not want us to have heroes. Heroes are against things-as-they-are. They break through the pattern of valetdom, the ruck that most of us accept out of indifference or weariness. They say that things aren't necessarily so, that they can be altered if we strain to change them. All heroes are rebels—which does not mean that all rebels are heroes—and as rebels they are spirited. Our times are dispirited.

We need to begin with a model.

When we think of the Elizabethan Age as heroic, it is not only a few exceptional men and women whom we recall, but a whole society that burst alive at the summons to a great enterprise, engaging the hearts and souls of all. The sea captains were joined in the same endeavor with the poet dramatists. . . .

(Henry Fairlie, "Too Rich for Heroes," *Harper's* Nov. 1978)

Dialogue Paragraphs Dialogue paragraphs set off the words of one speaker from those of another or from surrounding narration:

"John?" she whispered breathlessly.

Hoarsely he queried, "Wilma?"

"Oh, John!"

"Oh, ho, Wilma!"

"Hey," Frank called from the next room, "will you two knock it off? How can I learn to write dialogue paragraphs with you two out there having such a good time?"

The Parts of a Development Paragraph

The most frequent, most important, and most difficult paragraphs we write are the *development paragraphs* that present an idea, scene, or unit of action. They are the most frequent and important because they are what fill the middle of a writing and contain its substance. They are most difficult because they are generally the most complex, having more parts and more complexly related parts than other paragraphs. I said earlier that a paragraph is by its completeness of thought a kind of large sentence; it is also, by parts and design, something like an essay in miniature. Here are the sentences that comprise the parts of a development paragraph:

- *Introductory sentences.*
- *Topic sentences* are to paragraphs what thesis statements are to essays. They announce a subject and often make an assertion about it. Not every paragraph has a topic sentence, however, and a topic sentence may announce the subject and key idea for a series of paragraphs.
- *Development sentences* form the business end of a paragraph. They restate, elaborate, explain, illustrate, or support the key idea of the paragraph.
- *Conclusion sentences.*
- *Transition sentences* connect one paragraph with another.

In the following two-paragraph celebration of America and Americans these sentences work harmoniously to develop the subject matter and help readers make their way through it, exactly what well-developed and well-organized paragraphs should do.

Introductory sentences

Topic sentence

Development sentences: Facts

Quotation

An English economist once said that it was America that had taught the world that it need not starve. Consider that. It cannot be denied. The achievements of American agriculture are one of the wonders of the modern world. Americans consume each year only a third of the wheat which American farmers produce; there is no other valley in the world which has been made, by irrigation, as fertile as the Central Valley of California. But it is not only such facts and figures that tell the wonder. One must look down the vastness of the Middle West, as the English poet Louis MacNeice did in 1940, "astonished by its elegance from the air. Elegance is the word for it—enormous plains of beautifully inlaid rectangles, the grain running

Description different ways, walnut, satinwood or oatcake, the whole of it tortoiseshelled with copses and shadows of clouds. . . ." It is common for the American when he is in Europe to gasp at the hedgerows of England or the terraced vineyards of Italy, kept for centuries. But the gasp of the Englishman is no less when he gazes on a continent, immense in scale, still fabulous in its diversity, which not only is cultivated but has by its cultivation been given its own coherence; which unlike Europe has been made one. Who but the Americans would, so early, have made the Great Plains yield so much—those semi-arid lands which even they, at first, called "the Great American Desert"?

Closing question

Transition
Introduction   But let us return to small things. If America was to produce, it had also to invent. The English critic T. R. Fyvel once told a story of a friend, also English, who had "found himself for a fantastic weekend in a society of Texas millionaires who whizzed around in their private aircraft, dropping in on parties hundreds of miles away." The friend found this unexpectedly refreshing. He was even more impressed when he saw the children of his host "buzzing around in special little pedal motor cars which were air conditioned." But one night his Texan millionaire host turned to him and said something like: "You know, Bob, I ask myself if our machine civilization isn't shot all to hell." The Englishman, horrified, burst out to his host: "Don't have those decadent thoughts! Don't have any thoughts! Leave them to us— while you stay just as you are!" I understand his response. There seems to be nothing, however fanciful, that the American, with his unflagging inventive genius, will not attempt.

Development:
Anecdote

Topic sentence and
conclusion

(Henry Fairlie, "Why I Love America," *The New Republic* 4 July 1983)

Like essays in miniature, paragraphs create within themselves, by the arrangement of their parts, their own predictable patterns. There are two basic paragraph patterns you need to master, each illustrated by the preceding sample paragraphs. In the first pattern, illustrated by the first paragraph, the sentences develop *down from* a topic sentence coming early in the paragraph. After introductory and topic sentences, the remaining sentences, as it were, look over their shoulders at the topic sentence, careful to keep themselves in line with the topic given there.

↓ *Introduction:* America taught the world that it need not starve.
Topic: American agriculture is one of the wonders of the modern world.
↑ Facts of American agricultural production.
│ A description of the way American agriculture has ordered the continent.

In the second pattern, illustrated by the second paragraph, the introductory and development sentences look ahead, pointing *forward* to the topic sentence at the end.

Transition.
Introductory sentence announcing the need to invent.
An anecdote illustrating American inventiveness.
Topic: There is nothing that American inventive genius will not attempt.

Key idea early or key idea late: these are the two patterns readers expect when they read a paragraph. The good paragraph—that is, the predictable paragraph—is the one that plays its part in the larger pattern of the essay but is within itself predictable in subject, function, and design.

Writing Effective Paragraphs

The way to write good paragraphs is to write *for the eyes* as well as the brain. If your paragraphs are single in their subjects, clear in their designs, well developed, and connected smoothly to surrounding paragraphs, they'll fit your readers' minds like hand in glove. But they must not only *be* readable, they must *look* readable. Too short, and they'll look choppy, fragmentary, and disconnected, even when they're not. Too long, and they'll look forbiddingly complex. Pick up almost any piece of professional nonfiction writing and look at it rather than read it. See how the paragraph indentations come at regular intervals? I look at the narrow columns of my newspaper. Each paragraph runs from an inch-and-a-half to two inches long, column after column, page after page. I pick up a magazine. Here the paragraphs are longer, about three inches, three or four to a column—but no less regular in their length than my newspaper paragraphs.

If I look at these paragraphs more closely, I see that they are all skillfully organized. Ideas haven't been chopped to fit a prescribed length. These paragraphs have been designed this way, perhaps intuitively, to fit their writers' and publishers' guesses about how much paragraph complexity their readers can bear. The higher their reading level, the longer the paragraphs can run. With a little care and practice, you will learn to paragraph this way, so that your writing *looks* as readable as it really is. Here are three rules of thumb. For most college writers following them means learning to write longer, more fully developed paragraphs than they did before.

1. If you are writing by hand on standard-sized paper, design your paragraphs so that you break for a new one at least once per page, two or three times if your handwriting is small.
2. If you are typing double-spaced, plan to break three or four times per page.
3. If you are typing single-spaced, as in a letter, plan to break every inch and a half to three inches.

These are not inflexible rules, only guides, perhaps to be honored in the breach as often as not, but if you can organize your ideas to fit these patterns and surround them with white space, your writing will look as inviting as the professionals'.

In your concern for eye-appeal, however, don't forget "brain-appeal."

1. *Organize by the paragraph.* Use your outlines or other organizing schemes to identify your paragraph breaks for you. What you are doing as you make a map for yourself is marking off each leg of the journey you expect your writing will take.

2. *Write by the paragraph.* If you must stop while drafting, try not to stop in the middle of a paragraph without leaving a thread to pick up when you return. Complete your pattern or leave yourself clues to help you complete it. Your aim while you write is to keep your sentences flowing from beginning to end, no matter how often you stop.

3. *Revise by the paragraph.* Make sure each subject is clear and well developed, that you have written topic sentences for those paragraphs that need them, and that you have provided the necessary connections between paragraphs.

EXERCISES

1. From the exercises in Chapter 6, choose two that require you to write a paragraph. Follow the instructions for each exercise, but organize and write these paragraphs twice, once with the topic sentence at the beginning, once at the end. Beware: Writing a paragraph for the second time will require more than moving the topic sentence from beginning to end. The paragraph must develop *from* or lead *to* the topic sentence. That means a thorough reorganization. In the margins, identify the kinds of sentences you've used in each paragraph: introductory, topic, development, conclusion, and transitional.

2. Choose a three- to five-paragraph section from a recent writing you've done. In the margins identify each kind of sentence you've written: introductory, topic, development, concluding, transitional. Choose two of the paragraphs that could be better developed or organized and revise them.

WRITING PROJECTS

Topics

1. After doing library investigation, write a three- to five-page report on a person, event, institution, or concept important to your academic major or other field of interest. If a topic doesn't come to mind, ask an instructor in your major field to suggest one. Your reference librarian will guide you to the best sources of information. Your aims here are to introduce yourself to a subject of potential importance to you and to get the facts right. Write this report for yourself—you are your audience—but organize it according to an appropriate pattern from Chapter 6. Be sure to acknowledge any sources you borrow from; Chapter 17, "The Research Project," Step 6, pages 455–463, will show you how.

2. Ought/ought not: Write about things not as they are but as they ought to

be. Choose a community you belong to: your town, school, a class within your school, social class, age group, sex, ethnic group, special interest group, or nation. Then write a three- to five-page essay proposing a new law or custom that would improve life in your chosen community. Write to the members of that community. You may want to propose the modification of some law or custom or its abolition. Be original and insightful. If your law or custom, e.g., concerning the drinking age, abortion, or capital punishment, has already been proposed, find a new proposal—unless, that is, you have something new to add to the debate. Describe the need for change. If necessary, explain how your custom or law would work. Examine the consequences or benefits. You may, if you wish, suggest appropriate penalties for violators. You will probably follow the "problem/solution" pattern (see page 127).

3. We are surrounded by hidden messages, in the clothes we wear, the cars we drive, the gestures we make, the furniture we live with, the houses we live in. If you understand "body language," you know what is meant by hidden messages, the statements that one human being makes not obviously but just obviously enough to another human being, statements about identity, values, fears, hopes, status, class, and beliefs. Choose some area of human life in which you detect these hidden messages and write a three- to five-page essay describing what they are, how they are sent, and who receives them. Write to the people who send these messages or to those who ought to receive them. Consider organizing your essay according to a classification or "What is it?" pattern.

4. As citizens of the world, as well as citizens of a city, state, or country, we are obliged to know something about our world. What appear to you to be the three most important problems presently facing humankind? Look them up in the library, take notes, and write a three- to five-page essay describing them. Your reference librarian will guide you to the best sources of information. Write to your composition class. Organize according to one of the order-of-importance patterns. Be sure to acknowledge any sources you borrow from; Chapter 17, "The Research Project," Step 6, pages, 455–463, will show you how.

5. Analyze the communications strategy in an essay you have read recently; then write a three- to five-page essay explaining what you've found. What are the writer's thesis, persona, audience image, role, and design? In what ways are these features appropriate or inappropriate to the writer's purpose? You will probably use a version of the "What is it?" pattern to organize your essay.

THE WRITING PROCESS

1. Writing-in-progress.
   a. *Exploring:* Free association and freewriting.
   b. *Developing.*
      i. Take notes and freewrite to discover what you will say, take walk-around notes, write a letter to your audience (see pages 47–54).
      ii. Develop your subject: facts and statistics, examples, anecdotes, analogies, definitions, quotations, allusions.
      Try several figurative free associations: If _____ were a _____, it would/wouldn't be a _____. (See pages 91–92.)

Draw a picture of your subject; circle those parts your readers may not notice or understand (see page 83).

    c. *Planning a communications strategy:* Decide on a role, persona (distance and attitude), and thesis (*My point is that . . . What I mean to say is that . . .*).

    d. *Organize your essay* according to one of the eight patterns presented in Chapter 6: narrative, spatial, order of importance, comparison, pro/con, classification, descriptive analysis, causal analysis—or according to a mixed pattern. Write outlines, pie charts, flowcharts, sketches, or house tours to discover your design.

    →e. *New in this chapter:* Devise an introductory strategy to capture your audience's attention and focus their interest (see pages 135–141).

    f. *Revising:* Reconsider your ideas and communications strategy; create frictions in your thinking (see pages 55–56).

2. Writing: Write the preliminary draft of your project. Write freely, don't stop except to reread, give yourself room to revise (see pages 57–58).

3. Rewriting.

    →a. Be a zoom lens as you revise; add, delete, substitute, rearrange. *New in this chapter:* Examine your paragraphs to be sure they have topic and transitional sentences where necessary.

    →b. *New in this chapter:* Beware of self-conscious or wordy openings and conclusions that stop too soon or too late.

    c. Make your nouns and verbs as concrete and specific as possible (see pages 100–102).

    d. Copyedit for mechanical errors, recopy, and proofread (see pages 61–62).

4. Self-evaluation.

    a. What is your intention in this writing?

    b. What is your thesis?

    c. What did you do to help your readers read this writing? Will any parts be hard to follow? If so why? What would make them more readable?

    d. What do you like best about this writing?

    e. Did you try anything here that you hadn't tried before?

    f. What one change would most improve this writing?

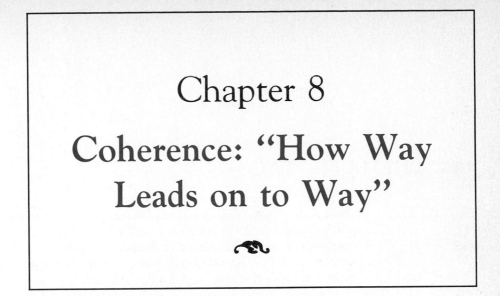

Chapter 8

Coherence: "How Way Leads on to Way"

If we consider writing from a fresh perspective, we see that this process we call composition actually proceeds as a process of de-composition. We may begin writing with a single idea in mind, but by the time we've developed, organized, and written it out, we've "de-composed" that single idea into any number of subtopics, several purposes, an introduction, body, and conclusion, page after page of paragraphs, dozens of sentences set off by capitalization and punctuation, and finally hundreds, even thousands, of individual words, each surrounded by white space. What we have created is an incredibly complex mosaic of bits and pieces of one kind or another; it's up to our readers, as they read, to re-compose our subject by putting those bits and pieces together. What enables them to do this is the principle of coherence. Coherent writing fits together, sentence to sentence, paragraph to paragraph, and part to part, so that readers sense not the fragments of an idea but a satisfying wholeness.

Coherence is a first cousin to the principle of predictability: both are principles of relationship. Prediction devices—introductions, designs, and paragraphs—help readers imagine a map of the reading journey that lies ahead and so anticipate where they are going. Coherence devices are sign posts and route markers that help them make that journey, guiding them as they read. Reading a piece of coherent writing feels like nothing so much as traveling a well-designed and clearly marked highway running smoothly to its destination. That readers will reach their destination is never in doubt, not even when it is momentarily obscured by a sharp turn of thought or the obstruction of a difficult idea. The coherence devices that create this confidence are the following:

155

Thematic tags.
Pronouns.
Transitions.
Punctuation marks.

THEMATIC TAGS

Thematic tags are key words that represent the subject of a writing. Repeated regularly, they are route markers that continually remind readers they are traveling the right road, still reading about the subject announced earlier in an introduction or at the beginning of a paragraph, still heading in the direction the writer has pointed them. In the following excerpt, the writer repeats thematic tags for her subject, marriage; see how they help her reassert a traditional view of that institution? The tags have been emphasized.

> *Marriage* is nothing more nor less than a permanent promise between two consenting adults, and often, but not always, under God, to cling to each other unto death. It sounds pretty grim, I know. But then we have a perfect model in our children and relatives for how *marriage* should be viewed. I cannot, at any time, send my children back to some other womb for a fresh start. I've got a few cousins, aunts, uncles, nieces and nephews with whom I might like to deny kinship, but I can't, any more than I can change the color of my eyes. My parents are my parents, whether I speak to them or not. In the same way, the husband and wife are one flesh, forever. If I divorce my husband, I am, in effect, cutting off part of myself. I think we have forgotten the fundamental basis of *marriage*, a notion that has nothing to do with moonlight and roses and my own personal wishes.
>
> *Marriage* is a partnership far more than a perpetual honeymoon. Anybody who stays *married* can tell you that. It may be made in heaven, but it is lived on earth. And because earth is the way it is, *marriage* is often irritating, hellatious, unsatisfying, boring and shaky. I myself, as a human being, am not always such a prize. Some days I wouldn't have *me* on a silver platter. But those seekers after the perfect *marriage* are convinced that the spouse will display perfection. The perfect mate, despite what *Cosmopolitan* says, does not exist, no matter how many of those tests you take.
>
> (Suzanne Britt Jordan, "Married Is Better," *Newsweek* 11 June 1979, emphasis added)

In only two paragraphs Suzanne Britt Jordan has repeated the thematic tags for marriage seven times! No doubt about this writer's subject. And by adding to her primary thematic tags all the words for partnership and family relations (*children, cousins, aunts, uncles, nieces, nephews, parents, husband, spouse,* and *mate*), she makes a point about that subject and underscores it: that marriage is a sobering and complex relationship, not a romantic affair between two perfect and footloose individuals.

Thematic Tags and the Reader's Memory

Besides announcing a subject, thematic tags perform a second valuable function. Because readers never remember all they read and because they store what they do remember in a nonverbal, nontemporal fashion, they need some indexing device to help them hold onto their memories and locate them in their minds. Thematic tags are that device. They are "sticky" terms that readers remember easily and that help them recall, by a process of association, the meaning of what they've read. Writing memorably certainly requires something good to say and an artful style to say it in, but it begins with nothing more difficult than the easy skill of strategic repetition. The most coherent writing, and often the most memorable, employs a small number of thematic tags and repeats them frequently in a variety of forms throughout the writing. The number of tags should be few; the number of repetitions, many. Too many *different* thematic tags usually means that a writing has too many subjects. The more subjects there are, the harder they are to keep track of and remember, the easier it is for a reader to become confused. Once more: *Few* tags, *many* repetitions.

Now this injunction to repeat words will rub some writers the wrong way. One of the few style rules they bring with them to college forbids repetition, and one of the few operations they perform when they revise is to root out repetition wherever they find it. They fear that it reveals a limited vocabulary or—worse—that they have little to say and can say that only monotonously. In two respects their impulse is sound. A broad and varied vocabulary *is* more useful than a narrow one, and certain kinds of repetition *do* become monotonous and distracting. But not *all* repetition is monotonous and distracting. Readers depend upon repetition of important words to keep themselves oriented. Besides, so essential is this repetition that readers are seldom bothered by it. Remember Suzanne Britt Jordan's paragraph on marriage? Were you bothered by her skillful repetitions of *marriage?* This is one kind of repetition to practice frequently.

Three Ways to Repeat Thematic Tags

In practice you'll discover that repetition of tags allows for and even encourages variety. Not only will you vary the grammatical form of thematic tags, as Suzanne Britt Jordan does with *marriage* and *married,* but often you will use *synonyms* for those tags to shade or qualify your meaning. This is what the writer does in the following report about a school-busing protest. The tags and their synonyms have been emphasized.

More than 10,000 *children* were *missing* in Los Angeles on September 19. By the end of the day, I could find only 300 of them. They were *hidden* away in a sort of *encampment* at the end of winding dirt roads and footpaths into the foothills of the Santa Susana Mountains. The *place,* protected by towering sandstone outcroppings, used to be a burying ground of the Chumash Indians; now it is called *neighborhood school number one*.

The *children* were in a *ring of modular buildings* clustered around an American flag, learning reading, writing, arithmetic, and a bit more in a *school* built by their *parents* on the outskirts of Chatsworth, a community that still has ranches, in the San Fernando Valley, at the northwestern corner of Los Angeles. *Mandatory school busing* had come to another city—and these *kids* were being *hidden* in what looked very much like what it really was, a *rebel camp* in the United States.

(Richard Reeves, "Another Citizens' Revolt in California," Esquire 7 Nov. 1978, emphasis added)

Thematic Tags: children ⟶ *Synonyms:* 300, kids
               missing ⟶ *Synonyms:* hidden
               parents
               school ⟶ *Synonyms:* encampment, place, Neighborhood School Number One, ring of modular buildings, rebel camp
            mandatory school busing

See how the synonyms for this school identify the protest it represents and help the writer portray the parents as the rebels he believes them to be? Without these synonyms Richard Reeves couldn't make his point.

A second way to create variety within thematic tags is *part-for-whole substitution,* replacing the term for a complete subject with one that refers to a part of it, one of its features, or a characteristic action. The following excerpt describes the human aging process by alternating the primary thematic tags, *body* and *aging,* with terms for parts of the body and aspects of aging. Again the thematic tags and their synonyms are emphasized.

Old men, old women, almost 20 million of them. They constitute 10 percent of the total population, and the percentage is steadily growing. Some of them, like conspirators, *walk all bent over,* as if *hiding* some precious secret, *filled with self-protection.* The *body* seems to *gather* itself around those *vital parts, folding shoulders, arms, pelvis* like a fading rose. Watch and you see how *fragile* old people come to think they are.

Aging paints every action *gray, lies heavy* on every movement, *imprisons* every thought. It *governs* every decision with a ruthless and single-minded *perversity.* To *age* is to learn the feeling of *no longer growing,* of *struggling* to *do* old tasks, to *remember* familiar actions. The *cells* of the *brain* are *destroyed* with thousands of unfelt tiny *strokes,* little pockets of clotted *blood wiping out memories* and *abilities.* The *body* seems slowly to *give up,* randomly *stopping,* sometimes *starting* again as if to *torture* and *tease* with the memory of *lost strength. Hands* become *clumsy,* frail *transparencies held together* with *knotted* blue *veins.*

(Sharon Curtin, Nobody Ever Died of Old Age [Boston: Little, 1972], emphasis added)

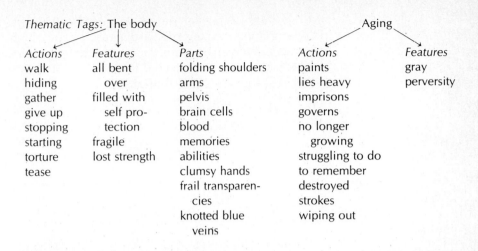

Thematic Tags: The body — Aging

Actions	Features	Parts	Actions	Features
walk	all bent	folding shoulders	paints	gray
hiding	over	arms	lies heavy	perversity
gather	filled with	pelvis	imprisons	
give up	self pro-	brain cells	governs	
stopping	tection	blood	no longer	
starting	fragile	memories	growing	
torture	lost strength	abilities	struggling to do	
tease		clumsy hands	to remember	
		frail transparen-	destroyed	
		cies	strokes	
		knotted blue	wiping out	
		veins		

A third way to write thematic tags without repeating is *member-for-class substitution,* replacing a tag with a class it belongs to or classes it can be divided into. Here a writer varies his primary thematic tags, *students* and *drugs,* with terms that denote members of these classes. Again, tags are emphasized.

> For most of the *students* who abuse them, *drugs* also provide the illusion of pleasurable connections to other people while serving to detach them from the emotions real involvement would arouse. *Drugs* were, for these *students,* the best available means of social relations. *Heroin abusers* found in the junkie underworld a sense of security, belonging, and acceptance derived from the acknowledgment and the shared need for *heroin. LSD abusers* felt their most intimate experiences involved tripping with another person. *Marijuana abusers* felt that *drugs* "took the edge off their personality" enough to permit them to be gentle and to empathize with other people. *Amphetamine abusers* were pushed into the social round on *amphetamine* energy, often being enabled to go through sexual experience they would otherwise have found unendurable.
>
> (Herbert Hendin, *The Age of Sensation* [New York: Norton, 1975], emphasis added)

Thematic tags: Students — Drugs

Class	Kind
drug	heroin
abusers	LSD
	marijuana
	amphetamines

Discovering Thematic Tags

Whatever repetition your writing requires—thematic tags themselves, their synonyms, or words for their parts or their classes—repeat frequently and emphatically. You'll write more clearly and memorably, and your readers will appreciate your care. You'll write more easily if you discover as many of these words as possible in advance, before you begin drafting. How? By sketching a *thematic tag tree,* a diagram listing all the tags you might use to present a topic, one tree for each topic. The little diagrams following the preceding sample paragraphs are each branches from this tree. Put together, they create a tree that looks like this:

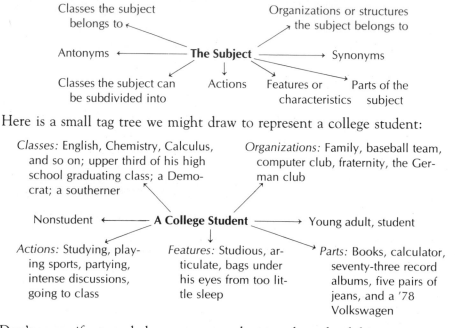

Classes the subject belongs to ← Organizations or structures the subject belongs to →

Antonyms ← — The Subject — → Synonyms

Classes the subject can be subdivided into   Actions   Features or characteristics   Parts of the subject

Here is a small tag tree we might draw to represent a college student:

Classes: English, Chemistry, Calculus, and so on; upper third of his high school graduating class; a Democrat; a southerner

Organizations: Family, baseball team, computer club, fraternity, the German club

Nonstudent ← **A College Student** → Young adult, student

Actions: Studying, playing sports, partying, intense discussions, going to class

Features: Studious, articulate, bags under his eyes from too little sleep

Parts: Books, calculator, seventy-three record albums, five pairs of jeans, and a '78 Volkswagen

Don't worry if a term belongs on more than one branch of this tree or you don't have terms for every branch. A thematic tag tree is not a neatly trimmed garden-variety tree. Its virtue is not its proportions but its fruitfulness. It is a simple, graphic instrument to help writers explore a subject and find the words to say about it.

EXERCISES

1. Draw thematic tag trees for the following passages. In the center of each diagram write the primary subject of the passage, and then at the end of the branches list any synonyms, antonyms, and terms that identify its parts, features, actions, or classes. The preceding diagrams will guide you. If a passage has more than one primary subject, draw a tag tree for each.

a. Television is being reinvented. In the next decade, the modern den will be pressed for floor- and shelf-space by the proliferation of communications technology. The television set itself—whether the conventional picture-tube box or the new, curved projection screen—will remain the focal piece of furniture, but it will no longer dictate the viewing agenda. Instead, the set will be the receiving unit for a range of components, converters, and special antennas by which the new entertainment-cum-information media may take the place of the neighborhood movie house, the home computer, the penny arcade, or the Sears Roebuck catalog. The television set may also serve as an electronic extension of the opera house, the football stadium, the town meeting, or the hospital emergency room.

(Les Brown, "Television vs. Progress," *Saturday Review* 16 Sept. 1978)

b. For the first time in 50 years, more Americans are moving to small towns than to cities. In the three decades prior to 1970, nine million people left small towns and moved to urban areas; but in three short years after 1970, 1.5 million left metropolitan areas behind and headed for homes in small towns. Clearly, the once magical attractions of cosmopolitan life—the arts, the sophistication, the promise of success—no longer have the allure [that simple country pleasures now do].

This trend is far too significant to be dismissed—along with organic gardens and communes—as nothing but a stale leftover from the Sixties. True, people who are moving from city to country are younger—by about 17 years—than those who are staying put; but statistics also show that they earn about $1,500 more annually, they have higher-status jobs, and they have on the average two years more education than their cohorts who have chosen to remain in urban areas. Nor are movers simply spilling over from city to suburb: People are heading for small towns that are independent of cities. Although some of these areas are within commuting distance of cities and suburbs, the most spectacular growth is taking place in towns far from urban centers.

(Susan Schiefelbein, ("Return of the Native," *Saturday Review* 26 Nov. 1977)

c. In Western history, craftsmanship, especially as it developed in the thirteenth and fourteenth centuries, constitutes one of the peaks in the evolution of creative work. Work was not only a useful activity, but one which carried with it a profound satisfaction. The main features of craftsmanship have been very lucidly expressed by C. W. Mills. "There is no ulterior motive in work other than the product being made and the processes of its creation. The details of daily work are meaningful because they are not detached in the worker's mind from the product of the work. The worker is free to control his own working action. The craftsman is thus able to learn from his work; and to use and develop his capacities and skills in its prosecution. There is no split of work and play, or work and culture. The craftsman's way of livelihood determines and infuses his entire mode of living."

With the collapse of the medieval structure, and the beginning of the modern mode of production, the meaning and function of work changed fundamentally, especially in the Protestant countries. Man, being afraid of his newly won freedom, was obsessed by the need to subdue his doubts and fears by developing a feverish activity. The outcome of this activity, success or failure, decided his salvation, indicating whether he was among the saved or the lost souls. *Work, instead of being an activity satisfying in itself and pleasurable, became a duty and an obsession.* The more it was possible to gain riches by work, the more it became a pure means to the aim of wealth and success. Work became, in Max Weber's terms, the chief factor in a system of "inner-worldly asceticism," an answer to man's sense of aloneness and isolation.

> (Erich Fromm, *The Sane Society* [New York: Holt, 1955])

2. Choose a recent writing you've done, circle your thematic tags and their variations, then draw a thematic tag tree, more than one if you have more than one primary subject. Compare a two-paragraph stretch of your writing with a passage of comparable length from Exercise 1. Did you repeat yourself as frequently as the professionals? Did you vary your thematic tags as they did? If not, rewrite your passage, repeating thematic tags and varying them whenever appropriate with synonyms and terms for your subject's features, actions, parts, and classes.

3. Make a thematic tag tree to help develop the subject of your current writing project. If you haven't yet chosen a subject, choose from those at the end of this chapter. A project with more than one primary subject may require more than one tag tree. When you have finished your tree, write an exploratory paragraph about your subject by using your thematic tags and any appropriate variations.

PRONOUNS

Imagine writing without pronouns. It wouldn't seem much of a loss, would it? After all, pronouns are mostly little substitute words, stand-ins for the larger, more important words that do the actual work of a sentence. What do they do but make a writing a little shorter? Right? Well, consider this sample paragraph that has been written without pronouns:

> In the folklore of the country, numerous superstitions relate to winter weather. Back-country farmers examine back-country farmers' corn husks—the thicker the husk, the colder the winter. Back-country farmers watch the acorn crop—the more acorns, the more severe the season. Back-country farmers observe where white-faced hornets place white-faced hornets' nests—the higher the nests are, the deeper will be the snow. Back-country farmers examine the size and shape and color of the spleens of butchered hogs for clues to the severity of the season. Back-country farmers keep track of the blooming of dogwood in the spring—the more abundant the blooms, the more bitter the cold in January.

You may be thinking right now, "If I have to read *back-country farmers* one more time. . . ." You see the problem, how awkward and needless the repetition. Obvious, too, is the choppiness, the disconnection—the *incoherence*. Each sentence seems to stand by itself, unrelated to those that precede and follow.

Now compare the preceding version with the original paragraph. Pronouns and their antecedents are emphasized.

In the folklore of the country, numerous superstitions relate to winter weather. *Back-country farmers* examine *their* corn husks—the thicker the husk, the colder the winter. *They* watch the acorn crop—the more acorns, the more severe the season. *They* observe where white-faced *hornets* place *their* paper *nests*—the higher *they* are, the deeper will be the snow. *They* examine the size and shape and color of the spleens of butchered hogs for clues to the severity of the season. *They* keep track of the blooming of dogwood in the spring—the more abundant the blooms, the more bitter the cold in January.

> (Edwin Way Teale, *Wandering Through Winter* [New York: Dodd, 1966], emphasis added)

This version reads more smoothly. Not only has the needless repetition been eliminated, but the sentences fit snugly together, the ideas of one sentence linked to the ideas of the next within an invisible pattern of pronoun-antecedent relationship. In this respect, pronouns are like the distance signs that mark the miles between cities and, by so doing, seem to draw those cities closer together. The guidelines for using pronouns well are the same ones for writing thematic tags: repeat and vary. Repeat pronouns frequently as substitutes for their noun antecedents; but occasionally interject those antecedents as reminders. In other words, don't let pronouns stray too far from the nouns they substitute for; especially do not use pronouns if their antecedents are unclear or ambiguous.

EXERCISES

1. Read each of the following paragraphs and substitute pronouns for nouns whenever pronouns seem appropriate. Be able to explain why you occasionally allowed the original nouns to stand in place of pronouns. Remember all the kinds of pronouns you have available to you: personal pronouns (*I, me, she, he, we,* and so on), possessive pronouns (*his, her, hers, mine,* and so on), relative pronouns (*who, which, that, whom*), indefinite pronouns (*each, anyone, every, everyone,* and so on), demonstrative pronouns (*this, that, these,* and *those*), reflexive pronouns (*himself, myself, herself,* and so on).

a. Consider the telephone. Nobody but an eccentric reactionary would dispute the fact that the telephone is one of the grand achievements of man. The telephone shrinks the globe. By facilitating dialogue, the telephone enhances the chances of peace. The telephone frees people to travel. By connecting people with emergency services, the telephone saves lives and alleviates fear. The telephone helps people to maintain relationships, to organize events, to accomplish more in people's lifetimes. And yet it is also indisputable that telephones discourage thought. Telephones rudely interrupt any conversation or calm. Unlike letters, telephones do not require people to think out people's messages in advance. Pressing people to fill the silence (for time is money), telephones encourage garrulity rather than concise, thoughtful expression. It is enlightening to browse through an anthology of great letters and ask oneself whether the writers would have written great letters had telephones been handy. Friendly letters, except as acknowledgments, have become almost quaint archaisms, like teatime and chaperones.

(Adapted from Carll Tucker, "Enemies of Thought," *Saturday Review* 18 Feb. 1978)

b. The next discipline of reality that children are subject to we might call the Discipline of Culture, of Society, of What People Really Do. Man is a social, cultural animal. Children sense around children this culture, this network of agreements, customs, habits, and rules binding the adults together. Children want to understand this network and be a part of this network. Children watch very carefully what people around children are doing and want to do the same. Children want to do right, unless children become convinced children can't do right. Thus children rarely misbehave seriously in church, but sit as quietly as children can. The example of all those grownups is contagious. Some mysterious ritual is going on, and children, children like rituals, want to be a part of that ritual. In the same way, the little children that I see at concerts or operas, though children may fidget a little, or perhaps take a nap now and then, rarely make any disturbance. With all those grownups sitting there, neither moving nor talking, it is the most natural thing in the world to imitate grownups. Children who live among adults adults are habitually courteous to other adults, and to children, will soon learn to be courteous. Children children live surrounded by people people speak a certain way will speak that way, however much people may try to tell children that speaking that way is bad or wrong.

(Adapted from John Holt, *Freedom and Beyond* [New York: Dutton, 1972])

2. Take a recent writing you have done and circle all pronouns. Are their antecedents clear and unambiguous? If not, cross out the pronouns and substitute their antecedent nouns. Read your writing at a natural pace. If you hear unnecessary repetition of nouns, change them to pronouns.

⬥ TRANSITIONS

Transitions are verbal signals that tell how one stretch of writing connects with another. They are like the road signs that guide a driver smoothly along a journey by announcing curves, turns, and hills, when to go slow, when to speed up. In contrast to thematic tags, transitions have little importance in themselves; their sole purpose is conjunctive, or joining. They create relationships between part and part, paragraph and paragraph, sentence and sentence, word and word and, by creating these relationships, produce the order indispensable to making sense. We use transitions to signal the following:

Addition or amplification (*and*).   Comparison (*similarly*).
Alternation (*or*).   Concession (*of course*).

Consequence or result *(so)*.

Contrast *(but)*.

Emphasis *(for example)*.

Place *(here)*.

Reason *(because)*.

Replacement *(rather)*.

Restatement *(in other words)*.

Sequence *(first)*.

Time *(then)*.

In the following example, transitions of all kinds bring together young people and old in a startling pattern of relationships. Transitions are emphasized; the marginal notations show the kinds of connections they make.

Addition

Reason
Alternation
Contrast
Concession
Addition
Time

Alternation

Addition
Contrast
Paragraphs linked
Reason and addition

Contrast and reason

Alternation
Addition

Consequence

Addition
Reason

The direct stare which passes between the young *and* the old is high up among the classic confrontations. It prefaces one of the great dialogues of opposites, *and* contains a frank admission of helplessness on either side, *for* nothing can be done to blot out the detail of what has been, *or* block in the detail of what is to come. *On the one side* is the clean sheet and *on the other* the crammed page, *although* the aged man knows only too well that youth isn't pristine *and* that some of the ugliest marks to be found on the record were made then. *As young and old survey each other*, there is no envy *and* little envy, respectively. The young do not want to be old, *nor* do they entirely believe that they ever could be, *and* the old, generally speaking, do not wish to be young. Once through the gamut of time is enough for most. What usually occurs is that an aged man finds life surprisingly sweet still *and* desires more agedness, *but* not a full repeat trip.

The young *and* the old are *also* sympathetically linked by their common awareness of the burdensome nature of life, *because* being strong, *and* facing the prospect before us, can be as daunting as being weak, *and* facing the end of the road. *In one respect, however*, the old have the advantage, *for* with agedness comes an amazing recall of the talk *and* actions of youth— exquisite, painful, shaming, triumphant, *or* whatever. The busy decades of work, parenthood, *and* adult drives of all kinds promise to have obliterated these immaturities, *and* one of the shocks *and* sensations of old age is the completeness of their recovery. If the young could understand the intensity of this recall, it would be enough to make them deliberately do things worth the recalling, a kind of burying of spring's trophies to be dug up for nourishment in the winter. *So* the main difference in the confrontation is that the young do not realize that they are accumulating the memories that in old age will often enough, alone, make them interesting *and* tolerable to youth. *For* it is a bitterness—one that no amount of common sense can lessen— that memories are about the only thing youth will want from age.

(Ronald Blythe, "Living to Be Old," *Harper's* July 1979, emphasis added)

Effective Transitions

So precise are his observations and so clear the relationships among them that the writer of the preceding paragraphs makes transitions seem easy, as if anyone could patch together almost any stretch of discourse and make it read smoothly. And in fact we *do* use transitions easily and often—but not always well. Transitions may even be the most difficult coherence device because we use them so easily. One problem is *imprecision*. The transitions we use most often—*and, also,* and *plus*—are the most imprecise. Because we use them so often in our speech, they lie closest at hand when we write. In relaxed, casual speech they pose no problems. They are ideally suited to its "add-on" character, impromptu and unedited. We're right there to sharpen any vague connection as soon as we see doubt begin to arch a listener's eyebrow. But in the silence of script, these terms are so broad in meaning and varied in their uses that they do not always create the precise relationships we intend.

Consider the relationships between these paragraphs:

> My first reason for opposing a legal drinking age of eighteen is the most obvious: the traffic accidents. The statistics have been in for a long time. Drivers sixteen to twenty-five are involved in drunk-driving accidents far out of proportion to their numbers in the total driving population. Too many people my age can't seem to hold their liquor. Given a low legal drinking age and our obsession with cars, we will drink and drive—and drive drunk. It's as simple as that. I don't want one of these young drunks running into me. The higher drinking age might keep at least a few teenagers sober—and safe.

> *And* I know many people younger than eighteen who get beer and wine with fake I.D.'s or because they look older than they are. Then there are the even younger high school sophomores and juniors, ages fifteen and sixteen, who know recent graduates. The younger teenagers get the older ones to buy beer for them. That's what I did when I was sixteen. And the older ones rarely object, even though many of them are as uneasy as I am now about kids that young—kids!—drinking. The higher drinking age may make it just a little more difficult for the youngest teenagers to begin drinking before they are ready.

What's being connected with what? Normally we would expect an *and* like the one that opens the second paragraph to connect something at the end of the first paragraph with something at the beginning of the next. But that's not what happens here. If we step back from these paragraphs, we see that the *and* actually joins the writer's first reason for opposing a low drinking age to his second. That little conjunction, however, is neither strong enough nor clear enough to make the connection. The writer should clarify the relationship between paragraphs with a complete transitional sentence: *My second reason concerns the age at which teenagers begin to drink. I know many people younger than eighteen. . . .* Now the connection is precise.

Here's a second example of imprecision, this time a vague relationship between sentences:

> When my deaf friends began signing animatedly, the family at the next table turned their heads suddenly, as if to avert their eyes. *Also,* one time the

four of us were eating at my father's restaurant when a group seated next to us began to stare.

Like the *and* in the first example, the *also* here signals little more than addition, although what the writer actually has in mind is a contrast between two impolite responses. A more precise transition might be *Another time the four of us were eating. . . .* The two occasions would then be connected, but the differing responses allowed to stand in contrast.

The second problem of easy transitions occurs when we depend on them to cover a *flawed or unconsidered design.* Once again speech is our misleading model. When we speak, we arrange our ideas as we go along, using our listeners' feedback to make sure we're clear, rephrasing as necessary. In writing, of course, it's harder to gauge our audience's understanding, and we have only one chance to put our ideas right. If they don't fall into predictable patterns, no number of transitions will reorganize them and make the connections we intend. Watch what happens in this brief paragraph:

> Kindergarten—what a giant step for a little kid to take! I remember the first day I took the bus to school. My mother, *however,* took me the first day to make sure I found my classroom. *But* on the second day I decided I was ready to make my way on my own. When the big yellow bus stopped at our driveway, I remember turning back just once to wave at mom, standing at the front door, a mixed-emotions smile on her face.

Trying to emphasize her feelings but get the facts straight at the same time, this writer confuses her chronology and then tries to fix it with transitions. But they won't work; after the second sentence readers expect to see the writer get on the school bus. When she doesn't, they become confused.

Now this kind of disorganization is natural enough in preliminary drafts when a writer is aiming more to get facts on paper than to communicate with an audience. Transitions at this stage are merely temporary framing, holding ideas together until rewriting begins. Then, thinking of readers and how they will read, this writer can reorganize her paragraph according to a predictable narrative pattern and scrap any unnecessary transitions, keeping only those that create coherence.

> Kindergarten—what a giant step for a little kid to take! On the first day of school my mother drove me to make sure I found my classroom. *But* on the second, I decided I was ready to make my way on my own and take the bus. I remember that big yellow bus stopping at our driveway for the first time. As I climbed on I turned back just once to wave at mom, standing at the front door, a mixed-emotions smile on her face.

The transitions in a finished piece of writing should assist a design, not compensate for it.

The third problem of easy transitions appears when writers organize well but then litter their prose with *unnecessary transitions,* perhaps in doubt that they're making connections, perhaps because the increased formality of public writing seems to require such fussiness. True, in public writing it's almost always better to be too clear than not clear enough, but if we have a good design, the logic of that design will often make connections for us. They won't have to be spelled out by transitions. Using them may only be confusing and distracting, as too many traffic signs at an intersection often distract and confuse drivers. Consider these two versions of a passage. The second—the original—is better than the first because it uses transitions only where necessary, depending everywhere else upon the logical order of the sentences to connect ideas. Transitions are emphasized.

> *In many respects* the world seems a very hazardous place. *For instance,* every day the newspapers announce that some chemical has been found to be carcinogenic, *or, equally important,* some catastrophic accident has occurred in some far-off place. This leads some of us *as a result* to hanker after a simpler world where there are fewer risks to life. *But* does such a world really exist?
>
> If, *by comparison,* we look back at the world of a century ago, we find that expectation of life was 50 years; *now, however,* it is 70 years. *Therefore* the sum of all the risks to which we are *now* exposed must be less than it was *then. All in all* we find that many of the larger risks of the last century have been eliminated, leaving us, *for that reason,* conscious of a myriad of small risks, most of which have always existed.

> The world seems a very hazardous place. Every day the newspapers announce that some chemical has been found to be carcinogenic, *or* some catastrophic accident has occurred in some far-off place. This leads some of us to hanker after a simpler world where there are fewer risks to life. *But* does such a world really exist?
>
> If we look back at the world of a century ago, we find that expectation of life was 50 years; *now it* is 70 years. *Therefore* the sum of all the risks to which we are *now* exposed must be less than it was. We find that many of the large risks of the last century have been eliminated, leaving us conscious of a myriad of small risks, most of which have always existed.
>
> (Richard Wilson, "Analyzing the Daily Risks of Life," *Technology Review,* The Alumni Association of Massachusetts Institute of Technology, 1979, emphasis added)

EXERCISES

1. Transition propositions: Following are ten sets of words.

Suburbs/community. Compassion/justice.
Big cities/community. Men/women.
Education/responsibility. Virtue/reward.
I or me/my family. Love/fear/respect.
Money/the good life. Past/present/future.

Choose five of these sets and explore your opinions about the relationship of one term to the other(s) it is grouped with. For each write a *transition proposition*, a sentence or clause using the first word in the series that leads to a sentence or clause using the next word. Connect these sentences or clauses with transitions from the following list. If necessary, change the order of the words in the set or their parts of speech. The examples following the list will show you several ways to write these propositions.

- *Addition or amplification:* additionally, again, also, and also, and then, as well, besides, beyond that, equally important, first (second, third, finally, last), for one thing, further, furthermore, in addition, likewise, moreover, next, now, on top of that, over and above that, too.
- *Alternation:* or, otherwise, nor.
- *Comparison:* in the same way, likewise, similarly.
- *Concession:* to be sure, granted, of course, it is true.
- *Conclusion, consequence, or result:* accordingly, as a consequence, as a result, consequently, for that reason, hence, inevitably, necessarily, that being the case, then, therefore, thus.
- *Contrast:* after all, although this may be true, and yet, be that as it may, but, conversely, even so, for all that, however, in contrast, in other circum-stances, in spite of that, nevertheless, nonetheless, on the contrary, on the other hand, otherwise, still, yet.
- *Emphasis:* as an example, as an illustration, for example, for instance, in-deed, in one respect, in other words, in particular, that is.
- *Place:* above that, at this point, below that, beyond that, here, near by, next to that, on the other side, outside, within, there, elsewhere, farther on.
- *Reason:* because, for, for this purpose, for this reason, to this end.
- *Replacement:* rather, instead.
- *Restatement or summary:* that is, in other words, in simpler terms, to put it differently, in conclusion, all in all, to summarize, altogether, as I have said, in sum, on the whole.
- *Sequence:* first, second, finally.
- *Time:* afterward, after a while, earlier, formerly, at last, at length, at the same time, simultaneously, at once, by degrees, eventually, finally, first (second, third), gradually, immediately, in a short time, in the future, in the mean-time, instantaneously, later, meanwhile, promptly, soon, suddenly.

Examples

Some people flee to the suburbs to find a community of people like them-selves, *but* what they discover is a community in name only.

A big city is not made up of one large community. *In contrast* to small towns, where people feel at home anywhere in their community, a large city is divided into many separate communities, whose citizens know about other parts of their city only what they read in the papers or see on television.

The good life is health, happiness, security, and love. *In other words,* money can add to or subtract from the good life, *but* it cannot be the sum total.

Too many judges show too little compassion for the victims of the criminals who stand before them; *for this reason* they rarely render complete justice.

2. Expand one of the transition propositions you wrote for Exercise 1 into a well-developed and well-organized series of two or three paragraphs. Do a free-writing to discover the subject matter that will support your propositions. Devote one paragraph to each subject or main idea. Connect your paragraphs with transitional words, phrases, or whole sentences.

3. Choose three to five paragraphs from a recent writing you've done and bracket [ ] all of your transitions: single words, phrases, or whole sentences. Do they make clear, precise connections of part to part? Is any unnecessary? Decide which need to be made more effective, which could be cut, and then rewrite.

✎ PUNCTUATING FOR COHERENCE

We generally think of punctuation marks as yield-right-of-way or stop signs; by signaling pauses, as the comma does, or a full stop, as the period does, they interrupt the flow of sentences and work against coherence. It takes skill with rhythm and language to move the writing smoothly from one idea to the next. There are, however, three marks of punctuation that help create coherence: the semicolon, colon, and dash. They ask the reader to pause, but they also signal particular relationships and bring together ideas that might otherwise stand in separate sentences, indistinctly related. In contrast to other punctuation marks, these are like road signs that announce conditions on the way ahead. (For the usage rules governing the semicolon, colon, and dash, see the sections under Punctuation in Chapter 18, pages 521–532.)

The Semicolon (;)

The semicolon is a kind of equals (=) sign. It balances what precedes with what follows; it signals more of the same, either the same ideas or the same patterns. Here a semicolon signals a restatement in the second half of the sentence that expands and clarifies the assertion of the first half:

> Americans do not build for the ages, or to gratify a royal vanity; our buildings, which must conform to a profitable expectancy, have impermanence built into them. They are planned to be torn down.
>
> (Adapted from Thomas Griffith, *The Waist-High Culture* [New York: Harper, 1959])

What the semicolon signals is "I'm going to say this again, but more fully and precisely." The next example expands this repetition from simple restatement into the pattern of the linked clauses:

> The old law of an eye for an eye leaves everybody blind. It is immoral because it seeks to humiliate the opponent rather than win his understanding; it seeks to annihilate rather than to convert.
>
> (Martin Luther King, Jr., *Stride toward Freedom* [New York: Harper, 1958]

Occasionally the semicolon functions like a compressed conjunction to signal balanced opposites.

> Stars, like people, do not live forever. But the lifetime of a person is measured in decades; the lifetime of a star in billions of years.
> (Carl Sagan, *The Cosmic Connection: An Extraterrestrial Perspective* [New York: Doubleday, 1973])

Professor Sagan could have substituted a connective like *while* for his semicolon: *But the lifetime of a person is measured in decades, while the lifetime of a star is measured in billions of years.* That would have belabored the obvious, however, and, by making the second half of the sentence dependent upon the first, it also would have blurred the contrast the present balanced opposition makes so sharply.

In this next example, semicolons connect and balance the many movements of a "sidewalk ballet" danced daily on a New York City street:

> When I get home after work, the ballet is reaching its crescendo. This is the time of roller skates and stilts and tricycles, and games in the lee of the stoop with bottletops and plastic cowboys; this is the time of bundles and packages, zigzagging from the drug store to the fruit stand and back over to the butcher's; this is the time when teenagers, all dressed up, are pausing to ask if their slips show or their collars look right; this is the time when beautiful girls get out of MG's; this is the time when the fire engines go through; this is the time when anybody you know around Hudson Street will go by.
> (Jane Jacobs, *The Death and Life of Great American Cities* [New York: Random, 1961])

To insert periods in place of semicolons and punctuate each clause as a separate sentence, as the writer could have done, would be to disrupt the unity and simultaneity of the actions she describes. Each clause introduces one or more of the dancers in her dance, all playing their parts, their harmony signaled by the semicolons.

The Colon (:)

The colon is often an *un*-equals sign. It signals imbalance, that what follows the colon is subordinate to or dependent upon what precedes it—but not necessarily less important. After a general statement it signals something specific: a list, an explanation, an example, a key point, or, in formal writing, a quotation. It is a compressed way of saying "for example," "that is," or "this is what I mean."

A Colon to Announce a List

While I sweep up the [candy wrappers dropped by students on their way to school] I watch the other rituals of morning: Mr. Halpert unlocking the laundry's handcart from its mooring to a cellar door, Joe Cornacchia's son-in-law stacking out the empty crates from the delicatessen, the barber bringing out his side-walk folding chair, Mr. Goldstein arranging the coils of wire which proclaim the hardware store is open, the wife of the tenement's superintendent depositing her chunky three-year-old with a toy mandolin on the stoop, the vantage point from which he is learning the English his mother cannot speak.

A Colon Preceding an Explanation
    Most of [the pedestrians] are heading for the bus and subways, but some hover on the curbs, stopping taxis which have miraculously appeared at the right moment, for the taxis are part of a wider morning ritual: having dropped passengers from midtown in the downtown financial district, they are now bringing downtowners up to midtown.

> (This example and the preceding taken from Jane Jacobs, *The Death and Life of Great American Cities* [New York: Random, 1961])

A Colon to Announce Two Examples
    The paradoxes [of American life] are everywhere: We shout that we are a nation of laws, not men—and then proceed to break every law we can if we can get away with it. We proudly insist that we base our political positions on the issues—and we will vote against a man because of his religion, his name, or the shape of his nose.

> (John Steinbeck, *America and Americans* [New York: Viking, 1966])

A Colon Preceding a Quotation
    Some people are so worn down by the yoke of oppression that they give up. A few years ago in the slum areas of Atlanta, a Negro guitarist used to sing almost daily: "Ben down so long that down don't bother me."

> (Martin Luther King, Jr., *Stride Toward Freedom* [New York: Harper, 1958])

The Dash (—)

The dash gives three distinct signals. More and more frequently it is used as an informal colon. It announces a list, explanation, and occasionally a quotation, but without the full stop those stacked periods seem to require. Instead, the reader slides along the dash from one part of a sentence to the next.

A Dash to Announce a List
    It is almost a ghost forest, for among the living spruce and balsam are many dead trees—some still erect, some sagging earthward, some lying on the floor of the forest.

> (Rachel Carson, *The Edge of the Sea* [Boston: Houghton, 1955])

A Dash to Connect a Generalization to an Explanation
    We [children of the sixties] knew each other's faces and bodies so well that any change was noticed at once, the fuel for endless notes exchanged in school. That's why I dressed so carefully mornings—I was about to face the scrutiny of fifteen gossip-seeking girls, ten only slightly less observant boys ready to imitate

my voice and walk, and one stern, prune-faced teacher who would check my spelling and long division with the care my enemies gave to my hems.
(Adapted from Joyce Maynard, *Looking Back* [New York: Doubleday, 1973])

Almost as frequently a dash signals a relationship opposite that signaled by a colon. It links a list to a generalization that *follows* it:

Choosing, defining, creating harmony, bringing that clarity and shape that is rest and light out of disorder and confusion—the work I do at my desk is not unlike arranging flowers.
(May Sarton, *Plant Dreaming Deep* [New York: Norton, 1968])

In its third function, a dash signals a curve ahead on the road of thought and carries the reader around that curve. It connects ideas that are related but that do not seem to be going in the same direction.

Dashes to Signal Sharp Turns of Thought
The average college freshman isn't ready for semicolons. He hasn't yet discovered any need for them, nor is he particularly eager to. To him they look forbiddingly exotic—about as tempting as a plate of snails. The literary gourmets can have them; he'll stick with his familiar comma and period—though if the truth be known, he isn't entirely comfortable even with these.
(John R. Trimble, *Writing with Style: Conversations on the Art of Writing* [Englewood Cliffs, NJ: Prentice, 1975])

A Pair of Dashes to Signal a Parenthetical Insertion
Sports are too much with us. Late and soon, sitting and watching—mostly watching on television—we lay waste our powers of identification and enthusiasm and, in time, attention as more and more closing rallies and crucial putts and late field goals and final playoffs and sudden deaths and world records and world championships unreel themselves ceaselessly before our half-lidded eyes.
(Roger Angell, *The Summer Game* [New York: Viking, 1972])

A Dash to Heighten Suspense
Then the picked and gutted carcass of the old car is shoved into a final death chamber—crushed flat by a five-ton press, which makes it scrunch like a stepped-on beetle.
(Edmund Wilson, *The American Earthquake* [New York: Doubleday, 1958])

EXERCISES

1. Most capitalization and punctuation have been removed from the following series of sentences; put them back and be able to defend your use of the semicolon, colon, and dash.

a. Why are Americans as a people unable to understand social accounting the costs in money of the mistakes we make organizing our society and caring for human beings?

Government and industry have very complex systems of cost-benefit analysis the "bottom line" is repeatedly invoked in policy discussions but when it comes to calculating the relatively minor expenditures necessary now to prevent some catastrophic social cost later we seem quite unable to do it.

(Adapted from Margaret Mead, "Social Accounting and the American Dream," *Business and Society Review* 19 [Fall 1976])

b. For the most part Americans are an intemperate people we eat too much when we can drink too much indulge our senses too much.

Even in our so-called virtues we are intemperate a teetotaler is not content not to drink he must stop all the drinking in the world a vegetarian among us would outlaw the eating of meat.

(Adapted from John Steinbeck, *America and Americans* [New York: Viking, 1966])

c. There is a stylized relation of artist to mass audience in the sports especially in baseball each player develops a style of his own the swagger as he steps to the plate the unique windup a pitcher has the clean-swinging and hard-driving hits the precision quickness and grace of infield and outfield the sense of surplus power behind whatever is done.

There is the style of the spectator also he becomes expert in the ritual of insult provocation and braggadocio he boasts of the exaggerated prowess of his team and cries down the skill and courage of the other he develops sustained feuds carrying on a guerilla war with the umpires and an organized badinage with the players while he consumes mountains of ritual hot dogs and drinks oceans of ritual soda pop.

(Adapted from Max Lerner, *America as a Civilization* [New York: Simon, 1963])

d. I once married a man I thought was totally unlike my father and I imagined a whole new world of freedom emerging five years later it was clear even to me floating face down in a wash of despair that I had simply chosen a replica of my handsome daddy-true the updated version spoke English like an angel but good God! underneath he was my father exactly wonderful but not the right man for me.

(Adapted from Anne Roiphe, "Confessions of a Female Chauvinist Sow," *New York* 30 Oct. 1972)

e. The inherent needs of children for at least a limited role in the world of work has been lost sight of in enthusiasm for other cultural goals production efficiency protection of children from inappropriate labor for overly long hours protection of the adult worker through unionization and equalization of economic status by minimum wage laws without adequate consideration for the salability of the services offered by the immature and inexperienced.

(Adapted from George A. Pettitt, *Prisoners of Culture* [New York: Scribner's, 1970])

f. Dense living conditions that are normal to a Japanese would be cramped to a Chicagoan and Chicago's density would be intolerable to a Nebraskan the teeming streets of Fez where native Moroccans know how to dodge the animals and each other to get where they are going make me feel anxious excited and if I'm jostled irritated the teeming streets of the Lower East Side where I know how to find bargains and blintzes make me feel energetic happy and if I'm jostled tolerant.

(Adapted from Carol Tavris, *Anger: The Misunderstood Emotion* [New York: Simon, 1982])

g. Every culture in every time throughout history has commemorated the transition of a human being from one state in life to another. Birth the emergence into manhood graduation from school at various levels birthdays marriage death each of these outstanding steps is acknowledged by a ceremony of some sort always public the guests in effect becoming witnesses to the statement of life's ongoingness of the natural order of history.

(Adapted from Marcia Seligson, *The Eternal Bliss Machine* [New York: Morrow, 1973])

h. Most of the lasting works of juvenile literature are thoroughly subversive in one way or another they express feelings not generally approved of or even recognized by grown-ups they make fun of honored figures and piously held beliefs and they view social pretenses with clear-eyed directness remarking as in Andersen's famous tale that the emperor has no clothes.

(Adapted from Alison Lurie, "Vulgar, Coarse, and Grotesque," *Harper's* Dec. 1979)

2. Choose a subject from the end of this chapter or from a recent reading and write three brief paragraphs about it. Use a semicolon in one, a colon in the second, and a dash in the third. You may use more than one of these marks and more than one kind in each paragraph.

WRITING COHERENTLY

The characteristics of good writing that you've studied in preceding chapters begin to appear in a piece of writing long before it reaches the drafting stage. A lively persona, an effective role, a clear thesis, supporting details, vivid words, and a predictable design—all of these evolve as writers explore, develop, and shape their materials. Not so with coherence. It doesn't appear until a writer puts things together, one word after another, in the process of drafting and revising. But this does not mean there's nothing you can do in advance to make sure your writing will flow smoothly, both when you write and your readers read.

The development strategies you learned in Chapters 4 and 5 will, among other things, provide you with thematic tags. The thematic tag tree you studied in this chapter is only the latest of these development strategies. Add it to your repertoire. Likewise, the organizing strategies you studied in Chapters 6 and 7 will help you know where to write transitions and what kind. The more fully you prepare for your drafts, the greater the chance you'll write with the increased confidence and relaxed concentration that are the hidden sources of coherent writing.

Writing in this absorbed state that some professional writers describe as almost like a dream state, you'll find words appearing more easily than they ever have before. You can cultivate this state once you begin drafting by writing for considerable stretches, without taking long breaks. Pause frequently, of course, as you learned in Chapter 3. But do so to reread, to see your ideas, hear your words, and feel the rhythm of your sentences. A writer at work is like a brick mason, pausing to look back, along a course of bricks he has laid, making sure they point him straight and true for the bricks he has yet to lay. Seeing where you've been, you'll have a better sense of where you're going. With your mind cleared of everything but your words and their momentum, you'll scarcely think of coherence; it will have become a natural part of your expression and habits of work.

When you turn to revision, however, coherence will require your conscious attention. Every change you make in subject matter, language, and design will require additional adjustments in your coherence devices. Even the best parts of your writing, where you make few changes, will still have an occasional choppy passage, a place where paragraphs or sentences look and feel abrupt, rough, disconnected. The following are some strategies for smoothing out the rough spots.

Circle Your Thematic Tags Circle thematic tags when you suspect you may have drifted from your subject. Circled tags are a graphic way to confirm or refute your suspicions. If you have too few tags or too many *different* thematic tags, you may have created a muddle for yourself and your readers. Keep the number of different thematic tags small by developing one subject at a time, but make sure you repeat them often at emphatic places in your sentences.

Write "Old-New" Sentences A sentence fits coherently with surrounding sentences when it repeats "old business" from earlier sentences while introducing "new business" to develop a subject one step further. The old business may be a thematic tag, one of its variations, a transition, or even a repeated grammatical pattern (a strategy we will take up in Chapter 11). Sentences that gave readers new business and nothing more would be incoherent; they would have nothing to link them to preceding sentences. See how the sentences in the following paragraph connect?

(1) Throughout the 1970s, teenagers preferred casual clothing made with natural fibers and down-played makeup and hair dye. (2) Now, many teenagers wear clothing made of heavily dyed artificial fabrics, and girls typically become interested in makeup at age twelve or thirteen. (3) New Wave youth ridicule "natural," or "health," food as tasting terrible, and identify it as the food that

their parents prefer. (4) Indeed, health food is to this generation of teenagers what spinach was to previous generations.

(Steve Barnett, "Brave New Wave of the '80s," *Across the Board* Dec. 1983)

Sentence 1: New = teenagers, clothing, down-played makeup and hair dye.

Sentence 2: Old = teenagers, clothing.
New = now, heavily dyed artificial fabrics, girls become interested in makeup.

Sentence 3: Old = teenagers/youth, natural.
New = New Wave, ridicule, health food tasting terrible, food parents prefer.

Sentence 4: Old = health food, this generation, teenagers, previous generations.
New = what spinach was.

Begin Rereading from the Beginning of a Paragraph   When you finish revising part of a paragraph, go back to its beginning and reread the whole paragraph through the revised part. You'll fall into the natural flow of ideas and sentences and be able to see and hear whether everything fits. Revise again, if necessary, until every sentence connects snugly with the next, a harmonious pattern of thematic tags, pronouns, transitions, and punctuation. You're reading now not with *your* eyes and ears but with your *readers'*.

Reread at a Natural Pace   When you've finished all your other revising and editing, reread once more, but at your readers' speed, listening for unnecessary repetitions of nouns and transitions. While composing we pause frequently, for all sorts of reasons. It's natural when we begin writing again to repeat a noun that appeared in a preceding sentence or make an explicit transition to a new idea. These help us find our way. Of course, readers rarely read this way, starting and stopping, so some of these repetitions and transitions will seem unnecessary. The pace of their reading and the design of your paragraphs will have already created coherence. Any additional signals will be distracting, making sentences seem choppy. There's where you should substitute pronouns and cut transitions.

EXERCISE

Turn back to Exercise 1, pages 160–162. If you've done this exercise, you've already identified the thematic tags in each passage. Now identify the other coherence devices: pronouns, transitions, semicolons, colons, and dashes. Doing so will show you how professional writers use all four coherence devices to make their writing flow smoothly from paragraph to paragraph, sentence to sentence, and word to word.

WRITING PROJECTS

Topics

1. Us and Them: Write a three- to five-page open letter speaking for a community you belong to. This community may be strictly or loosely defined: your town, state, or region; your sex, peer group, generation, social class; or some special interest group. Address your letter to those outside your community, especially those who belong to communities different from or opposite to your own. Here are several options for this letter.

   a. Explain what you see as you examine the members of the community opposite your own. Tell them (parents, children, teachers, parents, bosses, antagonistic or different social groups, the opposite sex, and so on) how they appear to you. By showing this group how you see them, you may help them better understand themselves. Base your essay on a thesis that asserts certain key traits, values, or attitudes of the members of this other group. Write from your experience and observations; develop and defend your thesis with vivid facts, examples, anecdotes, and details. Choose an appropriate pattern of organization from Chapter 6; especially consider one of the order-of-importance or pro/con patterns.

   b. Tell the members of this opposite community what they should know about you and your group. Your aim here is to help them better understand you. Base your essay on a thesis that asserts your group's key traits, values, or attitudes. Be detailed and specific in your self-analysis. Choose an appropriate pattern of organization from Chapter 6; especially consider one of the order-of-importance or pro/con patterns.

   c. Tell the members of this other community how they should behave or change their behavior toward you and your community. The underlying assumption here is that relations between communities are not as good as they should be. What's wrong? What would improve relations? Your thesis will propose the needed change. Organize your letter according to the problem/solution pattern. See Chapter 6, page 127.

   d. Compare and contrast your community with that one opposite yours. Look for key similarities and differences in aspirations, beliefs, traits, outlook, and behavior. Look especially for hidden or secret affinities between communities that may be the basis for improved relations. Your thesis will declare these hidden similarities or differences. Organize your essay according to one of the comparison or pro/con patterns in Chapter 6, pages 119–121.

2. When we think seriously about the world of work and careers most of us get about as far as the old proverb "A fair day's wage for a fair day's work." But is that all a job ought to provide? Since most of us will spend the majority of our waking adult lives at work, we ought to give it more extensive thought. What would be a "good" job—not a particular job, necessarily, but an ideal job worth having? What should a good job give a worker in return for his or her labor? On a good job, what should be the relationship between the worker and the work he

or she does? What about the relationship between employee and employer? What should be the relationship between the worker and the equipment to do the job? What about the working environment? What should the good employer expect from the good employee? To answer these questions look carefully at your own work experiences; interview friends and family. Develop your answers with details, examples, and anecdotes from the jobs you have had and observations of others' jobs. You may be describing an ideal job, but make your description as specific and practical as possible. Write out your description in a three to five-page essay. Address fellow workers in your situation or an employer, actual or potential. Don't feel that you must necessarily follow the order of these questions or answer them all. Choose an appropriate pattern of organization from Chapter 6; especially consider the "What is it?" pattern, page 127.

3. The Review: Write a three to five-page review of a book, movie, or recording that the members of your class should or should not read, see, or hear. Your primary purpose is not to summarize the work in question but to estimate its value and help your readers decide whether it's worth their time and money. See "The Critique," Chapter 13, pages 299–306, for guidelines to help you develop, organize, and write your review.

4. Choose a key passage other than the thesis from a recent reading you've done. It should be no longer than one paragraph. Write a three to five-page analytic essay explaining how your chosen passage contributes to the point or theme of the whole piece and how the writing leads to and unfolds from the passage. You should consider the work's thematic tags and design, also the writer's role and persona. Consider organizing your essay by combining the order-of-importance and process analysis patterns. The first half of your essay might explain, by examining thematic tags, how your passage supports the main idea and develops the writer's attitude. The second half might explain how this passage fits into the overall design and advances it one step.

THE WRITING PROCESS

1. Writing-in-progress.
   a. *Exploring:* Free association and freewriting.
   b. *Developing:* Discover all that you have to say about your subject. Use whatever methods and strategies seem appropriate.
   ——→*New in this chapter:*
      Write a thematic tag tree (see pages 159–160).

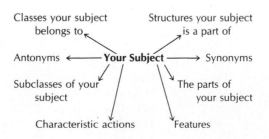

Write a transition proposition, two or more assertions about your subject linked by a transition (see pages 168–169).

c. *Planning a communications strategy:* Decide on a role, persona (distance and attitude), and thesis (*My point is that . . . What I mean to say is that . . .*).

d. *Organizing.*

   i. Organize your writing according to one of the eight patterns presented in Chapter 6—narrative, spatial order, order of importance, comparison, pro/con, classification, descriptive or causal analysis—or use a mixed pattern.

   ii. Write outlines, pie charts, flowcharts, sketches, or house tours to discover your design.

   iii. Devise an introductory strategy to capture your audience's attention and focus their interest (see pages 137–141).

e. *Revising:* Reconsider your ideas and communications strategy; create frictions in your thinking (see pages 55–56).

2. Writing: Write the preliminary draft of your project. Write freely, don't stop except to reread, give yourself room to revise (see pages 57–58).

3. Rewriting.

a. Be a zoom lens as you revise; add, delete, substitute, and rearrange. Examine your paragraphs to be sure they have topic and transitional sentences where necessary.

b. Beware of self-conscious or wordy openings and conclusions that stop too soon or too late.

c. *New in this chapter:* Circle thematic tags to check development and coherence; write "old-new" sentences; as you revise, begin rereading from the beginning of paragraphs; reread at a natural pace, listening for unnecessary repetitions and transitions.

d. Copyedit for mechanical errors, recopy, and proofread (see pages 61–62).

4. Self-evaluation.

a. What is your intention in this writing?

b. What is your thesis? What are your thematic tags?

c. What did you do to help your readers read your writing? Will any parts be hard to follow? If so why? What would make them more readable?

d. What do you like best about this writing?

e. Did you try anything here that you hadn't tried before?

f. What one change would most improve this writing?

Chapter 9

Clarity:
Making Meaning

"Literature," said the British writer Cyril Connolly, "is the art of writing something that will be read twice; journalism what will be grasped at once." The writing most of us do falls somewhere between these extremes, not literature, perhaps, but not journalism, either, yet taking something from both. Like literature, our writing often contains complex combinations of information, feeling, opinion, and motive. Its success depends upon our artistry, our ability to use words in varied and often complex ways. Like journalism, however, our writing is almost always done for readers who will read our writing only once. Its success also depends, therefore, on their ability to grasp it immediately. That means that despite all of its complexities of message and motive, our writing must be as clear as we can make it.

Good writing is almost always like this, as easy to read as possible, like a clear, clean window through which readers gaze on a panorama of ideas. As they read they're unaware of words or sentences, just as they're also unaware of the glass when they gaze out a window. The ideas themselves seem to become visible. Sometimes, of course, we want our readers to see our language first and foremost, just as windows are sometimes constructed out of stained glass. But for most public writing, communication is the first order of business, and the style that communicates our message most clearly and efficiently is the best style. This maxim does not mean that we should aim for a kind of stylelessness in our writing—far from it—only that in most public writing, we want our readers more aware of our ideas than the words and sentences that present them, and we choose our words and arrange our sentences to that end.

Nor does this maxim mean that we should always aim to make our writing *easy* to read. Adults shouldn't aim to write like first graders. Good writing is as clear as it can be yet still say *all* that needs to be said to a particular audience about a particular subject. Complex subjects thoroughly covered—or emotionally charged subjects delicately handled—will often make for difficult reading, no matter how many pains a writer takes to be clear. It is more difficult, for example, to write clearly about the causes of America's failures in the Vietnam War than the way to fly a kite. To make too easy an analysis of America's Vietnam involvement may be to oversimplify the subject and make it mean less than it should. The reader bears some responsibility here. If the writer has taken all the plains he or she can to write clearly, then the reader must take pains to understand.

The key to writing clearly is keeping readers oriented, free to devote their attention to your subject instead of groping among your words, trying to find their way. Readers have only so much time and energy to give to a writing. If it is vague, distracting in style, or difficult to follow, they will have to reread, perhaps several times, and the effort they devote to rereading a passage may be lost to obtaining a full understanding of it. That means following the guidelines given in preceding chapters:

- *Be clear about your thesis or main idea.* First, be clear to yourself about what you want to say; if you're not, your readers won't be clear, either. We may start with a point clearly in mind, but as draft leads to draft, it may become obscured. Use every stage of the composing process as an opportunity to compose *yourself,* to make up your mind anew about the point you want to make. The clarity of all your other ideas depends upon the clarity of this central controlling idea.
- *Formulate a communications strategy.* Give yourself the opportunity to make the change of roles that occurs to almost all public writers, from writing for yourself to writing for your readers. The clearer your design is to you, the more predictably you'll write for others. The clearer your image of your audience, the easier it will be to choose a persona and language that will put them at ease, ready to understand you. As well, you'll see more clearly what background information they'll need before they can grasp your subject.
- *Revise your writing.* Saying something clearly and well is almost always an evolutionary process: writing, revising, rewriting, and revising some more. Each version brings you a little closer to what you want to say and says it a little more clearly.

But sometimes, as you well know, writers do all this and more yet still end up writing obscurely. On these occasions, the problem—and the solution—probably lies in the smallest elements of a writing: its sentences and individual words. To write clearly is to keep readers oriented not only between sentences but also *within* them. And that is the subject of this chapter and the following: in Chapter 9, writing and editing clear sentences; in Chapter 10, choosing the clearest words.

WRITING CLEAR SENTENCES

Clear sentences make sense—at least what sense the writer intends. Because writing involves more than conscious thought, sentences may say *more* than a writer wants them to, but they ought never to say *less* or something *different*. Unclear sentences miss the mark and often make nonsense statements. The grammatical and logical relationships that keep readers oriented have been strained by words forced to do what they cannot do, be what they cannot be, or stand where they should not stand. No wonder such writing is unclear. Clear sentences, on the other hand, are clear because their words actually mean what their writers want them to mean, because their parts fit together in coherent, grammatical patterns, and because their writers practice the following guidelines. Try them out for yourself and see how much clearer, how much more emphatic, how much more interesting your sentences become.

Guidelines to Clear Sentences

Whenever Possible, Limit Your Sentences to One Main Idea The more that is happening in a sentence, the easier it is to become tangled as you write.[1] Even when you do write a complicated sentence clearly, you risk tangling your readers in words and phrases that do two things at once. Consider this sentence:

> Once upon a time we lived in a simple world controlled by understandable forces, a world of unrelenting struggle in which we pitted our talent, will and luck against nature, evil, and misfortune.

See the two main ideas here, the world's simplicity and the nature of our struggle in this world? The ideas are related, to be sure; nevertheless, they pull the sentence in two slightly different directions and make it that much harder to follow. Now consider the original version and the single ideas in each sentence:

Simple world
Struggle

Our fickle fates

Our response to
our fates
Life's clarity

> Once upon a time we lived in a simple world controlled by understandable forces. Life then consisted of the unrelenting struggle of talent, will and luck against nature, evil and misfortune. Sometimes we won, sometimes we lost. Sometimes fortitude and talent produced victory and pride, sometimes bad luck and weakness resulted in loss and shame. Sometimes we hated ourselves. Sometimes we hated our enemies. Sometimes we even hated God. But always the object and righteousness of our anger were clear and just a little bit uplifting.

The coming
of science
The power of
explanation
A change in
humankind's struggle
The disappearance
of evil

A change in
self-perception

Then, ever so slowly, came the specter of science, casting its shadow over all human problems. One by one, all the evils of the world fell prey to the most powerful of scientific weapons—explanation. Storms became weather fronts, crop growth became agricultural science and death became the product of microorganisms and a myriad of biochemical events. The grand struggle is no longer that of man against nature, but science against nature. The force of evil has disappeared from nature; sinfulness is no longer man's fate. The new "sciences" of sociology, psychology and psychiatry have cast aside such concepts as will, willpower, badness and laziness and replaced them with political and psychological repression, poor conditioning, diseased family interaction and bad genes. One by one, human failings have been redesignated as diseases.

(Rex Julian Beaber, "Stress—And Other Scapegoats," *Newsweek* 4 Apr. 1983)

Whenever Possible, Write Agent-Action Sentences   Grammarians call the agent-action pattern[2] *the active voice.* In active voice constructions, the subject of a sentence (the agent) commits the action of the verb, as in *"Bill sent the letter."* Bill, the agent, committed the action, sending the letter. This pattern—subject (agent) + active voice verb (action) + complement—is the most common English sentence pattern and the one readers most expect. To write active voice sentences is to write predictably, and to write predictably is to write clearly.

A corollary of this guideline is to put the agent-action pattern early in your sentences. Readers will know at the outset what your point is, and that knowledge will make your sentences even more predictable. See how many of the following sentences are built on an agent-action pattern that appears early and, consequently, how clear they are to read? Agent-action patterns are emphasized.

Starting about one million years ago, the fossil *record shows* an accelerating growth of the human brain. *It expanded* at first at the rate of one cubic inch of additional gray matter every hundred thousand years; then the *growth rate doubled; it doubled* again; and finally *it doubled* once more. Five hundred thousand years ago the *rate of growth hit* its peak. At that time the *brain was expanding* at a phenomenal rate of ten cubic inches every hundred thousand years. No other organ in the history of life is known to have grown as fast as this.

What *pressures generated* the explosive growth of the human brain? A *change of climate that set in* about two million years ago *may supply* part of the answer. At that time the *world began* its descent into a great Ice Age, the first to afflict the planet in hundreds of millions of years. The *trend* toward colder weather *set in* slowly at first, but after a million years *patches of ice began to form* in the north. The *ice patches thickened* into glaciers as more *snow fell,* and then the *glaciers merged* into great sheets of ice, as much as two miles thick. When the *ice sheets reached* their maximum extent, *they covered* two thirds of the North American continent, all of Britain and a large part of Europe. Many mountain ranges were buried entirely. So much water was locked up on the land in the form of ice that the *level* of the earth's oceans *dropped* by three hundred feet.

These *events coincided* precisely with the period of most rapid expansion of the human brain. Is the coincidence significant, or is it happenstance? . . .

In those difficult times, the traits of resourcefulness and ingenuity must have been of premium value. Which *individual* first *thought* of stripping the pelt from the slaughtered beast to wrap around his shivering limbs? Only by such inventive flights of the imagination *could the naked animal survive* a harsh climate. In every generation, the individuals endowed with the attributes of strength, courage, and improvisation were the ones more likely to survive the rigors of the Ice Age; *those who* were less resourceful, and *lacked* the vision of their fellows, *fell victim* to the climate and their numbers were reduced.

> (Robert Jastrow, "Man of Wisdom," *Until the Sun Dies* [New York: Norton, 1977], emphasis added)

Keep the Parts of Your Sentences Relatively Short Readers don't swallow sentences whole; they nibble them bit by bit. As they read, they store information temporarily in their short-term memories, an area of memory that remembers for only a few seconds. When they complete a statement that makes sense by itself—not necessarily a complete sentence—their minds transfer that information to their long-term memories, and the process begins all over again: read, store, transfer, read, store, transfer. But this short-term memory is a small pouch; it can hold only about seven bits of information. If it fills up before a passage makes sense, before what reading experts call *closure,* the reader will have to stop reading and start rereading. Thus this guideline: *not* short sentences but short *parts,* in sentences of whatever length. If you can make the parts of your sentences short, you will give your readers the opportunity to discover your meaning as they read along. See how you nibble the short parts of the following? The parts are separated by slashes (/).

> In World War II men died more or less willingly for the nation and the nation's honor,/and they were honored for it in return. Now we have become cynical about such things;/the nation lies,/fights unjustifiable wars,/the nation robs the poor to give to the rich. It is no longer sweet,/it is no longer fitting,/as Ezra Pound reminded us in "Hugh Selwyn Mauberly,"/ *pro patria mori.*
>
> But if not for our country, what shall we be willing to die for? When a nation loses its honor,/its citizens lose an anchorage,/a reference point,/one of their moral absolutes. We have always thought of ourselves as a special people,/better intentioned and much less corrupt than the rest of the world,/a nation that twice came to the rescue of a Europe dense with iniquity. It is as if, that illusion dead,/a victim of the last twenty-five years of our history,/we no longer know what was honorable. If as individuals we still have a sense of honor,/we don't know what to do with it,/when and where it applies. History has become an affair of powers and interests and sneers at the honor of nations;/it has thereby deprived us of models. A sense of honor has become the

moral equivalent of a vestigial organ;/it's there,/and we know it's there,/but it seems to have no function.

(Anthony Brandt, "A World without Honor," *Esquire* Aug. 1983)

Keep Related Words as Close Together as Possible   Keeping related words close together means, first of all, that you should put subjects as close as possible to their verbs. Putting subjects and verbs together helps readers reach closure quickly and get the main idea of your sentences. The sentences in the following passage are complex but easy to read, in part because subjects and verbs stand so close. Subjects and their verbs are emphasized.

When *I pulled* the trigger *I did not hear* the bang or *feel* the kick—*one never does* when a *shot goes* home—but *I heard* the devilish *roar* of glee *that went up* from the crowd. In that instant, in too short a time, *one would have thought,* even for the *bullet to get* there, a mysterious, terrible *change had come* over the elephant. *He neither stirred nor fell,* but every *line* of his body *had altered. He looked* suddenly stricken, shrunken, immensely old, as though the frightful *impact* of the bullet *had paralyzed* him without knocking him down. At last, after *what seemed* a long time—*it might have been* five seconds, *I dare say*—*he sagged* flabbily to his knees.

(George Orwell, "Shooting an Elephant," *Shooting an Elephant and Other Essays* [New York: Harcourt, 1950], emphasis added)

Equally important to clarity is the relationship between modifiers and the words they modify. *Modifiers* are words, phrases, or clauses that act as adjectives and adverbs. They provide additional information about other words, phrases, or clauses. Proximity poses no problem with single-word adjectives and adverbs, so-called bound modifiers that immediately precede or follow the words they modify; these words are bound together: "The *tall man walked slowly* from the room and *stood silently* at the foot of the *very steep stairs.*" The problem comes with *free modifiers,* those that can be put anywhere in a sentence. In the four versions of the following test sentence, see how the emphasized free modifiers can be moved and how moving these modifiers can affect meaning and clarity?

Freshly torn from its parent sun, the new earth was a ball of whirling gases *rushing throught the black spaces of the universe, intensely hot.* [In this version *intensely hot* is so far away from the *gases* it modifies that it seems to modify *universe* instead.]

The new earth was a ball of whirling gases, *freshly torn from its parent sun, intensely hot, rushing through the black spaces of the universe.* [In this version *intensely hot* is closer to *parent sun* than *whirling gases;* once again the modifier's relationship is uncertain.]

Intensely hot, freshly torn from its parent sun, rushing through the black spaces of the universe, the new earth was a ball of whirling gases. [In this version the opening series of modifiers appears to modify *new earth* and to have nothing to do with the whirling gases that compose the earth.]

Rushing through the black spaces of the universe, the new earth, *intensely hot, was a ball of whirling gases freshly torn from its parent sun.* [In this version the new earth is intensely hot; the gases have been torn from the parent sun.]

Now contrast these versions with the original sentence, completed and arranged to show the close relationship between the modifiers and the words they modify. Because its modifiers stand next to the words they modify, the sentence is clear, emphatic, and unambiguous.

>The new earth,
>   freshly torn from its parent sun,
>was a ball of whirling gases,
>   intensely hot,
>   rushing through the black spaces of the universe
>   on a path and at a speed
>   controlled by immense forces.

(Adapted from Rachel Carson, "The Grey Beginnings," *The Sea Around Us* [New York: Oxford UP, 1961])

Whenever Possible, Write Positive Statements   Negative statements almost always take more words to write than positive statements do. What complicates them further is the human brain's habit of first translating negative into positive statements before processing them. That slows reading time. Unless you want a negative statement for emphasis, prefer the positive.

Negative
There weren't any other members of the Schooner Club except Ishmael who didn't pay their dues before the date set by the club president.

Positive
All the members of the Schooner Club except Ishmael paid their dues before the date set by the Club President.

EXERCISES

1. Write a paragraph describing an accident and your reaction to it. It may be a serious accident or not, an auto accident or some other kind. As you write, try to follow the first guideline: Use one main idea per sentence.

2. Write a paragraph in which you predict the fate of your city, state, region, our country, or the world in the next decade. Try to follow the second guideline: Write agent-action sentences.

3. Write a paragraph describing a partnership in action. It may be two people working together on a job, a husband and wife talking to their children, two people playing a game, or another partnership of your choosing. Aim to show what the partners do together, what they do separately or alternately. Follow the third guideline: Keep the parts of your sentences relatively short.

4. Write a brief paragraph about one of the following topics. Follow the fourth guideline: Keep related parts together. Put subjects close to their verbs. Try using free modifiers to develop your subject, but make sure they're close to the words they modify.

dirt	a particular tool	a particular wild animal
money	the planets	a geographical feature from your
textbooks	poverty	state

5. Imagine you are a supervisor at a local company who must write a memo to a close friend whom you supervise. She has requested a raise, a promotion, a transfer to the Honolulu branch office, and a company car. You must say no to each of her requests. Say that in your memo, but follow the fifth guideline: Write positive statements.

EDITING SENTENCES FOR CLARITY

No matter how carefully you prepare and how well you master the preceding guidelines, you will seldom write many first draft sentences that are graceful little engines of clarity and light. Instead of going hum and whir, most first draft sentences go clink, clank, thud, mush. Knowing *what* you want to say, even *how* you want to say it, is not the same as actually saying it. More frustrating still, you'll know which sentences are wrong but be unsure how to spot the trouble or fix it once you find it. Here are two solutions to the problem, both phrased as questions. As you edit a draft, ask them about any sentences that seem unclear or awkward.

What's Happening Here?   *De*-construct the problem sentence into its individual assertions. For example: *I'd like to borrow an idea from Professor Niven, one that can be started now and that will produce results in only a few years.* Deconstructed into its assertions, this sentence looks like this:

I'd like to borrow an idea . . .
an idea . . . can be started . . .
an idea . . . will produce . . .

Ask if these barebones statements make sense. "An idea can be started"? Is it possible to "start" an idea? The action of every assertion ought to be clear and logical. If you find a non-sense statement, try rewriting it in other words or another arrangement of the original words. "I'd like to borrow a *proposal* from Professor Niven, one that can be *implemented* now and that will produce results in only a few years."

What Goes with What?   For example: *Stepping into the mansion's foyer, a small Tiffany lamp glowed in luxurious greeting.* Circle and connect related words or phrases.

> Stepping into the mansion's foyer,
> a small Tiffany lamp . . .

Are the relationships clear, close, logical, and grammatical? A lamp stepping into a foyer? If you spot non-sense, reword or rearrange. "*As we stepped into the mansion's foyer, a small Tiffany lamp glowed in luxurious greeting.*"

Here are some of the most common non-sense errors that these questions will uncover.

What's Happening Here?

Problems of Illogical Assertion   Illogical assertions occur when a subject does something it cannot logically do or when it is said to be something it cannot logically be.

Example
> My friend Sammy has recently undergone some moral changes and personal views.

What's happening here? *Sammy has . . . undergone some changes . . . and . . . views.* "Undergone some views"? Could this sentence mean that Sammy has changed—possibly been forced to change—his moral values and self-perception?

Revision
> My friend Sammy has recently had to change his moral values and self-perception.

Here's a second illogical assertion:

Example
> David is still too young for any major academic achievements. A prediction about his future, however, shows the potential of becoming every bit the scholar his brothers are.

What's happening here? *A prediction . . . shows the potential* and *A prediction . . . becoming . . . the scholar.* Can a prediction show potential? Surely a prediction can't become a scholar. The solution is to put David, the potential scholar, into the second sentence as a personal pronoun:

Revision
> David is still too young for any major academic achievements, but he has the potential of becoming every bit the scholar his brothers are.

Example
My experience as a hall monitor was a failure because I was new at the job and because the job was a classic example of a supervisor without authority.

What's happening here? *Experience . . . was a failure.* Can an experience fail?

Revision
I failed as a hall monitor because I was new at the job and because my position was a classic example of a supervisor without authority.

Mixed Metaphor
A mixed metaphor is a special kind of illogical assertion. A writer begins to make a metaphorical comparison but loses sight of it in a tangle of words and ends up making a second comparison that doesn't belong logically with the first.

An Example
The brush of Norman Rockwell has recently been silenced.

What's happening here? *The brush . . . has been silenced.* A silent brush? Noisy bristles, perhaps? The writer must have confused *silenced* with *stilled: The brush of Norman Rockwell has recently been stilled.*

A Second Example
The Beatles carved out new directions in popular music that were a springboard into the limelight of the public eye.

What's happening here? *The Beatles carved . . . directions; the directions . . . were a springboard; the directions sprang into the limelight; the limelight* (an early open flame stage lamp) *was in the public eye.* The solution to most mixed metaphors is to choose the best among them, but in this example, because all the metaphors are clichés, there is little to choose from. Flat statement is almost always better than a cliché.

Revision
The Beatles' new forms of popular music brought them sudden fame.

Mixed Construction
Mixed construction errors combine two ways of saying one thing. Many ideas can be expressed in more than one way. Non-sense results when two or more of these patterns are combined in one sentence.

An Example
The United States has the highest divorce rate than any other country in the world.

What's happening here? *The highest divorce rate than any . . . .* The solution is to choose *one* of the two patterns of comparison. By itself either is clear and correct.

First Pattern
The United States has the highest divorce rate in the world.

Second Pattern
The United States has a higher divorce rate than any other country.

EXERCISES

1. Here are non-sense sentences whose errors have been identified and under-lined. Rewrite them so they are clear.

   a. Illogical assertion: Fred's senses are keen, always noticing things, describ-ing, for example, the whole accident from the first moment the car began to skid.
   b. Illogical assertion: Another type of professional irresponsibility is when an employee declares, "I don't care whether the report is done on time. I will just tell the boss it has been lost."
   c. Mixed metaphor: If the underdeveloped nations would only wake up to the threat of totalitarianism, they might come in out of the rain and gather under Uncle Sam's wing.
   d. Mixed metaphor: As far as I can tell, Laura seems free of the shallowness that permeates the rest of the Sheridan family.
   e. Mixed construction: By removing the hood it makes it possible to take the engine out of the car.
   f. Mixed construction: By understanding the inevitability of death has en-abled Laura to understand life.

2. Here are more non-sense sentences. For each ask "What's happening here?" Identify the non-sense errors and then rewrite.

   a. Dim lighting in our office reflects a feeling of being smothered by an over-cast sky.
   b. In the last few months, Bill and Ruth's friendship has expanded to new depths. For a while there I was concerned about them, but now I'm confi-dent their friendship will span the test of time.
   c. My main interest in audio-visual electronics is a traveling audio-visual tech-nician.
   d. Back when I was a young woman, the economy seemed very plentiful.
   e. Yet it is not until an accident involving his car takes place does Mr. Bow-man realize what his true motives have been.
   f. A good rule to remember is never to assume when talking with a customer, do not take it for granted that the buyer knows what you are talking about when describing an item.
   g. The hospice concept is a program that provides skilled and compassionate care to terminally ill patients and their families.
   h. In comparison to the suburban judges and the view they take on traffic of-fenses make the Chicago court system a joke.
   i. Progress in the treatment of children afflicted with Down's syndrome ap-plies not only to their families and teachers but also to the taxpaying public that has paid for this progress.

j. The renaissance of hot air ballooning came in the early 1960s and has since then grown increasingly popular.

What Goes with What? (Part I: Parts That Don't Connect)

Faulty Pronoun Reference Faulty pronoun relationships occur when the relationship between a pronoun and its noun antecedent is obscure, ambiguous, or nonexistent. Three kinds of pronouns may be involved: personal pronouns (*he, she, it, they,* and so on), demonstrative pronouns (*this, that, these, those*), and relative pronouns (*who, which, that, whom*).

Example
What do you say to a friend who has just lost his job—especially when you've just been given a promotion and a raise? How do you express the sympathy you feel? *This* happened to me recently, and I had a great deal of difficulty handling *it.*

What goes with what? Do *this* and *it* in the third sentence refer to losing one's job, to giving sympathy, to receiving a promotion and a raise, or to some combination of these? The relationships are ambiguous, and so we can't be sure. The solution is to be more explicit. Here are two revisions that make clear the two possible meanings of the original.

One Revision
When my friend lost his job recently, I had a difficult time finding words to console him. It didn't help matters much that I had just received a promotion and a raise.

A Second Revision
When I lost my job recently, I felt that no one could find words to console me, not even my best friend, who had just received a promotion and a raise.

Here's another example:

When Fred reached Atlanta's airport, he quickly found a baggage cart to move his luggage, which was nonexistent at Chicago's O'Hare Airport.

What goes with what? . . . *his luggage, which was nonexistent* . . . Luggage nonexistent in Chicago? But wait, Fred had his luggage in Atlanta. How could it disappear? It was stolen by an ambiguous pronoun, *which.*

Revision
When Fred reached Atlanta's airport he quickly found a baggage cart to move his luggage—quite a contrast to Chicago's O'Hare Airport, where there were no carts.

To learn more about pronoun/antecedent relationships, see Chapter 18, pages 518–521.

Dangling Modifier A dangling modifier is a word or group of words that is supposed to be a modifier but that has nothing in a sentence to modify.

Either it "dangles," disconnected, or appears to make an illogical connection.

Example
After another hour of drifting down the river, the bridge came into view.

What goes with what? *After . . . drifting down the river, the bridge . . .* How many hours had the bridge been drifting down the river? The solution to the floating bridge is to put the actual river-drifters into the sentence.

Revision
After another hour of drifting down the river, we saw the bridge.

Example
It took a while for the audience to recognize it, but the actress's subtle, sensitive style gradually revealed the mother's character, an empathetic person.

What goes with what? *Character* in the context of this sentence means personality, but how can personality be *an empathetic person?*

Revision
It took a while for the audience to recognize it, but the actress's subtle, sensitive style gradually revealed the mother to be an empathetic person.

Misplaced Modifier   A misplaced modifier is a modifier located away from the term it is supposed to modify. This displacement slows reading time or creates an illogical relationship.

An Example
The dust begins to thicken as time passes on bookcases, files, and cabinets.

What goes with what? *. . . as time passes on bookcases . . . ?*

Revision
As time passes, dust begins to thicken on bookcases, files, and cabinets.

EXERCISES

1. Here are more non-sense sentences. The illogical relationships have been identified and underlined. Correct them.

a. Faulty pronoun reference: What are officials doing to students in public schools today? Too many of them cannot read or write. Instead of doing what they should be doing, they spend their time riding around town on buses. They argue that they do this because they must be in integrated schools in order to improve their educational opportunities.

b. Faulty pronoun reference: Once training was complete, our division was to move to South Carolina as part of the company's expansion plans. This accomplished, we received our new job assignments.

c. Dangling modifier: Although known by some for her work at City Hall and her interest in the arts, Heather Morgan Bilandic's name didn't really become a household word until she married the mayor of Chicago.

d. Dangling modifier: A bright new light has entered my life this year, <u>the joy of being close to a new life</u>, my nephew.

e. Misplaced modifier: The drive from Ohio to Chicago was a long and lonely one, about seven hours. My anticipation started to build, however, when I picked up a Chicago radio station <u>coming out of Fort Wayne, Indiana.</u>

f. Misplaced modifier: Two men walked into the diner <u>named Al and Max,</u> sat down at the counter, and gruffly ordered their food.

2. For each of the following non-sense sentences ask, "What goes with what?" Identify the errors and correct them.

a. Why should a black person take a job that doesn't interest him and that he may even be overqualified for just because of the color of his skin?

b. His real difficulties didn't begin until after he had been thrown out of his home town. This rejection must have been deeply embarrassing after having lived there for almost thirty years.

c. Another common insecurity is the feeling about ourselves when entering a new relationship, be it friend or lover.

d. When driving through downtown Arlington Heights, my grandparents' gray, two-story house looked drab and lonely, but it was still home.

e. I have already mentioned that our criminal justice system is a joke and that the media glamorize crime. Now I must ask, what shall we do about it?

f. After three hours of searching, Merlin was still no closer to finding the engagement ring he had dropped down the sewer, which greatly threatened his marriage proposal to Wilda.

g. Taken out of the department store showroom, I've found these new fashions to be about as practical for a working woman as a mink coat on a ski trip.

h. Some jobs are not satisfying but do pay good money, a supermarket, for instance.

i. None of us thought night would ever come after paddling our canoes for twelve straight hours.

j. When prices rise, consumers purchase less and production decreases; this causes higher unemployment and inflated prices.

What Goes with What? (Part II: Connections That Make No Sense)

Faulty Parallelism   Parallel structures are words or groups of words that are logically and grammatically similar, e.g., *hamburgers* and *french fries*, both nouns. Often parallel structures are joined by a coordinating conjunction (*and, but, for, yet, or, nor, so*): *Hamburgers and french fries are my favorite health foods.* Constructions that are logically parallel must also be grammatically parallel; if they are not, we call the error faulty parallelism.

Example
   My favorite health foods are hamburgers, french fries, and at the corner drive-in where I always order the strawberry milkshakes.

Grammatically the series in this sentence reads: noun *(hamburgers)* + noun *(french fries)* + prepositional phrase and clause *(at the corner drive-in where I always order the strawberry milkshakes)*. The third item in the series is not parallel to the first two.

Revision
    My favorite health foods are hamburgers, french fries, and the strawberry milkshakes I always order at the corner drive-in.

Here is a second, slightly different example:

    Lenore believes illegal immigrants should be deported and give their jobs to the American citizens we are now supporting on welfare.

What goes with what? The sentence makes two assertions: *Illegal immigrants should be deported* and *illegal immigrants should . . . give their jobs to the American citizens. . . .* The first is clear, but the second? Would the immigrants themselves give their jobs away? Not likely. *Should be deported* and *give* have been joined by a coordinating conjunction, making them seem to have the same subject, although, in fact, they are not related and not parallel. Someone *else* would give the immigrants' jobs to citizens on welfare. The solution: make *immigrants* the true subject of both verbs. Now the verbs are truly parallel.

Revision
    Lenore believes that illegal immigrants should be deported and their jobs given to the American citizens we are now supporting on welfare.

To learn more about parallel structure, see Chapter 18, pages 514–517.

Illogical or Incomplete Comparison   An illogical or incomplete comparison compares two subjects that are not logically comparable or creates an absurdity because the comparison is incomplete.

An Example
    The Road-Romper GLU has a basic warranty twice as long as any other American luxury car.

What goes with what? *a . . . warranty twice as long as any luxury car.* Can you imagine reading the fine print in a warranty twice as long as an automobile? That would be nearly forty feet of paper! The solution: put in the -'s that will compare car with car.

Revision
    The Road-Romper GLU has a basic warranty twice as long as any other American luxury car's.

A second example:

An Advertisement
    Don't let our sturdier products and broader guarantee fool you. Our prices are lower, too.

What goes with what? *Sturdier* than whose products? *Broader* than whose guarantee? *Lower* than whose prices? This advertisement refuses to compare itself to its competition, perhaps because it cannot prove the points of the comparison. Incomplete comparison is one way some advertisers seem to say more than they actually do.

Unmatched Numbers   In unmatched numbers there is not enough of something, a noun, usually, to go around; a word is singular when it should be plural.

An Example
Television has made people afraid to leave their home at night.

What goes with what? . . . *people afraid to leave their home* . . . If we're all in the same house together, as this sentence says, then why are we afraid? We can all leave together. The singular should be plural.

Revision
Television has made people afraid to leave their homes at night.

EXERCISES

1. The faulty connection errors in these sentences are identified and underlined. Correct them.

   a. Faulty parallelism: Now that Mike Royko has written a newspaper column slandering Walter Jacobson, perhaps Jacobson should do a TV commentary on Royko, pointing out that he is bald, four-eyed, has a huge nose with a colossal ego and no writing ability.

   b. Faulty parallelism: Throughout her twenties and thirties she was disappointed that she had not gone to college, but she read widely and became knowledgeable in history, English, and a love of poetry.

   c. Faulty comparison: The latest government report on cigarette smoking concludes that women have a harder time quitting smoking than men.

   d. Faulty comparison: After we leveled off at 9,000 feet, our flight became as smooth as any commercial jetliner.

   e. Unmatched numbers: She was the opposite of her husband, who made people's life unpleasant.

   f. Unmatched numbers: All of those who might normally be mistrustful changed their mind when they saw him.

2. For each of the following non-sense sentences ask, "What goes with what?" Identify the errors and correct them.

   a. Henry Clay, the Great Compromiser, solved the problem by proposing the Compromise of 1850. It abandoned the Wilmont Proviso, admitted California to the Union as a free state, all other new territories would be governed by popular sovereignty, abolish the slave trade in the District of Columbia, but popular sovereignty would decide whether slavery would be allowed there.

b. It took a severe illness and long hospital stay to break down Henderson's reserve and realize what he was missing in life.

c. It seems to me that husbands and wives ought to change places from time to time to balance their life.

d. Ron, a friend I had been close to in high school, was diagnosed as having a disease similar to Reverend Jones's wife.

e. Need I remind you that three of the major plants in Decatur have shut down and many others are decreasing their staff?

f. She suffered the suicide of her husband while she was still a teenager and trying to cope with the responsibility she assumed for it.

g. I was informed that the reason for experimenting with rabbits instead of cats or dogs is that rabbits have eyes similar to the membranes of the human eye.

h. Someone should invite those college and university professors down out of their ivory towers and accessible to the students, the way they should be.

i. I compare Laura's upbringing to myself.

j. Nobody appreciates mud wrestlers like me.

3. The sentences below contain all of the non-sense errors you have studied. Read each sentence, ask, "What's happening here?" and "What goes with what?" Identify the errors and correct them.

a. An example of a typical Christmas-rush customer is when Sally described the elderly woman at her check-out counter who gave her a difficult time.

b. I look at most automobile dealer service managers as a mechanic who is too old to crawl under cars.

c. She fashioned him into the image she wanted him to be.

d. Blanche, although not physically as strong as Stanley, her personality is tough.

e. Laura's immaturity is the fault of her parents and the way her mother, especially, hinders her from the lives of the others and the sorrows that everyone must face.

f. If I could take my vacation in Hong Kong I'd go gambling in Macau, horseracing, the kickboxing matches, and the Chinese New Year's celebration, which lasts four days.

g. She is why people are how they are today, keeping to themselves, minding their own business.

h. Two wires protruded from the pacemaker implanted in her chest and two from her back. A battery was taped to her chest which ran constantly. It had to be replaced every ten days.

i. Her irresponsibility led to one tragedy after another: fired from her studio because of her constant tardiness, alcohol and pills, which eventually took her life.

j. Responsible gun owners should perceive licensing or registration as a prized possession rather than an insult or document of suspicion.

k. With all of these facts before me, I now see that the author killed her protagonist very slowly, almost resembling Chinese water torture.

l. You may suspect that a man is an alcoholic if he spends more time drinking with his friends than his wife and children.

m. Out with television! Out! My wife and I will permit only limited radio listening, too. Back to books. Reading, thinking, loving, playing, living, and intellectual curiosity will help us grow back from the harsh blows civilization has placed upon us.

n. The climbers will then try to scale the south face to reach the summit, which has never before been achieved.

o. I walked into the Neighborhood Social Center a few days ago and found no supervision at all. Kids were drinking beer, and near one of the doors some gangster type was dealing drugs. The whole idea of the place has sadly dwindled.

p. When Joseph Sobek decided to pep up the game of paddleball back in the late 1940s, little did he realize what he was starting. He began by designing a racket with strings and a handle shorter than a tennis racket.

q. Chef Edgar has served dinners throughout Europe, including royalty.

r. When she came to her sister's in New Orleans, she did not find understanding; instead, she discovered an adversary who was the opposite of all she stood for by the name of Stanley Kowalski.

s. I was walking back to the courthouse after a lunchbreak where I was serving on jury duty.

t. Just recently a sixteen-year-old girl's life was brutally taken from her after being abducted only fifty yards from her home in Streamwood.

4. Choose one page from a recent writing you've done. In the margin identify the sentences you have written: one main idea sentences, agent-action sentences, short and related parts sentences, positive statement sentences. Each of your sentences may, of course, be more than one type. If any of your sentences do not follow the guidelines given earlier in this chapter, see whether you can improve them by rewriting. Does any sentence seem to make non-sense statements or seem obscure in meaning? If so, ask, "What's happening here?" and "What goes with what?" to spot the problem; then rewrite. Turn in the original page with your revisions.

WRITING PROJECTS

Topics

1. For the past several years parents, politicians, educators, and students themselves have been making a reappraisal of America's educational curriculum. Our educational system, it is often said, is ineffective. Supposedly, the students in today's schools—grammar school through college—are not being taught what they need to live successfully in an increasingly complex, increasingly technological, increasingly cosmopolitan society. Carry this discussion a step further by appraising part of the education you have received, or, if you are a parent, that of your children. Choose an educational level: grammar school, high school, or college. Describe the curriculum or, better yet, focus on one part of it: a grade level or course of study. What were you or your children taught? What was right or wrong with that course of study? What should be changed to update it and make it valuable for today's students? What would you keep and why? Do research, if

necessary, to gather facts and figures to support your conclusions. You may want to design a course catalog for your ideal school. In any case, your responsibility here is *not* to criticize or praise individual teachers or schools so much as to examine and evaluate the content and purpose of one level of American education as you know it. Write a three- to five-page essay. Address it to the persons most responsible for making your proposed changes: educational administrators, teachers, politicians, parents, taxpayers, or the students themselves. Consider organizing your essay according to the problem/solution pattern (see Chapter 6, page 127).

2. In a three- to five-page essay write the Ten Commandments for a New Age. Rewrite the original Commandments to update them, either to reflect the morals we actually hold or to set new standards for contemporary behavior. Your commandments should concern our most important emotions, beliefs, and actions. Address your essay to those most in need of these new commandments, either to better understand themselves or to reform their lives. Feel free to be satirical, if you wish. Consider organizing your essay according to an order-of-importance pattern (see Chapter 6, pages 118–119). Or organize your new commandments according to the original ones they replace.

3. In a three- to five-page essay write the Seven Deadly Sins for a New Age. The old ones were avarice, sloth, anger, gluttony, lust, pride, and envy. What should the new ones be? Also consider whether our definition of sin has changed. Address your essay to the sinners indicted by your list. Aim to reveal these people to themselves. Feel free to be satirical, if you wish. Consider organizing your essay according to an order-of-importance pattern (see Chapter 6, pages 118–119). Or organize your new sins according to those they replace.

4. One of the ways things get done in the modern world is through grant money, money given by one person or agency to another to fund some worthwhile project. Think of something worthwhile that you or a group you belong to would like to do and write a three- to five-page grant proposal requesting the money to do it. Grant money is generally given to fund community betterment projects, educational opportunities or programs (including educational travel), human welfare programs, artistic or cultural projects, recreational or personal development opportunities, and research projects. (You may be serious or fanciful, if wish, in the subject of your proposal.) Funding sources are usually individual philanthropists, government agencies, foundations, or businesses. Once you have a project to be funded, decide on an appropriate funding source; be as specific as possible (your librarian will help you identify funding sources). Address your proposal to this source. Decide carefully how much your project will probably cost. Organize your grant proposal like this:

    I. A description of the project.
       Reasons for proposing it.
       What you hope to accomplish with it.
   II. How you plan to accomplish your objectives, including procedures, facilities, equipment, supporting personnel, methods, location, and a project schedule.
  III. An itemized estimated budget.
  IV. A persuasive conclusion.

5. Write a three- to five-page essay defending what you understand to be the theme or thesis in a recent reading you have done. Explain how details, organization, point of view, and mood support your contentions. Consider organizing your essay according to the order of ideas in your thesis or according to one of the order-of-importance or "What is it?" patterns (see Chapter 6, pages 118–119 and 127).

THE WRITING PROCESS

1. Writing-in-progress.
    a. *Exploring:* Free association and freewriting.
    b. *Developing:* Discover all that you have to say about your subject. Use whatever methods and strategies seem appropriate.
        i. Write a thematic tag tree (see pages 159–160).
        ii. Write a transition proposition, two or more assertions about your subject linked by a transition (see pages 168–169).
    c. *Planning a communications strategy:* Decide on a role, persona (distance and attitude), and thesis (*My point is that . . . What I mean to say is that . . .*).
    d. *Organizing.*
        i. Organize your writing in a clear, predictable, coherent pattern; use whatever outlining or organizing strategy seems appropriate (see pages 128–132).
        ii. Devise an introductory strategy to capture your audience's attention and focus their interest (see pages 137–141).
    e. *Revising:* Reconsider your ideas and communications strategy; create frictions in your thinking (see pages 55–56).
2. Writing.
    a. Write the preliminary draft of your project. Write freely, don't stop except to reread, give yourself room to revise.
    ⟶b. *New in this chapter:* Whenever possible, write one main idea per sentence; write agent-action sentences; keep the parts short; keep related words together; write positive statements (see pages 183–187).
3. Rewriting.
    a. Be a zoom lens as you revise; add, delete, substitute, and rearrange. Circle thematic tags to check development and coherence.
    ⟶b. *New in this chapter:* Ask two questions of troublesome sentences.
        i. What's happening here? (See pages 189–191.)
        ii. What goes with what? (See pages 192–196.)
    c. Write "old-new" sentences; begin rereading from the beginning of paragraphs; reread at a natural pace, listening for unnecessary repetitions and transitions (see pages 175–177).
    d. Copyedit for mechanical errors, recopy, and proofread (see pages 61–62).
4. Self-evaluation.
    a. What is your intention in this writing?
    b. What is your thesis? What are your thematic tags?

c. What did you do to help your readers read your writing? Will any parts be hard to follow? If so, why? What would make them more readable?

d. What single sentence or paragraph do you like best in this writing? Can you explain what you like about it?

e. Did you try anything here that you hadn't tried before?

f. What one change would most improve this writing?

END NOTES

1. I am indebted for the "one main idea per sentence" guideline to Theodore M. Bernstein, *The Careful Writer* (New York: Atheneum, 1978).

2. For the term "agent-action" I am indebted to Maxine Hairston.

Chapter 10

Clarity: Proper Words in Proper Places

❧

❧ ECONOMY AND THE DEADWOOD FOREST

> Words are like leaves; and where they most abound
> Much fruit of sense beneath is rarely found.
> (Alexander Pope)

Clear sentences are clear not only because they make sense but also because they use the right number—not too many, not too few—of the right kinds of words. The first half of this maxim means that clear sentences are *economical:* they use as few words as possible to communicate their message. The fewer the words, the easier most sentences are to read. And, as I suggested in the last chapter, the less energy a reader spends reading a sentence, the more energy she will have to concentrate on its contents. One important caution: economy does *not* mean incompleteness. Economical writing uses the fewest words possible, but it says *all* that needs to be said to a particular audience about a particular subject. Brevity is no virtue when it leaves important parts of a subject undeveloped, unemphasized, or unconnected to related parts. This is especially true in college writing, which above all else requires writers to demonstrate in the clearest way possible what they know and can do. The writing process proceeds in this order: first finding ways to say all that needs to be said and then ways to say it most economically.

The greatest threat to economy is *deadwood,* great limbs of words, phrases, and whole sentences that may seem necessary when they are written but only weigh a writing down, bending it out of shape and obscuring meaning. Don't be concerned about deadwood while preparing or drafting; aim to be complete, concrete, and specific. But when you begin revising for style, remember the advice from Chapter 3: you can probably cut at least one word from each of your sentences. Brevity is almost always edited in *after* a draft has been written. One professional writer, William Zinsser, tells novice writers to revise by bracketing [   ] every word, phrase, or sentence that doesn't seem to be doing any work. After reconsideration, if it contributes nothing to the sentence, it should be cut.[1] The trick to skillful cutting is knowing what to look for.

Seven Kinds of Deadwood

Wordiness   The first species of deadwood to look for is the common garden variety, wordiness. Sometimes it appears only in an isolated word or phrase that can be easily pruned.

Example
[I see] the people of the world [as a whole] divided into three groups.

Revision
The people of the world are divided into three groups.

Other times, however, it is difficult to know what to bracket because the deadwood spreads throughout a passage. Simple pruning isn't enough. To restore these sentences to health is to reconstruct them.

Example
We are scheduling two alternate dates for an information session for any faculty members or administrative personnel who have not been previously involved with the first two orientation sessions or the Phase I workshop. The purpose of the meeting will be to bring everyone up to date about what has been going on in the process of redesigning the core curriculum.

Revision
Two sessions have been scheduled to update any faculty or administrators who missed the earlier meetings on the core curriculum. You may attend either session.

Relative Pronouns   Likewise, look for and cut any unnecessary relative pronouns (*who, which, that,* and *whom*).

Example
The other natural decorations in the cave are the flowerlike gypsum crystals, [which] cover the walls. The formations, [which are quite colorful], glow with the browns, oranges, and yellows of dissolved minerals.

Revision
The other natural decorations in the cave are the flower-like gypsum crystals, covering the walls with the glowing browns, oranges, and yellows of dissolved minerals.

Transitions   Cut unnecessary or wordy transitions. In Chapter 8 you learned to read at a natural pace, listening for unnecessary transitions. Especially listen for *the fact that;* it can almost always be cut.

Example
College is often so unsettling to recent high school graduates [because of the fact that] they don't know how to handle their new freedom.

Revision
College is often so unsettling to recent high school graduates because they don't know how to handle their new freedom.

Intensifiers and Qualifiers   Intensifiers and qualifiers are modifiers that express degree (*very, definitely, really, truly, uniquely, wonderfully, seems, perhaps, somewhat, quite,* and so on). Writers occasionally need them to shade meaning, but more often than not they use them like neon to make an idea flashy that would be more emphatic if left to stand alone. By their presence, intensifiers and qualifiers detract from the nouns and verbs that do the real work of the sentence.

Example 1
I [really] enjoyed our drive through the Colorado Rockies. For a midwesterner like me, used to [perfectly flat] prairieland, the granite and white peaks were [truly] breathtaking, especially the ones so [dazzlingly] high they pierced the clouds.

Revision
I enjoyed our drive through the Colorado Rockies. For a midwesterner like me, used to prairieland, the granite and white peaks were breathtaking, especially the ones so high they pierced the clouds.

Example 2
Now with one Chicago winter behind me, [it seems] I have become [somewhat] of a veteran midwesterner.

MISS PEACH

MISS PEACH by Mell Lazarus. Courtesy of Mell Lazarus and News Group Chicago, Inc.

Revision
    Now with one Chicago winter behind me, I have become a veteran mid-westerner.

Redundancy   In Chapter 8 you learned to repeat words to create meaning and coherence. *Un*-necessary repetition, however, produces the most insidious form of deadwood, redundancy. Most obvious is the needless repetition of words.

Example
    The [impression that was impressed on my mind] as I read the article was the extent of government interference in oil production.

Revision
    What impressed me most as I read the article was the extent of government interference in oil production.

Less obvious—and more pervasive for that reason—is the needless repetition of meaning. Upon his trade from the Cincinnati Reds baseball team to the Philadelphia Phillies, the great Pete Rose remarked, "Going to Philadelphia was like being reborn again." Born how many times? He meant to say twice, but *reborn again* means three times: born, reborn, reborn again. And John Brodie, the former football quarterback turned announcer, once remarked during a game featuring the Minnesota Vikings, "Frank Tarkington hasn't duplicated the same play twice." What he meant to say, of course, is that Tarkington, the Minnesota quarterback, hadn't called the same play twice, but in Brodie's redundant version, Tarkington hadn't called the same play *three* times: *duplicated* = twice; *duplicated twice* = three times.

Used by permission of Johnny Hart and News America Syndicate.

Passive Voice   In Chapter 9 you learned to write active voice, agent-action sentences, in which the subjects commit the action of the verb. Passive voice sentences are constructed in the opposite way: the subjects are acted upon; they *receive* the action of the verb, as in "The *letter was* *sent* by Bill." The letter, an object, is acted upon. Passive voice sentences are necessarily less economical than active voice, agent-action sentences because the passive voice requires more words to say the same thing:

Active voice: *Bill sent the letter.*

vs.

Passive voice: *The letter was sent by Bill.*

In more complex sentences than these examples, more words mean more reading time, more energy lost in the reading, less energy for the subject matter, and, therefore, less clarity.

The passive voice also poses a second, more subtle threat to clarity. It permits grammatically complete statements that omit the agents of an action—the actors—as in *The letter was sent.* Who sent it? Many times in our reading we would like to know who did what only to find this *who* omitted by a passive voice construction. Have you ever noticed, for example, how often bad news comes to us wrapped in the passive voice? *A tax-increase bill was proposed today. Tuition will be raised 10 per cent for the coming semester.* Neither of these passive voice sentences identifies the agents of the unpleasantness described, in contrast to active voice constructions that would necessarily name the senator who proposed the tax increase or the trustees who raised tuition. In other words, for those so inclined the passive voice is a way of avoiding responsibility for their actions. Once again, a problem of grammar becomes, as it so often does, a human problem; its solution requires wisdom, tact, and standards of conduct as well as knowledge of sentence structure.

Sometimes, of course, you will want to use the passive voice. It enables you to emphasize the receiver of an action by moving it to the beginning of a sentence: *"The letter was mailed yesterday."* Or you may have to use the passive because the agents of an action are unknown or irrelevant: *"The letter was returned unopened."* But whenever possible, avoid the passive voice; write agent-action sentences. Your writing will be clearer, more direct, more vigorous, and more complete. See how the following passage mixes emphatic passive sentences with more direct agent-action sentences? Passive voice constructions are emphasized.

The *link* between New Jersey and cancer *was supported* by studies made in the early 1970s, which indicated that cities tended to be more cancer-prone than other areas and that *up to 80 percent of all cancers were caused* by environmental factors, in particular, man-made chemicals. Ninety percent of New Jersey's 7.3 million residents live in urban areas. They live alongside sixty-five of some of the worst toxic waste dumps listed by the Environmental Protection Agency.

(Anthony DePalma, "State of Anxiety," *Harper's* Aug. 1983, emphasis added)

The two passive constructions enable the writer to emphasize, first, the connection between New Jersey and cancer and, second, the extent of environmentally caused cancer. Now contrast the effective passive voice sentence above with the following *in*-effective sentences:

Example
   Clothing obsolescence could be prevented by the refusal of men and women to substitute fad fashions for more traditional styles.

Revision
   Men and women could prevent clothing obsolescence by refusing to substitute fad fashions for more traditional styles.

A Second Example
   A large meeting was held in Bryan Hall at which Chicagoans dug deep into their pockets and *generous contributions were made.*

Revision
   At a large meeting in Bryan Hall, *Chicagoans dug deep* into their pockets and *made* generous contributions.

Impersonal Constructions   Related to the passive voice are impersonal constructions, patterns in which subjects are displaced by an expletive (*there*) or a pronoun (*it*): *There is a bug in my beer.* Generally they require more words than personal constructions to express the same idea, but sometimes, like passive constructions, they are necessary for emphasis or rhythm or because the agent of an action is irrelevant, e.g., *It is raining.* Just as often, however, they obscure or deemphasize the point of a sentence. In the following examples the first two use impersonal constructions effectively to move the main ideas to emphatic positions. In the third example, the impersonal construction only delays the main idea, pushing it into an unemphatic position.

An Effective Impersonal Construction
   Aside from the steps the country can take to protect water from contamination, *there are ways* to protect the public from the toxic effects of contaminants already in water. No contaminants appear to have an irreversible effect.
                    (Peter Rogers, "The Future of Water," *The Atlantic*
                    July 1983, emphasis added)

Two Effective Impersonal Constructions
   It is obvious that more is needed in education than the survival of the present system: the recruitment and training of a higher-caliber teacher, the achievement of excellence in the basic subjects, the expansion of the curriculum to develop neglected human capacities. And *it is ironic* that the public has suffered from amnesia on the subject of schooling just as computers are coming on-line that could help teachers impart basic knowledge and basic skills at a fraction of the time now required and in the individualized manner that would

please critics of lockstep education. But nothing is possible without the attention and concern of the public.

(George Leonard, "Car Pool; A Story of Public Education in the Eighties," *Esquire* May 1983, emphasis added)

An Ineffective Impersonal Construction
There is some land that is put aside every year but not nearly enough to equal the amount that is destroyed by us every time we put up a new subdivision or shopping center.

Revision
Some land is put aside every year but not nearly enough to equal the amount destroyed every time a new subdivision or shopping center goes up.

EXERCISES

1. The deadwood in the following sentences has been identified. Cut and revise.

a. *Wordiness:* The position of secretary falls more in the category of assistant than typist.

b. *Wordiness:* Professor Schwartz said leaflets would be sent to all union members in the near future to get more union involvement going.

c. *Wordiness:* The most scenic tour through Mammoth Cave is a strenuous four mile walk over a period of four hours. This tour includes a lunch stop in the Snowball Room and ends up at Frozen Niagra.

d. *Relative pronouns:* In front of us we had our duffel bags which were jam-packed with every piece of gear that we would need for the next twelve months.

e. *Transitions:* Dr. Thimble impressed the fact that young Joseph was "different" upon Joseph himself and his playmates.

f. *Intensifiers:* My English classes in grammar and high school were totally adequate for my needs.

g. *Intensifiers and qualifiers:* My growing love of opera really seems to be involuntary. A recent incident comes to mind that will certainly explain and dramatize this very great passion of mine.

h. *Redundancies:* The reason why the final chapter in American hijackings was finally written is because the federal government, combined together with local airport authorities, required stiffer passenger screening procedures.

i. *Redundancies:* In my opinion, I think capital crimes are often committed by people caught up in a state of extreme passion, confused by a crisis situation of some sort, or crazed by an insane fit.

j. *Passive voice:* Mr. Conklin's life was organized in a way that emphasized the simple pleasures.

k. *Passive voice:* When Helen redecorated her house, she had walls moved, rebuilt and repainted, new wall paper hung, and the woodwork stripped and revarnished. She did not stop until perfection was achieved.

l. *Impersonal constructions:* There is a definite need for private enterprise to become more involved and actively support non-profit community organizations. There are, of course, hundreds of ways in which these corporations can practice this social responsibility.

m. *Impersonal constructions:* Although our pontoon boat was fun to putt-putt around on, at times it was necessary to have a fast boat.

2. Identify the species of deadwood in each of the following, then cut and revise.

a. I somehow had the feeling that this committee was truly going to have an insurmountable problem.

b. In the short story "The Killers," I think the author Ernest Hemingway is trying to make a comparison between the two major characters, Ole Andreson and Nick Adams. Hemingway is trying to tell us that both men are running away from their problems.

c. The damage to the radiator produced an impairment in the function of the cooling system.

d. In the modern age of today, people go to hypnotists for help in the areas of quitting smoking, losing weight, and for other various health reasons.

e. Old Bilko has an inability to conform to society. His biggest problem stems from the fact that he does not realize what others do not want him to do.

f. Every once in a while, you meet a person who seems to be totally perfect, a person who has the right kind of wit, charm, intelligence, and looks— the totally adorable person.

g. Bob, the man whom I love, and I met when we were a very young age; we were lucky because of the fact that we had very few biased opinions about love.

h. The snow-capped mountains are an utterly fantastic work of art. Each peak has its own truly beautiful features of glistening snow and fresh-water streams rushing swiftly down the mountainsides in a way that can never, ever be duplicated by those scenes on travel posters.

i. When I reflect back on it, I must confess a factual truth: my success was caused more by dumb luck than any merit or skill.

j. Women think that men just want to stay single and fool around, but many men want to get married. They usually say no because of the fear of the fact that sometime in the future to come they may not be able to provide emotionally and materially for their families' well-being.

k. I would like to highlight the fact that my transition from a high school to college atmosphere was a very difficult process. Nevertheless, however, I passed the test successfully.

l. Reentry to the business world after being a housewife for eighteen years was really like entering the mysterious, awesome world of the unknown. Nerves frazzled, confidence dwindling down to an all-time low, and filled with feelings of fear, I nevertheless decided I had to give it a try.

m. This room is square in size and not too large, about sixteen by sixteen. There is a hanging chandelier hanging over the table and one window which faces to the east, through which the morning sun streams quite brightly.

n. In this pleasant garden is seen an amiable-looking old man dressed in a tattered tuxedo, seated under a linden tree.

3. Choose one page from a recent writing you have done. Reread it and bracket whatever deadwood you find. Cut and rewrite. Turn in the original with your revision.

❧ JARGON OF THE GOBBLEDYGOOK VARIETY, A SPECIAL SPECIES OF DEADWOOD

Jargon is the specialized language of a craft, profession, or discipline. By itself and in appropriate contexts, it is unobjectionable; it enables the members of a group to talk or write to one another directly, economically, and clearly. For example, words like *economy, passive voice, verb, thesis,* even *jargon* itself are part of the writer's jargon that enables us to talk intelligently about what we read and write. Here, in a second example, is a paragraph of computer jargon:

> The BLOAD command returns the contents of a Binary file to your Apple II's memory. BLOAD does *not* erase a BASIC program in memory, unless the data is BLOADed into the particular portion of memory containing your program. The syntax is BLOAD f [,Aa] [,Ss] [,Dd] [,Vv] where the S, D, and V parameters are as usual.
>
> (Apple Computer, Inc., *The DOS Manual* [Cupertino, CA: Apple Computer, 1980, 1981])

Now if that made no sense to you, well, it needn't make sense unless you're running a computer. That's the nature of jargon: insiders understand and use it; outsiders don't understand it and don't need to use it. Whenever human beings work together for very long at a complex task, jargon springs up to help them handle the work.

This special language causes trouble only when it is taken out of its proper context and loses its "shoptalk" function. Then it becomes a victim of its own features. But what seems to be a problem of language is, in reality, a problem of persona. Writers or speakers find themselves in situations that require distance between themselves and their audience, or they feel a need to elevate themselves and sound impressive. Perhaps they do not know how to shape a persona for a particular occasion, all those strategies for adjusting distance and attitude that you studied in Chapter 2. What they do know is some jargon, generally scientific and technical jargon, and they know, too, that it sounds faintly mysterious, intelligent, and impressive. And so they combine their pinch of jargon with an even smaller amount of linguistic savvy to try to solve their persona problem.

What results is not jargon anymore but a bloated, pompous, barely communicative, frustrating language called *gobbledygook,* a term given it by Texas Congressman Maury Maverick. In gobbledygook, deadwood litters the whole forest, the writing borne down by circumlocutions, swollen words, needless qualifiers, passive and impersonal constructions.

Prior to the Phase II Workshop, which is presently being formulated under the auspices of the TAD/CHUFA, there will be a series of various activities designed to acquire for the college community the most significant data obtainable regarding trends developing outside the immediate academic environment. For example, an attempt will be made to synthesize pertinent information on instructional computing from other educational environments, from business and industry sources, and from manufacturers and vendors of software and hardware. After these various activities have been scheduled, an extensive planning workshop will be convened very early during the Fall semester, hopefully prior to September 1. The assumption would be that by that time as many faculty and staff as possible would have had access to the available information regarding this vital area of instructional resources.

But the deadwood in gobbledygook such as this is not the only impediment to a reader's understanding.

- *Acronyms.* Acronyms are words formed from the first letters of a name, e.g., *FBI, CIA.* They should simplify meaning, but in gobbledygook they only obscure it: *Acdac, JUAD, Comcinpac, IJR, TAD/CHUFA.*
- *Few verbs but forms of* to be *and the passive voice.* These verbs slow sentences down, making them less vivid and emphatic: "There *is* no question that instructional computing will *be* vital to teaching in the future. The ultimate goal of this planning process *is* the design of a plan for the coordination of instructional computing that will allow us to take optimal advantage of our available resources—human, fiscal, and material. Therefore, everyone *is encouraged to be* at one of the two sessions that *are scheduled* to review what *is* now available and what *is* in the planning stage."
- *Excessive use of prepositional phrases.* Pieced together prepositional phrases string out sentences to obscure lengths, as the second sentence does in the preceding example: "The ultimate goal *of this planning process* will be the design *of a plan for the coordination of instructional computing* that will allow us to take optimal advantage *of our available resources*—human, fiscal, and material."
- *Nominals, especially* -tion *words.* Nominals are verbs turned into nouns; they, too, slow a sentence down: *conception, comprehension, adaptation, introversion, supportive, indicative, obtainable, information, instruction, assumption, coordination.*
- *Strings of nouns.* Noun strings link nouns into ambiguous phrases that obscure the subject of a passage: *student-faculty relationships, identifiable decision-making process, free-agent reentry draft, confrontation/crisis situation intervention center, demand analysis, research operations feedback report, tax schedule rate chart.*
- *Abstractions of all kinds.* Abstractions, especially words with a scientific ring, can impede clarity: *parameters, interface, input, throughput, meaningful associates, significant other, confrontation situation, counterproductive, ontological, gestalt, externalizing internals, nonverbal verbalizing.*

- *Latinate or "big" words for humble ideas.* Latin-derived and inflated words also interfere with meaning: *in-depth discussion, cognizant, facilitate, cognitive, intermodalist, dedomicile, educator, terminus, indices, encapsulate, appears to be suggestive of the fact that, in close proximity, has the capability of, give consideration to.*
- *Words transformed by derivational suffixes (-ize, -tion, -ate).* In gobbledygook, these transformations almost always exist to swell sentences to an impressive size when writers should be trying to trim them to economical directness: *maximize, minimize, verbalize, salarywise, prioritize, conferencing, commentate, actualize.*
- *Euphemisms or weasel words.* Euphemisms obscure the truth and therefore the meaning: *terminate* for *fire, expire* for *die, protective reaction* for *attack, the final solution* for *genocide, terminate with extreme prejudice* and *pacification of the enemy infrastructure* for *kill, substandard housing* for *slum, dentures* for *false teeth, preowned* for *used, senior citizens* for *old people, liberate* for *conquer, disadvantaged* or *underprivileged* for *poor, limbs* for *legs.*

THE WIZARD OF ID

Used by permission of Johnny Hart and News America Syndicate.

One or two of these features, perhaps even three or four, in a piece of writing do not automatically produce gobbledygook. Nothing is intrinsically wrong with any of these features; we wouldn't have them in our language if we didn't need them. But when you find several together and find them repeatedly, be suspicious. The writer's aim may be more to impress than communicate, the former aim probably defeating the latter. You would think the solution for such gobbledygook would be simple enough: public scorn for it wherever it appears, tireless praise for clarity by those who cherish clarity, and an attempt by writers who know better always to write economically, simply, appropriately, and directly. But the solution is neither this simple nor dramatic.

For one thing, as I suggested at the beginning of Chapter 9, writing cannot always be simple or direct, especially writing for business, political, or technical purposes. This writing often requires some of the features of gobbledygook, the passive voice, for example, or circumlocutions, abstractions, big words, and acronyms. The problem here is to avoid slipping over that fine line dividing appropriately complex writing from bombast. For another thing, much as we laugh at the most outrageous examples of it, there is something impressive about gobbledygook, just as many of us now admire those gigantic be-chromed and be-finned automobiles from the late 1950s. Big words *are* impressive, suggesting intelligence and learning even when there may not be much of either. Difficult writing strokes its audience, assuring them that since they are members of the audience they are "insiders," separate from the hoi polloi outside, privy to important ideas and masters of a special language.

Take, for example, the research done in 1981 at the University of Chicago.[2] Pairs of special essays were distributed among other essays to groups of readers. The content of the paired essays was the same; only the language and sentence style were different. One essay in each pair was written clearly, simply, and directly, the other with long words and complex sentences. Readers were asked to rate batches of essays that included these pairs, distributed far enough apart so that their similarities would not be noticed. With dismaying frequency, readers rated the inflated essays as better written and more intelligently thought out than the simply written essays. And here's the shocker: these readers were English teachers!

Once again: The problem of gobbledygook is more than a problem of language. As with most really important language problems, the issues are social, psychological, even ethical. How should we write when we know that clear, direct writing may be easier to read and remember but that inflated writing may be—on first reading, at least—more impressive? The answer lies in our respect for our readers and an understanding of their needs and expectations. Clarity and directness will communicate with them. If we must also impress them, speak tactfully, or shade our meaning, there are ways other than gobbledygook, namely, our grasp of our subject, our precision and thoroughness, the inventiveness of our communications strategy, and the grace of our sentences.

EXERCISES

The first three exercises ask you to do what you would never do in the real world, become a Jargonaut and write gobbledygook. The psychological principle is sound: knowing what gobbledygook is, how it is produced, and how it works, you will be less likely to let it infect your writing. You will need to use a dictionary and a thesaurus to find appropriately inflated synonyms.

1. Following are fifteen terms. Choose three and, using the symptoms for gobbledygook listed previously, translate these common terms into gobbledygook words and phrases. In the hands of a true Jargonaut, for example, a homely word like

jogging becomes *metronomic oscillation of the pedal extremities*. Use three words where one would do, an unfamiliar Latinate word where a familiar Anglo-Saxon word does just fine, four or five syllables where once there were one or two.

beer	student	fighting
freedom	teacher	dying
love	city	parents
friendship	talking	failure
home	happiness	success

2. Following are five familiar proverbs. Choose two and rewrite them into gobbledygook. Follow the suggestions given in Exercise 1.

a. A penny saved is a penny earned.
b. Waste not, want not.
c. A stitch in time saves nine.
d. A bird in the hand is worth two in the bush.
e. Birds of a feather flock together.

3. Imagine you are a Jargonaut in each of the following situations. How would you express yourself? Choose one scenario and a write a paragraph in the best—that is, worst—gobbledygook style.

a. You are proposing marriage.
b. You are asking a service station attendant to fill 'er up, check the oil, and clean the windshield.
c. You want to order a hamburger, fries, and a cola—to go.
d. You are a parent telling your child to clean his or her room.
e. You are a boss telling a lazy, incompetent employee he's fired.
f. You are the President of the United States declaring World War III.
g. You must write a job announcement for a chicken-plucker at the packing plant where you are the personnel manager.
h. You are a hobo writing your resumé before applying for the presidency of General Motors.
i. You are God giving the Ten Commandments to Moses.
j. You are a legislator introducing a law that pedestrians must walk only on the shady side of the street.

4. Dangerous announcements: This exercise asks you not to parody gobbledygook but to write seriously in hypothetical situations that may require you to adopt some of its features to be tactful yet complete or to create the proper persona. Choose one.

a. You are the personnel manager, chief supervisor, or boss at the company where you work. You must write a letter to a long-time friend and employee telling him he is being fired for incompetence.
b. You have just been elected president of your college dormitory's governing council. Your first item of business is the number of complaints regarding noisy parties, other late night disturbances, even destruction of school property that the council has received from college administrators. Write

an announcement to your fellow students—your equals in age, social standing, and academic rank—telling them that they must improve their behavior or face disciplinary action. Your dormitory is large, and not all of its residents know you well. Complicating matters, you are required to send a copy of this announcement to the dean of students.

c. You are the president of your college. You must write a letter to the student body warning them to stay away from the nightclub district in the local community. The clubs are wonderful places, filled every night with interesting people to meet and things to do. It is *the* place to go for fun and excitement, but several students have been mugged recently, and one was murdered. You are aware, however, that if you simply forbid students from going to this district, it will seem that much more enticing and exciting.

d. Write a paragraph proposing some change at your place of employment, a change that would make your work more efficient, comfortable, or simple. Address your paragraph to the authorities responsible for making this change. Use whatever jargon is appropriate but avoid gobbledygook.

5. Choose a recent writing you have done and reread it, looking for those characteristics of gobbledygook listed on pages 211–212. Bracket any examples you find; then see whether you can rewrite those sentences, eliminating the gobbledygook. Make sure your revisions create the appropriate persona—that is, the right distance and attitude—for the messages they contain. Turn in your original with your revisions.

PRECISION

Clear sentences use words that mean exactly what the writer intends. Sometimes, however, writers intend a word to mean one thing although in reality it means another. This frequently happens when writers are working with new subjects or trying to find a vocabulary suitable to a particular audience or occasion. The best defense against such inadvertent obscurity is to use familiar, not necessarily little, words whenever possible. With some experimentation and a good thesaurus, you can almost always find words you and your readers know well that are suitable to the occasion. This advice does not mean that a large vocabulary is unimportant. It is, and you should read widely to acquire it. But almost always the well-stocked vocabulary contains a larger store of familiar than unfamiliar words, familiar words right for writers, their readers, and almost every occasion.

Semantic Siblings

An especially troublesome problem of "right" words is semantic siblings, words related to one another by spelling, sound, or meaning, and therefore often confused.[3] Most writers are familiar with the most common of these siblings: *lie* and *lay*; *sit* and *set*; *to*, *too*, and *two*; *their* and *they're*; *site*, *cite*, and *site*; *affect* and *effect*; *threw* and *through*; *accept* and *except*. But

B.C.

Used by permission of Johnny Hart and News America Syndicate.

there are many, many others; to write clearly you must master the differences between them. Fail to recognize these differences and you will end up writing

> William has performed meretriciously for this corporation

when what you meant to write is that he has performed *meritoriously*. Don't be surprised if William never speaks to you again. After all, you've just said he is vulgar, tawdry, and insincere, for that is what *meretricious* means.

Such misuse of words is known as a *malapropism*, after Mrs. Malaprop, a character in Richard Sheridan's eighteenth-century comedy *The Rivals*, who habitually confused her words to the delight of her audience. For example, Mrs. Malaprop urges another character in the play to "promise to forget this fellow—to illiterate [obliterate] him quite from [her] memory." More recent audiences have been entertained by Archie Bunker's Bunkerisms on the television show *All in the Family*.

> I come home and tell you one o' the great antidotes [anecdotes] of all times, an item of real human interest, and you sit there like you're in a comma [coma].

> "Sorry" ain't gonna clench [quench] my thirst.

> How'd I know you had extensions to [intentions of] bein' an egghead?

> Let's take a look here and see what new subversion you got fermentin' [fomenting] here.[4]

Unidiomatic Expressions

A second problem of precision is unidiomatic expression. An idiom is an expression in a language that may not always make complete grammatical or logical sense but is never misunderstood by a native user. We say, *When you get to New York, be sure to look Lucille up, drop by, and say "Hi."* Native English speakers are never in doubt about how to *look up* or *drop by*. Similarly, certain words fall naturally into some contexts and not others, even though they may be logically and grammatically "right" in both contexts. Their positions are idiomatic. An unidiomatic expression, then, is not so much illogical as unexpected. Being unexpected, it is distracting. It draws attention to itself, slows reading time, and shifts attention from the point of the sentence.

Example
    A man by the name of John Wayne Gacy has been convicted of murdering over thirty young men and lodging them in various places beneath his home.

Used unidiomatically here, *lodging* makes this mass-murderer's house seem like a motel instead of the grisly charnal house it was. *Burying* is the familiar, obvious, and right choice. Unidiomatic expressions often suggest that writers lack knowledge, taste, or skill, although in fact they may only have produced a final draft without revising carefully enough. Once more the curious irony of good writing: freshness, simplicity, directness, and naturalness of language are almost always the products *not* of spontaneous expression but of careful revision. Give yourself the time to make your writing right.

EXERCISES

1. Correct the semantic siblings and unidiomatic expressions in the following sentences.

  a. It is hard for people to except kindness from strangers who behave erotically, especially when these perspective friends try to play the dominate roll.
  b. Religion was a bountiful commodity in Stacy's home, especially because her grandfather was religious beyond the point of sanity.
  c. Nick, not coherent to what was being realistically said to him, turned and sighed wispily, "All I want is a futuristic job, just something to give me a splattering of happiness."
  d. When R. J. Bowman thought of explaining his emotions, his need for love and understanding, he hesitated the intention, resisting to express his true feelings.
  e. Gamblers don't seem to care about the time; standing around the blackjack table dripping ringlets of perspiration, they're libel to be more concerned with some allusive person called "Lady Luck" then with the time of the night.
  f. The turning point in the movie was a wake-up realization that her daughter needed her help.
  g. He's like an angel. He visits the sick and affirmed, baring the pain along with the inflected. He even emphathizes with those in morning for ones who have past away.
  h. Another problem I foresee is the uncertain stability of keeping my job.
  i. Of coarse, that is exactly the affect capitol punishment is supposed to have. Potentially deviate individuals would imply that crime does not pay and altar their behavior quicker then you can say "Pull the switch!"
  j. But what happens if a parent achieves a very great age and becomes senile, too? This illness faces the children with a serious problem.

2. Following is a list of semantic siblings. Choose ten pairs and write a sentence for each pair that uses the siblings correctly. Example: *to, too, two: It was too late to go to two movies.*

ability/capacity	abjure/adjure	accelerate/exhilarate
accident/mishap	adapt/adept/adopt	adverse/averse
affect/effect	allusion/reference	apt/liable/likely
arbitrate/mediate	assume/presume	avaricious/voracious
avenge/revenge	between/among	blatant/flagrant
bow/bough	callus/callous	childish/childlike
closure/cloture	contagious/infectious	continual/continuous
convince/persuade	cord/chord	council/counsel
deadly/deathly	delusion/illusion	denote/connote
disinterested/uninterested	deprecate/depreciate	farther/further
fatal/fateful	fewer/less	flail/flay
flaunt/flout	fortuitous/fortunate	gambol/gamble
gantlet/gauntlet/gamut	grate/great	hail/hale
healthy/healthful	immured/inured	imply/infer
incredible/incredulous	lay/lie	mean/median/average
nauseous/nauseate	oral/verbal	peak/pique
practically/virtually	precipitate/precipitous	principle/principal
presumptive/presumptuous	prophesy/prophecy	purposely/purposefully
rack/wrack	raise/rise/raze	ravish/ravage
repulse/repel	seasonable/seasonal	sensuous/sensual
set/sit	tortuous/torturous	turbid/turgid
venal/venial		

3. Identify the deadwood, gobbledygook, semantic siblings, and unidiomatic expressions in the following and then rewrite.

a. It is, indeed, possible to drive through Boston, but one must be totally aware of the hazards involved. The streets are truly a menace, frighteningly narrow and congested. A map is absolutely essential, as you may have probably guessed.

b. Each building was in its original condition, standing just as it was the very first day it was built, which was over 100 years ago.

c. I had been insured that Norman was disinterested in both Gloria and Shirley, but last night I saw Shirley and him on a bus. When he cited her, he turned to her and cooed in a bemused voice, "Set over here with me, my pet."

d. Antigone is driven by her instincts and emotions while King Creon acts on the basis of principle and a reasoned analysis of each situation.

e. Mervin and Ervin were, it seems, already pretty drunk, and I wondered what might happen to the nauseous pair as the day wore on.

f. Our guide explained that because she was old, she worked less and less days each month in the fields. But she compensated for the amount of hours she spent in her hut by weaving baskets. She was very adapt at this even though she had a nervous tinge in her shoulder.

g. There are two significant causes responsible for the sharp increase in ruthless crime. The first reason for these dire emergency situations is the same reason that all crimes are on the rise, the movement toward a dehumanization of the individual throughout our culture. The recent Hearst kidnapping experience was a good example of this dehumanization.

h. Charlie is my brother, whom I live with, and who works as a plumber. He has his own truck, which is really a large van, and does all his work with the tools, equipment, and books which he keeps there.

i. There is so much advertising around us that children are growing up to believe that everything can be bought. There is nothing that will prevent this advertising, however, short of not buying the product.

j. The light infiltrates down into my room, revealing fragments of my past and present life.

k. Isaac says that due to the fact of his involvement with Tracy, she will not be able to experience much of life. After all, he is so much older than she. Needless to say, these weren't his real reasons for trying to break up with her. In actuality he is trying to avoid a commitment and using his age as an excuse.

l. As I tugged the ripcord and the parachute opened, I turned and the view of the mountains became clearly visible. The anxious feelings I felt before the jump disappeared, and now the only feelings felt were of peace and solitude.

m. The brotherhood he once felt for his fellowman was lost, and he developed an attitude of not wanting to get involved with anyone else's troubles.

n. As you may have guessed, young Smelt's biggest fault falls within the realm of telling the truth.

o. According to statistics, there is a new baby born in the United States every three minutes.

WRITING PROJECTS

Topics

1. Moral discourse: Write a three- to five-page essay in response to one of the following moral or ethical questions. Write to the members of your composition class.

a. When, if ever, is it permissible to lie, cheat, or steal?

b. Under what circumstances should an observer *not* report illegalities to the proper authorities?

c. Over what areas of human life should governments exercise no control?

d. To what extent are we obligated to be our brother's keeper? Who besides our families are we responsible for and in what ways: our friends, our fellow citizens, our fellow human beings?

e. When, if ever, is media censorship justified? Why or why not?

Develop your subject with definitions, examples, anecdotes, and explanations. Be as specific as possible. Consider the consequences of your recommendations. To deepen your understanding of the issues involved you may want to do some preliminary reading or interview parents, churchpeople, politicians, teachers, or professionals in the social sciences. Consider the order of ideas in your thesis for a possible organizing pattern or the order of importance, "What is it?" or problem/solution patterns.

2. The past two decades have been a period of great social change in America. Part of that process has involved a reappraisal of civic virtues, those values that in the past formed the social glue binding us into communities: honesty, duty, responsibility, compassion, respect, politeness, honor, thrift, order, humility, and industriousness. Continue the process of reappraisal by writing a three- to five-page essay on one of these "virtues" or some other social value not listed here. Explore what it used to mean in America by interviewing people older than you. Ask them to define this virtue and state its importance then and now. Then talk to your contemporaries. What do they have to say about the meaning of the virtue and its current importance? Ask your interview subjects for examples and anecdotes to illustrate their observations. If the virtue has changed its meaning or value, can you explain why? Consider how it might need to be redefined to be useful to contemporary life or whether, in fact, it is any longer necessary to the maintenance of a healthy community. Write to the members of your composition class. Consider organizing your essay according to a comparison/contrast or "What is it?" pattern.

3. One of the truisms of contemporary life holds that television is the great educator and communicator, more powerful than other media. Supposedly it tells the young, who do most of the watching, more about life than they get from any other source: the schools, the churches, their peers, other media, even their parents. If this is true, then television bears *serious* watching to discover just what it is teaching. Do that. Pick a particular kind of program: the sitcom, cop shows, adventure shows, the soaps, children's shows, the news, and so on. Watch several shows within your chosen category and take notes about what they say of human life. What values are celebrated or condemned? Who succeeds or fails? How? What goals are celebrated or condemned? What life-styles? What do these shows say about city, suburban, or country life? What do they say about religion, education, patriotism, sex, love, marriage, civic-mindedness? Write a three- to five-page essay in which you present your findings to your composition class, explain these findings, and draw any conclusions about television in general that seem appropriate. Consider organizing your essay according to one of the order-of-importance, pro/con, descriptive analysis, or "What is it?" patterns.

4. Write a three- to five-page essay defending what you understand to be the theme or thesis in a recent reading you have done. Explain how details, organization, point of view, and mood support your contentions. Consider organizing your essay according to the order of ideas in your thesis or according to one of the order-of-importance or "What is it?" patterns (see Chapter 6, pages 118–119, 127).

THE WRITING PROCESS

1. Writing-in-progress.
   a. *Exploring:* Free association and freewriting.
   b. *Developing:* Discover all you have to say about your subject. Use whatever methods and strategies seem appropriate.
      i. Write a thematic tag tree (see pages 159–160).

       ii. Write a transition proposition, two or more assertions about your subject linked by a transition (see pages 168–169).
    c. *Planning a communications strategy:* Decide on a role, persona (distance and attitude), and thesis *(My point is that . . . What I mean to say is that . . .).*
    d. *Organizing.*
       i. Organize your ideas in a clear, predictable, coherent pattern. Use whatever outlining and organizing strategies work for you (see pages 128–132).
       ii. Devise an introductory strategy to capture your audience's attention and focus their interest (see pages 137–141).
    e. *Revising:* Reconsider your ideas and communications strategy; create frictions in your thinking (see pages 55–56).

2. Writing.
    a. Write the preliminary draft of your project. Write freely, don't stop except to reread, give yourself room to revise.
    b. Whenever possible, write one main idea per sentence; write agent-action sentences; keep the parts short; keep related words together; write positive statements (see pages 183–187).
    ⟶**c.** *New in this chapter:* Whenever possible, use words familiar to both you and your audience.

3. Rewriting.
    a. Be a zoom lens as you revise; add, delete, substitute, and rearrange.
    b. Ask two questions of troublesome sentences.
       i. What's happening here?
       ii. What goes with what? (See pages 189–196).
    c. Write "old-new" sentences; begin rereading from the beginning of paragraphs; reread at a natural pace, listening for unnecessary repetitions and transitions (see pages 175–177).
    ⟶**d.** *New in this chapter:* Bracket [ ] deadwood of all kinds, reconsider, and then cut.
    e. Copyedit for mechanical errors, recopy, and proofread.

4. Self-evaluation.
    a. What is your intention in this writing?
    b. What is your thesis? What are your thematic tags?
    c. What did you do to help your readers read your writing? Will any parts be hard to follow? If so, why? What would make them more readable?
    d. What words or phrases will be most memorable in this writing? What will your readers like best about it?
    e. Did you try anything here that you hadn't tried before?
    f. What one change would most improve this writing?

END NOTES

1. William Zinsser, *Writing with a Word Processor* (New York: Harper, 1983).
2. Rosemary L. Hake and Joseph M. Williams, "Style and Its Consequences: Do as I Do, Not as I Say," *College English* 43 (Sept. 1981): 433–51.

3. For the term "semantic siblings" I am indebted to John Simon, "Sibling Rivalry," *Esquire* 15 Aug. 1978.

4. Mrs. Malaprop's and Archie Bunker's malapropisms were collected by Alfred F. Rosa and Paul A. Eschholz, "Bunkerisms: Archie Bunker's Suppository Remarks," *Journal of Popular Culture* 6 (Winter, 1972): 271–78.

PART IV

WRITING FOR STYLE

Chapter 11

Interest:
"It Don't Mean A Thing
If It Ain't Got That Swing"

The title of this chapter comes from the song of the same name by the great jazz composer and bandleader Duke Ellington. What it seems to say is that without rhythm and melody, lyrics make rather pale poetry, as anyone knows who has ever tried to read a song sheet without knowing the music. The message of a song is nothing by itself. And the same is true of the writing we do: "It don't mean a thing if it ain't got that swing." No matter how sound its ideas or thorough its development, if it doesn't make music of one kind or another, it will seldom mean much or be very satisfying, either to us or our readers. Consider, for example, this excerpt from an article that appeared in *Newsweek*, a magazine devoted above all else to making meaning:

> Caesar was right. Thin people need watching. I've been watching them for most of my adult life, and I don't like what I see. When these narrow fellows spring at me, I quiver to my toes. Thin people come in all personalities, most of them menacing. You've got your "together" thin person, your mechanical thin person, your condescending thin person, your tsk-tsk thin person, your efficiency-expert thin person. All of them are dangerous.
>
> In the first place, thin people aren't fun. They don't know how to goof off, at least in the best, fat sense of the word. They've always got to be adoing. Give them a coffee break, and they'll jog around the block. Supply them with a quiet evening at home, and they'll fix the screen door and lick S&H green

stamps. They say things like "there aren't enough hours in the day." Fat people never say that. Fat people think the day is too damn long already.

Thin people make me tired. They've got speedy little metabolisms that cause them to bustle briskly. They're forever rubbing their bony hands together and eyeing new problems to "tackle." I like to surround myself with sluggish, inert, easygoing fat people, the kind who believe that if you clean it up today, it'll just get dirty again tomorrow.

(Suzanne Britt Jordan, "That Lean and Hungry Look," *Newsweek* 9 Oct. 1978)

The meaning of the piece is clear enough: skinny people are unpleasant busybodies and fat people, pleasant, relaxed, and accepting souls. By itself, however, this message is next to nothing, hardly worth listening to and certainly not worth publication in a national magazine. But of course that's not the point; the message in this case doesn't mean a thing without its "swing," without, that is, the music of its style. Style is the point—and pleasure, the pleasure it gave in the writing and the pleasure it gives in the reading. The writer doesn't want to communicate with us, she wants to play, with stereotypes, with language, and with us her readers.

And how she does play! She opens with an allusion to Shakespeare's *Julius Caesar* that inflates her subject to mock-serious proportions:

Yond Cassius has a lean and hungry look;
He thinks too much: such men are dangerous.

She exaggerates the stereotypes of skinny and fat people until they become caricatures. She writes in a tone by turns deadly serious, paranoid, mocking, and praising. She hints at rhymes (*narrow fellows*), repeats sounds (*bustle briskly . . . rubbing . . . bony hands*), and manipulates her sentences so they create rhythms exactly appropriate to her mood of mock protest. The supposed message of the piece dissolves in, is absorbed by, and finally becomes the play itself. The *real* message is a delighted and delightful glorying in the joys of being fat. In contrast to many of us, this writer has retained that childhood joy in the look, sound, and feel of language. Remember when you used to talk to yourself, making up funny words and names, singing silly rhymes? She hasn't forgotten, and for that reason her writing is more interesting and more enjoyable to read. If you can learn to play with language, or remember how, your writing will be better, too.

Now you may be thinking, "Wait just a minute. What you're saying has nothing to do with me. I don't do this kind of 'stylish' writing. I'm a business [or psychology, or education, or accounting, or engineering] major. All I write now in college are serious reports, essays, exercises, and exams. And when I graduate, if I have to write it will be serious letters, memos, and more reports. Information is what is called for and what I give: facts and figures. What counts are clarity, brevity, and simplicity. Writing that swings? Childlike playfulness? You've got to be kidding." To those who think this way I say, consider the most serious, fact-oriented writing you can, writing that exists to inform and nothing more, writing dry as dust: the scholarly article published in a professional journal. Can you imagine anything less "stylish"? Here is the opening to a research study first published in *The Journal of Abnormal and Social Psychology:*

> Obedience is as basic an element in the structure of social life as one can point to. Some system of authority is a requirement of all communal living, and it is only the man dwelling in isolation who is not forced to respond, through defiance or submission, to the commands of others. Obedience, as a determinant of behavior, is of particular relevance to our time. It has been reliably established that from 1933–45 millions of innocent persons were systematically slaughtered on command. Gas chambers were built, death camps were guarded, daily quotas of corpses were produced with the same efficiency as the manufacture of appliances. These inhuman policies may have originated in the mind of a single person, but they could only be carried out on a massive scale if a very large number of persons obeyed orders.
>
> (Stanley Milgram, "A Behavioral Study of Obedience," 1963)

If you have read this paragraph with care, one thing should be clear: it is as stylish and musical in its own serious way as the preceding playful passage. Notice how the subject of the paragraph is repeated in measured and solemn precision from beginning to end (*obedience, obedience, obeyed orders*) and how that repetition emphasizes the subject. Notice how the varied sentence length and structure create rhythms that lead directly to the points the writer wants to make: an average length complex sentence that announces the subject, a compound/complex sentence that explains it, a short simple sentence that asserts the importance of obedience, and so on, an emphatic rise and fall of words and ideas. Notice that this writer, like the first, uses allusion, this time to the Nazi holocaust, to dramatize his subject and set the tone for his report. And notice that he repeats sounds (*systematically slaughtered, quotas of corpses*) and how, by connecting efficiency and murder, he intensifies our sense of the terrible consequences of thoughtless obedience.

Notice, finally, how the sentence about the gas chambers is shaped to imitate what it describes: *Gas chambers were built, death camps were guarded, daily quotas of corpses were produced. . . .* The clauses crank along, one after another, like the assembly line implied by the analogy that closes the sentence. They capture by look and by sound the numbed and routinized horror of corpses "manufactured" like refrigerators. This writer aims to do more than tell us that obedience is an important subject for contemporary scrutiny; he aims to make us *feel* that importance and to weight thereby the implications of the study that follows. All of this is his meaning, much more than flat statement of fact can say. And the stylishness of the passage helps to make that meaning. Even in serious, factual writing, then, "It don't mean a thing if it ain't got that swing."

For five chapters I've been celebrating the virtues of readability—predictability, coherence, and clarity. But important though it is, readability alone is almost never enough. Even in our most mundane writing we aim for more, to express our personalities and feelings, to command respect, to satisfy ourselves, even, if we have learned how, to please ourselves. Nor is mere readability enough for our readers. They must not only be able to read our writing; they must *want* to read it. Predictability, coherence, and clarity are no virtues if they lead only to obviousness, monotony, and inattention.

In a practical sense, then, this chapter and the following are about ways to promote reader interest. They will add to the "journalistic" skills you acquired in the preceding two chapters, skills that help readers grasp your message at once. In an impractical sense, however, Chapters 11 and 12 are about how to make music in your writing, how to make it a pleasure to do and a pleasure to read. Some ways of making music you already know. You know how a clear, vivid persona gives writing warmth and humanity and how a sense of audience draws readers into a subject. You know as well how to develop a subject in interesting and appropriate ways and how to use words that are vividly concrete, connotative, and figurative. In these chapters you will learn about repetition and variety, how writers manipulate sounds, words, sentences, and point of view to create a style that is rhythmic, emphatic, and interesting to read.

REPETITION

Repetition is the beat in the music of our writing. Drumbeat staccato in one passage, rolling surflike cadence in another—its patterns surprise readers by leveling out for a brief space the gentle rise and fall that predominates in most sentences. By this more insistent rhythm, it draws attention to an idea, emphasizes it, and connects it to related ideas in an undercurrent of sound and feeling. We can repeat sounds, words, and grammatical patterns.

Repeating Sounds

Alliteration   It may seem strange to talk about sound in writing meant to be read silently; nevertheless it is true that we listen with an auditory imagination to what we read and hear the sound of a silent sentence in our "inner" ear. What strikes that ear with greatest force is alliteration, the repetition of consonant sounds, usually at the beginning of words. That is what you heard earlier when you read Suzanne Britt Jordan's *bustle briskly*

. . . rubbing . . . bony hands. The effect of those repeated *b* sounds is to pull the paired words that much closer together and play one word off against the other. Hearing the alliteration, we see the meaning of each phrase more clearly. Even bolder—and funnier—is the alliteration later in her essay. Listen:

> Thin people are downers. They like math and morality and reasoned evaluation of the limitations of human beings. They have their skinny little acts together. They expound, prognose, probe, and prick.
>
> Fat people are convivial. They will like you even if you're irregular and have acne. They will come up with a good reason why you never wrote the great American novel. They will cry in your beer with you. They will put your name in the pot. They will let you off the hook. Fat people will gab, giggle, guffaw, gallumph, gyrate and gossip. They are generous, giving and gallant. They are gluttonous, goodly and great.

The *m*'s and *p*'s in the first paragraph bring skinny people to life, driven, obsessive, humming like little machines, puffing away at some task. By contrast, the pudgy alliterative *g*'s in the second paragraph celebrate the large-souled, hearty munificence of fat people.

Copyright © 1984 by United Feature Syndicate, Inc. Used by permission.

Now it is true that you will seldom alliterate this boldly, unless you, too, are writing humorously or satirically, but it is also true that serious writing uses alliteration. You heard it in Stanley Milgram's "systematic slaughter" and "daily quotas of corpses." You can hear it more obviously in this passage from an argument defending hunters:

> To the average contemporary city dweller or suburbanite, who associates guns with street crime and whose table meat arrives superbly packaged, the word hunting is likely to conjure up a vision of *b*eer-guzzling killers who *b*last away at *B*ambi with automatic wea*p*ons.
>
> (Jonathan Evans Maslow, "Stalking the Black Bear,"
> *Saturday Review* Dec. 1978, emphasis added)

The *b*'s and *p*'s sound like the gunfire in an antihunter's worst nightmare, the explosions exaggerated just enough by alliteration to suggest what Maslow is too tactful to say outright: the opponents of hunters and hunting are becoming just a little hysterical.

Assonance   Less insistent, less distinct, and less often used for these reasons is assonance, the repetition of vowel sounds. Generally it appears in descriptive writing, especially description designed to create a definite mood. Listen to novelist John Steinbeck set a scene in his novel *Cannery Row:*

> A well-grown gopher took up residence in a thicket of mallow weeds in the vacant lot on Cannery Row. It was a perfect place. The d*ee*p gr*ee*n luscious mallows towered up crisp and rich and as they matured their little cheeses hung down provocatively. The *ea*rth was p*er*fect for a gopher hole too, black and soft and yet with a little clay in it so that it didn't crumble and the t*u*nnels didn't cave in.
>
> (John Steinbeck, *Cannery Row* [New York: Viking, 1945], emphasis added)

See how the paired repetitions link related words and by so doing emphasize the subject and key details of the scene? Here's a second, more complex example, a description of the ballerina Anna Pavlova that is itself a ballet of gracefully repeated vowel sounds, different repeated sounds coming together in one word, separating, combining elsewhere in other words with other repetitions.

Short *i,* long *e*
Short *e*
Open *ä*
Long *i,* long *a*

> As her little bird body revealed itself on the scene, either immobile in trembling mystery or tense in the incredible arc which was her lift, her instep stretched ahead in an arch never before seen, the tiny bones of her hands in ceaseless vibration, her face radiant, diamonds glittering under her dark hair, her little waist encased in silk, the great tutu balancing, quickening and flashing over her beating, flashing, quivering legs, every man and woman sat forward, every pulse quickened.
>
> (Agnes De Mille, *Dance to the Piper* [Boston: Little, 1951] emphasis added)

More often than not, alliteration and assonance appear together, helping to emphasize a subject and evoke a particular feeling about it. Did you hear the alliteration in *bird body, trembling mystery, instep stretched?* Listen to the way this description of the Iowa State Fair emphasizes its praise by a litany of alliteration and assonance, even rhyme and half-rhyme.

> Year after year this rich and practical ritual of life is repeated. Animals whose ancestors competed many Fairs ago come back. So do people, returning by plane and automobile to the grounds their grandparents visited by train and buggy. Three-hundred-and-fifty-horsepower internal combustion engines have replaced the one-horse hitch or the two-horse team, but the essential objects of life are

the same: the den*ted ear* of corn, the *rounded rib* of s*teer* and *pig,* that nourishment of the human race which is the *prime purpose* of the *plowing* and harvesting State of Iowa.

(Paul Engle, "The Iowa State Fair," *Holiday* Mar. 1975, emphasis added)

EXERCISES

1. Write a sentence for five of the following topics in which you use **repetition of sound, alliteration or assonance,** to emphasize important words.

Examples

Whatever path its *vo*calists take, punk [rock] is *ve*hement, a *mu*sic of *mea*sured *vi*rulence. It arose at a time when rock had become "good music" *p*layed by *p*latinum acts. It revolted against musical expertise as well as the corporate machinery of pop.

(Jim Miller, "Some Future," *The New Republic,* 24 Mar. 1979, emphasis added)

Since memories begin with electricity, Francis Crick (co-discoverer with James Watson of the double helix) focuses his study of these evanescent impressions on the parts of the neurons that receive electric impulses—the dendrites. These little wisps at the tip of the neuron are studded with spines that connect to the next neuron in the circuit.

("How the Brain Works," *Newsweek* 7 Feb. 1983, emphasis added)

Whether you *b*orrow, *b*uy, or *b*uild them, *b*ookcases and their variously cantilevered *kin* eventually will share living space with you. That's not much of an assumption. Even video and computer freaks need a way to store the printed-and-bound word, if only for some reassurance that their intelligence isn't entirely artificial.

(Jeffrey Burke, "Lunacy and the Arrangement of Books," *Harper's* Apr. 1983, emphasis added)

a. Music.
b. Thinking.
c. Furniture.
d. Pocket change.
e. A pedestrian negotiating an intersection at rush hour.
f. A classroom full of students, an uninteresting lecture.
g. The good education.
h. Cooperation.
i. A subject from a recent reading.

2. Write a brief paragraph about one of the subjects of your recent reading, or choose a subject from the end of this chapter. Use sound repetition to emphasize important words.

Repeating Words, Phrases, and Clauses

In Chapter 8 you learned to repeat thematic tags for the sake of coherence. But you can also repeat words, as well as the grammatical patterns that contain them, for the same reasons you repeat sounds: for emphasis and mood. Listen to more about the Iowa State Fair:

> If all you saw of life was the Iowa State Fair on a brilliant August day, when you hear those incredible crops ripening out of the black dirt between the Missouri and Mississippi rivers, you would believe that this is surely the best of all possible worlds.
>
> You would have *no* sense of the destruction of life, only of its rich creativeness: *no* political disasters, *no* assassinations, *no* ideological competition, *no* wars, *no* corruption, *no* atom waiting in its dark secrecy to destroy us all with its exploding energy.
>
> (Paul Engle, "The Iowa State Fair," *Holiday* Mar. 1975, emphasis added)

Each *no* in the second paragraph helps emphasize just how far Iowa is from the threatful complexities of the modern world, and, by denying the world's destructive energies, the repeated *no*'s also affirm the life that Iowa nurtures.

To emphasize as this writer has done, we can repeat almost any word or grammatical pattern. What, for example, do you remember most about Lincoln's Gettysburg Address? First, perhaps the opening line, "Four score and seven years ago." But after that you remember the last line and its repeated prepositional phrases defining and celebrating republican democracy:

> that this nation, under God, shall have a new birth of freedom; and that government *of the* people, *by the* people, and *for the* people shall not perish from the earth.

Closer to our own time, we remember so much of John F. Kennedy's inaugural address because it, too, repeats words, here verb phrases:

> Let every nation know, whether it wishes us well or ill, that we shall *pay any* price, *bear any* burden, *meet any* hardship, *support any* friend, *oppose any* foe to assure the survival and the success of liberty.

We can also repeat larger structures, such as the *dependent clause* (a clause that cannot be punctuated as a complete sentence):

> But even if it could be demonstrated that the humanities contribute nothing directly to a job, they would still be an essential part of the educational equipment of any person who wants to come to terms with life. The humanities would be expendable only *if* human beings didn't have to make decisions that affect their lives and the lives of others; *if* the human past never existed or had nothing to tell us about the present; *if* thought processes were irrelevant to the achievement of purpose; *if* creativity was beyond the human mind and had nothing to do with the joy of living; *if* human relationships were random

aspects of life; *if* human beings never had to cope with panic or pain, or *if* they never had to anticipate the connection between cause and effect; *if* all the mysteries of mind and nature were fully plumbed; and *if* no special demands arose from the accident of being born a human being instead of a hen or a hog.

> (Norman Cousins, "How To Make People Smaller
> Than They Are," *Saturday Review* Dec. 1978,
> emphasis added)

This writer repeats the conditional *if . . .* pattern nine times to suggest the range of the humanities' concerns and to dramatize how fatuous it would be to diminish their role in higher education. He hems his opponents in with so many "if" conditions that we see their position is impossible.

For increased emphasis, we can detach repeated dependent clauses from their main clause and set them off as emphatic sentence fragments. Standing by themselves, they urge readers to pause a bit longer between each repetition and concentrate more carefully on its contents:

> For most women, abortion is a *pis aller,* a last resort, a necessary evil, chosen for want of a good alternative—and nothing more. It looms so large today *because* there is no decent alternative for many. *Because* an unwanted baby is an economic burden or a social shame, or both. *Because* of bad health or middle age or a truant husband or shocked and rejecting parents. Every normal woman's initial response to the thought of abortion is one of sadness, guilt, and revulsion.
>
> (Sydney J. Harris, "Protesters can't have it both ways
> in the fight against abortion," *Chicago Sun-Times* 12
> Oct. 1983, emphasis added)

We can even repeat *main clauses,* as the following does to point a contrast between what people expect about suicidal personalities and what the truth is:

> Twice in my life I have seen the expression on the face of a person who was soon to die by suicide. *It was not* the look of depression or despair. *It was* more the look of a person watching life from a great distance. *It was* an absorbed attention, as if the person were reviewing an elaborate show, of which he or she had once been the star. I hope I never see it again.
>
> (Hugh Drummond, "The Masked Generation," *Mother
> Jones* May 1981, emphasis added)

Antithesis   Antithesis is an especially dramatic kind of repetition, at once emphatic, complex, and surprising. It is a contrast made by pitting words, phrases, or clauses in one statement against matching words, phrases, or clauses in a second, parallel statement. The effect is that of reversing an idea or turning it inside out.

> Thin people want to face the truth. Fat people know there is no truth.
>
> (Suzanne Britt Jordan, "That Lean and Hungry Look,"
> *Newsweek* 9 Oct. 1978)

During the '70s we got liberated about everything that didn't matter and more conservative about everything that did. We were long on pleasure and short on self-denial. We were quick to give in to every passing fancy and slow to practice restraint. We were big on spending for ourselves and super-miserly about spending for others.
(Suzanne Britt Jordan, "The Joy of Abstinence," *Newsweek* 25 Feb. 1980)

Let us never negotiate out of fear. But let us never fear to negotiate.
(John F. Kennedy)

And so, my fellow Americans: ask not what your country can do for you— ask what you can do for your country.

My fellow citizens of the world: ask not what America will do for you, but what together we can do for the freedom of man.
(John F. Kennedy)

In each, the balanced repetition points up the contrast between the subjects yet their relationship as well: the great wisdom of fat people, the contradictions of life in the 1970s, the relationship of military power to a conciliatory attitude, and the relationship of individual to country and country to the world community.

Head-to-Tail Repetition   The verbal repetition you've studied so far has been created by parallel structure, a series of grammatically equal words, phrases, or clauses. The effect is a kind of vertical order, one emphatic statement after another, each repeating a pattern introduced earlier in the sentence or paragraph. But we can also repeat without parallel structure, connecting the end of one sentence to the beginning of the next—head-to-tail—in a horizontal order that aids coherence while emphasizing important words.

The decline of substantive women's roles in the movies has coincided with an increased emphasis on explicit *sex and violence*. *Sex and violence*, as even the most vigorous masochist will tell you, can be a very unhappy combination, and in the movies, as in life, it is the women who have been getting the worst of it.
(Andrew Ward, "Women of the Silver Screen," *The Atlantic* June 1978, emphasis added)

The common pattern on television detective shows suggests that murders tend to be carefully premeditated; but most legal and behavioral experts agree that careful planning is rarely a part of American *murders. The most typical murders* involve poor young minority males victimizing other minority males of the same age or older—friends, acquaintances, or strangers living in close, ghetto-slum proximity to the offender.
(Lynn A. Curtis, "What's New in Murder," *The New Republic* 26 Jan. 1980, emphasis added)

This thing called "human nature," as I conceive it, is like a musical instrument—say an organ. Now it cannot be changed, in the sense that the range of notes is given, and we cannot play the instrument outside that *range*.

But the *range* of possibilities is large enough so that we can play a nearly infinite number of melodies.

> (Sydney J. Harris, "Changing Human Nature," *The Best of Sydney J. Harris* [Boston: Houghton, 1975] emphasis added)

You might at first be dismayed to see repetitions so close together like this. The first impulse of many student writers, if they produced such sentences, would be to reorganize them or at least find a synonym for one half of the repetition and so obscure it. But yielding to either impulse would be wrong. These passages are coherent and emphatic *because* of the repetition. Each repetition identifies the key idea of the passage and links one sentence to the next. Keep this in mind as you write and revise: repeat to show that ideas in separate sentences, phrases, or clauses have equal value; repeat for emphasis; repeat for coherence; but *cut* or *reword* any repetition that does *not* contribute to emphasis or coherence.

EXERCISES

1. For five of the following write a sentence that uses the word, word ending, phrase, or clause in an emphatic series of repetitions.

Example

> Now the trumpet summons us again— *not as a call to* bear arms, *though* arms we need—*not as a call to* battle, *though* embattled we are—but *a call to* bear the burden of a long twilight *struggle* year in and year out, "rejoicing in hope, patient in tribulation"—a *struggle* against the common enemies of man: tyranny, poverty, disease and war itself.
>
> (John F. Kennedy, Presidential Inaugural Address, emphasis added)

a. No.
b. In the . . . , by the . . . , for the . . . (or any other series of prepositional phrases).
c. Love.
d. A word or words ending in *-ing, -ed,* or *-en.*
e. To.
f. _____(someone's name)_____ (or *she* or *he*) is/is not a . . .
g. The subject of a recent reading.

2. For each of the following write an antithetical sentence or sentences; use parallel structure and repetition to emphasize a contrast between two ideas.

Examples

> If a free society cannot help the many who are poor, it cannot save the few who are rich.
>
> (John F. Kennedy)

Imagination was given to man to compensate him for what he is not, and a sense of humor was provided to console him for what he is.
(Horace Walpole)

Man's capacity for justice makes democracy possible, and man's capacity for injustice makes democracy necessary.
(Reinhold Niebuhr)

a. Man/women.
b. Truth/falsehood.
c. Rich/poor.
d. Many/few.
e. Laughter/sorrow.

3. Choose one term from each of the pairs in Exercise 2 (5 terms in all) and write two sentences about that term. Connect the two sentences by head-to-tail repetition. Make sure that your repetition emphasizes key words as well as creating coherence.

Example
It is the tendency or wish to make *everything* difficult that *bothers me. It bothers me* because it makes a casualty of *simple truths. Simple truths* are simply and utterly true no matter how many mental somersaults one turns to deny them and cast them as problems.
(William J. Bennett, "Simple Truths," *Newsweek* 7 Jan. 1980, emphasis added)

4. Choose one of the subjects from your recent reading or choose one from the end of this chapter. Write a paragraph in which you use repetition (words, phrases, clauses, antithesis, or head-to-tail repetition) to emphasize the point you want to make.

❧ VARIETY

If repetition sets the beat in the music of our writing, variety makes its melody. Its devices interrupt patterns of language and sentence structure and help prevent monotony. By creating sharp changes—surprises, really—in our sentences, these devices draw attention to ideas and make them more interesting to read about. Here are two versions of a paragraph to show how these changes work, first, the unvaried version:

Consider what caused the current problems in American education. Several years ago people began to demand their rights. That is as it should be. They wanted equal education under the law. I would certainly be in favor of that. Social consciousness was aroused in Americans of all kinds. That was a valuable change in American life. Unfortunately, we made a number of strategic errors that had negative effects on our schools. We suddenly, naively, believed that by offering equal opportunities we could (1) make everybody happy,

(2) make everybody well-adjusted, (3) forgive everybody who failed, and (4) expect gratitude in return. Educators then decided they did not know how to teach when students became ill-tempered, uncooperative, complaining, and apathetic. Thus, these educators decided to make it easier on the poor, disadvantaged victims of broken homes, the mal-adapted, the unloved. They did what they should have done. The problem with these lofty theories is, however, evident. Poverty, ignorance, and ill-temper will always be present in young people. We look for every reason in the world for the declining test scores of our children, except for lack of intelligence and lack of diligence.

This paragraph is clear enough, predictable enough, and fluent enough, all right, but not very compelling to read. In fact, its montonous sameness makes it just a little bit dull and hard to concentrate on. For one thing, look at the length of the sentences: first, seven sentences of six to nine words, then a stretch of longer sentences, each about as long as the others. The choppiness is bound to put readers off. For another thing, see the sameness in sentence structure, for the most part subject + verb + complement. Each by itself may be a good sentence, but when they file lock-step down the page, one after another, they are bound to distract readers from the ideas they contain. For a third thing, the language and tone are all of a piece, formal and detached. Nothing breaks the tension this formality imposes and we're ready to quit the paragraph well before we're finished. Gimme a break! we cry.

Now contrast that version with the original:

> Consider for a moment what caused the mess [in American education]. A few years ago people began demanding their rights. Fair enough. They wanted equal education under the law. I'm for it. Social consciousness was born. Right on. Now, enter the big wrong turn, the one that sent our schools into never-never land. We suddenly, naively, believed that by offering equal opportunities we could (1) make everybody happy, (2) make everybody well-adjusted, (3) forgive everybody who failed, and (4) expect gratitude to boot. When students were surly, uncooperative, whiny, and apathetic, educators decided they themselves didn't know how to teach. So they made it easier on the poor, disadvantaged victims of broken homes, the misfits, the unloved. Well and good. But the catch to such lofty theories is evident. Poverty, ignorance and just plain orneriness will always abound. We look for every reason in the world for the declining test scores of our children except for stupidity and laziness.
>
> (Suzanne Britt Jordan, "I Wants to Go to the Prose," *Newsweek* 14 Nov. 1977)

This version is easy to read, a pleasure even, because of all the changes the writer rings in her language, sentences, and point of view. She varies the level of her words from the slangy and colloquial to the formal and serious. She varies her distance and attitude, detached one minute, enthusiastic the next, scornful and ironic the one after that. She exclaims, explains, and declaims in sentences that run from two to twenty-seven words. She varies the patterns of her sentences from one to the next: simple sentences, complex sentences, even a few fragmentary sentences. By these changes she makes us want to read, even if we disagree with her. You may not always want to write in a style this varied—such variety is not always necessary or appropriate—but by increasing the variety in your style, you'll take more pleasure in writing and give more in the reading. The rest of this chapter is devoted to variety in language; the next chapter, to variety in sentences and point of view.

Variety in Language

Most of us write words the way an old phonograph plays music, monophonically, with no tone control and little volume. We may choose words right for the audience and occasion, but too often we write unaware of ways we could modulate the music of our words to shade meaning, create interest, and give delight. We don't talk this way, however. Listen to yourself sometime in conversation, even serious conversation, to the way you play with words for effect or enunciate to lay special stress on an idea. There's no reason you shouldn't do the same in your writing.

Varying Distance Abruptly changing the distance between ourselves and our readers is one of the most useful ways to write for effect. We can shift suddenly from formal, ceremonial, or public words to informal, casual, intimate words, or vice versa, and by so doing emphasize a point or create a mood. Listen to a journalist admit in the opening of one column to mistakes he made in an earlier column:

> Nineteen seventy-nine isn't half over, and *I've already eaten more than a year's supply of crow,* simply because I made a public display of my skepticism over the existence of a certain 19th-century plumber and inventor. I have confessed my folly. Thomas Crapper did, in fact, exist, and several readers were kind enough to send me photographs of his London establishment, which is no longer standing. I also got a letter from Wallace Reyburn, the Englishman who wrote Crapper's biography, *Flushed with Pride.*
>
> *Now I have to down still another nibble of corvine ragout,* because in the same column I slandered *The People's Almanac,* that meaty compendium of general information written by David Wallechinsky and Irving Wallace. . . .
>
> (Thomas Middleton, "An Unserious Almanac, Seriously," *Saturday Review* 26 May 1979, emphasis added)

The *corvine ragout* this writer nibbles in the second paragraph is the same breed of bird he downed in the first: crow. But by stepping back suddenly from his readers and shifting his language to the ceremonial and formal— by becoming playfully stuffy and uncomfortable—he admits his errors, recognizes that others' criticism of him is all in good spirit, and shows he is

Used by permission of Johnny Hart and News America Syndicate.

not offended by their correction. Varying the language of the passage, he has gracefully and deftly set the mood for the rest of the article.

The cartoon above and the following example illustrate the more frequent shift in language, from formal to informal:

> Longevity, like literature, is a splendid teacher. By age 40, almost everyone has experienced enlarging sadness, such as the deaths of loved ones; enriching delights, such as introducing a child to Huckleberry Finn; deepening astonishments, such as contemplation of this fact of life: physically, *you ain't what you used to be. Every instant, every cell in your body is changing. This 40-year-old jumble of space and electricty is not the jumble it was at 30.*
>
> (George Will, "On Turning 40," *Newsweek* 27 Apr. 1981, emphasis added)

By shifting at the end to the informality of *ain't, you/your,* and *jumble,* George Will emphasizes the contrast between the lofty, impersonal generalizations about age he offered earlier and his genuine astonishment at his own advancing age. He knows that when one applies the great truths of life to himself, he is sure to sound pompous unless he takes the formal edge off them. Narrowing his distance toward the casual and intimate does that nicely.

Onomatopoeia   Onomatopoeia refers to words whose sounds echo their sense. *Mumble, murmur, hiss, slam, whir, squash, whip, buzz, sizzle,* and many, many other words imitate the sound or convey the feeling of their denotation. Listen to the words describing the opening of a TV game show.

> The show starts with the usual sudden *uproar.* "It's time for—'Family Feud'!!" someone *yells,* backed by a *screechy* din that sounds like *bluegrass music played by speed freaks.* We see the title, its dark red letters rendered in mock needlepoint across a yellow oval, like an *enormous* sampler, and then the title turns into some surname—PFISTER, say—also lettered in mock needlepoint. The studio audience goes nuts, the music *yelps and twangs,* as the oval *zips* leftward like a sliding door, revealing a sort of mock Victorian parlor, where the five immobile Pfisters pose in *wacky* imitation of some old-fashioned family por-

trait. After the announcer *shouts* their names, the Pfisters break out of this *tableau vivant* and line up, five *abreast, applauding back at the applauding crowd.* This rapid process then repeats itself, showing us the Pfisters' rival house—say, GRUBB—and then both little clans come *bounding* out onto the stage, a hectic edifice of lurid hues and tiny *winking* lights, and face off gaily, five abreast, each standing in a happy row behind a sort of elongated podium.

(Mark Crispin Miller, "Family Feud," *The New Republic* 18 and 25 July 1983, emphasis added)

Several of the descriptive words here are obviously onomatopoeic: *yells, screechy, yelps, twangs,* and *zips.* Others evoke a sound or feeling without being directly imitative: *uproar* sounds like a sudden clamor, as does *shout; enormous* sounds, well, enormous; and *bounding* has a bounce to it. The writer even employs individual letters in patterns of alliteration to create the atmosphere and sound of the show: *bluegrass music played by speed freaks* sounds too fast for its own good. And don't you hear the applause in *five abreast, applauding back at the applauding crowd?* If you doubt the powers of onomatopoeia, try substituting synonyms for these examples and see what happens to the paragraph. Try *turmoil* for *uproar,* or *moves quickly* for *zips.* The passage loses its energy and vividness. The writer has chosen the words he has because their sounds help dramatize the scene and evoke the faintly critical mood necessary to the analysis of the game show that follows. Onomatopoeia, like other variety devices, exists not for its own sake nor merely to "pretty-up" a piece of writing, but to help create mood and meaning.

Foreign Words   Almost every language, especially English, has a large store of foreign loan words. Some are borrowed because we need a word our native lexicon lacks. Most we absorb into the language and, with few exceptions, forget that they have been borrowed: *sauerkraut* from German, *algebra* from Arabic, *alligator* from Spanish, *moccasin* from the Algonquin Indians. The list runs into the many thousands of words. We borrow other foreign words not because we *need* them but because they are more economical ways to say something or because they offer delightful contrasts to our own words. When the GIs came home from Europe after World War II, for example, they brought with them a whole list of German substitutes for English words—*wunderkind, kaput, achtung, verboten*—that they had picked up to flavor their language.

Writers, too, borrow foreign words and for the same reasons, for emphasis and variety, to give their writing a certain *cachet.* (See that French word, denoting a small seal used by private citizens, now expanded to mean a distinguishing feature? *Cachet* lends a character that its ordinary everyday English equivalent, *distinction,* would not give in its place.) If such foreign words were ever absorbed into English, they would lose their emphatic value. We want them to continue looking and sounding foreign. Some are obvious, have been in our vocabulary for ages, and can be written without translation or explanation:

The do-it-yourselfer plans and works and sweats, and when he finishes his current project he has six more waiting. The don't-do-it-yourselfer accepts the status quo. And when the status quo breaks down, rusts out or grows dandelions, he accepts that too.

(Jack Conner, "Don't-It-Yourself," *Newsweek* 26 Oct. 1981)

No one needs to be told what *status quo* means; the phrase has been around so long we can even play with it, as Jack Connor does.

Other words are less familiar and need immediate translation, as Sydney Harris does to the French phrase in a passage quoted earlier.

For most women, abortion is a *pis aller,* a last resort, a necessary evil, chosen for want of a good alternative—and nothing more.

But, you might ask, if Harris must translate his phrase for readers who don't understand it, why does he use it? Because to use a foreign phrase and then repeat it in translation is to draw attention to an idea and emphasize it, in this instance, that abortion is a last resort. Here's another example:

Millions are being spent on videotape machines, toys to attach to toys (TV sets). A car is a necessity, but most cars are toys, too. They are built for *Homo ludens,* playful man. Why else call them "Stingrays," "Firebirds" and "Broughams"? Why else design dashboards that enable drivers to feel like Luke Skywalker?

(George Will, "Visions of Sugarplumbs," *Newsweek* 11 Dec. 1978)

The foreign phrase helps emphasize that playful adults, *homo ludens,* are a kind of subspecies of *homo sapiens,* reasoning human, and worthy of scrutiny therefore. To use foreign words this well you don't have to speak, read, and write twenty languages; you need only know those foreign words currently valuable in English, which need translating, and which to use with which audiences. A good ear, a good eye, and a good dictionary are all you need. You'll pick up the words and phrases just by reading and listening; and a good English dictionary will define most of them for you.

Emphasizing Devices Skillful writers write sentences that lead their readers naturally to their main points. Their structure creates their own emphasis and rhythm. But occasionally, in even the best of sentences, we may want to give readers an extra little nudge toward our meaning by drawing special attention to a word or phrase. Emphasizing devices do this. *Quotation marks* tell readers that a word is being used in a special sense:

I have been eagerly anticipating my "mid-life crisis," that moment when the middle-aged male does something peculiar—buys a Porsche or grows a mustache or takes up yoga or yogurt—to prove he is not a spent force.

(George Will, "On Turning 40," *Newsweek* 27 Apr. 1981)

The quotation marks here mock the "crisis" of middle age. George Will uses them to say to his readers, I may consider this to be a crisis and others like me might, but you are under no obligation to do so. Nothing very serious or "crisis"-like happening here, only the mild upsurge of anxiety that afflicts most who live to be forty.

Italics (underlining for all handwriting and typewriting) tell a reader to pay attention to whatever is so marked; they also bend the rhythm of a sentence and sharpen a stress point, giving to writing the emphasis that comes naturally in speech. Here italics point a contrast between children as they really are and our myths about them:

> I suspect that many adults are not so much interested in children, as in the *idea* of children—children as individuals hold less value for them than children as the mythic representation of all they feel is lacking in their own lives.
>
> (R. Keith Miller, "The Idea of Children," *Newsweek* 29 Aug. 1979)

Underline when you must and use quotation marks, too, but use both sparingly. Too many of them and your ideas will cry "Wolf!" demanding an attention they don't require. At the very least, overusing them will make your prose look cluttered and you, excessively finicky; at worst, you'll end up sounding melodramatic or false.

EXERCISES

1. Choose one of the following topics and write a paragraph in which you vary the distance between yourself and your audience to create emphasis or climax. Write in a formal language and then shift suddenly to the informal or intimate; or write informally, then shift suddenly to formal or public language.

    a. Work.
    b. Out of work.
    c. Loyalty or disloyalty.
    d. Libraries or other quiet places.
    e. Time.
    f. A subject from a recent reading you have done.

2. Choose one of the following topics and write a descriptive paragraph that uses onomatopoeia to dramatize its subject. Use words that imitate sound, use alliteration and assonance to imitate sound, use words associated with sounds, actions, things, or feelings.

    a. Candy.
    b. Traveling.
    c. Studying.
    d. A subject from a recent reading.
    e. Watching the opposite sex.
    f. A season of the year.
    g. Bookshelves, knicknack cabinets, or display cases.

3. Choose five of the following topics:

Authority.	Beauty.	Friends.	Memory.
Babies.	Good manners.	Law.	Books.
Fools.	Knowledge.	Clothes.	Sons/daughters.
Insight.	Religion.	Pleasure.	Husbands/wives.
Adversity.	Debt.	Honor.	Poetry.

Here are some of the most common foreign words and phrases used by English speakers and writers. Write a sentence about each of your topics by using one or more of these foreign terms or other foreign terms you are familiar with. Before you write, use a dictionary or foreign phrase book to check meanings you are unsure of.

à la carte	anima	ante	aplomb
à pied	après	a priori	à propos
au contraire	au courant	au fond	ad hoc
avant-garde	bête noire	très bien	blasé
bloc	brouhaha	Blitzkrieg	bravura
bonhomie	bon vivant	cachet	camouflage
canapé	cliché	capo	carpe diem
carte blanche	cause célèbre	caveat	chiaroscuro
cognoscenti	coiffeur	con amore	contretemps
cortège	coup	début	de facto
dégagé	déjà vu	de jure	dénouement
de rigueur	déshabillé	detente	de trop
distingué	dolce vita	donnée	Doppelgänger
double entendre	du jour	ecce	éclat
élan	émigré	en famille	ennui
ergo	esprit	exposé	façade
faux pas	flagrante delicto	gauche	guru
habitué	impasse	in toto	ipso facto
le mot juste	malaise	mêlée	nom de guerre
non sequitur	opus	passé	plus tôt
poseur	pro forma	protégé	raison d'être
rapport	rapprochement	savant	savoir-faire
sine qua non	sotto voce	têt-à-têt	vis-à-vis
Weltanschauung	Weltschmerz		

4. Choose one of the following topics and write a brief paragraph in which you use emphasizing devices—but not too many of them—to shade meaning or stress individual words.

a. Shadows.
b. Dancing.
c. Gifted students.
d. War.
e. Funny words.
f. Interesting people.
g. A subject from a recent reading.

WRITING PROJECTS

Topics

1. Good taste—almost everyone wants it, or what is equally important, wants to be thought to have it, but even those who do have it aren't always sure what it is. Clarify the subject by writing a three- to five-page extended definition essay. What is good taste, exactly? Is it only personal preference tricked out as if it were an absolute aesthetic or social law? Or are there genuine standards or characteristics peculiar to those who have good taste? Does good taste change from era to era, generation to generation, and region to region, or do only the objects of choice and judgment change? How does one know whether he or she has it? Can it be lost? Can one learn it, or is it innate, like athletic ability? What is its value? Write to the members of your composition class and answer any of the preceding questions that might be important to them. Consider organizing your essay according to the "What is it?" pattern (see page 127).

2. Write a three- to five-page character analysis of the personality best suited to your intended career. Are you "right" for the job you seek? Use this occasion to find out. Interview those who ought to know, observe people as they work, or research to find character profiles (see your librarian). You may want to make your essay more than an analytic report if you discover traits in workers that seem at odds with their jobs. Do some people choose jobs *in spite of* their personalities rather than because of them? Who? What traits are at cross-purposes to their work? What are the consequences of this conflict? Write this essay for yourself—you are your audience. Consider organizing your findings according to the "What is it?" pattern (see page 127).

3. Write a three- to five-page analytic argument in which you challenge a common assumption held by many of those you know. An assumption is the belief that something is true without the facts to prove it. This assumption may concern human nature, human communities, the animal kingdom, the physical world, a particular job, or some feature of the worlds of work or leisure. Make your subject and the false assumption about it as specific as possible. You don't want to be guilty of using unproven assumptions of your own to disprove others' assumptions. Write from your own observation, experience, and research; interview experts if necessary. Address your argument to those who hold this assumption. Consider organizing your essay according to one of the pro/con patterns or the problem/solution pattern (see pages 121–122 and 127).

4. Write a brief essay for publication (800–1,500 words). There are dozens of special-interest, limited-circulation publications in the United States that accept unsolicited manuscripts from nonprofessional writers. Pick one that publishes articles more or less exclusively about a subject you're interested in, for example, a bicycling magazine, a magazine for antique doll collectors, a spelunking magazine, and so on. (See the annual *Writer's Market,* if necessary, for a list of publishing opportunities.) Consider, too, the personal view columns in your newspaper's Op-Ed section, the "My Turn" column in *Newsweek,* the complimentary magazines published by airlines, or industrial publications. You can begin with either a subject or a market. Next, do a publication profile:

   a. What are possible sources of publication? What are their policies regarding unsolicited manuscripts and manuscript form?

    b. What kinds of articles do they publish: subject, length, style, point of view, documentation required?

    c. Who are your potential readers? How can you interest them?

When you've answered these questions, go ahead and write your article.

    5. Write a three- to five-page analytic essay identifying the theme or thesis in a recent reading you have done. Explain how the writer develops and supports that point. Consider especially persona or narrative point of view, methods of development, figurative language, design, and the emphasizing devices presented in this chapter. Consider organizing your essay according to an order-of-importance, descriptive analysis, or "What is it?" pattern (see page 127).

The Writing Process

1. Writing-in-progress.
   a. *Exploring:* Free association and freewriting.
   b. *Developing:* Discover all you have to say about your subject. Use whatever methods and strategies seem appropriate.
   c. *Planning a communications strategy:* Decide on a role, persona (distance and attitude), and thesis (My *point is that . . . What I mean to say is that . . .*).
   d. *Organizing.*
      i. Organize your ideas in a clear, predictable, coherent pattern. Use whatever outlining and organizing strategies that work for you (see pages 128–132).
      ii. Devise an introductory strategy to capture your audience's attention and focus their interest (see pages 137–141).
   e. *Revising:* Reconsider your ideas and communications strategy; create frictions in your thinking (see pages 55–56).
2. Writing.
   a. Write the preliminary draft of your project.
   b. Whenever possible, write one main idea per sentence; write agent-action sentences; keep the parts short; keep related words together; write positive statements (see pages 183–187).
   c. Whenever possible, use words familiar to both you and your audience.
   →d. *New in this chapter:* Repeat sounds (alliteration and assonance), words, phrases, and clauses for emphasis. Play with words (changing distance, listening for sound/sense relationships, using foreign words and emphasizing devices).
3. Rewriting.
   a. Be a zoom lens as you revise; add, delete, substitute, and rearrange.
   b. Ask two questions of troublesome sentences.
      i. What's happening here?
      ii. What goes with what? (See pages 189–196.)
   c. Write "old-new" sentences; reread at a natural pace, listening for unnecessary repetitions and transitions.
   d. Bracket [ ] deadwood of all kinds, reconsider, and then cut.
   e. Copyedit for mechanical errors, recopy, and proofread.

4. Self-evaluation.
   a. What is your intention in this writing?
   b. What is your thesis? What are your thematic tags?
   c. What did you do to interest your readers in your subject and emphasize your most important ideas?
   d. What words or phrases will be most memorable in this writing? What will your readers like best about it? What do you like best?
   e. Did you try anything here that you hadn't tried before?
   f. What one change would most improve this writing?

Chapter 12

Interest:
Variety's the Spice of Life—
and of Good Writing, Too

SENTENCE VARIETY

Varying Sentence Length (Sentence Combining)

Few features contribute more to an interesting, readable style than variety in sentence length. Long sentences, short sentences, sentences in between—in combination they create a a rhythm that lifts readers into a writing and carries them through it, line to line and page to page. The effect, someone has observed, is like riding ocean waves, rising, falling, rushing forward, rising, pausing poised, dropping, rising again. At the crests of the waves are relatively short sentences emphasizing important or dramatic ideas; in the long troughs between are middle length and long sentences, elaborating topics, explaining, restating, or making transitions. Consider this example; the numbers indicate words per sentence:

8	Play, and toys, are increasingly important to adults. Most work in law or
15	medicine or teaching, as on an assembly line, is repetitive. But variety is
6, 8	inexhaustible in play. Almost all work has almost always been drudgery. What
12	is new is that many people are surprised by the drudgery. They have be-
19	lieved that all of life, and *especially* work, can be fun, or, in the current argot, "self-fulfilling." Such a strange idea could only come from institutions of higher learning, and when it is refuted by reality, people assuage their
35	disappointment by turning with awesome intensity to the search for fun in consumption. In affluent societies, most people have acquired the "neces-

25   sities" (*very* broadly construed), and so the consumption that refreshes, briefly, is the consumption of adult toys.

> (George Will, "Visions of Sugarplums," *Newsweek* 11 Dec. 1978)

In short sentences (the average English sentence is now between seventeen and twenty words), George Will announces his subject: the differences between work and play that have turned adults' attention to adult toys. The longer sentences explain our illusions about work, the importance of play and toys, and the underlying reasons for our turn to toys. The short sentences declare; the longer sentences examine and restate.

Here is an exercise to check the variety of your sentences: Take a page from a recent writing you've done and count the number of words per sentence. Compare your numbers with George Will's. His sentences vary from six to thirty-four words, a difference of twenty-eight words. If you find paragraphs in your writing where your sentences fall repeatedly within four or five words of one another, you may suspect they lack a varied rhythm and are harder to read than they should be. Developing an effective style does *not* mean learning to write long, complex sentences exclusively—as some suppose—but learning to write sentences of all lengths and knowing what to put into each kind of sentence.

We can vary the length of sentences in two ways: by dividing up an idea that would otherwise lead to cumbersomely long sentences or, more frequently for most writers, by combining ideas that by themselves would lead to a series of short, choppy sentences. Here is how to combine ideas:

1. *Coordination:* We can combine parts or whole sentences by joining them with coordinating conjunctions (*and, but, so, for, yet, or*):

   Jack went up the hill. Jill went up the hill.
   + *and* =
   Jack and Jill went up the hill.

   Or:

   Jack went up the hill. Jill went out with Freddie.
   + *but* =
   Jack went up the hill, but Jill went out with Freddie.

2. *Subordination:* We can combine by putting a subordinating conjunction (*because, when, although, since, after, while,* and so on) in front of one sentence and joining it with another. What we have done is reduce the independent status of one sentence and make it, now a *dependent clause,* depend for the completion of its meaning on another sentence:

   Jack went up the hill. Jill went out with Freddie.
   + *when* =
   When Jack went up the hill, Jill went out with Freddie.

Or:

> + *while* =
> Jack went up the hill, while Jill went out with Freddie.

3. *Relative clauses:* We can replace the subject of one sentence with a relative pronoun *(who, which, whom, that)* and connect ("relate") that sentence to another:

> Jack and Jill went up the hill. Jack and Jill had nothing better to do.
> + *who* =
> Jack and Jill, who had nothing better to do, went up the hill.

Or:

> Jack and Jill drove up the hill. The hill was too steep to climb.
> + *which* =
> Jack and Jill drove up the hill, which was too steep to climb.

Or:

> Jack drove up the hill. Jack's car was a convertible.
> + *that* =
> The car that Jack drove up the hill was a convertible.

4. *Infinitive phrases:* We can combine sentences by changing the main verb of one sentence to its infinitive *(to)* form:

> Jack and Jill went up the hill. Jack and Jill were fetching a pail of water.
> + *to fetch* =
> Jack and Jill went up the hill to fetch a pail of water.

Or:

> Jack and Jill went up the hill to fetch a pail of water. That was a foolish thing to do.
> + *to go* =
> To go up the hill to fetch a pail of water was a foolish thing for Jack and Jill to do.

5. *Participial phrases:* We can change the verb of one sentence to its participial form *(-ing, -ed, -en)* and combine that sentence with another.

> Jack went down the hill. Jack discovered Jill and Freddie. They were seated by the well.
> + *discovering*
> or *having discovered* =
> Having discovered Jill and Freddie seated by the well, Jack went down the hill.

6. *Absolute constructions:* By removing part or all of a verb from one sentence, we create what is known as an absolute construction that can then be combined with another sentence:.

Jack struggled to the top of the hill. Jack's knees were wobbly. Jack's chest was heaving. Jack's shoulders were tense.

− were, − was, − were =

His knees wobbly, his chest heaving, his shoulders tense, Jack struggled to the top of the hill.

7. *Apposition:* We can combine sentences by turning one whole sentence or a part of it into a modifying noun or noun phrase, called an appositive.

Jack decided to go up the hill. Jack had been climbing hills for five years.

+ *a hill climber* =

Jack, a hill climber for five years, decided to go up the hill.

Or:

Jill was a gymnast. Jill came tumbling after Jack.

=

Jill, a gymnast, came tumbling after Jack.

With a little practice, you will be combining sentences and varying sentence length while you draft and revise, and you'll write more interestingly and emphatically as a result. At first, however, you'll do most of your combining *after* you have produced a draft, when you can play leisurely with your sentences, away from the heat of discovering ideas, language, and form.

- First, *look at your sentences;* if necessary count the words. Are they too frequently about the same length?
- *Read them aloud.* Do they sound choppy? If they do, find the dramatic or important ideas that belong in their own sentences, probably short. Then examine the others, looking for related ideas in short sentences that can be combined.
- When you've finished combining, *reread your writing aloud.* Do the stresses fall where they should, on the most important words? Can you give your reading the rhythms of measured but natural speech? If so, you've written varied, "musical" sentences.

EXERCISES

1. Combine the sentences of each set in three ways. Here are the operations you might perform: rearrange the order of the sentences, coordinate with conjunctions or punctuation, make subordinate clauses, reduce whole sentences to words or phrases. Feel free to add words, drop them or change their form in order to make your combinations.

Example

The railroad is bordered by a swamp.

The boys leap from a dead tree.

The boys are naked.
The water is warm and green.

Option 1

The railroad is bordered by a warm, green swamp into which naked boys leap from a dead tree.

Option 2

The boys, who are naked, leap from a dead tree into the warm, green water of the swamp that borders the railroad.

Option 3

Bordering the railroad is a swamp; boys, naked, leap from a dead tree into the warm, green water.

a. The whale dived.
   The dive was deep.
   The whale was attempting to evade the whalegunner's harpoon.

b. Albert was a carpenter.
   He was dependable.
   He had no imagination for design.
   He had no eye for details.

c. The mornings were bitter cold.
   Ruth put the key in the ignition.
   Ruth turned the key.
   Ruth hoped for the best.

d. Television has a huge audience.
   The audience is measured in the tens of millions.
   The size of the audience makes television the natural recipient of advertising dollars.

e. There was a rolltop desk.
   The desk stood in the corner.
   The desk had pigeonholes.
   The pigeonholes were stuffed with receipts.
   The pigeonholes were stuffed with letters.

f. A pet strolls through the house.
   The owners are away from home.
   The burglar alarm may go off.

g. Bravery is associated with courage.
   Bravado is associated with courage.
   Bravery is the expression of true courage.
   Bravado is the boastful pretense of courage.

h. John contemplated the boxes.
   The boxes contained pencils.
   The boxes were long and narrow.
   The boxes were covered with dust.
   John was waiting for his class to begin.

i. Disabled people may not always be independent in body.
   Their disability is unfortunate.

Most disabled people are independent in mind.
Most disabled people are independent in spirit.

j. Students expect success in college.
Students need accurate memories for success.
Students need discipline for success.
Students need inquisitive minds for success.
An inquisitive mind is the most important ingredient for success.

2. The following paragraphs read choppily because the sentences have approximately the same length, and too many share the same structure. Rewrite them, varying the length. Write short sentences for emphasis, longer for development or elaboration.

a. Racquetball is the newest of racquet games. It has been played in organized form for only a decade or two. The game is spreading quickly throughout the United States. Just last month the first televised game was broadcast on Chicago's channel 11.

b. Oahu is the island known as the "Gathering Place." This island was once a meeting ground for Hawaii's island kings. Since then this island has become known as the center of tourist life. Oahu has many exciting things to do and interesting places to go. A warm climate and beautiful scenery make it a year 'round vacation spot.

c. The Hotel Coronado's bar reminded me of a Frank Buck movie. The bar was a small room set off from the larger dining room. Behind the bartender hung a red clock that advertised "Drink Lion Beer." From the ceiling hung a huge fan that twirled slowly. My father sat down and ordered a drink. I ordered a Coke. I was served quickly and began to concentrate on the Coke label written in Spanish. The bartender did not seem to understand what my father wanted. At that point, a young man whose hair and beard were graying walked into the bar. He heard my father struggling to communicate. Then he stepped up to the bar and ordered the drink for him. The man was an American working as an engineer for the Spanish government. His name was Eric Martin.

Varying Sentence Patterns

Grammatical Patterns   We can classify sentences according to three grammatical patterns:

- *Simple sentences* are those that make one independent statement, e.g., *Jack loves Jill.*
- *Compound sentences* are those that make two or more independent statements, e.g., *Jack loves Jill, and Jill loves Jack.*
- *Complex sentences* are those that make one independent statement and at least one dependent statement, e.g., *Jack, who loves Jill, is loved by Jill in return.* Or: *Although Jack loves Jill, she does not love him.*

When we vary the length of sentences, we almost always vary their patterns as well. Consider this example; numbers identify words per sentence:

Simple sentence (4)
Compound (28)

Simple (29)

Complex (45)

Simple (16)

 I hate physical fitness. There is probably a more measured, thoughtful way of putting that, but I can't think of it just now—and anyway, we don't have a lot of time. You are about to reissue your annual Jan. 1 self-denying ordinance: no more smoking, no more Fritos, no more heavy drinking, no more anything except a no-excuses 2-mile daily run. I have spent the past fourteen months in one approximation or another of that condition, having cracked a lifelong smoking habit that was probably the sole support of at least four Kentucky families, gained the inevitable weight, lost it, gained it back, lost it again. At the moment I am holding my own—just barely and with no end of resentment.

> (Meg Greenfield, "Two Cheers for the Unfit,"
> *Newsweek* 2 Jan. 1978)

Simple sentences are not necessarily short, and complex sentences are not necessarily long, but more often than not they end up that way. This additional variety in the patterns of sentences enriches their rhythms and increases their power over readers' attention.

Cumulative and Periodic Sentences   Just as we classify sentences by their number of independent statements, so we can classify them by where they position their main ideas. In *cumulative sentences*, by far the more common English sentence pattern, the main idea comes early, almost always in the main clause. The remainder of the sentence builds on that main idea, shading meaning, adding details, adding details about details, as this sentence has done, flowing away from its main clause, often to considerable length. Here's another example, this about jury duty, its main idea emphasized:

> Several hundred other *men and women sit* on every side, as closely as in a movie theater, also waiting to be called for a jury, which they almost never are.
> (William K. Zinsser, *The Lunacy Room* [New York: Harper, 1970], emphasis added)

Here are two more examples, more complex than the first, arranged to show how the added elements develop from and modify what comes earlier in the main clauses of the sentences:

> *The writer*, at his desk alone, *must create* out of his own momentum,
> draw the enthusiasm up out of his own substance,
>   not just once,
>   when he may feel inspired,
>   but day after day
>   when he often does not.
> (May Sarton, *Plant Dreaming Deep* [New York: Norton, 1968], emphasis added)

> The concrete highway *was edged* with a mat of tangled,
>   broken,
>   dry grass,
> and *the grass heads were heavy* with oat beards to catch on a dog's coat
>   and foxtails to tangle in a horse's fetlocks,
> and clover burrs to fasten in sheep's wool;
>   sleeping life waiting to, be spread and dispersed,
>   every seed armed with an appliance of dispersal,
>   twisting darts and parachutes for the wind,
>   little spears
>   and tiny balls
> and all waiting for animals and for the wind,
>   for a man's trouser cuff
>   or the hem of a woman's skirt,
>   all passive but armed with appliances of activity,
>   still,
>   but each possessed of the anlage of movement.
>   (John Steinbeck, *Grapes of Wrath* [New York: Viking,
>   1939, 1970] emphasis added)

In each example, readers sense the unfolding of a subject, a flower blooming in their minds as they read. What follows the main idea is not less important than that idea, any more than a flower's petal is less important than the pistil and stamens at the center of the blossom. All parts work together to develop the writer's meaning.

By contrast, *periodic sentences* work *toward* a main idea, usually the most important and dramatic part of the sentence, coming near the end. The sensation for readers is one of mounting tension or suspense, building toward a climax or surprise that is held back until the very end. In this example, arranged to show its design, the main idea comes in the main clause:

> The erotic authority of Little Richard,
> the acrobatic dexterity of Chuck Berry,
> the bemused sexuality of Mick Jagger,
> the arrogant energy of Bob Dylan,
> above all the innocent pleasure in mastery shown by Elvis Presley amid the
>   mayhem of his first televised triumphs—
> *all this was made vivid* again in the finely picked images that comprised *The Heroes*
>   *of Rock and Roll,* a special aired February 8 by ABC-TV.
>   (Jim Miller, "Some Future," *The New Republic* 24
>   Mar. 1979, emphasis added)

We can't know the point of this list of descriptive judgments until we reach the main clause following the dash. Like this one, every periodic sentence is a little mystery drama, building suspensefully toward a climax.

Sometimes, however, this climax comes not in the main clause but in a final word or phrase:

> Having laid waste the wilderness,
>   skunked the waterways with toxics,
>   and decimated animal and Indian alike in the name of economic
>   development,
> we now indulge ourselves in an orgy of sentimentalism
>   for whatever comes labeled
>   *"natural."*
>
> (Jonathan Evan Maslow, "Stalking the Black Bear,"
> *Saturday Review* Dec. 1978, emphasis added)

We cannot understand the condemnation made by the opening series, know what the *orgy* is, or feel the blast of its sarcasm until we come to that last ironically placed word: *natural.*

A periodic sentence may even be written with its main clause early but its main idea or most dramatic point withheld until an emotional or logical climax:

> The mind has always been dumbfounded by the brain. That three-pound glob of matter hardly seems up to the task of writing "Paradise Lost," composing "Eroica" or discovering relativity. Yet for 2,400 years, ever since Hippocrates located the seat of the intellect inside the skull, the mind has been forced to admit that its greatest achievements, its loftiest thoughts, its deepest emotions all arise from *something with the consistency of Jell-O and the color of day-old slush.*
>
> (Sharon Begley, "How the Brain Works," *Newsweek* 7 Feb. 1983, emphasis added)

Those final ironically deflating descriptions of the brain's texture and color reinforce the paradox in the opening sentences of the passage, that all human achievement has come from such an unlikely looking source.

Whichever sentences you write, whether cumulative or periodic, they are both likely to be longer and more complex than your other sentences—necessarily so. Their structure is ideally suited to present complex subjects in all their details or to lead your readers through those details to a clarifying or dramatic climax. But because they are so long and complex, you'll seldom, if ever, write two such sentences back to back. Rather, you'll lead up to them, introducing their subjects with shorter, simpler, and more pointed sentences. And then, for the sake of rhythm and variety, you'll follow them with other short sentences. The following example judges the California governor's mansion built in 1975. See how the subjects and rhythms of the shorter introductory sentences prepare for the densely detailed cumulative sentence? And how the relatively shorter following sentence sustains the rhythm and language while capping the judgment of the cumulative sentence? Numbers indicate the length of the sentences.

11   The place has been called, by Jerry Brown [former California governor], a
19   "Taj Mahal." It has been called a "white elephant," a "resort," a "monu-

8

65

10

ment to the colossal ego of our former governor [Ronald Reagan, builder of the mansion]." It is not exactly any of these things. It is simply and rather astonishingly an enlarged version of a very common kind of California tract house, a monument not to colossal ego but to a weird absence of ego, a case study in the architecture of limited possibilities, insistently and malevolently "democratic," flattened out, mediocre and "open" and as devoid of privacy or personal eccentricity as the lobby area in a Ramada Inn. It is the architecture of "background music," decorators, "good taste."

(Joan Didion, *The White Album* [New York: Simon, 1979])

Rhetorical Questions   We can classify sentences not only by their parts and how they are arranged but also by what they do:

- *Declarative sentences* declare things, make assertions:

    Jack fell down and broke his crown.

- *Interrogative Sentences* interrogate, ask questions:

    Why did Jack fall down?

- *Exclamatory sentences* exclaim or cry out:

    Jack is such a clumsy fellow!

- *Imperative sentences* give commands:

    Pick yourself up, Jack!

Most of our sentences are necessarily declarative, because our writing is concerned primarily with making assertions of one kind or another: "Dear Mother, I'm broke. I need a few dollars to hold me till payday." Or: "There were four causes of the American Civil War." Or: "This raspberry ice cream is the best I've ever tasted." Such sentences are perfectly all right, unless we write a long string of them that falls into a monotonous, unemphatic pattern.

The easiest way to break the declarative pattern when it grips our sentences is to turn an assertion into a *rhetorical question*, a question that is in fact an assertion. The effect of such a question is to narrow the distance between reader and writer and make the writing into something of a dialogue. Watch how this passage attacks the way adults romanticize childhood:

We need to recognize that ideas have consequences. By granting a special status to children, we go far toward ensuring that they will be self-occupied and all too often, irresponsible. *If children are fundamentally different from you and me, how could we possibly expect them even to begin to measure up to the same standards? How can you discipline them when, by definition, they are supposed to be creative, natural, and free?* And so we find ourselves prone to make excuses where excuses are uncalled for—producing children that increasingly become sullen, spoiled and altogether unpleasant adolescents. We have forgotten that today's angry teen-ager was yesterday's celebrated child.

(R. Keith Miller, "The Idea of Children," *Newsweek* 27 Aug. 1979, emphasis added)

The first question, asking for an answer that must be negative, affirms that children are not *fundamentally different* from adults and therefore should have no special status. The second question follows from the first and even more emphatically asks us to examine for ourselves the writer's two points: that ideas have consequences and that our ideas about children are preventing us from raising them successfully. In other words, rhetorical questions invite readers to participate actively in ideas while shaping their responses to them.

Parenthetical Remarks   Parenthetical remarks are exclamations, asides, or explanations put into the middle of a sentence, one separate, complete thought inserted within a second complete thought. A parenthetical remark can be enclosed by parentheses, dashes, or commas. The effect is both surprising condensation and expansion. A sentence does two things at once and does them more compactly that two sentences would, for example, giving information but also judging its worth. Here a writer uses a parenthesis to expand and exclaim:

Already we have child-proof (and, often, adult-proof) containers for virtually everything.

(Philip Sellinger, "Mother Hen," *Newsweek* 5 Sept. 1977)

In this next example columnist George Will uses four parenthetical remarks to make his point. He inserts a qualifying phrase, enclosed by commas, in his second sentence. He follows his third sentence with a fourth, completely parenthetical sentence, itself containing a parenthetical aside. And his sixth sentence contains another parenthetical remark enclosed by commas. In combination, these parenthetical remarks are as much as anything else what gives this passage its warm conversational feeling.

1   . . . electric trains taught me the terrible weight of philosophic choice. In
2   the late 1940s, the world, or at least the heart of the habitable world, cen-
     tral Illinois, was divided into warring camps. On one side were loutish chil-
3   dren who preferred Lionel trains. (Lionel tracks had—and still may have for
4   all I know—*three* rails, for Pete's sake.) On the other side were precocious
5   and discerning children who rejoiced in American Flyers, like my model of
     a Pennsylvania steam locomotive. I believed then, and still do, that chil-
6   dren who embraced Lionelism had dark pasts and dangerous futures.

(George Will, "Visions of Sugarplums," *Newsweek* 11 Dec. 1978)

EXERCISES

1. Write a cumulative sentence from each of the following base clauses. Add words, phrases, or clauses to provide information about what precedes, either in the base clause itself or in one of the parts you have added. Here is an example arranged to show the process of addition:

> It is time for me to hurry to work too,
> and I exchange my ritual farewell
> > with Mr. Lofaro,
> > > the short,
> > > thickbodied,
> > > white-aproned
> > > > fruitman
> > > > > who stands outside his doorway
> > > > > > a little up the street,
> > > > > his arms folded,
> > > > > his feet planted,
> > > > > > looking solid as earth itself.

> (Jane Jacobs, *The Death and Life of Great American Cities* [New York: Random, 1961])

a. The rain fell all night long . . .
b. Coaxing their battered Oldsmobile, the Jonses headed west . . .
c. America is like a ship . . .
d. Give me the simple [or, *complex*] life . . .
e. Our hearts are fed on fantasies . . .

2. Finish these sentences in the periodic style. Adds words, phrases, and dependent clauses leading to a main clause or climactic statement.

Example

Behavior that in another time would have given rise to outrage and smoldering resentment is now too often shrugged off as being just the way things are.

> (Harry Stein, "On Not Turning the Other Cheek," *Esquire* Mar. 1980)

a. Behind my front door . . .
b. Gaudy neon lights . . .
c. Trusting in the generosity of our neighbors . . .
d. If we don't change our behavior . . .
e What most people fail to understand . . .

3. Choose two of the following subjects. For one write a brief paragraph containing a cumulative sentence; for the second, write a brief paragraph containing a periodic sentence. In both cases, plan carefully how to place these sentences for maximum variety and effect.

a. A deserted fairground.
b. The object that best expresses my personality.

   c. What bothers me most.
   d. Being a student.
   e. The good teacher.

4. Choose three of the following topics and write a brief paragraph for each, three paragraphs in all. For one write a paragraph containing at least one simple, one compound, and one complex sentence. For the second, write a paragraph that uses one or more rhetorical questions. For the third, write a paragraph that contains a parenthetical remark (surrounded this remark with parentheses, dashes, or commas, as they seem appropriate).

   a. His [or her] life was a sort of dream.
   b. Killing time.
   c. An almost sure sign of success [or, *failure*] is. . . .
   d. Stars, celebrities, and personalities.
   e. "In nature there are no rewards; there are consequences." (Horace Annesley Vachel)
   f. A subject from your reading or the end of this chapter.

VARIETY: POINT OF VIEW

Varying Persona

Eleven chapters ago I described the practical and ethical reasons for creating a persona in your writing that reflects your actual knowledge, experience, and feelings. It is this kind of persona that makes us sound authentic, sincere, and natural, the one we wear most comfortably. There will be times, however, when you will want to alter the features of that "real me" persona—perhaps even forsake it entirely—either to take yourself inside someone else's experience or to strike a closer relationship with your audience. Here, for example, a writer tries to dramatize a children's cancer ward for her readers by stepping out of her writing and describing the scene instead from their point of view:

> The first step into a children's cancer ward seems like a step into unreality. Images swim before you: A sign in boldface letters, "Remove Prosthesis Before Being Weighed." Mothers weary, waiting. A teenager with no more hair than the fuzz of a newborn; a tiny girl with ribbons tied to the two or three strands that are left. They look like small-sized veterans of some long-ago war, wraiths returned in a bad dream. Your eyes register them but your mind refuses them; for they are children, you think, who are waiting for death. The first step into a children's cancer ward brings with it a queasy feeling of hopelessness, and there seems to be only one way of coping with it: leaving.
> (Susan Schiefelbein, "Children and Cancer; New Hope for Survival," *Saturday Review* 14 Apr. 1979)

This example puts the reader into the writing. A more radical shift in persona puts the writer into the reader, erasing the distinction between "me" and "them," creating an "us" instead. Because this second shift in point of view is such a powerful strategy for persuasive writing, we will consider it in more detail in Chapter 14 (see pages 357–358). Here we need only observe that by abandoning our own point of view and adopting for the moment our readers' values, feelings, experiences, even their language, we create a relationship with them that will earn for our ideas and opinions a more sympathetic, fairer hearing. After all, we're enabling our readers to see *our* point from *their* point of view.

Here, in a paragraph quoted in Chapter 2, a writer tries to convince her readers, "we Americans," that we don't spend enough time in serious thought nor value intellectual activity. She does this by laying out her readers' mistrust of "thinkers" from their point of view:

> It is easy to understand the causes of this prejudice against thinking. One problem is that to most of us, thinking looks suspiciously like loafing. Homo sapiens in deep thought is an uninspiring sight. He leans back in his chair, props up his feet, puffs on his pipe and stares into space. He gives every appearance of wasting time; he reminds us more of Dagwood and Beetle Bailey than of Shakespeare and Einstein. We wish he would get up and *do* something; mow the lawn, maybe, or wash the car. Our resentment is natural.
> (Carolyn Kane, "Thinking: A Neglected Art," *Newsweek* 14 Dec. 1981)

Everything in the paragraph—the point of view, the language, the allusions to newspaper cartoons, the references to Shakespeare and Einstein, even the mood of the piece—belongs not to the writer but to those she wants to convince. Writing in this way, an act of imaginative sympathy, she invites readers into her discourse, demonstrates her understanding of their suspicions, dramatizes her fairness, and, by stating her readers' position so thoroughly, helps refine her own.

The most radical change we can make in our persona flattens its features into stereotype until we are playing a role in the theatrical sense, either for satire, humor, or both. Watch how this writer plays the happy, dedicated, but naive warrior in the battle against high energy prices:

> Last spring, in the privacy of my own home, I declared war on Big Oil. Actually, I had little choice. I'd already tried dialing down my thermostat to 62 degrees daytime, 58 at night. But, instead of a Presidential citation, all I'd received was a $1,500 heating bill. With fuel prices doubling, I had no option but to embark on a crusade calculated to free me forever from a dependence on foreign oil. Now, a year later, I'm happy to report that my campaign has succeeded beyond my wildest dreams. No longer OPEC's whipping boy, I thumb my nose at sheiks and multinationals. You see, the higher they raise their prices, the more money I save.
> How did I transform my porous old clapboard farmhouse into a multi-fuel home-heating center? Step by step, undaunted by cost, unswayed by sentiment. This is no game for softies, believe me. Take my old wooden storm sash. Charming? Sure. But, when the wind blew, my furniture rocked. So I set about

sacking those faithful old retainers in favor of the more efficient aluminum variety—30 windows and five big doors—for $3,000. A lot of money, you say, to pay for windows that fit on top of your windows? Not with home-heating oil pushing a dollar a gallon.

(Paul D. Zimmerman, "How to Beat the Energy Crisis," *Newsweek* 28 Apr. 1980)

Declared war on Big Oil, this persona declares, *embark on a crusade . . . succeeded beyond my wildest dreams . . . no longer OPEC's whipping boy . . . undaunted . . . unswayed . . . no game for softies . . . sacking those faithful retainers''*—by playing the role of a quixotic Knight Outrageous and playing it so broadly, the writer dramatizes the high costs of energy conservation and at the same time satirizes the foolishly expensive lengths that many—himself included, apparently—have gone to save a dime. The joke is on him and on all those others who have played the same role more naively but no less earnestly.

Irony

School teaches us a rational point of view; work, a practical one. Church teaches a moral point of view; popular entertainment, an emotional one. Unfortunately, we have no institutions to teach us the ironic point of view, although if we pay attention, that is the point of view life seems to teach most insistently. Things are seldom what they seem, events run counter to our best expectations, and we say one thing when we mean another—this is *irony,* the discrepancies between appearance and reality that the ironic point of view sees. The effect of this point of view is to pull us back from life just a bit, hold its surprises up to scrutiny, and help us manage them a little more gracefully.

The effect of irony in our writing is to make it more emphatic, complex, and interesting. When we state our observations as the opposite of what we mean, the discerning reader sees the opposition, recognizes the irony, and remembers. In the excerpt from his essay on the energy crisis,

Used by permission of Johnny Hart and News America Syndicate.

Paul D. Zimmerman gives examples of broad comic irony when he has his happy warrior against high energy prices boast: *No longer OPEC's whipping boy, I thumb my nose at sheiks and multinationals. You see, the higher they raise their prices, the more money I save.* And later:

> Already this past winter I've saved $2,000 in oil bills. And all it's cost me is slightly more than 5 grand. My wife and I would like to save twice as much next year, but we don't know whether we can afford to. So, instead, we're looking into freezing to death. Ecology-minded friends of ours who have been installing an icehouse say it's actually quite pleasant, like drifting off to sleep. And with the oil prices bound to break $10 a gallon by the end of the century, think of the money we'll save.

No longer a whipping boy? we ask. You've spent only *slightly more than 5 grand* to save two? You say you're thinking of freezing to death to save money? We've gotten Paul Zimmerman's ironic point.

Understatement and Hyperbole   These are special forms of irony. *Understatement* is just that, understatement for effect, making things out to be less than they actually are. *Hyperbole* is exaggeration, overstatement for effect, making mountains out of mole hills. Here is Paul D. Zimmerman with more on his campaign against "Big Oil." He has, he writes, just bought a woodburning stove *for a mere $350* (hear the understatement?):

Understatement   There is one hitch, I must warn you, with a woodburning stove: it requires wood. And not just a piece now and then. The kind of wood I'm talking about has to be cut, delivered and stacked. But, with enough wood *Understatement* on my land to sustain me for years, all I had to do was pay someone $50 a month to cut it and bring it in. You might think that's a lot of money to *Irony* pay for your own wood. Still, I get all the fun too: stoking the stove in the *Overstatement* freezing morning, feeding and tending it every twenty minutes, dragging in fresh logs from the frigid porch through my kitchen, in a trail of humus, *Understatement* bark, and slivers. And I've learned a lot—about the way rugs burn, about treating scorched hands and blood-tapping splinters.

Overstatement   Once I got the stove going, it turned our dining room positively equatorial. Flies thrived in profusion, as did the salamanders which fed on them. These tropical temperatures fooled our wall thermostat into thinking the rest *Overstatement* of the house equally cozy, when in fact life as we knew it had ceased to exist in some of the upstairs bedrooms. So I had the entire third floor equipped with baseboard heating. It cost $500. Now my 7-year-old daughter can dial her room to a comfortable 95 degrees and leave it that way, all day, while she's away at school. My electric bills have shot up by $60 a month. But *Irony* what's that when, within eighteen months, oil will be topping $2 a gallon?

The fun of this passage, as well as the exposure of the follies of those who would be energy sufficient, comes to us almost entirely through its ironies.

Sarcasm   Broaden irony enough and it is almost sure to become *sarcasm,* a form of jeering, sneering irony. It pretends to praise or agree when in reality it is scoffing. Here is a sarcastic protest against overregulation by the federal government:

> Surely we Americans are thrice-blessed—with a Mother Hen Congress and ever-growing Federal bureaucracy dedicated to saving us from ourselves. Rest easy (if you can find anything noncarcinogenic to wear, eat, sit or lie on). Mother Hen is determined to create for us the safest, most sterile and most orderly of all possible worlds—even if she is forced (reluctantly, of course) to "modify" our personal freedoms, one by one.
>
> Think of it! Eventually, we will be relieved of all personal responsibilities—including thinking for ourselves—and the need to make any personal decisions. The Great White Chicken in Washington, after all, knows far better than we what is best for us.
>
> (Philip M. Sellinger, "Mother Hen," *Newsweek* 5
> Sept. 1977)

The ironic blessing, the hyperbole, the understatement, the name-calling, the allusion to Voltaire's ironic line ("the best of all possible worlds"): all serve to dramatize this writer's opinion and, in the process, mete out a little verbal punishment to the federal government for what he sees as its unwarranted intrusion into our lives. Sometimes, as in this instance, mockery is the most direct, most emphatic way to make a point and be sure the audience gets it.

MISS PEACH

MISS PEACH by Mell Lazarus. Courtesy of Mell Lazarus and News Group Chicago, Inc.

EXERCISES

1. Choose a controversial subject, one you hold firm opinions about and write a paragraph about that subject as your opponents see it. Try to see through their eyes, feel through their feelings, understand from their perspective. Your aim here is not to change your mind—or theirs—but to enlarge your understanding and sympathy. Write this paragraph as a brief letter addressed to these opponents; let them know you understand.

2. Imagine you have just been fired from your present job. What would you say? Write an ironic letter in response. Use understatement and irony to avoid sounding melodramatic about big, urgent problems. Use hyperbole on small problems to make them seem larger than life. Praise by the way you condemn; damn with your praise, faint or otherwise.

3. Write an ironic protest to the latest action by some governmental body that affects your life, protest the latest overwhelming assignment by one of your instructors, or respond ironically to some outrageous request by a friend, neighbor, or member of your family. Write with overstatement, understatement, irony, and sarcasm.

❧ WRITING INTERESTINGLY

There are few hard-and-fast rules for writing interesting, emphatic, "stylish" prose. After reading this chapter and the preceding, you know *what* to do, but knowing *how* to do it and *when* are more the result of a characteristic point of view and the experimental urge than a set of rules. Often interesting writing results more from serendipity than anything else. The good word, the rhythmic sentence, the interesting approach to a subject often seem to come unbidden—although if the truth be told, the writer was probably searching for something new without being aware of it. When writers think about a writing they're groping not only for ideas but also for a style. The incubation stage is also a rehearsal stage, a time to work out in their minds or on paper the look and sound of the style right for their ideas. They usually begin to hear their writing in their mind's ear after a decent interval of preliminary thinking and writing, often when their minds are relaxed or occupied by something else. Suddenly they'll hear the "good" word, demanding to be written down.

Almost as frequently, an interesting style develops in the middle drafts of a writing. In first drafts writers are generally working out ideas and strategies, attempting to see what fits together. Occasionally the felicitous word or phrase will appear and pull things together, surprising and delighting. But in second or third drafts, writers are better able to turn to their style, listening to the sound of their words, feeling their flow, following the contours of an idea's shape. It is then, for most writers, that writing really begins to get interesting. If there are any lessons in this summary of the writing process, they're the same ones this text has come back to repeatedly:

- Effective writers stock their minds with ideas and then listen for the language their minds give back to them. They listen for these words in freewritings, doodles, sketches, notes, and outlines.
- Effective writers work for stretches long enough to begin hearing the

music in their writing. No composer writes a song one bar at a time; no good writer writes one line or one paragraph at a time.

- Effective writers reread their writing, either aloud or listening with their inner ear. They know that readers hear and feel the rhythm of a sentence before they understand its meaning, and so these writers look and listen for the right rhythms, the ones that stress what is most important and create the right moods. In good writing, idea, shape, and rhythm become one. Once more: "It don't mean a thing if it ain't got that swing."

A Cautionary Conclusion

Like spirited music, playful language has great carrying power. Therefore, in the academic and public writing you do, the playful language you'll use most effectively will probably be the quietest, most unobtrusive, like the background music that helps you concentrate as you work: a little alliteration to draw words together, two or three beats of parallel structure to link ideas, or perhaps a periodic sentence crafted to lead readers to a dramatic conclusion. More than half the examples used to illustrate interesting writing in these two chapters have come from humorous or expressive pieces, suggesting, I suppose, that these are the natural homes of playful prose. They are the most fun to write, verbal tours de force, in which self-expression, play, and experiment are the primary reasons for writing. And lucky is the writer who has opportunities to do such writing. You should look for such opportunities in whatever writing you do, keeping in mind the caveat that applies to most public and academic writing: they are written more to communicate, recommend, persuade, or demonstrate than to entertain.

We must gauge our readers carefully here, their temperaments and expectations. Some will have a sense of humor or ironic sensibility and would be delighted to read any writing, even practical public writing, that swings a little. But in most of your audiences these readers will be in the minority. The majority are more likely to be relatives of those writers I addressed at the beginning of Chapter 11, practical people without much fancy to tickle—at least while reading your writing as part of their jobs. All business themselves, they expect the same from you. To write playfully to them might suggest that you do not take the occasion or them very seriously, or that you are just showing off.

Writing interestingly, then, is a delicate balance between self-satisfaction and meeting the needs of readers. Occasionally we can do both at once; more often we have to choose how much to write for ourselves, how much to write for others. And in that search for the poised response, we end where we began twelve chapters ago, human beings making complex human choices about how to present ourselves to other human beings. The circle this book inscribes is the community circle, the boundaries of our humanity.

WRITING PROJECTS

Topics

1. Write a three to five-page satire of some institution, public person, event, or group. Your aim is to expose folly or evil doing and make fun of it by parody, exaggeration, humor, and sarcasm. Correct wrongful behavior by holding it up to ridicule; shame the subjects of your satire into mending their ways. Consider writing your satire as a persona who sees more than he or she understands. Such naiveté or gullibility will offer you all sorts of opportunities for irony and humor. Write to the members of your composition class.

2. An *encomium* is normally an essay of praise, but for this assignment write a *mock* encomium, a three to five-page essay of ironic praise designed to expose wrongful behavior, foolish ideas, or insensitivity by the person, group, agency, or institution that is the subject of your essay. Use a varied persona, irony (hyperbole or understatement), and sarcasm. Select the details and the language of your praise to show that your subject is more worthy of condemnation. Address either the person or persons you are condemning, those most likely to appreciate your irony, or those who most need to be enlightened about the true character of your subject.

3. Write a three to five-page essay analyzing the style of a recent writer you've read. How does this writer use connotation, honorific and pejorative terms, figurative language, devices of repetition and variety, sentence style, irony, and persona to create a mood, support a thesis, and fulfill his or her intentions? Consider organizing your essay according to an order-of-importance, classification, or "What is it?" pattern.

4. Write a three to five-page essay analyzing the uses of irony in a recent reading you have done. Explain the kinds of irony, how irony creates a particular point of view, what values are embodied by that point of view, what it enables a narrator to see of the subject, and what themes it helps the writer develop. Consider organizing your essay according to an order-of-importance or "What is it?" pattern.

THE WRITING PROCESS

1. Writing-in-progress.
    a. *Exploring:* Free association and freewriting.
    b. *Developing:* Discover all you have to say about your subject. Use whatever methods and strategies seem appropriate.
    c. *Planning a communications strategy:* Decide on a role, persona (distance and attitude), and thesis (*My point is that . . . What I mean to say is that . . .*).
    d. *Organizing.*
        i. Organize your ideas in a clear, predictable, coherent pattern. Use whatever outlining and organizing strategies work for you (see pages 128–132).

        ii. Devise an introductory strategy to capture your audience's attention and focus their interest (see pages 137–141).

    e. *Revising*: Reconsider your ideas and communications strategy; create frictions in your thinking (see pages 55–56).

2. Writing.

    a. Write the preliminary draft of your project.

    b. Whenever possible, write one main idea per sentence; write agent-action sentences; keep the parts short; keep related words together; write positive statements (see pages 183–187).

    c. Whenever possible, use words familiar to both you and your audience.

    d. Repeat sounds (alliteration and assonance), words, phrases, and clauses for emphasis. Play with words (changing distance, listening for sound/sense relationships, using foreign words and emphasizing devices).

————▶**e.** *New in this chapter*: Vary the length and patterns of your sentences, shift your point of view when appropriate, and use irony to emphasize ideas and command reader interest.

3. Rewriting.

    a. Be a zoom lens as you revise; add, delete, substitute, and rearrange.

    b. Ask two questions of troublesome sentences.

        i. What's happening here?

        ii. What goes with what? (See pages 189–196.)

    c. Write "old-new" sentences; reread at a natural pace, listening for unnecessary repetitions and transitions.

    d. Bracket [ ] deadwood of all kinds, reconsider, and then cut.

————▶**e.** *New in this chapter*: Look at the length of your sentences, count the number of words in each, and revise to vary pattern and length; reread your writing aloud to listen for rhythm, variety, and emphasis.

    f. Copyedit for mechanical errors, recopy, and proofread.

4. Self-evaluation.

    a. What is your intention in this writing?

    b. What is your thesis? What are your thematic tags?

    c. What did you do to interest your readers in your subject and emphasize your most important ideas?

    d. What sentences will be most memorable in this writing? What will your readers like best about it? What do you like best?

    e. Did you try anything here that you hadn't tried before?

    f. What one change would most improve this writing?

PART V

A GUIDE
TO PUBLIC
WRITING

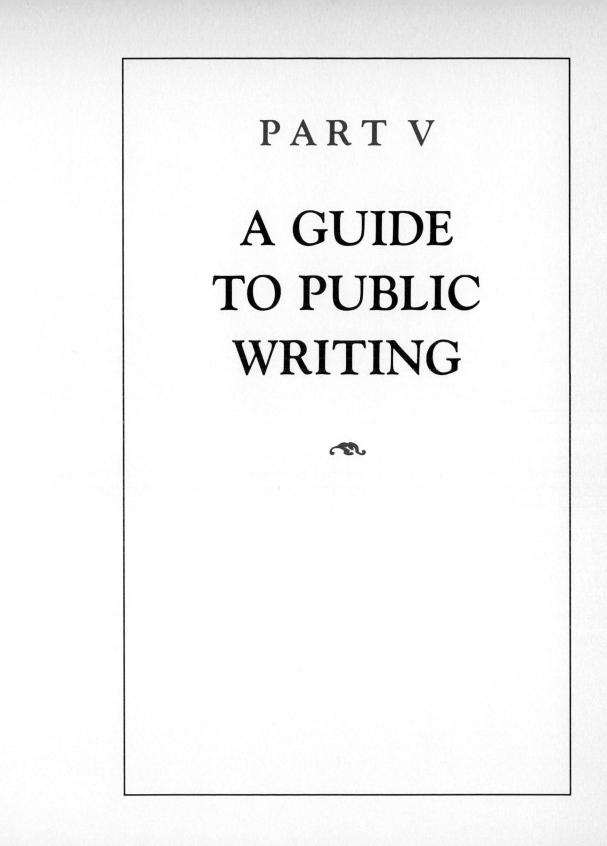

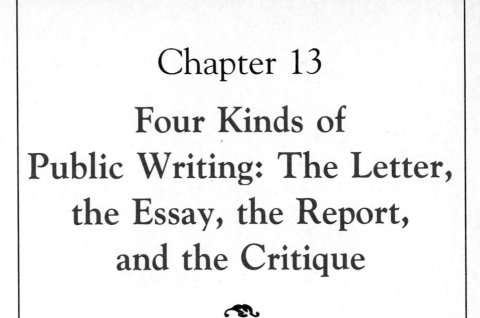

Chapter 13

Four Kinds of Public Writing: The Letter, the Essay, the Report, and the Critique

As you make your way through the chapters of Parts I, II, III, and IV, you will study the strategies and acquire the skills that will help you write more effectively no matter what kind of writing you do, no matter what audience you write for. There are, however, certain kinds of writing practiced by so many writers, including you, and common to so many writing situations, both in school and out, that they are worth studying in their own right. They are the primary subjects of Part V. They draw heavily upon the materials of the preceding chapters, but they also have their own purposes, conventions, formats, and styles that distinguish them from one another and from other kinds of writing. Each is worth particular attention. Therefore, you'll use Part V as a reference source while you read Parts I, II, III and IV, consulting the guidelines in Chapters 13–17 to help you complete individual writing projects.

THE PUBLIC LETTER

Letters to the editor, letters to public officials, complaint letters, order letters, query letters, informative letters, letters of congratulations, letters of application, letters of acceptance or rejection, letters of recommendation: the range of public letters written every day is incredibly broad. No wonder Americans write over 15 billion of these "business" letters every year. In the course of your academic, social, and working life, you're sure to write your share. You'll write good ones if you keep in mind the following guidelines to their look, sound, and contents.

Manuscript Form

First impressions count heavily in public letters. You have only a few minutes of your readers' time, so you must catch their eyes and their attention even before they begin to read. That means writing letters that look businesslike, like writing that can be read and understood effortlessly.

- *Paper:* Use good-quality, heavy bond white paper.
- *Typescript:* Whenever possible, type your letters. Use a black ribbon and standard typeface. If you use a computer or word processor, be aware that many readers object to dot matrix printers, especially when the ribbon is worn.
- *Length:* Whenever possible, limit your letters to a single page.
- *Balance:* Make your letter look readable by centering and balancing it on the page. Keep your paragraphs relatively brief, each surrounded by white space. List and enumerate wherever possible.
- *Nonsexist address:* Use nonsexist forms of address. Address your readers by name or specific title: *Dear Mrs., Mr., Ms., Miss, Dr., Professor,* and so on. When you do not know your readers' names, address them by title alone: *Dear Editor, Service Manager, Director of Admissions.* As a last resort: *Dear Sir (or Madam).*
- *Copies:* Save a copy of all your public correspondence.
- *Envelopes:* Mail your letters in standard number ten envelopes, 4 x 9½ inches. (For additional information on manuscript form, see Chapter 18, Manuscript Form, pages 511–512.)

Although there are several formats for business letters, they are all versions of one another. One of the most common and handsome is the "modified block" format, illustrated on the opposite page.

Just as the layouts of all business letters share a number of common features, so do the contents. First, the *persona* of public letters is almost always businesslike. The distance between writer and reader is neither chattily intimate nor woodenly ceremonial, but in between. The business of most public letters is business of one kind or another, and so they get down to business from the very first line and stick to it till the end. This purpose leads to a style that rarely employs frilly language or sentences. It is a style clear, concise, and direct.

Second, public letters are usually characterized by a *you attitude.* Effective letter writers try whenever possible to see their subjects from their

Return address (omitted with letter head stationery)

Dateline

2441 Dantzler St., NE
Orangeburg, SC 29115
Tel. (000) 000-0000
April 11, 1985

Inside address

Mr. Myron Hurdle
Service Manager
Super-Fast Electronics Company
4995 Silver Dollar Drive
Le Moyne, IL 60626

Body of letter: single
spaced, paragraph not
indented, double spacing
between paragraphs

Dear Mr. Hurdle: — Salutation

On April 1, 1985, I ordered a Super-Fast Quietline Dot Matrix Printer. It was delivered by AirXpress Delivery on April 10 (serial no. SFQ 35934).

While unpacking the shipping carton, I discovered that the printer's plastic cover was badly cracked and that 4 of the 6 transport screws were missing. I could not tell whether their absence might have led to the damage to the cover. When I then connected it to my computer, the printer seemed to run properly, that is, until I tried to superscript and print in the "emphasized" mode. The printer would do neither. I do not know whether this is a hardware or software problem. After I had tried three times without success to print in the "emphasized" mode, the machine stopped completely. Now it will not even run a self-diagnostic test. I have double and triple checked to see that the printer has been properly set up and connected.

Please advise me what to do. I cannot find a Super-Fast dealer listed in the local yellow pages. Is there a local computer service company that can help me, or should I return the printer to you for replacement or repair? As a free-lance writer who depends upon her computer and printer, I will very much appreciate your prompt response.

Complimentary close
aligned with return
address above

Sincerely,

Ella Anne Hathaway

Ella Anne Hathaway

readers' point of view and to write with readers' interests, needs, or benefits uppermost in mind. Even their *organization* reflects this "you attitude." In first paragraphs they generally announce the subjects of their letters, the reasons they have written, or other necessary background information. They want their purposes clear from the outset. When they have bad news to give, they save it until they have presented all the information and reasons explaining the bad news. When they want a response from readers, they make their requests clearly and put them in an emphatic position, often near the end, the most emphatic position of all. These writers do all they can to make it as easy as possible for their readers to understand and take appropriate action.

Four Kinds of Public Letters

Adjustment Letters   The adjustment letter is known popularly as the "complaint letter," but that name obscures its true purpose: not to sound off but to get a problem corrected. Your *role* in such letters will rarely be that of a critic and certainly not an enemy but rather a combination of reporter and persuader. The *audience* for adjustment letters is varied. Occasionally it will be the person who will actually solve your problem. More frequently it will be an intermediary who will pass your request along to those who will make the adjustment. Only rarely will it be the person responsible for creating the problem in the first place. The identity of your reader will greatly determine the contents of your letter—how much background and explanation you must give—and your persona. Because you want your reader to take the appropriate action, your *persona* should always be polite but firm, one who avoids emotional outbursts and threats. You don't want to complain or make a scene in an adjustment letter. You want results.

Application Letters   So, too, do you want results in this kind of letter, but results of a different kind. Here you want a job, a scholarship, grant money, or some kind of favor. Your *role* will be both as a reporter and as a persuader; your purpose, to describe exactly what you want and why you deserve it or why you're qualified. Quiet confidence is the best attitude for your *persona.* You want to sound calm, competent, concise, and well informed—but never boastful. This is the right persona to strike whether your *audience* is merely a screening official—say, a member of a personnel department—or the person with the final authority for granting your application. On the following pages are a sample application letter and the resumé that so often accompanies it.

Letters of Inquiry   You will write letters of inquiry to request services or information. The best interests of both you and your readers are at stake. If you're writing an order letter, say, for some mail-order product, your

1201 W. Chase Boulevard, Apt. 2c
East Lansing, MI 48824
April 14, 1984

Mary L. O'Grady, MSW
Director of Student Services
Harley Williams School
Institute of Child Psychiatry
709 W. Greenleaf Avenue
Chicago, IL 60620

Dear Ms. O'Grady:

Professor Farley Ashby, Chair of the Psychology Department at Michigan State
University, has informed me that you have three openings for Child Care Worker-
Summer Interns. I am applying for one of these positions.

As the enclosed resumé indicates, I am now a college sophomore studying for a
degree in child psychology. I plan a career as a child psychologist working
with institutionalized children. Most of my work so far has been with children.
For two years I worked as a summer counsellor at a camp for children with develop-
mental disabilities. My responsibilities were to provide tutoring, physical
therapy, and recreational supervision and to be a cabin supervisor for ten boys,
ages 8 to 10. For one year I worked as a Boys Club Recreation Supervisor. Of
course, my job often required me to do more than pass out basketballs and teach
table tennis. To many of the boys I was a "big brother" they could talk to
about their problems. My current job, besides helping to pay my tuition, room
and board, is providing me with a valuable introduction to institutional work.

I believe I am qualified by education and work experience to be a Child Care
Worker-Summer Intern at the Harley Williams School. I can be available for an
interview at your convenience, and if you wish, I will have my references and
academic records sent to you. I can be reached by mail at the above address or
at (000) 000-0000 between 9 and 11 a.m., Monday through Friday. I look forward
to hearing from you.

Sincerely,

Matthew Leigh

Matthew Leigh

Enclosure: Resumé

> Reference identifying initials of sender and typist
> (UPPER CASE/lower case), enclosures, or recipients
> of copies (cc: recipent's names)

Matthew R. Leigh
1201 W. Chase Boulevard
East Lansing, MI 48824

Social Security: 000-000-0000
Home tel.: (000)-000-0000
Work tel.: (000)-000-0000

Position desired: Child-Care Worker, Summer Intern

Career Objective: To become a child psychologist working with autistic
                        children in an institutional setting

Education:

    1982 to present: Michigan State University
                        Current standing: Sophomore
                        Major: Child Psychology
                        Honors: Dean's List, 1982-83
                            Leonard E. Frank Scholarship

    1978 to 1982:   Naperville Central High School, Naperville, IL
                        All-State Basketball and Track Teams, 1981 and 1982

Experience:

    1983 to present: Orderly, Weldon Memorial Hospital, East Lansing, MI

    1982 and 1983:   Camp Counsellor, Camp Onewata, Schroon Lake, NY
                            Tutored and supervised recreation at this
                            camp for developmentally disabled children,
                            ages 8-14.

    1982 to 1983:   East Lansing Boys Club, East Lansing, MI
                            Supervised group recreation

References: References and transcripts available from the
                        Placement Office, Michigan State University,
                        East Lansing, MI 48824

Dr. Farley G. Ashby   Ralph M. Runger, MSW
Professor of Psychology and Chair   Director
Department of Psychology   East Lansing Boys Club
Michigan State University   East Lansing, MI 48822
East Lansing, MI 48824

Steele N. Jones   Martha L. Wristen
Supervisor   Director
Service Staff Center   Camp Onewata
Weldon Memorial Hospital   Schroon Lake, NY 10212
East Lansing, MI 48820

readers stand to make a profit by fulfilling your request. Or, if you want information, say, in the form of a college catalog, they fulfill their job descriptions by serving you. Your *role* will probably be that of a friendly reporter with just a touch of the persuader so they will respond promptly to your request. The *audience* for such letters is often the most difficult piece of information to find. Be sure you direct your letter to the right agency, office, or person. Rerouting your letter if you misaddress it will waste your time and your readers'. As you write, anticipate their needs and questions. Give the necessary background information, and be specific about the information or service you want, itemizing if possible. Occasionally you'll want to tell your readers why you want the information or service, one way to help them see whether you've made the right request.

Response Letters   The range of response letters is broad, from letters to the editor written in response to public events and issues to business letters responding to other letters. At one end of this range your *role* will be that of a reporter-teacher-critic, as you present and explain your opinion. At the other end, you will write as a reporter-teacher-friend, answering another letter writer's request and promoting the good will of the organization you represent. The *persona* you adopt will speak, on the one hand, for you and people of like minds or, on the other, for your organization. In either case, you will want to sound courteous, responsible, understanding, concerned, and fair. In *no* case will you want to sound self-righteous or self-important. Your *audience* will be varied: neutral readers (for example, editors, not the subjects of your criticism), the actual subjects of you criticism (a government official), or interested readers looking to you for information or service. You must take pains to be clear about what your readers can do for you or what you can do for them.

❧ THE ESSAY

The essay is a moderately brief nonfiction prose writing on one subject or related subjects, unified by a specific mood, purpose, or thesis. The term *essay* comes from the same source as the word *assay*. Just as a metallurgist assays gold, analyzing it, weighing it, and discovering its worth, so does an essayist analyze a subject, weigh or evaluate it, and try to state its meaning and significance. The essay is one of the broadest, most varied and flexible forms of writing. And it is for these reasons that essays appear so frequently in college writing assignments and outside college in the books and magazines we read. They are suitable for many moods, purposes, and occasions, whenever men and women try to discover and present their thoughts, feelings, observations and experiences of themselves and their world.

Personal Essays

Despite their variety and flexibility, however, we can classify most essays into several broad kinds. The two kinds you'll write most frequently in college are personal and expository essays. Although they occasionally share features, they are distinct. The *personal essay* is just that, an essay about something personally important to the writer. Its subjects may be personal experiences, personally important ideas, or personally important people, places, and scenes. They may be big subjects or little, serious or humorous—crossing the threshold of adulthood by leaving home or taking a bike ride on a rainy fall day—but important to the writer in every case and worth writing about for that reason alone.

When you write a personal essay, your purpose is almost always expressive, to *express* your experiences, perceptions, and feelings in suitable words. Therefore, your *role* will primarily be as a participant. Occasionally you may also have to write as a critic, reporter, poet, teacher, friend, or enemy—but more than anything else you want to write your life, to translate it into words, to recapture it from memory, and to understand or appreciate it better thereby. You want to express what you felt when you saw the Grand Teton mountains the last time. You want to experience once more the shock of discovery you received when, standing in a market square in Marrakech, Morocco, you saw a Coke bottle, its label stamped in Arabic: for better or worse, America seemed to be everywhere! You want to describe your gratitude for the friends who sustained you when your father died.

But this expressive aim does not mean that personal essays are private writing, like diaries or journals. Whether written for a college composition class or publication in a magazine, personal essays have a *public audience*. The assumption that underlies the personal essay is that private experience has a value and an interest for more than the author alone. You may write first for yourself, but you also write for this public, and you'll judge the success of your essay in part by how well you enable readers to share your experiences, see your scenes, and feel your feelings. You'll use *I* frequently in your personal writing, an insistent *persona*, and you shouldn't feel self-conscious about it. All those *I*'s will be not only your personal reference point, your window on experience; those *I*'s will also be your readers' *eyes* (and every other sense, besides), the means for them to share your life with you.

You'll write your personal essays in the ways appropriate to the self-expression we share with others. Your *introduction* may provide the background information necessary to understand your subject, it may describe the setting, or it may plunge your readers directly into your subject at some dramatic moment: whatever will get them most involved with your writing and help them see where it is going. More often than not you'll *organize* your personal essays as stories (short autobiographical narratives), descriptive sketches of people and scenes, or reflective explanations of feelings, ideas, and discoveries. But your essays won't say everything about your subjects. Our lives are always too complex, even in the space of one moment, for us to describe all that is happening to us. Besides, you won't have room or time for it all. And so you will select from all that you *could* say about your subject and write only those details most important to the mood you want to express or the main idea you want to convey.

Consider a young woman trying to write about her parents' divorce. She's aware of not only her pain as her childhood home divides about her but also her parents' and brothers' and sisters' pain. Now, she could try to write about her parents' incompatibilities that led to their separation and, simultaneously, about her anger at their separation, but to do so may only confuse her account. She would have to manipulate two points of view (hers and her parents'), several roles (participant, reporter, critic, and teacher), and conflicting emotions (hers and the other family members'). So instead she will choose one primary role (participant rather than reporter, teacher, or critic), one set of details, perhaps one dramatic episode that sums up all she has gone through (the afternoon her father piled his personal belongings in the station wagon and took them to his new apartment). Her personal experience essay won't tell the *whole* truth but only *a* truth, the one that matters most to her, what *she* feels, watching the split in the home and family she loves. This focused role and subject are two more ways personal essays differ from journals and diaries. Personal essays have a definite purpose and design.

Expository Essays

The word *expository* comes from the Latin *expositorius*, meaning to set forth or explain. Implied by this word is the audience for that explanation. And therein lies the chief difference between personal and expository essays. Expository essays are written about subjects of immediate concern not only to writers but to their readers besides. Expository essays are fully public writing. The subjects of your expository essays may be important subjects or unimportant ones (the prospects for peace in the Middle East or how to bake a devil's food cake), general subjects or limited ones (race relations in America's major cities or the low-income subsidized housing debate in Arlington Heights, Illinois), serious subjects or humorous ones (capital punishment or the romantic blunders of contemporary couples). But in every case, your subjects will have more than immediate personal importance, and you'll develop them with more than personal details, experiences, and observations.

Your purposes are the obvious ones referred to in the preceding paragraph, to *expose* a subject by presenting information, analysis, and explanation of it. Suitable to such informative purposes, your *roles* will be those of reporter and teacher primarily. You may occasionally write as a participant, but to add information or understanding rather than self-expression. For example, in an essay about the enduring Arab-Israeli conflict, you might write an anecdote about your trip to Israel, not to share your experiences but to add the understanding you gained by first-hand observation. So, too, will your *persona* be more reserved and disengaged from your subject than it would be in a personal essay, more public writer-style than intimate talker-style. You may occasionally write as an *I*, but you don't want to get in the way of your information and explanation of it to your audience.

Appropriately to your informative purposes, you'll *introduce* your expository writing by describing the subject, providing necessary background information, or stating the significance of the subject—whatever will help your readers see the revelance of your essay to their interests. You'll *develop* your subjects with facts, figures, examples, definitions, analytic description, and the words of authorities—whatever will help your audience grasp your subject. And you'll *organize* your expository writing to the same end, occasionally in chronological order as instructions or the description of a process, but more often as an explanatory arrangement of the key parts or important features of your subject.

Three Student Essays

Immediately following are three brief essays that will introduce you to the range of personal and expository essays. All three were written by college freshmen. In subject they differ from the personal to the public, in mood from the humorous to the serious, and in purpose from entertainment to meditation and explanation. The first two essays are personal, the third expository. College requires that you master both kinds of essays, and the assignments that conclude the chapters in Parts I, II, III, and IV of this book will give you many opportunities for practice. Following in this chapter and later chapters are guidelines for writing three other kinds of essay: the critique, the persuasive essay, and the literary essay.

An imaginative title

Rank Has Its Privileges, but Revenge Is Sweet
by David Barts
(*A Humorous Personal Essay*)

An introduction that provides necessary background information and creates the writer's role and persona

Many, many moons ago, when I was in the fifth grade, our country was gearing up for another one of those contests we call presidential elections. I certainly didn't know much about the whole thing, but I decided I wanted Bobby Kennedy to win—he seemed like such a nice guy. My older brother, the big, bad high school freshman who knew it all, was rooting for some man named Nixon. As you know, Senator Kennedy was brutally murdered. After that, because my brother Denny knew so much, I started rooting for this Nixon, too. If I hadn't, then Denny probably would've beaten me up . . . again.

Four years later *I* was a big, bad high school freshman myself, now I knew it all, and Richard Nixon was a veteran President seeking re-election. He was having difficulties because of some bugging he had been caught at and something about a break-in at some place called Watergate, and I was having trouble convincing my brother and all my friends that he was a good President who just happened to get caught.

Two years after that, I had a tremendous argument with my English teacher because of a *D* I had received on an essay. The teacher had told us to write about the pardon President Ford had recently given former President Nixon. To this day I maintain that I received that *D* just because I was the only one in the class, including the teacher, who favored the pardon.

A transition to steer the reader to the actual beginning of the narrative

Additional background information to help readers understand the events to come

Six years later, and my story begins. I was stationed at the American Embassy in Paris, France, as a Marine security guard. Our detachment of Marines was divided into three "strings," each with a Sergeant of the Guard (SOG), an Assistant Sergeant of the Guard (ASOG), and six watch standers. Among other things, the SOG was responsible for driving the guard van around the city to post the watch at each of the several buildings we were assigned to guard. As the entire detachment had only one vehicle, the SOG always got off duty about an hour early so that he could get the van back to our quarters in time for the oncoming relief to use. Occasionally, though not as often as I would have liked, my SOG would let me, the ASOG, leave early and return the van.

During the middle of April in 1980, my string was working the graveyard shift. At about two o'clock in the morning, we received a message announcing that former President Nixon would be arriving at the Hotel George V at 8:15 that morning. Using every reasonable excuse and every unreasonable argument I could think of, I spent the next five and a half hours trying to convince the SOG that it would be a good day to let me be the one to take the van back. He simply had to let me because everything was on a very strict timetable: Whoever took the van would leave at 7:30, arrive at the Marine house at 7:45, and have a half-hour to make the ten-minute trip to the hotel and see the President at 8:15. Whoever didn't take the van would get off duty at 8:30, go home and go to bed, period. Well, rank does have its privileges. I lost. The SOG left early and assured me he would show me the pictures he was going to take. When I finally got home, I decided not to hit the sack but instead wait for that SOBSOG to find out what happened. He arrived with a smile on his mug and told me that he had indeed seen the President. He said that he couldn't get very close, but with his zoom lens he was sure he had gotten some good photos. I went to bed.

The writer describes in detail only those events crucial to his story; the rest he summarizes briefly

That afternoon my fiancée and I went to church to see the pastor about our rapidly approaching wedding. We finished our meeting and decided that since it was such a gorgeous spring day, we would walk home. We weren't in any particular hurry, so we walked slowly, admiring the sights. Our route home happened to include Avenue Alma Marceau, the street the Hotel

George V is on. I stopped my fiancée in front of the hotel and told her who was inside. We stood talking about Mr. Nixon for ten minutes. I was telling her how I had admired and respected him for so long. Once again: I ended up defending him.

Just as we were about to leave, I recognized a man walking out the hotel door. It was General Walters, one of the presidential aides during the Nixon years. Of course, I didn't know him personally, but I had seen him several times at the embassy. I assumed that if he was in the hotel, then he must have been with Mr. Nixon, so I crossed the street and asked him. He told me the President would be leaving the hotel at seven o'clock to meet his publisher for dinner and that possibly I could catch a glimpse of him then. I started to run home and get my camera and zoom lens, then remembered my fiancée standing across the street. I ran back to get her and then we ran to the Marine house.

While I was tearing apart my room and dumping out my drawers in search of my camera, I remembered that one of the other Marines had always preached Nixonism. I sped over to his room, woke him, told him the news, and then the three of us dashed back to the hotel.

Description to set the scene for the climactic episode

When we arrived we saw a limousine in front of the door and, naturally, a zillion cops, reporters, and photographers. A couple of Secret Service agents we knew were standing by the front door, so we went over to talk with them. When we told them why we were there, they just smiled and walked inside the hotel. They came back after a few minutes and we stood around making small talk. Suddenly, it dawned on me just how close to the door we were. I began to wonder if I would need that zoom lens after all. I sensed the crowd vibrating so I looked in through the glass doors and saw Mr. Nixon walking though the lobby directly toward those very same doors. I couldn't believe it—there he was, not twenty feet away.

Mind you, I've met my share of bigshots. On embassy duty there were so many VIPs visiting so often that we Marine guards actually began to dislike it when they showed up. For us, those visits usually meant extra duty and we weren't particularly fond of that. But this wasn't just another bigshot VIP, this was President Nixon.

That twenty-foot gap had narrowed to almost nothing and then he was practically in front of me. I was thinking that I couldn't believe all this as I fumbled with my camera. Then I almost went into shock when the Secret Service agent said, "Mr. President, I'd like you to meet a couple of the Marines from our embassy here."

Dialogue that dramatizes the most important moment

Knowing that this wasn't the time to make a blundering fool of myself, I tried to regain that diplomatic composure that had been so undiplomatically crammed down our throats in Marine Security Guard School.

Flashbulbs lit the sky as we talked. The President seemed genuinely interested in our tour of duty, how we liked Paris, and where we were originally from. I introduced my French fiancée and Mr. Nixon made a joke about the "French Connection." It was corny, but who cared? We began posing for pictures and the other Marine (we called him Lil Guy because he was only five feet tall) reached up and put his arm around the President. I figured, why not, so I did the same. We posed for a few thousand more pictures, talking as we posed, and then the President left.

Indirect quotation to summarize a dramatic scene

As his motorcade roared down the street, the three of us found ourselves in the middle of our very first press conference: Who were we? Where were we from? Did we realize that this was Mr. Nixon's first major public appearance since his resignation six years earlier? Did this mean that Mr. Nixon would be returning to public life? How did we feel about his presidency? As if we were presidential spokespersons. The reporters went on and on with their questions. We told them our names and hometowns, but with polite nonchalance we avoided the rest. When they were finished, we walked home in childish glee.

That night on duty, I told my SOG about the entire event. While I was being very, very specific about each and every detail, I noticed for the first time that he had green eyes. For one of those extremely rare moments in my life I thought of Shakespeare: "Jealousy is a green-eyed monster."

A small but telling detail

The next morning I saw three beaming faces with President Nixon on the front page of four different Paris newspapers.

The final event in the narrative, bringing the story to an ironic, humorous close

Having lived or been stationed in several places around our country and overseas, I've gotten to know a lot of people from a lot of places. During the next several weeks, I received newspapers from friends virtually everywhere that had pictures and stories about our rendezvous with the President. Among others, the *New York Times* arrived. The *McHenry Plaindealer* arrived. *The Stars and Stripes* arrived. The *Chicago Sun-Times* arrived.

I made sure my SOG got a copy of every one.

A Study of Leaves
by Carol Collins
(*A Reflective Essay*)

An introduction that gives the occasion for the writer's reflection

The main idea

Method of development: Analogy

Pattern of organization: Comparison

Tunnels of gold rise above us like cathedral walls. Torches of flame fill our eyes in the warm autumn sunshine. We gaze in wonder on this brilliant gift of nature. And then—with even more wonder and astonishment—I see how the pattern of these glorious leaves resembles our lives.

Even though each leaf may grow in its own shape and size, each is part of the larger organism, the tree. That small leaf is not only a delicate individual, interesting in itself, but takes its character from the tree and enables that tree to survive. We, too, are unique, growing in response to the shade, light, and nourishment that come our way, yet we are also part of that larger organism—society. And we have our own special gifts and talents essential to its life. The richer the gifts we offer by our involvement, the stronger that society becomes.

A topic sentence that
introduces the next
point in the
comparison

The writer's roles:
Teacher, poet, critic,
and reporter

Our lives unfold much as the life of the leaf. The leaf begins a tightly wrapped blade. As the blade is warmed by the sun and nourished by the rains, deliberately, unfalteringly, it unfolds and takes shape. It gains form, substance, texture, and color. We begin in a similar way, an undeveloped organism, eager to take in and absorb nourishment from the world around us. As we receive that human nourishment—love, caring, sharing, and learning—we begin to unfold and take on our form, substance, texture, and color—our personalities!

As the new leaf grows, its shape becomes fuller; its color changes from pale to deeper green. The leaf is maturing. Using nature's nutrients, the leaf assumes its characteristic form and begins contributing to the life of the tree. So, too, do we grow and mature, taking our love, experience, and knowledge and sharing them with others. By this action, we help sustain our human community. We become resilient, able to bend in the winds of fortune and survive. We mature.

The maturing continues. As the leaf witnesses the passing of summer, it becomes vulnerable to the dangers of time, less flexible, its connection with the tree more tenuous. But an amazing thing happens. About to die, the leaf blazes forth in color—its true color!—its brilliance bringing a special vision to us all. We, too, will grow old. We, too, will grow less flexible, less able to respond as life demands. Our hold on life will become more tenuous. But with our age and maturity, we, too, can burst forth in our own special brilliance.

We will gain greater freedom, freedom from family obligations, from our schedules, from social pressures to conform. We can fulfill all those dreams we've hidden and put aside for so long. We can take that planned trip, read those books we've always wanted to read, do what we've always wanted to but never had the time for. Like that brilliant autumn leaf, at the end of our lives we achieve our fullest individuality and are illuminated by that special brilliance we can share with others.

A natural conclusion:
A process completed
and a point made

At last, however, the leaf withers and falls to the ground. But even as it dies, it becomes the substance from which new life grows. The fallen leaves blanket the ground around the tree, protecting it from winter's harm. So, too, in our passing will we leave a legacy for those to come, a gift from the richness of our lives, the talents we have used, the wisdom we have shared. These essential elements will form the soil from which new generations will grow. Like the leaf, we live and die to bring forth new life.

Computers: What Are They?
by Paul Baker
(An Expository Essay)

A dramatic opening
that signals the

If you don't like the way this paper is written, blame my computer! And why shouldn't you? Doesn't everyone say computers are taking over every-

<table>
<tr><td>

writer's involvement
with a public subject

A description of the
causes of the attitudes
the writer opposes

The writer's roles:
Critic, teacher, and
reporter

The writer's thesis

The writer's commu-
nications strategy: To
begin with readers'
misconceptions and
then correct them

A transition that
guides readers to the
history that helps the
writer prove his point

A rhetorical question
that keeps the writer's

</td><td>

thing? Aren't they? That's what I hear frequently these days from people who really believe it—and I don't like what I hear. But is it any wonder this opinion exists? We see stories on television; we read them in the newspapers; we listen to our neighbors—all of them feed our misconceptions. Stories like these: A computer commandeered a commuter train and sent it on to the next station, leaving a surprised driver standing on the platform; or Mr. Adams' charge account was closed because the computer "decided" that he had passed on. Well, these stories are hogwash! Do we blame the plane for killing 247 people or the person who designed it? Or the person who piloted it? Or the person who serviced it? There's a great disparity between what too many people believe about computers and what is actually true. It's time to put the science fiction computer back in the paperbacks. Computers are tools, extensions of ourselves, to be used for the benefit of all people. They are not the twentieth-century kin of Frankenstein.

We all know what a computer is, right? On television we used to see the computer on *Star Trek,* which Captain Kirk commands: "Computer, give me all the references in your memory banks to a late nineteenth-century murderer known as Jack the Ripper." Within seconds the computer has the information for the Captain. Another favorite of mine is the computer aboard *Discovery,* a spacecraft traveling one hundred thousand miles an hour to "a planet on the farthest edge of the solar system." This Hal is described as "a chatty computer who ceasely guides your course [on board the *Discovery*] and your life." Then good old Hal blows a fuse in his memory circuits or something and begins killing the humans "he" is supposed to serve. In the novel and the movie *2001: A Space Odyssey,* the bad computer wins. Then, of course, there's that pretentious little computer in the *Star Wars* movies, R2D2. This futuristic version of Dorothy's Tinman is more of stand-up comic than a computer. Or maybe you are one of the few who take a more scholarly view of computers. In the words of Webster's *Dictionary,* a computer is "a device used for computing; specifically, an electronic machine which, by means of stored instructions and information, performs rapid, often complex calculations. . . ."

If you're like most people, one of the fantasy-land computers was your first encounter with them, and they just seemed to appear—on our TV screens, in the movies, in our books—overnight, as if left by some computer fairy. A little research, however, shows that historians trace the computer back 5,000 years to the beginnings of the abacus. The abacus is a kind of manual computer widely used in the Orient. This strange little device looks like a small jailhouse window with nine vertical bars and one horizontal. On each section of vertical bars is a number of bright colored wooden beads. Almost by sleight of hand, it seems, an expert can calculate the price of a six pack of Coke faster than you can say "Panasonic." Do you suppose the Chinese worried 5,000 years ago about the abacus taking over?

The next significant advance in computer history did not occur until the

</td></tr>
</table>

point before his
readers

early 1600s, when John Napier, a Scottish mathematician and inventor of logarithms, published his work on a mechanical means of computation. Using sticks made of bone or ivory and data tables, Napier described a method of multiplication and division. This was the first example of computation by mechanical means in recorded history. I doubt that people then were very worried about Napier's "bones" taking over anything.

The world's first digital computer was invented in about 1835 by the Englishman Charles Babbage. Babbage's device was called an "analytic engine." This device was only partially built because the techniques needed to produce the precision mechanical parts had not yet been invented. Still, this was the first device that could perform arithmetical procedures by decisions based on the value of a previously computed number. This mechanical computer, made of wheels, levers, cams, and gears would sit there— whirr, click, click, grind—and spit out the answer to a problem much as some of the old deck calculators still do today.

By the late nineteenth century, our nation, then just over a hundred years old, was growing rapidly. The census bureau was having trouble counting all the new heads, so in 1886 an American statistician, Herman Hollerith, developed the idea that holes in cards could be sensed by a machine. His idea was simple: by assigning a column, or group of columns, on the punched card to each question asked in the census and by creating a code for all the possible answers which would, in turn, be punched in the card, Hollerith could use a machine to accumulate the totals for the census. Using his idea, Hollerith reduced the amount of time necessary to complete the 1890 census by two thirds. Now, some people were probably awed and impressed by this feat, but most couldn't care less about Hollerith's machine.

The twentieth century finally brought the technology necessary to create the large electronic computer, and work was begun around the world to build these giant calculators. The first on record was the Mark I, built at Harvard University in 1939. This machine was a mechanical nightmare! It was approximately fifty feet long and eight feet tall and could add, subtract, multiply, and divide as well as look things up in a table.

In 1946, the ENIAC computer at the University of Pennsylvania was turned on and became the first truly all-purpose electronic computer. It was one thousand times faster than the Mark I at Harvard. It has been estimated that the nuclear calculations ENIAC did in two hours would have taken one hundred engineers an entire year to complete. As for what has happened since then, well, you have at least a vague idea. Computers since ENIAC have gotten smaller, faster, and more powerful. Today's technology, in fact, has made it possible to put the power of ENIAC into a single computer that will fit nicely in the palm of your hand.

The conclusion to the
writer's survey:

By reviewing briefly the history of computers, we can see that the computer is nothing more than a machine; still, it is a great invention, which

Computers as a
historical fact

Computers as a
social fact

Computers as an
emotional fact

A closing analogy that
echoes the writer's
thesis

has begun to change our lives in ways we are scarcely aware of. Today the computer is used in industry for increasing production; in business for controlling costs; in medicine for curing disease. Scientific fields such as nuclear research and space exploration could not exist without the computer. But as overwhelming as all this seems, we must remember that it is still people who drive these computers. Without people, the computer is nothing more than silicon, plastic, wires, some metal, a few switches, and several shots of electricity.

And it seems, because of those people, that computers are here to stay, an important part of our lives. Alvin Toffler, in his book *Future Shock*, tells us that "virtually every intellectual discipline from political science to family psychology" will be influenced by the "imaginative hypotheses triggered by the invention and diffusion of the computer" (27). As Toffler suggests in his book, the computer is just now beginning to affect us in important ways. But in the near future we will be using the computer throughout our lives as painlessly as we use the telephone today. Even now, we have small computers in our cars, our kitchens, and our rec rooms. Who knows, we might begin to see them in our bedrooms!

Most who come in contact with these super computers today form one of two attitudes. In *Information Technology: The Human Use of Computers*, Harry Katzan informs us, "People appear to be polarized: either they regard them [computers] as beneficial to mankind or they regard them as 'terrible' machines that dehumanize and threaten the individual" (307). I believe the computer is an extension of man's mind, as the automobile is an extension of his legs. Some will use the computer for evil, while others will use it to benefit us all. In the end, only people do right or wrong, *not* their machines.

WORKS CITED
Katzan, Harry. *Information Technology: The Human Use of Computers*. New York: Mason & Lipscomb, 1974.
Toffler, Alvin. *Future Shock*. New York: Random, 1970.

✎ THE REPORT

The report is a systematic presentation of specific information to an audience interested in that information. A student in an abnormal psychology class assigned to read Sigmund Freud's *Psychopathology of Everyday Life* and write a summary of it would probably use the report form. So, too, would a warehouse manager of a photo supply company "report" his year-end inventory to the vice president in charge of purchasing. A social worker at a community mental health center would use the report form to write up his interview with a client. A physicist would organize the results of her experiment in superconductivity as a report. And a magazine describing the quality of American fast-food restaurants would make its evaluation in report form. Reports are all around us, the staple of writing done in school, on the job, in the professions, wherever facts are at a premium.

The sources for this information may be a single book, as in a book report, or many books and articles, as in a research project. Or they may be first-hand observation, interviews, or experimentation. The report may draw conclusions about this information and may even make recommendations for action based upon it, but its primary purposes are informative rather than explanatory or evaluative. Because its subject matter is facts and figures, it often supplements its words with tables and other illustrations.

The Audience and Persona for Report Writing

The audiences for reports, both in school and out, are specialized, created by their specific interests in a subject and specific motives for reading. One social worker reads another's client case report in order to plan a course of treatment. Physicists read a colleague's research report to improve their understanding but also to evaluate its experimental results. Parents read a report on the quality of fast food because they want a healthy diet for their children. The audiences for your reports will be as specialized as these. They will come to your subject with definite interest in it and at least some knowledge, so you may not have to work very hard to capture their attention, although you will have to work to give them all the information they seek. You'll write most informatively if you begin your preparations with an audience profile:

- Who is my audience, exactly?
- What are their interests in my subject?
- What are their motives for reading?

The audiences for academic reports deserve one word of qualification. They will probably know most of what your reports will tell them and may even be experts about your subject. What would you say to a psychology professor about Sigmund Freud that she didn't already know? Academic audiences don't want to know about your subject; they want to know what you know. The trick when writing for them is to recognize their knowledge, not treat them as ignorant, and yet be as thorough and clear in the information you present as you would be for a less informed audience.

The persona for this kind of informative writing should usually be neutral in its attitudes and public in its distance from its readers. On most occasions you will avoid emotional content and beware of language charged with connotation. For informal reports and those in which you are an observer or source of information, write in the first person; otherwise, in the third person. In all cases, label opinions as such. Listen to this report of some of the information gathered during the 1980 U.S. Census.

> The divorce rate—the number of divorces per 1,000 Americans—doubled to 5 between 1965 and 1976. Largely as a result, the number of one-parent households has increased by 100 percent since 1970—and the number of married couples with children has actually declined. Today there are 109 divorced people for every 1,000 married ones, and among blacks, the ratio is even higher: 233 divorces per 1,000 married people. Nine out of every 10 one-parent families are maintained by Mom (and 48 percent of all black families with kids under 18 are headed by a mother alone). But over the past decade, the number maintained by single fathers has more than doubled, a trend many experts predict will accelerate as child-custody laws are reformed.
>
> (Merrill Sheils "A Portrait of America," *Newsweek* 17 Jan. 1983)

This reporter doesn't express dismay over the alarming increase in the divorce rate, even though he may be alarmed, nor does he offer his opinions about what might curb the divorce rate. His feelings about the facts are irrelevant here. More often than not, this is the persona you'll project in your reports.

However, if the occasion for the report is informal and your subject nonserious, you may relax your persona somewhat, write more personally, and use a vocabulary more familiar and connotative. Listen to the persona in this section from a report about beer published in *Consumer Reports,* a general-circulation magazine aimed at interested nonexperts.

> *Calories* A famed restaurateur was once asked if his latest culinary creation was fattening. "Only if you eat it," was the bland response.
>
> A brewer's answer could have been less evasive—"Only if you drink a lot of it." The imports averaged about 150 calories in a 12-ounce glass; so did the regular domestic beers. That makes beer less fattening than whole milk, which contains 150 calories in only eight ounces. A few individual brands went as high as 170 calories (*Kronenbourg*) or 175 (*Augsberger*). Then again, some were as low as 136 calories (*Hamm's*) or 140 (*Coors*).
>
> Still, the "beer-belly" image does attach to the product—hence the increasing popularity of light beers, with their aggressively promoted low-cal halo. Do you save significantly in calories by switching to a light beer? Maybe not.
>
> On average, the low-cal beers contained 98 calories, or one-third less than regular beer. Specific brands may be significantly higher or lower. A 12-ounce glass of *Pabst Extra Light,* for instance, contained only 68 calories. But 12 ounces of *Michelob Light* had 135 calories—about as much as in several regular beers.
>
> ("Beer," *Consumer Reports* July 1983)

With a subject like beer reported in a popular magazine, an informal public persona can appropriately crack jokes, address the audience directly, use contractions and slang, even write sentence fragments. But in most of your reports, your persona will be formal and reserved, keeping your personality and opinions out of the way of your information.

Gathering
Information

Whether you are writing a book report or direct observation report, begin by writing a *statement of the problem*. This is your reason for reporting. It may be a sentence identifying your aims, the question you want to answer, the actual problem you are trying to solve, or the assignment you must fulfill.

The purposes of this report are to describe the structure, summarize the contents, and state the conclusions of Henry Nash Smith's *The Virgin Land: The American West as Symbol and Myth*.

The purposes of this report are to compare and contrast American immigration now and as it was eighty-five years ago.

The purposes of this report are to describe the decline in the American auto industry during the 1970s and identify its causes.

The purposes of this report are to survey student attitudes at my college and to discover their thinking about the board of trustees' decision to eliminate pass/fail grades.

The purposes of this report are to describe the components of the basic personal computer and to inform potential buyers of what to keep in mind while they are shopping.

Writing this statement down early will help you stay on course as you search for your information. And, when you have finished gathering it, you will use a revised version of this statement in the report itself. Use the clause *The purposes of this report are . . ."* to start you off; you may not actually include it in your finished report, but writing it now will help you be precise and remind you to enumerate all your purposes.

Unless you're writing a single-source book report, your second step is to identify, design (in the cases of questionnaires or experiments), collect, and evaluate the sources for your information. Talk to experts in your field, instructors, corporations, agencies, anyone who can help you identify the sources you'll need and show you how to collect your information by the most thorough, reliable methods possible. Check with reference librarians to direct you to indexes, bibliographies, and other references that will help you identify book and periodical sources. Make sure that these sources are reputable by checking the credentials of the authors, compilers, and editors. If you cannot find these credentials in the frontmatter of the book, check book reviews (listed in several book review indexes that your librarian will direct you to). Remember, your report will be only as good as its information. If your sources are unduly biased or unqualified, your information may well be incomplete or unreliable. As you identify these sources, compile a bibliography listing them (see Chapter 16, "The Research Project," Step 3, pages 420–432). You will use this bibliography to help you document your sources and take credit for all the research you have done.

The information you take from books and articles you should record on note slips, the briefer the entry the better. You may also want to transcribe to note slips the information you gather from observations, questionnaires, interviews, and recordings, dividing the information into small pieces, one bit of information per note slip. You won't know as you gather your facts exactly how you will later present them. Short notes now will make it easier later to arrange your materials. If you're writing a book report, you should write down during your reading anything that will help you summarize the contents and describe the form of your book. (For more tips on note taking, see Chapter 16, "The Research Project," Steps 2 and 4, pages 405–412, 432–435.)

You will take most information in summary form. Any information you suspect your readers may not understand, you should *paraphrase* (a word-for-word translation from your source's words into your words). Quote sources when they are dramatic, when they sum up a point, or when you cannot summarize more economically. As you gather your information, remember that you are more than a human recording device. You must sift and weigh your facts, making sense of them as you go along. Look for information that several sources have in common; this may be a clue to its reliability, and you may want to combine these sources in your report. Look, too, for sources that supplement one another, one source providing what a similar source lacks. Look especially for contradictions or conflicts in your information. You can't simply dismiss a source when it contradicts another that you prefer. If you find contradictions or discrepancies, you've found a problem *within* your problem, and you're obliged to report it. The accurate, complete report must not only report information; it must also identify anything that obscures the facts or renders them suspect.

As you near the finish of your information gathering, begin to work out a statement of your conclusion. This conclusion may be one of the following:

A summary statement of your information.
Conclusions you have been led to draw that make sense of your information, that identify causes or consequences, that indicate significant points.
A solution to the problem.
Recommendations based on the information.

If you're writing a book report, your conclusions will be a brief summary statement of the book's subject, purpose, audience, and uses.

Organizing the Report

The two boundaries of all reports are the statement of the problem and the conclusion or recommendation. They may both appear at the beginning of the report, followed by the information of the report. Or the report may state the problem, give the information that develops or solves it, and then present the conclusion. However you organize your report, you'll want to introduce individual topics and subtopics with section headings. Use centered headings for major topics and headings flush with the left margin for subtopics.

Here are the conventional subdivisions of the report in their conventional order. Not every report will contain all these parts; nor are they always arranged in exactly this way. Make the design for your report logical, clear, easy to follow, and emphatic.

I. Statement of the problem.
II. Solution, if you are using the solution-first pattern.
III. Background.
   A. Causes of the problem or background information needed for readers to understand the problem.
   B. Other reports or work done on the problem, if relevant to yours.
   C. Conditions for information gathering: sources, credentials, reliability of information, methods used, and process followed to gather the information.
IV. The body of the report: the information gathered and presented in a logical, systematic way.
V. Solutions, conclusions, or recommendations, if not given earlier, or a general conclusion concerned with the implications or significance of your information.

A book report might follow this scheme or organization:

I. Introduction giving background information about the book: kind (genre), history of its composition, important facts about the author's life having a bearing on the book's contents, publishing information (length, publisher, editor, place of publication, publisher, and date of publication).
II. A systematic summary of the contents, describing the book's design, major ideas or subjects, its style or method of presentation, and its conclusions.
III. A systematic presentation of the book's positive and negative features (not required in all book reports).
IV. Your conclusion: an identification of the book's audience and uses,

a comparison with related works, and, if required, your judgment of its value.

Revising and Editing the Report

As you revise you will be concerned primarily with whether you have included all that needs to be said about your subject and whether you have stuck to your design. Be especially careful to see that you have organized clearly *within* each section; outline your paragraphs if necessary to determine whether they unfold logically. Then examine your language for its precision and for undue bias or inappropriate connotations; in the good report, exactness is nearly everything. See how precise and densely packed the information is in this description of a fast-food sandwich?

> We watched the "chef" carve paper-thin slices of beef off a large roast. But what we found in the sesame-seed bun we were served appeared to be pressed beef—gray in color, and very unappealing. It tasted like salty, steamed beef. And it was too soft for a real roast-beef sandwich. Perhaps the ketchup or horseradish sauces available would have improved—or, at least, hidden—the taste. We didn't try them.
>
> (*Consumer Reports,* "A gustatory guide to franchise alley," Sept. 1979)

The language makes us see and understand. The writers of this report don't depend upon big words to carry their information. Almost always the right words are small, familiar, and ready at hand—if we will only take the time to find them.

As you tinker with your sentences, make sure the most important information falls in the most emphatic positions. In informative sentences, these seem to be the ends of main clauses and the ends of complete sentences. Almost every sentence should begin by providing the introduction, context, or background for the information and then lead to the information itself. See these patterns at work in the informative/evaluative sentences describing a fast-food sandwiches?

> The *Whopper* was *one large burger with "the works"* (ketchup, tomato, lettuce, onion, pickle, and salad dressing) on a sesame-seed bun. It was *messy but tasty,* even though the meat was *a bit steamed in flavor and chewy in texture.*
>
> The *Whaler* didn't *fare as well.* The squre, breaded fillet seemed *lost amid the shredded lettuce and the over-sized bun.* What we could taste of the fish and tartar sauce was *pleasantly mild.*
>
> The oblong chopped-beef steak sandwich, with friend onion rings, barbecue sauce, and a toasted sesame-seed bun looked *very appetizing.* The meat was *striped* with dark charcoal-broiled marks to suggest that the glorified burger is cooked *on an open grill.* But the taste was *more steamed than broiled.* The texture was *dry and stringy.*
>
> (*Consumer Reports,* "A gustatory guide to franchise alley," Sept. 1979, emphasis added)

A Sample Report

Following is a report originally published in *Consumer Reports*. Appearing in a magazine devoted to helping consumers make informed choices about products, this report does more than inform; throughout it evaluates and recommends. The general audience and nonserious subject permit a relaxed, somewhat informal persona that occasionally goes so far as to play with the subject, but the wit never interrupts the business at hand: information and judgment.

Frozen Pizza

I. Statement of the problem: The popularity of frozen pizza that necessitates a survey

An informal persona

A standard for comparison

II. Summary of the findings

III. Background

A. The range of the survey

B. Methods, process, and standards of judgment

Topic heading
IV. The body

A. Methods to ensure reliable information

B. Findings
C. Specific standards of judgment

Pizza is as popular as blue jeans. It beats hamburgers as the favorite food of teenagers, and the frozen variety has become a staple of eat-at-home meals. Pizza is now the top-selling frozen food in the Midwest, number four nationally.

Going to the local pizzeria for fresh pizza is a fine old American custom. But when the craving hits, a pizza from the freezer is more convenient than a freshly made one from the pizza parlor. That may explain the high sales of the frozen variety. But how do frozen pizzas compete with pizzeria pies?

Few of the 43 frozen pizzas we tasted for this report could be called a taste treat, although all were nutritious as a snack or part of a meal. Many of the pizzas contained inappropriate ingredients (cheddar cheese, for one) that affected their taste and texture. Nearly all had one ingredient—insect fragments—that doesn't belong in any food. Some also contained bits of animal hairs.

We tested cheese and sausage pizzas—some with thin crusts, some with thick crusts (often called Sicilian style). Some have the topping on French or Italian bread instead of the traditional crust.

The pizzas come in a variety of sizes—from about 10 ounces to 28 ounces. Their price per 3 ½-ounce slice covers a wide range, too: from 20 to 66 cents.

Our Ratings are based on how the frozen pizzas tasted. Fresh pizzas from a local pizzeria were also rated. The taste tests were done by our sensory consultants . . . and covered flavor, aroma, texture, and appearance.

PIZZA AND THE PALATE

We repacked the 43 supermarket-variety frozen pizzas in unmarked containers and sent them off to our sensory consultants. We froze fresh pizzas (both cheese and sausage varieties) and packed them in unmarked boxes, too.

When our expert tasters' judgments came back, only the fresh pizzas were rated very good. The majority of the frozen pizzas were judged just fair.

An excellent pizza should consist of moderately thick, well-seasoned tomato sauce and melted mozzarella cheese (and, perhaps, some Romano or

Parmesan) on a bready, yeasty-tasting crust. A thin crust should be crisp. A thick one should be soft and chewy in the center.

D. Specific compara-
tive findings

A topic/transition sen-
tence to guide readers

Judgmental language
appropriate to an
evaluative report

The two fresh pizzas didn't quite live up to the ideal, but they were judged much better than most. Their faults: The crust lacked the right bready flavor and aroma, and the sausage on the meat pizza was a bit too greasy.

Among the frozen pizzas, variations from the ideal were legion. Most had a problem with crust. Some of the crusts tasted more like the cardboard boxes the pies came in than like a bread product. Some crusts were hard; some, soggy. Some were dry; others, too doughy.

Our sensory consultants noted bland or too-sweet sauces. Some sauces were too greasy or runny; others were dry or too thick. But the worst tasted and smelled as if they were on the verge of spoiling.

Mozzarella cheese was in short supply. Cheeses that were dry, mealy, and chewy were often used instead. Many of the sensory defects were related to the use of the wrong kind of cheese. When Romano was used, it tended to be overpowering, producing a sour flavor.

Several pizzas contain imitation mozzarella, and some have cheddar cheese in their topping. *Saluto* cheese pizza, for one, lists cheddar ahead of mozzarella in its ingredients list. Cheddar is the only cheese in *Ellio's* cheese pizza.

The sausage in the frozen pizzas rarely approached ideal Italian sausage, with its characteristic flavor of pork and spices. The pizzas' sausage varied from bland to too spicy. Some of the meat was dry; some was greasy.

PICTURES AND PROMISES

A second set of
judgments

An example to prove
a point about
misleading packaging

Factual language
appropriate to
technical description

Most of the frozen pizzas came in waxed cardboard boxes that feature mouth-watering pictures of pizza. After cooking, many of the pizzas looked anemic in comparison to those flattering pictures.

Some pizzas summarize the ingredients in large type on the front of the box. *Totino's Classic* sausage pizza, for example, begins its front-panel list with sausage and mushrooms. But on the back of the *Totino's* box, where the legally required list of ingredients appears in small type, pork is listed fourth, and mushrooms are sixth. It's not surprising that tomato purée and flour are that pizza's predominant ingredients. But the front-panel summary might lead a consumer to believe otherwise.

We noted some things in the various ingredients lists that don't belong in pizza, in our judgment. Among these were such additives as modified food starch, artificial gum, beet powder, beef stock, and monsodium glutamate (a flavor enhancer believed to cause uncomfortable reactions in some people).

Chef Boy-ar-dee Double Top cheese pizzas claim to have twice as much topping as crust. Uncooked, the samples we tested were about 59 percent topping by weight. Once the pizzas were cooked, the toppings shrank to about 46 percent of the pizza.

The *Celeste* regular-crust cheese pizza makes no special claims about the amount of topping. But, by our measurements, *Celeste* regular-crust was the most generous of the cheese pizzas: It had 53 percent topping after cooking. *Saluto French Bread* cheese pizza had the least topping—21 percent.

Besides weighing the toppings as a whole, we weighed the sausage from the meat pizzas before cooking. *Gino's, Oh Boy!,* and *Totino's Classic* had the least sausage—12 percent. *Totino's Party Pizza* and *Jenos Italian Bread Pizza,* with 22 percent, had the most.

JUST HOW NUTRITIOUS?

The topic sentence for an entire section

Pizza is nutritious, whether you eat it as a snack, a lunch, or part of a dinner. The tested cheese and sausage pizzas did not vary widely in nutrient content. All provided plenty of protein, for one thing. (The table below gives the average protein contribution of the cheese pizzas.)

The pizzas were also a good source of calcium. The cheese supplies that. The tested pizzas had a generous amount of Vitamin A, thanks to the tomato sauce. Thiamin and riboflavin content was adequate. Niacin, a nutrient usually associated with meat, was as plentiful in the cheese pizzas as it was in the sausage.

The cheese pizzas averaged 246 calories per 3½-ounce slice; the sausage pizzas averaged 253 calories.

As the table shows, a slice of pizza supplies a reasonable percentage of a teenager's Recommended Daily Allowance of protein, calcium, and some vitamins. And a light meal of salad, milk, and two slices of pizza would be nutritionally adequate for a youngster.

A judgment qualified for accuracy

But pizza doesn't have everything. The fact that a pizza is smothered in tomato sauce might make you think it contains a wealth of vitamin C. It doesn't. The high temperature at which pizza is cooked destroys much of the vitamin.

Another nutrient in short supply is iron. The American diet is often iron-deficient, probably because the foods that contain a lot of iron—calves' liver, prunes, lima beans—aren't among the most popular.

Pizza can also contribute a large part of a person's daily intake of sodium. According to the National Academy of Sciences/National Research Coun-

Pizza: nutritious snack or meal

The table below shows how a 3½-ounce slice of pizza contributes to the Recommended Daily Allowance of various nutrients for an 11- to 14-year-old boy. (Our percentages are based on the recommendations of the National Academy of Sciences/National Research Council.) The chart also shows the percentage of daily nutritional allowances for pizza eaten with a salad and a glass of lowfat milk.

	Calories	Fat	Sodium	Protein	Calcium	Iron	Niacin	Thiamin	Riboflavin	Vitamin A	Vitamin C
						Percentage of teen-ager's RDA					
Slice One 3½-ounce slice cheese pizza	246	9 gm.	615 mg.	26%	28%	4%	14%	14%	19%	10%	2%
Meal Two 3½-ounce slices cheese pizza Green salad (1 cup lettuce, cucumber, green pepper) One 8-fluid-ounce glass lowfat milk	625	21	1381	75	87	17	31	43	75	42	56

Ratings

Frozen pizza

Listed by types; within types, listed in order of estimated overall quality, based on sensory judgments by CU's consultants. Differences between closely ranked brands were slight. Sodium content is the average per 3½-oz. slice. Price is the average paid per package by CU shoppers.

Cheese pizza

Product	Size	Price	Cost per 3½-oz. slice	Sodium per 3½-oz. slice	Sensory defects
■ *The following was judged very good in sensory quality.*					
Fresh pizza	33 oz.	$3.75	$.44	473 mg.	A
■ *The following were judged good in sensory quality.*					
LA PIZZERIA (thick-crust)	18½	2.09	.37	702	V,X
ELLIO'S	16	1.52	.33	393	X
STOUFFER'S FRENCH BREAD	10¼	1.80	.66	614	U
LA PIZZERIA	20	2.18	.39	595	X,Y
SALUTO	20	2.46	.41	653	E,H
GINO'S	13	.98	.27	549	J,BB
FOX DE LUXE	13	1.04	.29	473	C,W,X
■ *The following were judged fair in sensory quality.*					
CHEF-BOY-AR-DEE DOUBLE TOP	21	2.11	.35	694	E,K,O,T,V,X
TOTINO'S REVOLUTIONARY PARTY	11¼	1.14	.33	562	C,K,O,BB
SALUTO FRENCH BREAD	11¼	1.75	.53	719	I,AA
SALUTO DEEP DISH	22	2.35	.39	630	E,X,V,BB
CELESTE (thick-crust)*	20	2.43	.39	404	I,W,CC
CHEF BOY-AR-DEE	13	1.29	.35	631	C,D,T,V,X
JENOS ITALIAN BREAD	12½	1.64	.47	707	H,X
JENOS	13	1.24	.39	546	G,H,S,V
ANN PAGE	12	.94	.20	487	E,R
CELESTE*	19	2.15	.41	661	M,T,W
JOHN'S ORIGINAL	13	1.07	.35	792	G,N,S,T,V
TONY'S	13¼	1.35	.38	702	C,D,T,V
OH BOY!	28	1.51	.20	579	B,D,E,L,Q,U,V
JENOS (thick-crust)	17	1.72	.41	705	E,I,T,X,BB
■ *The following was judged poor in sensory quality.*					
BEL-AIR	20	1.67	.30	734	E,L,Q

Sausage pizza

Product	Size	Price	Cost per 3½-oz. slice	Sodium per 3½-oz. slice	Sensory defects
■ *The following was judged very good in sensory quality.*					
Fresh pizza	35 oz.	$4.75	$.53	551 mg.	GG
■ *The following were judged good in sensory quality.*					
TOTINO'S REVOLUTIONARY CLASSIC (with mushrooms)	20¾	2.77	.46	706	T,BB
TOTINO'S REVOLUTIONARY PARTY	12½	1.19	.33	604	N
SALUTO DEEP DISH	26	3.09	.40	724	E
LA PIZZERIA	13	1.77	.48	713	Z,GG,JJ
	23	2.87	.45	713	Z,GG,JJ
■ *The following were judged fair in sensory quality.*					
CELESTE*	22	2.78	.45	699	D,H,HH
SALUTO	23	2.89	.42	700	G,T,V
CHEF BOY-AR-DEE DOUBLE TOP	22	2.85	.47	717	T,V,GG,JJ
STOUFFER'S FRENCH BREAD	12	2.31	.66	776	T,FF
CHEF BOY-AR-DEE	14	1.24	.32	698	F,G,T,V,DD
JOHN'S ORIGINAL	13½	1.00	.27	655	D,T,CC
BEL-AIR	23	2.10	.33	857	D,G,I
CELESTE (thick-crust)*	24	2.92	.42	723	E,GG,JJ
SALUTO FRENCH BREAD	13	2.18	.57	566	FF,JJ
FOX DE LUXE	13	1.12	.02	549	C,P,JJ
ANN PAGE	13	.84	.22	629	C,N,GG,JJ
JENOS ITALIAN BREAD	13½	1.76	.45	809	N,T
TONY'S	15	1.67	.42	580	C,D,E,G,T,V
JOHN'S PREMIUM	22	2.29	.40	1037	H,V,GG,JJ
GINO'S	13	1.01	.29	585	D,JJ
OH BOY!	28	2.01	.24	610	D,E,N,FF
JENOS	13	1.07	.33	627	C,D,P,Z,HH

* *According to the company, product has been changed.*

KEY TO SENSORY DEFECTS

CRUST
A–Not enough bread flavor and aroma.
B–Too thick.
C–Cracker like, or hard, or dry.
D–Tough.
E–Soggy, doughy, or raw.
F–Chemical flavor.
G–Cardboard flavor and texture.
H–Bland.
I–Aftertaste.

SAUCE
J–Not enough.
K–Too thin.
L–Too dry
M–Starchy
N–Bland.
O–Poorly blended flavor
P–Too sweet.
Q–Sour-tomato flavor and aroma.
R–Spoiled-tomato flavor and aroma.
S–Undercooked tomato flavor

CHEESE
T–Hard, dry, or mealy
U–Not enough.
V–Too chewy
W–Unmelted.
X–Not stringy enough.
Y–Not chewy enough.
Z–Bland.
AA–Sour
BB–Cheddar-cheese flavor
CC–Chemical aftertaste.

MEAT
DD–Not enough.
EE Tough, chewy
FF–Dry, or mealy
GG–Fatty or greasy
HH–Bland.
JJ–Too spicy

cil, the estimated *safe* consumption of sodium ranges from 900 to 1700 milligrams a day for an adolescent and from 1100 to 3300 milligrams for an adult. And even those levels are considerably above the 200 milligrams actually needed by most people. *Ellio's* cheese pizza had the lowest sodim content—393 milligrams per 3½-ounce slice. *John's Premium* sausage pizza had the most sodium—a whopping 1037 milligrams per slice. The ratings give the sodium content of each frozen pizza we tested.

EXTRANEOUS MATTER

First-person persona appropriate to this magazine report

Spices often contain minute insect fragments. These fragments are almost impossible to eliminate during harvesting and grinding. Since spices are an important part of pizza, we expected to find some insect fragments.

We found more than we bargained for. We tested six samples of each brand of pizza. All but three of 270 samples contained extraneous matter.

In most cases, the contaminants were insect fragments that probably entered the product with the ground spices. *Ann Page* cheese and *Saluto French Bread* pizza had the highest counts. But we found insect larvae, or even whole insects—thrips, mites, aphids—in *Saluto* cheese, *Celeste* thick-crust sausage, *Chef Boy-ar-dee* sausage, and *Chef Boy-ar-dee Double Top* sausage. That type of contamination indicates poor storage of ingredients.

We found animal hairs in some samples. These often come from rodents and are another indication of poor storage or unsanitary processing. Eight pizzas were guilty: *Celeste* regular- and thick-crust, *Jenos Italian Bread*, *John's Original*, and *Saluto French Bread* cheese pizzas; *Totino's Classic*, *Totino's Party*, and *Oh Boy!* sausage pizza.

The contaminants probably wouldn't make anyone ill. But their presence indicates lax control. Such conditions might permit other, possibly harmful, elements to contaminate the food.

RECOMMENDATIONS

V. General conclusions

A real pizza lover probably wouldn't be happy with any of the frozen brands. Your best bet is to buy fresh pizza from a local pizzeria, though it will probably be a bit more expensive than most frozen pizzas. If you like the convenience of frozen, then wrap and freeze the fresh pizza for later use. When that's impractical, choose a frozen pizza from among the brands we rated good. [See the chart on page 297.]

To cook frozen pizza, line your oven bottom with aluminum foil to catch drips. If your oven is gas, make sure to leave the vents uncovered. Put the pizza right on the rack, if you want a crisp crust—putting it on a cookie sheet gives a softer crust. Check the pizza at the shortest cooking time recommended by the maker. If the cheese isn't melted at the center, bake it a little longer.

(Adapted from *Consumer Reports*, Jan. 1980)

✍ THE CRITIQUE

The critique, also known as the review, is an evaluative essay. Its subject may be a tool or product, say, a new car reviewed in *Motor Trend* magazine. It may be an art object or performance: a book, movie, record album, play, art exhibit, or tv program reviewed in a newspaper column. It may be a restaurant. Occasionally the critique may take a particular kind of object for its subject rather than one object in particular, for example, American cars in general rather than one particular make or model, sci-fi movies of the 1970s and 1980s rather than *Star Wars*, Ernest Hemingway's novels rather than *A Farewell to Arms*. Whatever its subject and scope, the immediate aim of the critique is to judge the uses and values of that subject for an interested audience. The ultimate aim is to help readers make informed choices about the goods they buy or the entertainment they seek so they don't have to depend upon trial and error alone.

The Conventions of the Critique

In order to make its judgment, the good critique first of all describes its subject completely and accurately so that readers see and understand what it is. The critique may also classify it with similar subjects so that readers have the basis for an evaluative comparison; readers want to know what *kind* of movie they are reading about, what *kind* of novel, restaurant, or lawnmower. Then the good critique describes the aims, purposes, or uses of the subject under review. Most important, of course, the critique evaluates the subject, primarily in terms of the standards the subject sets for itself by its aims, claims, or design. No reviewer, for example, would judge a detective novel by quite the same standards she applied to a Shakespearean tragedy; nor would another reviewer judge an economy car by standards appropriate to luxury models. A reviewer tries to answer the question: Has my subject accomplished what it set out to do? Only later does she answer the larger question: Is it worth doing, or should it be doing something different?

The occasion and forum for a review determine the reviewer's persona, whether public and formal or intimate and informal. The persona of a record review in the campus newspaper, for example, will necessarily be different from the persona of a book review in *The New York Times*. But even in the most formal, detached review, the writer is still very much involved with his subject; after all, what is at issue is a human response to the subject, the reviewer responding on behalf of his readers. Thus, the reviewer always plays the participant's role as well as critic's, teacher's, and persuader's roles. In an intimate, informal review, he may base his evaluation almost exclusively on his responses. In more formal, public reviews, he may leaven personal response with impersonal, objective standards. But in the end, a review is always an exercise of personal taste, judgment, and discrimination, one writer sharing himself with readers in hope they will find his gesture of value.

Gathering Information and Making Judgments

A reviewer prepares for a critique by experiencing the subject: reading the book, seeing the movie, going to the concert, using the tool, eating at the restaurant, or studying and then driving the new car. As she "lives" the subject, this reviewer must always take a "two-eyed" view of it. On the one hand, she wants to experience it in the way any person might, so she can report accurately what her readers might expect if they were to have the same experience. At the same time, she must remain detached from her experience, the better to understand and judge it. That two-eyed view, an awareness of what's happening inside and an equal awareness of the subject that provokes her response, takes time and practice to acquire. Here's one method for developing this sensitivity.

Immediately after the experience, write down your responses in a free-writing. Aim for descriptive immediacy. Then, after your feelings have cooled, make a systematic response to your experience. Use the following instructions and questions:

1. Identify the work: its origins or producer (the creator, author, director, designer, or owner).
2. Summarize its contents or describe its layout, form, or design.
3. Identify its intended audience, customers, or users.
4. Describe its aims, purposes, or uses. Look for any assumptions that are implied by its construction or marketing.
5. Does it fulfill these aims? If not, where does it fall short and why?
6. Should it be doing something else? How does it compare to other objects in its class?
7. What is its value or use, now and for the future?

As you answer these questions in note form, begin to formulate a thesis for your review. Your thesis will be your judgment of your subject's value and uses: *My judgment is that . . . What I mean to say is that. . . .*

Organizing the Critique

Skillful reviewers design their reviews in many ways: for the sake of variety, to suit a particular audience, or to fit the space allotted to them. But whatever their layouts, they all include essentially the same parts. Here they are, arranged in one conventional pattern. Whatever pattern you devise, make sure that it is systematic and that one part leads smoothly and naturally to the next.

I. Introduction: This may be a no-nonsense opening that contains little more than an identification of the subject. Or if the space allows and the occasion requires, the reviewer may open imaginatively to capture the audience's attention and connect the subject of the review with some larger subject.

II. A thesis statement that offers a quick evaluation or another sentence that sets the mood and direction of the review

III. Background information about the subject, the reviewer's biases, the conditions under which the subject was experienced, or anything that has a bearing on the evaluation and the audience's understanding ot it.

IV. The subject's aims, purposes, and audience.

V. A detailed description of the work: its contents, layout, design, main ideas or features, and style.

VI. An examination of strengths and weaknesses.

VII. An elaborated statement of judgment: the uses or value of the subject and a comparison with related subjects, perhaps a ranking of the subject with others like it.

VIII. A conclusion that remarks anything unusual or noteworthy about the subject or comments on the introduction to the review in light of all that has been said.

Writing, Revising and Editing the Critique

As the statement of a reviewer's judgment, the critique will be filled with the reviewer, either in the first person or indirectly in its opinions and connotations. But take care in your critique to see whether your presence has obscured your true subject. After all, you're not writing a personal experience essay. You don't want your audience to watch you responding; rather, you want to draw from your responses to help readers understand your subject and determine whether they'd like to experience it.

Once you have determined that your focus is clear and steady and your design, logical and coherent, consider your language. Words rich in connotation will help convey your judgment; concrete and specific terms will support and enliven it. We might respond with terms like *good, bad, shoddy,* or *wellmade,* but without hard terms dense with feeling, our judgments will drift lifeless before our reader's eyes. See how this opening to a movie review not only conveys a sense of the judgment to come but gives us a feeling of the experience of the movie itself?

Now this is a movie. Alfred Hitchcock's "Rear Window" develops such a *clean, uncluttered line* from beginning to end that we're *drawn through it* (and into it) effortlessly. The experience is not so much like *watching* a movie, as like . . . well, like *spying* on your neighbors. Hitchcock *traps* us right from the start.

As his hero, Jimmy Stewart, idly picks up a *camera with a telephoto lens* and begins to *scan the open window* on the other side of the courtyard, *we look, too.* And because Hitchcock makes us *accomplices* in Stewart's *voyeurism,* we're along for the ride. When an *enraged man comes bursting* through the door to kill Stewart, we can't *detach* ourselves, because *we looked too,* and so we share the *guilt* and in a way we deserve what's coming *to him.*

(Roger Ebert, " 'Window' is simply a great film,"
Chicago Sun-Times 7 Oct. 1983, emphasis added)

The reviewer's words do not simply tell what happens in the movie; they make potential viewers feel what it's like to watch what happens. The aim here, as in all good critiques, is the sensation of the experience and an understanding of it.

Three Sample Critiques

Following are three critiques, of a record album, movie, and book. They will give you some idea of the range of styles, formats, and designs available to you.

Parting Should Be Painless
Roger Daltrey
(A Negative Record Review)

I. Background that provides a contrast

II. Thesis made with sarcasm and judgmental language

III. Background

A name-calling persona right for the audience and magazine

IV. An examination of the album's weaknesses

The reviewer's point of view

V. The few positive features

Parting Should Be Painless is Roger Daltrey's fifth record, but in a sense, it's his real solo debut: there's no Who to fall back on now. It's a good thing, then, he's got acting as a sideline, for this is a numbingly average record that lacks even the redeeming virtue of bad taste. With the Who, Daltrey is a belter; on his own, mysteriously, he's a whiner with MOR ambitions— and the middle of road, as any rock fan knows, is really nowhere at all. Well, as long as you're gonna stand still and watch traffic roll by, you might as well have some company. Daltrey's picked some fine hired hands to help him kill time—among them, guitar chameleon Chris Spedding, plus keyboardist Mickey Gallagher and bassist Norman Watt-Roy, both formerly of Ian Drury's Blockheads. All of them play as if embalmed.

The ten tunes come from all over—Bryan Ferry ("Going Strong"), Eurythmics ("Somebody Told Me") and various ballad-afflicted types not worth mentioning. They are, however, so stiffly and formally rendered that one is tempted to assume the tracks were laid down on different days in different studios. Daltrey himself sounds distanced from the songs, like he never warmed up to them—not that I'd exactly want them as neighbors, either. He frequently sings in a hypertasteful "beautiful music" croon, and he never, but *never,* attempts a robust, Who-like scream or growl, even on the few uptempo numbers.

Given something to work with, Daltrey gets a bit of a pop-funk groove going in "Looking for You" and "One Day," but mostly he gets swallowed up in the creaky uniformity of the arrangements. After a while, you begin looking for any little tic to break the mold: a clarinet solo in "Would a Stranger

Do," Daltrey's own harmonica fills on "Somebody Told Me," the sonorous horn charts in "Going Strong." All scant compensation, in the end. Parting with this album should not only be painless, but pleasurable.

(Parke Puterbaugh, *Rolling Stone* 26 Apr. 1984)

"The Right Stuff" Is Stuff That Makes a Great Movie
(A Positive Movie Review)

At the beginning of "The Right Stuff," a cowboy reins in his horse and regards a strange sight in the middle of the desert: the X-1 rocket plane, built to break the sound barrier. At the end of the film, the seven Mercury astronauts are cheered in the Houston Astrodome at a Texas barbecue thrown by Lyndon B. Johnson. The contrast between those two images contains the message of "The Right Stuff," I think, and the message is that Americans still have the right stuff, but we've changed our idea of what it is.

The original American heroes were loners. The cowboy is the perfect example. He was silhouetted against the horizon and he rode into town by himself and if he had a sidekick, the sidekick's job was to admire him. The new American heroes are team players. No wonder Westerns aren't made anymore; cowboys don't play on teams.

The cowboy at the beginning of "The Right Stuff" is Chuck Yeager, the legendary lone-wolf test pilot who survived the horrifying death rate among early test pilots (more than 60 were killed in a single month) and did fly the X-1 faster than the speed of sound. The movie begins with that victory, and then moves on another 10 years to the day when the Russians sent up Sputnik, and the Eisenhower administration hustled to get back into the space race.

The astronauts who eventually rode the first Mercury capsules into space may not have been *that* much different from Chuck Yeager. As they're portrayed in the movie, anyway, Gus Grissom, Scott Carpenter and Gordon Cooper seem to have some of the same stuff as Yeager. But the astronauts were more than pilots; they were a movie public-relations image, and the movie shows sincere, smooth-talking John Glenn becoming their unofficial spokesman. The X-1 flew in secrecy, but the Mercury flights were telecast, and we were entering a whole new era, the selling of space.

There was a lot going on, and there's a lot going on in the movie, too. "The Right Stuff" is an adventure film, a special-effects film, a social commentary and a satire. That the writer-director, Philip Kaufman, is able to get so much into a little more than three hours is impressive. That he also has organized this material into one of the best recent American movies is astonishing. "The Right Stuff" gives itself the freedom to move around in moods and styles, from a broadly based lampoon of government functionaries to Yeager's spare, taciturn manner and Glenn's wonderment at the sights outside his capsule window.

The actors

V. A comparison with
related movies

VI. Thesis

"The Right Stuff" is likely to be a landmark movie in a lot of careers. It announces Kaufman's arrival in the ranks of major directors. It contains uniformly interesting performances by a whole cast of unknown or little-known actors, including Ed Harris (Glenn), Scott Glenn (Alan Shepard), Fred Ward (Grissom) and Dennis Quaid (Cooper). It confirms the strong and sometimes almost mystical screen presence of playwright Sam Shepard, who plays Yeager. And it joins a short list of recent American movies that might be called experimental epics: movies that have an ambitious reach through time and subject matter, that spend freely for locations or special effects, but that consider each scene as intently as an art film. "The Right Stuff" goes on that list with "The Godfather," "Nashville," "Apocalypse Now" and maybe "Patton" and "Close Encounters." It's a great film.
(Roger Ebert, *Chicago Sun-Times* 21 Oct. 1983)

Climb Every Mountain
A Journey in Ladakh
by Andrew Harvey

(Houghton Mifflin, 236 pp., $13.95)

(A Mixed Review of a Book)

I. Introduction

Background information that will be used to explain and judge the book

II. Specific background information about the book's setting, and a history of its composition

The English have always been a traveling people. From their crowded islands, they have lit out for Patagonia, or the Mediterranean, equatorial Africa, or the deserts of the Middle East, performing all the while an imperial rope-trick: the Englishman temporarily sheds his Britishness, and enters to a troubling depth into the heart of another people. When he returns, he is a little skewed and troublesome, a man who is neither here nor there. Call it the Robinson Crusoe syndrome, a kind of wanderlust and plasticity of soul. There have been legendary travelers: Charles Doughty, T. E. Lawrence, Wilifred Thessiger. Like the antique travelers, they brought back stories to tell of extraordinary places and peoples, but also of themselves wrestling with their solitary natures. Such stories have often had the overtones of a spiritual progress: a travel story that is also a venture in self-remaking.

The young English poet, Andrew Harvey, has written a book in this tradition. Several years ago, he spent a few months in a region of the Himalaya Mountains near Tibet, known as Ladakh. Harvey had been drawn to Ladakh for several reasons: it is a remote area in which the traditional mountain life has managed to survive; in recent decades, it has become a refuge for a number of Tibetan Buddhist priests who have given new life to local Buddhist practice. Harvey's interest in Buddhism is not casual. He describes himself as an anxious, questing young man, ruffled by the contradictions of growing up, seeking some underlying truth that will reconcile himself to himself. As a child, he had lived in India, and now, as a man, he returns to pick up threads that had been lost.

III. A description of
the book:
Its style and purpose

Its subjects

IV. Weaknesses and
strengths
The author's inade-
quate self-revelation
and its effect on his
style

The book's best
feature

The reviewer's
language reveals
the mood of the
book's description

V. The "best parts" of
the book described,
leading to a conclud-
ing mixed judgment

He travels with his pen in his hand, and the book, a series of highly charged paragraphs, was probably assembled from his journal. His journey to Ladakh becomes a journey toward self-understanding, to which the vivid mountain scenes give substance. Ladakh, as Harvey describes it, is not a destitute realm of the high Himalayas, but a mirror in which the traveler sees himself renewed. The focus of the book, then, is double: it tells about Ladakh with its naked, gleaming peaks, and its rocky passes; its hardy white horses that stand beside tiny wheat fields; its ruined monasteries; its laughing, friendly people. It also tells about the traveler, and here Harvey does not always carry his reader with him. The spiritual crisis to which his journey is a response never becomes very real. Perhaps that is why Harvey is so relentless in his pursuit of signs and meanings which he seems to see, with an unfettered romantic urge, in every stone and every cliff. Harvey is rarely content to let a scene live apart from him. Everything must glimmer with foreshadowings of a higher consciousness. The result is a curiously programmatic and premeditated sort of writing. The very Buddhist expansion Harvey speaks of—a tenderly passive, unmolesting attitude, which lets things be in their completeness—is strangely lacking in *A Journey in Ladakh*.

Harvey is at his best with people, and his journey is marked by a series of vivid encounters with bus drivers and travelers, a fast-living Ladakhi guide, a loquacious hotel owner. He meets a Frenchman who spurters nihilistic tirades from Cioran about man's raving fantasy of holiness. He spends an evening with a melancholy Ladakhi scholar who sings holy songs to him, by moonlight, in a garden. He meets a psychologist who comes back to Ladakh year after year, ostensibly to interview the local people, but really as an act of love for this remote and pure place. Somehow these people seem more real than Harvey himself. They are not portentous and over serious; they do not spill out pious patches of "fine writing." It is as if Harvey, in these portraits, could speak with a freedom and a maturity which his own voice does not allow him.

We read about a Ladakhi "oracle," a frail old woman who spits and shrieks with bone-chilling authority when the trance is upon her. Later we read about an Indian couple, Dilip and Moneesha, who are funny, wise, and extremely touching. They have come to Ladakh to see a Tibetan master, Tucksey Rinpoche. Dilip is a wordly businessman educated in England who, late in life, has been possessed by a thirst for spiritual knowledge. Dilip is everything Harvey himself is not: funny and contradictory, touchingly personal, wise with a sad detachment, yet passionate too. Dilip is, perhaps, the most memorable presence in *A Journey in Ladakh*; more memorable even than the lovely figure of the Rinpoche himself who becomes the goal and fulfillment of Harvey's search. Tucksey Rinpoche is a happy, earthy man who gives off no glimmer of any higher state; he is solidly himself, whether he is acting his part in a public ceremony, or meeting Harvey with almost childlike pleasure in his private room. These meetings with Dilip and Rinpoche are perhaps inadvertently the culmination of *A Journey in Ladakh*. In them, Harvey manages to free himself of the portentousness which, unfortunately, mars so much of his book.

(Paul Zweig, *The New Republic* 24 Oct. 1983)

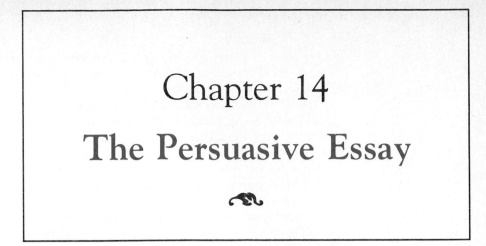

Chapter 14

The Persuasive Essay

Persuasion attempts to change minds, hearts, and actions. "You ought to think this way," it urges its audience. "Feel that way," it implores. "Do such-and-such," it pleads. When this change is not possible, persuasion proposes compromise between opposing sides or, at the least, a deeper understanding of one side by the other. It is one of the most frequent uses we make of language. At home, in school, on the job, or in public, in discussions, school papers, letters, books, and magazines, in political speeches and editorials, in lectures, sermons, and commercials—persuasion is everywhere a staple of our lives as language users and social beings.

Take a typical college student as an example. Let's call him John. In two weeks he has a paper on capital punishment due for his Criminal Justice class. He has to write a letter of application for a part-time job he wants at a record store. This weekend he's going to meet his Aunt Wilma and Uncle Fred for dinner, and he knows that sooner or later he and his uncle will get into a debate about what Fred believes to be the crisis of American education. He wants to convince his Aunt Wilma to give up her twenty-five-year smoking habit. He writes for the school newspaper and faces a deadline for his movie review of *Bruce Lee's Kung-Fu Killer Kousins*. And this evening he and his friends will meet to decide where they're going on their upcoming vacation. All of these are situations involving persuasion, the kind John and the rest of us find ourselves in every day. Because persuasion comes to us so frequently and naturally, you would think we'd all get good at it ourselves and rarely be misled by others' deceitful persuasion. That neither of these statements is always true suggests how important it is that we know a little more than common sense tells us about what persuasion is and how to express ourselves persuasively.

Let's begin with a few distinctions. All that goes by the name of persuasion is not really persuasion. Our word *persuasion* comes from the Latin

307

persuadere, "to advise thoroughly or urge." It is not coercion; nor is it seduction. In the nineteenth century and in movie slang of a few years ago, a "persuader" was a weapon, usually a gun. But the person staring down the muzzle of that gun was hardly being persuaded; he was being coerced. *Coercion*, from the Latin *coercere*, meaning "to restrain or hold in," uses threat or force to change people's minds. *Seduction*, from the Latin *seducere*, meaning "to lead aside," changes belief or behavior by tricking an audience to surrender their intellects and will. Although Vance Packard Called his enormously influential book on advertising *The Hidden Persuaders*, he really had in mind all the ways advertisers *seduce* us into making unintended purchases. Persuasion neither forces nor tricks; it calls upon its audience to use their full powers of intellect and emotion—knowing full well what they are doing—and give willing assent to an idea or proposal for action.

This chapter divides persuasion into two major parts. In the first part you'll learn to create the sound arguments that are the heart of almost every ethical and effective persuasion. In the second, you'll learn how to make these arguments persuasive by the force of your persona, by appropriate emotional appeals, and by a design that suits your intentions and the needs of your audience.

❧ THINKING LOGICALLY: ARGUMENT

As we use the word here, *argument* has none of the negative connotations of anger or hostility it so often has in popular use. When we think of argument in its popular sense, we hear two hostile people shouting at each other: *'tis! 'tisn't! 'tis too!* But in its narrower, strictly logical sense, an argument is nothing more—and nothing less—than reasons presented to defend a claim and the arrangement of those reasons in such a way that if an audience accepts one part of the argument, they are obliged to accept the plausibility or probability of the rest of the argument. Simply put, an *argument* is a process of reasoning. Our word comes from a Latin word meaning primarily to make clear, prove, or show, and that's what a logical argument aims to do.

The Elements of Argument

If you're like most people, the mention of logic and reasoning is just a little daunting.[1] We pride ourselves on our powers of intuition and common sense and admire others who have them. But people who are very logical, well, you've got to watch out for them. And logical thinking, well, you have to watch out for it, too; it takes so much care, attention, and practice. Both these attitudes are well founded. People who are logically minded often *do* seem one step ahead of everybody else. And reasoning well *does* require effort. But there are ways we can make the reasoning process a little easier for ourselves and at the same time gain the confidence that the arguments we construct are good ones.

One way is to understand what goes into an argument. Whatever its subject matter, length, or complexity, an argument contains no more than six elements. Two of these elements appear in nearly every argument: *claims* and *evidence*. We could scarcely have an argument without them. The other four may be necessary to make a particular argument plausible or convincing, but they don't appear in every argument: *reasoning principles, sources, qualifiers,* and *reservations*. Sometimes they are omitted entirely; other times they are implied, present but unseen or unheard in the argument as it comes to the audience.

Claims An argument is about a claim. It is the thesis of every argument, the point we want our audience to accept. More precisely, it is an assertion that something is true or probable, that a particular attitude is appropriate, or that such-and-such an action should be taken. Implied in every claim we make is our readiness to offer "reasons" to defend it. An argument begins when someone makes an arguable claim and ends when that claim is sufficiently defended or when it is sufficiently refuted.

We can make arguable claims about any subject open to differences of interpretation or opinion, *provided* that we can verify our interpretations or opinions in some way. Take, for example, some of the situations our student John finds himself in. Last summer, he, his girlfriend Nancy, and some other friends took a trip to the West. On their first day in the Colorado Rockies, John stood outside their lodge marveling at the trees.

> John: They're incredible! Look how tall they are! How massive! I didn't know redwoods grew in the Rockies.
> Nancy: They're not redwoods, John, they're Douglas firs.

Nancy's response is an arguable claim. So is the first line of John's movie review:

> Unless it is intended as a parody, *Bruce Lee's Kung-Fu Killer Kousins*, now showing at the Lakeview Theater, is perhaps the worst movie of any kind ever distributed for public consumption.

And, of course, the thesis for John's Criminal Justice paper on capital punishment is an arguable claim:

> Except for war crimes, the death penalty should be abolished.

The only claims we can't or shouldn't argue are (1) assertions of fact that can never be proved, (2) assertions of fact that can be verified without argument, and (3) purely subjective opinions. Consider this claim:

> Had he not been assassinated, President Kennedy would never have allowed the United States to become mired in a war in Vietnam.

Like genuinely arguable claims, this must be either true or false, but how could it ever be verified? It is fruitless to argue about it because its truth can never be discovered; nor could we ever reach a reasonable probability of its truth or falsity. Likewise, it would be a waste of time and energy to argue this second claim:

> When he was assassinated, President Kennedy was on his way to Dallas to resolve political differences within the Democratic party.

The public records will verify this claim or refute it, no need to argue about it. Here is a final unarguable claim:

> I didn't like *Bruce Lee's Kung-Fu Killer Kousins* at all.

We can't argue opinions based, as this is, on untestable feelings and beliefs. One person didn't like the movie, another did, and that is that. We might wish our feelings agreed with others' feelings more often than they do, but argument won't help us.

Another version of this last claim, however, is a bit uncertain:

> *Bruce Lee's Kung-Fu Killer Kousins* is a terrible movie.

If *terrible* means "I really didn't like the movie at all," then the claim is not arguable. But if it means "a terrible work of art," then it is an arguable claim, since objective standards of artistic value can be used to measure the quality of the movie and defend the opinion. Some people seem to think that opinions are never fit subjects for argument. "Well, it's *only* my opinion," they say. But that disclaimer is often a dodge, a way to believe things without being held responsible for them, a way of saying "I'm going to believe what I want, even if it's illogical or unfounded." Some opinions are purely subjective, of course, based on untestable beliefs known as *a priori assumptions,* and we aren't concerned with them here. They are the sources of some of our most important beliefs about ourselves, the purposes of human life, and the nature of the world, but they cannot be argued because they cannot be verified. Many of our other opinions, however, *can* be verified; through reasoning and evidence we can discover how sound they are. We owe it to ourselves to give those the best defense possible.

The good claim, then, is a *genuinely defensible assertion.* But it has three other characteristics besides that you'll want to remember whenever you argue. Like any good thesis, the good claim is *clear,* written in language its audience will understand and feel comfortable with. You want to make it as easy as possible for them to accept it. Also, the good claim is *precise,* unambiguous, its words meaning just one thing. Finally, the good claim is *limited but complete.* It never asserts more than the writer is prepared to defend, but it asserts *all* the writer has in mind. When you present an argument, you may not for tactical reasons state your whole claim at once, but when you're planning that argument, you should try to keep your whole claim before you to help you see all you have to defend and to help you chart any evolution in your thinking.

EXERCISES

1. Following are a number of assertions, some of them arguable claims, some not. Which are genuinely arguable? Be able to explain your choices. If any could be revised to make them arguable or to make them clearer or more precise, rewrite them.

a. I love Munchy-Crunchy Chocolate Bars.
b. Munchy-Crunchy Chocolate Bars are better than apples or carrots any day.
c. You can't teach an old dog new tricks.
d. Two times two equals four.
e. It looks like rain tomorrow.
f. All men are created equal.
g. A nationwide drinking age should be set at age twenty-one.
h. Teenagers, by and large, are terrible drivers, even when they're on their best behavior. Behind the wheel they tend to be as thoughtless, inconsiderate, and unnerving as a big puppy in a crowd of people dressed in their Sunday best.
i. Americans are tinkerers rather than thinkers. They set themselves to fixing this or that often without stopping to reflect on whether this or that is worth fixing.
j. Lee Harvey Oswald assassinated President John F. Kennedy on November 22, 1963.
k. The first *Star Wars* movie was the most influential sci-fi film ever made.
l. If all American high school students were required to take at least two years of a foreign language, they would better understand their own language and be better-informed citizens.
m. No more nuclear weapons!
n. Each year more crimes are committed in American suburbs than the year before.
o. Each year the suburbs become more and more dangerous places to live and and raise children.

2. Write one arguable claim for each of the following topics.

a. Urban, suburban, or rural life as you know it.
b. The causes or consequences of a prejudice you're familiar with.
c. A necessary change at your school.
d. The attraction, worth, or theme of a specific work of art, e.g., a book, movie, record, painting, or sculpture.
e. Human life today is like _____ (complete with an analogy).
f. A law (good, bad, actual, or proposed).
g. The causes, consequences, or significance of a specific historical event, public or personal.
h. One kind of food you know well.

i. A white-collar or blue-collar job you know well.

j. An *-ism* (e.g., Republicanism, humanism, sexism).

Evidence   Evidence is the proof for an argument, its grounds or foundation, what a claim is based upon. A piece of evidence is any specific statement about the physical world, human beings, or their creations that strikes us as true or probable. It may not always *be* a fact, but it has the force of a fact. Some of the evidence we use when we argue includes the results of experimental observation, reports, statistics, personal testimony, claims from other arguments already established as true, or other factual data. The key to using these facts well is making sure they meet what are known as the rules of evidence.

The first rule: the evidence must be *sufficient* to be convincing. There must be enough of it. Here is more of John and Nancy's argument about the fir trees. Following is a little diagram that lays out its elements.

Nancy: They're not redwoods, John; they're Douglas firs.

John: But look how tall they are and broad in their trunks.

Nancy: Look at the size and shape of the pine cones. See, this one's oval in shape and almost four inches long. Notice how pointed the needles are, and their blue-green color. And look at the dark brown color of the bark. And, after all, this is the Rockies, not the California coast.

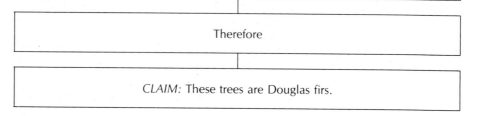

EVIDENCE: Because the trees have large oval cones, pointed blue-green needles, dark brown bark, and because this is the Rockies,

Therefore

CLAIM: These trees are Douglas firs.

Nancy offers several pieces of evidence, not just one or two, and together they are sufficient to be convincing.

Her argument also follows the second rule of evidence: her evidence is *representative*. She takes several kinds of evidence from a variety of locations. By contrast, consider the argument John's Uncle Fred made the last time he and Aunt Wilma visited:

What are schools teaching students these days? I swear these kids are all illiterate. Take the young people in my office, all of them two- and four-year college graduates. My secretary can't spell simple words like *receive* and *transferring*. I have an accountant who doesn't know the difference between *liable* and *libel* and a personnel manager who thinks Thomas Paine owns the Paine

Webber brokerage firm and *The Scarlet Letter* is an award given for advertising excellence.

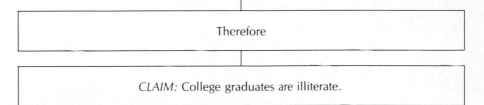

> EVIDENCE: Because the college graduate employees at my place of business can't spell, don't understand the differences between homophones, don't know American history, and haven't read widely,
>
> Therefore
>
> CLAIM: College graduates are illiterate.

Uncle Fred's evidence is neither sufficient nor representative. Three college graduates to support an argument against *all* college graduates? What schools did these students graduate from? What were their fields of study? Were they good students? Uncle Fred's case is not convincing.

The third rule of evidence: it must be *timely*. One of the first pieces of evidence John discovered when he began his Criminal Justice paper was a 1967 Harris Survey showing that a majority of Americans favored abolition of the death penalty. He wishes he could use it to support his claim, but he recognizes that old evidence from the 1960s has no value in the current debate. Times change, so does public opinion, and this evidence is useless.

The fourth rule of evidence: it must be *relevant* to the issues at hand. Here is more of John's argument against the death penalty:

> There seems to be little clear evidence that the death penalty deters murderers. In Wisconsin, a non–death penalty state, the murder rate per 100,000 people in 1965 was 1.5. In neighboring Illinois, which has a death penalty law, the murder rate was much higher, 5.2. In all the records I've checked, this lack of correlation between murder and capital punishment has appeared. This is just more evidence, therefore, that the death penalty ought to be abolished.

> EVIDENCE: Because statistics show that the death penalty does not affect the murder rate,
>
> Therefore
>
> CLAIM: The death penalty should be abolished.

Because proponents of the death penalty often claim that execution deters murderers from crime, John will strengthen his case by showing that, in fact, capital punishment does not deter. The evidence from his studies is directly relevant to his argument and that of his opponents. As you construct your arguments, make sure your evidence follows these same four rules: sufficiency, representativeness, timeliness, and relevance.

EXERCISES

1. Identify the claims and evidence in the following brief arguments. Then decide whether the claims are arguable and whether the evidence meets the four rules of evidence given previously.

a. Telephone calls to the White House after last night's Presidential address on Central American military policy favored the President's position by a four-to-one margin. Surely his position is a good one.

b. Senator Edward Kennedy has declared that "over 25,000 Americans die each year because of shooting accidents, suicides and murders caused by guns." He reported that in "1963, handgun murders totaled 4,200. Eleven years later, in 1974, handguns were used to murder 11,000 Americans. . . . The annual output of handguns increased from 568,000 in 1968 to over 2.5 million in 1974." Given this frightening increase in death and the instruments of destruction, I believe all long guns (i.e., rifles and shotguns) should be registered and handguns banned outright.

c. Book sales are down; newspaper readership has leveled off nationwide. People now get their news in snippets from TV. The texts of textbooks are being simplified and supplemented by more and more graphs, photos, and cartoons. You know what all that adds up to, don't you? Americans are degenerating slowly into ignorance.

d. (1) There is a cult of ignorance in the United States, and there always has been. The strain of anti-intellectualism has been a constant thread winding its way through our political and cultural life, nurtured by the false notion that democracy means that "my ignorance is just as good as your knowledge."

(2) Politicians have routinely striven to speak the language of Shakespeare and Milton as ungrammatically as possible in order to avoid offending their audiences by appearing to have gone to school. Thus, Adlai Stevenson, who incautiously allowed intelligence and learning and wit to peep out of his speeches, found the American people flocking to a Presidential candidate who invented a version of the English language that was all his own and that has been the despair of satirists ever since.

(3) George Wallace, in his speeches, had, as one of his prime targets, the "pointy-headed-professor," and with what a roar of approval that phrase was always greeted by his pointy-headed audience.

(4) Now we have a new slogan on the part of the obscurantists: "Don't trust the experts!" Ten years ago, it was "Don't trust anyone over 30." But the shouters of that slogan found that the inevitable alchemy of the calendar converted them to the untrustworthiness of the over-30, and, appar-

ently, they determined never to make that mistake again. "Don't trust the experts!" is absolutely safe. Nothing, neither the passing of time nor exposure to information, will convert these shouters to experts in any subject that might conceivably be useful.

(5) We have a new buzzword, too, for anyone who admires competence, knowledge, learning and skill, and who wishes to spread it around. People like that are called "elitists." That's the funniest buzzword ever invented because people who are not members of the intellectual elite don't know what an "elitist" is, or how to pronounce the word. As soon as someone shouts "elitist" it becomes clear that he or she is a closet elitist who is feeling guilty about having gone to school.

(Isaac Asimov, "A Cult of Ignorance," *Newsweek*
21 Jan. 1980)

e. Even more worrisome is what television has done to, rather than denied, the tube-weaned population. A series of studies has shown that addiction to TV stifles creative imagination. For example, a University of Southern California research team exposed 250 elementary students—who had been judged mentally gifted—to three weeks of intensive viewing. Tests conducted before and after the experiment found a marked drop in all forms of creative abilities except verbal skill. Some teachers are encountering children who cannot understand a simple story without visual illustrations. "TV has taken away the child's ability to form pictures in his mind," says child-development expert Dorothy Cohen at New York City's Bank Street College of Education.

(Harry F. Waters, "What TV Does to Kids,"
Newsweek 21 Feb. 1977)

2. List the evidence you would use to support one of the claims you wrote for Claim Exercise 2, pages 311–312. Make sure it satisfies the four rules of evidence. You may have to do some research or direct observation to gather your evidence.

Reasoning Principles

To the casual observer it may seem that a claim and its supporting evidence are all there is to an argument. Often that's all we see when we look at an argument. But of course there's more to it than that. Take John and Nancy's argument about the fir trees:

John:　　Sure, I see the pine cones, the needles, and color of the bark—so?

John doesn't see how Nancy's evidence supports her claim, and so she has to show him the connection between the two.

Nancy:　　Look, John, fir trees grow in the Rockies, redwoods on the California and Oregon coasts. Firs have large pine cones, redwoods quite small cones, only an inch long. Redwoods have grayish brown bark and flat yellow-green needles and are taller and older than fir trees.

What Nancy has done is present the reasoning principle she has used—in this case a definition—to make a claim based on the evidence before her.

If we diagram the elements of her argument as they stand now, they look like this:

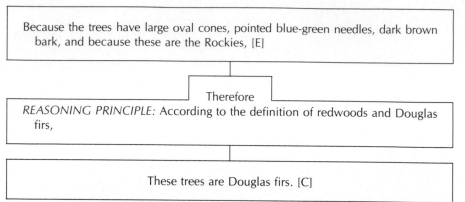

Because the trees have large oval cones, pointed blue-green needles, dark brown bark, and because these are the Rockies, [E]

Therefore

REASONING PRINCIPLE: According to the definition of redwoods and Douglas firs,

These trees are Douglas firs. [C]

Evidence consists of specific truths, individual facts; reasoning principles, on the other hand, consist of general truths or assumptions. These general truths or assumptions act as rules when we reason, and we rely on them the way we do the rules for a game. Just as the rules tell us how to play a game and whether particular plays are fair or foul, so do reasoning principles tell us what we can safely conclude about the evidence before us and whether a particular claim is justified or not. When we present an argument, we use these same principles as guidelines to show our audience that our evidence does indeed lead logically to our claim. If our evidence meets the conditions set by these principles, our claim is sound. In the preceding example, if Nancy's evidence is true, if it fits the terms of her reasoning principle-definition, and if that definition is true—then her claim must be true as well.

In our daily lives, at home, school, or on the job, we rely on hundreds, even thousands, of these reasoning principles. There is no room here even to begin to present them all. That's what parents, schools, books, and wise people are for. For the sake of simplicity, however, we can classify these principles into three broad categories: natural laws, principles of human life, and assumptions about the reliability of evidence.[2] *Natural laws* are general truths or assumptions about objects and events in the real world, like the "law" gravity, other rules of nature, scientific principles, and mathematical formulas. We use natural laws to determine why a toaster won't work, to reason that we have the flu rather than a bad cold, to discover the area of a circle, to explain why apes are similar to humans. *Principles of human life* consist of truths of human psychology, wise sayings, legal statutes and precedents, ethical standards, social customs, aesthetic standards, and rules of thumb. We rely on these principles to choose which college to attend, to know whether to tell the truth in a particular situation, to determine whether a person accused of a crime is guilty as charged, to decide whether a movie is worth seeing. *Reliability principles*, finally, are assumptions that the evidence of an argument is true or that its sources are credible.

Although you rely on these reasoning principles whenever you reason, you won't want to present them in every argument, only when you suspect your audience may not see how your evidence supports your claim. That's what Nancy does in her argument about the fir trees, and John must do the same when he argues that capital punishment should be abolished because it does not work. Even before he gives facts to show the death penalty does not deter murderers, he will want to introduce his reasoning principle: whatever else it accomplishes, effective punishment *ought* to deter potential criminals. Once he has laid down the rule he will argue by, he can present his evidence and the claim that his rule and evidence inevitably lead to. Here is an outline of his reasoning:

I. Effective punishment should deter crime [reasoning principle].
II. Statistics showing the death penalty doesn't deter criminals.
III. The death penalty is ineffective [a claim that, once established, becomes evidence in the next stage of the argument].
IV. It is unreasonable to do what is ineffective [reasoning principle].
V. The death penalty should be abolished [claim].

By presenting his reasoning principles in this way, John will anticipate the objections of opponents who might argue the contrary, that before deterrence or anything else, punishment should pay back a criminal for his crime.

The key to reasoning well—whether you show your audience your reasoning or not—is making sure that your reasoning principles meet the same standards applied to Nancy's argument. Obviously and first of all, these principles must be *true or at least credible;* otherwise, we can't be sure our evidence supports our claims. Nancy's natural law-definition of redwoods and fir trees is true, so she is confident that her evidence supports her claim. The human life-reasoning principles John uses in that part of his Criminal Justice paper we just examined are credible if not always true: many of us assume that punishment should deter potential criminals and that it is unreasonable to persist in doing what doesn't work.

The second standard for sound reasoning principles is *applicability*. Reasoning principles must actually apply to the evidence of the argument. Highway speeders sometimes reason: *I won't be stopped. I'm only going sixty, just five miles per hour over the limit.* Their reasoning principle? That the police give drivers a five-mile-per-hour leeway.

I am doing 60 mph. The speed limit is 55 mph. [E]

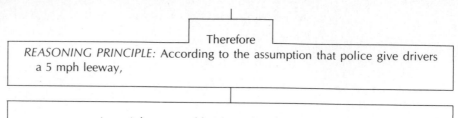

Therefore

REASONING PRINCIPLE: According to the assumption that police give drivers a 5 mph leeway,

I won't be stopped by the police for speeding. [C]

Now this general rule may apply in drivers' home towns or states, but—as they often find to their dismay—not in *every* town or state. By contrast, Nancy's definition certainly does apply to her evidence; so too do John's assumptions about the deterrent value of punishment and doing what is workable apply to the evidence of capital punishment.

EXERCISES

1. Write out the claims you can make on the basis of the following sets of evidence. You may be able to make more than one claim for each, and not all evidence will be relevant to every claim. Make sure your claims are arguable. Then write the reasoning principles you followed to make those claims, or explain the reasoning process you used to reach your claims. Make sure your reasoning meets the standards for effective reasoning principles given previously.

a. Oops, when I brought in the groceries from the car last night, I left a six-pack of cola outside on the porch by the door. The thermometer now says it's twenty degrees out there.

b. My car's engine will not turn over; the lights and radio don't work either. It is twelve below zero outside and one in the morning. I'm parked on a side street in a North Dakota town of eight hundred people. I have a bad case of the flu.

c. My ten-year-old has small red spots all over his face and body, fever, runny nose, and bloodshot eyes.

d. The radius of this circle is four inches.

e. A skydriver has just pulled the rip cord on his parachute, immediately after leaving the jump plane at 2,500 feet. The air is calm, the sky cloudless.

f. The Ponderous Pachyderm Steak House has three ingredients in its salad bar: brown lettuce, green carrots, and black tomatoes. Its steaks taste strongly of monosodium glutamate, come to the customers swimming in a pool of grease, are ringed with fat and as tough as shoe leather. The french fries are limp and salty. The sole dessert is blue jello that children generally consume through a straw.

g. Sybil made $150,000 last year as a tax lawyer. She has income from no other source. She is an American citizen, a widow, who lives in a twelve-room brick colonial in Greenwich, Connecticut, with her two children, ages eight and nine. She has never cheated on her income taxes, goes to church every Sunday, doesn't smoke or drink, mows her own lawn, and has a live-in housekeeper. Her children do well in school and are liked by their friends. She drives a two-year-old foreign-made sedan.

h. The President is a Republican, and the U.S. Senate is controlled by the Republican Party.

i. Each year one third of American households experience some form of violence or theft, for a total of some 41 million crimes. There are 35 million property crimes each year and 22,000 murders. Thirty-six to forty million people, sixteen to eighteen percent of the population, have arrest records for non-traffic offenses. Almost 2.5 million Americans are under some form of correctional supervision; 412,000 are in prison cells. In 1981, 124,000 convicts were released from prison. It costs $13,000 to keep a person in prison for a year. It costs $50,000 a bed to build a prison.

> (These figures and the following passage come from Richard Moran, "More Crime and Less Punishment," *Newsweek* 7 May 1984.)

j. Of every 100 felonies committed in America, only 33 are actually reported to the police. Of the 33 reported, about 6 are cleared by arrest. Of the six arrested, only three are prosecuted and convicted. The others are rejected or dismissed due to evidence or witness problems or diverted into a treatment program. Of the three convicted, only one is sent to prison. The other two are placed on probation or some form of supervision. Of the select few sent to prison, more than half receive a maximum sentence of five years. The average inmate, however, graduates into a community-based program in about two years.

2. Return to the argument you constructed for Evidence Exercise 2, page 315, and explain the reasoning that shows how your evidence supports your claim. You may have to use a different reasoning principle for each piece of evidence. Arrange your evidence and reasoning according to the model for arguments used earlier in this chapter (see page 316 for an example).

Sources In many arguments it isn't enough to present a claim and the evidence and reasoning it depends upon. It may not be clear that the evidence is, indeed, factual or that the reasoning principles are sound and actually do apply in the present situation. And so the arguer will have to identify the sources of the evidence or reasoning to back it up. The word *source* is used broadly here to mean a general body of knowledge from which reasoning principles come, general patterns in nature, regularities in human affairs, or documentation (the use of authorities' names, credentials or the titles of their works). Sources are anything that helps an audience accept our evidence and reasoning as true, credible, authoritative, or relevant.

Listen to more of John and Nancy's argument about the trees:

Nancy: Look, John, fir trees grow in the Rockies, redwoods on the California and Oregon coasts. Firs have large pine cones, redwoods quite small ones, only an inch long. Redwoods have grayish brown bark, flat, yellow-green needles, and are taller and older than fir trees.

John: How do you know all this? What are you, some kind of forest ranger or something?

Nancy: John, I've just had two semesters of botany, remember.

For her support Nancy has drawn on a general body of knowledge about botanical patterns in nature. If we diagram her argument to include her source, it looks like this:

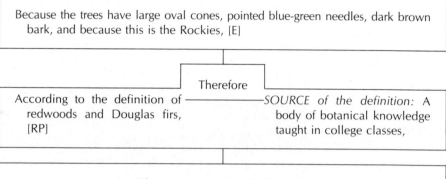

Because the trees have large oval cones, pointed blue-green needles, dark brown bark, and because this is the Rockies, [E]

Therefore

According to the definition of redwoods and Douglas firs, [RP]

SOURCE of the definition: A body of botanical knowledge taught in college classes,

These trees are Douglas firs. [C]

Or consider John's death penalty argument. He would summarize part of it this way:

I've just read four studies on the death penalty by three sociologists, all of them reputable researchers: Thorsten Sellin, Donald R. Campion, and Leonard D. Savitz. They provide statistics showing that the death penalty doesn't deter murder. It is unreasonable to continue doing what obviously doesn't work, and so I say the death penalty should be abolished.

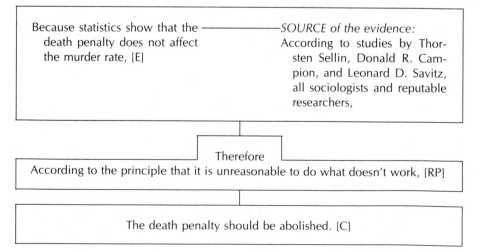

Because statistics show that the death penalty does not affect the murder rate, [E]

SOURCE of the evidence: According to studies by Thorsten Sellin, Donald R. Campion, and Leonard D. Savitz, all sociologists and reputable researchers,

Therefore

According to the principle that it is unreasonable to do what doesn't work, [RP]

The death penalty should be abolished. [C]

Nancy uses a source to establish her reasoning principles; John, to emphasize the truth of his evidence. Whenever you doubt your audience's confidence in you, you can support your argument by providing the names of the experts you've relied on, the books you've read, the witnesses you've examined, or the bodies of knowledge you've depended upon.

Qualifiers   In mathematics, the sciences, and formal logic it is often possible to argue with great precision and certainty, arriving at definite truth or at least a high degree of probability. This is seldom the case in the world outside the laboratory or logic classroom, however. The best we hope for out in the real world is to show that our arguments are plausible or probably true. As we construct these more tentative arguments we want to be clear just how strong we think our case is; we don't want to mislead others to take our claim for more than we intend it. And so we resort to qualifying words and phrases that indicate an argument's degree of force: *may, must, certainly, probably, necessarily, it is unlikely, as far as the evidence goes, it seems, as nearly as I can tell,* and so on. The number of these phrases is large, but for all practical purposes we use them to distinguish three degrees of certainty: a high degree of probability bordering on certainty, probability, and possibility.

Given the evidence and her botanical knowledge, Nancy can be very sure about her identification of the fir trees.

> *Nancy:*   John, I've just had two semesters of botany, remember? I know what the evidence tells me. Surely [qualifier] these are Douglas firs.

John has done some more research for his Criminal Justice paper and discovered studies of convicted murderers who were imprisoned, later paroled, and almost never again committed violent crimes or violated any other terms of their parole. They became model citizens. And so he reasons with confidence, if not certainty, that other paroled murderers will also pose little threat to their communities. If he were to diagram his argument, it would look like this:

Because studies show murderers rarely violate parole and almost never commit violent crimes, [E]

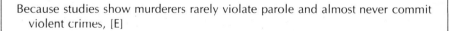

Therefore

According to the principle that what is true of individuals in a class is true of the whole class, [RP]

> QUALIFIER: It is highly probable that
> Paroled murderers pose no threat to their communities. [C]

John is less certain about one of the arguments he might use to convince his Aunt Wilma to give up smoking:

> Aunt Wilma, you've been smoking for twenty-five years. You know that all kinds of studies show cigarette smoke is full of carcinogens and that long-term smokers stand a five times greater chance of developing lung cancer than nonsmokers. I'm sorry to predict that cancer may well be in the cards for you.

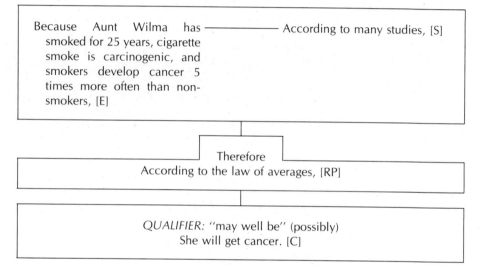

```
Because Aunt Wilma has ─────── According to many studies, [S]
smoked for 25 years, cigarette
smoke is carcinogenic, and
smokers develop cancer 5
times more often than non-
smokers, [E]

                    Therefore
         According to the law of averages, [RP]

         QUALIFIER: "may well be" (possibly)
              She will get cancer. [C]
```

Give your arguments the same careful qualification. With the exception of outright untruths, nothing discredits an argument faster than excessive claims.

Reservations   Just as arguments are rarely absolute, made without qualification, so are they rarely unreserved, applying in all situations without exceptions.[3] In effect, reservations are like the fine print at the end of a legal contract. They provide the exceptions to an argument, telling when and where it applies and when and where it does not. We can attach these reservations to our claims, evidence, or reasoning principles. Few people, for example, would claim that the death penalty should never be imposed for *any* crimes or criminals. They would modify that absolute claim with reservations. Our student John is no different. He claims that the death penalty should be abolished *except for war crimes.* As he has constructed it so far, his argument looks like this:

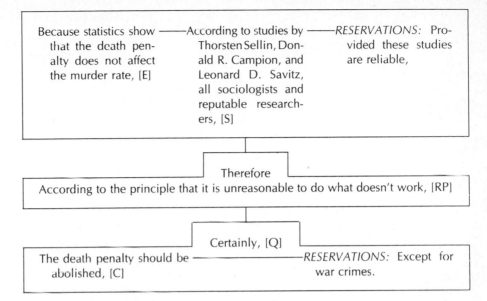

In similar ways, in examples we have already seen, John has added reservations to his movie review and his plea that his Aunt Wilma quit smoking:

> Unless it is intended as a parody [reservation], *Bruce Lee's Kung-Fu Killer Kousins*, now showing at the Lakeview Theater, is perhaps the worst movie of any kind ever distributed for public consumption.

> If you don't quit smoking soon [reservation], I'm sorry to predict that cancer may well be in the cards for you.

Argumentative Strings   As we have added one element to the next, the sample arguments we've been studying have grown quite complex, but if we compare them to the ones we have every day with friends, teachers, employers, or family, we see these examples aren't so complex after all, only parts of the arguments we would use if we were arguing in the real world. In real-life situations, we might have to make one claim and defend that before we could make and defend a second claim. The claim of the first argument, once defended, would become part of the evidence for a second argument, the two arguments now woven together into an argumentative string. We saw a brief example of this line of reasoning earlier in John's capital punishment argument:

Because statistics of murder rates in death penalty and non-death penalty states are similar, [E]

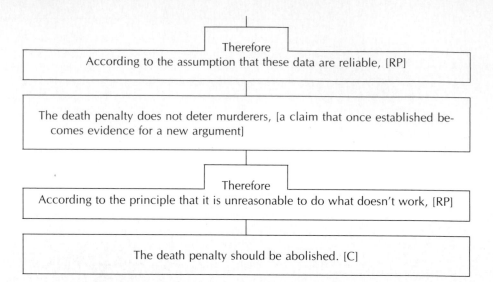

| Therefore |
| According to the assumption that these data are reliable, [RP] |

| The death penalty does not deter murderers, [a claim that once established becomes evidence for a new argument] |

| Therefore |
| According to the principle that it is unreasonable to do what doesn't work, [RP] |

| The death penalty should be abolished. [C] |

But as we've also seen, this is only part of John's complete argument against the death penalty. When he finally writes his Criminal Justice paper he will have to give many pieces of evidence for his central claim. And each piece of evidence will have to be presented in its own argument, complete with reasoning, sources, qualifiers, and reservations. Until he argues each of these argumentative strings separately, his larger argument will be neither plausible nor convincing. Here, on the opposite page, is the way all its major elements would look, arranged according to our diagram.

How detailed you make your arguments will depend, as most questions of development do, on your audience. Your aims, like those of our student John, are first to make your claims plausible to your readers, like something they *could* believe, and then convincing, like something they *should* believe. To achieve both, you'll say all you need to say—but not one word more.

EXERCISES

1. Beginning at the bottom of the following page are a number of arguments. Identify the elements of argument in each: claims, evidence, reasoning principles, sources, qualifiers, and reservations. As you read, look first for the major claims (there may be more than one argument in each example), then the evidence, and finally the other elements. Of course, not every argument will contain all six elements; identify only those elements actually present in each argument. It may help you keep them straight if you use the diagram for arguments given in the preceding pages. Decide whether these arguments are convincing, that is, whether their claims are genuinely arguable, their evidence reliable, their reasoning sound, their sources legitimate, and their qualifiers and reservations appropriate.

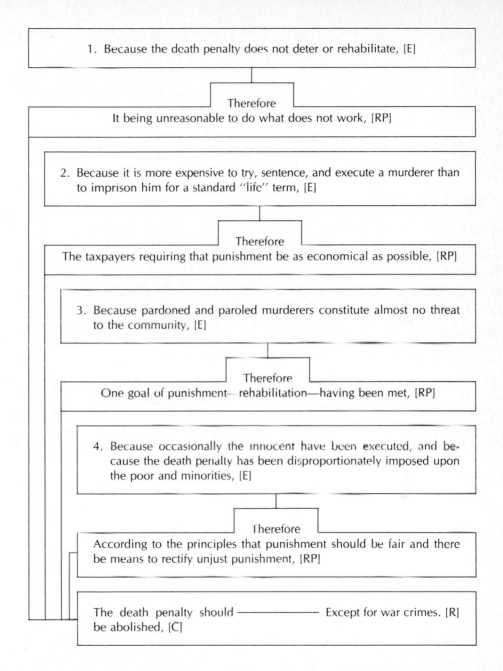

1. Because the death penalty does not deter or rehabilitate, [E]

Therefore

It being unreasonable to do what does not work, [RP]

2. Because it is more expensive to try, sentence, and execute a murderer than to imprison him for a standard "life" term, [E]

Therefore

The taxpayers requiring that punishment be as economical as possible, [RP]

3. Because pardoned and paroled murderers constitute almost no threat to the community, [E]

Therefore

One goal of punishment— rehabilitation—having been met, [RP]

4. Because occasionally the innocent have been executed, and because the death penalty has been disproportionately imposed upon the poor and minorities, [E]

Therefore

According to the principles that punishment should be fair and there be means to rectify unjust punishment, [RP]

The death penalty should ——————— Except for war crimes. [R]
be abolished, [C]

a. Don't be misled by his disheveled appearance and his relaxed manner; Harvey Dennim is certainly a first-rate student. He spends three nights every week in the library. He studies systematically according the survey-question-review method. He reads widely, outside his major and his assigned reading.

And he takes a variety of college courses. At least that's what his roommate tells me.

b. Tiny muddy footprints on the floor, books scattered by the door, jacket hanging from the stair railing, refrigerator door open, bread, empty milk carton, and peanut butter on the kitchen table, and back door open—Winnie must be home from school, that is, unless we've had a break-in by a ten-year-old vandal.

c. Now I know what I'm talking about because I've gotten it all from Professor W. E. Loughman, Harvard professor of education. A good school, he says, educates the whole person. Look at Gotham U. It requires liberal arts courses as well as courses in the physical and social sciences; it requires courses in physical education and the arts. It has a top-notch faculty and a fine library. Obviously Gotham U. is a good school.

d. Even if we assume that a right to smoke [cigarettes] exists—let's say it springs from the uniquely American notion that unless an activity is expressly forbidden, it is allowed—it does not follow that passengers have a right to smoke in airplanes. No right is absolute. We can't shout "Fire!" in a crowded theater, because somebody might get hurt in the resulting commotion. We ought not be able to smoke in an airplane, when to do so may leave an asthmatic 10 rows away gasping for breath.

(Lee S. Glass, "Fly the Smoke-Free Skies," *Newsweek* 16 Apr. 1984)

e. (1) . . . when I am asked . . . about registering women for the draft along with men I have to nod yes reluctantly. I don't want anyone registered, anyone drafted, unless it is a genuine crisis. But if there is a draft, this time it can't just touch our sons, like some civilized plague that leaves daughters alone to produce another generation of warriors.

(2) We may have to register women along with men anyway. Women may not have won equal rights yet, but they have "won" equal responsibilities. A male-only draft may be ruled unconstitutional.

(3) But at a deeper level, we have to register women along with men because our society requires it. For generations, war has been part of the rage so many men have held against women.

(4) War is in the hard-hat yelling at an equal rights rally, "Where were you at Iwo Jima?" War is in the man infuriated at the notion of a woman challenging veterans' preference. War is in the mind of the man who challenges his wife for having had a soft life.

(5) War has often split couples and sexes apart, into lives built on separate realities. It has been part of the grudge of self-sacrifice, the painful gap of understanding and experience between men's and women's lives. It is the stuff of which alienation and novels are written.

(6) But more awesomely, as a male activity, a rite of passage a test of manhood, war has been gruesomely acceptable. Old men who were warriors have sent young men to war as if it were their birthright. The women's role until recently was to wave banners and sing slogans, and be in need of protection from the enemy.

(7) We all pretended that war was civilized. War had rules and battlegrounds. War did not touch the finer and nobler things, like women.

(8) This was, of course, never true. The losers, the enemies, the victims, the widows of war were as brutalized as the soldiers. Under duress and in defense, women always fought.

(9) But, perhaps, stripped of its maleness and mystery, its audience and cheerleaders, war can be finally disillusioned. Without the last trappings of chivalry, it can be seen for what it is: the last deadly resort.

(10) So, if we must have a draft registration, I would include young women as well as young men. I would include them because they can do the job. I would include them because all women must gain the status to stop as well as to start wars. I would include them because it has been too easy to send men alone.

(11) I would include them because I simply cannot believe that I would feel differently if my daughter were my son.

(Ellen Goodman, "Drafting Daughters," *At Large*
[New York: Summit Books, 1981])

f. Many people believe that society's level of health depends primarily on medical treatment of the sick. But the relationship between increased investment in medicine and improvements in health is tenuous. Behavior usually has more to do with how long and healthily people live than does the soaring investment in medical treatments to restore health, or to slow its decline. Leon Kass of the University of Chicago notes that other animals "instinctively eat the right foods (when available) and act in such a way as to maintain their naturally given state of health and vigor. Other animals do not overeat, undersleep, knowingly ingest toxic substances, or permit their bodies to fall into disuse through sloth, watching television and riding in automobiles, transacting business or writing articles about health." For humans, health must be nurtured by "taming and moderating the admirable yet dangerous human desire to live better than sows and squirrels."

(George Will, "No 'Right' to Health," *The Pursuit of
Virtue and Other Tory Notions* [New York: Simon,
1982])

g. (1) The crisis of literacy is no fiction. Most young Americans now complete high school and at least attend college, yet few can read and write with a sophistication sufficient to justify twelve to sixteen years of schooling. At even the most elite colleges, a low standard of reading and writing has come to be taken for granted.

(2) Over the past decade, young Americans' command of English has consistently declined, from a standard that was none too spectacular to begin with. In 1973, 69 percent of 13-year-olds were able to write a "persuasive" letter as defined by the National Assessment of Educational Progress, mandated by Congress to monitor educational attainment around the nation; in 1978, 64 percent could demonstrate this very basic and trivial example of command of written language.

(3) As studies by the National Assessment and by John Goodlad, the author of *A Place Called School*, have shown, little writing is demanded of pupils in elementary and secondary school. The emphasis, in Goodlad's words, is on "mechanics—capitalization, punctuation, paragraphs, syllabication, synonyms, homonyms, antonyms, parts of speech—if teachers gave tests in-

volving writing paragraphs or essays, they seldom so indicated." Tests ask students merely for single words or short answers—identifications, "circle-the-verb" requests, and the like. The result is that pupils don't develop the habit of commanding language to express complex feelings or ideas, either in speech or in writing.

(From Leon Botstein, "Why Jonathan Can't Read," *The New Republic* 7 Nov. 1983)

h. (1) [The writer of the following essay is a former professional baseball player.] In 1939, Little League baseball was organized by Bert and George Bebble and Carl Stotz of Williamsport, Pa. What they had in mind in organizing this kid's baseball program, I'll never know. But I'm sure they never visualized the monster it would grow into.

(2) At least 25,000 teams, in about 5,000 leagues, compete for a chance to go to the Little League World Series in Williamsport each summer. These leagues are in more than fifteen countries, although recently the Little League organization has voted to restrict the competition to teams in the United States. If you judge the success of a program by the number of participants, it would appear that Little League has been a tremendous success. More than 600,000 boys from 8 to 12 are involved. But I say Little League is wrong—and I'll try to explain why.

(3) If I told you and your family that I want you to help me with a project from the middle of May until the end of July, one that would totally disrupt your dinner schedule and pay nothing, you would probably tell me to get lost. That's what Little League does. Mothers or fathers or both spend four or five nights a week taking children to Little League, watching the game, coming home around 8 or 8:30 and sitting down to a late dinner.

(4) These games are played at this hour because the adults are running the programs and this is the only time they have available. These same adults are in most cases unqualified as instructors and do not have the emotional stability to work with children of this age. The dedication and sincerity of these instructors cannot be questioned, but the purpose of this dedication should be. Youngsters eligible for Little League are of the age when their concentration lasts, at most, for five seconds—and without sustained concentration organized athletic programs are a farce.

(5) Most instructors will never understand this. As a result there is a lot of pressure on these young people to do something that is unnatural for their age—so there will always be hollering and tremendous disappointment for most of these players. For acting their age, they are made to feel incompetent. This is a basic fault of Little League.

(6) If you watch a Little League game, in most cases the pitchers are the most mature. They throw harder, and if they throw strikes very few batters can hit the ball. Consequently, it makes good baseball sense for most hitters to take the pitch. Don't swing. Hope for a walk. That could be a player's instruction for four years. The fun is in hitting the ball; the coach says don't swing. That may be sound baseball, but it does nothing to help a young player develop his hitting. What would seem like a basic training ground for baseball often turns out to be a program of negative thoughts that only retards a young player.

(7) I believe more good young athletes are turned off by the pressure of organized Little League than are helped. Little Leagues have no value as a training ground for baseball fundamentals. The instruction at that age, under the pressure of an organized league program, creates more doubt and eliminates the naturalness that is most important.

(8) If I'm going to criticize such a popular program as Little League, I'd better have some thoughts on what changes I would like to see.

(9) First of all, I wouldn't start any programs until the school year is over. Any young student has enough of a schedule during the school year to keep busy.

(10) These programs should be played in the afternoon—with a softball. Kids have a natural fear of a baseball; it hurts when it hits you. A softball is bigger, easier to see and easier to hit. You get to run the bases more and there isn't as much danger of injury if one gets hit with the ball. Boys and girls could play together. Different teams would be chosen every day. The instructors would be young adults home from college, or high-school graduates. The instructor could be the pitcher and the umpire at the same time. These programs could be run on public playgrounds or in schoolyards.

(11) I guarantee that their dinner would be at the same time every night. The fathers could come home after work and relax; most of all, the kids would have a good time playing ball in a program in which hitting the ball and running the bases are the big things.

(12) When you start talking about young people playing baseball at 13 to 15, you may have something. Organize them a little, but be careful; they are still young. But from 16 and on, work them really hard. Discipline them, organize the leagues, strive to win championships, travel all over. Give this age all the time and attention you can.

(13) I believe Little League has done just the opposite. We've worked hard with the 8- to 12-year-olds. We overorganize them, put them under pressure they can't handle and make playing baseball seem important. When our young people reach 16 they would appreciate the attention and help from the parents, and that's when our present programs almost stop.

(14) The whole idea of Little League baseball is wrong. There are alternatives available for more sensible programs. With the same dedication that has made the Little League such a major part of many of our lives, I'm sure we'll find the answer.

(15) I still don't know what those three gentlemen in Williamsport had in mind when they organized Little League baseball. I'm sure they didn't want parents arguing with their children about kid's games. I'm sure they didn't want to have family meals disrupted for three months every year. I'm sure they didn't want young athletes hurting their arms pitching under pressure at such a young age. I'm sure they didn't want young boys who don't have much athletic ability made to feel that something is wrong with them because they can't play baseball. I'm sure they didn't want a group of coaches drafting the players each year for different teams. I'm sure they didn't want unqualified men working with the young players. I'm sure they didn't realize how normal it is for an 8-year-old boy to be scared of a thrown or batted baseball.

(16) For the life of me, I can't figure out what they had in mind.
(Robin Roberts, "Strike Out Little League," *Newsweek* 21 July 1975)

2. Add qualifiers or reservations to the following statements to make them reasonable claims. Feel free to change the wording and attitudes to reflect your own thinking.

a. Abolish grades.
b. Raise the national highway speed limit.
c. Shut down America's nuclear power plants.
d. Playing frisbee is a wonderful pastime.
e. The ability to speak and write articulately leads to good grades.
f. Ours is a sexually permissive society.
g. The suburbs have more in common with the city than the country.
h. Modern poetry is difficult.
i. Compassion is more important than courage.
j. Saccharin causes cancer.

3. Choose three of the claims that you wrote for the preceding exercise. Write out your complete claims; then beneath each one list the sources that would provide you with reliable evidence and reasoning principles to argue that claim. You may list books, authority figures, bodies of knowledge, or general patterns in human beings or the world. You may have to do some research to identify these sources.

Four Kinds of Argument

Understanding the six elements of argument described in the preceding pages is one sure way to master the complexities of the reasoning process. With them you can tell whether an argument—yours or someone else's—is complete and plausible. A second way to master the process is understanding the basic kinds of argument. The subjects we argue about are nearly infinite, as are the situations in which we argue, and together these two facts mean that the combinations of our six elements into specific arguments will also be nearly limitless. Still, if we began classifying all these possible arguments, we would soon see that they fell into four kinds, each answering a particular question, each with its own characteristic strategies and design. If knowing the six elements of argument will help you construct complete arguments, knowing the four kinds will help you construct well-organized arguments.[4]

Categorical Arguments   Categorical arguments answer the question "What is it?" They show that their subjects (the "it") belong in a particular category (the "what"). We can argue that a subject belongs in a certain category in three ways: definition, comparison, and analogy.

Categorical argument by *definition* works like this: We create a category by making a definition of it and use that definition as the reasoning principle of our argument. Then we gather evidence showing that our subject either fits or does not fit the terms of our definition. That's the process John follows in one part of his Criminal Justice paper:

> Most people have little to fear from paroled murderers. If the statistics from the Ohio and New Jersey studies I have read are reliable, these men are wholly rehabilitated upon their release. They become law-abiding, nonthreatening, productive members of their communities.

Paroled murderers, he argues, belong in the category of rehabilitated criminals. In its elements, his argument looks like this:

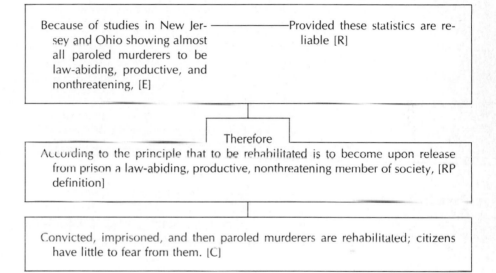

Because of studies in New Jersey and Ohio showing almost all paroled murderers to be law-abiding, productive, and nonthreatening, [E] ——————— Provided these statistics are reliable [R]

Therefore

According to the principle that to be rehabilitated is to become upon release from prison a law-abiding, productive, nonthreatening member of society, [RP definition]

Convicted, imprisoned, and then paroled murderers are rehabilitated; citizens have little to fear from them. [C]

The most straightforward way to write out such an argument is the *deductive pattern*. If John organized by this pattern, he would present his reasoning principle-definition early and establish that. Only then would he give his evidence showing that murderers fit the definition of rehabilitation. He might outline the argument like this:

I. Claim: that paroled murderers are likely to be rehabilitated.
II. Reasoning principle-definition: rehabilitation consists of being law-abiding, productive, and nonthreatening.
III. Evidence: showing that paroled murderers do, indeed, have the characteristics of rehabilitated criminals.

Because his definition is complex, however, John might just as well divide his argument into stages, first giving one part of his definition and the evidence covered by it, then the next, and so on, until the whole definition and all the evidence had been laid out.

   I. Part One.
      A. Definition-reasoning principle: Rehabilitated criminals are law-abiding.
      B. Evidence showing the low rearrest rate for paroled murderers.
   II. Part Two.
      A. Definition: Rehabilitated criminals are nonthreatening.
      B. Evidence showing that paroled murderers are almost never involved in violent behavior.

Or, for dramatic impact, John may choose the *inductive pattern* for his argument. According to this pattern, he would present his evidence first, then the claim it leads to, and finally, if necessary, the definition-reasoning principle. This pattern usually works best when the definition is obvious and noncontroversial. In an outline, John's argument would look like this:

   I. Evidence about paroled murderers from Ohio and New Jersey studies.
      A. The studies show they are law-abiding.
      B. The studies show they get and keep jobs.
      C. The studies show their presence is nonthreatening.
   II. The claim that paroled murderers are rehabilitated.
   III. The reasoning principle that defines rehabilitation as being law-abiding, productive, and nonthreatening upon release from prison.

The effect of this design would be to give John's argument a spontaneous feeling, as if he were creating the category as he went along, considering each piece of evidence he has observed. That may not actually be the case, but often that is the way inductive categorical arguments work: they create a category by assembling evidence rather than assembling evidence to fit a preestablished category.

Nancy's argument about the fir trees is one example of the second type of categorical argument, *comparison/contrast*. She has, in effect, two reasoning principle-definitions, one for redwoods and one for Douglas firs, and she supports her claim by showing that the evidence fits the Douglas fir trees category better than the redwoods category. For his capital punishment paper John constructs a comparison/contrast argument that works in the opposite way. As he does more research into the behavior of paroled murderers, he uncovers evidence about the behavior of other paroled felons, those not convicted of murder, and this enables him to make a comparison. Nancy has two definitions and one set of evidence; he has *one* definition and *two* sets of evidence. He aims to show, by comparison, that one set of evidence fits his reasoning principle-definition better than the other. His argument now looks like this:

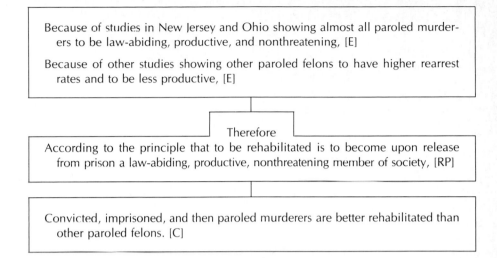

Because of studies in New Jersey and Ohio showing almost all paroled murderers to be law-abiding, productive, and nonthreatening, [E]

Because of other studies showing other paroled felons to have higher rearrest rates and to be less productive, [E]

Therefore

According to the principle that to be rehabilitated is to become upon release from prison a law-abiding, productive, nonthreatening member of society, [RP]

Convicted, imprisoned, and then paroled murderers are better rehabilitated than other paroled felons. [C]

In essay form, this comparison/contrast argument would probably follow one of the conventional patterns for definition arguments:

I. Claim: that paroled murderers are better rehabilitated than other paroled felons.
II. Reasoning principle-definition: rehabilitation consists of being law-abiding, productive, and nonthreatening.
III. Block comparison of the two sets of evidence.
   A. Evidence showing rearrest rates and job figures for paroled felons not convicted for murder.
   B. Evidence showing lower rearrest rates and higher employment figures for paroled murderers.

The third version of categorical argument, *argument by analogy*, makes a claim about a subject and defends it by comparing that subject imaginatively with some simpler or more familiar subject. Put another way, an argumentative analogy reasons that if two subjects are similar in certain obvious ways listed as evidence, then they may also be similar in other, more crucial respects asserted in the claim. While doing his research John came upon the following analogy in a death penalty argument by the late FBI Director J. Edgar Hoover:

> A judge once said, "The death penalty is a warning, just like a lighthouse throwing its beams out to sea. We hear about shipwrecks, but we do not hear about the ships the lighthouse guides safely on their way. We do not have proof of the number of ships it saves, but we do not tear the lighthouse down."[5]

In its elements, we can arrange the analogy this way:

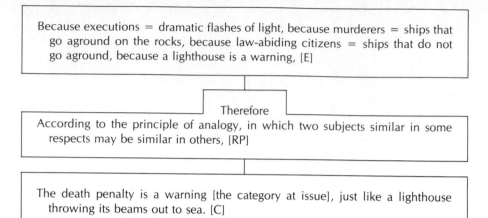

Of course, analogies never prove anything conclusively, because the comparison between the two subjects is incomplete or merely figurative rather than literal. We can't say that the death penalty is like a lighthouse in the same way we say a paroled murderer is like other paroled criminals—John's argument. Nevertheless, analogical comparisons do dramatize a subject and help show how it fits in a particular category, in this example, how the death penalty is a sufficient warning to potential murderers. Neither Hoover nor the judge he quotes is interested in lighthouses but in finding a way to demonstrate their claim that the death penalty is a deterrent to crime. Comparing executions to a lighthouse helps them "illuminate" their claim.

EXERCISES

1. Write arguable categorical claims for each of the following. No matter how your finished sentences look, make sure that in each instance you assert that your subject *is* something, is *not* something, is *like* something, is *unlike* something, or is one thing *rather than* another.

a. The religious beliefs of Americans your age.
b. The use of drugs by Americans your age.
c. An author or film-maker preferred or disliked by Americans your age.
d. The musical tastes of people your age and people your parents' age.
e. A time in American history most like or unlike the present decade.

Some Examples of Categorical Claims
Most of America's Great Lakes are too polluted to permit unrestricted sport and commercial fishing.

You'll find little coliform bacteria pollution in Lake Superior.

Lake Erie was once a wide, shallow sewer dumped in by both Canada and the United States.

Lake Erie is no longer the open sewer it once was, but it is not yet the angler's paradise that environmentalists want it to be.

The sailing on Lake Michigan is more challenging than the sailing on Lake Huron or Erie.

2. Write definitions for the categories given in the following claims. If you were to argue these claims, your definitions would become your reasoning principles. Be sure your definitions can actually be applied to the subjects of your claims.

  a. Mary McLeod Bethune is the kind of person anyone could admire as a hero.
  b. The writing we do in college and on the job is as much a science as an art.
  c. The inexpensive tract house and townhouse developments thrown up in America's suburbs over the past twenty years will probably become the ghettos of tomorrow.
  d. Most of today's young people have little sense of the alienation felt by so many in the 1960s.
  e. To the dismay of parents, administrators, and even many students some college dormitories are more like zoos than residences.
  f. Although some critics would deny it, Tennessee Williams' play *A Streetcar Named Desire* is as much a tragedy as *Hamlet* or *Oedipus the King*.

3. Gather the evidence that will support one of the claims you wrote for Categorical Claim Exercise 1. You may have to do some research to identify this evidence. If it's not clear how a piece of evidence supports your claim, be sure to give the reasoning principle that shows how. Outline your argument according to one of the patterns of categorical argument given on pages 331–333.

Causal Arguments   Causal arguments answer two questions: "What caused it?" and "What will be the effects of it?" That is, causal arguments defend claims about causes *or* effects. They work in two directions. In the first, we reason backward from effects to discover their probable causes. This is what John did as he tried to reason out the causes of the typical murder for his capital punishment paper.

In the vast majority of cases, over two thirds of them, murders are crimes of passion.

Effect: murder————was caused by————→ *Cause:* passion

His argument with his Aunt Wilma about her cigarette smoking requires reasoning in the other direction, from a present cause into the future to discover potential effects.

Aunt Wilma, you've been smoking for twenty-five years. . . . Cancer may well be in the cards for you.

Cause: smoking————will cause————→ *Effect:* lung cancer

In either direction, causal arguments aim to demonstrate a relationship between the causes and effects given in the evidence of the argument.

Unfortunately, this relation often looks more obvious or easier to demonstrate than it is, and for this reason, you'll want to remember the following three cautions when you construct causal arguments.

First, sound causal arguments distinguish among the kinds of causes that produce an effect. Not all that we call causes work to produce an effect in the same way and with the same force; therefore, in our search for causes we have to know what kinds of causes we're considering. There are three kinds: necessary, sufficient, and contributory causes. *Necessary causes* are the conditions necessary so that an effect can occur. Recall for a moment the forest fire illustration presented in Chapter 6, in which causal analysis is presented as a pattern of organization. The necessary cause of most forest fires is tinder-dry trees and vegetation. A dry forest in the closing weeks of a rainless summer doesn't guarantee a forest fire, but there are few fires in rainy seasons or the winter. *Sufficient causes* are, in a simple sense, the "true causes" of an effect. They can produce an effect by themselves, although other sufficient causes may produce the same effect in other situations. The carelessly dropped match, the unextinguished cigarette or campfire, the lightning bolt—all these are sufficient causes of forest fires, each capable of starting a fire by itself. *Contributory causes* cannot produce effects by themselves, but they can influence other causes. Carelessness with matches, cigarettes, and campfires or an extended drought will not by itself cause fires, but it can lead to them.

Second, sound causal arguments identify as many of the causes of an effect as possible. Causes and effects rarely occur in tidy one-to-one relationships, one clear cause producing one definite effect. Preparing for his Criminal Justice paper, John discovered that two thirds of all murders were crimes of passion, that more than three quarters of all murderers had been drinking before their crimes, and that two thirds of all murderers knew their victims In most murders it seems that *multiple causes*—anger, alcohol, familiarity, provocation, motivation, and the presence of a weapon—act on a murderer all at once to produce the crime. But causes may also be linked in a "causal chain" of *remote to immediate causes,* one cause producing an effect that itself becomes the cause of another effect. It is this causal chain many have in mind when they claim that poverty, overcrowding, and broken homes are the "root causes" of crime. People who reason this way recognize that remote contributory crimes sometimes underlie and lead to more obvious immediate and sufficient causes. Sound causal arguments follow out the links in this chain, careful to distinguish between false and true causes. After all, not everything that precedes an effect helps to cause that effect.

Third, sound causal arguments allow for reciprocal causes. In some cases one cause produces an effect that in turn produces an effect in the original cause. Sound confusing? Remember the comedians Laurel and Hardy? Stanley would do something foolish (cause); Oliver would respond (effect) by shoving Stanley (cause); Stanley would respond (effect) by shoving back (cause), and so on, back and forth, cause-effect-cause-effect, until both men had lost their derbies and their dignity and ended up taking a pratfall. For a sobering example, our student John discovered some slight evidence that reciprocity may work in ironic ways in death penalty laws. A study made in nineteenth-century England revealed that of 167 persons executed in 1866, 164 had witnessed a public execution. It is just possible that one execution was the remote contributory cause of a murder that became the sufficient cause for another execution, and that, in turn, became a contributory cause of another murder, and so on, back and forth, death begetting more death in a pattern of reciprocal cause and effect.

The design we give to causal arguments almost always depends upon the time sequence that links causes and their effects into a chronological pattern, the same pattern presented in the discussion of causal analysis in Chapter 6. This pattern applies whether we reason back from effects to causes or forward from causes to probable effects.

I. Effect-to-cause claim [reasoning backward].
II. Immediate cause closest to the effect.
III. Next closest cause.
IV. And so on, to the remote, underlying causes farthest from the effect.

I. Cause-to-effect claim [reasoning forward].
II. Remote, contributory, and necessary causes.
III. Immediate and sufficient causes.

Occasionally, however, we may use a third pattern to organize a causal argument, when multiple causes all act at once to produce an effect. The organization here is not chronological, from remote to immediate causes, but logical: from the most important to the least important causes, from the least to the most important, or from the obvious to the not so obvious yet equally important causes:

I. Multiple cause claim.
II. Most important cause.
III. Next most important, and so on.
IV. Least important cause.

I. Multiple cause claim.
II. Obvious but least important cause.
III. Next most obvious or important cause.
IV. Least obvious but most important cause.

EXERCISES

1. Based on your observation, reading, or experience, write an arguable cause/effect claim for five of the following subjects. Your claim should assert either the specific causes of a particular effect or the specific consequences of a particular

cause. You may want to use qualifiers to indicate the force of the cause, e.g., "directly caused," "contributed to," "was essential to," and so on.

    a. Your choice of a college or a career.
    b. Virtuous behavior, e.g., honesty, fidelity, courage, compassion.
    c. Teenage rebellion.
    d. Academic success in your chosen major.
    e. A successful marriage that you know.
    f. The success or failure of a recently introduced product or service.
    g. The success or failure of a particular sports team or individual performer.
    h. Increasingly violent or sexually explicit movies.
    i. The extinction or decline of a species of plant or animal.
    j. Current relations between the United States and another country.

2. Look up one of the following in an encyclopedia or biographical dictionary and list its causes. (See the Appendix, pages 546–551.) Whenever possible, identify the kinds of causes you discover; necessary, sufficient, or contributory; reciprocal; remote or immediate. If you discover a chain of causes, arrange them in chronological order.

    a. The Great Chicago Fire of 1871.
    b. World War I.
    c. The American dustbowls of the 1930s.
    d. The defeat of the Confederate forces at the Battle of Gettysburg, July 1–3, 1863.
    e. Ernest Hemingway's death.
    f. The Boston Tea Party of 1773.
    g. Volcanic eruption.
    h. The common cold.
    i. The execution of Joan of Arc.
    j. The decline of the Aztec civilization.
    k. The extinction of the dinosaurs.
    l. The Russian Revolution of 1905.
    m. The Great Depression.
    n. The successes of the German Nazi Party in the 1920s and 30s.
    o. The flight of an airplane, propeller-driven or jet.

3. Choose one of the claims you made for Cause/Effect Exercise 1 and gather the evidence to support it. If the relationship between a cause and effect is not clear, you will have to explain your reasoning. Outline your argument according to one of the models on page 337.

Value Judgments

Value judgments answer the question "What good is it?" If we study them more closely, however, we see that these judgments really involve three answers to three slightly different questions, each depending on a definition of the word *good*. When we ask "What good is it?" we're really asking whether a subject is useful or not, pleasing or displeasing, ethical or unethical. Consider some of the value judgments our student John has made as part of his arguments:

Bruce Lee's Kung-Fu Killer Kousins is perhaps the worst movie of any kind ever distributed for public consumption. = The movie is not aesthetically pleasing.

Aunt Wilma, smoking is bad for your health. = Smoking is not useful to Aunt Wilma's health.

The death penalty is criminologically unsound. = The death penalty is not useful to criminals or society.

The death penalty is vindictive, mere revenge, pure and simple. = The death penalty is morally wrong.

To argue each of these claims John must show that the subject in question meets or fails to meet certain utilitarian, aesthetic, or moral standards of value (definitions of *good*) contained in the reasoning principles of each argument. In some instances, that smoking is bad, for example, the definitions of good health are so obvious they aren't open to question and may only have to be implied. It would be enough to give only the claim and the evidence that defends it. In other instances, that the death penalty is vindictive, one might have to begin the argument by establishing the reasoning principle, the moral judgment that revenge is wrong. Only after that reasoning principle has been established as sound could the argument continue. Some value judgment arguments, in other words, are as much about their standards of value as they are about the subjects they judge. Arguing effectively here depends upon clear, complete, appropriate standards of value and knowing when to present them directly, when merely to imply them.

In design, value judgment arguments look very much like either categorical arguments or causal arguments because the judgment itself always contains a categorical or causal claim along with its evaluation.

Bruce Lee's Kung-Fu Killer Kousins is . . . the worst movie = This movie belongs in the category of worst movies.

. . . smoking is bad . . . = smoking (cause) will have bad effects on one's health.

Here is a capsule summary of John's movie review and the design he would follow if he were to write it out, a design based on the pattern for categorical arguments.

Unless it is intended as a parody, *Bruce Lee's Kung-Fu Killer Kousins*, now showing at the Lakeview Theater, is perhaps the worst movie of any kind ever distributed for public consumption. We don't ask for much from B-grade adventure movies, a barely plausible plot, characterization only slightly more complex than that for cartoon characters, and production values that permit viewers at least occasionally to forget they are watching a movie. This movie does not even come close to meeting the least of these standards. We are asked to believe, for openers, that a ten-year-old boy swam the China Sea in ten days searching for his father. Didn't the tiny fellow ever get tired? Eventually he and his father just happen to bump into each other on a street corner in downtown Hong Kong, one of the most populous cities in the world. Together they defeat a gang of twenty-five Kung-fu killers with only their wits, fists, feet, assorted sticks, and a whole lotta heart and then win 3 million pounds in the local lottery. Oh, come on! The acting was wooden throughout. When the father squeezed his kid at their first meeting, you could see the man was about to suffocate the boy. The production values were terrible. Every shot was predictable. The scene of Hong Kong's burning was clearly done with cellophane and cardboard on a sand-table. The language dubbing was so poor that characters were continually heard speaking when their lips were not moving. And, in the climactic fight scene, a Boeing 747 could be observed taking off in the background—this in a story supposed to take place in 1925.

   I. Value judgment claim.
  II. Reasoning principle-definition of the standards for judging a B-grade adventure movie.
 III. Applying the standards to the evidence.
    A. A wholly implausible plot line.
      1. Human impossibilities.
      2. Absurd coincidences.
    B. Ineffective acting.
    C. Poor production values.
      1. Predictable shots.
      2. Poorly done special effects.
      3. Poor dubbing.
      4. Poor scene setting.

On the other hand, if John were to marshall all his arguments against his Aunt Wilma's smoking and organize them in a logical design, they might look like a causal argument, in particular, the pattern that reasons from causes to their immediate and then long-term effects.

   I. Value judgment claim that smoking is bad for his aunt's health. (Implied rather than stated directly are the reasoning principles that what has happened to others could, by the law of averages, happen to her and that whatever injures the body is bad for it.)
  II. Minor immediate effects of smoking: gum irritation, skin pallor, premature aging of the skin, lack of energy and breath.
 III. More serious effects: impairment of circulation, high blood pressure, and possible heart disease.
 IV. Very serious long-term effects: emphysema, lung cancer, and death.

EXERCISES

1. Choose five of the following categories and write the standards of value (reasoning principles) that you might use to help you defend specific value judgments about specific subjects. For example, what standards for effective political behavior would you use to judge individual politicians? In effect, you are writing definitions. In each case, identify whether your standards of value are utilitarian, aesthetic, or ethical.

a. The effective politician.
b. The best/worst place to live.
c. The ideal college or university.
d. Good music.
e. The well-dressed person.
f. The best/worst automobile.
g. The ideal friend.
h. The ideal game for college students.
i. The good restaurant, book, or movie.
j. The good society.

2. Choose one representative from five of the categories listed in Value Judgment Exercise 1, e.g., a specific politician, specific place to live, specific college or university, specific kind of music, specific musician, and so on. Write a value judgment claim about each of your choices. Make your evaluations detailed and specific.

3. Choose one of the claims you wrote for Value Judgment Exercise 2 and construct an argument to support it. Gather the evidence that will demonstrate your claim. If your standards of value are not obvious, you will have to present them. Outline your argument according to one of the models on pages 331–340, or create a logical design of your own.

Propositional Arguments Propositional arguments answer the question "What should be done about it?" and sometimes "Who should do it?" The first three kinds of argument you've studied are about belief; this fourth kind is about action.

> The death penalty should be abolished in the United States.
>
> Aunt Wilma, you should stop smoking.

Like value arguments, however, propositional arguments consist of other arguments to establish their reasoning principles and evidence. These arguments within arguments often make propositional claims the most challenging to support. For example, you earlier studied John's complete argument in favor of abolishing the death penalty (page 325). Each of those separate, subordinate arguments, some of them depending upon additional argumentative strings, would have to be presented before John's defense of his proposition would be complete.

Not surprisingly, the pattern for such a complex argument is also complex. But we can simplify it somewhat if we envision it as shaped like an hourglass.[6] Like the thick upper body of the hourglass, preliminary arguments come first, demonstrating that *a problem* or *need for action* exists, in this case, that the death penalty is not doing what effective punishment should do. These arguments may be arranged for dramatic effect or logical force, least dramatic first, the more dramatic later on, but instead of each argument leading to the next, they all funnel to the central propositional claim in the middle. Funneling out from this proposal are new arguments about the *benefits* of taking the proposed action, in this case, what will be gained by abolishing capital punishment and substituting new penalties. On some occasions, this third section will also consider alternative courses of action and show that the course proposed by the claim is the simplest, most practical, most ethical, or only choice under the circumstances.

I. The need for action: A. Possible executions of the innocent; B. Murderers posing no threat to the community; C. The expense of executions; D. The nondeterrence of the death penalty; E. Its inconsistency and unfairness; F. Its dehumanization

II. Claim that the death penalty should be abolished in the United States

III. Benefits: A. Rehabilitated criminals returned to society; B. The sanctity of life upheld; C. The adoption of effective alternatives; D. The recognition of the social bond between the community and its criminals

Complex though it may still be, if we imagine the propositional argument in this way, it has a clear form and, like the sand that flows to the bottom of the glass, a clear direction.

EXERCISES

1. Choose five of the following topics and write a propositional claim for each. Be as specific as possible. In your claim try to indicate the reason action is necessary or the benefits of acting upon your proposal. Identify those persons who are to make your proposed change. Address them directly.

   a. A change at your home.
   b. A change in your community.
   c. A change that motorists or other travelers should make.
   d. A change most Americans should make.
   e. A bad habit you should break.
   f. A prejudice or stereotype that should be abandoned by someone you know.
   g. A product or service many people should buy.
   h. A change in the law or by some government agency.
   i. A change at the movies, on radio or TV, in the music industry, at a magazine, newspaper, or other publisher.
   j. A change at some organization or place of business.

2. Choose one of the propositional claims you wrote for Exercise 1. Construct a needs/benefits argument that might convince the appropriate audience to make your proposed change. Gather the evidence that will demonstrate needs and benefits. If necessary, identify the reasoning that connects evidence and claim. Outline your argument according to the three-part "hourglass" pattern on this page.

3. Summing Up: Four Kinds of Argument.

a. Turn back to Claim Exercise 1, page 311, and identify the kinds of arguable claims listed there: categorical, cause/effect, value judgment, or propositional.

b. Turn to Evidence Exercise 1, pages 314–315, and identify the kinds of arguments you find. There may be more than one kind of argument in each sample.

c. Turn to Exercise 1, pages 324–330, and identify the kinds of arguments in each example. Here, too, you may find more than one kind of argument used to support a claim.

❧ LOGICAL FALLACIES: WHEN ARGUMENTS GO WRONG

Arguments are such delicate creations, often difficult to create and ruined by the least misstep in their construction.[7] When they don't perform as we intend them, that is, when they don't successfully support their claims, the most frequent cause is an error of reasoning, called a fallacy. A *fallacy* is a reasoning strategy that may be sound in another situation—with different evidence, reasoning, sources, qualifiers, or reservations—but in this instance it will not do what the arguer wants it to. What's worse, fallacies often don't look wrong. Until examined, they may seem convincing to arguer and audience alike. For this reason, every arguer risks falling victim to honest, accidental errors of reasoning. For the same reason, audiences risk falling victim to deliberate fallacies perpetrated by deceitful people who recognize that hoodwinking an audience is the only way to defend their claims. To avoid fallacies in your arguments and spot them in others', you need to understand the most common and important of these fallacies, presented on the following pages in alphabetical order. Even without knowing their names, however, you can spot most errors of reasoning if you ask these questions whenever you find a suspicious argument:

1. Is the claim clear and arguable?
2. Is there any actual evidence to support the claim?
3. Is there enough evidence?
4. Is the evidence relevant?
5. Are all assumptions justifiable?

Ad Hominem ("To the Man"—or the Woman)

Occasionally, by mistake or design, an arguer will shift attention from the issues of an argument and, instead of arguing about those issues, attack his or her opponent. It is easy to assume, but not always true, that the quality of a claim depends upon the character of a claimant. In court, of course, an attorney is justified in attacking the character of a witness who for reasons of self-interest or incapacity may be unreliable. And there may be times in our own arguments when we will want to oppose a claim by disputing the ability of our opponents to make true statements or sound claims. But it is a fallacy to attack the character of the arguer simply to avoid the real issues at hand. This is the fallacy we detect in name-calling and in many examples of guilt by association. Hear the ad hominem attack in the following claim?

> The misguided, weak-kneed, liberal opponents of the death penalty fail to recognize that their most fervent allies in their opposition are the bestial residents of every death row in the country.

Whether one is weak-kneed, a liberal, or under sentence of death has nothing to do with the quality of an argument against the death penalty, but if listeners are distracted by this name-calling, they may be led to oppose the abolitionists without ever considering their argument.

Ad Populum ("To the People")

Like the ad hominem fallacy, the ad populum fallacy is one of evasion. Here the arguer appeals to the irrational fears and prejudices of an audience instead of addressing the issues. We detect it in "the sob story"—the irrelevant appeal to pity—and in the thick use of honorific or pejorative words to rouse feeling instead of thinking. Consider these two passages, the first from a pro-death penalty essay, the second from an anti-death penalty essay.

> Was not this small, blonde six-year-old girl a child of God? She was choked, beaten, and raped by a sex fiend whose pregnant wife reportedly helped him lure the innocent child into his car and who sat and watched the assault on the screaming youngster. And when he completed his inhuman deed, the wife, herself bringing a life into the world, allegedly killed the child with several savage blows with a tire iron.
> (J. Edgar Hoover, *F.B.I. Law Enforcement Bulletin* 30 [June 1961])

> There is a record of an early English hanging of a half-starved female criminal who dropped through the trap and dangled at the end of the rope, eyes bulging with dread, because she was not heavy enough—she was a small 12-year-old girl—for the fall to break her neck. The hangman had to go down the 13 steps, grab her legs and add his weight to hers to carry out the sentence.
> (Michael V. DiSalle, "Capital Punishment: The Barbaric Anachronism," *Playboy* May 1966)

Murder and an execution are both horrible events, true, but the charged language that depicts the horror in these passages is not always relevant to the issues at hand. It's there largely as an incitement to our fears and passions.

small, blond six-year-old girl	half-starved
child of God	dangled
sex fiend	eyes bulging with dread
innocent child	small 12-year-old girl
screaming youngster	13 steps
inhuman deed	grab her legs
savage blows	

Whether we favor or oppose the death penalty, shouldn't we be as concerned about the death of a three-hundred-pound, dark-haired, sixty-year-old as we are about the deaths of a little blond six-year-old or a half-starved twelve-year-old? As we shall see, the appeal to an audience's emotions has a legitimate place in a persuasion—but *not* when it serves to cloud a person's reasoning powers or take the place of argument.

Appeal to Authority

Authorities or experts are almost always useful support for the evidence and reasoning of an argument. Their superior knowledge and judgment add weight to almost any case, and you should cite them as sources. But they are no substitutes for the argument itself. The appeal to authority becomes fallacious when that authority is used as the final word—in place of the evidence—or when the authorities make claims outside their areas of expertise. This fallacy is harmless enough in magazine and TV advertisements that use movie actors and sports figures to sell everything from beer to underwear; their only "expertise" is their fame. It is a more significant error in the following serious argument about the death penalty:

> I favor retention of the death penalty for two reasons: The first is that J. Edgar Hoover and all subsequent heads of the FBI have favored it. They ought to know what they're talking about. My second reason is that my minister favors retention. He reminded me that the Bible, in Exodus 21:12, speaks of evil-doers being executed. "He that smiteth a man, so that he die, shall surely be put to death."

The FBI chiefs may all have had good reasons for their support of the death penalty, and so may ministers and Old Testament patriarchs, but the fact of their support is no substitute for a systematic presentation and evaluation of their reasons. Authorities can strengthen a claim, but their good names alone are never proof for that claim.

Appeal to Force

The appeal to force is the use or threat of force rather than reason to change the belief or action of an audience. Force may be moral, psychological, or physical. Here it is psychological:

> If you want to keep this job, let's hear no more antisocial remarks from you about the abolition of the death penalty.

Such intimidation has no place in argument.

Begging the Question

The fallacy of begging the question assumes the truth of a claim without evidence. A claim is, remember, an assertion whose truth or probability is in doubt. None of its terms can be assumed to be true; they must be *shown* to be true. Begging the question is reasoning in circles, supporting a claim with reasons that merely restate the claim.

> Such a cruel, unusual and barbaric punishment as the death penalty must not be permitted in a civilized society like ours.

Distilled to its essence, the claim opposes the death penalty, and if that were all it did, it would be a perfectly acceptable claim, capable of being defended with evidence and reasoning. But in its present version here, it offers in addition several unproven assumptions without the slightest suggestion that they are only assumptions: that the death penalty is cruel, unusual, and barbaric; that civilized societies do not practice the death penalty; and that our society is somehow more civilized than others that practice the death penalty. Now it may be true that the death penalty *is* barbaric, true that civilized societies do *not* practice it, and true that we become less civilized by executing fellow human beings—but the truth of these buried claims cannot be taken for granted, or "begged." They must be laid out, argued, and supported, each in its turn, and *then*, once the probability of these claims has been established, the arguer can proceed to argue the central claim against the death penalty. If these buried claims cannot be supported, then the central claim must be abandoned or modified.

Either/Or Fallacy

Arguments often deal in alternatives, but the either/or fallacy, instead of recognizing and considering all possible alternatives, restricts them to just two, one of which is clearly unsound. The either/or fallacy is a process of oversimplification. It backs an audience into a corner and then allows only one way out.

> If murderers are allowed to live, we have as much as confessed that human life has no value.

What this claim asserts in other words is, *either* murderers are executed and the value of human life is affirmed, *or* they are allowed to live and the value of human life is denied. It is true that sparing a murderer may show callousness toward the victim of the crime, but it may also show other things besides: an awareness of mitigating circumstances, of sound puni-tive policy, even of compassion. The claim may, finally, be true, but in its present form it is unsound because it has failed to consider all alterna-tives.

Equivocation

To shift the meaning of a term during the course of an argument is to equivocate. The result for the audience is ambiguity, confusion, or, if they fail to spot the equivocation, a mistaken belief that a claim has been prop-erly defended. Sound arguments depend upon words that mean the same at the end of an argument as they did at the beginning.

> The executioners and even the judges and juries who do the sentencing are all killers, are they not? That makes them no better than the wretched killers they destroy.

This argument equivocates about the term *killers* in order to make all kill-ers look like murderers. Obviously, one may take a life in our society, even a human life, and not be a murderer. All murderers are killers, certainly, but not all killers are murderers.

Faulty Analogy

An analogy, remember, compares two subjects, using the simple or famil-iar to explain the complex or unfamiliar. An argumentative analogy uses similarities between subjects to suggest that there are other similarities be-sides. Analogies are often effective in both informative and persuasive writing. They become suspect only when the two subjects are not truly comparable or when their similarities are trivial or irrelevant. In these cases the analogy is faulty; the argument, fallacious. Consider:

> We are members of the body politic, are we not? If a diseased or infected part of the human body—the appendix, for example—is incurable or threatens the rest of the body, we remove it and destroy it. The same should be true in the body politic, for the murderer, by his poisonous deed, threatens the life of the community as surely as the appendix does the body. Like a diseased organ, the murderer should be removed and destroyed.

The reasoning principle for this argument, that human bodies and politi-cal bodies are similar in ways significant to the argument, is false. Mur-derers, despite the character of their deeds, do not threaten the body pol-itic in quite the same way an infected appendix threatens the human body. Society can survive the murderer's presence, isolated by prison walls, in a way the human body cannot survive the continued presence of a diseased appendix.

Hasty Generalization

The fallacy of hasty generalization involves jumping to conclusions from evidence that is incomplete, irrelevant, or unrepresentative.

> We are reasonable men and women; we seek pleasure and avoid pain. Therefore, it is reasonable to assume that the death penalty will deter murderers.

What this argument fails to consider is that the capacity for reason does not mean that human beings will always behave reasonably; nor does the absolute quality of the second sentence recognize that although the death penalty may deter certain murderers—those who do reason out actions and consequences—it will not deter all. The argument has moved too hastily and carelessly from evidence to claim. It will not be sound until qualifiers and reservations are added to state when it applies and how probable its claims are.

Post Hoc Fallacy

The full name for this special form of hasty generalization is the *post hoc ergo propter hoc fallacy*. The Latin means "after this, therefore because of this," and the fallacy comes from assuming that because *A* precedes *B*, *A* must have caused *B*. But temporal sequence does not always signal a causal relationship; nor does every effect have only one cause.

> When Delaware abolished the death penalty, murder in that state decreased significantly. It is apparent, therefore, that judicial killing, far from being a deterrent to murder, is actually an incitement to it.

Perhaps there is a causal relationship here, and the death penalty *does* incite rather than deter murderers. We saw this possibility suggested earlier in our discussion of causal reasoning. But we can't be sure without sufficient evidence and appropriate reasoning principles. The decline in the murder rate in this instance may have been only coincidental, the actual causes lying elsewhere. Even if the abolition of the death penalty did play some part, it may have been only a contributory cause, a host of other causes also helping to pacify the citizens of Delaware. Only a carefully laid out argument will identify all causes and distinguish between contributory and sufficient ones.

Red Herring

A red herring is a diversionary tactic. Its name comes from the British trick of dragging smoked herring across the path of hunting hounds. The strong odor of the fish diverted the dogs from the pursuit of their quarry and saved the hare or fox for another day. In argument a red herring diverts an opponent from a weak or unsupportable claim by introducing irrelevant issues. This fallacy involves changing the subject or ducking the issues.

You opponents of the death penalty apparently don't want to see murderers punished, do you? By your opposition to the death penalty you show more regard for the criminals than for their victims.

These two red herrings divert the debate from capital punishment to punishment in general and to compassion for criminals. If opponents take the scent of this diversion, they will soon find themselves no longer arguing about the original subject, and the arguer will be free from the obligation to support his or her claim.

EXERCISES

Here are a number of fallacious arguments. Identify the fallacies in each (there may be more than one fallacy per argument), describe the errors of reasoning, and, if you can, tell what changes might make the arguments more plausible.

1. Obviously Addie cannot be lazy, or she wouldn't be the straight-A student she is. So Edgar must be lazy, because if he had any ambition at all, he'd get high grades, too.

2. Please don't give us a final exam, Professor Moe. We've studied so hard all semester long, we're tired now. And you're such a hard grader. Besides, examinations don't teach anything, and we're here to learn, aren't we? Examinations have no place in a true learning environment.

3. Sure Donny Doowell can propose that a minimum income be provided for all Americans, funded by tax dollars. What does he have to lose? He's a high-living, filthy-rich, overintellectual liberal who made millions selling "Peace-Now!" T-shirts. He's got a battery of high-priced tax lawyers, and I'll bet they guarantee he pays hardly a dime in taxes. So much for his stupid proposal.

4. What fallacy can be found in the cartoon below?

5. I don't know why they require students to take literature courses, anyway. So much literature is bad for growing minds. It's filled with sex, violence, fantasy, and outlandish adventures.

MISS PEACH

Miss Peach by Mell Lazarus. Courtesy of Mell Lazarus and News Group Chicago, Inc.

6. Human beings we call "Man." A woman is not a man. Therefore, a woman is not a human being.

7. I say abortion is wrong, an evil, bloody rite conducted in homage to the false gods of self-interest and self-gratification. Come with me and I will prove it to you. Come with me to the crowded waiting room of your local abortion mill. See the rows of unthinking young women staring vacantly at the floor or idly flipping through magazines selling beauty and sex. What do they care about the lives soon to be torn from them? Come with me into the operating room, scene of destruction of human life after human life by bloody-handed surgeons. Watch them coolly take these tiny lives, dismember these half-formed bodies with their steel instruments, and throw them out like yesterday's trash. To see such a place and its horrors is to know why this unspeakable practice must be stopped now.

8. I just have to get myself a pair of Thomas Tookas designer jeans. I saw the President of the United States wearing a pair! Yes, the President! And Paul Newman and Robert Redford, too, in those ads. And now I hear they're the world's largest selling jeans. Everybody's wearing them—and they only cost $79.95.

9. It's as plain as the nose on your face. Anyone riding the train to work is going to be late. Jane's late. Therefore, she must have ridden the train.

10. Alf is a Republican and never votes for any Democratic candidates. Therefore, it's easy to see he doesn't believe in democratic principles. That makes him unpatriotic, since patriots defend their country, and America is a democracy. Thus, Republicanism is unpatriotic and un-American.

11. You say you want to raise the drinking age to twenty-one in order to reduce traffic deaths, but look at yourselves. You're all over thirty. It's obvious you just want to oppress young people, keep them in their places, and prevent them from enjoying themselves.

12. The vast majority of men and women who are successful today wear suits. If you want to be a success, you'll wear a suit, too.

13. You want to know why the Tarrytown Turtles lost the full-contact badminton championship? I'll tell you why. Because they're losers, that's why. And losers never win.

14. Our college should not give grades, and graduation should be automatic. We have paid good money for our education, and as consumers we ought to get what we've paid for. You take a suit to the cleaners, put your money down, and it comes back clean. Go to the grocery store, put your money down, and get back fruits, vegetables, meat, and bread in return. Buy a ticket to a baseball game, and get entertained in return. The same should be true of a college education. You've paid good money; you ought to get your degree without delay—and no hassles about grades.

15. In the past two years I have given every student in my classes nothing but D's and F's. Now I see admission test scores have gone down again, for the tenth straight year. Obviously, students are getting dumber and dumber.

16. Look at yourself! Either you start exercising everyday and eating more fruits, grains, and vegetables, or you're going to be a physical wreck before you're twenty-five.

17. Sure, the Q-8000 Sportster's gasoline tank is in the trunk and its bumpers only withstand a one-mph collision. So? But, hey, don't you see how aerodynamic its styling is? The Q-8000 is a car designed to knife through the air, to turn heads. Imagine yourself darting down the freeway, cutting across lanes, in and out of traffic, that eight-speaker stereo just a-rockin' and a-rollin'. And look at those pin-stripes and that paint job. Now, if you'll just sign this contract right here.

❧ WRITING PERSUASIVELY

If we all were like Dr. Spock, the thoroughly rational Vulcan of *Star Trek* fame, the effective persuasion would end with a good argument. Being reasonable men and women, we would never ask for anything more from our opponents nor feel required to give them anything more than sufficient evidence and appropriate reasoning to defend a claim. Sound argument would be enough. But think of some of the arguments you've been in. You may have been silenced by the logic of your opponents, you may have recognized that there were no fallacies in their reasoning—yet still you were not convinced. Or remember those times you were persuaded to do or believe something you later realized was neither reasonable nor wise: childhood mischief, perhaps, a prejudiced opinion, or an impulsive purchase? You see the point. Even the most reasonable among us are not always reasonable. Sometimes we remain unconvinced by the best of arguments; other times we are easily won by the worst. Unlike effective argument, effective persuasion depends on more than reason.

Good persuasion is not only logically sound; it is also moving. It contains an argument at its core that looks reasonable, but—something more—it *feels* believable, like something an audience can accept without difficulty. More, it is an argument they *want* to accept. Over two thousand years ago the Greek philosopher Aristotle identified three kinds of "proof" present in almost every good persuasion. The first and most important is *logos*, the logical argument. But its success depends heavily upon *ethos*, the character of the person making the argument, and *pathos*, the feelings roused in the audience by the argument. The good persuasion, then, is a sound argument presented in a powerful way by a credible persona.

Ethos: The Persuader's Persona

We can have the soundest arguments in the world, but if we don't strike our audiences as credible, as someone readers can believe in and trust, our arguments won't have much chance. Consider former President Richard Nixon. He was a skillful arguer in many ways but never very successful persuading many of his opponents because he could never shake the persona of "Tricky Dick" acquired early in his political career. The character of the arguer, or at least the character as the audience perceives it, is the ultimate support for an argument. If we can't trust the arguer, we won't trust the argument. By the force of his personality he evokes in his audience the good will that prompts them to listen with attention and suspend the suspicion with which they naturally greet their opponents. Before the persuasive argument, therefore, must come the persuasive persona. What does an audience look for in a persuasive persuader?

- *The Good Argument:* A plausible, complete argument creates its own good will by revealing the care, diligence, and intelligence of the arguer. Audiences are more susceptible to writers who have spent some effort to reach them.
- *Knowledge:* Reveal the quality of your ideas by the texture of your argument, by using quotations, references, and allusions to reinforce your claims. Too much "learning" and you may become intimidating or seem to be showing off, but an appropriate demonstration will help convince your readers that you do, indeed, know what you're talking about.
- *Fairness:* Show your fairness. Give an accurate statement of your opponent's position. Doing so will demonstrate that you have listened to the other side. It is easier to listen to someone who has herself listened well.
- *Reasonability:* If there is a possibility for compromise, you ought to recognize it and state your flexibility. The aim of persuasion, after all, is not the demolition of your opponents but their cooperation. You may have to give to get.
- *The common bond:* If you can, speak the language your audience speaks, and demonstrate your interest in what they're interested in. They will listen more comfortably to someone who sounds like them and shares their outlook and values. But remember, too, that almost anyone can spot a phony, unless that phony is very, very slick.
- *The common good:* Most important, make it clear whenever possible that you argue not for your benefit but the common good. We are necessarily self-interested creatures, but the more we recognize ourselves united with our opponents by concerns larger than self-interest, the easier it is to create that community of good will essential to our audience's assent.

The most important place to present this persona and create its good will is early in a persuasion, often in the introduction. Readers listen to the arguer before they hear his or her argument. Listen to the way a supporter of the death penalty introduces himself and his argument:

A man like his audi-
ence, unconcerned

Until recently, my business did not require me to think about the punishment of criminals in general or the legitimacy and efficacy of capital pun-

with punishment (a community created)

His opponents' position stated in words his audience would be comfortable with

A reference that shows the writer's learning

The writer connects his position with a cause most readers would support

Thesis

ishment in particular. In a vague way, I was aware of the disagreement among professionals concerning the purpose of punishment—whether it was intended to deter others, to rehabilitate the criminal, or to pay him back— but like most laymen I had no particular reason to decide which purpose was right or to what extent they may all have been right. I did know that retribution was held in ill repute among criminologists and jurists—to them, retribution was a fancy name for revenge, and revenge was barbaric—and, of course, I knew that capital punishment had the support only of policemen, prison guards, and some local politicians, the sort of people Arthur Koestler calls "hang-hards" (Philadelphia's Mayor Rizzo comes to mind). The intellectual community denounced it as both unnecessary and immoral. It was the phenomenon of Simon Wiesenthal [the hunter of Nazi war criminals] that allowed me to understand why the intellectuals were wrong and why the police, the politicians, and the majority of the voters were right: we punish criminals in order to pay them back, and we execute the worst of them out of necessity. Anyone who respects Wiesenthal's mission will be driven to the same conclusion.

(Walter Berns, "For Capital Punishment," *Harper's* Apr. 1979)

Here for comparison is the thesis paragraph from an abolitionist's essay against capital punishment. See how this author establishes his credentials for arguing his case and demonstrates his interest in the welfare of others?

Although as governor of Ohio I reluctantly allowed six men to die in the electric chair in accordance with my oath of office, I am totally opposed to the death penalty. I am thoroughly convinced that capital punishment is a relic of barbarism, that it is immoral, that it usurps for society the exclusive privilege of natural laws, that it is futile because it does not deter the homicidal criminal, and its finality precludes any possibility of correcting an error.

(Michael V. DiSalle, "Capital Punishment: The Barbaric Anachronism," *Playboy* May 1966)

He impresses us that, in the past, he put his oath of office before his opinion, and that makes us feel, given what his office required him to do, that here is a person who weighs his beliefs and responsibilities very carefully. We are more likely to listen willingly and attentively to someone this dedicated to the public good. No mere self-interest here. Later in his essay he offers personal experience that both argues his claim indirectly and impresses upon us his compassion, magnanimity, even his courage—just the sort of qualities we look for in a trustworthy persona.

I lived with these [paroled] murderers for the four years of my term as governor. They were assigned to staff the Executive Mansion—gardeners, chauffeurs, laundrymen, housemen, cooks and yardmen. My wife and I lived with these men, killers all, not as keepers and prisoners, but as human beings with whom we shared their many problems as errant members of society who had paid their penalty with 20 years of their lives. We trusted them completely. My wife had no fear of going into the kitchen and arguing over a recipe with a cook who was sharpening carving knives at the same time, even though the cook was serving time for murder. She felt quite at ease being driven by a felon, or dressing down an ex-lifer houseman who left dust in the corners. The greatest display of trust, I suppose, was our leaving these homicidal staffers as baby sitters for our grandchildren when they came to Columbus for the Christmas holidays. The only risk we ever ran was that the felonious baby sitters would spoil our small fry—feed them forbidden ice cream or otherwise surreptitiously overindulge them.

As we read this argument, the ethos created by its author urges us to conclude to ourselves, if this Ohio governor, with all his knowledge and experience, can believe as he does, perhaps we can too. And that is what the effective persuasive persona should do.

Pathos

Logos and ethos are "external proofs." They lie outside the audience, within an argument or the character of the arguer. They remove objections that the audience might have, lower defenses, and show the way to the acceptance of a claim. But full acceptance of that claim almost always depends upon something *within* the audience. And that is *pathos*: the emotion, desire, and will roused by a persuasion. There is no conflict here between reason and emotion. In the effective persuasion, as in the healthy personality, the two work together, harmoniously, to make change possible and then bring it about. The well-constructed persuasion always urges us to make a value judgment about the belief or action proposed by its argument. Its argument says to readers, "This is the logical thing to do or believe." But its language and details say, "You want to do or believe this because it is the useful, pleasing, or good thing to do." Effective persuasion makes us *desire* the belief or action that reason has led us to agree to. How? By the use of anecdotes, description, figures of speech, connotative language, satire, sometimes even sarcasm.

See how this anecdote that opens Governor DiSalle's attack on the death penalty creates an aversion to executions and prepares us to desire the abolition he will propose in his thesis? We are in the mood to agree to his argument even before we hear it.

Ironic language

The opposing position made to look cruel

Pity evoked

The Lord Chief Justice wondered if the death penalty might not be a trifle severe in view of the prisoner's age. The trial judge argued against mercy on the ground that William York's punishment would be an example deterring others from a life of crime. So William York was hanged for stealing a shilling from the man to whom he was apprenticed. He was ten years old. The place was London. The time was 1748.

The second most valuable place for an emotional appeal is the end of a persuasion, after an argument is finished. The aim here is not unlike putting a turbo-charger on an automobile, to take the power that is already in the engine and give it greater force. Coming at the end, after an argument has created intellectual assent to a claim, an emotional appeal can charge a reader to action. Earlier you read Walter Berns's introduction to his argument that righteous anger—expressed by the death penalty—is the proper response to those whose murderous crimes threaten human and communal life. Now consider his conclusion and how it links support for the death penalty with good citizenship and the associated emotions of pride, patriotism, and fellow feeling. Notice, too, how the skillfully used honorific and pejorative words pique those emotions and prod us to assent.

> To exclude anger from the human community is to concentrate all the passions in a "self-interest of the meanest sort," and such a place would not be fit for human habitation.
>
> When, in 1976, the Supreme Court declared death to be a constitutional penalty, it decided that the United States was not that sort of country; most of us, I think, can appreciate that judgment. We want to live among people who do not value their possessions more than their citizenship, who do not think exclusively or even primarily of their rights, people whom we can depend on even as they exercise their rights, and whom we can trust, which is to say, people who, even in the absence of a policeman, will not assault our bodies or steal our possessions, and might even come to our assistance when we need it, and who stand ready when the occasion demands it, to risk their lives in defense of their country. If we are of the opinion that the United States may rightly ask of its citizens this awful sacrifice, then we are also of the opinion that it may rightly impose the most awful penalty; if it may rightly honor its heroes, it may rightly execute the worst of its criminals. By doing so, it will remind its citizens that it is a country worthy of heroes.

This conclusion reinforces its claim by reminding us of our national and personal ideals—concern for others, dependability, trust, honor, courage, sacrifice, and justice—pressing us to recognize that who we are and what we want to be depend upon our willingness to do what the claim requires. To desire the virtues of good citizenship, Berns concludes, entails that we also accept the necessity of capital punishment for those who by their murderous crimes repudiate that citizenship.

Planning a Communications Strategy

Identifying an Audience and Defining a Purpose   Everything you've read so far about argument and persuasion has been a prologue to the actual writing of a persuasive essay. Now, at last, you're ready to begin. Preparing to write persuasively means designing a sound argument that will be (1) plausible and (2) moving for a particular audience. Begin there, with your potential readers and a freewriting description of who they are and what you want from them. Most of what you say in your persuasion and the way you say it will be determined by your discoveries now. Persuasions never exist in a vacuum; we're trying to persuade certain people of certain things.

- Who is your audience? What is their age, sex, politics, and class? Where do they come from? Young liberal women from New York City will respond to different appeals than retired male farmers from Nebraska. You may want both groups to accept the same claim, but you won't argue with both groups in the same way.
- What is their position on your claim? Are they potential allies who need only some rousing encouragement before they will give their assent? Are they disinterested observers, the position most of your instructors will take to your arguments? Are they on the fence, divided in their opinions? Or are they on the other side of that fence, clearly your opponents? Their attitude toward your claim will have much to do with the way you phrase it.

Gauging the Opposition   Once you understand your audience, turn to their argument or that of your actual opponents.[8] *Before* you prepare your own argument, sketch theirs. What are their claims? Are these claims qualified in any way? What evidence proves their claims? What reasoning authorizes that proof? Do they depend upon sources for their evidence or reasoning? Are there any situations in which your opponents' claims might actually be true, probable, or appropriate, where you would have to yield to them? In what situations would they be clearly false, improbable, or inappropriate?

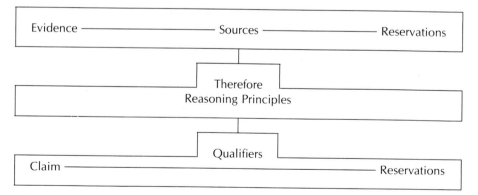

Drawing out your opponent's argument in this way will make it easier to spot any weaknesses and help you know where to direct your argument and rebuttal and how to organize them for greatest impact.

Such a careful description of your opponents' position will also help you identify their priorities, often the real issues of contention. In many arguments, the sides disagree not because they disagree about evidence or reasoning but because their priorities are different. These priorities are given many names, but more often than not they all come down to the same three standards we considered earlier under value judgment arguments: standards of utility, morality, and aesthetics. Different people order these standards in differing ways, and that explains their different opinions. Those who approach a subject with standards of utility uppermost in their minds will necessarily see that subject in a way different from those with moral or aesthetic values uppermost. One subject, three different sets of priorities, and, as a result, three different positions. Take the debate about capital punishment. As our student John studied the arguments for both sides while preparing to write his Criminal Justice paper, he was struck again and again by how much the often bitterly divided abolitionists and retentionists had in common: both oppose dehumanization and brutality, both insist upon justice, both are concerned for the economics of punishment, both are concerned with the welfare of the community, both seek effective measures, both often argue on religious grounds.

What seems to divide them is the scale of their values. They arrange their common evidence in different ways according to different priorities and reach different conclusions. Those *opposed* to the death penalty are more practical and utilitarian in their concerns; the evidence they return to most frequently and emphasize most heavily concerns the cost and effectiveness of punishment. Those *in favor* of the death penalty are more concerned with justice and morality; their arguments pose most frequently the questions of what is "fair" and what is "right." Any argument with one side or another would have to begin by recognizing this difference in priorities. In fact, argument would probably consist of reasoning about what should take precedence, utility or morality, whether effective criminology is more important than absolute justice. The conflict here is not between a right standard and a wrong one but between two right ones, the useful vs. the good.

Alternatives to Persuasion   Often in this search for priorities an arguer will find so much common ground between herself and her opponents that compromise is not only possible but perhaps the easiest way to resolve the differences between them.[9] Argument then consists not so much in trying to win the other side over as in extending the common ground until there is room on it for both parties to stand and support their separate claims. At this point, persuasion turns into negotiation, showing how both sides can win. It proceeds by the following steps:

1. Defining the issues in a way both sides can accept.
2. Making a fair statement of both sides' positions, first the opponents' and then the arguer's.

3. Describing common grounds, goals, and values.
4. Enumerating possible compromises that recognize the interests of both sides.

Or another arguer may discover as he draws out his opponent's arguments that, common ground notwithstanding, the two sides are so divided by their values and priorities that compromise and even rational argument are impossible. Such is often the case in the debate over capital punishment. One claim elicits a counterclaim, which in turn prompts another claim by the first party, and so on, back and forth, the two sides no longer listening to each other but shouting, now arguing in the popular rather than logical sense of the word. Persuasion is impossible. Even to try would be an incitement to hostility. All that a wise writer can do is try to reach an understanding with his opponents about the issues that divide them. John may argue his death penalty case fully in a Criminal Justice class, but if he disagrees with family or friends and recognizes that deep feelings are at stake, he may take this less contentious approach. This agreement to disagree proceeds in a two-step process. The writer first lays out the other side of the argument as carefully, fairly, and nonjudgmentally as possible; then he lays out his side, but in the same manner as he presented his opponents' position, as nonjudgmentally and *nonthreateningly* as possible. The aim is neither persuasion nor accommodation but simple understanding. A change of mind or negotiations will have to wait for another day, when the seeds of understanding have taken root and grown in both the arguer and his opponents.

Designing the Persuasion Once you're sure of who your audience is and what your opponents' position is, then you can plan the contents of your persuasion. What arguments will be most persuasive? Not all the arguments you might make to defend your claim will have an equal appeal. You won't present *all* your arguments, only those that will appeal most forcefully to your audience and speak to their priorities.

- If they are interested in the moral issues surrounding your subject, then you may want to argue that accepting your claim will promote justice, fairness, honor, virtue, integrity, loyalty, or patriotic values.
- If utility heads their list of priorities, then your argument will be strongest if it emphasizes the ease, health benefits, practicality, simplicity, effectiveness, or efficiency associated with acceptance of your claim.
- If their concerns are primarily aesthetic, your arguments should probably emphasize the emotions of pleasure or displeasure associated with your subject.

Obviously, not every subject can be tailored to fit an audience's priorities this neatly; still, if you can construct your argument to appeal their priorities wherever possible, you'll have a far easier time finding the supporting details and language that will be most persuasive.

Once you're sure of the argument you want to make, begin planning the overall design of your persuasion. What opening will establish your credibility and create an atmosphere of good will? What conclusion will be strongest in its motivating power? Try to arrange your persuasion so that it rises to a climax, both argumentative and emotional. Save your best till last. The body of your persuasion will probably be a logical defense of your claim, following the conventional design appropriate to the argument you're making: categorical, cause/effect, value judgment, or propositional. You studied these designs earlier. If your thesis consists of multiple claims, however, you may opt for another design to embrace them all. The simplest is the spare pro/con design:

I. An introduction stating the problem or the issues.
II. The argument pro: in favor of a claim.
III. The argument con: against the claim.
IV. A thesis/conclusion that chooses between the pro and con positions.
V. A defense of the conclusion as the best choice.

The classical argumentative design, descended to us from the ancient Greek and Roman deliberations, will help you be sure that your argument has included all the necessary elements:

I. Exordium: the introduction setting the mood and establishing a persona.
II. Division of proofs: a summary of the problem and a statement, at least partial, of the claim (the thesis or conclusion).
III. Narration: the facts of the case (the evidence).
IV. Confirmation: the argument of the claim.
V. Refutation: answering the opponents.
VI. Peroration: the conclusion, making new appeals, reinforcing the original appeals, or summarizing the claim.

Similar in form to the proposition argument is the argumentative version of the problem/solution design presented in Chapter 6:

I. An introduction describing the problem.
II. The causes of the problem.
III. The consequences if the problem is unsolved.
IV. The solution put forward as the best solution possible.
V. A conclusion describing how the solution might be enacted.

The rebuttal design makes no new proposals but does reveal weaknesses in opposing arguments. Such a pattern is appropriate when solutions do not exist or present ones are not feasible.

I. A review of opposing arguments.
II. A claim stating their weaknesses.
III. A point-by-point rebuttal.
IV. A restatement of the problem or what is needed to solve the problem in light of the rebuttal.

Or you may choose *not* to present your argument logically. For some audiences and issues, a vivid narrative or extended analogy may have more force than a line of reasoning. Such a pattern is not necessarily illogical or fallacious for abandoning a logical design. Here the argument is absorbed into the form and made subordinate to the language and imagery. It becomes what the British Renaissance poet Sir Philip Sidney called "a speaking picture." The audience is convinced by reasons contained in the dramatization, moved rather than led to new belief or action.

Writing,
Revising,
and Editing

The soundness and plausibility of an argument depend as much on coherence as anything else. What is an argument, really, but a series of connections between data and statements? The coherence devices described in Chapter 8, especially thematic tags and transitions, make those connections. Just as they do in every other kind of writing but of special importance to argument, they lead readers along and enable them to say, "I get it; I can follow what you're saying." After writing a preliminary draft and determining that the design of your persuasion is sound, examine its flow. Outline your draft, if necessary. Check to see that your tags and transitions reveal the logical relationships. What is the equivocation fallacy but a surreptitious or unintended substitution of one thematic tag for another? What is the post hoc fallacy if not putting the wrong transition between statements and so making an unwarranted connection? Remember, too: What seems clear, logical, and self-evident to you will surely not seem so to your opponents nor, perhaps, to your undecided readers. Help them understand.

Extend the same attention to your language. The two dangers confronting every arguer are vagueness and ambiguity. How can an audience respond as you want them to if your argument doesn't say what you mean or offers unintended options? What, for example, does it mean to claim that elimination of the death penalty "will weaken justice"? How are we to understand the metaphor in that verb? Will abolition make our society less just, less capable of rendering justice, both, neither? The metaphor is vague; it needs a sentence of explanation. Or what does it mean to claim, as some do, that society has the right to execute its "uncontrollable members for the protection of others"? Do we destroy those who can't control *themselves*, those whom *we* can't control, both, neither? This claim is both vague and ambiguous. As such, it gives its audience no certain direction. The good persuasion tells its readers precisely what it wants from them, gives all the necessary grounds for their response, and moves them to action.

Here is a brief persuasive essay. Whether or not its claims are compelling as you read is less important—in this context, at least—than your understanding of its elements, methods, and design.

Introduction appealing to the reader's horror and indignation (pathos)	(1) Events are conspiring lately to give the death penalty a bad name. First the revival of the electric chair in Alabama was fouled up by technical difficulties; it took three pulls of the switch to execute the first death warrant there in 20 years. Then racial overtones incited an international controversy over the hanging of three black nationalists convicted of bombings in South Africa.
	(2) Meanwhile, the Khomeini regime in Iran defended the religious purity of its revolution by executing 17 members of the Bahai faith.
The response the author would like from his readers	(3) It is almost enough to make one reassess his support for local experiments with lethal injection.
A summary of one opposing argument using the language of the writer's opponents (ethos)	(4) Or is it? Capital punishment, like any other legitimate instrument of state power, can be misused. But what does that prove? We have learned much from the state's abuse of the mental health process in the Soviet Union, but only a fool would counsel that we must close our mental hospitals because they abuse theirs. Isn't an assault on the death penalty similarly misdirected? The answer is no.
Reasoning principle	(5) Sometimes you can judge the morality of a practice by the company it keeps; executions hang out in the world's seediest neighborhoods. The liberal democracies that we normally use as points of reference will not execute, even under substantial pressure. Contrasting those nations still engaged in capital punishment with those that abstain is a course in moral geography that we cannot ignore.
Evidence	
Claim	
Source of the evidence	(6) A recent survey of capital punishment by Amnesty International provides an excellent starting point. South Africa, for example, is ranked as one of the world leaders in executions, averaging well over 50 a year in the period studied. Of the 132 persons the government reported executed during 1978, one was white.
Evidence	
A possible objection to the evidence	(7) South African leadership in executions may just be a product of punctilious reporting. Many nations, including the Soviet Union (and, until very recently, China) have been understandably reluctant to acknowledge widespread executions. Many other countries would have difficulty sorting out informal government killing from officially sanctioned execution: Argentina, Cambodia under Pol Pot and Idi Amin's Uganda must be excused from such a detailed census.

Rebuttal

(8) Still, the officially reported patterns do speak forcefully to the contrast between countries that execute and those that refrain. Western nations show wide variation in laws on capital punishment but nearly all avoid exacting the ultimate penalty.

Evidence

(9) Only three of 15 nations in Western Europe reported any executions during the 1970s: France, Greece and Turkey. In Great Britain, a proposal to bring back execution was decisively defeated this summer.

Evidence

(10) But South Africa is hardly isolated in its executions. Many of its African neighbors execute with some regularity, as do nations across the Third World. The large group of developing nations that reject execution is still a minority.

Evidence

(11) And while the trend in most countries is away from execution as a tool of government, there are exceptions. Authoritarian military coups provide opportunities for new death penalties in many nations. Dictatorships of the left and right, in countries as disparate as Haiti and Cuba, find common ground on capital punishment. And the executioner is reputed to ply his trade, quietly, through much of the Eastern bloc.

An *a fortiori* ("all the stronger") argument: If these countries can foreswear executions, how much more should the United States be able to do the same

(12) Two non-executing nations merit special attention because of the provocation they have endured without resort to capital punishment. Israel exists in fear of external force and domestic terror, and its government can hardly be called soft-hearted; yet not since the death of Adolf Eichmann has the prospect of an execution become real.

(13) West Germany, of course, has a special legacy in the department of government violence. Small wonder its citizens suffered through a decade of kidnapping and assassination without being exhorted to fight fire with fire.

Answering possible objections

(14) But what if Western Europe is wrong and our proponents of execution are right? The unanimity of Europe's pacifism toward Hitler was no substitute for correct policy. Might this be another mass mistake?

A conclusion that restates the case

(15) The case for capital punishment might survive the hostility of its enemies but never the enthusiasm of its friends. It is possible that the West Germans and Scandinavians are missing out on a policy to enhance the social value of human life. But is it possible that Idi Amin embraced it as such? Are there other areas of ethical propriety in which it is suggested we take instruction from South Korea and Uganda?

Rhetorical questions

(16) The correlation between capital punishment and human-rights violations is so strong that the list of countries with active executioners matches Amnesty International's other scorecards concerning torture and political repression. Can this be a coincidence? Or have we stumbled on a shorthand method of taking a society's moral temperature?

Claim posed as a rhetorical question

Emotional appeal made through word choice

(17) Much of the rhetoric in favor of American execution seems arid and provincial, a species of neobarbarian chic. The pattern resembles an iron law of political economy: Capital punishment thrives only where life is cheap.

(Franklin Zimring, "Capital punishment's getting bad name lately—and it should," *Chicago Sun-Times* 29 Sept. 1983)

The Elements of the Argument

Because authoritarian, racist, despotic ————————According to Amnesty
   governments all practice capital pun-   International Reports, [S]
   ishment, [E]

Because undeveloped nations do the
   same, [E]

Because Western nations, in general, do
   not execute, even those who might be
   presumed to have good reasons for
   doing so, [E]

Therefore

According to the principle that one can sometimes judge the morality of a practice by the company it keeps (guilt by association), [RP]

The death penalty is immoral, ——————Except for war criminals like
   [C]   Adolf Eichmann, [R]

The Design of the Persuasion: A Reworking of the Classical Form

I. Introduction setting the mood, dramatizing the problem, and sug-
   gesting the claim to be made.
   A. The problem (1–2).
   B. The response that the reasonable person would make (3).
   C. Qualifications that the opposition might make (4).

II. The argument.
   A. Reasoning principle and claim (5).
   B. Executions in South Africa, an immoral, racist government (6–
      7).
   C. Practices in Western nations (8–9).
   D. Practices in the Third World (10–11).
   E. Practices of two nations who might be presumed to use capital
      punishment but who do not (12–13).

III. Conclusion: Restatement of the case in light of the evidence.
   A. Consideration of possible error by those nations who do not
      practice capital punishment (14).
   B. An assertion that those authoritarian governments who prac-
      tice capital punishment can be viewed only as the preceding
      argument has viewed them (15).
   C. Restatement of the claim (16–17).

EXERCISES

1. Here are two more brief persuasive essays. Identify the claims, the kinds of argument used in each, and the elements each writer uses to construct his argument. Outline the essays. If the writer uses more than one argument, each argument may be outlined under one major topic heading (I, II, III, and so on). Identify where the writer's persona is clearest and what he does to appear trustworthy. Where does the writer appeal to the audience's emotions? Which emotions? What emotional strategies or language can you find? Finally, just how persuasive are these essays? Can you spot any weaknesses in either writer's argument, persona, or uses of language?

Behind the Cockpit Door

(1) Are you as white knuckled as I am when traveling as an airline passenger? What's it worth to save a buck? It's become fashionable to question the cost of an airline ticket, especially if it's more than $49. No one questions the ticket price at a rock concert or ball game. So I say the price to step on board a $70 million airplane to be flown through the night and brought safely to dock even in the worst weather should carry a certain premium.

(2) The big complaint nowadays is that labor costs are too high. Seems the airlines would really like to lower the fare to $29, but they can't afford to do that. The story going around is that greedy airline workers extracted bloated contracts and the airlines had to pass this through to the public by raising fares. If you believe that's all there is to it, then maybe you'll also believe the airlines would like to do a complete 180 and make all the tickets free.

(3) Pilots are reasonable people. And reasonable people don't work hard, study and apprentice for years to fly just for fun. My training involved more input in terms of time and money than that of a brain surgeon. I'm not paid for sitting up there when things are routine, but for the other times. I've earned my year's salary—no, more—in just two minutes on more than one occasion, and I'm sure the passengers strapped to the iron beast behind my cockpit door would have gladly voted me that amount when we all reached solid ground together.

(4) During the last 10 years the dollar cost of having me in the cockpit about doubled (but, like yours, so did my cost of living); over the same period fuel cost went up five times (from less than 20 cents a gallon to around a dollar, where it hovers . . . temporarily). Do the beleaguered airline bosses put the heat on the oil companies? No. Suddenly the buzzword is labor cost—it's me who's out of line. It doesn't matter that today I generate more revenue. Ten years ago, in a 707 I hauled 185 passengers at 550 mph. Today, my 747 carries 385 passengers at 600 mph. If my airline still flew 707s, they'd have to employ more than twice as many of me to do the same job. So already they're ahead.

(5) But whether it's a long haul or air shuttle, one huge myth needs to be abolished: pilots don't all make $100,000 per year. A few very senior captains may be in that league, but most are not, and more than half the pilot rosters consist of copilots and second officers at far lower levels. We have all watched the strengthening economy reward others while we gave back huge chunks of earnings. [In 1983 the pilots of some airlines agreed to reductions in wages and benefits to help those airlines avoid predicted bankruptcies.] For me it's already

been an aggregate 35 percent. Yet I'm told it's not enough. It now seems the guns are all pointed just one way. It doesn't make any difference what any worker may be worth if his employer can go to bankruptcy court on the conjecture he may be broke some time in the future and then use that argument to shred supposedly good-faith contracts and dictate streetsweeper wages for all, take it or leave it.

(6) I'm fed up with being the culprit. Labor represents 34 percent of my "established" airline's total cost. Not bad. Maintaining and flying airplanes properly is labor intensive. The figure was not much different years ago when the airlines were coining money. "Low cost" airlines have seen their labor costs reach as much as 27 percent. So the spread is not that devastating: only the approach taken. The airline bosses go up to Capitol Hill and extol the virtues of today's deregulated blood bath but come back to the troops in the line and cry poor. You need a wide-angle lens to see them talking out of both sides of their mouths. They beg the employees for relief—and worse—but where is the first with enough guts to ask that stability, structure, and sanity be reimposed on our industry?

(7) Travelers are being ambushed, too. Fares to cross one state line on many routes far exceed those to the coast. Absurd but true. Not all the extravagant promises of lower fares are being kept. For the industry's problems are much greater than my salary. Our current fleet is getting old. There are new planes out there that get better gas mileage, but they have price tags starting above $50 million and going up to nearly $100 million. Unlike the worn-out, hand-me-down rolling stock most start-up airlines depend on and even some established airlines are using, these new planes, if widely flown, might actually net a profit—even at discount fares. But how do we get from here to there?

(8) The airlines collectively must disburse more than $10 billion in debt payments over the next five years before they spend the first dime for new airplanes or improve safety. At $49 a ticket with Mom and the kids free, there's no way to generate the billions they need to regain their health and remain viable. Already Boeing must go to Japan and Singapore for orders; not too many U.S. airlines have ordered 757s or 767s in recent years. Will the turmoil in our airlines gut the airplane industry as well?

(9) There's no free lunch. If you want to ride on the cheap, then expect cheapness. Trouble is, flying is a game that's very unforgiving. Passengers would be appalled if they knew what the new economic reality has made standard practice: minimum fuel, minimum rest, minimum equipment list, minimum engines. The risks are increasing. Several emergency landings in recent months attest to it. Few people know of the effective ground work pilots have done to keep our industry honest. In working with these men I've come to realize that we have not just a union but a true professional association. If what is going on now succeeds in breaking that, and we lose that all-critical dialogue on air safety, it will be tragic not only for me but for you, the flying public. Such cost cannot be measured in dollars.

(10) It takes profit to buy new planes and to provide the safety, well-being and stability the industry needs. To heap the current crisis entirely on labor's shoulders is eminently unfair and ultimately unrealistic. The cost for competent labor is just as much a reality as other costs. I'm sure the white-knuckled

passenger who buys extra insurance when he flies would rather have his plane and crew meet the highest standards. That's the best policy. And you'll never get it for $29 or $49 round trip.

(Thomas G. Foxworth, "Behind the Cockpit Door," *Newsweek* 31 Oct. 1983)

Limiting Handguns

(1) We buried Donald Brown in May. He was murdered by three men who wanted to rob the supermarket manager he was protecting. Patrolman Brown was 61 years old, six months from retirement. He and his wife intended to retire to Florida at the end of the year. Now there will be no retirement in the sun, and she is alone.

(2) Donald Brown was the second police officer to die since I became [police] commissioner here [in Boston] on Nov. 15, 1972.

(3) The first was John Schroeder, a detective shot in a pawnshop robbery last November. John Schroeder was the brother of Walter Schroeder, who was killed in a bank robbery in 1970. Their names are together on the honor roll in the lobby of Police Headquarters.

(4) John Murphy didn't die. He was shot in the head last February as he chased a robbery suspect into the Washington Street subway station. He lived, but he will be brain-damaged for the rest of his life, unable to walk or talk.

(5) At least two of these police officers were shot by a handgun, the kind one can buy nearly everywhere for a few dollars. Those who don't want to buy one can steal one, and half a million are stolen each year. There are forty million handguns circulating in this country; two and [a] half million are sold each year.

(6) Anybody can get a gun. Ownership of handguns has become so widespread that the gun is no longer merely the instrument of crime; it is now a cause of violent crime. Of the eleven Boston police officers killed since 1962, seven were killed with handguns; of the seventeen wounded by guns since 1962, sixteen were shot with handguns.

(7) Police officers, of course, are not the only people who die. Ten thousand other Americans are dead as the price of our promiscuous right to bear arms. Gun advocates are fond of saying that guns don't kill, people do. But guns do kill.

(8) Half of the people who commit suicide do so with handguns. Fifty-four percent of the murders committed in 1972 were committed with handguns. Killing with handguns simply is a good deal easier than killing with other weapons.

(9) Rifles and shotguns are difficult to conceal. People can run away from knife-wielding assailants. People do die each year by drownings, bludgeonings and strangulation. But assaults with handguns are five times more likely to kill. No one can convince me, after returning from Patrolman Brown's funeral, after standing in the rain with hundreds of others from this department and others, that we should allow people to own handguns.

(10) I know that many people feel deeply and honestly about their right to

own and enjoy guns. I realize that gun ownership and self-protection are deeply held American values. I am asking that people give them up.

(11) I am committed to doing what I can to take guns away from the people. In my view, private ownership of handguns must be banished from this country. I am not asking for registration or licensing or outlawing cheap guns. I am saying that no private citizen, whatever his claim, should possess a handgun. Only police officers should.

(Robert di Grazia, "Limiting Handguns," *The New York Times* 26 Sept. 1974)

2. Devise a communications strategy for a persuasive essay. Choose one of the topics you developed for the argument exercises earlier in this chapter, or come up with a topic of your own. Your communications strategy should include the following:

a. A statement of your claim (your thesis) and purpose (the kind of arguments you will use to defend your claim).

b. A one-paragraph sketch of your audience, including a list of their priorities and your analysis of what appeals might be most persuasive.

c. A description of the persona you will use to gain your audience's trust.

d. A list of elements of your opponents' arguments, including a description of the strengths and weaknesses of their position and a statement of whether any compromise is possible.

e. A list of the elements of your argument.

f. An outline of the essay you might write.

END NOTES

1. For the six elements of argument, I have adapted Stephen Toulmin's *The Uses of Argument* (London: Cambridge UP, 1958) and Stephen Toulmin, Richard Rieke, and Allan Janik's *An Introduction to Reasoning,* 2nd ed. (New York: Macmillan, 1984).

2. For the three kinds of reasoning principles I'm grateful to James C. McCroskey, *An Introduction to Rhetorical Communication* (Englewood Cliffs, NJ: Prentice, 1968) 83.

3. For the term "reservations" I'm grateful to McCroskey, p. 80.

4. For my description of the four kinds of argument I am indebted to Manuel Bilsky, et al., "Looking for an Argument," *College English* 14 (Jan. 1953): 210–16; rpt. in *Teaching Freshman Composition,* ed. Gary Tate and Edward P.J. Corbett (New York: Oxford UP, 1967). I am also indebted to Jeanne Fahnestock and Marie Secor, "Teaching Argument: A Theory of Types," *College Composition and Communication* 34 (Feb. 1983): 20–30.

5. This analogy was quoted in "Statements in Favor of the Death Penalty," *F.B.I. Law Enforcement Bulletin* 29 (June 1960); rpt. in *The Death Penalty in America,* ed. Hugo Adam Bedau (Chicago: Aldine, 1967).

6. I'm indebted for this image and its explanation to Jeanne Fahnestock and Marie Secor, "Teaching Argument: A Theory of Types," *College English* 34 (Feb. 1983): 28.

7. For my introduction to logical fallacies I have borrowed from Toulmin, Rieke, and Janik's *An Introduction to Reasoning,* 2nd ed. (New York: Macmillan, 1984).

8. For these suggestions abour reconstructing an opponent's argument I am grateful to David S. Kaufer and Christine M. Neuwirth, "Integrating Formal Logic and the New Rhetoric: A Four-Stage Heuristic," *College English* 45 (Apr. 1983): 380–90.

9. These alternatives have much in common with Rogerian Argument. For a thorough discussion, see Maxine Hairston, *A Contemporary Rhetoric,* 3d ed. (Boston: Houghton, 1982) 340–46.

Chapter 15

The Literary Essay

The literary essay is the record of a reader's encounter with a work of literature: a novel, story, play, poem, essay, or film. It is the final "oooh," "aaah," or "oh . . ." in the process of artistic appreciation, the most insightful "Now I've got it," the most complete "Let me explain it to you." It transforms the reader from passive spectator of an imaginative world to active participant, helping him discover in depth and detail the impression that world has made on his thinking and feeling. The literary essay is also a test of that understanding. By making his thoughts visible and giving them an order and permanence they wouldn't otherwise have, it helps the reader *see* whether those thoughts add up to anything and make sense of his experience. Finally, the literary essay is one of the fullest ways of sharing that experience. Reading these days is one of our most private acts. When was the last time, besides your childhood, that someone read aloud to you or you read to someone else? Almost never, of course, do two people read the same work together, but silently, to themselves. Even in the movies, we may sit with friends in a theater filled with hundreds of others, but there in the dark, we're all basically alone with our thoughts. The literary essay, however, unites silent, solitary readers and viewers into a genuine audience. It turns up the lights and gets people talking to one another, one reader or viewer adding by the expression of his understanding and pleasure to the understanding and pleasure of others.

READING LITERATURE

The good literary essay begins with good reading, and good reading is almost always a dual process, two things happening at once. To read literature, it is not enough to read the way we would a newspaper or textbook, for the facts alone. The facts—the details—of literature provide us with

369

Feiffer

WHY DOESN'T ANYTHING EVER GET SETTLED?

WHY DO THINGS GO ON AND ON AND NEVER WIND UP?

SONGS END BOOKS END PLAYS END MOVIES END. CARTOONS HAVE PUNCH LINES

BUT IN LIFE THERE'S NO BEGIN- NING AND NO END NO LOGIC NO RULES NO CONSISTENCY

JUST LOTS OF UPS AND DOWNS.

AND MIDD

© 1978 JULES FEIFFER

the immediate pleasures of characterization, event, surprise, sound, and rhythm. But the interpretations we make of them provide the deeper pleasures of understanding. Therefore, *Reading rule 1:* When you read literature, you must focus on two things at once, its facts and what they are adding up to. And you must hold this double focus without the picture getting blurry. That takes some getting used to. You know the old cliché about perception: "He couldn't see the forest for the trees." When you read literature, you must look closely at each tree in the forest, yet see the whole forest at the same time.

And there are other contraries in the reading process. Half the pleasure of literature is confusing it with real life, forgetting for the moment that we are seeing nothing more than words on a page or images on the screen, imagining instead that we are standing there in a yellow wood, peering down two diverging paths, smelling the leaves, wondering where the poet will take us. And we *should* escape into the artist's world in this way—as long as we keep one eye peeled on the artistry that has lured us into the world. As the cartoon makes clear, art is not life after all. And so we must be aware of the conventions of art—its rules of characterization, form, and language—that very much distinguish it from life. The other half of art's pleasure come from these differences. *Reading rule 2:* Read literature first as life, then as art.

A third contrary has to do with literary characters. As with all its other details, most literature tempts us to see characters as somehow real. Of course they are not. They are always simpler than real people and bolder in their thoughts, actions, personalities, relationships, and morality. What is a character, after all, but one or two personality traits, a few articles of clothing, one or two speech patterns, and a conflict or two? Consider the most complex of characters, a Hamlet, for example. How little we know about him. Was he in danger of flunking out of Wittenberg University? We don't know. What was really going on between Ophelia and him? We can't be sure. How much simpler was his life! Sure, he had problems with Ophelia and worse ones with his mother. And of course there was the problem of his indecision. But compare his relatively simple "complexities" with those we face everyday, juggling relations with far more people, divided by many more motives, balancing several obligations against one another. All he had to do, basically, was follow the command of his father's ghost and kill the new king his uncle. Simple.

To see these characters well, we must not lose sight of their grand simplicity, even as the literature tries to fool us about how complex they are. It is through their simplicity that we understand their role in the work and their contribution to its themes. *Reading rule 3:* Read literary characters first as real people, then as artistic creations. First identify with them, feel the quality of their lives, look at life through their eyes, but then stop. Don't surrender yourself to them completely. When we first meet real people, we usually greet them with healthy skepticism, withholding acceptance until we know them better. Do the same with literary characters. Do *not* believe everything they say. Often they understand themselves and their world less than we do. Note discrepancies between what they say and what the narrator says, between what they say and what they do. This ironic discrepancy is one of the devices an artist has for making characters seem more lifelike than they are. It will point the way for you to see them in their other capacity, as artistic creations, two-dimensional figures, sharply limited in personality and behavior, each playing a prescribed role in a drama of action, feeling, and idea larger than they are and containing them. (At the end of this chapter, pages 388–395, is a brief list of terms that will introduce you to the basic elements and conventions of literature. Study them. They will help you read—and write about your reading—with greater insight and pleasure.)

WHAT THE LITERARY ESSAY IS NOT

A literary essay is not a book report. A book report is primarily a summary of a work, recounting the details of character, fact, background, and plot. A literary essay, however, is an explanatory interpretation of a work or some part of it. A literary essay may use summary but never for the sake of summary alone. It summarizes to help explain something or prove a point.

A literary essay is not a book review. A book review is primarily a recommendation or condemnation: reasons to read or not read a book, to see or not see a movie. You will surely state your likes and dislikes in the literary essays you write, but your aim is not to recommend or condemn so much as to explain what makes the good work good or the not-so-good work not so good.

The literary essay is not necessarily a research essay. There are thousands of outstanding books and periodicals weighing down the shelves of almost every library in the world that will help you understand authors, their lives, and times. You may want to look at some of them to help you understand your reading, but before you do, first try your own thinking. It may be every bit as insightful as what you would find in the library. If you turn to these sources before you make your response, their superior style may overwhelm your feelings and confuse your thinking. Respond on your own; *then*, if you wish, check to see what professional literary scholars have to say. Use them to help you explain *your* responses more precisely than you could without them. Be sure to acknowledge all borrowing. (Chapter 16, "The Research Project," Step 3, pages 416–432, and the lists of references in the Appendix will tell you how to find these sources. Chapter 17, Step 6, pages 450–464, will show you how to weave them into your own style and document your borrowing.)

❧ THE SUBJECTS OF LITERARY ESSAYS

Literary essays focus their explanatory powers on the three essential elements of the artistic experience: the work itself, the reader or viewer, and the artist.

The Work Itself

To write about literature is almost always to become something of a historian, psychologist, or detective. A novel or poem, a play or film unfolds to us a world whole and contained, with its own scenery, particular characters, and mood; its own events, crises, and meaning. The literary essay tries to explain this world as we have experienced it. Created as a reflection of one artist's imagination, this world has an order and coherence. It adds up and in so doing makes a dramatic commentary on the life that inhabits it. The sum of this commentary is its themes; we write literary essays trying to describe them. This search for understanding is *not* the search for a "moral to the story," however, although some literary works do have morals. A moral says, in effect, "Do this or don't do that." A theme says, "Life is like this." We write about literature believing that if we can understand its neatly ordered world, we may better understand our own disordered one.

But here's the paradox again: despite all of its lifelikeness, a work of literature is always something made up, not life at all but a *fiction*. If half the fun of literature is experiencing its life, the other half is knowing how the fiction works, how it uses language, pattern, and a particular style of presentation to create its world and express its ideas. We enjoy a magician's tricks and illusions, but we also like to know how she does them. In the same spirit, we write about literature trying to explain its magic, the tricks it uses to make it do what it does.

And here is one other thing we know about literature that affects the way we read it: even the greatest examples never stand alone. They come out of a tradition of other works similar to them in form and subject, a tradition that contributes to lesser and greater works alike. There may have been only one Shakespeare or Mark Twain, but there were dozens of other Renaissance playwrights writing tragedies and equal numbers of nineteenth-century American journalists trying to describe the changing West. We write comparisons of one work with similar works, exploring them as products and representatives of a particular time and place.

The Reader

Reading is almost always an encounter that takes place somewhere midway between readers and their texts. The literature offers its words, patterns, and style, and the readers bring their own vocabulary, experiences, and values. What they read depends as much upon what they bring to the literature as what the literature gives to them. The "meaning" of a work is the result of this cooperation. This does not imply that a novel or film can mean whatever we want it to. To say that is to say words have no generally agreed upon meanings and to miss the traditions artists draw from. There are many, many "wrong" ways to read a literary work, and they almost always result from not seeing what is there on the page or screen or from expecting a work to do something it is not trying to do.

But there are also many "right" readings of a work of art. The mysteries of a poem or a play can be viewed, legitimately, in a number of ways. One reader views a literary character as "strong" because of past experiences with real people, other literary characters with the same traits, and the words that describe those characters. To another reader that strong character seems only "domineering," and she responds this way because of *her* past experiences with people, characters, and language. Both readings are right, authorized by the cooperation between the reader and the work. We write literary essays about this cooperation as it occurs for each of us, exploring what in the literature provoked our responses and what in our lives will account for those responses.

The Writer

It is an error in reasoning known as the biographical fallacy to assume that a writer's work offers consistent and reliable information about that writer's life. Literature is always "made up" in some way, a combination of the real and the imagined, mixed together, shaken up, and arranged to suit that artist's vision of experience and whimsy. So we have to be very careful about drawing parallels between artists and their art. Yet no one would deny that those parallels exist, and it is the aim of one kind of literary essay to trace them out as carefully as possible. To understand the parallels is to understand a work of art more fully and appreciate it more deeply. To know about Charles Dickens's childhood spent working in a blacking factory, for example, is to read more sensitively the portraits of deprived, suffering children in his novels. To understand the poet Sylvia Plath's relationships with her father and then her husband is to read the images of her poetry with greater understanding. Some artists, of course, separate themselves almost completely from the works they create, but most works contain real-life historical truth along with their fiction, and it is legitimate for an essayist to investigate the experiences and influences that have shaped the artist and the art.

SEVEN PATTERNS OF THE LITERARY ESSAY

Whichever element of your artistic experience you choose to write about—the work itself, its impact on you, or the artist—you'll probably choose one of the following patterns to help you make your presentation.

The Question of Interpretation

The question of interpretation is the basic literary essay and the most common. The writer's aim is to answer a question that readers have about a work. These questions customarily have to do with features of the literary work: character, plot, style, and so on. Here are the questions most frequently asked:

- *Characterization:* Who is this character? What kind of person is he or she? What are this person's values, motives, conflict, typical responses, and fate? What details of appearance, speech, behavior, or gesture reveal personality? How does this character contribute to the mood or theme of the work in which he or she appears? Is the character major or minor, flat or round, static or dynamic, protagonist or antagonist, foil or blocking character? (For a definition of these terms, see the brief list of Basic Terms for Writing about Literature, pages 388–395.)

- *Setting:* Where does the work take place? How does the environment influence character, provoke conflict, or determine the course of the plot? What mood does the setting inspire in the characters and readers? What repeated details are used to create the mood of a setting and to evaluate it?

- *Plot:* What is happening, exactly? Identify the change or action taking place. Beneath every obvious event are undercurrents of action and reaction. What are they and how do they affect the course of the plot? What are the causes and consequences of the change taking place? How many parts are there? What is the relationship between them; that is, what in one part prepares for or leads to the next?

- *Tone or mood:* What is the mood of the work: happy, sad, optimistic, pessimistic, satiric, ironic, celebratory, or another? What details of characterization, setting, or plot create this mood?

- *Symbol and image:* What characters or details of setting resonate with a deeper meaning that suggests they may symbolize themes, values, or conditions? What do they symbolize? What images are repeated throughout the work? How do these images help present character, setting, mood, or theme?

- *Point of view:* Who is the narrator? Is the narrator inside the work (an *I*) or outside it, disembodied, writing in the third person? How does the narrator try to convince the reader of the importance, value, or interest of the story? What does the narrator know that the reader does not upon a first reading? What does the *reader* know that the narrator does not? How do the narrator's knowledge, relationships with characters, and values affect the plot, characterization, and theme of the work? What is the narrator's motive for telling the story? What is the narrator's point? Is it the same conclusion the reader draws?

- *The key passage:* How does this passage sum up the theme, characterization, language, style, tone or imagery of the work in question?

The question of interpretation essay generally follows the design of an argument: it makes a claim about its subject—the thesis that answers the question—and then supports that claim by systematically presenting evidence from the work and reasoning about that evidence. Often the design of the interpretive essay looks like this:

I. Introduction leading to the thesis that answers the question of interpretation.
II. Subthesis 1 supporting, defending, or explaining the thesis (with appropriate evidence, conclusions, and explanations).
III. Subthesis 2.
IV. Subthesis 3, and so on, until the thesis has been fully supported.
V. Conclusion that connects the question answered to related questions or to subjects it has a bearing upon.

The Exploration of Solutions

The exploration of solutions is a more complex version of the question of interpretion essay. It recognizes that a work or a part of it may be explained validly in more than one way. The writer's goals are to survey these alternative solutions and, when possible, choose the best. The introduction often poses the problem of interpretation; the body of the essay examines the merits of various solutions. The conclusion may argue that one solution is the most plausible or makes best use of the evidence, or it may argue that several interpretations, though different from one another, each explain the work equally well. In this respect good literature is like life: rich, complex, impossible to explain in only one way. This kind of essay recognizes that fact.

The Refutation

The refutation is yet another version of the question of interpretation essay. Here the question has to do with another's interpretation, whether from a member of your class or a professional literary scholar. The aim of this essay is to show that the interpretation in question is unsound or incomplete and then to correct it. The design of the essay often looks like this:

I. An introduction summarizing the opposing interpretation.
II. A thesis that identifies problems in the opposing interpretation, posing refinements, corrections, or new interpretations.
III. A point-by-point refutation of the original interpretation, often following the pattern of the original.

The Bond Between Art and Life

The essay examining the bond between art and life is a comparison essay. It assumes that there is a relationship between art and real life and that information from one can help explain the other. According to this pattern, a writer may draw upon her own experiences or observations of life and use them to explain character, plot, or theme in a literary work. Or another writer may write more personally and use the characters, events, or subject matter of a work to help make sense of some person, event, or period in his own life. Or, a third writer may compare details from an artist's life with those in the literature, using the facts of biography to help readers better understand the "facts" of the fiction. The goal in all cases is to create parallels between life and art. The design for one version of the essay might look like this:

I. Introduction leading to a thesis assertion about what the work has to reveal of life in the real world.
II. A brief explanation of the work or part of it to show that it does, indeed, mean what the thesis says it does.
III. A point-by-point application of the events or meaning of the work to the writer's real world to help explain that world.

Impressionistic Criticism

The reader himself rather than the literary work is the true subject of this essay, and his goal is self-discovery, to explain why he responded to the work as he did. The essay answers three questions: (1) What are my responses? (2) What in the literary work provokes these responses? (3) What in my experiences, observations, or beliefs will explain these responses?

Then and Now

The then and now essay recognizes that our perceptions, understanding, and feelings about a work change the more we read, discuss, and think about it. The writer traces the evolution of that understanding by answering three questions: (1) What did I originally think or feel and why? (2) What caused the change in my thinking? (3) What do I now think and feel? The design of the essay often follows the order of these questions.

Appearance and Reality

The essay treating appearance and reality may occasionally be a version of the then and now essay in which a reader begins by exploring what she expected about character, plot, mood, theme, or style as she was reading. She explains what caught her attention and what conclusions she drew from these details. Then she tries to account for the discrepancies between what she expected and what really happened. The writer of this essay recognizes that some works of art present us with surprise endings, so she attempts to discover what the artist has done to mislead us about the course of the work and, contrarily, what ambiguous or obscure clues the artist has provided to foreshadow the surprising conclusion, if only we were attentive enough to spot them. In sum, this is an essay that describes artistic form.

In its other version, this is a study of irony, that discrepancy between the ways characters view their world, the way *we* view their world, and the consequences of these characters' limited or distorted understanding. This essay proceeds by examining what these characters think, why they think as they do—whether from motivation, misinformation, or upbringing—how they behave in terms of their thinking, the trouble they get into because of their limitations, their discoveries of "reality," and any changes that result from their discoveries.

❧ PREPARING TO WRITE

Gathering Materials

When you think you have a subject for a literary essay—a key question that needs answering; a character, episode, or theme that needs explaining; or a response that needs describing—do an exploratory freewriting. Pose your question in detail, describe your response and what provoked it, or explore how one of the seven essay patterns might help you present your subject. Then discover what you will say to develop your subject by using any of the following methods of development.

Note Taking   Reread the work in question and take notes on your subject. These notes will be most useful if you introduce each with its context. What's happening? Who's speaking to whom? Where and when? Quote, summarize, or paraphrase as appropriate. Then explain your note to yourself. How does it develop your subject, support your thesis, or answer your key question? Do you have an idea where you will use it in your essay?

A Thematic Tag Tree   The thematic tag tree device from Chapter 8 is especially useful for discovering details about characters, groups of people, and setting. It will provide evidence to support your thesis and key words for your essay. Sketch out a thematic tag tree as you reread, being sure to use quotation marks to distinguish between your judgments and what the work actually says about your subject. You don't have to find details for every branch of the tree, and don't be concerned if one detail could go on more than one branch. Here's a thematic tag tree about Laura Sheridan, the major character of Katherine Mansfield's story "The Garden Party":

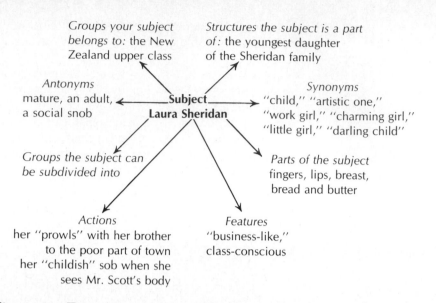

Groups your subject belongs to: the New Zealand upper class

Structures the subject is a part of: the youngest daughter of the Sheridan family

Antonyms mature, an adult, a social snob

Subject Laura Sheridan

Synonyms "child," "artistic one," "work girl," "charming girl," "little girl," "darling child"

Groups the subject can be subdivided into

Parts of the subject fingers, lips, breast, bread and butter

Actions her "prowls" with her brother to the poor part of town her "childish" sob when she sees Mr. Scott's body

Features "business-like," class-conscious

Figurative Free Associations   The device of making figurative free associations from Chapter 5 is useful for discovering your feelings about your subject; it will give you analogies, metaphors, and similes to dramatize your opinions. Try several until you find ones that are vivid, fresh, and true to your responses.

If ___(my subject)___ were ___(choose from one of the following categories)___, it would/wouldn't be ___(make up a term to complete the formula)___ .

a place
a means of transportation
a toy
the weather
a plant or tree
an animal

a piece of furniture
a movement
a musical instrument
a color
a tool or device
a sound
an article of clothing

a beverage
a building
a shape
a smell
a food
a road

Example
  If Stanley Kowalski of Tennessee Williams' *A Streetcar Named Desire* were a place, he'd be a toy store the week before Christmas.

Thesis Statements   Try several versions of your thesis as you develop your subject: *My point is that . . . What I mean to say is that . . .* Each new version will show your increasing understanding of your subject. But beware of "So?" thesis statements that merely assert a fact about some feature of a literary work: "Laura Sheridan, of Katherine Mansfield's 'The

Garden Party,' lives in a dream world." So? So what's the writer's point about this fact? A good thesis for a literary essay makes an assertion about the causes, consequences, meaning, or significance of the facts it contains. Compare this "So?" thesis to the following:

> *A Thesis for a Study of Plot and Conflict*
> My point is that throughout the first part of Katherine Mansfield's "The Garden Party," Laura Sheridan is a character in her mother's dream play, a play in which the characters—the Sheridan family—only play at life. During the story, Laura gradually awakens from this dream play, abandons the role her mother has scripted for her, and discovers what it means to be fully alive.

> *A Thesis for a Character Study*
> My point is that there are two reasons Sammy quits at the end of John Updike's "A & P." What I mean to say is that he wants to be a hero and impress the girls who have invaded his store, but he also wants to flee a confining, conservative world that prevents the full exercise of his human powers.

> *A Thesis for a Study of Imagery*
> My point is that the imagery of Eudora Welty's "Death of a Travelling Salesman" creates patterns of opposition that describe R. J. Bowman, the major character, and define his fate. What I mean to say is that the images of dream and reality, youth and age, darkness and light, mystery and clarity, highway and pathway, point the way to the story's themes.

Organizing the Literary Essay

Perhaps the most startling fact for writers just beginning to write about literature is this: Your essay is *not* directly about the story, novel, poem, play, essay, or film that you have just experienced. It is about your *thesis*. Everything you say in your essay should lead to or follow from it. The design of your essay should be based upon its logic and language rather than the plot of the work. The only exceptions are *process analyses* that trace a conflict or pattern of change through a work, or the line-by-line explanation of a poem. These necessarily follow the pattern of the work. For all other essays, follow the pattern in your thesis. As you organize your ideas by outline or some other means, be sure that each part of your intended essay supports one of the assertions in your thesis and repeats its thematic tags. In this way you will ensure that your writing is both logical and coherent.

Plan for a title and introduction that will capture the attention of your readers. Unless your thesis is startling, you probably won't want to begin there; that would be too bald. Nor should you begin by summarizing the work in question. Assume your audience has read it but perhaps not recently. They don't want mere summary; they want careful explanation. That means you'll want an introduction to set the mood for your essay, identify its subject, and put your readers into a frame of mind to understand your analysis. They'll find your essays easier to read and you'll find them easier to write if you put your thesis at the end of your introduction.

Capture your readers' attention and then lead to your point. Occasionally, you may want to put your thesis at the end of your essay, for suspense or dramatic impact, but be sure the design of your essay leads clearly to your thesis from the very beginning. Here are some common opening strategies.

The Question You Want Your Essay To Answer
Just what is Ernest Hemingway trying to tell us in his sparely narrated short story "The Killers"? He must be saying more than that two men want to kill a Swede boxer they don't even know. He must be saying more than that two nasty gunmen types enjoy themselves intimidating the occupants of a small-town diner. He must be saying more than the old saw about people too afraid to get involved. Yet these few details are almost all there is to this story. Is that all there is? Let's look closer, especially at the details that create the setting and those exchanges in which the characters talk about the events that we readers have been watching unfold.
—Lorraine Nelles

A Key Quotation That Sums Up the Point You Want To Make
"Our wills conflict head on. No chance of reconciliation." These two sentences, spoken by Antigone to Creon, are the threads from which are woven Sophocles' tradegy *Antigone*. The two main characters, Antigone and Creon, are the tragic protagonist and antagonist. They are tragic in the sense that one leads to the other's destruction, whether directly or indirectly. The warp and woof of every episode of the play is their violent struggle: between the supposedly subservient woman and the supposedly superior man, between the representative of divine laws and the representative of man-made laws, between Antigone's love and Creon's arrogance.
—Loretta Nuesslein

The Imaginative Opening
Reading about Preacher Jones in Joy Williams' "Taking Care" affected me like listening to an entire song played one half-tone out of key. The story is about a man who loves. He loves everyone and everything to such an extent that it seems nearly to consume him. And yet, as he looks around him at the people upon whom he has bestowed his love, he sees illness, confusion, emptiness, and pain. Jones himself can make no sense of it. It would appear either that love is not enough or that love creates misery and unhappiness. I can find no space at all in my brain to entertain the second assumption. I love, and on the whole, the people I love seem to thrive and grow. Others have loved and left legacies of greatness and humanitariansm behind them. But poor Preacher Jones loves and reaps mostly grief and failure. I also happen not to believe that it is simply some errant stroke of fate that decrees some people will suffer terribly in their lives while others do not. Abraham Lincoln once said, "Most folks are about as happy as they make up their minds to be." Therefore, I am forced to conclude that there is something missing from Jones' life. Why isn't his love enough?
—Christina Stauffer

A Well-Known Quotation

"Yea, though I walk through the valley of the shadow of death, I shall fear no evil. . . ." Most of us are familiar with this phrase, and not simply because we read the Bible. Most of us have taken that walk through the valley when we first encountered death, usually as children and, if we were lucky, with the guidance of our parents. In Katherine Mansfield's "The Garden Party" we watch young Laura Sheridan take her walk through the valley. But she receives no guidance from her parents; she must take that walk alone.

—Donald Uhlmeyer

A Generalization About Life That Applies to the Work in Question

All the fun and games aside, childhood is about learning how to be an adult. The examples set by authority figures and the guidance they give mold children's personalities and determine the adults they will be one day. Using these examples as they endure the crises of childhood brings them, step by step, closer to adulthood, wisdom, and independence. In the short story "The Garden Party," Katherine Mansfield dramatizes the quandary of young Laura Sheridan, struggling to do the right thing, struggling to follow the guidance of her authority figures, but suspecting all the while that their examples and their guidance are insufficient. Laura has to learn to grow up almost all by herself.

—Stephen Craig

An Illustrative Anecdote from Real Life

There are some people who never learn to stand up for themselves. I know a woman who underwent unnecessary surgery because she did not wish to inconvenience her revered physician. No matter how great her misgivings, how racked with indecision she was, how indefinite the evidence that surgery was necessary, she could not bring herself to postpone or cancel the operation. To have done so would have been against hospital policy, and she was very intimidated by policies. So, on a dreary, cold March morning, she allowed herself to be wheeled into an operating room where she allowed her doctor to carve away what later proved to be a perfectly healthy breast. In her indecisiveness, in her suffering, in her stoic endurance of the life that others have determined for her, my friend reminds me of Reverend Jones in Joy Williams' story "Taking Care."

—Chris Lindley

At the same time, plan your conclusion. Don't just restate your thesis. Aim to unify your essay by referring to the subject of your opening or connect your subject to larger, related issues. Some examples:

A Conclusion That Coincides with the End of the Work

Laura Sheridan's transformation is complete when she stands beside the carter's deathbed. Until now, her need for security and approval has prevented her from displaying any feelings that might set her apart from her family. She has come to the death-bed from a life of garden parties, pretty dresses, and extravagant hats, entirely removed from anything having to do with human suffering or tragedy. When she cries, "Forgive my hat," she leaves behind the frivolous trappings and illusions of her childhood and replaces them with the realities of life, of which death is the final and irreversible reality. She accepts this life and, by so doing, discovers her identity.

—Janice Kramer

A Generalization About Life Based on the Work

Life is more than garden parties and proper manners and Sunday Socials. There are good people and bad. There are rich people and poor. There are free people and oppressed people. When a baby is born, someone else is dying. All this is common knowledge to most adults. The point is that a child needs to learn and experience the real world in all of its astonishing variety so that she can cope with it as an adult. Certainly there is hope for the Lauras of this world. But many of them will have to spend a good part of their adult lives learning lessons that should have been taught them in their childhood.

—Stephen Craig

An Imaginative Close

Eventually, a person must experience the unpleasant parts of life. But by experiencing the difficult along with the easy, a person grows and develops. After all, how does a flower ripen and blossom without the rainstorms that threaten to bend it but end up giving it nourishment and life.

—Laurie Wayne

A Personal Reflection

Preacher Jones's story jarred my emotions because it tells of waste, of a man capable of deep caring who can't care about himself. If he is truly going to stop surrendering, if the end of the story is really to be a new beginning, Jones will have to stop apologizing and start to live. He will have to bring the love of himself into harmony with his love for others. Love is never something to be apologized for. Faith is nothing to be ashamed of. These are things we offer along with ourselves, the people we are inside, risking error, pain, and rejection on the chance that we just might leave the mark of our passing on the people around us.

—Christina Stauffer

❧ WRITING, REWRITING, AND EDITING

Every draft, no matter how well prepared, is always in some sense exploratory. That is especially true with the complex process of literary interpretation. It is not unusual for a writer to begin with a thesis that seems clear and complete but later discover all sorts of new things to say while she writes, despite all her planning. Nor is it unusual for another writer to begin with one thesis and end up with a second, new thesis that he mistakes for a conclusion. Write your preliminary drafts assuming you will make discoveries and have to revise, reorganize, and rewrite in order to incorporate them.

As you revise, check to be sure you've included sufficient evidence, either in summary or direct quotation, to support all of your claims. Be sure, too, that you've explained that evidence so its support for your thesis will be clear. See how this writer introduces her evidence, presents it, and then explains it?

Topic sentence

Subtopic assertion

Introduction to a quotation

Explanation

Transition and subtopic assertion

Summary of evidence

Quotation

Explanation
Conclusion

It is these journeys, these passages beyond themselves, that really develop their characters. Nick [the major character of Ernest Hemingway's "The Killers"] does not seem able to surrender himself completely to the risk of helping someone else. After visiting Ole Andreson and having his offer to go to the police rebuffed, he returns to the diner, deciding he must leave town. He must erase the image of the day: "I'm going to get out of this town. . . . I can't stand to think about him waiting in the room and knowing he's going to get it. It's too damned awful." He does not seem to realize that although no risk means no loss, it also means no gain.

Laura's fate is different [Laura, the major character of Katherine Mansfield's "The Garden Party"]. She wonders if she can overcome the obstacles along her way—her upbringing, the smoky dark lane, the mean little cottages, the dark knot of people, the dead Scott lying in his bed. She does overcome the obstacles. She holds the sensation of the moment beyond its climax—" 'It was simply marvelous,' " she remarks to her brother—in order to incorporate it into her life. By doing so, she gains a mature consciousness which will enable her to handle other obstacles in her life. Nick goes out, confronts life, and retreats; Laura confronts life, persists, and grows.
—Kathy Iwanowski

When you're satisfied with your evidence and explanation, be sure your readers can follow your interpretation. Outline your draft if necessary to be sure. Check your transitions and repetition of thematic tags. Try to see your design through your readers' eyes; they won't always see your subject as you do. Does each paragraph or part announce by word or phrase where you've been and where you are going? Do these transitions make clear how each subtopic supports your thesis? You don't want to be too obvious about transitional signals, but better to be too obvious than not obvious enough.

When you're sure of your analysis and form, be sure of your language. Your aim in a literary essay should be a fully human response to the work. Your language should not only say what you want to say but feel the way you want it to feel, as in the following example. Notice how many words are concrete, specific, and filled with connotative meaning, how they evoke the mood of the scene as well as describe it.

When R. J. Bowman enters the cabin in the sky, he feels he has found a haven. In the midst of its austere surroundings, it darkness, its stillness, there is hope for him at last. Nothing that is said within the walls is very important; the conversation, sparse and strained, is almost meaningless. It is that which remains silent that really matters: the emotions, the feelings, the colors, the sounds. R. J. Bowman is absorbing it all. At first he is baffled by this strange new world in which he has intruded, but the more he perceives it, the more his soul awakens. The pride in the woman's eyes when she looks at Sonny, her complete confidence in his physical strength, her conviction about the goodness of his heart, her proud dependency on him—the humanity of it all. R. J. Bowman can hardly stand it. There is so much in these four walls around him, so many things he never knew existed. Without realizing it, he is experiencing a long-overdue rendezvous with his bewildered soul, and he likes the feeling. For a fleeting moment, in his rapture, he comes close to declaring his humanity to the silent woman sitting across from him, but instead, he retreats in shame. How can he express the loneliness, the emptiness, the pain, and yet maintain his dignity?

—Hilda R. Bamberger

Finally, edit your essay to conform to the conventions of literary interpretation:

- Identify the author and title of the literary work in your introduction.
- Use quotation marks around titles of short stories, essays, and poems; underline the titles of novels, plays, and films, e.g., *The Old Man and the Sea* (a novel), "The Garden Party" (a story).
- Use quotation marks around any exact quotations, whether one word or several sentences (see Quotation Marks, pages 529–530).
- Quotations of more than four lines should be indented ten spaces from the left margin, double-spaced, and quoted *without* quotation marks, unless there are quotation marks in the original.
- When writing about literary works, describe the action in the *present* tense, even though the work is written in the past tense. The story may say *When Laura walked down the hill . . .* , but unless you are quoting, you should write: *When Laura walks down the hill. . . .* We treat the action of a literary work in the present tense because that is the impression it gives us as we read. Any actions that occur *before* the opening of a story should be put into past tense.

TWO LITERARY ESSAYS

Laura's Light Flickers
by Ann Thomas
(*A Question of Interpretation*)

Opening generalization that leads to a theme statement

Author and title of the literary work given in the opening

In her story "The Garden Party," Katherine Mansfield presents two extremely contrasting worlds. The reader sees these worlds through the eyes of young Laura Sheridan, the main character. The garden (representing Laura's world and the setting for the Sheridan's "most successful party") is filled with well-groomed green lawns, brilliant flowers, and blooming trees. There are no clouds in the sky, only a "gold haze." To Laura, everything in her world seems to be bright and lovely. There is no darkness or disorder. But across the lane from Laura's home, where the poorer cottages are situated and Laura has gone exploring with her brother, life is dark and sordid. Here nothing grows in the gardens but "cabbage stalks, sick hens, and tomato cans." The cottages bear no beauty, pattern, or tidiness about them. As Laura sees these two worlds, so she sees the aspects of life, contrary and alien to each other. Laura's world consists of black and white, with no grays. It is the author's intention to prove to her readers, by proving to her main character, that these two realms of light and dark, life and death, happiness and sorrow are woven together inseparably.

We first encounter the Sheridan's domain, Laura's childhood world, in the family garden. Filled with magnificent bright flowers, fruit-laden trees, and well-trimmed emerald lawns, the garden is a most effective setting. Everything seems perfect and orderly, except for the "dark flat rosettes where the daisy plants had been." Has something died in this wonderful, lively garden? Even the overnight appearance of a legion of roses as though by divine intervention makes one suppose that they were not blooming yesterday and may not bloom tomorrow. But at this point in the story, Laura does not see that the fading of flowers is as much a part of the garden as their budding.

The story moves from the garden into the Sheridan's house where preparations are being made for the party that afternoon, and here occurs a disturbance that shakes Laura's perspective of her well-groomed, orderly life. At the back door of the house a delivery man mentions the death of a man named Scott who lived in the nearby cottages. Death is not unknown in the real world, but in her world it is unfathomable that happiness and sorrow can exist side by side. Since she cannot bring the dead man back to life, she tries to do the only thing that will reconcile the conflict in her viewpoint. " 'Jose,' " she asks her sister, " 'however are we going to stop everything?' " But Jose and the rest of the family have a broader if superficial understanding of the real world. There is no need to sacrifice their happiness for others' sorrows. They label Laura's response as "extravagant." Since no one seems to be of the same mind as poor Laura, she grows confused. Trying to picture "that poor woman, those little children, and the body being carried into the house" is too much for her understanding; the image seems "blurred, unreal." Not ready to confront her confusion, Laura retreats from the edge of the real world into the family world of garden parties.

And so the party begins. The party-goers, who are "all happy," promenade across the lawn eating ices and stopping only to "press hands, press cheeks, and smile into eyes." Still, here the narrator questions the immortality of both the guests and the party: "They were like bright birds that had alighted in the Sheridan's garden for this one afternoon, on their way to— where?" The guests will not linger forever in the garden; nor will they live forever. Likewise, the "perfect afternoon [and the party itself] slowly ripened, slowly faded, slowly its petals closed."

Part II: Laura's move-
ment from one world
to another, from igno-
rance to knowledge

Presentation of images
that reveal Laura's
state of mind

Laura's discovery of a
larger world that
includes both life and
death, garden parties
and wakes

A conclusion that
returns to the subject
of the introduction
and thesis

A well-known quota-
tion that sums up the
writer's reading of the
story

Introductory quotation
dramatizing the
writer's thesis

After the party, Laura's father recalls the death. And her mother sends her to the mourning Scotts with a basket of leftover food from the party. As she nears the dead man's house in the approaching darkness, her distinctions between life and death, happiness and sorrow, are still quite clear. The road separating the two worlds "gleamed white," and Laura in her shining white dress, carrying "kisses, voices, tinkling spoons, laughter, the smell of crushed grass" within her, is untouched by the dark, smokey lane and cottages. But life does exist within the darkness and gloom, if only Laura could see it. Inside the cottages lights flicker as Laura approaches another kind of party, a party of mourners grouped outside the Scotts' home. Her bewilderment increases as she enters the dim house. At first blurting out, "I only want to leave—," meaning the basket of food, she falls silent as the widow faces her. It is apparent that Laura does want to leave; she is afraid to face the pain and sorrow that she believes she will find there. The widow, on her part, cannot understand Laura's appearance. "Why was this stranger standing in the kitchen with a basket?" Knowing that death and darkness are a part of life, she expects no sacrifices from the Sheridans.

Before Laura can flee the house, she is drawn into the room where Scott lies in state. Looking upon his face, she finds no tears of sadness as she expected. "Happy . . . happy . . . All is well, said that sleeping face. This is just as it should be. I am content." The contentment on the dead man's face reveals to Laura that death is very much a part of life. "What did garden-parties and lace frocks matter to him?" Laura sees that in death all the features of life are equalized and harmonized. There are no black and white, only a smooth blending of gray.

Perhaps Miss Mansfield has proven nothing to her readers that we don't already know, but to Laura Sheridan an altogether new world has bloomed in her garden. She can return to her home and her parties ready to accept the dark challenges and sadness she may face as she grows older. The story of "The Garden Party" may be summarized in the lines of Aristophanes, who wrote over two thousand years ago:

Perhaps death is life and life is death,
And victuals and drink an illusion of the senses;
For what is death but an eternal sleep?
And does not life consist in sleeping and eating?

Antigone Did It Without the ERA
by Adrienne Klumpp
(*The Bond Between Art and Life*)

" 'I'm bound to say,' " says Ismene to her sister Antigone, " 'you're being very loyal but very silly.' " And *I* am bound to say, "You're being very strong-willed, Antigone, and very modern." I am also bound to say that, viewed in light of the feminist movement and the campaign to see an Equal Rights

Amendment adopted for the U.S. Constitution, Sophocles' Antigone is a most inspiring character and that both opponents and proponents of feminism might do well to notice her.

Antigone could be the ideal of every contemporary, free-thinking, liberal-minded woman, for though many forces threaten to limit her life, what she asserts above all else is what women of today seek above all else—freedom. Not freedom to sit in bars or go braless or refuse to make the office coffee—those are the freedoms of the small-souled—but instead the freedom to actively determine and participate in one's own fate. Antigone is satisfied with nothing less. No one should have to be.

The details of Antigone's dilemma are, of course, unique. None of us will ever be concerned with burying a brother in defiance of a tyrannical king's edicts. The principle that has been violated by Creon's command to leave Polyneices unburied is one of justice. It is an edict challenged by no one and accepted as being the nature of things. But it results in an injustice to which Antigone cannot passively submit. She *must* bury her brother. She is firm in her purpose, willing to die if that is what God commands. In guaranteeing to Polyneices the eternal life to which he, as a human being, is entitled by the unwritten laws of heaven, she acts simply, lucidly, directly, and reasonably.

Antigone looks for no reason or excuse, as Ismene does, to rescue her from the death that she knows is to be her fate for disobeying Creon. She wastes no time in justifying her position or in seeking an identity. She affirms the identity that is already hers—not that of a woman, not that of a subject, not that of a self-proclaimed inherent weakling—her sister's lament. She is, first and foremost, Antigone, a creature of noble blood, who is forced by circumstances to show her mettle. That is enough.

Her goal is simple. She does not apply pretentious higher motives to her action, is not out to change the world or to save mankind. She wishes only to bury her brother's body so that he may smile on her when she meets him in eternity. It's as simple as that, but it is a simplicity that gives her own life significance and dignity.

So, too, is Antigone's action direct. When Ismene shows by refusing to assist her sister that noble blood does not necessarily nourish a noble spirit, Antigone is not further deluded by hope for help from elsewhere. She seeks no permission, appeals to no one's mercy, asks for no aid, garners no support, not even from Haemon, her betrothed, who, besides loving her, has unlimited access to Creon as his son. She has made up her mind. What does it matter anymore who is with her and and who is not? Justice, human decency, and duty matter, and they pour forth from her like the libations she pours over her brother's body. She burns no bras, utters no curses, screams no slogans—and offers no apologies. She is reasonable in both intent and deed. And if fate decrees that she suffer for it, she is of great enough soul to suffer as she has lived—with honor, purpose, and dignity.

Part II: Applying the
lessons of the play to
contemporary life

Many of those who would deny the modern woman her freedom do so on the premise that the family would invariably suffer. But it is interesting, I think, that Antigone, a young woman in love, engaged, and looking forward to a royal life as the wife of the future king, places her current role as a family member above all else. She has watched her father be destroyed, her mother commit suicide, her brothers kill each other. She has seen her sister shirk her duty and has seen Polyneices defeated in life and dishonored in death. But her loyalty to them does not falter. It remains important to her that she save her brother and that she be warmly welcomed by her father, mother, and her other brother Eteocles to eternal life. Acting in complete freedom then, she does not deny or reject her family but instead clings to its roots for sustenance and life.

A. Antigone's defense
of her family

Transition that
reminds readers of the
logical order of impor-
tance pattern of
organization

Most assuring and edifying is the selflessness with which Antigone's spiritual freedom enables her to act. She thinks first of Haemon's sorrow when she speaks of their marriage which can now never be. Under sentence of death herself, she consoles Ismene: " 'Don't go and die as well as me,' " she says. " 'One death's enough. Save yourself. . . . I don't grudge you that.' " And she willingly sacrifices her life for her brother. "Greater love hath no man. . . ." There's something so eternal about her and the love that enables her to go outside herself, a love that gives her happiness because she is helping those she knows she should help, a love that at no time allows her to consider that, when she dies, there will be no one to do for her what she has done for Polyneices.

B. Antigone's
selflessness

C. The meaning of
Antigone's action ap-
plied to the actions of
contemporary women

As the Chorus sings, those possessed by love *can* lose control. Those who are completely free, however, are not possessed of love but instead possess it. It is the difference between the small-souled and the great-souled. We are not, most of us, destined to die nobly in pursuing our goals—and I thank God for that. But if the freedom the modern woman seeks will enable her to love so completely and selflessly, then that freedom is a worthy goal and need not necessarily be flaunted in "men only" bars where she insists on being called "Ms." Antigone, it is true, dies in exercising her freedom, which is tragic. But at least she dies the master of her own fate, and that is enviable.

❧ BASIC TERMS FOR WRITING ABOUT LITERATURE

Characters   The actors in a literary work. Almost always, of course, they are human beings, but they need not be so. Lassie is as much a character in her animal stories as the white spider is in Robert Frost's poem "Design" or R2D2 or Jabba the Hutt in *Star Wars*. A character, then, can be anything—person or not—that has personality, the traits of human beings.

We expect that writers will bring their characters to life through description and narration so that we can participate imaginatively in their lives, and we often judge a work by the lifelikeness of its characters. But we shouldn't forget that the characters of literature are also devices—mechanisms, really—to help writers dramatize their vision of experience. We can understand how these characters work in literature, both to tell a story and create a theme, if we classify them according to their roles and complexity.

- *Protagonist:* The main character of a literary work, not necessarily a virtuous or sympathetic person.
- *Antagonist:* The force or forces opposing the protagonist, not necessarily evil or unsympathetic. The antagonist may be human, the natural elements, or something in the social environment.
- *Normative character:* A character representing the standards by which other characters are to be judged.
- *Mouthpiece:* A character who speaks for the author. But do not assume that a virtuous or appealing character necessarily represents the artist's views.
- *Narrator:* The person telling the story. It may be an actual *I* in the story or some disembodied voice that speaks in the third person. Do not confuse the narrator with the writer or assume that the narrator's view of a story is the "correct" view.
- *Blocking figure:* A character who obstructs the normal desires of the protagonist, not necessarily the antagonist.
- *Foil:* A character who, by direct contrast of action and personality, illuminates another character's personality. The most famous example is Shakespeare's impulsive Laertes, who acts in constant contrast to the indecisive Hamlet. Laertes' character helps us better understand Hamlet's.
- *Confidant(e):* A character in whom another character confides, thus permitting readers to see inside a character's mind or emotions.
- *Flat and round characters: Flat* characters are stereotyped creations. Their traits are few, obvious, and consistent. They lack the complexity and divided motivations of rounded characters. Their responses are generally predictable. Often they are portrayed by the use of an identifying gesture, action, article of clothing, or characteristic of speech. We see these characters most in minor roles, in the background, or on the fringes of an event. *Round* characters are complex, with something of the full personalities we associate with real people. They have individual traits in abundance and complex motivations and feelings. Main characters tend to be round.
- *Static and dynamic characters:* Static characters do not change or grow; dynamic characters do. This change may be positive or negative. Flat

characters may be static or dynamic; round characters may be static or dynamic.

Setting   The time and place in which the plot of a literary work occurs. Setting includes the natural and social environments, anything that provides the background and milieu for a character. Setting may be merely background or directly influence the lives and behavior of characters.

Conflict   A clash of opposing forces, ideas, actions, desires, or wills. Conflict is often the energizing power of a literary work, the fuel for a plot. A character may be in conflict with him- or herself, another character, society, the natural world, or a combination of these. The conflict may be physical, mental, emotional, or a combination.

Plot   The pattern of events or incidents in a story, novel, play, film, or dramatic poem. Although coincidence may occasionally move them along, the plots of most significant literary works result from cause and effect born of conflict, one event leading to and causing another and so on until the forces contained within the action and reaction have worked themselves out. We don't have a plot unless we have conflict. Put another way, a plot is the pattern of a particular conflict, one action, "single, whole, and complete." A plot generally moves from stability to instability, points of mounting tension, a crisis, resolution of the tensions, and new stability. More than anything else, plot distinguishes literature from life by giving the former an order and meaning that life seldom has.

Although some plots are *circular*, ending where they began, or repeating the same event again and again, the most common plots are *linear* and follow a course much like the design presented on the opposite page.

Point of View   All literary works are told and thus have a narrator—not to be confused with the writer—who does the telling. Point of view identifies the narrator's relationship to the action and to other characters; it also defines what the narrator knows about the action narrated. There are five basic points of view:

- *Omniscient:* This is the narrator as God. Narrators from this point of view know everything and have all the prerogatives. They can go anywhere, see everything. They can take us into one character's mind and heart, tell us what they want us to see and then, the next moment, take us inside another character half way around the world. These narrators are generally free to interpret and explain the action to readers, although they need not do so.
- *First-person participant:* The protagonists tell their own stories (an *I*

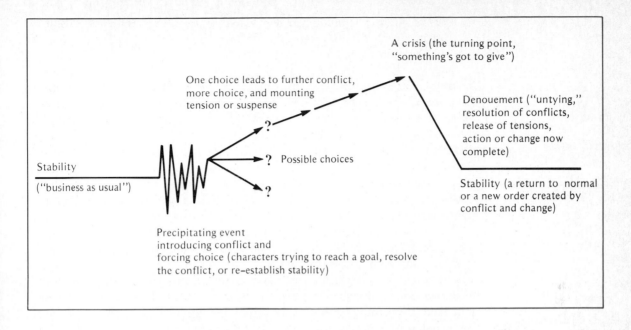

telling about *myself*) and are limited in their storytelling by their physical location, their knowledge of events, biases, motives, morality, and personality traits. What these characters do not know does not get told. Often their incomplete knowledge or lack of wisdom creates an ironic gap between the readers' judgments of their stories and their own. An example of this kind of narrator telling his own story is Mark Twain's Huckleberry Finn.

- *First-person observer:* These narrators tell someone else's story they have witnessed (an *I* telling about *him* or *her*). Like first-person participant narrators, observer narrators are limited in their knowledge. Often their observations and judgments are at odds with those of the characters they describe, creating many possibilities for ironic observation. Perhaps the most famous example of this point of view is Nick Carroway, who tells Jay Gatsby's story in *The Great Gatsby*.

- *Third-person dramatic:* The action is told as if a play were being described. Narrators from this point of view present the action without explanation or evaluation, without revealing a character's thoughts or feelings, except as they are revealed by the character's gesture, action, or direct statement.

- *Third-person sharp focus:* The action is told in the third person (*he* or *she*) but from the point of view of one of the characters. The audience knows only what this character knows and sees what that character sees. Any explanation or evaluation is presented as that character would give it, in terms of his or her values, biases, emotions and limitations.

As first-person points of view do, this one allows many possibilities for ironic discrepancy between the character's way of looking at events and the audience's.

Theme   The theme of a work is more than its subject, e.g., love, hatred, patriotism, the nature of evil, and so on. It is more than a moral platitude about the subject, e.g., love is good, evil is bad, or patriotism is in woefully short supply these days. And it may be more than a generalization about the meaning of a work. A theme is all that a work dramatizes about its subject, a combination of idea, feeling, and moral perspective. Theme is a central insight conveyed not simply by flat statement but by the whole texture, fabric, and design of the literary work. Theme is embodied by the characters, setting, action, plot, imagery, even by style.

A statement of theme is the single most important observation a reader can make about a work of literature, summing up as it does in one small space the meaning, mood, and moral perspective of a work of literature. The way to state the theme is to ask yourself the subject of a literary work. This will not be a person but some concept, condition, or situation. When you have determined the subject, then reexamine the work to discover just what it dramatizes or asserts about that subject.

Theme = Subject of a work + what the work dramatizes about that subject

When you write out a theme statement it should observe the following conventions: [1]

- Because the statement of theme is a generalization about that part of life the writer has chosen for a subject, theme statements never name the characters of the work in question. Characters are embodiments of the theme, illustrations of it. To identify a character in a theme would turn that statement from a generalization to a specific instance.
- A theme statement is a complete declarative sentence, never a fragment or a question.
- A theme is a conditional rather than categorical generalization; therefore, it uses words like *may, perhaps, seems, probably,* rather than *never, ever,* or *always.*
- A theme statement for a significant work of literature will always be more complex and insightful than a trite saying like "Love conquers all."
- A significant work of literature will probably dramatize more than one theme, and those themes may be stated in more than one way.

Eudora Welty's "Death of a Travelling Salesman" dramatizes that love between two human beings is the most crucial element in human life; without it, there is no "real" life.

The theme of Eudora Welty's "Death of a Travelling Salesman" is that some people fail at life because they've worked too hard at success and misunderstood the importance of the simple things like love, home, family, warmth, and communion that anyone can have but many do not.

Eudora Welty's "Death of a Travelling Salesman" portrays the plight of modern materialistic man, cut off by his own fear and mistrust from the fulfillment offered by natural and human life. Though he desires union with nature and other human beings, the mistrust born of his material values keeps him apart, isolated, alone with his breaking heart.

- As a unifying generalization about a work, a theme statement should not contradict any major details of that work.

Image (Imagery)   Words used to portray what we perceive with any of our senses. Writers use imagery to present character, describe setting, and dramatize events. It is through the imagery that we recreate a literary work in our minds as we read. And it is by the careful selection and presentation of imagery that writers create mood and theme. The images of a literary work exist not just for their own sake or their liveliness but for their contribution to the whole work. Be especially aware of repeated words or images (iterative images) and images in combination with metaphors and similes. The writer is probably using these motifs with significant intentions.

Symbol   A symbol is something that plays its own part in a literary work yet at the same time represents something else. It may be a natural or manufactured object, an event, an animal, a scene, or even a person that stands for a set of ideas or emotions. Take a farmer's bull, for example. The bull is just a bull, an animal in a pasture, eating, mating with cows, eliminating waste, eventually becoming tough pot roast and shoe leather. But for thousands of years we humans have seen in the bull a symbol of physical and sexual power and have even made it a divine figure in some societies. If that bull appeared in a short story, it would be just a bull, playing whatever part the writer assigned it, but she could also describe that bull in such a way that we couldn't read about it without awareness of its symbolic dimensions.

> Mrs. May's bedroom window was low and faced on the east and the bull, silvered in the moonlight, stood under it, his head raised as if he listened— like some patient god come down to woo her—for a stir inside the bedroom. . . . Clouds crossing the moon blackened him and in the dark he began to tear at the hedge. Presently they passed and he appeared again in the same spot, chewing steadily, with a hedge-wreath that he had ripped loose for himself caught in the tips of his horns. . . . The bull, gaunt and long-legged was standing about four feet from her, chewing calmly like an uncouth country suitor.

. . . The bull lowered his head and shook it and the wreath slipped down to the base of his horns where it looked like a menacing prickly crown.
(Flannery O'Connor, "Greenleaf," *Everything That Rises Must Converge* [New York: Farrar, 1956])

Often what a symbol represents cannot be stated with absolute certainty, although it is clear that the symbol points directly toward meaning and theme. In this respect, symbols are evocative devices that create a mood or background of ideas that enrich a literary work. Writers use symbols when they want to tell a story or present an experience too complex for literal representation. Yes, they could stop and explain their ideas, but they wouldn't be creating art anymore; they'd be preaching or teaching. A symbol has all the vividness appropriate to imaginative writing, but it has also that fourth dimension that makes it resonate with extra meaning and significance.

Motif   Any significant pattern of repeated ideas, imagery, symbol, language, or incident. Motif is a device of emphasis, one of a writer's chief means for creating and signaling a theme.

Tone   The mood created by characterization, description, setting, plot, language, and the pace of presentation. Tone usually supports theme in some way.

Irony   One of the most important devices a writer has for giving literature something of life's complexity, for creating surprise, and for ordering experience. Irony almost always involves an incongruity between appearance and reality, expectation and result, intention and action, feeling and thinking. In most works of literature, things aren't always what they seem and don't always turn out as expected, either for the audience or for the characters. There are three kinds of irony:

1. *Verbal irony:* A discrepancy between what people say and what they really mean, saying the opposite of what is intended.
2. *Dramatic irony:* The discrepancy between what a character says or believes and what the audience knows to be true. We in the audience often have superior wisdom or get knowledge from the narrator that is withheld from the characters.
3. *Irony of situation:* The discrepancy between appearance and reality or between what one expects and what actually happens. If a character intends to do one thing but ends up doing the opposite, if the audience expects one thing to happen but something quite different occurs, that is irony of situation.

A summary of Ernest Hemingway's short story "The Killers" illustrates these forms of irony. The story opens when two gangsters enter Henry's

Diner in the town of Summit. They have come to kill a boxer, Ole Andreson, who has apparently double-crossed someone in the Chicago mob. The killers know that Ole comes nightly to Henry's to eat his supper. In the kitchen they tie up Sam the cook and the one patron, a drifter named Nick Adams. George, the counter-man, is stationed at his usual place to give the look of "business as usual." Time passes but Ole doesn't show. At last, the killers leave as abruptly as they came.

After George unties Nick and Sam, the three discuss the near tragedy, and George urges Nick to go warn Ole. Disregarding Sam's caution to "stay way out of it," Nick agrees to go immediately. Sam's response: "Little boys always know what they want to do." That is *verbal irony* as well as sarcasm, the opposite of what Sam actually means to say. Young Nick most certainly does *not* know what he should do if he wants to save his skin.

At Ole's apartment, Nick discovers the boxer lying on his bed with his clothes on, his face to the wall, knowing the killers are coming, waiting for them. He is, he tells Nick, "through with all that running around." This is the opposite of what Nick and the reader expect and an example of *irony of situation*. We expected a fighter and a fight; we find a man who has given up, resigned to die.

Stunned and confused by Ole's passivity, Nick returns to the diner, where he recounts his discovery to George. "It's a hell of a thing," he says at the story's conclusion. "I'm going to get out of this town. . . . I can't stand to think about him waiting in the room and knowing he's going to get it. It's too damned awful." George's advice is, "Well, . . . you better not think about it." That exchange is an example of *dramatic irony*. Nick thinks he can flee the knowledge of evil and human powerlessness he has learned in this town. Knowing more about Nick than he does himself, *we* know he cannot. No matter where he runs, he will no more be able to "not think about it" than Ole can escape his killers. There lie the irony and the theme of the story.

END NOTE

1. For the conventions of theme statements I have followed Laurence Perrine's *Story and Structure* (New York: Harcourt, 1974).

Chapter 16

The Research Project:
Searching and Re-searching

❧

❧ GENERAL INTRODUCTION: A REDEFINITION OF RESEARCH

Research writing is the center of academic and professional life, the spring from which come many of our best ideas and greatest achievements. It is the tie that binds informed men and women into an intellectual community. It is their town meeting, their supermarket, factory, warehouse, newspaper, and telephone network. For these reasons, the research paper is the most important and one of the most frequent college writing assignments. It is your passport to that same community of informed men and women, one of the most efficient methods for acquiring information about a subject, organizing it, and testing its usefulness and value.

The research papers you will write now and in terms to come will fall into the same five patterns professionals use to present their research:

1. *The report:* You may do reserach to discover, present, and explain information about a subject new to you. Or you may present the results of direct experimentation or observation.
2. *The problem/solution essay:* You may state a problem; do research to understand its causes, consequences, and significance; then pose a solution to it.
3. *The review of research:* You may survey and evaluate the research done by professionals. Your interest is less in information about a subject

than in the state of the information. After reading professional research on a subject, you will describe what these researchers know about that subject, how they have gathered their information, how reliable it is, what conclusions they have drawn about it, what controversies surround it, who agrees with whom, and who has the best interpretations of it.

4. *The directive essay:* You may do research to discover how to do something and present your discoveries as a set of how-to instructions.
5. *The argumentative essay:* You may do research to gather the evidence and reasoning that will prove a claim.

You may have thought the research paper was a big book report, a library exercise in which only facts count and success is measured by the number of footnotes. But as you can tell from the foregoing list, that is not the case. College research papers are at once more interesting, more challenging, and more varied. You will gather information in a variety of ways: by reading, yes, but also perhaps by observation, experiment, interview, electronic recording, questionnaires, even certain forms of introspection. You'll gather this information from a variety of sources in a variety of locations from the library, certainly, but also perhaps from the lab or fieldwork. And you'll do a variety of things to that information: explain it, evaluate the methods that have produced it, add to it, test its truth, apply it to new situations, and organize it. The aim of college research writing is not facts for the sake of facts but learning to do research in the professional sense of the word, learning a new method for finding, handling, and using knowledge.[1]

The form your research papers take, their length, the number and location of your sources will all vary—as professional research projects vary—depending on your subject, the time available for research, the occasion, your knowledge, and the materials available. The only general restrictions placed on all research projects are these: (1) Your subjects must be truly researchable; that is, you must be able to find and assemble genuine facts about your subjects. (2) These subjects must be sharply limited so you can present your research in detail yet have room to defend your conclusions and show how your limited subjects illuminate larger subjects. (3) You must present the results of your research in a systematic way. (4) You must document the sources of your research.

Now, early in your career as a research writer, you may be approaching this most important, complex, and lengthy of college writing assignments with just a little apprehension and all sorts of questions. The aim of this chapter and the following is to put you at ease and give you confidence. Chapters 16 and 17 will answer all your questions, give you the strategies and information necessary for successful research writing, and lead you step by step through the seven steps of the research process.

Chapter 16
1. Charting the territory of your subject: choosing a subject, limiting it, framing a problem, posing a tentative hypothesis.
2. Investigating: doing primary source research.
3. Investigating: using the library, discovering secondary sources, and preparing a bibliography.
4. Investigating: doing secondary source research.

Chapter 17
5. Devising a communications strategy and organizing.
6. Composing, revising, and documenting research.
7. Preparing the final draft.

Followed carefully, these steps will help you master the complexities of research writing, manage the chaos that inevitably accompanies successful research, discover a few shortcuts to speed your work, and, most of all, achieve the chief objective of all significant research: better understanding of ourselves and our world.

Step 1: Charting the Territory of a Research Project

❧ THE GOOD RESEARCH TOPIC

You know the truism that goes, to get a good answer you've got to ask the right question. With only slight modification we can say the same about the research project: to do good research you've got to have the right topic. Choosing the right topic will largely determine whether your research challenges and informs you or is a frustrating, time-consuming chore, whether you work efficiently or confusedly, whether your project succeeds or not. Even if a college instructor gives you a list of topics to choose from—all of them the "right" topics—you still have to make one of them right for you. Here are some suggestions.

What to Choose and How

Choose Selfishly   Choose a subject that piques your curiosity, one you'd like to learn about but have not had the chance until now. Make your research a learning process and your writing a report of your discovery. If you choose a subject of wide interest, say, prison sentences and their effect on crime rates, you'll do most of your research in the library. But you may instead choose a subject of personal and local interest, say, a correlation of crime rates with the fear of crime in your community. You'll do most of your research for this topic in interviews "on the street" and at city hall.

Choose a problem you'd like to see solved. If you're writing a literary research essay, you'll tackle a problem in interpretation, say, the major theme of a literary work, a complex character, a difficult episode or scene, or a series of images that seem important but whose meaning is obscure. Your research will show you how literary scholars have reasoned their way through the same problem. If you're writing a nonliterary research essay, you may consider some particular human, social, or environmental problem. It may be a large problem of general concern, childhood malnutrition in America, or an immediate and local problem, the need for traveling food kitchens to feed the homeless in your community. Your research will be an attempt to understand the problem and find solutions, and your essay, the systematic description of problem and solutions.

Choose a theory—scientific, social, or psychological—that you'd like to test. You may try to validate this theory by conducting an experiment or gathering primary source information. However, make sure it is a theory you have the time, knowledge, and skill to test. For the sake of simplicity you may want to limit your test to some part of a theory or to a method of testing you know well from college courses or general reading. For example, you may test a theory about the effect of open spaces on human behavior—part of the science of proxemics—by observing various areas of your campus and comparing human behavior there. Of course, before you begin your experiment, you may have to read the research of professionals to help you make your test. When you finish your research, you will probably produce a report weighing evidence and drawing conclusions, pro or con, about how well your evidence confirms the theory in question.

Choose an opinion you'd like to support. You will research for evidence to support that opinion and use the opinions of experts to sharpen it. Your writing will be an argumentative essay. Or you may want to do direct observation research to form an opinion. You may gather a "panel" to try consumer products, sample their findings, and draw some conclusions about the products. You will write a comparative report, weighing the merits of similar products and reporting your evaluations.[2]

Choose Challengingly   The best subject for a research project will hold your interest for all the time it takes to complete. But keep in mind that you won't exhaust your interest when you finish. If you choose your subject well, you'll do research that raises more questions than it answers, questions that will stimulate further thinking, reading, and writing long after this particular project is finished. The best research projects lead not only to a finished piece of writing but to more learning.

Choose Practically   Challenge yourself, yes, but be realistic about the time, skill, and background knowledge necessary to meet this challenge. You may have a fascinating plan for taking a "fear of crime" survey in your community, but if you do not have the money, time, transportation, or knowledge necessary to conduct a valid survey, your work will be frustrating at best and incomplete or flawed at worst. Especially should you spend some time, before you get too deeply into your project, visiting libraries or other sources of information to see if they have what you'll need.

Choose Quirkily   It is surprising how often beginning researchers dismiss their most interesting, freshest, and most insightful topics: aboriginal dream religion, the psychological value of wilderness, horror stories as "real" literature, to name a few. These they put down as "foolish," "weird," "not very important," "just something I've been thinking about." What they don't recognize is that what interests them may also interest others.

Some Research Topics to Beware Of

Beware of *"easy-chair" subjects*, the ones you're tempted to choose only because you might do well writing about them. In your desire to be realistic and practical, don't forget that an easy topic may dull you into complacency. You'll lose interest and show it by the declining quality of your thought, research, and writing.

Beware of *subjects you think you ought to choose*, the ones you think might interest an instructor or the ones the crowd is choosing this term. Drug abuse, schizophrenia, and alcoholism are perennial favorites. Now, all of these have important research that could be done about them, but if you choose them only because everyone else does, you'll find it difficult to discover your own purpose, point of view, or thesis to help direct your research.

Beware of *"headline" subjects*, the ones that fill today's front pages and the agendas of tv talk shows: the latest form of computer crime, the most recent trend in modern marriages, this week's war in some corner of the world, the hottest new novelist, recent discoveries in cancer research, or an impending sale of vast amounts of federal land. True, these are interesting subjects, but often they are too new to have received the serious attention of the experts. They are unresearchable unless you have the time and talent to do your own direct-observation research. What you want is a subject that has been around long enough to capture the interest of a broad—not necessarily large—audience of specialists and nonspecialists alike. This audience creates the demand for the serious, detailed, and sound general interest books and articles in which you will do most of your research. But don't drop headline subjects too quickly. With a little concentration you may turn them into truly researchable topics. Computer crime may lead to ethical issues in the management of electronic information; the sale of federal lands, to a history of federal land policies. Research demands flexibility, and this is nowhere more important than in the identification of a topic.

Beware of *subjects that require great amounts of background information*, e.g., Albert Camus's novel *The Stranger* as a representative of existentialist philosophy. To develop a subject like this a writer commits himself to enough research for three essays: a biographical study of Albert Camus's youth and early writings, a study of French existentialism in the 1920s and 1930s, and an analysis of the novel itself. All that in ten to twenty pages? Hardly. Choose what you have the time to do well.

Beware of *"the life and times of . . . "* biographical subjects, e.g., Reverend Martin Luther King's life as a civil rights leader. Any subject that focuses primarily on the life of a historical figure risks that the essay to come of it will be more a summary narrative (. . . *and then* . . . *and then* . . .) than an analysis, more a report of dates, events, and people than a judgment of that person's motives, conflicts, thought, and achievements. If you want to write about a historical figure, you may begin by looking at this person's life, but try to make an interpretation of part of that life or examine some issue raised by this person's activities or beliefs, e.g., the influence of Martin Luther King's pacifism on his Alabama civil rights campaigns. Good biographies do more than just summarize and narrate; they explain, draw conclusions, and evaluate.

Beware of *one-word topics or one-phrase topics* like *cancer, genetic engineering, William Faulkner's character Joe Christmas, the Civil War,* or *interferon.* These may contain good subjects, but in their present form they are too broad, too inclusive, too disconnected from a particular researcher's interest or opinions. If you have some topics like these in mind, limit them to fit your interests or skills. Add a noun or verb to identify your interest, express an opinion, or pose a problem, e.g., *treating the emotional side effects of cancer* or *Joe Christmas, the rebel with a cause.*

❧ FROM SUBJECT TO HYPOTHESIS

Finding a Subject

Now that you know which subjects are right and which to beware of, the trick becomes finding the one just right for you. Some writers know from the very beginning what they want to write about. If that describes you, skip this section and go to the next. If you're not one of these fortunate few, what you need are some good options, the more the better. No need to choose just yet. You are an explorer surrounded by uncharted country. If you stake a claim to the first territory you come to, you may miss more fertile territory a little farther on. Here are some exploratory strategies; come up with a list of five to ten possible topics.

Talk to the Experts   Go talk to professors or other experts in subjects that interest you. Tell them you're looking for a research project to pursue and you have just so many weeks for it. Ask them what topics might be suitable to your interests and skills.

Write   Do an *exploratory freewriting* to discover possible subjects. Or try a *free association*. Put several of these headings at the top of a page: *human question, social question, environmental question, past, present, near, far, persons, places, things, doing things.* See what topics they bring to mind. If you already have some unshaped subjects in the back of your mind, do a focused freewriting to define your interests or identify issues worth investigating.

Read   Go to the library and look up possible subjects in an encyclopedia, biographical dictionary, or general interest book and do some background reading. You're not doing research yet, just serious browsing, looking for what is generally known about these subjects and what their enduring problems or issues are. Note interesting subtopics, issues, or personalities. The Appendix lists some of the most important encyclopedias, biographical dictionaries, and reference sources (see pages 546–551).

Look up possible subjects in bibliographic indexes. Once again, the Appendix will help you (pages 540–546). The citations beneath the headings in these works will give you an idea of what interests professional researchers, how they have divided up your subject, and what sources you will find when it comes time to use the library.

Look up your subjects in the card catalog. Look for book titles that identify controversies and pinpoint subtopics worth considering. Look up your subjects in the *Library of Congress Guide to Subject Classification.* There you will find the descriptors used to classify books in American libraries. Not only will this list help you use the card catalog and bibliographic indexes, but its divisions of major subject areas will give you subtopics to narrow your thinking and help you recognize researchable topics.

Look through magazines in your field or serious general interest magazines. They will show you current controversies surrounding your subject or subtopics on which you could focus your research.

When you've finished your exploratory talking, writing, or reading, you'll probably have given yourself more than enough choices for research subjects. Now you can use the guidelines at the beginning of Step 1 and choose the best subject, the one that is most interesting, specific, controversial, and researchable. But remember, your decision here is preliminary. As you do your research, you will narrow, sharpen, and rethink your subject in light of what you discover—or fail to discover. This change is natural; almost never will you end up with quite the subject you begin with.

Posing a Key Question and a Hypothesis

Professional researchers don't wake up in the morning, yawn, and muse to themselves, "I wonder what I'll discover today about acid rain"—or South African terrorists, federal land management policy, superconductors, William Faulkner's *Light in August,* or Reverend Martin Luther King's pacifism. No, they begin with definite objectives and, often, definite expectations. So should you. Once you have a research subject, you should begin to limit it and draw the line of inquiry you'll follow as you research your subject. Doing so will give you some idea what you're looking for, why, and what you'll do with what you find.

Pose *the key question* you want your research to answer. To frame this question, begin by deciding which of the following questions apply to your subject and which most deserve answering.

- What is my subject: a person, place, thing, process, or belief? What is it for?
- What does it belong to? How is it different from or similar to other members of its class?
- What are its parts and how do they work together?
- What is its scene, environment, or background? Where does it come from?
- What is happening to it or what is it doing? What are the causes of its change? What are its effects or consequences? What will stop the process?
- Whom does it affect? How does it affect me? Why?
- What good is it? Should anything be done about it? What and how?

Combine the most interesting and important of these questions into a specific key question you will try to answer.

Examples

What is the effect of acid rain on the fish and game population of the upper Midwest?

What effects is "privatization" of federal lands having on the amount of American wilderness available for recreational use?

What elements do horror stories have in common? What explains their enduring popular appeal? Can they be classified with "serious" literature?

What is interferon, how does it work, and what is its impact on contemporary medicine?

What influence does television as a medium have on the news it presents?

Identify your *purpose* for researching and writing. It may change later, but thinking about it now will help you know what you're looking for and why. Is your purpose informative: to discover a body of information, then explain and organize it for your knowledge and others'? Is it directive: to discover and state the procedures for doing something? Is it critical: to present, explain, and evaluate a subject in order to discover the truth about it and determine its use or value? Is it argumentative: to gather, organize, and present evidence in support of an opinion or claim? Is it some combination of these purposes?

Example

My purposes are to discover the extent and sources of acid rain in the Midwest [informative], to lay the blame for this pollution where it belongs, and propose a solution [critical-argumentative].

State your *tentative hypothesis*. This is a statement of what you actually expect to discover or prove about your subject. If you're beginning your research in ignorance, you'll have nothing to say here, but if your purposes are critical or argumentative, you probably already know something about your subject and have some ideas about what you'll find. Your actual research may modify this hypothesis heavily, even disprove it, but stating your goal now will emphasize the direction of your research and help you begin planning for a sound thesis. Write your hypothesis as a declarative sentence:

I expect to discover/prove/explain/demonstrate/show that ___(make an assertion about your subject)___ .

Examples

I expect to prove that nuclear waste disposal dumps are now almost full and that the U.S. has not adequately planned for new disposal methods when these sites are no longer available.

I expect to discover similarities between nineteenth- and twentieth-century American feminists.

I expect to explain how television as an electronic entertainment medium necessarily distorts the news it presents.

EXERCISE

Chart the territory of your research project by listing your decisions about your subject and making a schedule.

1. My general subject area.
2. My specific research subject.
3. My key question.
4. My purposes (report, explanation, critique, instructions, or argument).

5. My tentative hypothesis (if possible).
6. What terms in my question or hypothesis are vague, too general, or unclear? What objections could be made or questions raised about my hypothesis? Ask friends, instructors, or fellow students to answer these questions for you.
7. The date this project is due.
    a. Number of days for researching.
    b. Number of days for organizing.
    c. Number of days for writing.
    d. Number of days for revising and preparing the final draft.

Step 2: Investigating—Taking Primary Source Notes

If you've written a research paper before, you already know how time-consuming note taking can be. Still, there's no way around it. For the sake of completeness, you have to take notes. There's no way to remember all the information you'll need for a paper as long and complex as the one you're now planning. For the sake of accuracy and documentation, as well, you have to take notes. You must get everything exactly right and be fair to your sources. And for the sake of organization, you have to take notes. Most of your information will come from sources with purposes and designs different from your own. To make it useful to you, you must reduce it to manageable bits and pieces you can arrange to suit *your* purposes and design. Your care, patience, and thoroughness are crucial at this stage of your project. What shortcuts there are, the following pages will give you.

❧ AN INTRODUCTION TO NOTE TAKING

If your sources are few and your research paper brief, you can be somewhat casual about your note taking. With only a small number of notes to take, you can jot them down on one or two pieces of paper and organize them with lists or by drawing arrows. Or you can photocopy your sources, highlight important passages, and write marginal notes. However, if your sources are many and your paper long—probably your present situation—these informal methods won't help you manage what is sure to be first a blizzard and then an avalanche of information. You need a system: brief notes taken on regular-sized note slips.

The Mechanics of Note Taking

You'll take four kinds of note slips. 1. Bibliography slips: The term *bibliography* means, literally, "writing about books." On bibliography slips you'll record the publication or other identifying information for all the print and nonprint sources you consult for your research. You'll use these slips to locate your sources and, later, after you've written your project, to document your borrowing.

2 and 3. Primary and secondary source slips: These are the notes we most associate with the research paper. On them you'll record the information, explanations, and judgments that will develop your subject and support your thesis.

4. Planning slips: These notes are *not* about your topic but about the paper itself, the plans you'll follow to organize and present your research. For a paper this complex, you may not be able to plan it all in your head.

Note Slip Size   Simplicity and ease of handling require that you use the same size slips for all your note taking. Buy a package of four-by-six inch cards, or better yet, make your own by cutting notebook paper sheets into four squares. Or draw lines dividing them now but cut them later, after you've finished your research. Avoid noteslips smaller or larger than four-by-six (three-by-five or five-by-eight). One is too small for complete notes; the other is too large and will tempt you to economize and save time by filling the slip from top to bottom.

The Length of a Note   Generally speaking, the shorter the note the better. Put only *one* idea or bit of information on each slip. Beginning researchers often put too much on a slip. To write more than one idea per slip, however, is to make that slip useless when it comes to sorting and organizing your information. When in doubt, divide an idea or piece of information in two and put each on a separate slip.

Methods of Note Taking   Write your notes in ink, type them out if you can get the research materials to a typewriter, or photocopy your materials, cut out what you need, and tape it to the note slips.

Where Not To Take Notes   *Never* take notes on the backs of note slips. If you do, you may forget. If you have a rare lengthy note that requires more than one slip, write on only one side and clearly label each note in the series: "note 1 of 2," "note 2 of 2," and so on.

The Contents of Note Slips

Take notes on everything that will develop your subject, answer your key question, and prove or disprove your hypothesis. When in doubt, take a note. Always take too many notes rather than too few. If you're like most researchers, you'll end up taking two or three notes for every one you actually use. That's not sloppy thinking or poor planning; that's not being uneconomical or inefficient. That's the way research works. You don't know at the beginning exactly what you'll need, no matter how clear and precise your key question or hypothesis is. Taking many notes will keep your options open. It is easier to throw away what you don't use than trudge back to the library, relocate a source, reread, and take the note you should have taken in the first place. And be fair. If you find something that tends to disprove your hypothesis, take it down. Revise your hypothesis to incorporate this contradictory evidence. What count, remember, are truth and sound judgment. Professional researchers learn as much from wrong hypotheses corrected by their research as they do from hypotheses that don't change at all. Besides, your research paper will be richer, subtler, and more interesting for making use of all relevant and significant information.

Every primary and secondary source slip should contain the following:

- A subject heading to identify the contents of the note and help you sort your slips.
- A bibliographic reference to identify the source of the note.
- A page number, if a print source.
- An introduction to the note.
- The note itself.
- Your commentary on the note: an explanation or directions about how you intend to use it.

(See the basic note slip layout at the bottom of the page.)

Subject heading → *Cronkite on superficiality of tv news*   *Barrett, News 196-97* ← Bibliographic reference and page number

Clearly marked quotation → *"We fall far short of presenting all, or even a goodly part, of the news each day that a citizen would need to intelligently exercise his franchises in this democracy. So as he depends more and more on us, presumably the depth of knowledge of the average man diminishes. This clearly can lead to disaster in democracy."*

A good quotation to open with — it sets up my thesis. ← The writer's purpose for the note

Note-taking Strategies

Whatever your sources of information, print or nonprint, you'll take information from them in four basic ways: direct quotation, summary, facts and figures, and paraphrase.

Direct Quotation A direct quotation is just that, an *exact* reproduction, word for word, punctuation mark for punctuation mark, of the original source. Quote often but quote briefly; the lengthier your quotations now, the more difficult later to work them into the fabric of your ideas, design, and style. If you put long quotations on your note slips, you may find yourself in a week or two, as you're organizing, staring at them, wondering why you quoted in the first place. Brief quotations will reveal their purposes to you more quickly and easily.

What Should You Quote?
- Passages that sum up a key point in a condensed, emphatic way.
- Passages whose meaning or feeling would be lost in a summary.
- Dramatic, memorable, or well-known passages.
- An authority's judgments or conclusions about your subject.
- Passages whose contents cannot be presented any more economically.

To quote readably, gracefully, and accurately, you will need to know how to use these punctuation marks:

- Quotation marks, double (". . .") and single (for quotations of quotations: " '. . .' ").
- Colons (:) and commas (,) to introduce quotations.
- Ellipsis points (. . .) to signal omissions.
- Brackets ([. . .]) to insert your editorial explanations or corrections within a quotation.

The Punctuation section of Chapter 18, pages 521–532, will give you full instructions for these punctuation marks. Review them before you begin note taking. At the top of the opposite page is a direct quotation note for a literary research essay on Katherine Mansfield's story "The Garden Party."

Summary As you may already know, a summary is a condensation or digest of the original in your own words. When you summarize, you're concerned not with the language, examples, stylistic flourishes, or design of the original but only with its meaning and essential details. You may summarize in complete sentences, in fragments, even in single words. But summarize with care. Your words must not distort the sense or mood of the original. And take care that your summary doesn't gradually drift into a direct quotation. If you quote key words or phrases, surround them with quotation marks. As with direct quotations, write an introduction that gives the background and context for your note. What to summarize:

- Background information.
- Commentaries, explanations, and evaluations.

Mrs. Sheridan's insensitivity   "Party" 543

    When Laura tells her mother of Scott's death, Mrs. Sheridan's first response is, " 'Not in the garden?' interrupted her mother . . . 'Oh, what a fright you gave me!' "

    Mrs. Sheridan's first response has nothing to do with the dead man and his family. She is only concerned with herself: where Scott died (a possible lawsuit if he died in her garden) and how the news has affected her.

Bibliographic reference and page number

Quotation within a quotation and an ellipsis to signal an omission

Writer's character analysis

- Arguments.
- Whatever you need the sense of but not the actual language.
- Data, if your project does not require exact figures.
- In literary works: description, characterization, episodes, and lengthy exchanges of dialogue.

Below is a summary noteslip based on the following paragraph analyzing the problem of grade inflation:

> Another mechanical contrivance that has caused the raising of grade-point averages is the greater leniency of rules permitting students to withdraw from courses. Withdrawals were always possible, but formerly the conditions under

Early withdrawals   Aristides "Inflation" 494

    Withdrawal policies are another of what this author calls the "mechanical contrivance[s]" promoting grade inflation. In earlier days, students could withdraw, but they had to do it early in a term and have good reasons. Now they can withdraw late and for trivial reasons. They don't even have to give their reasons.

    How widespread is this policy? The author is vague here. S.C. State doesn't require reasons for withdrawal, but our deadline has been moved up in the last year from the last week of the term to the tenth week. Is this change in policy occurring elsewhere?

A quotation made to fit the grammar of a passage by a bracketed insertion

Evaluation of the source and questions raised

which a student could withdraw from a course were rather stringent, and the decision to seek a withdrawal had to be made fairly early in the term. Now withdrawals can not only be made fairly late in the term at most schools, but no reason for the withdrawal need be given. Frequent (if unstated) reasons for withdrawals are that a professor is too dull, the reading load in a course is too heavy, or the student finds himself out of his depth and calls for the withdrawal as for a life preserver to pull him to safety. Used as a means of avoiding boredom, strenuous work, and failure, withdrawals can only have further contributed to the inflation of grades.

("Aristides," "The Other Inflation," *The American Scholar* 54.4 [Autumn 1976]: 492–97)

Facts and Figures   There will be times, many of them, when you'll want facts and figures from lists, charts, tables, polls, questionnaires, summaries, and nonprint sources. But remember, these data are seldom as "raw" as they may appear. Almost always they have been selected, filtered, edited, and arranged to support a writer's thesis. Make sure your note includes a context for these facts and figures: the kind of source and the source's thesis or purpose, if you can determine it. Including a context statement is one small way to protect yourself in the event the information is distorted or erroneous. And be sure to take only a few facts and figures for each slip. You probably won't use them all, anyway; nor will you organize them in quite the same way as your source or use them for the same purposes. The fewer the facts on each slip, the more useful they will be. On the opposite page is a table of figures from a government document and below is a note slip taken from it.

Black executions for rape   Nat'l Prisoner St. 110–11
    Between 1930 and 1962 446 people were executed for rape in the U.S. 45 were white, 399 were black. These figures supplied by Federal and State prison officials.
_____

    During this period blacks constituted 10-15% of U.S population, yet almost 10 times as many blacks as whites were executed for rape. Match this with the approximately equal numbers of blacks and whites executed for murder and it begins to seem not only that the death penalty was executed unfairly but also that it was an agent for social control and an expression of racial prejudice.

Primary source bibliographic reference and page number

Writer's synthesis and conclusions— an interpretation of the evidence

Prisoners Executed under Civil Authority in the United States, by Race and Offense: 1930 to 1962

(The figures in parentheses show the number of females. For years 1930–1959 excludes Alaska and Hawaii except for two Federal executions in Alaska, one in 1948 and one in 1950.)

Year	All Offenses				Murder				Rape				Other Offenses[a]		
	Total	White	Black	Other	Total	White	Black	Other	Total	White	Black	Other	Total	White	Black
All years	3,812	1,722	2,049	41	3,298	1,640	1,619	39	446	45	399	2	68	37	31
Percent	100.0	—	—	—	86.5	—	—	—	11.7	—	—	—	1.8	—	—
Percent	100.0	45.2	53.7	1.1	100.0	49.7	49.1	1.2	100.0	10.1	89.5	0.4	100.0	54.4	45.0
1962	47	28	19	—	(1) 41	(1) 26	15	—	4	2	2	—	2	—	2
1961	42	20	22	—	33	18	15	—	8	1	7	—	1	1	—
1960	56	21	35	—	44	18	26	—	8	—	8	—	4	3	1
1959	40	16	33	—	41	15	26	—	8	1	7	—	—	—	—
1958	49	20	28	1	41	20	20	1	7	—	7	—	1	—	1
1957	65	34	31	—	(1) 54	(1) 32	22	—	10	2	8	—	1	—	1
1956	65	21	43	1	52	20	31	1	12	—	12	—	1	1	—
1955	76	44	32	—	(1) 65	(1) 41	24	—	7	1	6	—	4	2	2
1954	81	38	42	1	(2) 71	(1) 37	(1) 33	1	9	1	8	—	1	—	1
1953	62	30	31	1	(1) 51	(1) 25	25	1	7	1	6	—	(2) 4	(2) 4	—
1952	83	36	47	1	71	35	36	—	12	1	11	—	—	—	—
1951	105	57	47	1	(1) 87	(1) 55	31	1	17	2	15	—	1	—	1
1950	82	40	42	—	68	36	32	—	13	4	9	—	1	—	1
1949	119	50	67	2	107	49	56	2	10	—	10	—	2	1	1
1948	119	35	82	2	95	32	61	2	22	1	21	—	2	2	—
1947	153	42	111	—	(2) 129	(1) 40	(1) 89	—	23	2	21	—	1	—	1
1946	131	46	84	1	(1) 107	45	(1) 61	1	22	—	22	—	2	1	1
1945	117	41	75	1	(1) 90	37	(1) 52	1	26	4	22	—	1	—	1
1944	120	47	70	3	(3) 96	45	(3) 48	3	24	2	22	—	—	—	—
1943	131	54	74	3	(3) 118	(1) 54	(2) 63	1	13	—	11	2	—	—	—
1942	147	67	80	—	(1) 116	(1) 57	59	—	24	4	20	—	7	6	1
1941	123	59	63	1	(1) 102	(1) 55	46	1	20	4	16	—	1	—	1
1940	124	49	75	—	105	44	61	—	15	2	13	—	4	3	1
1939	159	80	77	2	144	79	63	2	12	—	12	—	3	1	2
1938	190	96	92	2	(2) 155	(2) 90	63	2	25	1	24	—	10	5	5
1937	147	69	74	4	(1) 133	67	(1) 62	4	13	2	11	—	1	—	1
1936	195	92	101	2	(1) 181	(1) 86	93	2	10	2	8	—	4	4	—
1935	199	119	77	3	(4) 184	(2) 115	(1) 66	3	13	2	11	—	2	2	—
1934	168	65	102	1	(1) 154	(1) 64	89	1	14	1	13	—	—	—	—
1933	160	77	81	2	151	75	74	2	7	1	6	—	2	1	1
1932	140	62	75	3	128	62	63	3	10	—	10	—	2	—	2
1931	153	77	72	4	(1) 137	(1) 76	57	4	15	1	14	—	1	—	1
1930	155	90	65	—	(1) 147	(1) 90	(1) 57	—	6	—	6	—	2	—	2

[a] Armed robberies, 19 kidnapping, 11 burglary, 8 espionage (6 in 1942 and 2 in 1953), 6 aggravated assault.

Adapted from "Executions 1962," *National Prisoner Statistics*, No. 32 (April 1963); rpt. in *The Death Penalty in America*, ed. Hugo Adam Bedau (Chicago: Aldine, 1967).

Paraphrase   A paraphrase is a word-for-word, line-by-line translation of a passage, usually a difficult one, into your own words. It is usually as long as the original, includes all examples and explanations, and respects the design of the original. Paraphrase any passages that you find difficult to understand or that you suspect may trouble your readers if quoted directly. If within your paraphrase you quote any key words or phrases, be sure to enclose them in quotation marks. Below is a paraphrase slip based on an interpretation of Katherine Mansfield's story "The Garden Party":

> When Laura figuratively exorcises childhood by apologizing to the dead man for her festive party hat, the act is intrinsically moral, not only as an assertion of human solidarity, but also because it projects her beyond her mother's way of life. For it is not fanciful to remark that in the story Mrs. Sheridan's "dream" is meant to be, quite literally, immoral.
>
> (Don W. Kleine, " 'The Garden Party': A Portrait of the Artist," *Criticism* 5 [1963]: 363–71)

Laura's apology   Kleine "Portrait" 363

When Laura apologizes to the dead man for her hat, she purges herself of her immaturity. Her act, in Kleine's words, is "intrinsically moral" both because it asserts her recognition of and union with mankind — *Key words quoted*
and because it enables her to step outside her mother's "immoral" dream world.

This world is immoral because it denies the existence of people outside it. This view is similar to — *Explanation of the note and a comparison with a complementary source*
the point D. Taylor makes in "A Dream – A Wakening," but Taylor uses the term "unreal dream" instead of "immoral." Kleine's term is more significant. Kleine also provides more explanation and evidence.

PRIMARY SOURCE NOTE TAKING

You may think that once you have a subject you should head off to the library and begin your research and note taking there. Not necessarily so. You already know that not all research takes place in the library. You will almost certainly end up there, of course, but before you go, you should confront your subject directly, in primary source research. Essentially there are two kinds of research sources. *Primary sources* are direct sources: observation, questionnaires, interviews, experiments, or the original works of a writer. Primary source information is *raw data,* unselected, unfiltered, unedited, and unexplained. *Secondary sources* are indirect sources of information. If primary sources provide raw data, secondary sources digest those data and explain them, interpret them, or support opinions about them. Secondary sources are usually books and magazine articles *about* a subject. You will use both kinds of sources, perhaps secondary more than primary. But in the beginning, at least, and perhaps throughout most of your project, you should try to get your hands on raw data. Do your own thinking *before* you see what others have to say. Where should you look for primary source information? The following sections will show you. Read the ones appropriate to your topic.

Looking Inside Yourself

Chances are you already know enough about your subject to have some tentative opinions. If your ideas are sound, you ought to take credit for them in your essay, but you can't do so if they end up tangled with the ideas you discover in secondary sources. A good reason, then, for writing down what you already know and believe before you read the complex writing of professional researchers. Equally importantly, by writing down what you know now, before you begin your research, you are more likely to uncover weaknesses in your thinking, unwarranted assumptions, or gaps in your knowledge that you will try to repair with your research.

Buy or make yourself a stack of four-by-six note slips and start writing, freewriting style. What you are doing is a more focused version of the exploratory writing you did to find a topic. You may even find that you repeat some of the things you wrote earlier. That's okay. Write down about your subject whatever you know, think, feel, believe, have heard, or have experienced. If you've chosen a subject about which you know little, you'll write only a few slips; if you know a lot, then many. Because you are putting each idea on a separate slip, you don't have to worry about the order of ideas. Now your only concerns are completeness, accuracy, and the dividing up of your ideas. Put your initials in the upper right corner to identify yourself as the source of the information. Rethink your key question and hypothesis in light of what you discover in these notes.

Looking Outside Yourself

Observation   If you have the right kind of topic and the right skills, you may get much of your information through direct observation or experiment. Working with teachers or other experts, you should begin planning now to make these observations. That means locating or identifying your sources of information, writing up reliable questionnaires or other survey instruments, and devising valid experimental procedures. You must take great care that the methods you use to gather your information don't distort or cloud it. Thus your dependency on experts. The notes you take as the result of primary source research should always give the following:

- The context of the information—who did the observing, when, where, under what circumstances.
- Tentative explanations of the causes, consequences, significance, or meaning of the information and your intended uses of it.

Don't let your data remain raw. You'll use much of this commentary later in the paper itself.

Interviews   Some direct observation information may come by interviewing witnesses or other people who have "lived" your subject. Plan your interview carefully. Be clear in your own mind about your objectives and write out your questions. Then make clear and complete arrangements with the interviewee; these include giving your reasons for the interview, the information you want, and your uses of it. The interview itself, like an essay, has a definite shape, a beginning, middle, and end.

- *The beginning* contains the introductory courtesies, a reminder of the purposes for the interview and its subject. Make sure you ask whether the interviewee objects to note taking or a recorder.
- *The middle* consists of questions and answers. Some will be primary: "How long have you worked in the news department at KRKL television?" Some will be follow-up: "What did you mean when you said just now that advertisers exert '*almost* no control' over a news broadcast?" Some questions are closed, like the first example. They ask for specific answers. Others are open-ended: "What changes would you like to see TV news departments make?" In your notes be sure to identify clearly all direct quotations.
- *The end* of an interview is a time for final clarifications, interpretive questions, summing up the interview, and parting courtesies. Ask whether the interviewee objects to being identified and quoted directly in your paper.

After the interview, do an interpretive freewriting in which you explain to yourself, on note slips, your conclusions about the interviewee and the interview. And because you will almost never use a complete, unedited interview, you should divide it into small question/answer episodes, either transcribed from tape, highlighted in the original notes, or cut and pasted onto note slips.

Printed Primary Source Information   Generally we think of books and magazines as secondary sources, "about" a subject rather than the subject itself. There are, however, a number of printed primary sources of raw information:

Newspapers.
Yearbooks.
Almanacs and other fact books.
Atlases and gazetteers (geographical dictionaries).
Census documents and other statistical abstracts.
Biographical dictionaries.

The Appendix (pages 539–551) identifies the most important of these, your library card catalog or reference librarian will help you locate them, and Step 3 will show you how to prepare bibliographic references for them (pages 424–428).

Literary Research

If you're writing a literary research essay, your primary source is the short story, play, novel, poem, or essay that provides your topic. The notes you take from the dialogue, description, figurative language, or plot will provide the evidence to support your interpretive thesis. Gathering this evidence before you read secondary source literary criticism will help you draw your *own* conclusions before you're confronted by others' interpretations and will make you a better judge of their interpretations. Before you start note taking, however, make a bibliography slip for your primary source (see the example below). You will use this slip later to document your borrowing from this source and to prepare your bibliography. See Step 3, pages 424–428, for sample bibliographic entry forms. Find the one appropriate to your source and follow its layout and punctuation exactly.

"Party" — Bibliographic reference

Mansfield, Katherine. "The Garden Party." *The Short Stories of Katherine Mansfield.* New York: Alfred A. Knopf, Inc., 1962. — Complete publication information in correct format

When you begin note taking, take notes by the paragraph. That is, read the *complete* paragraph before you take notes on it. This way you will understand the context of any ideas, images, or dialogue and not risk distorting them. Before you write your note, jot down a brief introduction describing the setting, what's happening, who is speaking to whom about what, the mood. You'll use this information later in your actual essay when you introduce your evidence. After your note, beneath a solid line, give its point: an explanation, a statement of its significance, or the use you intend for it. Of course, you won't be able to explain much in the beginning, but keep after yourself. Your understanding will increase along with your knowledge, and you'll soon be able to write the detailed commentaries that you'll use to explain your evidence in your essay. Finally, give your note a subject heading, bibliographic reference, and page number.

EXERCISE

When you've finished your primary source notes or you're ready to begin using secondary sources, pause to take stock of how far you've come. Give yourself the opportunity to redefine your subject and revise your key question, purpose, and hypothesis. Take note of shifts in your perspective, incorporate discoveries, and rethink your objectives. Get everything as clear in your mind as possible before taking the next step. Complete the following:

In light of my primary source research:

1. I can now phrase my specific research topic as:
2. My key question is now:
3. My purpose is now:
4. What I've discovered about my subject is that:
5. My tentative hypothesis, if different from 4: What I expect to discover/prove/explain/demonstrate/show about ____(my subject)____ is that _____.

I now have _____ days left to finish my research before I begin organizing, writing, and revising my project.

Step 3: Investigating—Using the Library and Preparing a Working Bibliography

AN INTRODUCTION TO LIBRARY RESEARCH

Now you're ready to do what we most associate with research writing: go to the library and gather the printed materials you'll use to write your paper. By writing a key question, hypothesis, and primary source notes beforehand, you've focused and limited the research that lies ahead, and you have a better idea what sources you're looking for than if you had gone to the library as soon as you picked a topic. If you're doing a nonliterary research project, you're looking for the facts, figures, explanations, and opinions that will develop your subject or support your hypothesis. If you're writing a literary research essay, you're looking for explanations and opinions to bolster your interpretation. Once you get to the library, the following guidelines will help you define your search even more precisely and ensure that it goes efficiently and successfully.

How Many Sources?

Although your instructor may announce at the outset a minimum number of sources for you to examine, there is no way you or anyone else can say now the actual number you'll search for and read. If your search goes like most people's, you'll look for four sources before you find one good one. Some you won't be able to find, some that at first seem appropriate won't be, and some will say only a little about your subject. But you'll still want to read as much as possible in the time you have; that will probably mean more than the minimum number of sources. Keep researching until your responsible common sense tells you, "Enough! You've read enough to develop your subject and have just enough time left to organize and present what you've discovered."

What Kinds of Sources?

Try to divide your research as evenly as possible among the following:

- Books.
- Essays in books.
- Articles in magazines or journals.
- Nonprint or unpublished library sources (when appropriate).

Books have room for the long and broad views of a subject. They can offer sense-making generalizations and all the facts and figures to support them. But because they take so long to produce, they're occasionally dated soon after they reach library shelves. This is especially true of books in the sciences. Articles in periodicals are more current and focused. Often they take the narrow and short views of their subjects. But what they gain in limited subjects, density of detail, and timeliness, they often lose in the generalizations that organize, unify, and make sense of a subject. Check both kinds of sources; they complement each other. Essays in books, especially collections of essays by different authors, often turn out to be the best articles published during a certain period, now all gathered together under one roof, so to speak. If not outdated, these may well be your most valuable, trustworthy sources. Nonprint and unpublished materials are the forgotten members in the cast of library sources: television and radio tapes; pictures and graphs; recordings and films; and letters, diaries, and doctoral dissertations. In most research projects they play minor roles, but they may be just what you need to prove a point or to dramatize or illustrate it.

Which Sources?

Spend your time with sources that treat your subject in depth and detail rather than superficially. Before you're finished, you'll probably look at three kinds. (1) Use *popular general sources* with care. They may be written by experts, but they may not be. General encyclopedias like the *Encyclopaedia Britannica* or *World Book,* general interest news magazines like *Time* or *Newsweek,* and "best-seller" books usually fit this category. You may use them for background or introductory reading; however, their information may be dated, oversimplified, or of uncertain authority.

Your most useful sources will probably be (2) *serious general sources,* written by experts for a broad, educated audience. These are articles published in serious general interest magazines like *The Smithsonian, The Atlantic,* and so on, or books put out by major publishers. (3) *Specialized sources* are written by experts for experts. These are articles published in scholarly journals and books brought out by university or specialized presses. If you begin not knowing much about your subject, you'll find these tough going, but once you get a grasp of your subject you may turn to them. The most recent generally contain the most current information and the best-informed opinions.

Spend your time with *the right writers.* Check their credentials whenever possible. Usually you'll find them listed on the dust jackets of scholarly books, at the beginning or end of scholarly articles, or in book reviews (see the Appendix, pages 542–543, for indexes to book reviews). Make sure your writers are experts working in their own fields and that their books have been well received by knowledgeable readers. Popular general interest books and articles may be easy to find and read, but their contents, shaped by current fashions, the pressures of early deadlines, and the attention span of their nonspecialized audience, may not prove the most reliable or informative. Whenever possible, read what the experts write and read.

Try whenever possible to use *the most recent sources.* Especially in the sciences, sources become obsolete quickly. A good practice is to begin searching for materials published in the present and work backward for five to fifteen years, the length of your search depending on your subject. More often than not, the experts you'll read have, as a matter of professional responsibility, studied the most important earlier sources and incorporated them into their own more recent writing. Only if you're doing historical research should you violate this practice. If, for example, you're investigating what Americans knew of Nazi persecution of the Jews, of course you would want to read newspapers, magazines, and books published before World War II. But these you would treat as primary rather than secondary sources.

If yours is a controversial subject, strive for *balance in your research.* The experts are biased, too, sometimes unduly so. Do not depend too heavily on one author, publisher, or school of opinion. Divide your investigation among competing opinions. Read those you disagree with. You'll end up with a clearer, fairer presentation of your subject and a better defense of your thesis. One of your aims, remember, is to sample a range of expert opinion and then make a judgment about which seems most sound.

Which Libraries?

Like sources, libraries are not all created equal. Local community libraries may be rich in local archival materials, but they don't always have the scholarly sources specialized research requires. If you don't find what you want in the card catalog or reference room of a community library, check to see whether it has a lending program with other, larger libraries. Of course, you'll spend most of your time in college or university libraries, but even these have their specializations and limitations, and you may need to visit several. You may also want to contact nonacademic organizations (businesses, religious and political organizations, legal and medical offices, and museums). Often they have specialized but excellent libraries. In any event, always call ahead to a library you intend to visit for the first time; not all libraries are open to everyone at any time. Finally, get to know your reference librarians. Their expertise is the library itself: knowing where everything is, how to find it, and how to use it. If you're having trouble, don't hesitate to check with them. Their job is helping you.

❧ IDENTIFYING SOURCES

Begin looking for your sources even before you get to the library. When professional researchers have to find the right sources for a project, many begin by talking to other experts, in person, by phone, or letter, to see what they recommend. Why should they waste valuable time? Why should you? Get in touch with a professor or other expert.[3] If you have to write a letter, your reference librarian will help you locate a directory of corporate names, officials, and addresses.

When you get to the library, resist the temptation to do what you usually do: head straight for the card catalog. It will tell you only what that one library contains. At the beginning of your search you want to know about *all* that is available on your subject—in your library and elsewhere—so plan to spend some time in the reference room with *bibliographies* and *indexes.* These are systematic listings of books, articles, and nonprint materials on particular subjects and authors. Most are book length and published monthly or annually. Some now appear on microfilm, as well, and many are included in the computerized information retrieval services subscribed to by many libraries. The Appendix, pages 540–546, lists the most important of these bibliographies and indexes and shows you how to use them; spend a few minutes browsing through its pages and identify the ones you want to consult. Your reference librarian will help you locate and use them.

PREPARING BIBLIOGRAPHY NOTE SLIPS

As you search bibliographies or indexes and find titles that sound relevant, write them down on note slips, along with the accompanying publication information. Put down all you'll need now to find your sources and later to document your borrowing. Sometimes, however, a bibliography will not give you all you need to make a complete entry; when that happens, leave blank spaces on your note slips to be filled in when you locate the actual book or article. Use slips rather than lists on sheets of paper because individual slips, each with its own source, will be more useful as you search for titles, add and drop sources, and arrange them for your documentation. One shortcut is to mark off sheets of paper, write your entries within the lines, and cut the sheets when you begin to search for the sources themselves. List as many sources as you can find. You won't find them all or use all you do find, so at the beginning you want to give yourself as many as possible to choose among. On pages 421–422 are three bibliographic entries for the most common kinds of sources, first as they appear in indexes and then as you will translate them onto bibliography slips.

Standard Bibliographic Formats

As you can see from the these three examples, bibliographic entries do not all have quite the same format. They differ in the information they contain, their arrangement, and punctuation. The various indexes you consult will use several formats, you'll use another to make entries on your note slips, and later, in other courses, you may use still others. Your responsibilities as a researcher are to know which formats are appropriate for your present project, to follow them faithfully in all their particulars as you write your entries, and to make your entries complete. You *must* be exact here, first so that you can use your entries to find and document your sources and then so that your readers can use them. The formats you'll learn in the following pages have been authorized by the Modern Language Association and are widely accepted for academic and professional writing. They'll stand you in good stead for most of your college writing. But if you write papers for courses in mathematics, the biological or phys-

A Book

Tanaka, Jack. Classroom Management; A Guide for the School Consultant. Springfield, Ill.: Charles C Thomas, 1979. 199 pp. [Bibliog. and glossary incl].

LB 3013
.T35

Consultant

Tanaka, Jack. Classroom Management; A Guide for the School Consultant Springfield, IL: Charles C Thomas, 1979.

Library: Harper's - yes

Read ✓

An Essay in a Book Length Collection of Essays

11525. Boyer, Paul. "Minister's Wife, Widow, Reluctant Feminist: Catherine Marshall in the 1950's," 253-71 in Janet Wilson James, ed. Women in American Religion. Philadelphia: U of Pennsylvania P. 274 pp.

"Wife"

Boyer, Paul. "Minister's Wife, Widow, Reluctant Feminist: Catherine Marshall in the 1950's." In Women in American Religion. Ed. Janet Wilson James. Philadelphia: U. of Pennsylvania Press, 1980. 253-71

Library:

Read:

An Article in a Periodical

```
Acid rain and gray snow. G. R. Hendrey. bibl (p 100-1) il
        Natur Hist 90:58-65 F '81
```

"Acid"

Hendrey, G. R. "Acid Rain and Gray Snow." ————— Title of article
Natural History ————————————————————— Title of periodical
90 (February 1981): 58-65 ————————— Volume number, date,
and page numbers

Library: S. C. State – yes   Read: ✓
Harper – no

ical sciences, or psychology, you'll want to check with your instructors to find out which formats they require. Each of these subjects has its own.

The Modern Language Association bibliographic entries contain the following information, arranged and punctuated in the ways shown.

The Author's Name   Always write the first author's name *last name first*, then the given name, followed by a period. This arrangement enables entries to be organized alphabetically. Use square brackets to indicate parts of a name that are known but not given or to identify the true name when a pseudonym is given, e.g., *T[homas] S[tearns] Eliot* or *Mark Twain [Samuel Langhorne Clemens]*.

Chapter or Essay Title   Enclose chapter and essay titles in quotation marks, closed with a period.

The Title of the Work   Always take the title from the title page. Separate the title from the subtitle by a colon. Underline the complete title and close it with a period. But when a normally underlined title appears within another underlined title, do not underline the shorter title. For example, here is a book title that contains another book title: *The Popular Imagination, Southern History, and* Gone with the Wind.

Editors, Translators, or Compilers Follow the names of editors, translators, or compilers with a period. If you are using statements made by the editor of a book, e.g., the introduction or notes, list the editor's name at the beginning of the entry. Do the same if you find only an editor's name given in a bibliographic index. Later, if you use an author's work in the anthology compiled by that editor, you will put the author's name at the beginning of the entry and move the editor's name to its customary position following the title.

Edition and Volume Numbers List the edition you have used whenever it is not the first, followed by a period. List the number of volumes with this particular title, followed by a period, e.g., 5 vols.

Series If the book is part of a series, write the title of the series and an arabic numeral indicating its place in the series, followed by a period. Do not underline the series name or enclose it with quotation marks.

Publication Information (1) A *book:* list the place of publication, colon, publisher, comma, date of publication, and a period. If several cities of publication are given, list only one, the one in which the book originated or a major city. If the city is not well known, give the state or country as well. In bibliographies and works cited, you may shorten the publisher's name: use the publisher's last name; use the *first* last name if the publisher's name includes more than one person; or use the first key word, e.g. *Random,* for Random House. Use the original publication date unless you are using an edition other than the first. If you are using a reprint by a different publisher, give the original and reprint dates of publication. If you are using only one chapter or essay from the book, follow the date of publication with a period, two spaces, the inclusive pages of that section, and another period. (2) An *article:* the title of the periodical, underlined, followed by the volume number, the date of publication (see the sample entries for the appropriate use of parentheses), a colon, and the page numbers of the article.

Incomplete Entries If an index does not give complete bibliographic information, do not simply skip that part of the entry. The only exception to this rule is an anonymous or unsigned work. If no author is given, begin the entry with the title of the work (see the following sample entries). In every other case, think of an entry as a series of pigeonholes. Every pigeonhole must have something in it. If you do not find the information you need, use the following abbreviations.

- No publisher given = *n.p.*
- No place of publication = *n.p.*

- No date = *n.d.*
- No page numbers = *n. pag.*

In its most extreme form, an incomplete entry would look like this: *The Autobiography of an Unknown Man.* N.p.: n.p., n.d. N. pag. Obviously, you must do everything you can to locate complete bibliographic information. Generally all you have to do is examine the front- or backmatter of a work.

Spacing and Indentation   When you have finished a project and are writing your bibliography or list of works cited, double-space within and between entries. The first line of an entry begins at the left margin; second and subsequent lines of an entry are indented five spaces (see the sample bibliography, pages 431–433).

Punctuation   Close each block of information in an entry with a period: *Author. Title. Editor. Edition. Number of volumes. Series. Publication information.*

Use the following models to prepare your bibliographic note slips. If you don't find the exact model you need for a particular entry, the list of conventions given in the preceding paragraphs will enable you to determine the proper format.

Bibliographic Entries for Books

A Book with One Author
Tanaka, Jack. Classroom Management: A Guide for the School Consultant. Springfield, IL: Charles C Thomas, 1979.

Two Authors
Van den Haag, Ernest, and John P. Conrad. The Death Penalty: A Debate. New York: Plenum, 1983.

Three or More Authors
Frampton, Merle E., et al. Forgotten Children. Boston: Sargent, 1968.

    [*et al.* is short for *et alia* ("and others").]

A Pseudonym (Pen Name)
Twain, Mark [Samuel L. Clemens]. The Adventures of Tom Sawyer. New York: Macmillan, 1962.

Committee or Group Author
Consumer Reports Books. The Medicine Show. Mount Vernon, NY: Consumers Union of the United States, Inc., 1955.

Anonymous Author
Sir Gawain and the Green Knight. Ed. J. A. Burrow. Baltimore: Penguin, 1972.

A Short Work in a Collection

Landes, William M. "An Economic Analysis of the Courts." Essays in the Economics of Crime and Punishment. Ed. Gary S. Becker and William M. Landes. New York: National Bureau of Economic Research, 1979. 164–214.

> [Each essay in this collection is considered a separate source. If a researcher used five essays from this one book, she would, in fact, have five different sources.]

An Essay Reprinted in a Collection of Essays

Lind, Ilse Dusoir. "The Calvinistic Burden of Light in August." New England Quarterly 30 (Sept. 1957): 307–29. Rpt. in Light in August and the Critical Spectrum. Ed. John B. Vickery and Olga W. Vickery. Belmont, CA: Wadsworth, 1971. 79 95.

> [The original source of publication is given first, then the reprint source. You will usually find original sources listed on an acknowledgments page at the beginning or end of the collection or at the bottom of the first page of each essay.]

A Book That is a Volume in a Series

Durrell, Lawrence. Mountolive. Vol. 3 of The Alexandria Quartet. 4 vols. New York: Dutton, 1959.

A Book Published in Several Volumes (One Title for All Volumes)

Walker, Ernest, et al. Mammals of the World. 3 vols. Baltimore: Johns Hopkins UP, 1964.

Introduction, Foreword, Preface, or Afterword

Kalisch, Beatrice J. Introduction: "Putting Child Abuse and Neglect into Perspective." Child Abuse and Neglect. By Ray E. Helfer, M.D. Westport, CT: Greenwood, 1978.

An Editor's Comments in a Book

Fromm, Erich, ed. 1984. By George Orwell. New York: Harcourt, 1949.

Revised or Englarged Edition

Parker, Rolland S. Emotional Common Sense: Avoiding Self-destructiveness and En-hancing Personal Development. Rev. ed. New York: Harper, 1981.

A Series

Doyle, Edward, and Samuel Lipsman. America Takes Over, 1965–67. The Vietnam Experience 1. Boston: Boston Publishing, 1982.

An Edition Other Than the First

Hart, James D. The Oxford Companion to American Literature. 4th ed. New York: Oxford UP, 1965.

> [UP identifies a university press.]

Reprinted Edition

James, Henry. Hawthorne. 1879. Ithaca: Cornell UP, 1966.

A Translation
Camus, Albert. The Stranger. Trans. Stuart Gilbert. New York: Random, 1954.

The Bible
The Holy Bible. The King James Version.

> [Do not underline Bible titles.]

A Dictionary
The Random House Dictionary of the English Language: College Edition. 1968 ed.

Pamphlets

Heinl, J. Lawrence. How to Grow Better House Plants. 11th ed. Toledo, OH: A Green Thumb Product, 1971.

Reports or Bulletins

Agency Bulletin. Vol. 26, no. 1. Springfield, IL: Independent Insurance Agents of Illinois, 1983.

Periodical Articles

An Article in an Annual, Semiannual, or Quarterly Journal
Joyce, Christopher. "Safer Aircraft Fuel." New Scientist 3 (1981): 680–780.

> [In this type of periodical, pages are numbered consecutively throughout a volume, from one issue to the next.]

An Article in a Journal Numbered Separately for Each Issue
Dubois, Paul E. "Promoting Physical Fitness in the Fire Service: A Statewide Effort." Fire Journal 78.3 (May 1984): 51–55.

> [The first number after the journal title is the volume, the second, the issue number.]

An Article in a Weekly or Monthly Periodical
Magnuson, Ed. "Child Abuse: The Ultimate Betrayal." Time 5 Sept. 1983: 20–22.

> [Begin entries for unsigned magazine articles with the title of the article. Abbreviate months of publication except May, June, and July. When an article is not printed on consecutive pages, give the first page and a plus sign, e.g., 36+ .]

A Review
Ellmann, Richard. "The Nation's Conscience." Rev. of An American Procession, by Alfred Kazin. The Atlantic June 1984: 121–24.

Newspaper Articles

Newspaper Article
Watson, Jerome. "Reagan Assures Nation on Gulf." Chicago Sun-Times 23 May 1984, sec. 1: 1–2.

> [Begin entries for unsigned newspaper articles with the title of the article.]

Editorial
"Exit Polls No Threat." Editorial. Daily Herald [Arlington Heights, IL] 7 May 1984,
  sec. 1: 8.

Letter to the Editor

Hyman, Lawrence W. Letter. The New Republic 4 June 1984: 4.

Government or Corporate Publications

Commission Report
President's Commission on the Assassination of President Kennedy. Hearings before
  the President's Commission on the Assassination of President Kennedy. 26 vols.
  Washington: GPO, 1964.

Government Report
United States. Cong. House. Sub-Committee on Science, Research and Technology.
  Genetic Engineering, Human Genetics and Cell Biology. 96th Cong., 2nd sess.
  Washington: GPO, 1980.

  [The formats for government publications are many and varied. The order of
  an entry is usually: Government body. Subsidiary body. Title of document. Author if known (By . . .). Identifying numbers and publication information.]

Corporate Publications
Rand McNally & Company. All about Bicycling. Chicago: Rand, 1975.

Encyclopedia Articles

Brodman, Estelle. "Special Libraries." The Encyclopedia Americana. 1983 ed.
  [Begin entries for unsigned encyclopedia articles with the title of the article.]

Unpublished Sources

A Dissertation
Hine, William Cassidy. "Frustration, Factionalism, and Failure: Black Political Lead-
  ership and the Republican Party in Reconstruction Charleston, 1865–1877." Diss.
  Kent State University, 1979.

A Personal Letter
Bresnahan, Roger J. Letter to the author. 7 May 1984.

Nonprint Sources

Official Testimony
Stienmetz, Suzanne. Testimony before the Select Committee on Aging. The Serious
  Problem of Elder Abuse. U. S. House of Representatives. 97th Cong., 1st sess. 3
  Apr. 1981.

Lecture or Speech

Lowe, John W. "The Forward March of Wharton's A Backward Glance." American Literature II: Literature after 1870, Midwest Modern Language Association. Minneapolis, 4 Nov. 1983.

Interview

Munro, George. Telephone interview. 9 May 1984.

Radio or Television Program

"Hunger in America." Narr. Charles Kuralt. Writ. Peter Davis. Prod. Martin Carr. CBS Reports. WBBM, Chicago. 21 May 1968.

Play (a performance)

The Country Wife. By William Wycherley. Dir. Peter Hall. With Albert Finney. Olivier Theater, London. 27 Dec. 1977.

[Cite the text of a play as you would a book.]

Film

Hiroshima Mon Amour. Dir. Alain Resnais. Argos-Daiei-Como-Pathe Productions, 1959.

Recordings

Ellington, Edward Kennedy ["Duke"]. "Harlem Airshaft." The Duke Ellington Carnegie Hall Concerts, December 1947. Prestige, P-24075, 1977.

Computer Software

Lutus, Paul. Apple Writer II. Computer Software. Apple Computer, Inc., 1982. Apple IIe, 64KB, disk.

❧ LOCATING SOURCES

When you've prepared bibliography slips for all the sources you think you'll want to consult, you're ready to locate them and begin reading. But as you read, always keep an eye out for new sources that weren't listed in the indexes you consulted. Check bibliographies at the backs of books and the ends of articles; check foot- and endnotes. Make new note slips as you go along.

Periodicals

To see whether your library has the articles you're looking for, you'll have to find out how it catalogs its periodicals. Some libraries include them in the regular card catalog, but most list them separately in their own catalog or more simply in looseleaf folders, binders, pamphlets, computer printouts, or metal filing wheels. In these lists you'll find what periodicals the library carries, how long it has been accumulating them, what volumes it has of each, and which are available only on microfilm or microfiche.

Recent issues you will most often find, unbound, in a periodicals room. Back issues are collected at the end of a year or complete volume, bound in hard cover, and placed into a special section of the library's stacks—or, with increasing frequency, back issues are microfilmed and filed in cabinets. "Bound periodicals" are often arranged alphabetically by title, but in some libraries they are now arranged, like books, by call numbers. Be sure to look for call numbers when you consult the periodicals catalog and, if you find them, write them on your bibliography slips. When you've located the articles you want, you will either have to take your notes there, in the reading room, or photocopy them; most libraries do not permit periodicals to circulate.

Books and Nonprint Sources

To see whether your library has the books, records, tapes, or films you want, you will, of course, check the card catalog or its equivalent computerized catalog. Each work in a particular library is listed on at least three cards:

1. An author card.
2. Title card.
3. Subject card.

If you're doing a nonliterary research project, you'll look up books by first finding your subject heading. If you're doing a literary research essay, you'll begin with the author's name, since in the broadest sense he or she is your subject. If the card catalog doesn't have the subject heading you want, check the *Library of Congress Guide to Subject Headings*. You may need to search under a cross-reference. On pages 430–431 are examples of the three kinds of cards you'll find. As you can see, they are all versions of the same card. Only the headings differ.

To find a book once you've located its card, you must use the call number that classifies it, either a Dewey Decimal or Library of Congress number. Most libraries arrange their holdings according to one or the other system of classification but not both—although the cards in their catalogs may have both numbers printed on them, as the samples do. When the latter is the case, write both call numbers in the upper left corner of your bibliography slips. That way, you can find the books no matter what library they're in. The libraries you visit will probably have brochures introducing you in detail to their catalog systems; be sure to ask.

If when you get to the stacks you can't find a book you're looking for, check with the librarian. The book may be in a preshelving area, about to be put back on the shelves. If it is checked out, a call for it can be sent to the current borrower, or another copy may be available through interlibrary loan. If you have no luck there, then on to another library. Continue until you've gathered as many sources as possible. You may have to

Subject Card

Author's name   Subject   Title

Library call number

Place of publication, publisher, and date

Number of pages, portrait, size of book

Includes a bibliography

Subject classification

Library of Congress classification number   Dewey Decimal System number

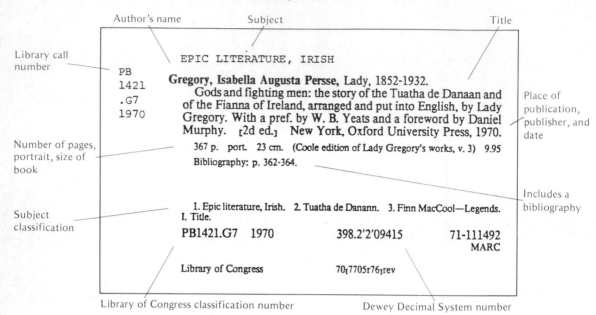

```
         EPIC LITERATURE, IRISH
PB
1421     Gregory, Isabella Augusta Persse, Lady, 1852-1932.
.G7          Gods and fighting men: the story of the Tuatha de Danaan and
1970      of the Fianna of Ireland, arranged and put into English, by Lady
          Gregory. With a pref. by W. B. Yeats and a foreword by Daniel
          Murphy.  [2d ed.]   New York, Oxford University Press, 1970.
             367 p.  port.  23 cm.  (Coole edition of Lady Gregory's works, v. 3)  9.95
             Bibliography: p. 362-364.


             1. Epic literature, Irish.  2. Tuatha de Danann.   3. Finn MacCool—Legends.
          I. Title.
             PB1421.G7   1970        398.2′2′09415         71-111492
                                                              MARC

             Library of Congress        70[7705r76]rev
```

Title Card

```
         Gods and Fighting Men
PB
1421     Gregory, Isabella Augusta Persse, Lady, 1852-1932.
.G7          Gods and fighting men: the story of the Tuatha de Danaan and
1970      of the Fianna of Ireland, arranged and put into English, by Lady
          Gregory. With a pref. by W. B. Yeats and a foreword by Daniel
          Murphy.  [2d ed.]   New York, Oxford University Press, 1970.
             367 p.  port.  23 cm.  (Coole edition of Lady Gregory's works, v. 3)  9.95
             Bibliography: p. 362-364.


             1. Epic literature, Irish.  2. Tuatha de Danann.   3. Finn MacCool—Legends.
          I. Title.
             PB1421.G7   1970        398.2′2′09415         71-111492
                                                              MARC

             Library of Congress        70[7705r76]rev
```

430

Author Card

> PB
> 1421
> .G7
> 1970
>
> **Gregory, Isabella Augusta Persse,** Lady, 1852-1932.
>   Gods and fighting men: the story of the Tuatha de Danaan and of the Fianna of Ireland, arranged and put into English, by Lady Gregory. With a pref. by W. B. Yeats and a foreword by Daniel Murphy. [2d ed.] New York, Oxford University Press, 1970.
>   367 p. port. 23 cm. (Coole edition of Lady Gregory's works, v. 3) 9.95
>   Bibliography: p. 362-364.
>
>
>   1. Epic literature, Irish.   2. Tuatha de Danann.   3. Finn MacCool—Legends.
> I. Title.
>
> PB1421.G7   1970   398.2'2'09415   71-111492
>   MARC
>
> Library of Congress   70[7705r76]rev

interrupt your reading later to locate new sources, but try to keep these distractions to a minimum.

EXERCISE: A WORKING BIBLIOGRAPHY

When you've made bibliography slips for all the sources you think you'll want, write a "working bibliography." This is a kind of wish list, a systematic presentation of all the sources you'd like to look at if you had the time and could find them all. By writing it out, you'll demonstrate to yourself and your instructor that you know what sources are available and how to present bibliographic information in a conventional format. Later, having deleted unused or unavailable sources, you'll use this working bibliography to prepare the final bibliography or works cited list that will accompany your finished project.

To prepare a bibliography, arrange your slips in alphabetical order according to the last name of your authors and copy out your entries. Remember these conventions: (1) Do *not* number your entries. (2) If an entry has no author, alphabetize it along with your other sources, but use the first key word of its title (excluding *A, An,* and *The*). For example:

Schelling, Thomas C. The Strategy of Conflict. Cambridge, MA: Harvard UP, 1963.
"Servants of a Higher Ideal," *New Life* 29 Sept. 1983: 47–50.

(3) If you have two or more sources by the same author, arrange them alphabetically by the first key words in the titles. Give the author's name for only the *first* entry. Before all other entries by the same author, put three hyphens followed by a period.

Kleine, Don W. "An Eden for Insiders: Katherine Mansfield's New Zealand." College English 27 (1965): 207–09.

---. " 'The Garden Party': A Portrait of the Artist." Criticism 5 (1963): 360–71.

On the opposite page is a brief example of a working bibliography.

Step 4: Investigating—Taking Secondary Source and Planning Notes

✎ READING SECONDARY SOURCES

Reading for research is different from most reading you do, even other reading for your college classes. Most reading, after all, is a passive sort of activity. You're not doing anything special, just waiting for what your reading will do *to* you, whether inform you, move you, sway you, confirm you in an opinion, or entertain you. When you read for research, however, you're reading actively, with a sharp focus and immediate purpose. You're looking for something specific, even when you don't always know quite what it is. You're not waiting to see what your reading will do to you; you're trying to see what you can do with it. Therefore, you must read in a different way.

What to Look for When You Read

Reading for research, you're looking for all the "matter" of your subject. But this subject matter is probably broader and more complex than you think. You're looking for six kinds of information:

Evidence   Evidence is the facts and figures that will develop your subject and prove your hypothesis. Evidence will fill the majority of your secondary source note slips.

Inferences   Inferences are the conclusions and judgments that your sources have made about their evidence. Some you will use to support your conclusions, others you will quarrel with and try to show as erroneous or incomplete.

Explanations   Facts and figures alone are never enough to complete a project. You want to understand their meaning and significance and then communicate both to your readers. You'll look to secondary sources for these explanations.

Title centered 1 inch from top of page

Working Bibliography

Two works by the same author

Birren, Faber. Color Psychology and Color Therapy. Rev. ed. New Hyde Park, NY: University Books, 1961.

Double-space throughout the bibliography

---. Light, Color and Environment. New York: Van Nostrand Reinhold, 1969.

A work by two authors

Bornstein, M. H., and L. E. Marks. "Why Colors Look Different." Psychology Today Jan. 1982: 68.

A standard book entry

Halse, Albert O. The Use of Color Interiors. New York: McGraw, 1968.

Journal entry

Kane, L. "The Power of Color." Health 14 (July 1982): 36-37.

Libby, William Charles. Color and the Structural Sense. Englewood Cliffs, NJ: Prentice, 1974.

Unsigned article

"The Many Voices of Color." House Beautiful Feb. 1976: 51.

Nassau, K. "Causes of Color." Scientific American 243 (Oct. 1980): 124-25.

Packard, Vance. The Hidden Persuaders. New York: Simon, 1957.

Magazine article

"Raise Your Color Consciousness--an Expert Tells You How." Redbook Feb. 1978: 70-72.

Seebohm, C. "Color--the New Prescription for Health." House and Garden Mar. 1976: 34.

Indent 5 spaces

Illustrations   You'll want to make clear and vivid both your evidence and explanations, and so you'll be looking for examples, striking details, anecdotes, and analogies that will dramatize your subject for your audience.

Authoritative Pronouncements   Backing by authorities makes your evidence look more trustworthy and your opinions more credible.

The State of the Knowledge of Your Subject   In its broadest sense, your paper is not only about a subject but also about the knowledge of that subject. As you research, you want to look for answers to these questions:

- What is not yet known about my subject?
- Who believes what? How have my sources arrived at their conclusions? Are their methods sound? What are the strengths and weaknesses of their positions?
- Who agrees with whom? Where are the controversies? Whose side am I on? Why?
- Which sources complement or supplement other sources?
- Who are the reigning authorities?

Your research objective should be to draw sound conclusions about your subject *and* about what are the best information and opinions. The challenging research subject is never cut-and-dried. Facts are in doubt, opinions conflict, and you must make decisions.

Where to Begin Reading

Although you'll end up something of an expert on your subject, you're not an expert yet, so you want to begin your research with the general and introductory sources that do not require an expert's knowledge but will provide you with the background necessary to understand more specialized studies later on. Before you begin reading, spend a few minutes arranging your sources from introductory to advanced, general to specific. Examine tables of contents, forewords, and introductions. Consider where articles have been published; read one in *Psychology Today* before one in *The Journal of Orthopsychiatry*. Arranged in this way, your reading will be systematic rather than haphazard, and you'll read your way gradually into the complexities of your subject.

How to Read

Rarely will you read a source—especially a book—from beginning to end; nor will you always read at the same pace. With a book, begin by looking at the table of contents for chapters relevant to your subject or those that provide necessary background. Or turn to the index at the back and look up key words associated with your subject, taking note of synonyms. After reading the introduction to give you an overview and a feel for the author's bias, you'll probably spend the rest of your reading in the chapters you've identified. With a periodical article, read the introduction, then begin to skim, looking for topic sentences and key words that identify your subject. Often you need to read only the first lines of paragraphs to tell whether they're of value. When you find something relevant, slow down and read those parts with care, taking in every word. Beware, however, of reading out of context. Be sure you see how the part you're reading fits with the author's larger purpose, design, or explanation. One of the most common errors made by student researchers is misrepresentation of a source. The best way to prevent it is always to read by the paragraph: read through the *entire* paragraph before you take a note, and make sure your note tells how your borrowed information fits the scheme of ideas in that paragraph. And beware, too, that your reading may reveal new gaps in your knowledge. To fill them you may have to return to the library, gather new sources, and read some more.

COPING WITH THE CHAOS OF RESEARCHING

As you take secondary source notes, something unsettling will happen. Some of the doubts you had in the beginning about your topic, the library, and finding sources will begin to disappear, but in their place will come all sorts of new questions. More disturbingly, you may also discover that the topic you originally wanted to research has little written about it, that what you expected to find is different from what you're actually finding, or that you've found far more than you expected, more than you'll ever be able to digest in the time available. If you're the kind of person who folds your socks, sorts them by color, and arranges them neatly in your dresser drawer—or even if you aren't—the chaos that is part of any research project will sometimes be difficult to bear. What you need is a method for managing it, a way to manage your mounting stacks of notes, your new questions, and new ideas.

The first half of this method is really a state of mind more than a method, an openness to change. Be prepared to change your mind about any part of your project and adapt it to what your sources supply. After all, you can only do what they will let you. You can't bend information or ideas to fit the preconceived notions you had at the beginning of your project. That would be distortion. There's nothing wrong with narrowing, expanding, or shifting your subject in the middle of your research if your materials require it. Nor is there anything unusual about discovering that a first hypothesis is wrong or that preconceptions are just that. You may have thought at the outset that this was your subject, all nice and neat and symmetrical:

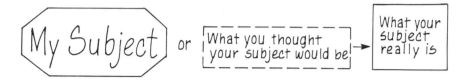

Now you know from your research that your subject is like this:

This evolution in the shape and content of your project is natural to every investigative process. Researching well is like walking on ice: you won't get across unless you have great balance and the ability to change direction and pace quickly.

The second half of this method for managing chaos is *planning slips*, the fourth kind of note taking. The human mind is such a messy marvel. It never works in nice, neat stages, and that's part of the reason for the chaos you feel. One part of your mind will be working on one problem while another is doing something else. You'll get ideas for one part of your project while working on another or when not doing anything at all, just standing in the shower perhaps. Don't put them aside, telling yourself you'll remember them later; you won't. Jot them down on primary or secondary source notes. At the same time you'll be getting all sorts of other ideas, not about the contents of your paper so much as the paper itself, ideas about the following:

- Introductions and conclusions.
- Patterns of organization.
- Illustrations and other devices to communicate your ideas.
- New versions of your key question or tentative thesis.
- Topic sentences that will organize parts or paragraphs.
- Transitional strategies that will get you from one part to the next.
- Good lines that bring ideas into focus.
- Persuasive strategies for your persona, role, or style.

Write these ideas on planning slips. They'll provide you with the opportunity to plan the script for your paper and conduct a preliminary rehearsal before you get down to the serious dress rehearsal and preview performances of outline and preliminary drafts.

Your aim as you take all four kinds of notes—bibliography, primary, secondary, and planning—is to get down on paper *everything* you'll use to write your paper, all of your plans, information, explanations, and interpretations. You will not, in the end, take notes on all your paper will say, but the more you write down now, the less you'll have to think of later and the more time you'll have to do what the composing step is all about: getting your ideas to flow together in a coherent style.

EXERCISE

When you reach the halfway point of your secondary source note taking, pause once again to take stock of your project. Give yourself the opportunity to evaluate its most important elements and fix your purposes clearly in mind.

In light of my secondary source research:

1. I can now state my specific research topic as:
2. My key question is now:
3. What I'm discovering about my secondary sources:
   a. Who agrees with whom? What are the controversies?
   b. Which sources complement or supplement each other?
   c. What I expected to find that I did not? What I am finding instead?
   d. Which sources are the best? What makes them so?
4. My tentative thesis:

   What I want to prove/explain/demonstrate/show about _____(my subject)_____ is that _____. What I mean to say is that _____.

I now have _____ days left to finish my research before I must stop, organize my notes, write and revise my paper.

END NOTES

1. For a fuller redefinition of college research projects, see Richard L. Larson, "The 'Research Paper' in the Writing Course," and Robert Schwegler and Linda Shamoon, "The Aims and Process of the Research Paper," *College English* 44 (Dec. 1982): 811–24. See also Thomas Tryzna, "Approaches to Research Writing: A Review of Handbooks with Some Suggestions," *College Composition and Communication* 34 (May 1983): 202–07.

2. For the suggestion of an evaluative research project I am grateful to Dean Memering, *Research Writing: A Complete Guide to Research Papers* (Englewood Cliffs, NJ: Prentice, 1983).

3. For this networking suggestion I am grateful to Thomas Tryzna, "Approaches to Research Writing: A Review of Handbooks with Some Suggestions," *College Composition and Communication* 34 (May 1983): 202.

Chapter 17

The Research Project: Writing and Revising

❧

Step 5: Organizing—Getting Ready to Write

As you've been taking notes, your concentration has probably been divided between the subject of your paper and its design. Even before you've discovered all you want to say, you've been thinking about how to say it. And that's as it should be. You already know that writers produce good writing not all at once, in one draft, but little by little, each idea and draft bringing them closer to the ideal they see in their mind's eye. Your objective now, somewhere in the middle of this evolutionary process, is discovering a design that will carry your project to a successful finish, one that will make meaning out of the jumble of slips on your desk and enable you to say all you want to. As you try out possible patterns for your paper, use these standards to decide which is best. The good design is:

- *Appropriate,* suitable to your purpose and audience.
- *Clear in its divisions,* its subtopics clearly related to one another but also clearly separate.
- *Logical,* that is, systematic in its arrangement of your subtopics, one topic leading naturally to the next.
- *Emphatic,* stressing what is most important by locating it in important positions near the beginning or end.

PLANNING FOR FORM

Finding a Design

Begin looking for the good design in the same three places you'd look if this were any other writing project: in the subject itself, your purposes for writing, or your readers' reasons for reading.

The Parts   Like a neatly peeled and sectioned orange, some subjects fall naturally into their parts. If you've been taking careful note slips, your subject headings will probably reveal these parts to you. Thumb through your notes, make a list of these headings, and sort them out.

The Thesis   You know from Chapter 6 that some thesis statements contain in their assertions a mini-outline for a whole paper. Each assertion provides a major topic heading. For example:

> The nature of the television medium creates disadvantages that prevent it from providing complete news coverage. Besides these inherent disadvantages, there has been a trend toward popular, entertaining news shows, and this trend has further reduced the amount of significant information presented.

> I. Inherent disadvantages of TV as a news source.
> II. The trivialization of news by the need to entertain.

The Classic Organizing Patterns   If you're clear about your purposes, you'll probably see your materials begin to fall into one of the classic patterns described in earlier chapters. If your purposes are informative and explanatory, see Chapter 6, pages 117–127, especially the order of importance, classification, analysis, and problem/solution patterns. If you're writing a scientific, technical, or fieldwork report, see Chapter 13, pages 292–293. If you're writing an argument, see Chapter 14, pages 358–360, especially the pro/con and rebuttal patterns. If you're writing a review of research, you may organize it according to this standard pattern: first a classification of sources into groups, an explanation of their differing views, and then an evaluation of these groups, to establish the most informative, insightful, and useful.

The State of Our Knowledge   You may find a design by examining the evolution of our knowledge of a subject, say, what scientists once thought of the atom and sub-atomic particles, what they now know, and how they have made their discoveries. Or you may trace the evolution of your own understanding of a subject, organizing your paper by comparing appearance with realities, what you once thought, what you think now, and the process of your enlightenment.

The Gimmick   You may find a pattern in some imaginative ploy, possibly a hypothetical story that will organize and present your information. For example, one way to examine the damage acid rain has inflicted upon the United States would be to take a series of boat trips, first in the less severely damaged waters of the Midwest and then in the virtually dead lakes of the Northeast.

Whatever you do, however, by all means *avoid* organizing your paper in terms of your sources, first what one has to say, then another, then the next, and so on. Your paper is about your subject and thesis, *not* about your sources. Perhaps the hardest part of research writing is taking other people's ideas, information, and opinions and making them serve your purposes. You'll have little chance of success if you fail to incorporate them to your design. Remember our nation's motto: *E Pluribus Unum,* from many, one. That's your goal, to integrate your sources into one coherent presentation. You'll reach that goal if you keep this organizing hierarchy in mind:

1. Organize your major ideas into a logical pattern.
2. Sort your note slips so they support each major idea.
3. Then, and only then, sift your sources, select those that provide the best support, and arrange them according to the topics they support.

Creating a Communications Strategy

The crush of information and the complexities of organization are so great for many beginning researchers that they forget the importance of a communications strategy. Here as elsewhere, however, a pattern will organize your ideas, but it won't communicate them. As you take primary and secondary source notes, you should be writing planning slips to develop this strategy.

A Finished Thesis   Make sure you've evolved your thesis into a statement that is clear, precise, complete, and sound. If you don't understand clearly what you want to say, your readers won't either. Revise on planning slips until you get it right. Statements that are too general will not give you much direction; nor will they help your readers make clear predictions about the contents of your paper.

An Overgeneral Thesis
   If humanity continues to pollute the air the way we are today, we will certainly destroy our planet.

Revision
   If humanity continues to pollute the air as we are today, this planet could become like our sister planet, Venus: hot, lifeless, desolate. By increasing the amount of CO_2 in the atmosphere through air pollution, we are also increasing the "greenhouse effect" and overheating the atmosphere. If we reach a critical

point, the "greenhouse" effect" could trigger a runaway heat increase and destroy life on the planet.

An incomplete thesis has the same effect as an overgeneral one. There is no sense of purpose; things don't add up.

A So? Thesis
Women have been on the march campaigning for equality since the American Revolution.

Revision
Women have been on the march compaigning for equality since the American Revolution. Their progress can be marked by several landmark cases decided in the U.S. court system. Without these legal decisions, women today would have no basis on which to continue their pursuit of equality.

A question thesis is a contradiction in terms. Thesis statements don't ask questions, they answer them.

A Question
Does the evidence reveal that the Shroud of Turin could possibly be the burial garment of Jesus Christ, or is it a fraud of some sort?

Revision
Using the evidence available to us through photography, the Gospels, medical science, and other scientific technologies, we can show that the Shroud of Turin is not a fraud, that it contains the images of a human being, that these images were caused by means not known to us, and that it could be the burial Shroud of Jesus Christ.

An ill-formed or imprecise thesis makes it hard for a writer to organize a research project and harder for the reader to understand.

A Poorly Designed Thesis
In "Greenleaf," by Flannery O'Connor, symbolism is used to explain Mrs. May's conflicts and death. What I mean to say is that by studying the symbolism of the bull and sunlight throughout the story, one can gain a better understanding of Mrs. May.

Revision
In "Greenleaf," by Flannery O'Connor, the symbols of the bull and sunlight are used throughout the story to represent Mrs. May's loneliness, her conflict with the natural world, and her desire for control. In ironic ways these symbols foreshadow her violent death.

Audience   Your instructors are always your primary audience for your research project, and your aim is to communicate to them your understanding of your subject and the research process. But you are also writing to a larger secondary audience whose makeup depends on your purposes. Those are the people you want to inform, the ones you want to persuade, or the scholars whose information you've borrowed and whose work you're evaluating. Construct a profile of these readers: Who are they? What don't they know about your subject? What do they need to know? What might they like to know? Who is the most sympathetic member of this audience you can imagine? Plan to write to this member of your audience.

Persona   Generally speaking, the persona for research papers writes in public, writer-style sentences rather than talker-style. This persona is no cold fish but is nevertheless somewhat reserved. State your opinions, certainly, and argue your case vigorously; even make an emotional appeal if necessary. But the impression you want to create is that of a writer who is fair, interested in a thorough presentation of the facts however they affect the issues, and aware that these issues have more than personal importance.

Introduction   Plan now for an opening that will set the mood and direction for what follows. The good opening for the research paper is the same as any good opening: it captures your audience's attention, leads to your thesis, and creates a bridge between the real world and the world of your essay. Almost any opening strategy from Chapter 7 can be adapted here. However, the technical, informative, and evaluative purposes of research writing make these strategies especially appropriate:

- Begin with a *summary* of earlier research to narrow your subject and provide background. Then describe the evidence you will examine and the methodology you will use. This is the standard opening for a scholarly research report.
- Begin with an *analogy* to help readers imagine or understand your subject.
- Begin with a *definition* of a term crucial to your subject, but be original.
- Begin *personally*, with what you once thought about your subject or what piqued your interest in it.
- Begin with the *problem* you want to solve for which your thesis is the solution.
- Begin by presenting the *position of those you're quarreling with*; your thesis will be your opinion.

Here is an effective introduction:

Dramatization of the conditions in which the problem appears

Take a look through any contemporary "woman's" magazine and what you're likely to see on almost any page are diet ads of one kind or another. "Lose pounds fast!" they exclaim. "Eat what you like while still losing weight!" The models glamorized in these magazines are exclamation point thin, long, gaunt celebrations of the results of fasting. Diet and exercise books written by famous personalities such as Victoria Principal and Jane Fonda only feed the anti-food craze. Running, aerobics, tennis, and other sports are today's leisure time activities; those who aren't involved are bound to feel lazy, fat, out of style. Thinness is definitely the fad—in fashion, in Hollywood, in everyday U.S.A. And it is true that watching one's weight and keeping in

Transition statement to the true subject
shape are both healthy ideals to live by. But like other good things, they can be abused. When thinness and dieting are taken to extremes, they can result in a disorder called anorexia nervosa.

Definition of the subject
Anorexia nervosa is a dieting disease in which the afflicted becomes obsessed with the idea of staying slim. Excessive dieting and exercise continue until the dieter's body is nothing more than a weakened, bent skeleton. Ironically, even though the dieter fears food and weight gain, she thinks about both constantly. I say *she* because 95 percent of all anorexics are women who come from the upper middle and upper classes. Because anorexia is on the increase, or at least being diagnosed more frequently, much has been

Narrowing the subject
written about it in newspapers and popular magazines. The symptoms are familiar to most. Less well known are the causes.

After studying patients with anorexia nervosa, experts have formed four theories about its causes: psychological, familial, sociological, and biological. A "true cause" has not yet been found, because some patients have not been clearly influenced by forces within any of these four categories. Never-

Thesis paragraph
theless it is generally accepted that some combination of psychological, familial, and sociological influences helps create the anorexic. A few experts believe that there are direct biological causes, but their theories appear quite weak.

The body of the essay
The psychological cause is the anorexic's desire to gain self-control. Dieting seems to her to be a gesture of discipline and power. . . .

Conclusion It is difficult now to anticipate the mood and contents of your conclusion, but at least you can plan what kind of close will be appropriate to wrap up your paper. Professional researchers often employ these strategies:

- Close with an *anecdote* that dramatizes or sums up the point you've been trying to make.
- Close with a *look into the future* of your subject; identify the paths future investigators should follow.
- Close with a *warning* about what will happen if something is not done about your subject.
- Close with a *personal word* about your relation to your subject.
- Close with a *generalization about life* implied by your treatment of your subject.
- Close with a *quotation,* provided that you don't just quote and then stop. It is your paper; you ought to have the last word, if only to explain a powerful closing quotation.

- Close with the *long view*, a statement of how your subject fits into a larger subject of which it is a part.
- Close by giving the *limitations of your research*, stating what it hasn't done or where it may be unreliable or invalid.
- Close by *referring* to something you said in your introduction.

Illustrations   Invent any illustrations you will need to explain or dramatize your subject.

Emotional Appeal   If an emotional appeal is appropriate to your project, plan for it now. Rousing your readers' emotions may be necessary if they are to do what your thesis proposes and your paper reasonably argues.

Your Good Character   Plan ways to demonstrate your fairness, learning, and wisdom, so your readers will recognize you as trustworthy and be more inclined to accept your opinions.

A SHORT COURSE IN OUTLINING

You know from Chapter 6 that outlining is not the only organizing strategy, but it is especially useful for projects like research papers that contain large amounts of information and depend heavily on logical designs. Whatever the contents and purposes of your writing, you can use outlines in four ways: as a tool for preliminary planning, a device for testing the logic of your thinking, a guide for writing, and a test of your organization *after* you've written a draft. For research projects you'll write two and possibly three outlines, each a version of the others: a sketch, working, and final outline.

The Sketch Outline

A sketch outline is just that, a preliminary sketch of your design, the outline of an outline, a logical list of major points, the bare bones you want to cover with the body of your essay. And that's all—no introduction, no conclusion, no minor topics, no presentation of any parts of your communications strategy. All you want to do in your sketch outline is discover and test the order of your major ideas. You'll probably try a number of these brief outlines before you find the one that meets all the standards for a good design listed at the beginning of Step 5.

When you think you've hit on a pattern that may work with your subject, try sketching it on a planning slip. List the major topics or parts of your essay after roman numerals; put subtopics after capital letters. An example:

I. Positive aspects of TV news.
   A. More timely than print news sources.
   B. Visual impact greater than that of print sources.
II. Problems inherent in the medium.
   A. Misleading visuals.
   B. Lack of time.
   C. Confusing news show formats.
III. Problems of the push for ratings.
   A. Competition prompted by the desire for profits.
   B. Entertainment consultants hired to reshape shows.

Now see whether your sketch outline actually does organize your subject by sorting your primary, secondary, and relevant planning slips into piles according to your outline's major divisions. Then subdivide the slips for each topic heading into subtopic piles. If you can't decide where a particular slip should go, make a copy of it and put the original in one pile, the copy in another. Decide later, when you make the final arrangement you'll follow as you write your paper, where that note really belongs. If all your important note slips do not fit onto your piles, your design is wrong. Try again. Slips that seem irrelevant or unimportant or that don't fit what is otherwise a good design should be put onto a discard pile. But don't throw them away just yet. You don't know now what you may suddenly need while writing your rough draft.

Three Secrets of Effective Outlining

You Cannot Divide a Topic into Only One Subtopic If you have a I, you must also have a II, if an A, then at least a B, if a 1, then a 2, and so forth. An outline slices the pie of your ideas. If you slice the pie once, you have halves, I and II. If you then slice one of those halves, you have two smaller slices, I. A. and I. B. If you are trying to divide a subject and discover that you have only one subtopic, what you really have is not a subtopic but a restatement of the original topic. *Not:*

III. The use of color associations to influence behavior.
   A. Advertisers' uses of color.
      1. To distort the images of products.
      2. To evoke positive color associations.
IV. The use of color by interior decorators to influence perceptions.

But:

III. The use of color by advertisers to influence behavior.
   A. To distort the images of products.
   B. To evoke positive color associations.
IV. The use of color by interior decorators to influence perceptions.

Avoid Long Coordinate Columns of Topics or Subtopics   These usually indicate that you've failed to see relationships among individual topics in the series. What you must do is group related subtopics and list (subordinate) them under major topic headings. *Not:*

    I. Mrs. Sheridan's manipulation of her daughters' experiences.
    II. Her manipulation of their thoughts.
    III. Her manipulation of their feelings.
    IV. Her manipulation of their actions.
    V. Her confinement of her daughters in a "dream world."
    VI. The features of this dream world.
    VII. The motives of her behavior.
    VIII. Her eldest daughter's failure to escape this dream world.
    IX. Laura's escape.

But:

    I. Mrs. Sheridan's manipulation of her daughters.
      A. What they see.
      B. What they think.
      C. What they feel.
      D. What they do.
    II. The "dream world" to which Mrs. Sheridan would confine her daughters.
      A. Its features.
      B. Mrs. Sheridan's motives.
    III. The success of her daughters in escaping this world.
      A. Her eldest daughter's failure.
      B. Laura's success.

Subdivisions Must Be Logical   Because subtopics represent divisions of the topics that they stand beneath, they must reflect the form amd even repeat the language of those larger topics. To fail to make subtopics fit their topics is like slicing a cherry pie and discovering that one of the slices is cherry, another boysenberry, one spinach quiche, one pepperoni pizza, and one lemon meringue—not a very appetizing or logical pie! The individual slices of a subject must have the same ingredients as the whole subject; that is, subdivisions should repeat thematic tags from the headings they divide. *Not:*

    I. Women in eighteenth- and nineteenth-century America.
      A. Jobs.
        1. The Revolutionary War.
        2. The Civil War.
        3. Discrimination.
      B. The vote.

It is not clear how "Jobs" and "The vote" are proper subdivisions of "Women in eighteenth- and nineteenth-century America," or what two the wars have to do with "Jobs." *Instead:*

  I. The social standing of women in eighteenth- and nineteenth-century America.
    A. As workers.
      1. No job discrimination during the Revolutionary and Civil wars.
      2. Pervasive job discrimination after both wars.
    B. As political participants.

Both the headings and subheadings have been reworded to reflect the true purpose of this section, a descriptive analysis of women's social standing. Now it's clear how one topic leads to the next and how subtopics divide the topics they stand beneath.

The Working Outline

Having organized the major topics and subtopics of your essay into a sketch outline and sorted your note slips accordingly, you're ready to make the working outline that, with those slips, you'll use to write the first draft of your paper. Your working outline will be the longest and most detailed of your three outlines. It should account for *all* that you want to say.

- Introduction.
- Thesis.
- All major topics, subtopics, and their subdivisions, including evidence, illustrations, explanations, and quotations.
- Transitions.
- Conclusion.

Your working outline is the dress rehearsal for your first draft, in turn a kind of preview performance of the finished project. The more detailed and complete you are here, the more insightfully and coherently you'll write later.

Prepare your working outline by subdividing your piles of noteslips—already divided once or twice when you made your sketch outline—into successively smaller piles. Arrange the notes in the smallest piles into the order you'll actually follow as you write your paper. Then, using these piles, write a fully expanded version of your sketch outline, now your working outline. When you have completed dividing and subdividing, arranging, and planning your working outline, you're ready to write your first draft.

The Final Outline

In some college classes a final outline is required for the finished research project. If it is, you'll prepare this outline *after* you've completed all your other writing and revision. The first two outlines were for your benefit; the last is for your readers, to give them at a glance an overview of the contents and design of your paper. It should include your thesis, account for the major topics and subtopics of your paper, and follow these conventions exactly.

Omit Introduction or Conclusion Headings   Because an introduction and conclusion in your paper are taken for granted, these headings are unnecessary. If you write something substantive in either place, indicate it in your outline by labeling its subject matter or function, e.g., I. *Review of Research*, I. *Description of the Problem*, and so on.

Use Either the Topic or Sentence Outline Format   Be consistent in outline format. A *topic outline*, comprising only single words and phrases, looks easier to do; in fact, it is harder. At any one level of subdivision, the topics are understood to be coordinate or equal in value. Idea I is equal in value to idea II, idea A is equal to B, idea 1 is equal to 2, and so on. Because these statements are logically equal, they must also by convention be made grammatically equal. That is not always so easy to do. *Not:*

  I. The Sheridan family's "dream world" [noun phrase].
    A. Orders reality [verb phrase].
      1. Arranging the garden [participial phrase].
      2. Mrs. Sheridan manipulates her children [clause].
    B. In the "dream world" [prepositional phrase].

But:

  I. The Sheridan family's "dream world" [noun phrase].
    A. Its nature: an ordering of reality [noun phrase].
      1. The arrangement of the garden [noun phrase].
      2. Mrs. Sheridan's manipulation of her daughters [noun phrase].
    B. Laura's life in the "dream world" [noun phrase].

For a *sentence outline*, on the other hand, you need not worry about the intricacies of grammatical parallelism. Here every statement is grammatically equal to every other because no matter how brief, all statements are complete sentences.

  I. The Sheridan family lives in a "dream world."
    A. It is a reordering of reality.
      1. It rearranges the natural world to suit the family's fancy.
      2. It rearranges the social world to suit the family's aristocratic class consciousness.
    B. Laura lives happily in this world until she reaches young adulthood.

The sentence outline has one other benefit besides its ease. With only a little revision, its complete sentences often become the introductory, tran-

Sketch Outline

Double-space twice

    That colors provoke powerful human reactions, sometimes highly subjective, is nothing new. What is new is the extensive and sometimes unsettling use made of this knowledge. In advertising, interior design, medicine, even in prisons, color is used to influence moods, attitudes, and behavior, sometimes for questionable ends.

Double-space twice

I.   The physical properties of color: hue, saturation, and brightness

II. Factors determining color preference

   A. Physiology: age and sex

Double-space throughout

   B. Culture

   C. Family and social standing

III. The uses of color

Topic outline format

   A. In advertising to influence behavior

      1. To distort the images of products

      2. To evoke positive color associations

   B. In interior design to influence perceptions

      1. To change impressions of size and shape

      2. To change impressions of heaviness and brightness

      3. To change impressions of room temperature

      4. To give prison inmates illusions of reduced strength

   C. In medicine to change attitudes and behavior

      1. To speed healing after surgery and enhance exercise therapy

      2. To calm manic-depressive patients

      3. To reduce suicide rates

Note that numbers are outdented rather than indented

449

sitional, topic, or explanatory sentences of the actual paper. In this respect, a sentence outline is a kind of rough draft for a rough draft.

Standard Outline Subdivisions

I. A. 1. a. (1) (a)
II. B. 2. b. (2) (b)

EXERCISE

Find an appropriate pattern for your research project, sort your slips into topics and subtopics, and then write a sketch outline. Your outline will test the logic of your thinking, prepare you to write a working outline, and demonstrate your understanding of the conventional outline format. An example sketch outline appears on the previous page.

Step 6: Composing

❧ DRAFTING

Rough drafts, like the finished ones they precede, may be good or not so good, depending on the way they are written. The good rough draft is one that makes revising easiest and creates those features of good writing that appear most naturally at the drafting stage. You'll make the rough draft of your research paper a good one if you're prepared for the special challenges it will throw before you. The most obvious is one of space and organization, arranging all your notes, outlines, books, and other materials so that everything you need to write your draft is comfortably available at your fingertips. You don't want to risk breaking your concentration or coherence to rummage for a misplaced note or source. A greater challenge is the length of your project. Your research paper may be so long you'll have to write it in several sessions, posing one more risk to coherence. You'll reduce that risk if you leave yourself convenient starting places for the next session. Conclude one session when you reach the end of a major section but not before you've written the transition or introduction to the new section you'll write at the next session. Give yourself that thread to pick up when you return.

Integrating Source Materials

Your greatest challenge will occur in integrating source materials: introducing facts, figures, quotations, and opinions; weaving them with other facts, figures, quotations, and opinions; stitching them into the fabric of your ideas; explaining them, handling several sources at once; and then documenting all of your borrowing. No matter how closely you follow your outline and note slips, if you don't take care, your paper could end up like a raggedy coat, tatters of this idea and that held loosely together by frayed transitions.

The Pattern for Borrowing You'll make your writing easier if you keep in mind two pieces of advice: First, be clear in advance about your reasons for borrowing. Every fact, opinion, or quotation ought to contribute clearly to your intentions. You will borrow for four reasons:

1. To support an idea or opinion.
2. To dramatize a subject.
3. To illustrate or explain it.
4. To sum up.

It's always easier to know *how* to present a piece of information if you know *what* it's there for. Second, most borrowing is a three-step process, one you will learn to vary into interesting, artful patterns.

1. *Introduce your borrowing.* Put others' words and ideas in context. Tell how they fit into your essay and how they fit the sources from which they've come. If you need to earn respectability for a piece of information, if it is a fact that may be in dispute, or if it is an opinion, begin by giving the author's name (full name for first references) and, if necessary, the author's credentials or the name of the work you're borrowing from. Try using a variety of words to characterize your sources. It is boring to write only *Author A says . . . , Author B says . . . , Author C says . . . ,* Instead, try introductions like these:

> According to Irene Herr, president of BioSystems International, . . .

> Daniel C. Locker suggests . . .

or advises, argues, asserts, believes, declares, defines, denies, describes, hints, hopes, indicates, reports, responds, reveals, urges, warns. Here are two examples of well-introduced borrowing:

Assertion
Introduction of a
supporting source

Topic sentence

Source's credentials

Explanation of the
evidence

Television has also become America's most trusted news source. According to a Roper Poll, 51 per cent of Americans find TV news most believable, compared to only 22 per cent for newspapers (Barrett, *Rich News* 7).

Hospitals are also leaning toward the use of brighter, more brilliant colors. On the advice of Marcella Graham, a medical technologist, color consultant, and interior designer, one hospital achieved "immediate and positive" results when it repainted each floor (Kane 36). Use of pumpkin orange, strawberry pink, emerald green, and lavender produced surprising results: elderly men were encouraged to get out of bed and shave, female patients requested makeup and combs and visited in the halls, and the morale of the staff improved (Kane 36).

2. *Present the quotation, summary, or paraphrase itself.*

3. *Explain the borrowing.* Don't assume your readers will get your meaning by themselves. Don't belabor the obvious, but help them understand how your borrowing supports the point of your paragraph or thesis. Here are two examples:

Topic statement

Source elaborates on topic

Explanation of a term from the source

Because the family plays such an important role in the anorexic's life, family therapy is often used in conjunction with other types of treatment. "Family therapy focuses heavily on challenging the enmeshed styles within the family" (Garfinkel 293). An "enmeshed" family is one in which members often seem to intrude on each other's thoughts and feelings, creating too much sharing, togetherness, and a lack of privacy (Garfinkel 182). Overprotection by the family discourages independence and increases the normal apprehension accompanying adolescence.

Topic

Supporting source and her credentials

Explanation of evidence from the source

In building interiors, deep colored walls appear heavy; pale, pastel walls appear light (Halse 47). This also applies to objects. In an experiment performed by Bonnie Bender, color marketing manager at Pittsburgh Paints, workers had "considerably" more difficulty when lifting physically light boxes painted black than heavy boxes painted white (Kane 36). Further research of my own to explain this phenomenon only produced similar results. Could this response be explained by the fact dark colors seem "perceptually heavier" due to their absorption of more light than lighter colors? I believe so.

Taking Credit for an Idea   Occasionally you'll get an idea about your subject only to discover later that some of your sources have already had the same idea. You want to take credit for your original thinking, but you don't want to appear guilty of plagiarism. What to do? Begin by presenting the idea as your own, in your own words. Then, in a sentence or two, acknowledge that your sources have had the same idea. Perhaps quote the best among them and explain, if necessary, how your idea differs from theirs. In this way you take credit for having the idea on your own but demonstrate you are not alone in your thinking. Your sources will give your idea added weight. An example:

The writer makes an assertion

Using a source for support

Using other sources

Disagreement with sources

Yet, as we shall see, Joe Christmas is as much a foil to characters like Joanna Burden and Reverend Hightower as Lena Grove is to him. Unlike Joanna and Hightower, the Joe we meet at the beginning of *Light in August* is, in Alfred Kazin's words, still "trying to become *someone*, a human being, to find the integrity that is so ripely present in Lena Grove" (99). A number of other readers have also noticed this potentiality and aspiration in Joe, but none seems fully aware that his striving for an identity is the key to his character and central to the design of the novel (Howe 68; Chase 104). Abused though he may have been, Joe still has not lost completely the healthy qualities Lena possesses so abundantly.

Working with Several Sources at Once Presenting source materials is for most research writers like pinning clothes to a clothesline. We hang them one at a time until we reach the end. There will be times, however, when you'll need to handle several sources at once: when comparing and contrasting, presenting both sides of an argument, reviewing research, or summarizing complementary sources. You have to be careful here or you'll end up with your sources, like wet wash, tangled together, a confusing knot for your readers. There are two ways to solve this problem gracefully. The first is to summarize all your sources at once, without mentioning their names. Follow the summary with an endnote number referring readers to the end of your paper and a note that lists their names. This way you give credit to your sources but do not clutter your text with a list of their names.

Summary statement
Endnote number

Conclusion about findings

Explanation of the conclusions

From my research I have found the causes of anorexia nervosa to fall into three major categories: the psychological, familial, and sociological.[3] The physical causes I looked for seemed to be symptoms or by-products of the illness, not actual causes. One important conclusion I have reached is that all cases vary. A model of the anorexic family does not fit all patients' families. Many people live in families that meet the anorexic family type but do not develop the illness, while some patients have families radically different from the model yet do develop anorexia. Anorexia doesn't simply happen because all the predisposing factors are present. Even though a patient has many of the characteristics common to anorexia, a tragic event, such as separation from parents, a death in the family, personal illness, or a disruption of the homelife, may be necessary to trigger the illness.

The second way to handle multiple sources is to nominate a spokesperson, perhaps the best known, to speak for all the sources in a group. Again, you would document all your sources in a single group endnote.

The writer's position

A spokesman for the opposition and his opinion

Writer's rebuttal

Reverend Hightower's is a failed life, contrasted at the end of *Light in August* by Joe's tragic affirmation and Byron Bunch and Lena Grove's comic triumph. He is anything but the redeemed man that so many readers, among them Cleanth Brooks, take him to be[5]. Brooks argues that Hightower is reborn, brought back into the life of the community by his aid at the birth of Lena's child: "He has finally dared something and has broken out of his self-centered dream" (*Country* 69). I argue, however, that his rebirth is a miscarriage and that Hightower soon returns to the "self-centered dream" he has served for so many years.

Quotations The most important advice for weaving sources into your paper is to quote briefly. Quote often if you wish, but keep quotations short. Few readers read long quotations, they interrupt the flow of your sentences, and you must use or explain every word you quote. Whenever possible, make your quotations less than a sentence and connect them grammatically to your own ideas and sentences. Use ellipsis points where required to signal that you've omitted words from your source. If a quotation does not fit grammatically with your introductory sentence, precede the quotation with a colon (:). Two examples:

Introduction
Elipsis to signal
an omission

According to Richard Salant, former president of CBS News, "Anyone who has ever prepared to deliver a television broadcast, as I have . . . knows how difficult it is to make facts known or events understandable" (Diamond 63). He continues, "I'm afraid we compress so well as to almost defy the viewer and listener to *understand* what we say. And when that becomes the fact we cease to be communicators."

Source's credentials

The color pink, specifically a shade known as Baker-Miller pink, has been widely used but with "mixed results," according to research conducted by Alexander Schauss at the American Institute for Biosocial Research in Tacoma, Washington. Dr. Schauss's study suggests that pink is especially effective in calming manic and psychotic juveniles" (Miller 227). Another study, of 153 men at the U.S. Naval Correctional Center, showed similar results: "Baker-Miller pink can curb aggressive tendencies, and actually reduce strength. At last count . . . more than 1,400 hospitals and institutions in America are using pink for its tranquilizing effects" (Kane 37).

Introductory colon

A Source Within a Source   Occasionally you'll read a source (A) that quotes or summarizes another source (B). You want to take information from the second source (B). Whenever possible, try to find the original (B). It is possible something has been lost in transmission and that source (B) is inaccurate or incomplete as it appears in (A). If you cannot find the original, however, announce the secondhand nature of your borrowing in your paper. For example, in his essay opposing capital punishment, Charles S. Milligan (source A) quotes the theologian Reinhold Niebuhr (source B).

To take a Christian approach [to the death penalty] we must find out what the situation is. This amounts to saying that the good Samaritan must use his eyes and his head as well as have compassion. He must see what is wrong and use his best reasoning to deal helpfully and effectively with the problem, using the means available. As Reinold Niebuhr says:

A community may believe, as it usually does, that reverence for life is a basic moral attitude, and yet rob a criminal of his life in order to deter others from taking life. It may be wrong in doing this; but if it is, the error is not taking the life but in following a policy which does not really deter others from murder. The question cannot be resolved on *a priori* grounds but only by observing the social consequences of various types of punishment.

If you wanted to use the original Niebuhr source (B) but could not find it, you might write, "In his argument against capital punishment, Charles

S. Milligan quotes Reinhold Niebuhr . . .," quote Niebuhr from Milligan, and then document Milligan (A) as your source. In your bibliography or works cited you would acknowledge first the original source (B) and then your source (A).

Niebuhr, Reinhold. <u>Moral Men and Immoral Society</u>. New York: Scribner's, 1932. Quoted in Charles S. Milligan. "Capital Punishment: A Christian Approach." <u>Social Action</u> Apr. 1961: 19.

Avoiding Plagiarism

Only the unethical or ignorant writer would borrow information without acknowledging its sources, but conscientious writers sometimes plagiarize unaware because they are uncertain what borrowing must be documented and what need not be. The absolute but often vague rule: *You must document in a note or the text of your paper the source of any quotations, ideas, or information not in the common domain.* Did you get that? You must document your borrowing whether you take an author's actual words or only the ideas. Both belong to the author. To fail to document a borrowing is plagiarism, a form of theft.

Of course you will always acknowledge the sources of all opinions and interpretations you borrow, but it's not always easy to tell about facts. Columbus's discovery of the New World in 1492 is a fact that presents no problem, but what should a writer do with the fact that television news shows present an average of 16 ½ minutes of news per half hour? Should she document that? Well-known facts, quotations, and proverbs are considered in the common domain and need not be documented. Even facts and quotations new to you need not be documented if they are repeated unattributed from one source to the next. If your sources treat a fact as common knowledge, you may, too. If many sources cite without documentation that TV news shows spend only 16 ½ minutes on the news, then that is common domain information and need not be documented. But if only one source presents that fact, it is original information and must be documented. One caution: if you *quote* or *paraphrase* one writer's presentation of public domain information, you must document that. The facts may belong to everyone, but the words or organization that contain them belong to the source.

If you've chosen a subject about which you know little, you will have to document often. Your aim is not to churn out pages and pages of documentation; your aim is to master a subject. But if most of your paper is borrowed, you must acknowledge that fact. You want to lend credibility and authority to your writing, and if it takes many borrowings and much documentation to do so, then so be it. When in doubt, document.

One final caution about inadvertent plagiarism: Beware of letting summaries and paraphrases drift into direct quotations presented without quotation marks. If you have taken careful notes, you'll know when you're quoting and when not. Even single words taken from the original source must be quoted if the author has invested them with significant or personal meaning. Always, of course, you will put quotation marks around phrases, clauses, and complete sentences quoted from the original.

You will document your borrowing, take credit for your research, and avoid plagiarism by providing parenthetical documentation or endnotes. Footnotes, once the standard, are now used rarely. Both parenthetical documentation and endnotes are appropriate for all your college writing, but each is not appropriate for every course, and there is more than one format for each method. Be sure to find out which methods and formats your instructors prefer.

PARENTHETICAL DOCUMENTATION

Parenthetical documentation is the simplest, most contemporary documentation method, the one you saw in many of the preceding examples. If you use this method, you will document your borrowing parenthetically in the text of your paper. With slight alterations of format this method is acceptable for writing in almost every academic discipline. The Modern Language Association format, used for papers in the humanities, consists of four variations.

1. Give only the *page number* of the source when you introduce a borrowing with the author's name and when you're using only one source by that author. Always place parenthetical documentation at the end of a borrowing, after quotation marks, but *before* the final period, like so: (57). With block quotations, place the parentheses two spaces after the last punctuation mark. For example:

> It is Frank N. Magid who dictated the hard-and-fast rule that no news item be more than ninety seconds in length, no matter how important. A ninety-second story is called a minidocumentary. It is also Magid who brought us "Happy Talk." According to Ron Powers:
>
>> Happy Talk owes much of its identity to the bantering remarks made among anchormen, reporters, weathermen and sportcasters during transitions from topic to topic. But the concept has a much broader scope. It defines a newscast that is weighted toward the trivial . . . and away from the abstract, the disturbing, the vital. . . . (26)

2. Give *a shortened version of the title and the page number* when you introduce a borrowing with the author's name and you're using *more* than one source by that author. Use this same form of documentation when citing unsigned or anonymous works. No punctuation separates the title and page number. In the following example, a student documents a quotation from a periodical article.

Thus, as Walter Slabey suggests, when Joe Christmas flees the sharecropper's cabin, he comes near to the end of his "night journey, a ritual of death and rebirth, of withdrawal and return" ("Ritual" 334).

3. Give *the author's last name and the page number* when you do *not* introduce your borrowing with the author's name and when you use only *one* source by that author. No punctuation separates the author's name and the page number.

Stories that can reach TV audiences almost instantly may not appear in newspapers until the following morning. In this sense, "the news . . . on television makes the front page of the morning's paper obsolete" (Schwartz 86).

4. Give the *author's last name, a shortened title, and the page number* when you do *not* introduce your borrowing with the author's name and when you are using *more* than one source by that author. A comma separates the author's name and the title; no punctuation separates the title and page.

Along with political coverage, news consultants discourage use of any stories that are hard to explain or visualize. Their excuse is that the public doesn't want them (Barrett, *News* 120).

Preparing parenthetical documentation is simple. Just include it in the appropriate places as you write your rough draft. Later, when your readers read your paper, this documentation will refer them to the "Works Cited" at the end of your paper, where you'll list complete publication information for every source you've used. If they wish, interested readers can use this list to locate and read your sources. The layout of the "Works Cited" is the same as for the working bibliography described in Step 3, pages 431–433, with one difference: the "Works Cited" contains *only* works you've actually used in your paper. To prepare your "Works Cited," cross off from your working bibliography any sources you don't actually use in your paper, change its title, and recopy. Everything else remains the same. If you wish to take credit for additional background reading, list alphabetically *all* the works you've consulted, whether you've cited them in your paper or not, and title this list "Works Consulted."

The only notes you'll need in a paper with parenthetical documentation are content notes. The convention of research writing is to avoid these notes whenever possible. But there may be times when you'll need to provide information or explanation that cannot be worked into the body of your paper:

- Definitions.
- Formulas.
- Explanations.
- Translations.
- Cross-references.

- Opinions.
- Group documentation of several sources.

When this is the case, put raised numbers in your text (like so[3]) to refer your reader to a page headed "Notes" containing all your notes in consecutive order. This page immediately follows the text of your paper and precedes your "Works Cited." Center its heading one inch from the top of the page, double-space throughout, and indent the first line of each note five spaces. Raise the note number one-half space and leave a space between the number and the note. Here's a sample passage you read earlier containing a note number and parenthetical documentation:

> Reverend Hightower's is a failed life, contrasted at the end of *Light in August* by Joe's tragic affirmation and Byron Bunch and Lena Grove's comic triumph. He is anything but the redeemed man that so many readers, among them Cleanth Brooks, take him to be.[5] Brooks argues that Hightower is reborn, brought back into the life of the community by his aid at the birth of Lena's child: "He has finally dared something and has broken out of his self-centered dream" (*Country* 69). I argue, however, that his rebirth is a miscarriage and that Hightower soon returns to the "self-centered dream" he has served for so many years.

On the notes page, this group documentation note would read:

[5] For the opinions of these readers see Langston 60; Williams 205; Sandstrom 542; Abel 78; Lind 80; Pitavy 24; and Olga Vickery, The Novels of William Faulkner 111.

ENDNOTE DOCUMENTATION

Endnotes give a project the neatest, least cluttered look and make the text easiest to read. Because all notes—documentary and content—appear together in one place at the end of the paper, there is nothing in the text to distract a reader except the raised note number placed at the end of a borrowing or reference. It is for this reason that many prefer this method. If you plan to use endnotes, however, don't number your borrowings while writing your rough draft. You'll do that when you prepare the endnote pages of your final draft. You can't foresee now whether you'll want to add or drop notes later; numbering them now will only complicate revision. Instead, weave your source materials into your paper and, at the end of each borrowing, where you will eventually put a note number, write your note between parallel lines exactly as it will appear on your notes page (see the example on the opposite page).

When you've finished revising your paper and everything is set the way you want it, write your note numbers and prepare your notes pages:

1. Reread your paper and number your borrowings in brightly colored ink (so you won't miss them while recopying).

Color is produced when "light energy of various wavelengths is reflected from surfaces or emitted by luminous objects."

M. H. Bornstein and L. E. Marks, "Why Colors Look Different," Psychology Today Jan. 1982: 68

Short wavelengths are blue; longer waves run toward green; the longest are red.

2. Number them consecutively from the beginning to the end of your paper (do *not* assign each source its own number; use a new number for each borrowing, 1, 2, 3 . . . 33, 34, 35, even if several numbers refer to the same source).
3. Use arabic numerals without periods, parentheses, or slashes. Raise these numbers one-half space above the line and put them at the first break *after* the borrowing, outside all punctuation except dashes, like so.[25]
4. Copy out the final draft of your notes pages from the notes in your text. Your notes should conform to the following conventions.

The Standard Endnote Format

Because notes are just that, notes, they are intended to read as complete sentences. Thus, the format for endnotes differs somewhat from that for bibliographic entries.

- *Indentation.* Indent the first line of each note five spaces. Make second and succeeding lines flush with your left margin.
- *Note numbers.* Raise note numbers one-half space and place them at the beginning of each note, without punctuation, separated from the note itself by one space.

    [1] Virginia DeMoss, "All about Anorexia Nervosa," Runner's World Sept. 1981:78.

- *First References.* The note that documents your first borrowing from a source must, like the preceding example, include complete bibliographic information.
- *Second and later references to a source.* The forms *Ibid.* ("in the same place"), *op. cit.* ("from the work cited"), and *loc. cit.* ("in the place cited") are no longer used. For successive or later references to a source you've already cited in full, you need give only the author's last name

and page numbers of the borrowing. A later reference to the source cited previously:

   2 DeMoss 79.

However, if you use more than one work by an author, you will also have to use a shortened form of the title to distinguish between the works.

   2 DeMoss, "Anorexia" 79.

- *Capitalization and punctuation.* Begin all notes with capitals and end them with periods; do not use internal periods.
- *Author's name.* Give the author's name in normal word order, first name first.
- *Publication information.* For books, enclose the place of publication, publisher, and date of publication in parentheses.
- *Page numbers.* Always give the exact page number(s) of a borrowing.
- *Spacing.* Double-space between and within entries.

Following are the most common note forms. Using these, the conventions given previously, and the bibliographic entries in Step 3, pp. 424–428, you can determine the form for every kind of note.

Endnote Entries for Books

A Book with Two Authors
   1 Ernest Van den Haag and John P. Conrad, The Death Penalty (New York: Plenum, 1983) 13.

Committee or Group Author
   2 Consumer Reports Books, The Medicine Show (Mount Vernon, NY: Consumers Union of United States, Inc., 1955) 29.

An Essay Reprinted in a Collection of Essays
   3 Ilse Dusoir Lind, "The Calvinistic Burden of Light in August," New England Quarterly 30 (Sept. 1957): 307–29; rpt. in Light in August and the Critical Spectrum, ed. John B. Vickery and Olga W. Vickery (Belmont, CA: Wadsworth, 1971) 82.

A Book That is a Volume in a Series
   4 Lawrence Durrell, Mountolive, vol. 3 of The Alexandrian Quartet, 4 vols. (New York: Dutton, 1959) 99.

A Book Published in Several Volumes (One Title for All Volumes)
   5 Ernest Walker, et al., Mammals of the World (Baltimore: John Hopkins UP, 1964) 2: 52.

      [The numeral 2 followed by a colon refers to the number of the volume cited.]

Introduction, Foreword, Preface, or Afterword
   6 Beatrice J. Kalisch, Introduction: "Putting Child Abuse and Neglect into Perspec-

tive," Child Abuse and Neglect, by Ray E. Helfer, M.D. (Westport, CT: Greenwood, 1978) 102.

An Edition Other Than the First
    [7] James D. Hart, The Oxford Companion to American Literature, 4th ed. (New York: Oxford UP, 1966) 321–22.

Reprinted Edition
    [8] Henry James, Hawthorne (1879; Ithaca: Cornell UP, 1966) 66.

A Translation
    [9] Albert Camus, The Stranger, trans. Stuart Gilbert (New York: Random, 1954) 130.

The Bible
    [10] Deuteronomy 2: 12 (the King James Version).

A Dictionary
    [11] The Random House Dictionary of the English Language; College Edition, 1968 ed.

Periodical Articles

An Article in an Annual, Semiannual, or Quarterly Journal
    [12] Christopher Joyce, "Safer Aircraft Fuel," New Scientist 3 (1981): 682.

An Article in a Weekly Magazine
    [13] Ed Magnuson, "Child Abuse: The Ultimate Betrayal," Time 5 Sept. 1983: 21.

Newspaper Articles

Signed Newspaper Article
    [14] Jerome Watson, "Reagan Assures Nation on Gulf," Chicago Sun-Times 23 May 1984, sec. l: 2.

Editorial
    [15] "Exit Polls No Threat," editorial, Daily Herald [Arlington Heights, IL] 7 May 1984, sec. 1: 8.

Government Publications

Government Report
    [16] U.S. Cong., House, Sub-Committee on Science, Research and Technology, Genetic Engineering, Human Genetics and Cell Biology, 96th Cong., 2nd sess. (Washington: GPO, 1980) 47.

Encyclopedia Articles

Signed Article
    [17] Estelle Broadman, "Special Libraries," Encyclopedia Americana, 1983 ed.

Nonprint
Sources

Official Testimony
   [18] Suzanne Stienmetz, Testimony before the Select Committee on Aging, <u>The Serious Problem of Elder Abuse</u>, U.S. House of Representatives, 97th Cong., 1st sess., 3 April 1983.

Radio or Television Program
   [19] "Hunger in America," narr. Charles Kuralt, writ. Peter Davis, prod. Martin Carr, <u>CBS Reports</u>, WBBM, Chicago, 21 May 1968.

Play
   [20] William Shakespeare, <u>Othello</u>, <u>The Complete Pelican Shakespeare</u>, ed. Alfred Harbage (Baltimore: Penguin, 1969), II.iii, 1–22.

Film
   [21] <u>Hiroshima Mon Amour</u>, dir. Alain Resnais, Argos-Daiei-Como-Pathe Productions, 1959.

Special
Endnote
Entry Forms

An Author Cited in the Text of a Paper
   If in the text of your paper you give the author of a source, you need not restate the author's name in the first full endnote reference. For example, a sentence from a paper reads:

> Thomas Carlson argues that Mrs. May "lives in constant fear that it [her land] will turn against her, which explains her need to rule with an 'iron hand.' "[12]

The entry on the endnote page begins with the title of the source and includes everything but the author's name:

   [12] "Flannery O'Connor: The Manichaean Dilemma," <u>Sewanee Review</u> 77 (1969): 267.

Group Notes
   For the sake of simplicity, clarity, and unity, consolidate your notes in a group entry whenever possible: (1) when borrowing from several sources within a paragraph, (2) when borrowing from one source several times in a paragraph without borrowing from other sources, (3) when several sources speak on the same subject, or (4) when you wish to cite a group of authorities to support an idea. For example, a passage in a paper reads:

> There are two prevalent theories about why Joe Christmas flees his arraignment in Jefferson. The first, held by Lawrence Thompson, Richard Adams, and Walter Slatoff,[10] follows the suggestion bandied about by Jefferson's townspeople the night of Joe's murder: "It was as though," they speculate, Joe "had set out and made his plans to passively commit suicide."

The endnote for this entry would read as follows:

   [10] Lawrence Thompson, <u>William Faulkner: An Introduction and Interpretation</u> (Baton Rouge: Louisiana State UP, 1964) 73; Richard Adams, <u>Faulkner: Myth and Motion</u>

(Princeton: Princeton UP, 1968) 78; Walter Slatoff, Quest for Failure: A Study of William Faulkner (Ithaca: Cornell UP, 1960) 103.

Extensive Borrowing From One Source

When borrowing extensively from one source, especially a primary source for a literary research essay, indicate in the first reference to the source that future references will be cited parenthetically in the text of your paper. In this way you need cite a frequently used source only *once* on your endnote page. In the text of an essay, these references would appear as follows:

> Feeling that the party should be canceled, Laura tells Jose it is not right to have a party and celebrate when there are people in mourning, but Jose thinks Laura extravagant.[3] Next, Laura goes to her mother and asks, " 'Of course, we can't have our party, can we?' " (543). But Mrs. Sheridan responds just as Jose has done and even seems amused by her daughter (544).

On the notes page, the reference would look like this:

[3] Katherine Mansfield, "The Garden Party," The Short Stories of Katherine Mansfield (New York: Knopf, 1962) 543; future references will be cited parenthetically in the text.

REVISING

When you've finished drafting and are ready to revise and edit, remember that you'll be making five changes: addition, deletion, substitution, rearrangement, and correction. Here is a revision checklist to guide your work:

_____ Have you said all you need to develop and communicate your subject?

_____ Have you introduced and explained the materials you have borrowed? Is your documentation complete and conventional?

_____ Does your thesis appear somewhere in your introduction? Is it clear and complete?

_____ Does your essay make sense? Does one part lead logically to the next? Check thematic tags and transitions.

_____ Is your language clear, precise, economical, and vivid?

_____ Do your sentences flow smoothly and rhythmically from one to the next? Read your paper aloud.

_____ Have you prepared correct rough drafts for a final outline, endnotes if required, and a list of works cited or a bibliography?

When you can say yes to these questions, you're ready to go back through your paper and write marginal instructions to yourself about the spacing, indentation, and block quotations you'll use in the final draft. They will speed your work at a point in your project when you'll want every minute you can spare.

Step 7: Writing the Final Draft

❧ MANUSCRIPT FORM

Typing   Type your research paper, have it typed, or use a word processor. Generally, handwritten research papers are unacceptable. Use good-quality twenty-pound 8½ x 11 inch white paper and standard typefaces. Be aware that some readers object to dot-matrix printers.

Margins   Leave one-inch margins on the top, bottom, and both sides of the text.

Titles   Do not put the title of your paper in quotation marks; do not underline or capitalize in full. Underline or quote words in your title only if you would underline or quote them in your text. If your title is more than one line, double-space between lines.

If *title and outline pages* are required: On the title page, center your title one third of the way down the page. On the outline page, center the heading two inches from the top; double-space twice before and after the thesis statement. On the first page of text, center your title two inches from the top and double-space twice before the first line of text.

If title and outline pages are *not* required: Type your heading and title on the first page of text, as you would for any other college paper. Put a double-spaced heading in the upper left-hand corner, one inch from the top and left side; include your name, instructor's name, course and section numbers, and date. Two spaces beneath the heading, center your title; double-space twice before the first line of text.

Headings for notes, appendix, bibliography, or works cited pages: center the heading one inch from the top of the page and double space before the first line of text.

Copyright © 1981 by United Feature Syndicate, Inc. Used by permission.

Spacing and Indentation   Double-space throughout the text of your paper, including quotations. Indent the first lines of new paragraphs five spaces from the left margin.

Subdivisions   Except for the report format, avoid breaking the flow of your paper with headings and subheadings. Your research project should read like a carefully organized, coherent essay. If you must group related paragraphs, double-space twice between sections.

Illustrations   There are two kinds of illustrations. The first is visual and consists of pictures and charts; the second is numerical and consists of tables. Present both in the body of your paper as near as possible to the ideas they illustrate. Label *pictures* and *charts* as *figures*, number them consecutively throughout your paper by using arabic numerals (e.g., *Fig. 1, Fig. 2, Fig. 3*), and give them a brief descriptive caption. Put this information beneath the illustration, flush with the left margin. Label *tables* as such, number them consecutively with arabic numerals (e.g., *Table 1, Table 2, Table 3*), and give them an explanatory title. Put this information above the illustration flush with the left margin. If you borrow illustrations, document your borrowing in a note immediately beneath the table. Any content notes should follow, preceded by consecutive lowercase letters (e.g., *a, b, c*) instead of numbers. Indent the first line of content notes five spaces. Double-space throughout. An example of a chart appears below, and a sample table is illustrated on the following page.

An Appendix   If you have a number of illustrations or extensive explanatory information too long for notes, place it into an appendix im-

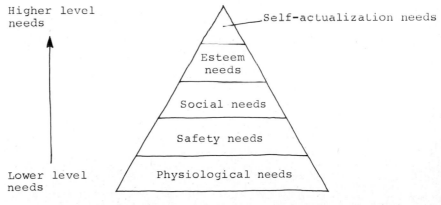

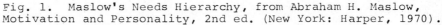

Fig. 1.   Maslow's Needs Hierarchy, from Abraham H. Maslow, Motivation and Personality, 2nd ed. (New York: Harper, 1970).

Table 1

Comparative Evaluation of Fast-Food French Fries (Small)

Fast-food chain	Price	Serving size[a]	Calories	Sodium
Arby's	55¢	2 1/4 oz.	195	31 mg.
Burger King	59	1 3/4	158	56
Hardee's	50	2 1/4	202	48
Jack in the Box	59	2 1/4	217	117
Kentucky Fried Chicken	65	3 1/2	221	92
Long John Silver's	58	3 1/2	282	59
McDonald's	62	3	268	45
Roy Rogers	56	3	230	161
Wendy's	72	3 1/2	317	110

Source: Adapted from Consumer Reports July 1984: 369.

[a] Rounded to nearest 1/4 oz.

mediately following the text of your paper and preceding notes and bibliography. An appendix should be headed by "Appendix 1," "Appendix 2," and so on, and given a title. Place the centered heading one inch from the top of the paper, double-space, and then give the title. Double-space between the title and the text.

Pagination   Begin counting the pages of your paper from the first page of text, *not* from the title or outline page. Put page numbers on your paper beginning with page 2 and continue to the end, including *all* notes, appendix, and bibliography pages.

Place page numbers in the upper right corner one-half inch from the top and one inch from the right side. Put your last name before each number (e.g., *Jones 5*). Do *not* punctuate numbers with periods, dashes, parentheses, or asterisks.

Corrections   Make corrections neatly in ink or typescript after erasing or using correction fluid. Do not write in margins or below the line. Make insertions with a caret (∧).

The Order of Pages   Arrange the parts of your research project in the following conventional order:

1. Title page, if required.
2. Outline, if required.
3. Text.
4. Appendix, if necessary.
5. Notes, if required or necessary.
6. Works Cited, Bibliography, or Works Consulted.

❧ QUOTATIONS

Block Quotations   Quotations of more than four lines should be blocked, that is, introduced by a comma or colon, indented ten spaces from the left margin and none from the right, and typed with double-spacing. If you quote two or more paragraphs, indent the first line of each complete paragraph an additional three spaces; thirteen spaces total. Do *not* enclose a blocked quotation with quotation marks, *unless* there are quotation marks in the original, for example, if you are quoting someone's speech, in which case quotation marks should appear as in the original. Do *not* begin a new paragraph after a block quotation unless you make a genuine shift in subject matter.

Dialogue in Fiction   When you quote exchanges of dialogue, you must follow the paragraphing of the original and use the block quotation form, even if you quote fewer than four typed lines. Incorporate single speeches of fewer than four lines into the text of your paper. Here is an example of dialogue from an essay on Katherine Mansfield's "The Garden Party":

Laura and Jose nowhere more clearly reveal their fundamental differences than when they quarrel about stopping the garden party:

> "Oh, Laura!" Jose began to be seriously annoyed. "If you're going to stop a band playing every time some one has an accident, you'll lead a very strenuous life. I'm every bit as sorry about it as you. I feel just as sympathetic." Her eyes hardened. She looked at her sister just as she used to when they were little and fighting

[Indent 13 spaces]

[Indent 10 spaces]

[Double-space throughout]

Quotation
marks as
they appear
in the
original

together. "You won't bring a drunken workman back to life by being

sentimental," she said softly.

    "Drunk! Who said he was drunk?" Laura turned furiously on Jose.

She said, just as they had used to say on those occasions, "I'm going

straight up to tell mother."

    "Do, dear," cooed Jose. (242)

Documentation 2 spaces after
last punctuation of the quotation

Dialogue in Plays or Films

When you quote an exchange of two or more speakers, block the entire exchange, giving each speaker a separate paragraph introduced by the speaker's name and a colon. Do not use quotation marks for dramatic dialogue unless they appear in the original. Incorporate single speeches of fewer than four lines into the text of your paper and surround them with quotation marks. Here is a block quotation from an essay on Tennessee Williams' *A Streetcar Named Desire*:

The pressures of Blanche's presence in the Kowalski household force Stanley

from the very beginning, and in every scene thereafter, to reveal his cultural

and emotional immaturity. His is truly a case of arrested development:

Indent
13 spaces

Stanley: . . . Hey, Stella!

Double-space throughout

Stella [faintly, from the bathroom]: Yes, Stanley.

Underlining
to indicate
original italics

Stanley: Haven't fallen in, have you? [He grins at Blanche. She

tries unsuccessfully to smile back. There is a silence.] I'm afraid

Indent
10 spaces

I'll strike you as being the unrefined type. Stella's spoke of you

a good deal. (31)

Quotation of Poetry

Unless you want to give special emphasis, you should incorporate from one to three lines of poetry into the text of your paper, enclosed with quotation marks. Separate individual lines with a slash (/) preceded and followed by a space. Block-quote poetry of more than three lines. Introduce it with a colon and indent ten spaces. Indent more or less if the passage would look unbalanced on the page. Double-space within the quotation and arrange the passage so it looks as much like the original as possible. If you omit one or more lines from a block quotation, use a single line of spaced periods the same length as the immediately preceding line.

The sixteenth century English poet Robert Herrick may not have had research
paper writers in mind when he wrote:

> Only a little more
>
> I have to write,
>
> Then I'll give o'er,
>
> And bid the world good-night.
>
> (Hesperides)

But research paper writers would certainly feel a kinship upon reading his lines.

Punctuation   Use ellipsis points (. . .) where required to signal omissions. Use brackets ([. . .]) to insert explanatory information within a quotation. See Chapter 18, page 522 and 526–527. If your typewriter does not type brackets, you will have to draw them.

Editorial Commentary   Use [sic], meaning "thus," after errors or illogical statements to assure your readers that you have quoted accurately. Unless you say otherwise, by [emphasis added], your readers will assume that whenever you underline a quotation, it was underlined or italicized in the original.

On the following pages is the final draft of one of the most common kinds of research project: an argumentative and informative essay with title and outline pages, parenthetical documentation, and a list of works cited arranged according to the Modern Language Association format.

A SAMPLE RESEARCH ESSAY USING PARENTHETICAL DOCUMENTATION

Title centered 1/3 of the way down the page

Television News--Is It Enough?

by

Martha J. Hazen

Double-space

English 102

Dr. Walter Ballou

October 31, 1983

Two-thirds of the way down the page

Sentence outline format

Heading centered 2 inches from top

Outline

Double-space twice

Single space

Thesis: The nature of the television medium causes disadvantages that keep it from providing complete news coverage. Besides these inherent disadvantages, there has been a trend towards popular, entertaining news shows which further reduces the amount of significant information presented.

Double-space twice

I. TV news has some positive aspects.

   A.   TV news is more timely than print.

   B.   Visuals have an impact unavailable in print.

II. There are problems inherent in the medium that keep it from being

   completely effective.

   A.   Visuals can be misleading.

Double-space throughout the outline

   B.   There is not enough time.

   C.   The format of a news show is confusing.

III. The push for ratings has made TV news even less effective.

   A.   Increased profitability during the 1960s and 70s led to

        competition.

   B.   News consultants were hired by stations to make news more

        entertaining.

        1.   Showbiz tactics instead of hard news

        2.   Condescending attitude of news consultants

Indent 5 spaces

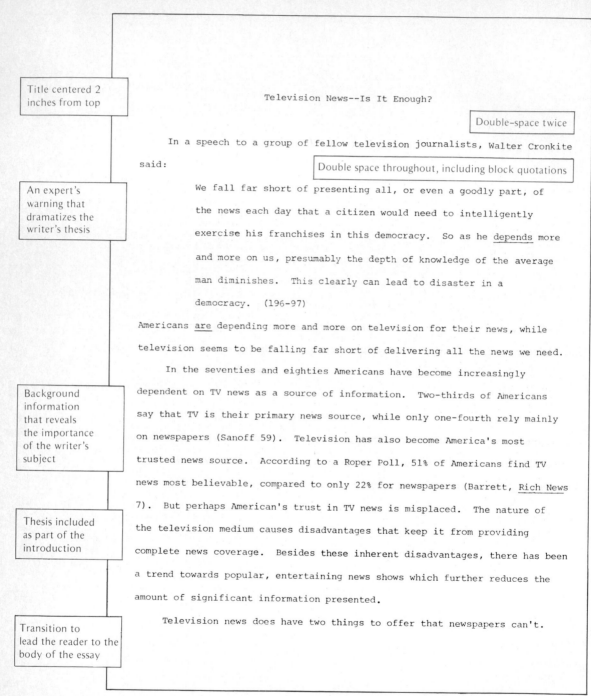

Title centered 2 inches from top

Television News--Is It Enough?

Double-space twice

In a speech to a group of fellow television journalists, Walter Cronkite said:

Double space throughout, including block quotations

An expert's warning that dramatizes the writer's thesis

> We fall far short of presenting all, or even a goodly part, of the news each day that a citizen would need to intelligently exercise his franchises in this democracy. So as he <u>depends</u> more and more on us, presumably the depth of knowledge of the average man diminishes. This clearly can lead to disaster in a democracy. (196-97)

Americans <u>are</u> depending more and more on television for their news, while television seems to be falling far short of delivering all the news we need.

Background information that reveals the importance of the writer's subject

In the seventies and eighties Americans have become increasingly dependent on TV news as a source of information. Two-thirds of Americans say that TV is their primary news source, while only one-fourth rely mainly on newspapers (Sanoff 59). Television has also become America's most trusted news source. According to a Roper Poll, 51% of Americans find TV news most believable, compared to only 22% for newspapers (Barrett, <u>Rich News</u> 7). But perhaps American's trust in TV news is misplaced. The nature of

Thesis included as part of the introduction

the television medium causes disadvantages that keep it from providing complete news coverage. Besides these inherent disadvantages, there has been a trend towards popular, entertaining news shows which further reduces the amount of significant information presented.

Transition to lead the reader to the body of the essay

Television news does have two things to offer that newspapers can't.

Author's name and page number ½ inch from top,
first line of text 1 inch from top

Hazen 2

Topic sentence to introduce Part I

First, it can be more timely. Before they can be read, newspapers have to be written, edited, typeset, printed, and distributed. Stories that can reach TV audiences almost instantly may not appear in newspapers until the

Ellipsis points

following morning. In this sense, "The news on . . . television makes the front page of the morning's paper obsolete" (Schwartz 86). Another advantage of television news is the availability of visuals such as film and graphics to illustrate a story. Visuals can not only add interest to a story, or explain it graphically, they also add to its credibility. People trust TV news because it seems unbiased--it's there on film for everyone to see.

Transition to introduce Part II

But these visuals can be a disadvantage to viewers seeking significant news. Since visuals are considered essential to sustaining interest in a newscast, a sensational story with an exciting piece of film will often be shown in place of a more significant, but visually dull story (Patterson 30).

Thematic tags to create unity: "visual," "see," "graphics," "graphically," "film," "videotape," "shown," "visually," "shots," "talking heads," "on the air"

"Tell" stories (news stories simply read by anchor persons) are less attractive than stories accompanied by film or videotape. And film or videotape of action such as a protest, fire, or battle scene, is preferred over "talking heads," shots of news sources who are simply speaking, (Patterson 40). This means that sensational news is more likely to be on the air than visually dull political or financial news.

Quotation woven into a sentence

Those who trust TV news' objectivity (66% rank it, along with consumer protection groups, as "the most ethical of U.S. institutions" [Barrett,

Part II. A.

Rich News 7]) should remember that although a piece of film or videotape makes a story seem more credible, that film may be shown out of context or edited to the point of meaninglessness. Walter Cronkite illustrated this

A block quotation woven into the writer's paper by an introduction

problem by pointing out in his speech that if that speech were to be reported on the news,

    the best to be hoped for . . . would be the presentation of one

Hazen 3

single idea, one claim, or one denunciation, and that without any, <u>any</u> of the qualifications, reasons, or background that led me to make that assertion. . . . If our medium chose to present me with a filmed or taped excerpt . . . this, too, would be shortened to only a sentence or two, and while no more complete than a "tell" item, would, by presenting me in person, place the stamp of authenticity on my words. (191)

This lack of completeness is not the result of a deliberate effort by news directors to restrict information. It is simply the result of television news' greatest weakness: there simply isn't enough <u>time</u> to present the news in depth or detail. Television journalists make no attempt to deny the limitations of their medium. As newsman John Chancellor says, "We can't tell the whole story. A television news program is a special sort of front page" (Diamond 63).

According to a survey of news shows taken by the American Association of University Women, the average half-hour news show has only about 16 1/2 minutes left for presenting news items, after commercials, sports and weather are accounted for. Into those 16 1/2 minutes, reports Marvin Barrett, are squeezed about 14 news stories (<u>Moments</u> 63).

The average news story, according to Edwin Diamond, is only 20 to 30 seconds long, and a newscaster speaking at normal broadcast quality pace can deliver no more than 120 words per minute (63). This severely limits the amount of information that can be included in each story. At 120 words per minute, there just isn't the time to make even a one-hour newscast more than a "headline service."

Richard Salant, former President of CBS News, once set an entire script of a <u>CBS Evening News</u> telecast into newspaper type. He found that it

---

Place parenthetical documentation of block quotations two spaces after the last punctuation

Part II. B.

A quotation to sum up a point

Introduction giving the source of the information

An authority and his credentials

The use of an
authority's words
to dramatize the
writer's problem

filled less than the equivalent of two columns of page one of the New York Times (Barrett, Moments 63). According to Salant, "Anyone who has ever prepared to deliver a television broadcast, as I have . . . knows how difficult it is to make facts known or events understandable" (Diamond 63). He says, "I'm afraid we compress so well as to almost defy the viewer and listener to understand what we say. And when that becomes the fact we cease to be communicators" (Barrett, Rich News 196).

A paragraph unified
by a single subtopic:
The difficulty of
watching TV
news well

The fast pace of TV news compounds the problem of informing viewers effectively. Most stories are the same length, regardless of topic or significance (Patterson 83). The viewer can't tell which stories are important by the amount of time devoted to them, and more importantly, the viewer can't determine their significance on the basis of a thorough understanding of the story because too little information is made available

Transition

to him (Patterson 83). Added to this disadvantage is another: unlike newspaper readers who can read what they want in the order they want, TV

Part II. C.

viewers can't go back to review what is unclear the first time around. Strict attention must be paid, or the meaning of a story is lost. This

A quotation to
make a point

makes television not a "boob tube," but a "very demanding mode of communication" (Barrett, Moments 64).

In spite of its limitations, TV does a fairly good job as a "headline service," presenting brief, up-to-the-minute summaries of the day's news events along with some visual illustrations. But the trend has been for

Part III. A.

Americans to rely on TV as their primary source of information. And instead of leading to improved news coverage, this trend has had the unfortunate effect of making the news even more superficial. TV news has become a victim of its own success. Stations once provided news telecasts as a means to satisfy FCC requirements for "public affairs" programming. It

wasn't seen as profitable, merely as "one of those things you had to do
to keep your license" (Barrett, Moments 90). But as viewing increased in
the late sixties, stations found that news could be one of their most
profitable commodities. For one thing, it was found that if local news
outdraws its competition, it often means those viewers will stay tuned to
that station all evening (Barrett, Moments 90). One rating point can mean
from 1.2 to 1.6 million dollars of income per year (Barrett, Rich News 117).

Applying an
authority's words
to a new situation
to create a fresh
point of view

Part II. B. 1.

The great broadcast journalist Ed Murrow once said, "If news is to
be regarded as a commodity, only acceptable when saleable, then I don't
care what you say, I say it isn't news" (Barrett, Rich News 22). His
remark seems tailor-made to today's "news," which has itself been tailor-
made as a saleable commodity by "news consultants." Consulting firms such as
McHugh and Hoffman and the Frank H. Magid Association have been hired by
the majority of U.S. news stations to make news shows as entertaining as
possible in order to boost ratings. They engage in market research to
discover what local news audiences find most entertaining and then tailor
the news accordingly (Barrett, Moments 90).

The hallmarks of a show after the news consultants have "improved"
it include "young and beautiful anchor persons, matching blazers,
designer haircuts, news desk badinage, socko short items, and seductively
soft short items" (Barrett, Rich News 120). It is Magid who dictated
the hard-and-fast rule that no news item be more than 90 seconds in length,
no matter how important. A 90-second story is called a "mini-documentary."

Colon to introduce
a block quotation

It is also Magid who brought us "Happy Talk." According to Ron Powers:

> Happy Talk owes much of its identity to the bantering remarks
> made among anchormen, reporters, weathermen and sportscasters
> during transitions from topic to topic. But the concept has a

Hazen 6

much broader scope. It defines a newscast that is weighted

toward the trivial . . . and away from the abstract, the dis-

turbing, the vital. . . . (36)

Along with political coverage, news consultants discourage use of any

stories that are hard to explain or visualize. Their excuse, according to

Marvin Barrett, is that the public doesn't want them (Rich News 120).

The apparent attitude of news consultant firms toward the public

to which they aim can be illustrated by a sign placed on the wall of a

newsroom by a Magid consultant. It reads:

Remember, the vast majority of our viewers hold blue collar

jobs . . . never went to college . . . have never been on an

airplane . . . have never seen a copy of the New York Times . . .

do not read the same books and magazines that you read . . . in

fact, many of them never read anything. (Barrett, Moments 89)

Regardless of the accuracy of this advice, it certainly does a disservice

to the viewers who depend on a news service produced with such a condescending

mentality.

This attitude, along with the trivia it presents, seems reason enough

to decrease reliance on TV news. Combined with the inherent inability of

even serious news shows to present more than a superficial summary of the

day's news, it seems that America's increased dependence on TV news is a

mistake. Perhaps Americans should rely on TV only as a "headline service"

to summarize and illustrate the stories they will read in the next day's

paper. But since a full scale defection from TV news seems unlikely, it

is important that TV news be improved. TV stations should devote more

effort to the integrity of their news content than to the entertainment

value of their news production. Walter Cronkite has advice to give on

the subject:

Period and ellipsis to end a quotation

Part III. B. 2.

A quotation used as primary source of evidence to support the writer's point

The logical conclusion to the writer's research

A potential solution to the problem

Hazen 7

A conclusion that
offers an expert's
description of a
solution

The solution quite simply is, for the network newscasts, more time,

and for the local newscasts . . . a better utilization of it . . .

Doing what experienced news directors would like to be doing

instead of what news consultants and non-news-oriented station

managers want to do. In other words, it means covering the

meaningful, the genuinely important, relevant, and significant

news of your communities--city hall, county courts, the

state house--whether there is a picture story there or not,

whether the resulting story can be told in 20 seconds or not. (197)

The writer's
final challenge

TV news cannot do everything, but what it does do, it could do better.

Hazen 8

Heading centered 1 inch from top

Double-space between heading and text   Works Consulted

Two works by the same author

Barrett, Marvin. Moments of Truth. New York: Crowell, 1975.

---. Rich News, Poor News. New York: Crowell, 1978.

Cronkite, Walter. Remarks at the RTNDA Conference, Miami Beach, Florida,

13 Dec. 1976. Rpt. in Rich News, Poor News. By Marvin Barrett.

New York: Crowell, 1978. 191-98.   Double-space throughout

Reprinted source

Standard book citation

Diamond, Edwin. The Tin Kazoo: Television, Politics and the News.

Cambridge: The MIT Press, 1975.

Epstein, Edward Jay. "The Logic of News Operation." News from Nowhere.

New York: Random, 1973. 100-111. Rpt. in The TV Establishment.

Ed. Gayle Tuchman. Englewood Cliffs, NJ: Prentice, 1974. 44-52.

Alphabetical arrangement

Magazine article

Funt, P. "Television News: Seeing Isn't Believing." Saturday Review

Nov. 1980: 30-32.

Mickelson, Sig. The Electric Mirror. New York: Dodd, 1972.

Patterson, Thomas E., and Robert D. McClure. The Unseeing Eye. New York:

Putnam's, 1976.

Two authors

Powers, Ron. The Newscasters. New York: St. Martin's, 1977.

Sanoff, Alvin P. "TV News Growing Too Powerful?" US News and World Report

9 June 1980: 59-61.

Schwartz, Tony. Media, The Second God. New York: Random, 1981.

Small, William. To Kill a Messenger: Television News and the Real World.

New York: Hastings, 1970.

Indent 5 spaces

PART VI

A HANDBOOK FOR COLLEGE WRITERS

Chapter 18

A Guide to
Edited American English

Every chapter in this text except this one is about good writing and how to produce it. This is a chapter about "correct" writing. As I suggested in Chapter 1, good public writing is almost always correct writing, too, but good writing and correct writing are *not* necessarily the same. To see how they differ, you need to know the differences between two terms, *grammar* and *usage*. Together they have caused more confusion, distraction, and dismay among more writers than any others having to do with language and writing.

A NOTE ON GRAMMAR AND USAGE

Grammar

Grammar is the set of rules the native speakers and writers of a language use to produce their sentences. *Rules* may be a little misleading, however, since the word implies a conscious adherence to a standard. The native users of a language learn most of these rules without thinking and follow them unconsciously. The rest they learn from friends or family. No English teacher, linguist, or grammarian decides what they shall be. We, the actual speakers and writers of English, decide what our language shall be and what rules it shall follow. Our grammar is not a set of inflexible and changeless rules imposed upon us but part of our lives as individual and social beings, changing and developing according to our practices, needs, and whims. We can do anything to our language we want—provided we can find a few million others to go along with us.

According to this sense of the term, "correct" or "good" grammar is the grammar of every native speaker and writer of English. "Ain't nobody here by that name" is a grammatically correct English sentence for some speakers of English. The rules of their dialect allow them, even require them, to produce that sentence. For speakers who speak other English dialects, "There is no one here by that name" is a grammatically correct sentence, although grammatically incorrect for the speakers of the first group. In this sense, then, native users of a language don't have to "watch their grammar"; they're always right.

Usage

But that definition is *not* what people have in mind when they advise someone, "Watch your grammar!" What they mean is another set of language rules known as usage. *Usage* is the rules of language etiquette that determine what is proper for specific classes of people on specific occasions. Grammar says, in effect, "This is what a native speaker actually does to produce a particular sentence." Usage says, "This is what a speaker *ought* to do to produce a sentence appropriate for this occasion." What we call good grammar, good English, or standard English has less to do with English grammar than with the language etiquette generally observed by the best educated, most successful, and most powerful of English users. Theirs is the dialect of English used in the schools, in the professions, in the business world, and in the media. It is, therefore, the set of standards taught as "correct English" to everyone, regardless of class, position, or dialect. It is a language a little more formal than other English dialects, a little fussier about the relationships between words, a little more obvious in its logic, a little more complete in its statements, and more often written than spoken. Frequently referred to as *Edited American English,* its "rules" have come to provide the standards by which most public speakers and writers are judged.

What follows in this chapter is a guide, in alphabetical order, to the most important and most troublesome of these rules. They are most important because they are the rules most important to the majority of Edited American English users; lapses here are what they notice most quickly and condemn most strenuously. They are most troublesome because they are often at odds with the rules of other, usually spoken dialects we use at home and with friends. Mastering these rules will not directly make you a better writer. As I suggested in Chapter 1, knowledge of usage bears the same relationship to writing that a knowledge of the rules of baseball bears to an actual World Series game. Knowing the rules and playing well are not the same. Still, if one expects to play well . . . Mastering the conventions of Edited American English will increase your ability to play well the role expected of educated men and women and to reap their rewards.[1]

ABBREVIATIONS

An abbreviation is a shortened form of a word (*vol.*, *bro.*, *inc.*) or a word from which the middle has been omitted (*dept.*, *Mr.*, *Sr.*, *Mrs.*). More and more frequently, abbreviations are being written without periods (e.g., *MA*, *PhD*, *NY*, *rpm*, *mph*). But you will almost always use periods after single letters and after abbreviations ending in lowercase letters (e.g., A.M., *introd.*, *pag.*). When an abbreviation comes at the end of a sentence, use only one period.

Avoid most abbreviations in public writing, except for "in-house" writing, e.g., memos, letters, reports, and proposals to people thoroughly familiar with your subject matter.

Always abbreviate: *Mr.*; *Mrs.* (*Ms.* is not technically an abbreviation but is written as one); *Dr.* before a name; scholarly degrees after a name (*BA*, *MA*, *PhD*); *Jr.*, *Sr.*; and time designations such as A.M., P.M., AD, BC. Do *not* abbreviate given names: not *Tho. Tucker*, but *Thomas Tucker*.

Titles. Spell out titles when used with surnames alone, e.g., *General Eisenhower*, *Senator Stevenson*, *Reverend Hightower*. But abbreviate titles when they precede full names, e.g., *Gen. Dwight Eisenhower*, *Sen.*, *Adlai Stevenson*, *Rev. Gail Hightower* (but when preceded by *the*: *the Reverend Gail Hightower*).

Company names. In the body of your writing, spell out company names. In notes or documentation, abbreviate consistently for *Co.*, *Corp.*, *Bro.*, *Inc.*, and *Ltd.*

Geographical terms. Spell out the names of countries (except for the USSR), states, territories, and possessions when they stand alone in the body of your writing or follow city names, e.g., *Chicago, Illinois*. In notes or documentation, use Zip Code and other standard abbreviation forms, e.g., *IL* for *Illinois*, *NJ* for *New Jersey*, *UK* for *United Kingdom*, *Sp.* for *Spain*, *Swed.* for *Sweden*, and so on.

Dates. In the text of formal public writing, write out months and days, e.g., *Thursday, October 31st*. You may abbreviate in less formal writing. In notes and documentation, abbreviate months and days, except *May, June, July*.

Units of Measure. Do not abbreviate units of measure in the body of your writing: not *gal.*, *in.*, *yd.*, *sq. mi.*, *pt.*, or *bbl.*, but *gallon, inch, yard, square mile, pint,* or *barrel*. You may abbreviate in the text of technical writing.

ACRONYMS

An acronym is a word formed from the first letters of other words, usually the titles of organizations, agencies, and other groups: *FBI, CIA, AFL-*

CIO. Often acronyms are pronounced as words: *OPEC, CORE, SALT, SNCC.* Generally all the letters of acronyms are capitalized, and they are written with *no* internal or closing periods: *CBS, NBC, UNICEF,* but *Nazi, MiG, laser, sonar.*

✎ ADJECTIVES AND ADVERBS

Users of Edited American English are particular about the way they use adjectives and adverbs. An *adjective* modifies (provides information about) a noun or pronoun. In sentences these nouns or pronouns act as subjects, objects, or indirect objects.

> *An Adjective Modifying a Subject*
> *Simple* Simon met a pie man.

> *An Adjective Modifying a Direct Object*
> Simon met a *crafty* pie man.

> *An Adjective Modifying an Indirect Object*
> Simon gave the *crafty* pie man all his money.

An *adverb* modifies a verb, another adverb, or an adjective.

> *An Adverb Modifying a Verb*
> That male chauvinist Peter the Pumpkin Eater *suddenly* decided to imprison his wife in a pumpkin shell.

> *An Adverb Modifying an Adverb*
> There he kept her *very* well.

> *An Adverb Modifying an Adjective*
> His reputation among women was *deservedly* poor.

It is an error to use one kind of word in a position reserved for the other. Casual spoken English is much less fussy about this distinction than Edited American English.

> *An Adjective in Place of an Adverb*
> The police gave me my ticket and drove away. After watching them disappear, I took off *slow* and didn't go over fifty-five the rest of the way. (*slowly*)

> *An Adjective in Place of an Adverb*
> The night of the prom everything went *perfect.* (*perfectly*)

> *An Adjective in Place of an Adverb*
> No matter how hard he tries, Melvin dresses *sloppy.* (*sloppily*)

A special problem occurs when writers get too fussy:

> Velma felt *badly,* but what could she do?

Because *badly* follows the verb, where adverbs often appear, it seems to be appropriate. But the verb in this sentence is a *linking verb,* a verb that "links" a subject (Velma) to information about it, called a subject complement. What follows a linking verb should be an adjective or noun, *not* an adverb:

> Velma felt bad, but what could she do?

When you're not sure whether to write *bad* or *badly*, remind yourself that you'd never write *Velma felt goodly*. Other linking verbs are *act, appear, become, grew, look, seem, sound, taste, turn*.

❧ AGREEMENT

Agreement describes the similarities between words of different grammatical forms. Words that "agree" are in different parts of speech (nouns, verbs, and pronouns), yet because they are involved with each other, they share certain formal characteristics:

- Person: first *(I, we)*, second *(you)*, or third person *(he, she, they)*.
- Number: Singular or plural.
- Gender: masculine, feminine, or neuter.

Edited American English is careful about agreement; words that are involved with each other must signal their relationship by grammatical agreement.

Subject-Verb Agreement

Subjects must agree with their verbs in *number*: Singular subjects take singular verbs (1 = 1); plural subjects take plural verbs (2 = 2).

> *Singular*
> *Jack is* nice to Jill (1 = 1).

> *Plural*
> Those *mittens were lost* by three little kittens (2 = 2).

Separated Subjects Don't be misled by nearby nouns; no matter how far apart, the true subjects should determine the number of their verbs.

> *Not*
> Little Miss Muffet, as well as her fourteen suitors, *were eating* curds and whey.

> *But*
> *Little Miss Muffet*, as well as her fourteen suitors, *was eating* curds and whey.

> *Not*
> Learning how to make pies from four and twenty blackbirds *are* easy.

> *But*
> *Learning* how to make pies from four and twenty blackbirds *is* easy.

Delayed Constructions   Occasionally the subject *follows* rather than precedes its verb; still, the true subject determines the number of the verb.

Not
   There *is* already too many men in the tub to suit the butcher, the baker, and the candlestick maker.

But
   There *are* already *too many men* in the tub to suit the butcher, the baker, and the candlestick maker.

Not
   All I can see from here *is* the King's horses and the King's men using Zippy Glue to put Humpty-Dumpty together again.

But
   All I can see from here *are the King's horses and the King's men* using Zippy Glue to put Humpty-Dumpty together again.

Compounds   Ordinarily, compound subjects take a plural verb: *Jack and Jill are* going up the hill (1 and 1 = 2). But if the compound is thought of as a unit, then its verb is singular ([1 and 1] = 1):

   Curds and whey doesn't sound like snack food to me.

or

   The horse and buggy is a thing of the past.

If compound subjects are joined by *or, nor, either . . . or, neither . . . nor,* the verb is singular when both subjects are singular (1 or 1 = 1), plural when both subjects are plural (2 or 2 = 2):

   Neither Jack nor Jill is going up the hill today.

   Either Bo Peep's sheep or the three little kittens are spending the day lounging in the basement rec room.

However, if one subject is singular and the other plural, then the number of the subject *closest to the verb* determines its number. This is called a proximity rule.

   Neither Bo Peep nor *her sheep are* anywhere to be found. (1 nor 2 = 2)

   Neither her sheep nor *Bo Peep is* anywhere to be found. (2 nor 1 = 1)

Collective Nouns   Collective nouns are words like *class, committee, couple, dozen, group, herd, jury, public, remainder,* and *team*. They are singular but refer to groups of things, people, and actions. They take a singular verb if their members are acting together collectively. But if their members are acting individually, they no longer refer to a collective, and their verb is plural.

Singular
The *group* in the tub *is singing* "Rub-a-dub-dub."

Plural
The *remainder* in the tub *are disagreeing* about who should pull the plug. (Each has his own opinion and argues individually.)

Plural Nouns   Plural nouns take a singular verb if they are singular in meaning or understood as a unit.

Three dollars is all that Simple Simon has left after meeting the pie man.

Fifteen miles is a long way to walk when you're broke and alone.

Economics is the next course Simple Simon should register for.

Relative Clauses   The subject of a relative clause—always the relative pronoun *who, which,* or *that*—determines the number of its verb. But because relative pronouns have no singular or plural endings, you must determine their number by identifying their *antecedents,* the nouns for which they substitute.

Not
Little Tommy Tucker is one of those people who *sings* for supper.

But
Little Tommy Tucker is one of *those people who sing* for supper.

Not
The Grosso Grande XJ is one of the few cars on the road today that *gets* good mileage.

But
The Grosso Grande XJ is one of *the few cars* on the road today *that get* good mileage.

Not
The mountains are covered by a blanket of trees that *look* like softest velvet.

But
The mountains are covered by a *blanket* of trees *that looks* like softest velvet.

Indefinite Pronouns   Indefinite pronouns refer to indefinite, unspecified antecedents:

each	everybody	anyone
no one	nobody	neither
every	anybody	everyone
someone	either	

The sense of these words is often plural; for example, *everybody* obviously refers to more than one person. But because the form of these words is singular, indefinite pronouns take singular verbs.

- *Each* of the men *is singing* "Rub-a-dub-dub."
- *Every sheep has returned* to Miss Peep.
- *Either* of the boys *is willing* to help Miss Muffet repair her car.
- *Someone has stolen* the kittens' mittens.
- *Neither has* ever *climbed* that hill to fetch a pail of water.
- *Anyone who wants* to ride a cock horse to Banbury Cross *is supposed* to sign a rental form before noon.

Pronoun-Antecedent Agreement

Pronouns should agree with *their* nouns in person, number, and gender. In the preceding sentence, for example, *their* is third-person plural, and so is its antecedent, *pronouns.*

Compound Antecedents   Compound antecedents are nouns joined by *or, nor, either . . . or, neither . . . nor.* If both antecedents are singular, so is the pronoun (1 or 1 = 1). If both antecedents are plural, so is the pronoun (2 or 2 = 2).

> *Neither Miss Muffet nor little Bo Peep* is carrying *her* purse this evening (1 nor 1 = 1).

> *Either the Tuckers or the Muffets* are sure to make fools of *themselves* when *they* come to Tommy and Missy's wedding (2 or 2 = 2).

A proximity rule: If one antecedent is singular and the other plural, the antecedent *closer to the pronoun* determines its person, number, and gender.

> Neither Humpty-Dumpty nor *the three little pigs* will invest *their* savings in tax-free municipal bonds (1 nor 2 = 2).

> Neither the three little pigs nor *Humpty-Dumpty* will invest *his* savings in tax-free municipal bonds (2 nor 1 = 1).

Indefinite Pronouns   When indefinite pronouns (always singular) act as antecedents for definite pronouns, the definite pronouns are also singular.

> The three little pigs decided that *each* would build a tri-level ranch-style home for *himself.*

> *Every one* of the three little kittens claims *she* has lost *her* mittens.

A problem arises, however, when an indefinite pronoun or collective noun refers to a group made up of both men and women. Imagine this situation: Several executives receive a memo requiring their presence at a board meeting. The memo contains this sentence:

> Each officer will bring ___(definite pronoun)___ copy of the year-end corporate financial statement.

If all the executives are men, the memo will read *his copy;* if they are women, it will read *her copy.* But if they are both men and women, what should be done? Informal English has solved the problem by permitting noun-pronoun disagreement: "*Each* will bring *their* copy." Edited American English hasn't solved the problem yet. The old legal and social custom—never a grammatical rule—required the use of the masculine pronouns (*he* and *his*) as generic pronouns to refer to both men and women in situations like this, but this custom is now properly objected to by many, since *he* and *his* disregard the women in the group. We could put *his or her* or *his/her* into the memo, but to some that sounds ponderous. The graceful, nonsexist solution to the problem of gender is rewording. The sense of the sentence is plural, so the grammar should be made plural throughout.

The *officers* will bring *their copies* of the year-end corporate financial statement.

(For more on the problem of gender in English, see Sexist Language, page 533.)

EXERCISES

1. The errors of subject-verb agreement in the following sentences have been identified and underlined. Correct them.

   a. Separated subject and verb: Vestiges of an elegant and romantic past remains in the fine architectural examples preserved from the wrecker's ball.
   b. Separated subject and verb: The livelihoods of virtually all its 25,000 residents depends upon or is enhanced by the commerce stimulated by the summer theater festival.
   c. Compound subject, singular verb: I was disappointed that I could barely see the race from where I sat, but the crowd and the excitement in the air was almost enough to compensate for my disappointment.
   d. Compound subject, singular verb: Neither Bill nor his friends was satisfied by Abner's excuse.
   e. A collective noun subject, plural verb: Statistics, never among the easiest subjects, have always been especially difficult for me.
   f. Relative pronoun subject, singular verb: Walter is one of those students who is not satisfied with merely satisfactory work.
   g. Indefinite pronoun, plural verb: He even noticed the color and style of the Bermuda shorts that each of them were wearing at the time of the accident.

2. Identify and correct the errors of subject-verb agreement in each of the following.

   a. The chief justice, in addition to the associate justices, were present for the dedication of the monument to President Fillmore.
   b. Neither of those statements are true of life in big cities.
   c. The days before Laura's wedding ceremony reveals her trying to find a way to postpone it.

d. His moral principles and wholehearted dedication to fair play is what led him to his destruction.

e. With just a little more diligence and careful thought, any one of those students are capable of doing A work.

f. The negative consequences of Melvin's spontaneity and enthusiasm was apparent to anyone who cared to look for them.

g. When you have finished building your deck, all you should be able to see beneath it is the pilings supporting the beams and joists.

h. The dress and equipment for racquetball is similar to that for tennis.

i. When she arrived in New Orleans, she began to put on the curious and outlandish airs that was objected to at once by Stanley.

j. I am one of the few people I know who actually likes airports.

3. The errors of pronoun-antecedent agreement in the following sentences have been identified and underlined. Correct them.

a. Noun-pronoun agreement: As the story makes clear, a person almost always makes it their duty to go out of their way to help others feel as they themself do.

b. Noun-pronoun agreement: When I was in high school, I never knew drugs existed, and even if I had, I never would have been able to afford them. Teenagers today, however, don't need to worry about affording it. He can always wheedle money out of his parents or brothers and sisters.

c. Noun-pronoun agreement: Having only a short time to do all the things I'd like to do with my family gives me tingly sensations deep inside. It feels like a bad case of nerves: joy, anxiety, and fear all mixed together.

d. Noun-pronoun agreement: I feel that a person who is capable of such brutal crimes should be taken out of society for good. They shouldn't be put into a mental hospital or released on probation.

e. Noun-pronoun agreement: The waves were crashing onto the shore with such power that it was propelling our boat faster than we could row it.

f. Indefinite pronoun antecedent: Notice how every time Mr. Johnson tries to help someone, they initially respond with hostility or suspicion.

g. Indefinite pronoun antecedent: The author seems to be saying that everyone who lives with such terrible hardships in their lives cannot understand all the good they are capable of.

h. Indefinite pronoun antecedent: When the day was nearly over and the races were finished, everyone was so tired they could barely walk. In fact, most of them were lying there sleeping in the grass.

i. Indefinite pronoun antecedent: The company has mandated that each of them must contribute one per cent of their income to any three charitable organizations of their choice.

j. Indefinite pronoun antecedent: Knowing from the very beginning that Wilson wasn't on the up and up, James did what anyone would do in that situation to protect themselves from a con man.

4. Identify and correct the errors of pronoun-antecedent agreement in each of the following.

a. It seems to me that all the violent acts attributed to addicts occur when the addict is trying to get drugs. In that case, why prevent them? Why not legalize all drugs but strictly control its sale and distribution?

b. Whether they are salespeople or not, most people go through life presenting an image to sell oneself to the world.

c. Mr. Morton was going to see to it that everybody took their time, stopped to enjoy themselves, and learned all that life had to offer them.

d. A cutting is a leaf and stem of plants that a gardener places in damp soil; they soon root and grow into a new plant.

e. It seems to me that our young people have become increasingly confused about themselves. No one is really sure who they are, what they're going to do for a career, or how they should live their lives.

f. My intentions were to write a lighthearted essay about my nephew and me. I had hoped to get an amused and sentimental response from my readers. After all, I thought, everyone can relate in some way to a small child and the things that happen to them.

g. Anybody staying at the lodge could ride the horses twice a day if they chose. There were plenty to go around because the ranch owned their own herd.

h. As soon as teenagers turn sixteen, they are able to start driving, and of course they want their own cars. At this time parents don't argue too much because they would rather have their child drive his own car than have to drive them wherever they want to go. Unfortunately, his first car is usually a hazard for him and the rest of us.

i. Over the years we have come to recognize them as a company that not only offers a fine annuity program but continues to serve the client after their enrollment.

j. The strike can never be settled as long as everyone is clamoring to express their opinion.

☙ CAPITALIZATION

The tendency of Edited American English is to keep capitals to a minimum. Even so, we capitalize many words besides personal names, the first words of sentences, and the pronoun *I*.

Personal Names and Titles

Capitalize civil, military, religious, and professional titles when they immediately precede a personal name, e.g., *President Lincoln, General Grant, King George.* Do *not* capitalize titles following a name or used in place of a name, e.g., *Senator Stevenson,* but *Adlai Stevenson, senator from Illinois.* One exception: for toasts or introductions, capitalize titles used alone in place of a name.

Capitalize a kinship name only when followed by a given name, e.g., *Uncle Scrooge replied to Huey, Dewey, and Louie, "Thank you, nephews."*

Capitalize abstractions when they are *personified,* that is, given the attributes of persons, e.g., *I am happy that Nature has smiled at last and that on this final day of the semester Spring has arrived.*

Capitalize the names for the various groupings of humankind, e.g., *Africans, Indians, Englishman, Caucasian,* and so forth. But do *not* capitalize designations based on mere color, size, or other physical characteristic, e.g., *white, black, aborigine, highlander,* and so forth.

Place Names

Capitalize geographical names for countries, regions, or parts of continents, e.g., *United States, Spain, Europe, the Arctic, the Southern Hemisphere, the South* (but not the direction, as in *birds fly south for winter*), *New England, North Pole, the Badlands of South Dakota, the English Channel, the New World, New York's Lower East Side.*

Capitalize the names of cities, counties, states, empires, colonies, and kingdoms:

New York City, but *the city of New York.*
the Roman Empire, but *the empire of the Romans.*
Naperville Township, but *the township of Naperville.*

Capitalize the names of mountains, rivers, lakes, oceans, islands, and so forth, but capitalize generic terms like *lake, river,* and *island* only when part of a name, e.g., *Long Island, the Isle of Wight,* but *the islands in the north of Lake Michigan.*

Capitalize the names of buildings, thoroughfares, and monuments, e.g., *the Capitol, the White House, Flitt Hall, the Midway, Stonehenge, the New York Thruway, the Empire State Building, Sears Tower, Route 66.* Do not capitalize proper nouns or personal names that have become common nouns, e.g., *arabic numerals, brussels sprouts, diesel engine, french fries, manila envelope, plaster of paris, roman numerals, scotch whiskey, venetian blinds.*

Names of Organizations

Capitalize the full names of organizations, institutions, and companies, e.g., the *United States Congress,* the *House of Representatives, Chicago City Council,* the *State Department, U.S. Supreme Court,* the *Democratic Party,* the *Nazi Party, Republicans, Chicago Cubs, Hudson's Bay Company,* the *Boy Scouts of America.* But do *not* capitalize generic names, e.g., *adoption court, the cabinet, the legislative branch, the executive branch, the government, fascism, nazism.*

Historical and Cultural Terms

Capitalize the names of historical, political, and cultural events, e.g., *the Fall of Rome, the Civil War, the New Deal.* Capitalize historical periods only when they are proper names or to avoid ambiguity, e.g., *the Restoration,* but *the seventeenth century; the Roaring Twenties,* but *the twenties; the Great Depression,* but *the thirties.*

🐌 CASE

Case is the form nouns and pronouns take to identify their function in a sentence. In this respect, English is simpler than other languages, having only three cases: the subject case, object case, and possessive case. Nouns are especially simple, because the subject and object cases are the same:

Jack and Jill's *dog* bit the three little pigs' *dog*.

To form the possessive case all we do is add -'s or -s', as in *Jill's* dog and the three little *pigs'* dog. Where case is sometimes troublesome, however, is with the seven pronouns that have different forms for each case:

Subjective Case	*Objective Case*	*Possessive Case*
I	me	my/mine
he	him	his
she	her	her/hers
we	us	our/ours
they	them	their/theirs
who	whom	whose
whoever	whomever	

Subject Case

Use the subject case for the subjects of sentences and clauses:

When *she* saw the three little pigs in their new convertible, *she* laughed so hard *she* burst into tears.

Not
The three little pigs and *me* are going driving in their new car.

But
The three little pigs and *I* are going driving in their new car.

Use the subject case for pronouns that complement or complete the subject of a linking verb:

For formal public writing: *It* is *I* who am going driving, but *it* is *he* who bought the car.

For casual and general public writing, "*It* is *me*" is appropriate.

Use the subject case for pronoun appositives that refer to the subjects of clauses or sentences. An *appositive* is a noun or pronoun that gives information about another, preceding noun or pronoun.

Not
We, Jill and *me*, have just had a terrible accident.

But
We, Jill and *I*, have just had a terrible accident.

Object Case
- Use the object case for direct objects: *Miss Bo Peep saw* me *sitting comfortably on my front porch.*
- Use the object case for indirect objects: *Miss Bo Peep gave* me *her sheep to watch while she went for a ride with the three little pigs.*
- Use the object case for objects of prepositions: *With* them *beside* her, *Miss Bo Peep felt safe from Humpty-Dumpty's advances.*
- Use the object case for pronoun appositives that refer to direct objects: *The three little pigs gave* us, *Miss Bo Peep and* me, *their car keys.*

Who and Whom

Who, whom, whoever, and *whomever* pose special problems. Even the most fluent of Edited American English users are occasionally confused about which case to use. Consider *Who did you give it to?* Because *Who* is in the position normally reserved for subjects and the preposition *to* is at the other end of the sentence, the subject case *Who* seems appropriate. Only the most particular writer recognizes that *Who* is in fact the object of the preposition, and so the sentence should read *Whom did you give it to?* There is, however, an easy formula to help you solve these problems of case quickly and almost infallibly.[2]

1. Consider only the words after the place where the pronoun should go.

The three little pigs did not know *who/whom* should be given the car keys. = *who/whom should be given the car keys*

The three little pigs would give the keys to *whoever/whomever* they thought would have the most fun. = *who/whomever they thought would have the most fun*

Who/whom do you think should have the keys?

They gave the keys to little Bo Peep, *who/whom* many consider to be the best driver in town. = *who/whom many consider to be the best driver in town*

2. Rearrange the part of the sentence you're considering to make a new sentence; leave a blank where the pronoun should go.

_____ should be given the car keys.

They thought _____ would have the most fun.

You think _____ should have the keys.

Many consider _____ to be the best driver in town.

3. Substitute *he/she* or *him/her,* whichever is correct, in the blanks.

She should be given the keys.

They thought *he* would have the most fun.

You think *she* should have the keys.

Many consider *her* to be the best driver in town.

4. The subject case *he/she* = *who/whoever*; the object case *him/her* = *whom/whomever:*

The three little pigs did not know *who* should be given the keys.

The three little pigs would give the keys to *whoever* they thought would have the most fun.

Who do you think should have the keys?

They gave the keys to little Bo Peep, *whom* many consider to be the best driver in town.

Possessive Case

Use the possessive case to signal possession, ownership, or relationship:

Little *Bo Peep's* angora mittens didn't fit the *kittens'* pretty paws.

One's paws were too tiny; the *others'* were too large.

Remember, however, that the possessive case of personal pronouns does *not* use the apostrophe, e.g., *its, hers, ours, yours, theirs.*

Use the *of the* possessive form for inanimate objects that are never personified (given human attributes); use *-'s* for inanimate objects that can be personified:

When he reached the *end of the road* he came to his *journey's end.*

Use the possessive case for a pronoun that acts as the subject of a gerund. A *gerund* is an *-ing* verb acting as a noun.

His standing there in that precise spot explains why he was struck by the cow that jumped over the moon.

Going driving with little Bo Peep was surely the reason for *their missing* the Big Bad Wolf when he came to call.

Comparatives and Case

Informal speaking and writing permit an object pronoun after the comparative *than*, e.g., *Little Bo Peep is taller than me.* Edited American English, however, requires a subject pronoun after a linking verb like *is*, e.g., *Little Bo Peep is taller than I [am].* Occasionally the meaning of a sentence can be affected by the choice of case:

Little Bo Peep thinks more of the three little pigs *than me.* (She likes the pigs better.)

Little Bo Peep thinks more of the three little pigs *than I.* (I don't like the three little pigs as well as little Bo Peep does.)

Reflexive Pronouns

Reflexive pronouns are formed by adding *-self* to the possessive or object forms: *myself, himself, herself, itself, ourselves, yourself, themselves.* Use reflexive pronouns when referring to what has been named by a preceding pronoun, noun, or noun phrase:

> *He* taught *himself* to drive.

> I am finally going with the three little *pigs themselves.*

Do *not* use reflexive pronouns when the simple subject or object cases are appropriate.

> *Not*
> The three little pigs and *myself* will be delighted to accept the dinner invitation.

> *But*
> The three little pigs and *I* will be delighted to accept the dinner invitation.

Nonstandard Forms

Edited American English *never* recognizes *hisself, themself, theirself,* or *theirselves* as correct pronoun forms. Use *himself, herself,* or *themselves.*

EXERCISES

1. The case errors in the following sentences have been identified and underlined. Correct them.

a. Incorrect object case: You and <u>me</u> are going to finish this semester if it's the last thing we do.
b. Incorrect subject complement: The first singer on tonight's program will be <u>her</u>.
c. Incorrect object case for an appositive: We, Marty and <u>me</u>, had been separated for so many years that when I first saw him again, <u>I</u> wasn't sure who it was.
d. Incorrect subject case: Please help my wife and <u>I</u> solve a problem.
e. Incorrect object of a preposition: Could you settle a bet between my mon and <u>I</u> about the TV show *Mork and Mindy?*
f. Incorrect subject case for an appositive: The friendly farmer gave us each, Harry and <u>I</u>, two free bushels of rutabagas.
g. Incorrect subject case: This was the woman *who* we used to know as a real fighter against injustice.
h. Incorrect object case: <u>Whom</u> shall I say is calling?
i. Incorrect object case with a comparative: My mother has always been happier than <u>me</u>, perhaps because she likes knock-knock jokes more than <u>me</u>.
j. Incorrect reflexive pronoun: The Snead brothers play miniature golf with Edna and <u>myself</u> every Wednesday evening.
k. Nonstandard form: For us to spend one more penny helping the Weeble family is foolish; they have to learn to help <u>theirselves</u>.

2. The following sentences contain case errors, sometimes more than one per sentence. Identify and correct them.

a. I'll go with whomever asks me first.

b. It should be obvious that us students would prefer not to take the test today.

c. Professor Spritzer, whom many people thought would soon retire, has decided to teach his popular course, The Essentials of Film, for one more semester.

d. Between you and I, learning the rules about the case of pronouns is the most fun I've ever had, but remember, now, that's just between you and myself.

e. Was it her who you blamed for him being late?

f. There is great curiosity about whom the next Democratic nominee will be.

g. Among we Americans, it is not uncommon to find people who are at once generous but bigoted, sentimental but cruel, fun-loving but hardworking.

h. Rudolph and myself have just opened a new business and have surprised ourselves by our success.

i. The First Brigade, which includes myself, will be leaving on the first merchant marine troop ships.

j. In a democracy it's up to we the people to decide whom should be given the power to lead us.

k. Among the many whom we hope will be there are Earl and Leslie Diamond.

l. Although I'm fifteen years younger than my supervisor, I'm just as qualified as her and certainly more intelligent.

COMMA SPLICES AND RUN-TOGETHER SENTENCES

Comma Splices

A comma splice is two or more grammatically complete sentences joined by a comma instead of being separated by a period or other mark of punctuation. Two sentences are "spliced" together as if they were one. Occasionally, these sentences are so closely related by subject and design that a comma splice is the best way to signal their relationship. Consider:

> When you live on a dirt road, you can always tell when a car is coming. *First you see the dust trails, then you hear the engine.* There is an art to guessing who is coming; *the best can tell by the dust trails, the rest can tell by the sound of the engine.*
>
> (Bryant Steele, "Dirt Is Beautiful," *Newsweek* 21 Oct. 1981)

> *These people cherished something here that he could not see, they withheld some ancient promise of food and warmth and light.*
>
> (Eudora Welty, "Death of a Travelling Salesman," *A Curtain of Green and Other Stories* [New York: Harcourt, 1941])

You, too, will occasionally use the comma splice as an effective punctuation strategy. But be sure that such informal punctuation is appropriate for your audience, as is seldom the case in college writing. Be sure, too, that your sentences are similar to these examples. First, the sentences you connect must be relatively short. Second, their subjects must be the same or closely related. Third, their patterns must be similar (called parallel structure). Finally, the sentences must be closely related in some way, or one must lead to the next.

More often than not, however, comma splices are errors of sentence structure and punctuation. A comma is the "weakest," least precise mark of punctuation. If the spliced sentences are long or their relationship indistinct, the comma will not be strong enough to make the connection the writer intends, and the comma-spliced sentences won't communicate clearly. The way to fix the comma splice is to punctuate or reword so that the relation between the sentences is clear and grammatical. Consider:

> One man does not have the right to decide the fate of another, we create our own destinies, and they suit us because they are God's judgments, not another man's.

Revise with a Period
> One man does not have the right to decide the fate of another. We create our own destinies, and they suit us because they are God's judgments, not another man's.

> People who do not live life fully are often unhappy and frustrated, they are usually not as healthy as active people.

Revise with a Conjunction that Produces a Compound Sentence
> People who do not live life fully are often unhappy and frustrated, and they are usually not as healthy as active people.

> She was talking to Mr. Greenleaf, telling him that his boys should treat her more respectfully, after all, she was the one who had allowed them to live on her farm and had given them hand-me-down clothes to wear.

Revise with a Semicolon
> She was talking to Mr. Greenleaf, telling him that his boys should treat her more respectfully; after all, she was the one who had allowed them to live on her farm and had given them hand-me-down clothes to wear.

> It all began like this, I had just received my driver's license and rushed to call my friend in Chicago and tell him I was coming for a visit. Out the door I ran, leaped into my car, and turned the key.

Revise with a Colon
> It all began like this: I had just received my driver's license and rushed to call my friend in Chicago and tell him I was coming for a visit. Out the door I ran, leaped into my car, and turned the key.

> I asked my girlfriend whether she knew where they were, she didn't.

Revise with a Dash
> I asked my girlfriend whether she knew where they were—she didn't.

At last Stanley took his revenge on Blanche, I mean he presented her with a one-way ticket back to the hometown that had driven her out in disgrace.

Revise by Rewording to Produce One Grammatically Complete Sentence
At last Stanley took his revenge on Blanche, a one-way ticket back to the hometown that had driven her out in disgrace.

A special instance of the comma splice may occur when two sentences are joined by a conjunctive adverb. A *conjunctive adverb* is an adverb that does what a conjunction does: it connects words, phrases, and clauses. Here are the most common:

accordingly	also	anyhow	besides
consequently	furthermore	hence	however
indeed	likewise	moreover	nevertheless
otherwise	still	then	therefore

But although a conjunctive adverb does what a conjunction does, a conjunctive adverb is *not* a conjunction and cannot be punctuated as a conjunction is. You can write the following:

Jack and Jill went up the hill to fetch a pail of water, *but* they went home when they discovered they had forgotten the pail.

But you create a comma splice if you write this:

Jack and Jill went up the hill to fetch a pail of water, *however*, they went home when they discovered they had forgotten the pail.

The key to correct punctuation is knowing the difference between these two kinds of words. How to tell them apart? A conjunctive adverb can be moved within its sentence; a conjunction cannot:

However, they went home when they discovered they had forgotten their pail.

They went home, *however*, when they discovered they had forgotten their pail.

vs.

They went home *but* when they discovered they had forgotten their pail.

The best way to correct this kind of comma splice is to replace the comma with a semicolon:

Jack and Jill went up the hill to fetch a pail of water; however, they went home when they discovered they had forgotten their pail.

Run-Together Sentences

A run-together (or fused sentence) is two or more grammatically complete sentences run together, with no punctuation separating them. The effect is similar to making two brush strokes of fresh watercolor, side by side. The two run together and muddy the picture. Consider:

> The boy told Mr. Philips that he was moving to Vermont at that time Mr. Philips offered the boy's mother the name of a Vermont friend, should they need help when they arrived.

The result of this run-together: confusion. We can't be sure when the boy is moving and when Mr. Philips made his offer. Correct a run-together in the same way you would a comma splice, by effective punctuation.

> *Revise with a Period*
> The boy told Mr. Philips that he was moving to Vermont. At that time Mr. Philips offered the boy's mother the name of a Vermont friend, should they need help when they arrived.

Other examples:

> I figured that as long as I had money I wouldn't be as dependent on my mother therefore she couldn't give me a hard time whenever she disagreed with the way I was living my life.

> *Revise with a Semicolon*
> I figured that as long as I had money I wouldn't be as dependent on my mother; therefore, she couldn't give me a hard time whenever she disagreed with the way I was living my life.

> Miss Jackson has explained to us that Mr. Philips is the embodiment of goodness he knows no evil and even lacks that so-called enlightened self-interest that can sometimes degenerate into evil.

> *Revise with a Colon*
> Miss Jackson has explained to us that Mr. Philips is the embodiment of goodness: he knows no evil and even lacks that so-called enlightened self-interest that can sometimes degenerate into evil.

EXERCISES

1. Here are sentences punctuated almost entirely by commas, some necessary for clarity, some unnecessary, some producing comma splices. Repunctuate to eliminate commas splices and unnecessary commas. Before you begin, review the rules for the colon, dash, and semicolon (see Chapter 18, pages 522, 526, and 530).

a. I'm not going to college, because I've been pressured into it, I'm going, because I want to go, because there are subjects I want to study.

b. Such behavior is ridiculous, either Piltdown wants to get married, or he doesn't, it's as simple as that.

c. Delphinia felt no great attraction to this person, all she did was write a letter for him, because he was unable to find the words, that would convey his message.

d. Reverend Hightower's isolation is the result of living too long in his selfish dream land, where he doesn't have to care for others, however, Joe's isolation is a result of his flight from himself, his attempt to escape, rather than resolve the conflict of his dual identities.

e. The members of the neighborhood block club feel they no longer have to go it alone, no longer are they outnumbered by the bureaucrats and street thugs, by banding together, however, they sometimes lose sight of the true purpose of their alliance, and begin to get a little giddy with the power of their numbers.

2. Here are short passages punctuated almost entirely by commas, some necessary for clarity, some unnecessary, some producing comma splices. Repunctuate to eliminate comma splices and any unnecessary commas. Review the rules for the colon, dash, and semicolon before you begin (see Chapter 18, pages 522, 526, and 530).

a. Gertrude Stein, the expatriot American writer of the 1920s, once dismissed Oakland, California, with the remark, "There's no 'there' there," about most cities, however, just the opposite is true, "there" is always there.

b. Live in a large city for five months, five years, or five decades, the length of your stay makes little difference, the city will never become so familiar, and dependable that, like a partner in a comfortable marriage, you can take it for granted, it won't keep regular hours, it won't stay out of your way.

c. Lock your doors, pull the shades, turn up the stereo, spray the air freshener, put on a night shade, even, no matter, the city's sights, smells, sounds, flavors, and textures will still be insistently, persistently, jarringly, invigoratingly, enervatingly, overwhelmingly there.

d. Most of all, a large city impresses with its noise, not sound, noise, a sound is distinct, patterned, with a definite pitch and source, ending as it began, in silence, noise is indistinct, cacophanous, sourceless, noise rings with its own undertones, overtones, and sprung rhythms, its own backbeat, backfire, and backtalk, noise is the sound of the city.

e. Silence in the city is but a pause between individual sounds, sharp and close at hand, even then, however, in the background, from the next room, the next flat, down the block, around the corner, or just a block away will come the noise, the murmur of a hundred languages, the rumble of a thousand buses, the shriek of as many subways and sirens, the honk of a million cars, the hum of innumerable electric motors, the rattle of coins on a counter, the rush of coats in a doorway, the click and thump of footfalls, and everywhere at once your rhythm and my melody, his station and her channel, our woofers and their tweeters, this laughter and that cry.

3. Here are sentences from which almost all punctuation has been removed. Repunctuate for clarity and to correct run-together sentences. Review the rules for the colon, dash, and semicolon before you begin (see Chapter 18, pages 522, 526, and 530).

a. The holiday season will soon be upon us again once more most of us will squander this valuable opportunity to share ourselves and our possessions with the less fortunate.

b. He couldn't understand the relevance of the prosecutor's line of questioning his mother was long dead and buried what could she have to do with the murder in question?

c. To an emotional person he sounds cold without feelings but what if the telegram he received was incomplete he wasn't about to respond until he was sure of all the facts.

d. I like to cook all right but cleaning up after last night's cookout was horrible my fingernails will never be the same again as for my hands well you don't want me to describe what they look like.

e. Too many politicians these days are not content with convincing the public they are the best qualified for office they want instead to crush their opponents with the weight of innuendo and irrelevant charges bury them beneath an avalanche of distorted information obviously reform of the campaign process is in order.

4. Here are short passages from which almost all punctuation has been removed. Repunctuate for clarity and correctness. Review the rules for the colon, dash, and semicolon before you begin (see Chapter 18, pages 522, 526, and 530).

a. If city sounds combine to form a dissonant democracy of noise its sights smells and flavors threaten anarchy a riot of things to see inhale and savor objects seem always to be crowding into view elbowing each other for attention pulling your glance this way and that running from the corner of a gabled turn-of-the-century brownstone house electric and telephone wires draw your gaze back to a telephone pole in the alley and then off to a squat blond brick warehouse a red garage blocks half a handsome old brown apartment building.

b. The aromas of city life are more subtle than its sights but no less insistent as you walk by an open window curry from an Indian kitchen fills a brief space on the sidewalk with its aura from the next flat its windows also flung open to the summer air you might catch the steely waft of chiles simmering or the pickled pungency of sausages in a skillet and because oil is the lubricant that smooths every urban complexity its smells and flavors are everywhere slick from the buses in the street heavy in the factory air bubbly around the fries at the corner grill and finally thick at the bottom of a catchbasin.

c. The texture of city life is the one urban sensation you can never avoid you can stop your ears or buy a machine that produces white noise you can close your eyes wear fashionably dark glasses or turn away you can hold your nose you can eat out of a can or the freezer but even if you wear gloves move to a high-rise and take a cab everywhere you cannot escape the feel of the city on your skin in your hands underfoot in your chest.

d. The texture of the city rakes your face with sandy summer winds and salty winter winds it wilts you in its humidity the sweat of city life

e. You feel the texture of city life in the rusty scales from the railing on your stoop you feel it on your finger drawn across a grimy window pane you feel it on city lots twenty-five feet wide six-flat apartment buildings crowding on either side you feel it on the sidewalk at five o'clock rubbing shoulders with all those strangers bumping jockeying for position at bus stops nudging ahead at crosswalks a few of you bound to rub each other the wrong way no matter what your reserves of politeness indifference or self-absorption.

CONTRACTIONS

We use contractions in our writing (*can't, won't, should've, I'll, they'd*) to capture the rhythms and sounds of speech. They are proper and effective in all forms of public writing when the aim is to narrow the distance between writer and reader by creating a relaxed, informal persona. On more formal public and ceremonial occasions, whenever there is a large gap in social standing, age, or knowledge, contractions are inappropriate. Whether you use them or not depends, as almost always, on your decisions about purpose, occasion, and audience.

THE DOUBLE NEGATIVE

A double negative says no twice. It uses two negative terms where Edited American English uses only one:

> There *ain't nobody* here.
>
> I *don't* have *nothing* to lose by staying here.
>
> He *can't hardly* swim.
>
> She *didn't* get *no* presents from Santa Claus.

Logical-minded people insist that one negative cancels the other and turns what was intended to be a negative statement into a positive. But of course no reader ever misunderstands a double negative in that way. For hundreds of years it has been one way for English speakers to say no emphatically. It is part of English grammar. *However,* most Edited American English users strongly object to double negatives, probably because they are such clear markers of class and education. Therefore, avoid double negatives in formal public speaking and writing, but for social rather than grammatical reasons.

ETC. (NOT *ECT.!*)

Etc. is an abbreviation for the Latin phrase *et cetera*, meaning "and others." We use it for economy's sake at the end of a list to signal that more could have been included if we had chosen to do so. Use *etc.* in less formal public writing. In more formal public writing, use *and so on, and so forth.* For lists of people, use *and others*. Whatever form you use, take care that your readers know what terms are covered by *etc.* or *and so forth.* If they are unfamiliar with your subject and won't know what you've omitted, then complete your list. Never take a shortcut that might confuse your readers.

✑ FRAGMENTARY SENTENCES

No rules are more important to Edited American English than those requiring grammatically complete sentences. The "correct" Edited American English sentence is built upon an *independent clause,* a group of words that can stand by itself and be closed by a period, exclamation point, or question mark: *Jill jogs. Jill jogs? Jill jogs!* An independent clause contains a main subject, a main verb, and often other grammatically related words, phrases, and clauses, e.g., *In my opinion, my next door neighbor Jill jogs with the most fluid stride of any runner I've ever seen, amateur or professional.* In serious, nonimaginative public writing you will almost always write complete sentences.

A *sentence fragment* is just that, part of a sentence left to stand by itself, punctuated as if it were a complete sentence. Writers write fragments partly because they come so naturally in our speech: *Coming? Where? My house. When? Now. Maybe.* These are grammatically incomplete, genuine fragments, but they didn't feel incomplete. Such logically complete fragments linguists have begun to call "minor sentences" and to recognize as legitimate and proper in Edited American English. They enable writers to write with greater economy, rhythm, clarity, and emphasis than grammatically complete sentences would permit. In the following examples, fragments have been emphasized.

Emphatic Fragments
Beatings. Bayonetings. Beheadings. Torchings. No food. No water. No rest.
And it all happened after the battle of Bataan ended.
(Television ad for "NBC Reports: Bataan, The Forgotten Hell," Aug. 1983, emphasis added)

A Fragment for Economy
Of the two calamities that have recently befallen intellectual life in America, one, the American League's "designated hitter" rule, could be repealed easily. *Not so the trivialization of higher education.*
(George F. Will, "Freedom To Learn," *Newsweek* 29 May 1978, emphasis added)

A Fragment for Clarity and Sentence Length
It is a man's singular fate to know that he is an incomplete creature, a kind of monster and angel joined together, with the monster forever betraying the angel and bringing him lower than the beasts. Nothing that other creatures do to each other is nearly as wicked as what we do to our fellows.

The pain is in the knowing. *In the feeling that we have all the ingredients for a lovely life, except one: the reaching out toward each other in amity, instead of the clenched fist, the rock, the club or, worst of all, the monumental indifference toward our own kind.*

> (Sydney J. Harris, "Human tragedy: knowing the best but doing the worst," *Chicago Sun-Times* 18 May 1983, emphasis added)

A Fragment for Rhythm and Emphasis

Every parent knows how inadequately the phrase "I want the best for my child" sums up the real feelings in his or her heart. Beyond trying to ensure healthy bodies and happy homes for our children, we mean that we want to offer them the abundance of life. *Not an abundance of material possessions, but of the curiosity, adventure and joy that will do so much to add satisfaction to their lives when they are grown.*

> (Deborah Fallows, "What Day Care Can't Do," *Newsweek* 10 Jan. 1983, emphasis added)

Fragments that *don't* work we call broken sentences. Almost always they are phrases or clauses disconnected from a main clause to which they should be connected. Sometimes they occur because novice writers fear long sentences and break up a group of words that has grown too long, even when the two new groups of words are grammatically incomplete by themselves. Less frequently, they are potential independent clauses from which something is missing. To fix broken sentences, connect the fragment to its main clause, supply the missing words, or reword. If you can teach yourself to hear the way the human voice rises or falls at the end of a grammatically complete sentence, you'll find it easier to spot fragments in your writing. Whether you complete them depends upon whether they are "minor" or "broken" sentences and upon your audience. Most Edited American English readers object strongly to fragments, even though they read good ones all the time in magazines, books, letters, and business writing. Read the following fragments and their revisions aloud. Listen to your voice. Fragments are emphasized.

A Long Sentence Fragment

I wonder when I get older whether I'll feel about life the way my father does. *Losing any hope of accomplishing his dreams, looking at life as all work and little reward for that work, forgetting his troubles by submerging himself in a TV show, and abusing his body with drink and smoke in hopes that life will not last any longer than it has to.*

Revise by Combining

I wonder when I get older whether I'll feel about life the way my father does, losing any hope of accomplishing his dreams, looking at life as all work and little reward for that work, forgetting his troubles by submerging himself in a TV show, and abusing his body with drink and smoke in hopes that life will not last any longer than it has to.

A Fragmentary List
I love making plans. Everything should be neat, simple, and precise. *One month for basics, one month for learning the school songs and other intermediate marching routines, and one month for advanced kickoff and half-time shows.*

Revise by Combining with a Colon
I love making plans. Everything should be neat, simple, and precise: one month for basics, one month for learning the school songs and other intermediate marching routines, and one month for advanced kickoff and half-time shows.

A Fragmentary Verb Phrase
One of my year-old son's favorite tricks is to take the keys from the table. *Then walk around and try to unlock all the doors.*

Revise by Combining
One of my year-old son's favorite tricks is to take the keys from the table, then walk around and try to unlock all the doors.

A Fragmentary Modifier
Antigone has an acerbic wit. *An ability to combine the sharp word and the telling insight and so shred Creon's kingly pride that he can only sputter in response.*

Revise by Combining
Antigone has an acerbic wit, an ability to combine the sharp word and the telling insight and so shred Creon's kingly pride that he can only sputter in response.

A Fragmentary Dependent Clause Headed by a Subordinating Conjunction (e.g., after, although, as, as if, as though, because, before, if, since, though, until, when where, while, why)
Although Stanley is occasionally capable of love, tenderness, and insight. He is more often a man given to crude exchanges, casual cruelties, and blind self-absorption.

Revise by Combining the Dependent Clause with the Independent Clause
Although Stanley is occasionally capable of love, tenderness, and insight, he is more often a man given to crude exchanges, casual cruelties, and blind self-absorption.

A Dependent Clause Following an Independent Clause
The jobs I found that paid the most money not only were the hardest but had the highest lay-off rate. *Especially when the worker was at the bottom of the seniority list, as I was most of the time.*

Revise by Combining
The jobs I found that paid the most money not only were the hardest but had the highest lay-off rate, especially when the worker was at the bottom of the seniority list, as I was most of the time.

A Dependent Relative Clause (a clause with a relative pronoun—who, which, or that—for its subject)
Last night I turned off the air-conditioner and opened the window to the fresh night breezes. *Which unfortunately blew in every particle of ragweed pollen from the surrounding five square miles.*

Revise by Combining
Last night I turned off the air-conditioner and opened the window to the fresh night breezes, which unfortunately blew in every particle of ragweed pollen from the surrounding five square miles.

EXERCISES

1. These exercises will help you better understand the parts that make up a complete sentence and teach you to recognize fragments. Rewrite each of the following sentences into as many different fragments as you can. To help you, here is a sentence rewritten in all its possible fragments.

Example
Jack and Jill went up the hill.

Subject + Predicate
Jack and Jill. Went up the hill.

Main Clause + Phrase
Jack and Jill went. Up the hill.

Changing Main Verb to -ing or -ed Form
Jack and Jill, going up the hill.

Inserting Relative Pronouns
Jack and Jill, who were going up the hill.

Adding a Preposition and the To- Form of the Verb
For Jack and Jill to go up the hill.

Adding a Subordinating Conjunction and Changing the Verb Form
While Jack and Jill were going up the hill.

a. Yosemite Valley, in California's Yosemite National Park, is surrounded by huge gray granite cliffs, some smooth and sheer, some topped with domes or spires.
b. El Capitan, which rises about 3,000 feet above the valley floor, is the most famous of the cliffs.
c. Half Dome, about 1,800 feet high, dominates the upper end of the valley.
d. The cliffs have a particular kind of allure.
e. The first white men to ascend the mountains around Yosemite often compared them to the Swiss Alps.

(Adapted from David Schonauer, "Fixed-Object Jumping," *The Atlantic* May 1983)

2. Now choose five of the fragments that you've created and turn them into original complete sentences by adding words and ideas of your own.

    a. Original sentence: *The cliffs have a particular kind of allure.* + a subordinating conjunction *(although)* = a fragment: *Although the cliffs have a particular kind of allure . . .*

    b. + a main clause to complete the sentence = a complete sentence: *Although the cliffs have a particular kind of allure, it is unnoticed by most tourists.*

3. The following passages contain almost all fragments, some effective, some not. Combine or rewrite the ineffective fragments into complete sentences; let the effective fragments stand as they are. In most instances, all you will have to do is repunctuate. Review the rules for the colon, dash, and semicolon before you begin (see Chapter 18, pages 522, 526, and 530).

    a. Life. In the country. Images of peace. Freedom. Community. Contentment. And dignified grace crowd your mind's eye. Right? Now there *is* some truth to these images. Even though they come to you from the sentimental story lines of commercial television. Or the manipulative narratives of advertisers. But not much truth.

    b. Listen to someone. Who has lived in both city and country. Our images of country life are like an amateur's photograph. Slightly blurred and crudely cropped. So we don't see the whole picture. Take the much-praised peacefulness of country life. Sure, there's peace. Lots of it. But often it is the peace of a country cemetery. On a mid-July afternoon. And there's freedom, too. But to do what? Is anything so empty of possibility and barren of imagination as the thin line of a country road? Or the square of a country acre? As country dwellers have recognized for ages. The greatest freedom of country life is the freedom to leave. Which they have done in enormous numbers.

    c. Urbanites, unaware of these refugees from the country, imagine that in the country people live together. Not in the compressed agglomerations of city blocks. But in genuine communities. Villages united by shared values.

    d. However, like our other notions of country life, what little truth there is to the ideal of country communities is ironic. True. There is a homogeneity to small-town and rural life. Most of your country neighbors will be German like you. Or Swedish. Or Irish. Or Italian. And community spirit is the cream of this homogeneity. At its best this spirit nourishes the contentment and dignified grace. That are the virtues of rural life. But like cream, this community spirit can curdle. Into an oppressive conformity. To dress alike, believe alike, live alike, build alike.

    e. The curves that so often shape rural life. The depthless arc of the open sky. The constraining sweep of the community circle. The narrow parabolas of job opportunity. Can sometimes bend against the young lives growing there. Preventing them from reaching their potential stature. No wonder so many young men and women flee. To stand straight. No matter how strait the city sidewalk on which they stand. To breathe deeply. No matter what the pollution index.

✒ *I* IN FORMAL PUBLIC WRITING

Many writers enter college assuming that they should never refer to themselves in their writing. And it is true that in some kinds of writing—especially scientific, technical, and report writing—the writer should remain not invisible, exactly, but at least unobtrusive. If the occasion is ceremonial or formally public, if the subject is the center of attention, or if objectivity is at issue, then unnecessary *I*'s will make the writing sound too informal, distract the reader, or create an appearance of undue bias. But whenever you are involved with your subject or want to create an informal persona, you should feel free to refer to yourself as *I* and *me*. Almost never will the occasion be so formal or your persona so detached that you will have to labor over such phrasing as *this writer has observed . . .* or *one may conclude that . . .* when what you would really like to say is *I have observed* or *I believe*.

There is one kind of *I*, however, that you will almost always want to avoid in the final drafts of your writing, the one that often appears in self-conscious introductions: *In this essay I want to explain. . . .* This is an example of a writer trying to find himself a role and thesis, a perfectly acceptable strategy in exploratory writing, but unnecessary and distracting in finished writing. Don't tell your readers what you're going to do; just do it.

✒ MANUSCRIPT FORM

Edited American English puts the best possible face on itself. Most public writing is, after all, down to business and addressed to relative strangers we hope to impress. Therefore, it ought to look as professional and businesslike as possible. The idiosyncrasies of handwriting, stationery, and format that give personal writing some of its charm are merely annoyances in public writing. You want your readers to pay attention to your content, not yourself.

Paper Use clean white paper of high quality, 8½ by 11 inches. If you write by hand, use good-quality lined theme paper. Do not use spiral notebook paper; it never looks anything but messy. Always write on only *one* side of the page. Be aware that many college instructors will not accept handwritten work.

If you type, make sure the type face is clean and your ribbon fresh. If you write by hand, use permanent ink. If you use a word processor and printer, make sure your ribbon is fresh, and avoid the all-capitals format. Note that some readers object to dot-matrix printers.

Paragraphs   Indent new paragraphs five spaces. Do not leave extra space between paragraphs. Indent block quotations ten spaces from the left margin, none from the right.

Spacing and Margins   If you type, double-space throughout the text of your paper, including block quotations (quotations of more than four lines). If you write by hand, single-space if the lines are widely spaced and your handwriting clearly legible; otherwise, double-space. Leave a one-inch margin on the top, bottom, and both sides of the text.

Titles and Headings   If a title page is required, see Chapter 17, "The Research Project," Step 7, page 474. Most college writing does not require a formal title page. Use a heading instead: On the first page of text, one inch from the top and left side, put your name, instructor's name, course, section number, and date, double-spacing between lines. Two spaces beneath that and centered in the middle of the page, write your title. Double-space throughout all titles and headings. Double-space twice between your title and text. Divisions within the text of your paper: center major headings; place subheadings flush with the left margin. Double-space twice between headings and text. Use headings to increase the readability of your paper, but beware of the fragmentation and incoherence that will occur if you use too many of them.

Pagination   Do not number the first page of your paper. On the second and following pages, put your last name and the page number (e.g., *Munro* 6) in the upper right corner, one-half inch from the top and one inch from the right side. Do *not* punctuate numbers with periods, dashes, parentheses, or asterisks.

Corrections   Correct all errors you discover while proofreading. Erase or use correction fluid or special adhesive strips. Anything you cannot erase, neatly strike out, like so: ~~an error.~~ Correct transposed letters with a curved line: trans̲o̲s̲ed. Insert missing words or letters above the line, over a caret (∧): insert∧on. If you must insert a sentence or more, rewrite or retype the page.

❧ NUMBERS

Numbers Written As Words

• Numbers of less than one hundred: *three, nine, thirty-nine* (note the hyphen in two-word numbers). Be consistent, however. If you write several numbers in a passage, and they apply to the same category, make them all either words or figures:

On Monday Little Jack Horner and his friends ate 3 pies, on Tuesday 14, on Wednesday 29, on Thursday 12, on Friday 43, for a grand total of 101 pies.

- Dollar amounts and percentages expressed in no more than two words: *four hundred dollars, fifty-nine cents, twenty-six percent.*
- Round numbers: *twenty thousand.*
- Numbers at the beginning of a sentence: *Three hundred twenty-nine realtors tried to sell condominiums to the old woman who lived in a shoe.*
- The time of day: *two o'clock.*
- Ordinal numbers: *first, second, third.*
- Fractions that stand alone: *After his party little Jack Horner had only one-third of a pie remaining.*

Numbers Written As Figures

- Dates: *July 20, 1944,* or *20 July 1944.* But spell out centuries and decades: *Growing up in the forties, immediately after World War II, was an exhilarating experience.*
- Page numbers and book references: *page 331, pages 32–41, figure 13, Act III, scene ii, line 39 (III.ii.39).*
- Very large numbers: *2.6 billion years ago.*
- Numbers used with abbreviations and symbols: *3:30 P.M., 14 mi., 20 lb., 35-mm film, 47°F., 12 mph, 6 hr., $400, 26%.*
- Numbers followed by fractions: *37⅝, 12½, 3⁹⁄₁₀.*
- Decimal fractions: *2.3, 3.14159.*
- Dollar amounts expressed in more than two words: *$3.49, $299.00, $18,245.39.*
- Street addresses and highways: *1317 W. Pratt Blvd., Route 59.*

Plurals of Numbers

When you write them out, form the plurals of numbers as you would the plurals of other nouns: *Although they looked much older, the three little pigs were only in their twenties.* Form the plurals of figures by adding *-s* alone: *In the 1950s, when they played in the major leagues, the three little pigs had batting averages that ranged from the high .280s to the low .170s.*

Punctuation of Numbers

In figures of one thousand or more, put a comma between every group of three digits: *$14,029,376,000.00.* The exceptions are page numbers, addresses, decimal fractions, Zip Codes, telephone numbers, and year numbers of four digits: *page 2003, 1045 S. Halsted, 3.9145, 60626, (312) 555-2107, 1985.*

❧ PARALLEL STRUCTURE

As grammarians use the word, *parallelism* refers to words, phrases, or clauses that are grammatically equivalent to each other. That is, they can be labeled as the same part of speech: noun, verb, prepositional phrase, noun phrase, verb phrase, relative clause, subordinate clause, and so on. *Faulty parallelism* occurs when two or more parts of a sentence or paragraph should be equal in grammatical form but are not. Here are four rules to help you master the complexities of parallel structure. (For more on faulty parallelism, see Chapter 9, pages 194–195.)

Rule 1   When you join words by coordinating conjunctions (*and, but, yet, for, so, or, nor*) make them parallel in grammatical structure.

Not

Jill likes *to fish and hot-air ballooning.* (Here an infinitive verb is connected to a noun phrase.)

But

Jill likes fishing and hot-air ballooning.

Not

The third filming was uneventful except *when the dog barked before each take and this strange feeling of déjà vu.* (A subordinate clause is connected to a noun phrase.)

But

The third filming was uneventful except for the dog's barking before each take and this strange feeling of déjà vu. (Both are now noun phrases, objects of the preposition *for.*)

Not

Two minutes after we stumbled into what seemed to be a clearing, I found myself chest-deep in *green slime, weeds six feet high, and hundreds of bugs all over me.* (Although the three noun phrases are grammatically parallel, they are not logically parallel: chest deep in weeds six feet tall? Chest deep in hundreds of bugs?)

But

Two minutes after we stumbled into what seemed to be a clearing, I found myself chest-deep in green slime, lost in six-foot weeds, and covered by hundreds of bugs. (The series consists of three grammatically and logically parallel adjective phrases.)

Rule 2   When verbs describe the same event put them in the same tense. Otherwise, they produce a *shift in tense* error, a form of faulty parallelism. (For more on tense, see pages 536–538.)

Not

    Our baby Tommy *began* to walk at Christmas time, even though all our relatives *told* us Tommy *is* too young to walk. (The shift is from past to present tense.)

But

    Our baby Tommy began to walk at Christmas time, even though all our relatives told us Tommy was too young to walk.

Not

    At the beginning of the story, Mr. Jackson *leaves* his house loving the world; he *set* out to make others happy. After buying his newspaper, he *cut* across an avenue and *took* a side street uptown. (The shift here is from present to past. When writing about the action of a story or novel, use the present tense.)

But

    At the beginning of the story, Mr. Jackson leaves his house loving the world; he has set [present perfect tense] out to make others happy. After buying his newspaper, he cuts across an avenue and takes a side street uptown.

Rule 3   Be consistent in point of view. When you use several pronouns referring to the same person, do not shift grammatical point of view from one pronoun to the next. Usually an erroneous *shift in point of view* involves a shift from first person (*I, me, we, our*) or third person (*he, she, they, them, theirs*) to second person (*you, yours*).

Not

    One reason *I* like rock 'n' roll is the sense of invigorated relaxation it gives *you.*

But

    One reason I like rock 'n' roll is the sense of invigorated relaxation it gives me.

Not

    I enjoyed working as a dishwasher because nobody ever bothered *you* while *you* were working.

But

    I enjoyed working as a dishwasher because nobody ever bothered me while I was working.

Not

    The first step in making paint is staging the chemicals. When the stager begins, *she* must be careful to use the right chemicals so *she* does not ruin the paint. That means reading the production formulas to see what *you* need.

But

    The first step in making paint is staging the chemicals. When the stager begins, *she* must be careful to use the right chemicals so *she* does not ruin the paint. That means reading the production formulas to see what she needs.

Rule 4 Do not shift voice without good reason. *Voice* refers to the relationship between a subject and its verb. In *active voice* constructions, the subject commits the action of the verb: *The boy hit the ball.* In *passive voice* constructions, the subject is acted upon by the verb: *The ball was hit.* As long as you're writing about one subject, keep to one voice or the other. (For more on active and passive voice, see Chapter 9, pages 184–185, and Chapter 10, pages 205–207.)

Not

Alice and Jane *sighed* with satisfaction because all their goals *had been achieved.* (a shift from active to passive voice)

But

Alice and Jane *sighed* with satisfaction because they *had achieved* all their goals.

Not

When I *wasn't* horseback riding, many other activities *were made* available to choose from (a shift from active to passive voice).

But

When I *wasn't* horseback riding, I *had* many other activities *to choose* from.

EXERCISES

1. Rewrite the following sentences to correct problems of faulty parallelism. The errors have been identified and underlined.

a. Faulty parallelism: He declares that his principles are not those of a "do-nothing" politician. His views are very rigid and intends to bring his country back from the edge of ruin.

b. Faulty parallelism: Now that I am almost thirty-five and with only a high school diploma, I see an uncertain future for myself and my family.

c. Faulty parallelism: The room is decorated with Colonial furniture: a round, dark pine dining table with matching chairs and on the south wall is a dark pine, two-story hutch with glass doors.

d. Faulty parallelism: I sometimes imagine myself as one of those patients I used to care for: a stroke, heart attack, failing kidneys, or, worst of all, cancer.

e. Shift in tense: Most people will do all they can to defend themselves and prove they were innocent.

f. Shift in tense: Throughout the day he offered assistance to anyone in need and even gave money away. But then he goes home and treats his wife badly.

g. Shift in tense: For an hour and a half I was running around the house, jumping up and down, squealing delightedly, and started calling all my friends.

h. Shift in point of view: The Boston matrons in their 1955 Studebaker Hawks are unlike any other women I've ever seen. When they hit the open road, they floor it. I was doing seventy on a freeway when one of them zipped past me and left me in her dust. They'll occasionally acknowledge <u>your</u> presence with a glance, but don't be fooled into thinking they're concerned about <u>you</u>.

i. Shift in point of view: Whenever <u>Alma</u> visits Maria's house, <u>she</u> feels as if <u>she</u> wants to stay there forever. It's the sort of place that makes <u>you</u> want to arrive for <u>your</u> next visit with everything <u>you</u> own in <u>your</u> arms.

j. Shift in voice: Senator Stubble reminded his staff that when preparing their report <u>they should limit</u> themselves to observed facts and <u>care should be taken</u> not to include unsubstantiated evidence.

2. Identify and correct the problems of faulty parallelism in the following sentences.

a. With greater attention the lectures could be understood, and I would not have to ask Professor Sterno to explain himself after class.

b. When I plan out my life these days, I invariably divide it into three unequal categories: academic, work, and pleasure.

c. Mildew filled out registration forms until he had signed up for all the classes he wanted and most important that the classes did not overlap.

d. Students should also be encouraged to spend more time at the local library and using its facilities, reading newspapers and magazines, and watching television.

e. All my months of practice have paid off. Now, the audience applauds, chills of giddy delight run down your spine, and the sweet feeling of success overwhelms you.

f. He spends the whole day walking around in his comfortable resoled shoes and his pockets full of change.

g. Some names in automotive history are surprising: Thomas Alva Edison is responsible for many inventions that aided the growth of the industry, and Edward V. Rickenbacker, known principally for his aviation exploits, but who also was a prominent race car driver and founder of the Rickenbacker Motor Company in 1926.

h. Most Germans visit Holland in the summertime for the annual streetfairs. Counters are set up in the streets in front of huge tents. Behind these counters homemade bread and cheese were sold, and in the tents people are drinking and dancing.

i. My group chose anxiety for its class project. It was to be graded on how interesting and informative your report is. Sounds simple enough, right? That's what our group thought.

j. I can picture him now. He's probably about fifty-three, attractive, but overweight, thick gray hair, overwashes it so it tends to be dry and fly-away, and this poor fellow is desperately insecure about himself.

❧ PLURAL FORMS

Add -s or -es to form the plurals of names and other capitalized words: *Three Jacks, four Jills, and thirteen Joneses held hands as they climbed the hill.*

Add -s alone to letters, coinages, and numbers. Use an apostrophe only when confusion might result: *In the early 1960s, the three little pigs studied their three Rs very thoroughly and earned their PhD's.*

Add -s to the end of compounds and group words, whether they are one word or hyphenated: *checkbooks, scholar-poets, citizen-soldiers.* In some compounds, however, add -s to the first word, the noun, rather than the modifier following it: *mothers-in-law, attorneys general, passersby, courts martial.*

PRONOUN REFERENCE

A pronoun takes the place of a noun, its *antecedent. Antecedent* means "to go before," but a noun does not necessarily have to go before its pronoun:

A pronoun preceding its antecedent

If *she* paid more attention, *Bertha* could see that
Fred likes kumquats more than *he* pretends.

A pronoun following its antecedent

Whatever their arrangement, the lines of relationship between pronoun and antecedent must be clear and unbroken. If the relationships are obscure or ambiguous, we call the problem *faulty pronoun reference.* (For more on faulty pronoun reference, see Chapter 9, page 192.)

Rule 1 Make sure every pronoun has a definite antecedent, a noun or noun phrase that you can put your finger on. This rule makes *it, this,* and *they* among the most difficult English words to use well, because we often use them to refer vaguely to what has gone before or to imply an antecedent that isn't actually there in a preceding sentence.

There are now at least two four-wheel-drive tracks in Wisconsin where *they* hold races on a large muddy oval. Although there are no prizes, *it's* still a lot of fun. The fire departments from surrounding communities will even hose your truck down for you before you go home, that is, if *they* haven't run out of water making the tracks muddy.

We get the point here, certainly, but only the second *they* has an actual antecedent, *fire departments.* The first *they* refers by implication to the operators of the tracks and the *it* in *it's* to racing in general. The solutions to the reference faults? First, eliminate pronouns when their antecedents are unknown or unimportant by using the passive voice verb form (see pages 205–208). Second, be specific:

There are now at least two four-wheel-drive tracks in Wisconsin where *races are held* on a large muddy oval. Although there are no prizes, *the racing* is still a lot of fun. . . .

Rule 2 Avoid ambiguous pronoun reference. A pronoun is ambiguous when it seems to refer simultaneously to two different antecedents.

> Sometimes people do not know how to distinguish moral law from governmental law. Governmental law, or the law of the people, is literal and specific; it lacks compassion for human frailty or error. *This* seems to be King Creon's problem in Sophocles' play *Antigone*.

What is the king's problem, his inability to distinguish between moral and governmental law, his lack of compassion, or both? We can't be sure. The solution to ambiguous reference? Specify the relationship: *Bad judgment and lack of compassion are King Creon's double problems in Sophocles' play* Antigone.

Another example:

> The criminal, acting according to his strange code of conduct, chose the road to prison instead of freedom, *which* I found difficult to understand.

What was difficult to understand, the criminal's code of conduct, his choice, or both? The solution is to be specific: *The criminal, acting according to his strange code of conduct, chose the road to prison, a choice I found difficult to understand.*

Rule 3 Beware of sentence and clause antecedents. It used to be that an antecedent *always* had to be a noun or noun phrase, because that's what pronouns stand for. But on occasion English writers and speakers make entire sentences or clauses the antecedents for pronouns. Shakespeare did it:

> To be or not to be: *that* is the question.

Contemporary writers do it, too:

> *A Sentence as Antecedent*
> Places to visit in July and August: The Greek Islands of the Ionian Sea, Corfu, Zakinthos, and Ithaki. The people of these islands are the most civilized of Greeks. *This* may be because they were never conquered by the Turks.
> (*Esquire* 5 June 1979, emphasis added)

> *A Paragraph as Antecedent* ·
> I now come to windows, the cleaning chore that has probably struck more anomie into more hearts than any other household task save oven cleaning. Still, clean windows can make a dramatic difference in how a room looks. And there's a trick to them. Forget all you've read and been told about waiting for a cloudy day, wiping with newspapers, and all that. Buy a squeegee. Just mix up a bucketfull of warm water with a little ammonia (in this case homemade brew *is* called for), wash the window with the sponge end of the squeegee, and wipe it dry with the rubber end. Done.
> *This*, however, leaves open the question of how to deal with the *outside* of the window. . . .
> (Ben Yagoda, "What Every Man Should Know,"
> *Esquire* Aug. 1983, emphasis added to *this*)

What Rule 3 means, therefore, is this: Use a pronoun to refer to an entire clause or sentence, *provided* the whole clause or sentence is the antecedent. Don't use a pronoun to refer vaguely to only part of what precedes:

> This man was a complete fake. He didn't mean any of the nice things he said. The very next day he turned around and spoke disparagingly about those he had complimented. *That's* why we can't trust first appearances.

Why can't we trust first appearances? Because the man spoke disparagingly, because he contradicted himself, or because he turned out to be a fake? We can't be precisely sure from the preceding sentences. This writer should be more specific: *Such hypocrisy explains why we can't trust first appearances.*

EXERCISES

1. Rewrite the following sentences to solve the problems of faulty pronoun reference. The errors have been identified and underlined.

a. Implied antecedent: Old Bilgewater's Bar and Grill has a large clientele because of its attractive decor, the type of food they serve, and the kind of music they play.

b. Implied antecedent: Only in the last few years have they begun to build color televisions that don't require viewers to get up and adjust them every few minutes.

c. Implied antecedent: He had no desire to taste the goat's milk, and he was certain he didn't want to milk it.

d. Ambiguous antecedent: I was the last kid on the bus every morning, but I was also the first one off. This was fine with me because then I got to spend a little more time with my friends.

e. Ambiguous antecedent: Raymond told Frank the good news about his lottery ticket.

f. Sentence antecedent: Company morale is low because employees don't know one another or understand jobs besides their own. This makes it hard to increase productivity.

g. Sentence antecedent: The roles are then reversed. The parents are now cared for by the children, sometimes twenty-four hours a day, an ironic contrast to the time years ago when the parents cared for their children. This is when a nursing home, if it is a good one, might be considered.

2. Identify and correct the problems of faulty pronoun reference in the following sentences.

a. Once inside the amusement park I could see lines of food stands down every path. That's why they didn't let me bring my own food, which added up to many extra dollars of profit for them.

b. Jill bent closer, trying to catch the old woman's voice, who was mumbling of old, long-gone beaus, dead for thirty years or more.

c. You should get down to Grubber's Stuffo Food Town as soon as possible; they're having a fantastic sale on snack pies.

d. The king cannot comprehend that the princess would risk his royal wrath by a gesture of love and respect toward the condemned rebel. This is typical of many people in our day and age as well.

e. A father would never hit his child unless he was bad.

f. Japan was all that I expected it to be, a place where simplicity was the key to all things. It was reflected nowhere more clearly than in their pen and ink drawings, little jewels of grace and economy.

g. Overcrowding is now so great in America's prisons that in some states they pack them in four or five to a cell.

h. Teachers who care more for their field of study than their students are often the ones who complain most loudly when they have to do some work like answering a few of the questions they ask or reading what they write.

i. When my grandfather was sick last year, all he ever said was that he wasn't dead yet, wasn't worrying about it, and we shouldn't worry about it either.

j. Mr. Johnson treats people equally, even those he disagrees with. This was his response even when he discovered his favorite nephew was joining the Democratic Party.

PUNCTUATION

More than any other feature of the writing system, punctuation compensates for the silence of script and gives writers back their voices. When we speak, we have all the vocal resources of stress, pitch, rhythm, and pause to help listeners catch our meaning. When we write, we have none of them. Without punctuation, readers couldn't begin to understand even a relatively simple sentence like this:

> When Michael returned the car was parked near the drive in the restaurant where the fast moving vans drivers like to eat.

Imagine the difficult time English readers must have had in the fourteenth and fifteenth centuries, when manuscripts and the first printed books used punctuation haphazardly, sometimes not at all! Here is our sample sentence effectively punctuated:

> When Michael returned, the car was parked near the drive-in, the restaurant where the fast moving-vans' drivers like to eat.

The fifteen marks of English punctuation are presented in the following sections in alphabetical order. As you study and experiment with them, keep two points in mind. First, despite the occasional complexity of punctuation rules, these fifteen marks perform only four roles: introducing, ending, separating, and enclosing. Second, the best writers tend to use fewer punctuation marks than other writers. For them, punctuation is organic, part of the language, design, and rhythm of their sentences, not rules to be followed blindly but an aid to meaning. They punctuate as much by sound and feeling as by rules and make their sentences as clean, forward-moving, and direct as possible.

The Apostrophe (')

Use an apostrophe to signal possession by nouns and indefinite pronouns.

- A singular noun: *the little kitten's mittens, the kitty's mittens.*
- A plural noun: *three little kittens' mittens, the kitties' mittens.*
- An indefinite pronoun: *anyone's mittens, nobody's mittens.*
- A proper noun: *Little Miss Muffet's tuffet, IBM's tuffet* (names of more than one syllable ending in *-es* take an apostrophe alone, without an *-s*: *Moses' tuffet, Aristophanes' tuffet*).
- Use an apostrophe in contractions: *can't, won't, I'll, it's.*
- Do *not* use an apostrophe with coinages, letters, numbers, and abbreviations, unless confusion would result by omitting the apostrophe.

> Not: *the three Rs, the 1980s, at sixes and sevens, PhDs.*
> But: *a's, b's, and c's.*

- Do *not* use an apostrophe with possessive pronouns: *its, hers, theirs, ours, yours.*

Braces { }

Braces are the most inclusive sign of enclosure and are most often used in mathematical formulas and tables: {[( )]}.

Brackets [ ]

Insertions. When quoting use brackets to make editorial corrections, explanations, and comments. The brackets separate the words of one writer, the one doing the quoting, from the words of the writer being quoted.

Corrections
"Jack and Jill went up the hill to fetch a pile [sic] of water." (Whenever you quote, quote exactly, even an obvious error. To signal to your readers that you are aware of the error, write the Latin word *sic*, meaning "thus," in brackets following it.)

Explanation and Comments
"Jack and Jill [currently the United States' best hope for a gold medal in next year's Olympic hill-climbing event] went up the hill to fetch a pail of water."

Parenthetical elements. Use brackets to signal parentheses within parentheses, especially when documenting sources: (*Jack and Jill,* Hill-Climbing Made Easy [*New York: Fifth Story Press, 1983]*).

The Colon (:)

Lists, explanations, quotations. Use a colon before a list, explanation, or quotation that is not grammatically a part of the introductory sentence preceding it.

A List
The three little kittens have lost their mittens: the pink woolen mittens, the pigskin mittens, and the skiing mittens.

An Explanation
Frankly, no one believes them when the three little kittens tell us they have lost their mittens: everyone knows they are pathological liars.

A Quotation
The third kitten made her confession sheepishly: "I hocked my mittens to get money for a trip to Las Vegas."

Introductions and salutations. Use a colon after a speaker's introductory remark or after the salutation of a formal letter:

Ladies and gentlemen:

Dear Ms. Muffet:

Numbers. Use a colon between chapter and verse in a biblical reference (*John 1:1*), between hours and minutes (*3:43*), between volume and page number (*34: 426–27*).

Colons, quotations, and complete sentences. When you use a colon to introduce a quotation or a passage of more than one sentence, capitalize the first letter of the first word. Otherwise, do *not* capitalize: *It is clear why Ms. Muffet left her tuffet: a spider had sat down beside her.*

Do *not* use a colon after introductory phrases like *like* and *such as*. (For more on the colon, see Chapter 8, pages 171–172.)

The Comma (,)

Compound sentences. Use a comma before the coordinating conjunction that joins the independent clauses of a compound sentence. The exception is the short compound sentence.

Jack and Jill went up the hill to fetch a pail of water, but when it began to get dark and they still had not found the well, they came home again.

Jack and Jill went up the hill but soon they returned.

Series. Use a comma between items in a series and before the conjunction that precedes the last item: *Jack fell down, broke his crown, and lost all the change he had in his pockets.*

Nonrestrictive and restrictive modifiers. Use commas to set off nonrestrictive modifiers from the rest of the sentence. A *nonrestrictive modifier* is a word, phrase, or clause that adds nonessential information to a sentence.

A Nonrestrictive Word
Jack and Jill, lovers, married suddenly.

A Nonrestrictive Phrase
Jack and Jill, having dated for five years, decided to marry soon after their terrible tumbling accident.

A Nonrestrictive Clause
Jack and Jill, who had been planning to install plumbing for years, went ahead with the job soon after their terrible tumble.

Do *not*, however, use commas around a restrictive word, phrase, or clause. A *restrictive modifier* provides information essential to the meaning of a sentence; the sentence could not be understood without it. The absence of the commas is one way of signaling the importance of a restrictive element to the rest of the sentence.

A Restrictive Word (emphasized)
Jill's brother *Phil* laughed uncontrollably as he watched his sister tumble down the hill.

A Restrictive Phrase
The elderly woman *sitting on the bench next to Phil* struck the oaf with her umbrella.

A Restrictive Clause
The report *that Jill submitted to her insurance company* cited cuts, contusions, and psychological anguish.

Here are three simple rules that will help you know whether to punctuate these modifiers.[3]

Rule 1: If a relative clause begins with *that,* do not punctuate.

The boy [that] Jill chose was Jack.

Rule 2: If you can substitute *that* for *who, whom,* or *which,* do not punctuate:

The girl [whom] Jack liked best was Jill.
The hill [which] Jill fell down was Old Baldy.

Rule 3: If you can omit the *who, whom,* or *that,* do not punctuate:

The hill [that] Jack climbed is higher than any other.
Jill has told everyone that she is madly in love with the handsome young man [whom] she has chosen to be her husband.

Introductory elements. Use a comma to set off an introductory phrase or clause from the rest of the sentence; this comma may be omitted if the introduction is short and the meaning clear.

An Introductory Phrase
Looking up the hill and thinking to himself that he would never get to the top if he had to stop and rest with Jill every five minutes, Jack wondered whether he should leave her.

An Introductory Clause
When Jill detected the condescending tone in Jack's voice, she vowed she would beat him to the top of the hill no matter what.

A Comma Omitted
Glancing at his watch Jack decided they had rested long enough.

Direct address, interjections, transitions, and parenthetical elements. Use commas to set off direct address, interjections, transitional adverbs and parenthetical elements that have a close relationship to the rest of the sentence.

"Jack, this is the last hill I'm ever going to climb with you."

"Oh, be quiet!"

Jill, however, would not be quiet.

Jack and Jill, once lovers but now not even civil to each other, argued bitterly the final hundred yards to the summit.

Coordinate adjectives. Use a comma to separate two or more adjectives if each adjective modifies the noun by itself: *Jack is the tall, dark stranger standing over there on the hill.* If you can reverse their order or put *and* between them, they are coordinate adjectives and should be separated with a comma; otherwise, do not punctuate: *Jack is the tall black man standing over there on the hill.*

Titles. Use a comma to set off titles or positions following a person's name: *Jack Jones, Hill-Climber Extraordinaire; Jill Jones, BA, MA, PhD.*

Dates. Use a comma between the day of the month and year: *February 9, 1944.* Do not use a comma for *9 February 1944* or *February 1944.*

Omissions. Use a comma to signal an omission for brevity: *Jack took the right-hand fork on the way to the summit, Jill, the left.*

Quotations. Use a comma to set off a direct quotation from the rest of the sentence:

Jack sighed, "Jill, you're never going to make it."

"Just watch me," Jill responded.

Do *not* use a comma if the quotation is the subject or complement of the sentence:

"Just watch me" was Jill's response.

Jill's response was "Just watch me."

Place the comma *inside* quotation marks but *outside* closing brackets or parentheses: *"I don't think you can keep up with me," Jack remarked (although if the truth be known he was as tired as she), and then he turned back to the trail rising before him.*

Clarity. Use a comma for clarity: *To Jack, Jill remained an enigma.*

Do *not* use a comma between subject and predicate: *The pail that they had carried together for four hours and twenty-five minutes [,] had now become so heavy they were in danger of dropping it.*

The Dash (--)

Type a dash as two hyphens with no space before or after: *word--word.* Use it to signal an abrupt change of thought: *Tom, Tom, the piper's son learned to play when he was young--too young, if you ask me.*

Faltering speech. Use a dash to signal faltering speech: *I--I--don't think I know how to play "Rock Around the Clock."*

Explanations. Use a dash to introduce and emphasize an explanation: *The music instructor spent a half-hour explaining to Tom the proper methods for removing his pipe from its case--an explanation he hoped would not be lost on his dense pupil.*

Parenthetical elements. Use a dash to set off and emphasize parenthetical material: *Now Tom with his pipe did make such a noise--such a hooting, screeching, and squawking--that the city council voted to declare Tom an environmental hazard.*

Lists. Use a dash to introduce a list: *Tom and his pipe have been banned in all the major cities--New York, Boston, Chicago, Dallas, and Los Angeles.*

Use a dash after an introductory list: *"Teen Angel," "You Light up My Life," and "Dead Man's Curve"--these three songs were the whole of Tom's repertoire.*

Do *not* use a comma after a dash, except when the comma separates a quotation from words that identify the speaker: *"I--I--," Tom stammered.* (For more on the dash, see Chapter 8, pages 172–173, and Chapter 12, page 257.)

The Ellipsis (. . .)

Type ellipsis points as three evenly spaced periods, with one space before and after each. Use them to signal the omission from a quotation of a word, phrase, sentence, or whole paragraph.

"Little Bo-Peep has lost her sheep and can't tell where to find them."

". . . Bo-peep has lost her sheep and can't tell where to find them."

"Little Bo-Peep . . . can't tell where to find them."

"Little Bo-Peep has lost her sheep. . . ."

When an ellipsis ends a sentence, use four periods, three for the ellipsis and one for the period. It is not logical, perhaps, but the *first* dot is considered the period. Therefore, there is no space between the last letter of the last word and the first dot: *"sheep. . . ."* If the sentence closes with a question mark or exclamation point, that mark is retained, followed by three ellipsis points: *"Do you mean to tell me little Bo-Peep has lost her sheep? . . ."*

Use a full line of ellipsis points to signal the omission of a full line or more of poetry.

> Little Bo-Peep has lost her sheep,
> . . . .
> Leave them alone, and they'll come home,
> Bringing their tails behind them.

Use ellipsis points to signal a pause in speech or an unfinished statement that trails off: *When the police interrogated her, Miss Peep seemed disoriented: "I'm . . . they're gone, and I'm all alone. . . ."*

Do *not* use ellipsis points when quoting what is obviously an incomplete sentence: *Miss Peep claims she "has lost her sheep."* Use ellipsis points only when the quotation would appear to be complete without them or when something has been omitted from the middle of a passage. For the same reason, do *not* use ellipsis points at the beginning of a block quotation that opens with a complete sentence or at the end of a block quotation that closes with a complete sentence.

The Exclamation Point (!)

Use the exclamation point to make an outcry: *Old King Cole was such a merry old soul!*

Use the exclamation point for emphasis or irony: *Old King Cole is merry, sure!* But avoid its overuse. Too many exclamation points make a writing sound melodramatic or false in tone. When everything is exclamatory, nothing is emphatic.

Place the exclamation point inside quotation marks and parentheses when it is part of the quoted or parenthetical matter: *Old King Cole cried, "Bring me my fiddlers three!" (Old King Cole wasn't so merry when he later discovered his three fiddlers had made off with his pipe and his bowl!)*

The Hyphen (-)

Use a hyphen to divide a word at the end of a line: *hy-phen.* Be sure to divide words only between syllables. Do not allow single letters to stand alone, as would be the case with *e-licit, a-cre,* or *u-nite.* Divide after a vowel but according to pronunciation: *Neu-ron, educa-tion.* Divide words spelled with a hyphen *only* at the hyphen: *well-disposed, mother-in-law.*

Use a hyphen to join compound words: *soldier-statesman, two-thirds, dust-catching.* But note that some compounds are *open compounds* that have no punctuation between words: *decision making, problem solving.* Others are *closed compounds,* joined as if they were one word: *checkbook, greenhouse, catlike.*

Use a hyphen between a prefix and proper name: *pre-Kennedy years, post-Super Bowl depression.*

Use a hyphen between compound adjectives that precede a noun: *fast-moving van, well-known poet, cross-eyed baseball player.*

Hyphenate written numbers *twenty-one* to *ninety-nine.*

Parentheses ( )

Use parentheses to set off explanatory or amplifying remarks that are not closely related, grammatically or logically, to the sentence or paragraph where they appear:

Little Jack Horner (an actual sixteenth-century Englishman) sat in the corner eating his Christmas pie; he put in his thumb and pulled out a plum (the estate he created on lands seized by Henry VIII from the church), and said, "What a good boy am I."

Of the ways to enclose remarks—commas, dashes, and parentheses—the parentheses signal the greatest separation between the ideas inside the punctuation and those outside. Dashes tend to emphasize what they enclose, parentheses to deemphasize.

If one sentence contains another sentence enclosed by parentheses, do not open the parenthetical sentence with a capital or close it with a period: *He put in his thumb and pulled out a plum (had he delayed much longer it would have been a prune).* When a parenthetical sentence stands by itself, open it with a capital and close it with a terminal punctuation mark: *Sing a song of sixpence, a pocket full of rye; four and twenty blackbirds baked in a pie. (By the time of Shakespeare in the sixteenth century, this rhyme was already an old favorite in England.)*

Always put other marks of punctuation *after* the parentheses: *Simple Simon met a pie man (reportedly selling lemon meringue pies), and the poor soul promptly lost his shirt. At the time, Simon was going to the fair (the local county fair); had he continued on his way instead of allowing himself to be hypnotized by the pie man's neon sign, he wouldn't have squandered his life's savings ($29.30).*

Use parentheses to enclose numbers or letters in enumeration: *This small drama has a cast of two: (1) Simple Simon, (2) the pie man.* (For more on parentheses, see Chapter 12, page 257.)

The Period (.)

Use a period at the end of a sentence, like this. Do *not* use a period for a sentence contained within another sentence:

Parenthetical Sentence
Seesaw, Margery Daw, Jenny shall have a new master (after all that seesawing, I'll bet she has an upset stomach, too).

A Quotation
"Rub-a-dub-dub, three men in a tub" was all the laundry man could sing.

Use a period after numbers or letters that enumerate items in a list:

My corner bakery should consider adopting recipes for
  1. Jack Horner's plum pie
  2. The good king's four and twenty blackbirds pie
  3. Simple Simon's pie

Use periods after abbreviations ending in lower case letters (*Mr., Mrs.*), between dollars and cents (*$19.95*), and before decimals (*3.141592*).

Do *not* use a period after items in a vertical list unless one or more items is a complete sentence. Do *not* use a period after titles and headings. Do *not* use periods after the letters of an acronym: *FBI, SPCA, BMW, CIA.*

Place periods *inside* quotation marks, whether single or double, whether the quotation is a single word or a complete sentence: *"Pease-porridge hot" sounds only slightly more appetizing than "pease-porridge in the pot, nine days old."*

The Question Mark (?)

Use a question mark to indicate a question or doubt:

Baa, baa, black sheep, have you any wool?

"Yes, Sir, yes, Sir, three (?) bags full (in today's recessionary economy?)."

Put a question mark at the end of a complete sentence included parenthetically within another sentence: *One for my master, one for my dame, and one for the little boy (guess who will get the smallest bag?) who lives in the lane.*

Do *not* use a question mark after an indirect question: *He wanted to know whether Baa Baa Black Sheep had any wool.*

Place the question mark inside quotation marks or parentheses only when the question is part of the quoted or parenthetical matter.

Did he say, "Three bags full"?

He asked, "Have you any wool?"

Quotation Marks (" ' ' ")

Direct quotations. Use double quotation marks (" ") as the standard signal of quotation, whether the quotation is a word, phrase, paragraph, or more. Put them around all direct quotations:

While Humpty-Dumpty was sitting on the wall, he wondered suddenly, "What am I doing up here?"

Do not use quotation marks around indirect quotations reporting the words or thoughts of another:

While Humpty-Dumpty was sitting on the wall he wondered suddenly what he was doing doing up there.

Use quotation marks to signal that a word is being used in a special sense: *These three little pigs have certainly made little "pigs" of themselves, haven't they?* (For more on this use of quotation marks, see Chapter 11, pages 241–242.)

Use single quotation marks (' ') *only* for quotations within quotations, *never* for words quoted alone or for a special sense of their meaning. For quotations of quotations within quotations, alternate marks of punctuation (double, single, double, and so on), making sure that you close with as many quotation marks as you opened with.

Jane complained to Bill, "John said, 'I don't love you any more, not since Betty winked coyly at me, whispered huskily, "Come over here, big boy," and sang sweetly in my ear, "Row, Row, Row Your Boat." ' "

Quotations and paragraphing. When a quotation runs for more than one paragraph, open each paragraph with quotation marks, but close only the last.

For *block quotations,* those indented and set off from the rest of the text, do *not* use quotation marks unless there are quotation marks in the original (see Chapter 17, "The Research Project," Step 7, pages 467–469).

Quotation marks and other punctuation. Always put periods and commas inside quotation marks; put colons and semicolons outside. Put exclamation points and questions marks either inside or outside: *inside* if the quotation itself is an exclamation or question, otherwise outside.

Humpty-Dumpty told his lawyer he had suffered what could only be called a "great fall"; then he asked, "Do you think we could sue for personal injury liability?"

His lawyer responded with a resounding, "No, you egghead!" He drummed his fingers nervously on his desk while Humpty mumbled disconsolately to himself. "What's that?" the lawyer asked. "Did I just hear you say, 'I think I'm going to pieces'?"

"But I can't cope," Humpty moaned.

"Don't let me hear any more of this 'can't cope'! Too much talk like that and you'll end up nothing more than an empty shell of a man. Pick yourself up; pull yourself together!"

Titles. Use quotation marks around the titles of short works: articles, essays, chapter titles, lectures, short stories, poems, songs, and individual episodes of TV programs. Do *not* use quotation marks around the titles for your school or business writing unless they contain actual quotations.

The Semicolon (;)

Independent clauses. Use a semicolon in place of a conjunction to join related independent clauses:

Old Mother Hubbard went to the cupboard to get her doggie a bone, *but* when she got there, the cupboard was bare, and so the poor doggie had none.

Old Mother Hubbard went to the cupboard to get her doggie a bone; when she got there, the cupboard was bare, and so the poor doggie had none.

Conjunctive adverbs. Use a semicolon before a conjunctive adverb joining two independent clauses (see page 501): *Old Mother Hubbard's cupboard was bare; however, she did have some wieners in the refrigerator.*

Coodinating conjunctions. Use a semicolon before a coordinating conjunction (*and, but, for, or, so, yet*) to join two long independent clauses, especially if they contain internal punctuation:

Old Mother Hubbard was clearly a victim, a victim of the War on Poverty that had lofty aims but precious few funds to wage it; for while the President and Congress were hailing an end to poverty and hunger in America, they were, in fact, channeling a large portion of the federal budget into defense spending on the real war then being waged in Southeast Asia.

Series. Use a semicolon between items in a series when one or more items contain internal punctuation:

The old woman who lived in a shoe had so many children: Cosmo, her thirty-seven-year-old eldest child, a former zeppelin pilot; Melvin, her twenty-eight-year-old son, who had squandered her life savings on a scheme to pinstripe the Golden Gate Bridge; Constance, a burnt-out professional golfer; and Gilda, the baby of the family at eighteen, whose only aim in life was to grow up and become a TV game show host.

Semicolons and other punctuation. Place the semicolon outside closing quotation marks or parentheses:

Little Tommy Tucker sings for his supper (it was an aria and quite well sung); what shall we give him? Some say, "Give him the business"; I say we should give him a hamburger and fries, to go.

(For more on the semicolon, see Chapter 8, pages 170–171.)

Underlining (__)

Underline wherever italics would appear in printed matter. Underline titles of longer or complete works: books, magazines or periodicals, plays, pamphlets, long poems, TV series, records, and movies. Underline the titles of paintings, ships, airplanes, and trains. Underline foreign words or phrases that haven't been anglicized: de trop but not raison d'être or status quo. Underline words for emphasis, but be sparing. Design your pragraphs and sentences so the most important words and phrases come at the most emphatic positions, the beginning and the end. (For more on underlining, see Chapter 11, pages 241–242.)

EXERCISES

Most punctuation has been removed from the following sentences. Punctuate each sentence so that it is clear and emphatic in meaning as well as correct.

1. Murder mysteries comic books cook books even auto repair manuals my dancing teachers reading tastes are more eclectic than anyone elses I know

2. When I saw the money flying to Topeka in an old biplane was the last thing on my mind

3. There are three reasons Christine has been successful she studies four hours every day rain or shine weekdays and weekends usually by herself she reads constantly and she never speaks to strangers especially those who look like they might be volley ball players

4. Bondos history paper opened with this sentence When Christopher Columbus landed in the New World at 329 pm in 1942 sic his first words were This appears to be Spains golden opportunity to corner the market on beachfront fast food franchises

5. Ernest Applewort has recently published an autobiographical novel Rocky Mountain Hideaway its first chapter Over the Cliffs and into the River would make a great movie

6. Im glad however that my pet Japanese beetles didnt escape from their cage they cost me a fortune

7. Mr Moses challenge which he announced in a booming bass voice startled all of us Whos going to join me on my round the world hang glider flight he cried

8. Mother youll be happy to know that Ive appended to this letter my estimated budget for the four years of my undergraduate career and the following seven years of graduate school see the attached spreadsheet. You'll send the check by registered mail wont you and oh by the way make it a certified cashiers check

9. Abraham Lincoln began the Gettysburg Address with these well known words Four score and seven years ago our forefathers brought forth on this continent a new nation

10. The burglar who just climbed through my bedroom window appears to be my high school algebra instructor Prof E B Dunkle Id better call the police right away or maybe the FBI

11. The mid term examination 50 true false questions and 3 essay questions will probably take most of the hour to complete but if you move right along you should finish before time is up

12. Oh Bill isnt it necessary to sign ones own name to the wedding license Judy asked her husband to be. Youve signed John Doe why is that

13. Wasnt it Harvey who said My lifes goal is to sell vanilla ice cream in a banana republic

14. Four mothers in laws wedding rings were found by Stephens father in laws bloodhound not the first time that hounds nose has benefited someone

15. Having decided to eat the boys basketball rather than play with it the ape a real gorilla no mere chimp lumbered off the court

SEXIST LANGUAGE

Many people, both men and women, rightly object to the gender bias expressed by certain English words, especially occupational titles, official titles, and generic terms: *steward/stewardess, policeman, businessman, chairman, congressman, mankind, common man, man,* and so on. Even though a writer may not intend it, these terms appear to exclude women, involve a person's sex where it is irrelevant, or devalue an occupation. If you're describing positions filled by both men and women or if your readers would be offended by gender-biased terms, you'll want to find more appropriate words. Generally, these will be slightly more specific or general words: *steward/stewardess* = *flight attendant; policeman* = *police officer; businessman* = *business person, executive, accountant, vice president,* and so on; *chairman* = *chairperson* or *chair; congressman* = *senator* or *representative; mankind* = *human kind; common man* = *people* or *populace.* (For more on the problem of gender in English, see Pronoun-Antecedent Agreement, pages 490–491.)

SPELLING

If you're one of the many people who don't spell as well as they think they should, you can begin solving your problem by recognizing two facts: First, even the poorest speller still spells correctly three quarters of the time. You don't have to solve your problem by learning spelling from the ground up. Second, poor spellers generally misspell the same words or the same kinds of words over and over and misspell them in the same ways. Their misspelling system is as regular as the spelling system. They are following rules when they spell, but they're the wrong rules.

The next thing to do is make an inventory of your errors; learn what you have misspelled and how. When a paper is returned to you by an instructor or when you are working with a friend, before you turn the paper in, write up a list of your spelling errors *exactly as you have misspelled them.*

Wrong	*Right*
thier	their
convient	convenient
forfilling	fulfilling
grammer	grammar
were	where
reconize	recognize
goverment	government

When your list grows to a page in length, sort your errors into categories. Add to these categories whenever you discover new misspellings. Here are the twelve types of common English spelling errors used to sort the preceding list.[4]

1. Long vowel sound.
2. Short vowel sound.
3. Final consonant or consonant cluster: *grammer*.
4. Silent *e*.
5. Homophone (similar sounds, different spellings).
6. Suffix.
7. Prefix.
8. Double consonant.
9. Missing letter or syllable: *convient, reconize, goverment*.
10. Word confusion: *forfilling* (?), *were/where*.
11. Letter reversal: *thier*.
12. Others.

When you have sorted your errors, begin to investigate them, looking for similarities or reasons for misspelling. The maker of the preceding short list leaves letters out of words. Does he not listen carefully? In two words he omits *n* or a syllable with *n* in it. Does he have trouble hearing that sound? And although he has put *forfilling, were, thier,* and *grammer* into different categories, each of these involves an *r* sound, and three involve an *er/air* sound confusion. Does he have trouble distinguishing among the vowels in these *r* syllables? (Every dictionary contains a pronunciation guide that will help you sound out words and learn which sounds you misspell.) Discovering (1) which words you misspell and (2) how you misspell them will often be enough to help you catch many of your errors in future writing or at least tell you what to look for as you proofread.

The third step is to buy yourself a word guide. These are small books—easy-to-carry, usually soft-cover—that list only words, no definitions. With them you will be able to check your spelling in less than one quarter the time it takes to use a dictionary. There are even poor speller's guides for those whose spelling is so bad they don't even know where to begin looking up a word. These guides give a word twice, as it is misspelled and spelled correctly. Look a word up as you normally misspell it, and the guide will give you the correct version.

Fourth, your spelling will improve if you can master these few simple tricks that good spellers know:

• *Compare spellings:* Correctly spelled words look right and feel right as you write them. Write out alternative versions and compare.
• *Disassemble words:* Listen to the sound of their parts. Make yourself see, sound out, and hear the word as you've actually spelled it. Is it *tra-deg-y, lon-li-ness, ne-ccess-ary?* No, it's *tra-ged-y, lone-li-ness, ne-cess-ary.* This practice will help you decide whether you need single or

double letters when you add those tricky prefixes and suffixes: *mis-spell, dis-serv-ice, dis-a-gree, fin-al-ly, re-al-ly, hap-pi-ly.*

- *Look for related words* to help you spell the unaccented vowels that almost always sound like the *u* in *but*, no matter what their spelling. There are almost two dozen ways to spell this *uh* sound, but if you can find a related word in which the unaccented vowels are accented, you can find the correct spelling.[5]

comp ? tition + comPETE =
democr ? cy + autoCRATic =
prev ? lent + VALue =
rel ?tive + reLATE =

exhil ? rate + hiLARity =
gramm ? r + gramMARian =
monot ? nous + monoTONE =
mir ? cle + mirACulous =

The final line of defense against misspelling is learning the most important English spelling rules.

I Before E   Everyone knows the beginning of this rule: *i* before *e* except after *c*. Not too many know its indispensable remainder:

1. *i* before *e* except after *c* when pronounced long $\bar{ee}$,
2. *e* before *i* when pronounced like long *ā* as in *neighbor* and *weigh*

Thus, we spell *relieve, conceive,* but *conscience, vein,* and *freight*. You can keep track of the few exceptions to this rule if you remember this nonsense sentence: *Neither sheik seized weird leisure.*

The Silent E   English generally puts a silent *e* at the end of words to keep a preceding vowel long in sound: *mat/mate, met/mete, kit/kite, hot/hotel, cut/cute.*

1. Drop the silent *e* when adding a suffix that begins with a vowel: *grate/grating, retrieve/retrieving, love/lovable, prime/primal, cute/cutest.* The vowel in the suffix keeps the preceding vowel long.
2. Keep the silent *e* when adding a suffix that begins with a consonant: *lone/lonely, care/careful, sincere/sincerely, live/livelihood.*
3. For words ending in *-ce* or *-ge*, keep the silent *e* when adding a suffix that begins with an *a* or *o*: *charge/chargeable, service/serviceable, courage/courageous.* We retain the silent *e* to keep the *g* and *c* sounds "soft" (a *j* and *s* sound). Try pronouncing *chargable, servicable,* or *couragous.*
4. Other exceptions keep the *e* to avoid confusion: *singing/singeing, dying/dyeing, shoeing, hoeing, toeing.* The remaining exceptions you must memorize: *mileage, wholly, argument, judgment, truly, awful, duly.*

Changing Y to I   The rules for changing *y* to *i* are simple, but you must also remember a number of exceptions to the rules.

1. When a word ends consonant + *y*, change *y* to *i* and add the suffix: *busy/business, penny/penniless, lonely/loneliness, community/communities.* Exceptions: *babyish, cityless, fairylike, secretaryship.*
2. When a word ends vowel + *y*, simply add the suffix: *donkey* + *s* = *donkeys; valley* + *s* = *valleys, boy* + *ish* = *boyish, employ* + *er* = *employer.* Exceptions: *paid, laid, daily, gaily, said.*
3. If the suffix is *-ing* or *-ist* do *not* change the *y: lobby* + *ist* = *lobbyist, copy* + *ing* = *copying, study* + *ing* = *studying.*

Doubling the Consonants at the End of a Word   Double the consonant only when a word meets *all three* of these rules.

1. The word ends vowel + consonant: *war, begin, prefer, fog, cut, glad.*
2. The suffix begins with a vowel: *-ing, -ed, -y, -en.*
3. The word has one syllable or is accented on the final syllable:

> warring, beginning, preferring,
> foggy, cutting, gladden
> *but:* benefited, honorable, concealed, gladdened

☙ TENSE

Broadly speaking, *tense* refers to the time indicated by a verb; more precisely it refers to the forms a verb can take. Few native English writers have trouble with the three simple tenses of Edited American English:

Past	*Present*	*Future*
she laughed	she laughs	she will laugh

Verbs get trickier, however, when we combine them with auxiliary verbs to make complex statements about the quality of events or their relation to other events:

- Past perfect tense: *she had laughed* (an event in the past completed before another past event).
- Present perfect tense: *she has laughed* (an event begun in the past completed in the present).
- Future perfect tense: *she will have laughed* (an event to be completed in the future).
- Emphatic tense: *she did laugh; she does laugh.*
- Progressive tense: *she is laughing; she was laughing; she will be laughing.*
- Conditional tense: *she would laugh; she would be laughing; she would have been laughing.*

Edited American English is precise about keeping its tenses straight and using them to arrange events in a clear order. It is scrupulous, too, about using conventional forms; that means not confusing tense markers at the end of *regular* verbs with the internal changes that mark the tenses of *irregular* verbs. Here is a sampling of regular and irregular verbs whose tenses have been formed incorrectly:

Not	*But*
drawed	drew
drug	dragged
binded	bound
blowed	blew
brung	brought
catched	caught
costed	cost
creeped	crept
drived	drove, driven
had went	had gone
growed	grew
sweared	swore

Here are other common tense errors and the ways to correct them:

Sound Confusion
    He was *suppose* to go to Memphis at the beginning of the month (the past tense -*d* sound is lost in *to*).

Revision
    He was *supposed* to go to Memphis at the beginning of the month.

Sound Confusion
    I *use* to see them twice a week.

Revision
    I *used* to see them twice a week.

Sound Confusion
    If I had thought of checking the spare tire before I left, I *would of* made it to the game on time (the contracted form of *have* [-*ve*] is confused with *of*).

Revision
    If I had thought of checking the spare tire before I left, I *would've* made it to the game on time.

Tense Marker Unpronounced and Unwritten
    Whenever I am *frighten*, I wish I were back in high school, where everything was safe, secure, and simple.

Revision
    Whenever I am *frightened*, I wish I were back in high school, where everything was safe, secure, and simple.

Confused Tenses

I am writing you because of an opportunity that has opened in my office. Recently my manager *has asked* me to find one or two individuals interested in a sales career (past tense required for an event in the past).

Revision

I am writing you because of an opportunity that has opened in my office. Recently my manager *asked* me to find one or two individuals interested in a sales career.

Confused Tenses

All of a sudden my head started spinning as I thought of all the chores I *forgot* to do (past perfect tense required for an event completed before another past event).

Revision

All of a sudden my head started spinning as I thought of all the chores I *had forgotten* to do.

Confused Tenses

I never *forgot* those words of wisdom (because the writer probably still remembers those words of wisdom, the present perfect tense is required).

Revision

I *have never forgotten* those words of wisdom.

END NOTES

1. Wherever possible I have followed the conventions of the *MLA Handbook for Writers of Research Papers*, 2nd ed. (New York: The Modern Language Association of America, 1984) and *The Chicago Manual of Style*, 13th ed. (Chicago: U of Chicago P, 1982).

2. For the rules to discover pronoun case I am grateful to Maxwell Nurnberg, *Questions you always wanted to ask about English* (New York: Pocket, 1972).

3. For the rules to punctuate non-restrictive modifiers I am grateful to Louis E. Glorfeld, et al., *A Concise Guide for Writers* (New York: Holt, 1974).

4. The spelling error classification is adapted from Mina Shaughnessy, *Errors and Expectations* (New York: Oxford UP, 1977).

5. For the suggestion to look for related words I am grateful to Maxwell Nurnberg, *Questions you always wanted to ask about English* (New York: Pocket, 1972).

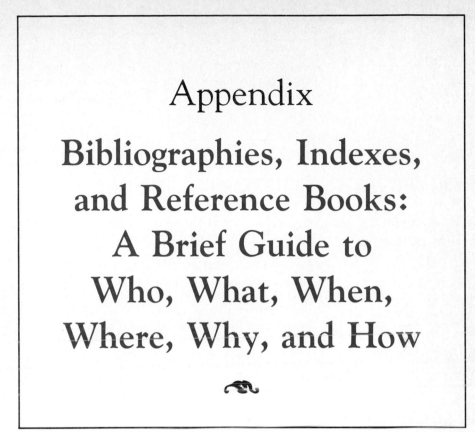

Appendix

Bibliographies, Indexes, and Reference Books: A Brief Guide to Who, What, When, Where, Why, and How

GENERAL INTRODUCTION

This appendix consists of two lists that will help you with many of your college writing projects. Use them whenever you need to find information. The first list, "Finding Sources," contains the most important bibliographies and indexes in your library. These periodicals, books, microfilm, and computer services will guide you to sources of information on almost every subject imaginable. The second list, "Finding Information," begins on page 546 and contains the most important reference sources in your library. These books are direct sources of information on every subject. Both lists are divided by subject.

Finding Sources
General bibliographies and indexes.
Abstracting services.
Reference guides.
Book reviews.

Finding Information
Almanacs and atlases.
Biographies.
Dictionaries and word books.
Subject dictionaries.

Government publications.
Newspaper indexes.
Subject indexes.

News summaries and digests.
General encyclopedias.
Subject encyclopedias.
Quotations.
Statistics.

ᖲ FINDING SOURCES

General
Bibliographies
and Indexes

Access: *The Supplementary Guide to Periodicals.* Syracuse, NY: Gaylord, 1975. [Indexes 130 popular and nontechnical magazines not cataloged in *The Reader's Guide to Periodical Literature.*]

Computerized bibliographies. [There are two kinds. One—the OCLC system is an example—is a super-sized card catalog, enabling you to find books, periodicals, and authors in your library or any other that uses the system. To use it you need an author or title to start with. The second—such as the Dialogue Information Retrieval Service—will for a fee help you find sources when you have only a subject. Your computer librarian will connect you with over 200

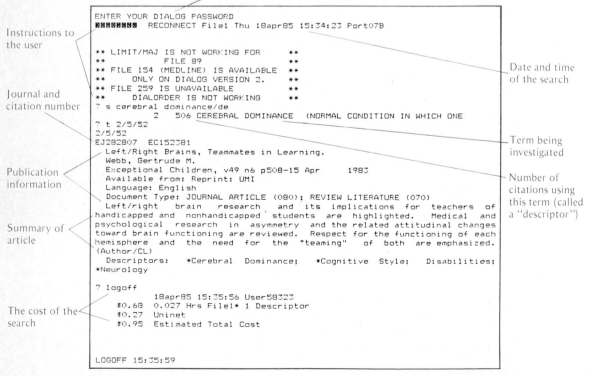

The name of the computer service

Instructions to the user

Journal and citation number

Publication information

Summary of article

The cost of the search

Date and time of the search

Term being investigated

Number of citations using this term (called a "descriptor")

```
ENTER YOUR DIALOG PASSWORD
████████  RECONNECT File1 Thu 18apr85 15:34:23 Port07B


** LIMIT/MAJ IS NOT WORKING FOR    **
**          FILE 89                **
** FILE 154 (MEDLINE) IS AVAILABLE **
**     ONLY ON DIALOG VERSION 2.   **
** FILE 259 IS UNAVAILABLE         **
**     DIALORDER IS NOT WORKING    **
? s cerebral dominance/de
            2    506 CEREBRAL DOMINANCE   (NORMAL CONDITION IN WHICH ONE
? t 2/5/52
2/5/52
EJ282807  EC152381
  Left/Right Brains, Teammates in Learning.
  Webb, Gertrude M.
  Exceptional Children, v49 n6 p508-15 Apr     1983
  Available from: Reprint: UMI
  Language: English
  Document Type: JOURNAL ARTICLE (080); REVIEW LITERATURE (070)
    Left/right  brain  research  and  its  implications  for  teachers  of
handicapped  and  nonhandicapped  students  are  highlighted.  Medical  and
psychological  research  in  asymmetry  and the related attitudinal changes
toward brain functioning are reviewed.  Respect for the functioning of each
hemisphere  and  the  need  for  the  "teaming"  of  both  are  emphasized.
(Author/CL)
  Descriptors:  *Cerebral  Dominance;  *Cognitive  Style:  Disabilities:
*Neurology

? logoff
         18apr85 15:35:56 User58323
  $0.68  0.027 Hrs File1* 1 Descriptor
  $0.27  Uninet
  $0.95  Estimated Total Cost


LOGOFF 15:35:59
```

data bases, extensive bibliographic listings organized by subject, and you will get back a printout with the number of sources available on your subject, full publication information, and even brief summaries. Ask your computer librarian for help with these services. On the opposite page is a printout from the Dialogue Service.]

Essay and General Literature Index. New York: Wilson, 1900–33, 1933 to present. [Indexes essays from anthologies and chapters from books on a wide variety of subjects. An indispensable guide to literary and nonliterary subjects discussed in books.]

Humanities Index. New York: Wilson, June 1974 to date. [Catalogs scholarly articles in a variety of fields published in 260 journals. This and the *Social Science Index* replace *Social Science and Humanities Index*, 1920–65, which replaced the *Reader's Guide Supplement and International Index*, 1907–19. Check here if your subject has to do with art, architecture, folklore, history, language and literature, philosophy, or religion.]

The Magazine Index. [This microfilm index contains references to articles in 354 popular American magazines, 1979 to date. For more recent articles it

Arrangement by subject and author

Cross-references

Title of article — Author's name

Publication date — Volume and page number

Contents of article

Contains bibliography

Publication

Contains illustration

Subheading

Subject

Author

Achepohl, Keith
        about
  Keith Achepohl. M. E. Stegmaier. il por *Am Artist* 48:62-5 Jl '84
Acheulean hand ax *See* Axes
Achievement *See* Success
Achievement tests *See* Educational tests and measurements
Achievements, Student *See* Student achievements
Achondroplasia *See* Dwarfs and dwarfism
Acid precipitation (Meteorology) *See* Acid rain
Acid rain
  Acid rain [discussion of May 28, 1984 article, Maybe acid rain isn't the villain] W. M. Brown. *Fortune* 110:11-12 Ag 6 '84
  Acid rain annual report [report of the National Acid Precipitation Assessment Program] *Sci News* 125:392 Je 23 '84
  Acid rain costs millions in visibility alone [Environmental Protection Agency study] *Natl Parks* 58:43-4 Jl/Ag '84
  Acid rain: ionic correlations in the eastern United States, 1980-1981. E. Gorham and others. bibl f il *Science* 225:407-9 Jl 27 '84
  Acid rain: unproved threat or deadly fact? C. E. Riemer and J. W. Miller. il *Good Housekeep* 198:236 Je '84
  Camel's Hump revisited [H. Vogelmann's study] Blair Ketchums Ctry J 11:21 S '84
  Forests in a fossil-fuel world. S. Postel. il por *Futurist* 18:38-46 Ag '84
  How scientists are tracking acid rain. R. Gannon. il map *Pop Sci* 225:67-71 Ag '84
  Is acid rain eating our gardens? W. Schultz, Jr. il map *Org Gard* 31:53-7 Je '84
      Laws and regulations
  Acid rain's political web. I. Peterson. il *Sci News* 126:58-9 Jl 28 '84
  Dumping garbage on neighbors [EPA rejects plea by N.Y., Pa. and Me.] *Time* 124:18 S 10 '84
  Superfunding acid rain controls: who will bear the costs? S. L. Rhodes. bibl f il map *Environment* 26:25-32 Jl/Ag '84
  Watchdog with a limp [W. D. Ruckelshaus] J. McGowan. por *Macleans* 97:5 Ag 13 '84
Acids, Fatty
    See also
    Prostaglandins
Ackermann-Blount, Joan
  The waiting is over. il *Sports Illus* 61:44+ Jl 23 '84

supersedes *The Reader's Guide to Periodical Literature*. Start here to look for popular sources; then, if you need older materials, go to the *Reader's Guide*.]

The Reader's Guide to Periodical Literature. New York: Wilson, 1900 to date. [Indexes articles on a wide variety of subjects published in 175 popular periodicals intended for general, rather than scholarly, audiences. The format for cataloging and arranging entries is the same for this H. W. Wilson publication as for all other H. W. Wilson Indexes. On the previous page are examples of *Reader's Guide* entries.]

Social Sciences Index. New York: Wilson, 1974 to date. [Lists scholarly articles in 260 journals on subjects such as anthropology, economics, environmental science, education, law, medicine, political science, psychology, and sociology.]

Abstracting Services

Abstracting services briefly summarize the contents of the sources they catalog; often you can determine without looking at the actual source whether it will be useful to you.

Abstracts in Anthropology. Westport, CT: Greenwood, 1970 to date.

Biological Abstracts. Philadelphia: Union of American Biological Societies, 1926 to date.

Chemical Abstracts. Columbus, OH: American Chemical Society, 1907 to date.

Child Development Abstracts and Bibliography. Chicago: The U of Chicago P for the Society for Research in Child Development, 1927 to date.

Historical Abstracts, 1777–1945. Santa Barbara, CA. [Indexes articles on world history appearing in thirteen-hundred periodicals and thirty languages.]

Language and Language Behavior Abstracts. Ann Arbor, MI: U of Michigan, 1967 to date.

Psychological Abstracts. Washington, DC: American Psychological Association, 1927 to date.

Sociological Abstracts. New York: Sociological Abstracts, 1953 to date.

Reference Guides

Bibliographic Index. New York: Wilson, 1937 to date, semiannual. [Includes bibliographies published as parts of books as well as those published in pamphlets, articles, and complete books.]

Sheehy, Eugene P. *Guide to Reference Books*. Chicago: American Library Association, 1968. [This guide supersedes Constance M. Winchell, *Guide to Reference Books*, 1967.]

Book Reviews

Book Review Digest. New York: Wilson, 1905 to date. [The primary source for locating reviews; gives digests of reviews and citations for the complete reviews.]

Book Review Index. Detroit: Gale Research, 1965 to date. [Indexes reviews in major scholarly journals and arts magazines.]

An Index to Book Reviews in the Humanities. Williamson, MI: Phillip Thomson, 1960 to date.

Technical Book Review Index. New York: Special Libraries, current.

Government Publications

Congressional Information Service/Index. Washington, DC: Congressional Information Service, monthly. [Indexes nearly all U.S. Congressional publications except the *Congressional Record.*]

Congressional Record Index. Washington, DC: Government Printing Office, biweekly. [The daily record of the proceedings of Congress.]

Leidy, William Philip. *A Popular Guide to Government Publications.* 4th ed. New York: Columbia UP, 1976.

Monthly Catalog of United States Government Publications. Washington, DC: Superintendent of Documents, monthly.

Parish, David W. *State Government Reference Publications: An Annotated Bibliography.* Littleton, CO: Libraries Unlimited, 1974.

Winton, Harry N.M. *Publications of the United Nations System: A Reference Guide.* New York: Bowker, 1972.

Newspaper Indexes

The Chicago Tribune Index

The National Newspaper Index. January 1, 1979 to date. [Microfilm index to the *New York Times, Christian Science Monitor,* and the *Wall Street Journal.*]

The New York Times Index. New York: The New York Times, 1851 to date. [The index is divided into citations and summaries of the actual news stories. Here are sample citations and a cross-referenced summary.]

Subject reference

A cross–reference directs the reader to the summary of a major story

ACHITOV, Avraham. See also Israel—Pol, Ag 13, D 15
ACHORN, Robert C. See also Associated Press (AP), Ap 23
ACID Rain. See also Statue of Liberty, My 19. Water Pollution, Ja 28, F 1, Mr 2,7, Mr 9,12,15,20,22, Ap 10,21,22, My 19,29, Jl 18,29, Ag 5,7,18, S 7, O 6,29, N 8,12,15, D 19. Weather—NYS, D 19. Weather—US, Mr 2,7,9, Jl 20, O 29, N 8,12
ACIDS. See also Teeth, D 16. Names
ACK-Ti-Lining Inc
   Collins & Aikman Corp names Alan S Lerner president of subsidiary (S), Ag 28,IV,2:4
ACKER, C Edward. See also Airlines—Intl Services, My 27. Westgate California Corp, O 31
ACKER, Jack. See also Baseball—NL, New York Mets, O 10

WATER Pollution
   NYS Gov Carey says Northeastern states are seeking Federal action against acid rain and wind-transported pollution from south and west; says acid precipitation, which occurs when sulfur and nitrogen pollutants from smokestacks combine with rain and snow, has destroyed over 7,000 acres of prime Adirondack habitat for brook trout; other fisheries are threatened (S), Ja 28,II,2:2

Cross-references

Location of original story (date, section, page, column)

Subject Indexes (A Selected Guide)

ART
Art Index. New York: Wilson, 1964 to date.

BUSINESS, ECONOMICS, AND STATISTICS
Business Index. [A microfilm index to 375 magazines and periodicals.]
Business Periodicals Index. New York: Wilson, 1958 to date.

CONSUMER INFORMATION
Consumers Index to Product Evaluation and Information Sources. Ann Arbor, MI: Pierian, 1973 to date.

EDUCATION
Current Index to Journals in Education. New York: Macmillan Information, 1969 to date. [Indexes 700 education or related publications.]
Education Index. New York: Wilson, 1929 to date.

HISTORY
America: History and Life. A Guide to Periodical Literature. Santa Barbara, CA: American Bibliographical Center, Clio Press, 1964 to date.

Alphabetical list of authors

Subject headings

MLA indexing number

Periodical article

Book

Author of an essay in a book

Editor of a book

MILLER, WALTER MICHAEL, JR. (1923-)

Novel/A Canticle for Leibowitz (1960)

[9398] Wagar, W. Warren. "Round Trip to Doomsday." 73-96 in Rabkin, Eric S., ed. & introd.; Greenberg, Martin H[arry], ed.; Olander, Joseph D., ed. *The End of the World*. Carbondale: Southern Illinois UP; 1983. xv, 204 pp. (Alternatives.) [†Treatment of history as cycle.]

MITCHELL, JOSEPH (1908-)

Prose

[9399] Perrin, Noel. "Paragon of Reporters: Joseph Mitchell." *SR*. 1983 Spring; 92(2): 167-184. [†Journalism.]

MITCHELL, MARGARET (1900-1949)

Novel/Gone with the Wind (1936)

[9400] Dwyer, Richard. "The Case of the Cool Reception." 21-31 in Pyron, Darden Asbury, ed. *Recasting:* Gone with the Wind *in American Culture*. Miami: UPs of Florida; 1983. x, 232 pp. [†Reception study.]

[9401] Goodwyn, Frank. "The Ingenious Gentleman and the Exasperating Lady: Don Quixote de la Mancha and Scarlett O'Hara." *JPC*. 1982 Summer; 16(1): 55-71. [†Relationship to bestsellers. Treatment of tradition compared to Cervantes Saavedra, Miguel de: *Quijote*.]

[9402] Harwell, Richard, ed. Gone with the Wind *as Book and Film*. Columbia: U of South Carolina P; 1983. xxi, 273 pp. [Prev. pub. material †And film adaptation by Fleming, Victor.]

[9403] Irvin, Helen Deiss. "Gea in Georgia: A Mythic Dimension in *Gone with the Wind*." 57-68 in Pyron, Darden Asbury, ed. *Recasting:* Gone with the Wind *in American Culture*. Miami: UPs of Florida; 1983. x, 232 pp. [†Role of myth. Treatment of Earth Mother; relationship to O'Hara, Scarlett (character). Archetypal approach.]

[9404] Jones, Anne Goodwyn. "'The Bad Little Girl of the Good Old Days': Gender, Sex, and the Southern Social Order." 105-115 in Pyron, Darden Asbury, ed. *Recasting:* Gone with the Wind *in American Culture*. Miami: UPs of Florida; 1983. x, 232 pp. [Revision of sect. of 1981 Bibliog. 1.6205 †Role of gender in social order of Southern United States; O'Hara, Scarlett (character). Feminist approach.]

An essay in a book-length collection

Abbreviation of periodical title

Publication date, volume number, and page numbers

Total pages in volume

Subject of article and cross-reference headings used in the Subject Index

International Bibliography of Historical Sciences. New York: International Publication Service, 1930 to date.

Krickman, Albert. *The Woman's Rights Movement in the United States, 1848–1970: A Bibliography and Source Book.* Metuchen, NJ: Scarecrow, 1972.

LANGUAGE AND LITERATURE

The Critical Index: A Bibliography of Film, 1946–73.

Modern Language Association of America. *International Bibliography.* New York: MLA, 1922 to date. [Since 1981 published in two parts: *Subject Index* and *Classified Listings and Author Index.* On the opposite page are sample citations from the *Classified Listings and Author Index.*]

Twentieth Century Short Story Explication. Hamden, CT: Shoe String, 1976, Supplement, 1979, 1981. [Arranged alphabetically by author and then story title. See *Studies in Short Fiction,* Summer issue, for an annual index to sources published after 1981. Below are sample citations from *Twentieth Century Short Story Explication.*]

LIBRARY SCIENCE

Library Literature. New York: 1921 to date.

LAW

Index to Legal Periodicals. New York: Wilson, 1952 to date.

Legal Resource Index. Menlo Park, CA: Information Access Corp. [A microfilm index to over 680 periodicals and newspapers.]

MASS MEDIA

Blum, Eleanor. *Basic Books in the Mass Media.* Urbana, IL: U of Illinois P, 1972.

Story titles

Book title
(see index
for a full
citation for
a book)

Periodical
article

Essay in a
collection
of essays

Periodical essay
cited in full
earlier
under another
story title

"Frau Brechenmacher Attends a Wedding"
   Berkman, Sylvia. *Katherine Mansfield* . . . , 43-44.
   Daly, Saralyn. *Katherine Mansfield,* 32-34.

"Frau Fischer"
   Daly, Saralyn. *Katherine Mansfield,* 35-36.

"The Garden Party"
   Bloom, Edward A. *The Order* . . . , 176-179.
   Brewster, Dorothy, and Angus Burrell. *Modern Fiction,* 361-362.
   Daly, Saralyn. *Katherine Mansfield,* 99-100.
   Davis, Robert M. "The Unity of 'The Garden Party,'" *Stud Short Fiction,* 2 (1964), 61-65.
   Fricker, Robert. "'The Garden Party,'" in Göller, Karl H., and Gerhardt Hoffmann, Eds. . . . *Kurzgeschichte,* 203-213.
   Friis, Anne. *Katherine Mansfield* . . . , 105-106.
   Halter, Peter. *Katherine Mansfield* . . . , 127-133.
   Hughes, Derek. "Katherine Mansfield . . . ," 29-30.
   Iverson, Anders. "A Reading of Katherine Mansfield's 'The Garden Party,'" *Orbis Litterarum,* 23 (1968), 5-34.
   Kleine, Don W. "An Eden . . . ," 207-209.
   ———. "'The Garden Party': A Portrait of the Artist," *Criticism,* 5 (1963), 360-371.
   Lawrence, Margaret. . . . *Femininity,* 351.
   Lesser, M. X., and John N. Morris. *Teacher's Manual* . . . , 19-20.

Two articles
by the same
author

MUSIC
Music Index. Detroit: Information Service, 1949 to date.

PHILOSOPHY AND RELIGION
Philosopher's Index. Bowling Green, OH: Bowling Green University, 1967 to date.

POLITICAL SCIENCE
Harmon, Robert B. *Political Science: A Bibliographic Guide to the Literature.* Metuchen, NJ: Scarecrow, 1965 and 1974.

SCIENCE
Applied Science and Technology Index. New York: Wilson, 1958 to date.
Biological and Agricultural Index. New York: Wilson, 1964 to date.
Malinowsky, Harold R. *Science and Engineering Reference Sources.* New York: Libraries Unlimited, 1967.

SOCIAL SCIENCE
Index to Literature on the American Indian. San Francisco: Indian Historian Press, 1970 to date.
Index to Periodical Articles By and About Negroes. Boston: Hall, 1950 to date.
Public Affairs Information Service Bulletin. New York: Public Affairs Information Service, 1915 to date. [PAIS is the indispensable guide to the social sciences.]
Social Science Index. New York: Wilson, 1965 to date.

❧ FINDING INFORMATION: REFERENCE GUIDES TO INFORMATION OF ALL KINDS

Almanacs and Atlases

Barone, Michael. *Almanac of American Politics.* Boston: Gambit, 1972 to date.
The Book of States. Lexington, KY: The Council of State Governments, 1935 to date.
Goode's World Atlas. 14th ed. Chicago: Rand, 1976.
Information Please Almanac, Atlas and Yearbook. New York: Information Please Almanac, annual.
McWhirter, Norris, and Ross McWhirter, eds. *The Guiness Book of World Records.* New York: Stirling, annual.
The Municipal Year Book. Washington, DC: International City Management Association, 1934 to date. [Provides up-to-date information about cities.]
The Negro Almanac. 3rd rev. ed. New York: Bellwether, 1976.
The Statesman's Year-Book. New York: St. Martin's, 1864 to date. [Provides information about nations.]
Times Atlas of the World. Comprehensive ed. New York: Quadrangle/The New York Times Book Co., 1975.
The West Point Atlas of American Wars. 2 vols. New York: Praeger, 1959.
The World Almanac and Book of Facts. New York: Newspaper Enterprise Association, 1868 to date.

Biographies

Current Biography. New York: Wilson, 1945 to date, monthly.

Dictionary of American Biography. New York: Scribner's, 1964.

Dictionary of National Biography. London: Oxford UP, 1945. Supplement: 1951–60, 1961–70. [For Great Britain.]

Dictionary of Scientific Biography. 16 vols. New York: Scribner's, 1970–80.

International Who's Who. London: Europa Publications, annual.

The McGraw-Hill Encyclopedia of World Biography. New York: McGraw, 1973.

Webster's Biographical Dictionary. Springfield, MA: Merriam, 1967 [Includes living persons.]

Dictionaries and Word Books

American Heritage Dictionary of the English Language. William Morris, ed. Boston: American Heritage and Houghton Mifflin, 1969.

Bernstein, Theodore M. *The Careful Writer.* New York: Atheneum, 1965.

Evans, Bergen and Cornelia Evans. *A Dictionary of Contemporary American Usage.* New York: Random, 1957.

Fowler, Henry Watson. *Dictionary of Modern English Usage.* 2d ed. Rev. by Sir Ernest Gowers. Oxford: Clarendon, 1965.

Funk & Wagnalls New Standard Dictionary of the English Language. New York: Funk, 1963.

Partridge, Eric. *Dictionary of Slang and Unconventional English.* 7th ed. New York: Macmillan, 1970.

Random House Dictionary of the English Language. Ed. by J. M. Stein. New York: Random, 1966.

Roget's International Thesaurus. 4th ed. New York: Crowell, 1977.

Webster's New Dictionary of Synonyms. Springfield, MA: Merriam, 1977.

Webster's New World Dictionary of the American Language. Ed. by David Guralnik. New York: Popular Library, 1979.

Webster's Third New International Dictionary. Ed. by Philip Babcock Gove. Springfield, MA: Merriam, 1961.

Subject Dictionaries

ART AND ARCHITECTURE

Cowan, Henry J. *Dictionary of Architectural Science.* New York: Wiley, 1973.

McGraw-Hill Dictionary of Art. New York: McGraw, 1969.

BUSINESS AND ECONOMICS

Kohler, Eric L. *A Dictionary for Accountants.* Englewood Cliffs, NJ: Prentice, 1952 and following.

McGraw-Hill Dictionary of Modern Economics: A Handbook of Terms and Organizations. 2d ed. New York: McGraw, 1973.

EDUCATION

Page, G. Terry, and J. B. Thomas. *International Dictionary of Education.* Cambridge, MA: MIT Press, 1980.

GEOGRAPHY

The Columbia Lippincott Gazetteer of the World. Ed. Leon E. Seltzer. New York: Columbia UP, 1962.

Larousse Encyclopedia of World Geography. New York: Odyssey, 1965.

Webster's New Geographical Dictionary. Rev. ed. Springfield, MA: Merriam, 1972.

FILM

Dictionary of Films. Berkeley: U of California, 1972.

HISTORY

Dictionary of American History. 7 vols. New York: Scribner's, 1976.

Dictionary of Dates and Anniversaries. Robert Collison, comp. New York: Transatlantic Arts, 1967.

JOURNALISM

Kent, Ruth Kimball. *The Language of Journalism: A Glossary of Print-Communications Terms.* Ohio: The Kent State UP, 1970.

LAW

Black's Law Dictionary. St. Paul, MN: West, 1979.

LITERATURE

Holman, C. Hugh. *A Handbook to Literature.* New York: Odyssey, 1972.

Shipley, Joseph T., ed. *Dictionary of World Literary Terms.* Boston: The Writer, 1970.

MATHEMATICS

James, Glenn, and Robert C. James. *Mathematics Dictionary.* New York: Van Nostrand, 1976.

MUSIC

Grove, Sir George. *Dictionary of Music and Musicians.* Ed. by Eric Blom. 5th ed. 9 vols. New York: St. Martin's, 1954.

MYTHOLOGY

Funk & Wagnalls Standard Dictionary of Folklore, Mythology, and Legend. New York: Funk, 1972.

POLITICAL SCIENCE

Plano, Jack C., and Milton Greenberg. *The American Political Dictionary.* Rev. and expanded. New York: Holt, 1967.

RELIGION

Brandon, S. G. F., ed. *A Dictionary of Comparative Religion.* New York: Scribner's, 1970.

SOCIAL SCIENCE

English, Horace B., and Ava Champney English. *A Comprehensive Dictionary of Psychological and Psychoanalytical Terms.* New York: McKay, 1958.

Gould, Julius, and William Kolb, eds. *A Dictionary of the Social Sciences.* New York: Free Press, 1964.

SCIENCE AND TECHNOLOGY
McGraw-Hill Dictionary of Scientific and Technical Terms. New York: McGraw, 1974.
Steen, Edwin B. *Dictionary of Biology.* Totowa, NJ: Barnes, 1975.

News Summaries and Digests

CQ Weekly Report. Washington, DC: Congressional Quarterly, Inc., 1943 to date. [Summarizes U.S. Congressional activities.]
Editorial Research Reports. Washington, DC: Congressional Quarterly, Inc., 1965 to date, weekly. [Analyzes current issues, gives background, lists bibliographies for further reading.]
Editorials on File. New York: Facts on File, 1970 to date. [Reprints of newspaper editorials on controversial issues.]
Facts on File. New York: Facts on File, 1941 to date, weekly. [Summarizes news stories from around the world.]

General Encyclopedias

Collier's Encyclopedia. New York: Macmillan Educational Corp., 1981.
Encyclopedia Americana. New York: Encyclopedia Americana, 1978. [Emphasizes subjects relating to the United States.]
New Columbia Encyclopedia. New York: Columbia UP, 1975.
New Encyclopaedia Britannica. 15th ed. Chicago: Encyclopaedia Britannica, 1974.

Subject Encyclopedias

ART AND ARCHITECTURE
Encyclopedia of World Art. New York: McGraw, 1959–68.

ASTRONOMY
Cambridge Encyclopedia of Astronomy. The Institute of Astronomy, University of Cambridge. New York: Crown, 1977.

BIOLOGY
Encyclopedia of Biological Sciences. 2d ed. New York: Van Nostrand, 1970.

BUSINESS AND ECONOMICS
Dictionary of Economics and Business. 4th enl. ed. Totowa, NJ: Littlefield, 1978.
University Dictionary of Business and Finance. New York: Crowell, 1957.

CHEMISTRY
Encyclopedia of Chemistry. 3d ed. New York: Van Nostrand, 1973.

COMPUTER SCIENCE
Computer Dictionary and Handbook. Indianapolis: Sams, 1972.
Encyclopedia of Computer Science. New York: Van Nostrand, 1976.

ECONOMICS
Encyclopedia of Economics. New York: McGraw, 1982.

EDUCATION
Encyclopedia of Education. New York: Macmillan, 1971.

ENGINEERING
Engineering Encyclopedia. 3d ed. New York: Industrial Press, 1963.

ENVIRONMENTAL SCIENCE
Encyclopedia of Environmental Science. New York: McGraw, 1974.

FILM
International Encyclopedia of Film. New York: Crown, 1972.
Oxford Companion to Film. New York: Oxford UP, 1976.

HISTORY
Encyclopedia of World History: Ancient, Medieval, and Modern Chronologically Arranged. 5th ed. Boston: Houghton, 1972.

LANGUAGE AND LITERATURE
Cassell's Encyclopedia of World Literature. Rev. ed. New York: Morrow, 1973.
Hayes, Curtis W., Jacob Ornstein, and William W. Gage. *The ABC's of Language and Linguistics.* Rev. ed. Silver Spring, MD: Institute of Modern Languages, 1977.
McGraw-Hill Encyclopedia of World Drama. New York: McGraw, 1972.
Modern World Drama: An Encyclopedia. New York: Dutton, 1972.

MATHEMATICS
Prentice-Hall Encyclopedia of Mathematics. Englewood Cliffs, NJ: Prentice, 1982.

MEDIA
Rivers, William L. et al. *The Mass Media and Modern Society.* 2d ed. New York: Holt, 1971.

MUSIC
New Grove Dictionary of Music and Musicians. Washington, DC: Grove's Dictionaries of Music, 1980.

PHILOSOPHY
Encyclopedia of Philosophy. New York: Macmillan, 1973.

PHYSICS
Encyclopedia of Physics. 2d ed. New York: Van Nostrand, 1974.

POLITICAL SCIENCE
American Political Dictionary. 5th ed. New York: Holt, 1979.
Worldmark Encyclopedia of the Nations. 5th ed. New York: Worldmark and Harper, 1976.

PSYCHOLOGY
The Encyclopedia of Human Behavior: Psychology, Psychiatry, and Mental Health. New York: Doubleday, 1970.

RELIGION
Encyclopedia of Religion and Ethics. New York: Scribner's, 1961.

SCIENCE
McGraw-Hill Encyclopedia of Science and Technology. New York: McGraw, 1966 and supplementary yearbooks.

SOCIAL SCIENCE
International Encyclopedia of the Social Sciences. 17 vols. New York: Macmillan, 1968.

SOCIOLOGY
Encyclopedia of Social Work. New York: National Association of Social Workers, 1977.
Encyclopedia of Sociology. Guilford, CT: Dushkin, 1974.

SPORTS
Menke, Frank G. *The Encyclopedia of Sports.* 6th ed. New York: Barnes, 1977.

Quotations

Bartlett, John. *Familiar Quotations.* Boston: Little, 1968.
Stevenson, Burton. *Home Book of Quotations, Classical and Modern.* New York: Dodd, 1967.

Statistics

American Statistics Index: A Comprehensive Guide and Index to the Statistical Publications of the United States Government. Washington, DC: Congressional Information Service, 1973 to date. [Includes abstracts of statistical publications.]
The Gallup Opinion Index: political, social and economic trends. Princeton, NJ: The American Institute of Public Opinion, 1965 to date.
Statistical Yearbook. New York: United Nations Department of Economic and Social Affairs, Statistical Office, 1949 to date.
U.S. Bureau of the Census. *Statistical Abstract of the United States.* Washington, DC: Government Printing Office, 1878 to date. [Summary of figures on social, political, economic, and cultural activities.]

INDEX

THE ELEMENTS OF WRITING

WRITING SAMPLES